International Strategy of Emerging Market Firms

T0295991

Emerging economies are expected to be in the driver's seat of the global economy in the medium and long term. Large multinational corporations will account for much of this activity.

In this textbook, Andrei Panibratov explains how emerging market firms accumulate and exploit market knowledge to develop competitive advantages while operating globally. Chapters dedicated to the key emerging economies – Brazil, Russia, India and China (BRIC) – are enhanced by detailed case studies of large firms' activities. The book is divided into four parts, focusing on the following:

- An outline of the relevant terminology and the context of the international strategy of emerging market firms, providing an introductory foundation for the whole book.
- A guide to the evolution of perspectives regarding international strategy, designed to illustrate the changes and trends in the recent academic research on internationalization.
- A country-by-country illustration of the internationalization of BRIC economies and firms, providing an overall picture of each country's global integration, outward investments and strategies.
- The concepts and practices behind the strategies employed by different firms.

Written by an established international business scholar, this book is essential reading for students of international strategy who wish to understand the importance of the emerging economies.

Andrei Panibratov is Professor of Strategic and International Management at the Graduate School of Management and Deputy Director of the Center for the Study of Emerging Market and Russian Multinational Enterprises at St. Petersburg State University, Russia.

International Strategy of Emerging Market Firms

Absorbing Global Knowledge and Building
Competitive Advantage

Andrei Panibratov

Routledge
Taylor & Francis Group

LONDON AND NEW YORK

First published 2017
by Routledge
2 Park Square, Milton Park, Abingdon, Oxon OX14 4RN

and by Routledge
711 Third Avenue, New York, NY 10017

Routledge is an imprint of the Taylor & Francis Group, an informa business

British Library Cataloguing in Publication Data
A catalogue record for this book is available from the British Library

Library of Congress Cataloging in Publication Data
A catalog record for this book has been requested

ISBN: 978-1-138-90379-1 (hbk)
ISBN: 978-1-138-90380-7 (pbk)
ISBN: 978-1-315-69666-9 (ebk)

Typeset in Bembo
by Apex CoVantage, LLC

MIX
Paper from
responsible sources
FSC
www.fsc.org   FSC® C013056

Printed and bound in Great Britain by
TJ International Ltd, Padstow, Cornwall

Contents

Figures

Graphs

Tables

Acknowledgements

During the past eighteen years of teaching and studying international business in the context of emerging markets, the urge to disseminate at least part of what I have learned from other people (my tutors, colleagues and students), and absorbed from multiple international projects in which I was a part, has grown, until I finally decided to encapsulate this wealth of knowledge in the present book.

In retrospect, having suffered through the editorial process, I look back and realize the extent of the efforts of many people who contributed to this project in their own way. I therefore wish to express my gratitude to all those who made a contribution to the successful completion of this book.

Traditionally, I felt tremendous support and help from professor Marina Latukha during my work on this title (and, of course, beyond the book). I send her my warm and heartfelt thanks. I hope Marina will always accompany me in my other adventures!

Students whom I teach at the Graduate School of Management inspired me in their own individual ways and subconsciously contributed a large amount to the content. A little bit of each of them will be found here, weaving in and out of the pages.

This book was given impetus by the establishment of the Center for the Study of Emerging Market and Russian Multinational Enterprises at St. Petersburg State University, which I see as a logical continuation and development of my previous investigations in the area. I have invited professor Lilac Nachum to become a director of the Center, and I am grateful for her strong commitment and patience.

My extensive thanks to Chris Fodor for his hard editorial work. He has not only helped me out with much excellent advice while polishing the text of the book, but also brought his creativity and personality into many fragments of the edited text.

Lastly, I wish to express my endless gratitude for their love to my beloved parents, Yuri and Tamara, to whom I dedicate this book.

Introduction

Why do we continue reading books on emerging market firms?

This book is about the internationalization of emerging market firms. Right here the reader may ask: yet another one? There are already several books! They encompass many topics: from entry strategies and foreign investments to talent management and cultural integration. In fact, a short review of some selected books is provided in our first chapter.

Although traditionally undervalued by scholars in terms of their competitiveness, knowledge, speed and outcomes, emerging market firms have in reality shown not only strong positions in their home countries, but they are also demonstrating an ability to play a critical role on the global scene. The proof of their increasing multinational status – significant scope of operations, employment of large multinational workforces, outstanding financial figures and recognizable brand names – accompanied their geographic expansion into international markets. This explains why they are often referred to as to emerging multinational enterprises (EMNEs). Although many of these firms are relatively mature and can be compared to established multinationals from developed economies, many of the EMNEs are younger, of lesser size, less experienced and more restricted in their assets, both material and intangible.

The limitations of previously published books on international business become more flagrant when serious readers delve inside them. Literally all of these studies focus on China as the sole or the main context. Rarely are examples from Brazil, India or Mexico analyzed. As to the context of other emerging economies such as Kazakhstan, Nigeria or Russia, this becomes the exception rather than the rule. Learning about the international strategies of companies from these areas is difficult.

This book gives equal hearing to all countries in the BRIC quartet (Brazil, Russia, India, China). Although the BRIC concept has been widely criticized (with which I fully agree), this approach allows us to maintain a formal balance between the most important global economies in the developing world. Referring to the BRIC framework allows comparisons, evaluations and even benchmarking of empirical evidence from emerging multinationals, and enables the reader to understand the most important trends as these firms develop outside their home-country borders.

Given my position as head of the Center for the Study of Emerging Market and Russian Multinational Enterprises at the St. Petersburg University Graduate School of Management in Russia, the reader will understand (and hopefully forgive) our emphasis on the Russian context. The increasing importance of Russian multinationals provides interesting insights. There are three main reasons for this. To start with, Russia remains one of the largest outward investors among emerging economies, with affiliates almost all over the world, and Russian firms pursue an unusually wide range of strategies in going abroad and thus deserve careful examination. Second, Russia is one of the least examined economies in business and management literature and therefore readers should benefit from this new knowledge and widen their experience of emerging markets based on the case studies covering Russian multinationals. Third, my past almost two decades of study of corporate internationalization in emerging economies provides additional insight based on Russian experiences.

Many emerging market firms are well-known leaders in their home markets, but not all of them have been satisfactorily treated as multinationals. This is not surprising: in many cases, their internationalization only became possible when overbearing political regimes collapsed or changed, leading to privatization processes and the introduction of legislation to promote overseas investments, including foreign direct investment (FDI). Hence, most emerging multinationals (EMNEs) are still weaker than their Western counterparts and lag behind.

At the same time, these EMNEs display not just the sheer ambition to compete in foreign markets and sufficient funding to invest abroad but also the competitiveness and ability to generate competitive advantages that were believed to be possessed by developed market firms alone. How do they do this? What helps them? Why do they demonstrate different results? These and other related questions are answered in this book.

The organization of the book reflects the most important historical, economic, institutional, managerial and political perspectives of emerging market firms, with international strategy being our main focus. This book consists of twelve chapters and is organized in the following manner.

Chapters 1–3 provide the terminology and define the context for international strategy of emerging market firms, and hence provide the foundation for the whole book.

The first chapter starts with the most important definitions and terminology related to internationalization, entry strategy and ownership modes. In analyzing the choices companies make when going international, the discussion concentrates on differences in the internationalization of emerging market firms.

The second chapter sets the stage by describing emerging economies, starting with the BRIC quartet, yet also covers other countries that are not part of that group. The analysis includes both important historical background and outward investment, more specifically the motives, destinations and institutional determinants for outbound foreign direct investment (OFDI). Special attention is given to Russia, which received short shrift in previous emerging market studies.

Chapter 3 shows how emerging markets and EMFs have learnt from "Western" experiences. Several cases illustrate how multinationals from developed countries established themselves in various BRIC markets and examines their operations, brands, networks and value chains. What explains the different results, with some developed multinationals successfully gaining foothold while others failed? Such experiences gave the incoming multinationals valuable knowledge on emerging economies, but just as importantly, they gave the EMFs valuable management insights.

Chapters 4–6 present the evolutionary perspective regarding international strategy, and hence are rather theoretical. These three chapters aim to explain the changes and trends in the recent academic research on internationalization.

Chapter 4 exposes the more "established" theories – resource-based view, transaction cost approach, institutional perspective, Uppsala model and eclectic paradigm – that are often used as the foundations for internationalization theories.

Chapter 5 switches to more focused internationalization concepts and provides the dynamic perspective of international strategy, showing how firms move from simple export strategies to more complex foreign direct investments. Why do some multinationals rely on M&A (mergers and acquisitions) transactions, and what do they really acquire when purchasing firms abroad? The role of intangible strategies that are often critical for successful international expansion is also covered.

Chapter 6 concentrates on some younger perspectives in international strategy. Bringing together two concepts – internationalization and competitive advantage – this chapter shows the environmental effects on MNEs, discusses the competitive advantages and disadvantages of emerging market firms and provides illustrations using Russian multinationals.

Chapters 7 to 10 are devoted to a thorough illustration of the internationalization of BRIC economies and firms, with one full chapter per country. After providing an overall picture of each country's global integration and outward investments, each chapter describes the international strategies of emerging MNEs.

Chapter 7 describes international strategies of Brazilian multinationals, with case studies of Embraer and Vale, where the first demonstrates more selective targeting of overseas markets and the second follows a more global approach in its foreign operations.

Chapter 8 deals with Chinese multinationals, distinguishing between automaker Geely and mobile handset manufacturer ZTE, both very knowledge hungry, but behaving very differently. While Geely captures knowledge, ZTE prefers to cultivate it.

Chapter 9 explores the Indian market using case studies on Tata Motors and Wipro, both active acquirers yet with different twists. Through its M&A strategy, Tata acquires brands, which facilitate future sales, whereas Wipro purchases know-how and knowledge.

Chapter 10 presents case studies of Russian multinationals in industries such as metallurgy, petroleum and banking. Our three examples are Severstal, Gazprom Neft and Alfa-Bank, each illustrating different motivations and methods for international expansion: securing resources, or integrating in the markets or servicing home-country clients.

Chapters 11 and 12 discuss concepts and practices that make the final shape of international strategy of emerging market firms. Sometimes companies expand abroad for non-market reasons. Chapter 11 presents three such motivations: government involvement in internationalization, the liability of foreignness while expanding abroad and political connections as a foundation for competitive advantage.

Chapter 12 discusses the intangible side of EMNE internationalization, in particular, the move from natural resources to technology, knowledge absorption and exploration and organizational and cultural integration. These three phenomenon accompany the successful international strategy of many emerging market firms.

Taken together, these twelve chapters attempt to provide a general understanding and specific highlights of the international strategy of emerging market firms. During their internationalization process, what knowledge did they accumulate and then exploit, and what new competitive advantages did they build?

Part I

Contemporary meaning and context for international business

1 Four questions about international strategy

International business has mimicked international air travel. Fifty years ago, flying abroad was a private club, with a few gentleman operators, sophisticated service and a mostly elite clientele. Companies operating internationally were also a select few. As international business activity turned into its current maelstrom of frenetic activity over the past decades, the strategies for doing international business also became more complex.

This is reflected in the number of textbooks that cover topics such as emerging markets and emerging multinational enterprises, the volatility of economic conditions and distance between markets (both physical and institutional), the institutional voids to emerging multinational enterprises' competitive advantages and the role of government in the internationalization of emerging market firms. These books vary in their definitions of international business (IB) and international strategy (IS), and more specifically in their recognition of the importance of emerging economies (EEs), and their perspective on emerging market firms (EMFs) or emerging multinational enterprises (EMNEs).

The basics of international business are well covered by two books. The first, Alain Verbeke's *International Business Strategy* (2013), combines analytical rigor and practical managerial insight on the functioning of multinationals (MNEs). With a critical view of important theoretical articles, he shows how these can be applied by real companies engaged in international expansion, especially when entering unfamiliar, distant markets. For Verbeke, international strategy means effectively and efficiently matching company strengths with the opportunities and challenges found in geographically dispersed environments.

The second book, David Collis's *International Strategy: Context, Concepts and Implications* (2014), examines how the heterogeneity of markets, the volatility of economic conditions, the increased scale of activities generated by global expansion and other phenomena create tensions and trade-offs for firms. Which product should be offered abroad? In which countries? Where should various activities be located? How can operations across the globe be organized best? For Collis, international strategy is how multinationals create value across countries and what principles and constraints guide their decisions.

The emerging market perspective is introduced in two books worth mentioning. The first, Yadong Luo's *Multinational Enterprises in Emerging Markets* (2002), provides a series of lessons on how to reap maximum returns while mitigating related risks arising from the economic, socio-cultural and regulatory environments of emerging markets. The author covers critical issues for emerging markets: government policy, corruption and personal networking, liability of foreignness and more. The book is empirically grounded on case studies including Walmart in Mexico, Sony in Poland and Brazil and Philip Morris in Russia.

The second book, Tarun Khanna's and Krishna Palepu's *Winning in Emerging Markets: A Road Map for Strategy and Execution* (2010), advances the discussion about emerging markets themselves and how organizations can best leverage the potential of these countries. The authors argue that proper market evaluation is more than collecting data points related to size, population and growth potential. In fact, they suggest that firms should first assess the area's lack of institutional infrastructure and then formulate strategies around what the authors call institutional voids that may benefit the firm. Such voids are the primary exploitable characteristic of emerging markets, and even though they mean challenges, they also provide major opportunities for both multinationals and local companies.

The environment for international business is reflected in three other books worth mentioning. *Institutional Theory in International Business and Management* (2012), edited by Laszlo Tihanyi, Timothy Michael Devinney and Torben Pedersen, assembles the most prominent journal articles from recent years. The main focus is on institutional theory, as opposed to transaction cost theory and neoclassical economics, leading to the suggestion of a new theoretical framework regarding the roles of institutions in international business.

Another collection of articles is gathered in *International Business: New Challenges, New Forms, New Perspectives* (2012) edited by Simon Harris, Olli Kuivalainen and Veselina Stoyanova (2012). The book combines existing studies with new in-depth knowledge about some recent challenges for international businesses. It also presents new perspectives from the experience of successful business experts in managing large international projects, the issues faced and the strategies used to confront them.

Leslie Hamilton and Philip Webster in *The International Business Environment* (2015) delve into the challenges of the international business environment. The authors define this environment as a heady mix of dynamic socio-cultural, technological, political, legal and ecological factors, and identify the core issues faced by firms. Case studies are sourced from many countries, including emerging markets in Africa, South America and Asia. Moreover, these case studies are updated to include recent events such as the Arab Spring, economic sanctions against Russia or changes in specific global market sectors.

Among these books, even those including emerging market perspectives, the emerging star remains China, with India, Brazil and other emerging economies of South Asia, Latin America and sub-Saharan Africa explored to a lesser extent. Russia and its new breed of multinationals remains largely behind the scenes, despite Russia's huge size, substantial inbound foreign investment and active foreign investment and colorful institutional environment.

Unleashing Russia's Business Potential: Lessons from the Regions for Building Market Institutions (2002), edited by Harry Broadman, analyzes the Russian market and its institutional environment. The book is based on in-depth case studies of more than seventy companies across Russia. It addresses four key areas marked by institutional influence: the policy structure governing corporate competition and market structure; the regulatory regime governing the price, supply and access to local infrastructure services; the access to corporate finance in regional markets; and the legal system for resolving commercial disputes.

One of my previous books, *Russian Multinationals: From Regional Supremacy to Global Lead* (2012) focuses on Russian multinationals and emphasizes the role they play in the world economy. The variety of strategies and policies is depicted with case studies from the oil & gas, metallurgy, banking and high-tech industries. The influence of institutions on these companies is examined, with particular attention paid to special treatment from the Russian government and the consequences of government involvement on international results.

This short bibliographical summary illustrates how scholars have switched their focus from international strategy to internationalization. The key argument behind this is that while strategy is mainly the process, internationalization covers both process and phenomenon. Sometimes it is easy to understand *what* emerging multinationals do (what their strategy is) but difficult to understand *why* they do it (the motivations and resources behind their international expansion). As a result, although both developed and emerging market firms may follow similar strategies, their internationalizations will differ.

In this book, international strategy is closely linked to emerging economies and multinational companies from emerging countries. Moreover, our empirical background extends to firms originating not only from China (typical for the vast majority of strategy textbooks) but also from Brazil, India, Russia, South Africa and other countries that are usually less studied as breeding grounds for emerging market firms.

One of the tectonic shifts in international business is the recent appearance of emerging multinationals. Thirty years ago, who had heard of Gazprom, Embraer, Wipro or Haier? Most previous books on international business were written based on evidence from large corporations originating in developed countries. With the rising importance of emerging markets and their presence in global business (with China, India, Russia, Brazil still solid bricks in worldwide commerce), this approach does not work anymore. A new context is required.

To kick off, this chapter briefly explains what business internationalization means. It is then logical to proceed to examining which entry modes are most frequent for companies that seek to expand geographically. Which entry solutions work best for contemporary international business and which should be reconsidered based on environmental changes? Thereafter, the most "popular" ownership strategies are presented. Finally, the key features of the internationalization process of EMFs are analyzed as well as their differences with respect to the internationalization of multinationals from developed countries.

1.1 What is internationalization today?

More than forty years ago, some academics postulated that internationalization was basically concerned with the interaction between actual behavior and attitude, but it is more commonly understood as international activities undertaken by a business.[1] It was also mentioned that the outward movement of a firm's cross-border operations could be termed internationalization. Other authors have widened the meaning of internationalization to mean the process of increasing international activities and the organizational changes that can be associated with those activities.[2] The outward growth and inward performance of multinationals are linked through countertrade in its many forms. This explains the international growth of some companies through international tie-ups. Based on this countertrade phenomenon, other researchers[3] defined internationalization as the process of increased involvement in global operations. However, they clarify that even once a business takes up international activities, its international involvement is not necessarily ongoing, since de-internationalization can occur later on.

In the late 1980s, internationalization was considered a process involving incremental stages, meaning that a company could become international step by step. Academics tended to clearly define those stages as well as the boundaries between them. On the other hand, the critics of this approach pointed to the limited connection of theory and practice and the questionable ability to identify stages and processes that lead the movement from one stage to another.[4]

Therefore, there is no exact and commonly used definition for the notion of "internationalization," although in general it is described as "the degree to which firms depend on foreign markets, or their foreign market penetration in terms of sales revenue."[5] In other words, internationalization can be described as the process of increasing the involvement of firms in international markets. The concept reflects the evolution of a company moving from operating in its domestic market (often referred to as home market) to additional foreign international host markets.[6]

In the 1990s and later, internationalization extended beyond operational expansion to include the indirect and direct effects of international transactions on corporate operations and the process of creating and managing transactions with other countries.[7] Some academics went so far as to define internationalization as the process of adapting a firm's operations (i.e. strategy, structure, resources) to international environments.

The fundamental studies of the internationalization process refer to various approaches and concepts, including, among others:

- Kravis's non-availability approach (1956);
- Posner's technology gap theory of trade (1961);
- Rogers's diffusion of innovations, seeking to explain the forms, reasons and speed of the new ideas and technologies spreading through cultures (1962);
- Hymer's advantage theory, explaining why firms can compete in foreign settings against indigenous competitors (1976);
- Dunning's eclectic paradigm, binding three basic forms of international activities and three categories of company advantages (1980; 2000); and
- Porter's diamond model (1990), describing the reasons why particular industries become competitive in particular locations.

When observing internationalization from a more practical viewpoint, it is possible to find many external factors that influence both decision making and process flow. These factors may be classified as product specific, industry specific, firm specific and environmental.[8] So even such a brief overview of the theories and viewpoints demonstrates the huge amount of information regarding internationalization.

Product versus service internationalization

An important issue for scholars is whether the internationalization of physical goods differs from that for services. Whereas some researchers acknowledge that theories described for manufacturing products are applicable to services,[9] other scholars suggest that direct applicability is questionable.[10] For these academics, so-called hard services where production and consumption are decoupled and soft services (e.g. information technology [IT]) for which production and consumption occur simultaneously differ in their internationalization processes.[11] Hard services can be internationalized in the same way as manufacturing industries, while soft services cannot. Hence, IT services should follow different strategies.[12]

Most laymen ignore the fact that service companies from emerging economies are capable of growth and internationalization.[13] To improve the understanding of service firms' internationalization, a framework including certain key elements was developed:[14] company-level resources, management characteristics, firm characteristics along with competitive and international advantages, degree of involvement/risk and host-country factors. These elements help define the service company's unique competitive and international advantages, which then establish its rate of return. Company-related resources and characteristics lead to the choice of entry mode, taking into consideration host-country factors, which in turn affect the choice of entry mode.

Some academics found that, for service firms, international experience does not significantly affect the choice of entry mode, thus questioning the sequential approach for a company's internationalization process. Another finding is that capital-intensive services adopt more flexible and less risky methods of expansion in environments where the level of economic and political instability is high and where the cultural distance is greater.[15]

One academic study[16] examined the influence of external and internal factors on service firms' choice of entry mode and concluded that service firms tended to use more integrated (higher control) entry modes for larger foreign markets, either in cases of unavailability of suitable host-country partners or in cases of companies having strong corporate policies on retention of control. On the other hand, service firms tended to use less integrated (lower-control) entry modes when facing greater restrictions on foreign ownership, or internal aversion to environmental risk, or when needing to get rapidly established or, finally, when constrained by resources.

Service firms from emerging economies are increasing their efforts to integrate into the global economy, and they have already started expanding abroad. What has driven the considerable worldwide growth of the services sector? Suggestions include tense competition in domestic markets, profit margin pressure and the opportunity to develop business in foreign markets.[17]

How do emerging market firms go international?

Having proven the point of academic interest in emerging markets, the most critical question remains: how do companies from emerging markets internationalize?

One traditional means for the international expansion of companies from emerging markets is producing at home and exporting goods to foreign markets.[18] These companies follow both the internationalization[19] and international product life-cycle models.[20] They first go overseas by exporting and then, when market knowledge is obtained, commit in the form of more investment-oriented entry modes, such as joint venture (JV) or foreign direct investment (FDI). Some researchers consider the majority of emerging market firms to still be in the early stages of the internationalization process, wherein export is dominant.[21]

As a strategy process, internationalization implies many challenges for a company, including economic, cultural, political or environmental ones. Managers must address these factors not only if the company goes physically abroad but also when it remains domestic. Companies that limit themselves to domestic operations face competition from international entrants into their market. These domestic firms should be aware of how to create a brand that will be strong internationally, or how to maintain competitive advantages against foreign intruders or how to build a corporate asset that will withstand strong rivals.

Why do emerging market firms go international?

Considering both the positive and negative aspects of internationalization, it is rational to think that the potential advantages and benefits must exceed the costs and risks. Internationalization can help a company to reach several goals: increasing firm size or profitability, or balancing firm strategy. How do these expansion drivers involve emerging markets?[22]

First, overcoming stagnation in the domestic market via expansion into new markets can be an easier task when the new markets are less saturated and have lower entry barriers, which can be the case for emerging economies. This makes for revenue growth.

Second, growing the bottom line can be simpler in emerging markets, since this simply requires expanding the customer base with existing products, where consumers are less sophisticated and more loyal to foreign brands and therefore ready to pay more for foreign goods.

Third, a company's strategic balance can be improved as a result of decreasing its uncertainty in its domestic market by including emerging markets in its country portfolio, thus hopefully also improving overall company sustainability.

What motivates international expansion is a major theme in academic literature. Multiple academic studies have been conducted to figure out the motivations and determinants.[23] Probably, this stream of studies originated with Stephen Hymer (1960), who concluded that not only companies but also their foreign subsidiaries use firm-specific advantages to enter and operate in foreign markets.

Most scholarly works, after Hymer's seminal effort, have sought to uncover the motivations to set up theoretical frameworks and to reveal the determinants of internationalization strategies. One study on the causes of company internationalization[24] identifies proactive and reactive types of drivers. Proactive reasons include profit advantage, unique products, technological advantage, exclusive information, managerial urge, tax benefit and economies of scale. Reactive reasons include competitive pressures, overproduction or excess capacity, declining domestic sales, saturated domestic markets and proximity to customers and ports.[25] Applying this dichotomy, companies can be divided into two simple categories: passive internationalizers (mostly driven by reactive factors) and active internationalizers (driven mostly by proactive factors).

What drives active internationalizers?

Proactive motivations generally cover corporate actions made to improve current performance – for example, to improve efficiency or production capacity, to decrease average operational costs and so forth. In general, active internationalizers are trying to predict future market circumstances and plan their actions accordingly. By doing so, these companies are making efforts to develop long-term competitive strategic advantages. There are four motivating factors at work here:

- *Market seeking* is, probably, the most common reason for foreign expansion and is often the response to domestic market saturation. Tata Motors (Chapter 9) is a prominent example of this approach.
- *Resource seeking* is another important driver and uses resources in a broad sense, referring to the corporate need for certain factors (or inputs) which are critical to its business. The case of Severstal (Chapter 10) fits well to illustrate this.
- *Risk avoidance* or *business diversification* drivers appear when companies face rapidly changing external factors such as political conflicts or civil commotion. The more assets you have in different locations, the lower the risks because they are spread out. (Never place all your eggs in one basket!) The external factors that exert influence on the business environment can be described using the PESTEL model (political, economic, social, technological, environmental or legal factors). For example, when operating in an unstable and economically declining market proves risky for a company,

then diversifying abroad may lower the risks. This motive is extremely popular for emerging multinationals and is reflected in most of the company cases in Chapters 7 to 10.

- *Cost reduction* is also a motivational factor for companies to go abroad. There are several ways to cut operational costs when going global – for example, by outsourcing functional tasks through the access to cheap labor or other resources, scale or scope economies (especially in production, average costs might be decreased when increasing the production capacities), taxes or import-export tariffs, etc. This motive is popular for developed multinationals that expand into less-developed economies and is supported with the set of examples in Chapter 3.

What drives passive internationalizers?

Reactive motivations can also provoke internationalization, but they are mostly about actions taken in order to counteract undesired environmental changes (competitive threats, political changes, economic dynamics, etc.). This reactive motivation to internationalize could be described as either "pushed from home" or "pulled from abroad," when a company is either forced to expand outside its home market or is attracted by forces in foreign markets.[26] Many companies driven by reactive motivational factors could be described as "passive," since they were actually forced into expanding abroad.

When operating in highly competitive markets, companies should monitor and react quickly to competitors' actions in order to preserve market share.

Three motivating factors influence passive international expansion:

- *Pursuing the competitor:* the company restricts competitors from gaining significant competitive advantage from international expansion by entering the same markets and targeting the same goals (customers, firms, projects). The examples of Embraer (Chapter 7) and Geely (Chapter 8) show that a company often follows competitors into foreign markets to preempt them from gaining a dominant position there.
- *Following the client:* this refers to situations when companies are obliged to enter foreign markets in pursuit of key customers. This situation is especially relevant for Russian MNEs (see Chapter 10) due to rapid internationalization of Russian business in general during the last two decades. The example of Alfa-Bank illustrates this.
- As for *meeting the demand*, this refers to situations when companies expand abroad in order to satisfy external requests for its products or services. Typically, however, such situations only represent minor revenue contributions, and therefore export operations can handle them. It is only when the demand reaches a certain threshold that companies consider establishing a subsidiary or sales offices to better meet customer expectations. Chinese telecom company ZTE (Chapter 8) is a good illustration here.

Is foreign expansion reasonable?

Once a company is motivated to enter a foreign market, it should evaluate the extent to which this decision is reasonable. The difficulty in understanding the differences between home and host countries should not be underestimated. These differences define whether the product should be adapted to local needs or not. The theory of gradual internationalization is based on "distance" parameters. This concept was once applied to study Internet companies in the United States and some evidence was found, although the cultural and socio-cultural distance indexes were poorly correlated with internationalization.[27] How can the "distance" be measured? The CAGE distance framework[28] is useful for comparing the environments of different countries. The CAGE analysis includes four main parameters:

1   *Cultural distance*, including language, social customs and traditions, mentality, values, religion, etc.
2   *Administrative distance*, including government relations and support, legislation, corruption, etc.
3   *Geographic distance*, including transportation costs, time zone, climate, etc.
4   *Economic distance*, including taxes and tariffs, cost of capital, interest rates, exchange rates, inflation, etc.

Stages of internationalization

Many scholars attempted to not only understand what internationalization is but also how active or intensive it is. One difficulty here is that the level (or extent) of internationalization is not a quantitative dimension. There is still no reliable method to measure internationalization, although distinguishing between stages of internationalization has been suggested.[29] While stage models are behavior models rather than assessment tools, it is possible to compare the levels of internationalization of different companies and use this as the assessment tool.

One of the best-known frameworks regarding stage internationalization is the Uppsala model, introduced by Johanson and Vahlne in 1977. The authors suggest that firms gradually enlarge their international involvement. Companies start by choosing markets close in physical distance. As its international experience and knowledge increases, the firm approaches new markets characterized at greater geographic distances. Thus the authors perceive experiential knowledge as essential for internationalization. The initial Uppsala model is presented in Figure 1.1.

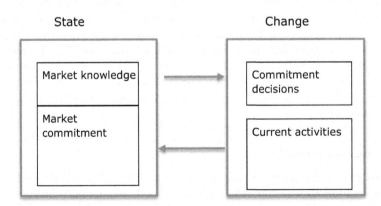

Figure 1.1 Uppsala model: the dynamic nature of the knowledge

Source: Johanson and Vahlne 1977, p. 26

Table 1.1 Ansoff model of internationalization

Stage	Activity	Conditions that determine need of activity
Exporting	Agent sales	Small ratio of export in sales, no barriers for import, local demand exceeds supply/capacity
	Foreign subsidiary	Substantial ratio of export in sales, no barriers for import, demand equals supply, significant competition, importance of after-sales service
International	Local marketing	Different conditions, differentiated marketing strategies, fierce competition
	Local R&D and manufacturing	Barriers for import, lower costs
	Local diversification	Local opportunities of growth, local financing
Transnational	Global optimization of the manufacturing, R&D	World competition, advantages of multiplication in global scale
	Global diversification, global management of a whole range of activity	Competition from globally optimized firms

Source: Ansoff, 1989

One study[30] used different incremental stages of internationalization, defining the characteristics of each stage. A simplified version of this staging model is presented in Table 1.1.

Here another issue arises: how should managers define the optimal or desired level of internationalization? Based on the advantages listed, companies can opt for the level of internationalization that corresponds to the foreign market conditions listed in the third column of the table. Each switch from one stage of internationalization to the next implies greater costs and therefore risks. This approach assumes that the firm is independent in its decision making in choosing the entry mode.

Theoretical approaches to international expansion

Some scholars have defined internationalization as a process of knowledge development and incremental commitment,[31] the outward movement in a company's international operations,[32] a process of increasing involvement in international operations[33] and the crossing of national boundaries in the process of growth.[34] Summing up those definitions, internationalization strategy can be defined as where, when and how firms expand into foreign markets.

Many studies explain why and how firms internationalize, some of which became background for many consequent theories and approaches.[35] The two key theories for internationalization strategy are the eclectic paradigm and transaction cost approach. The eclectic paradigm, also called OLI theory,[36] sets up a main framework to explain FDI decisions with ownership, location and internalization (OLI) advantages. Transaction cost approach (TCA) led to the development of several FDI theories[37] and set up the framework which explains how international expansions occur. The core concept of the theory is that the transaction is made with the lowest cost available. The optimal timing for switching ownership mode – for example, from simple export to FDI – is determined, according to TCA, when the cost of the mode becomes lower.[38]

These two approaches are definitely not sufficient to fully explain internationalization, and firms surely have other motivations to expand abroad. Many companies try to increase existing capabilities through international expansion, but they also build up new capabilities by acquiring foreign assets.[39] For example, acquisitions allow firms to obtain new technological resources.[40] Firms also venture abroad to increase profitability, which offsets unexpected costs and risks in foreign countries.[41] Yet another motivation is the latecomer perspective: to catch up with early movers, firms are willing to obtain technology or brands through acquisitions.[42] Internationalization can only represent a "springboard," to increase resource accessibility, find growing foreign markets and overcome constraints in the domestic market.[43]

Once motivated to expand internationally, companies confront challenges and risks which they need to mitigate and overcome. The most well-known risk is the liability of foreignness, which is defined as additional costs for firms when they do business in other countries.[44] Uncertainty is another important risk facing companies when they expand abroad.[45] One social aspect to the challenge is suggested by the concept of "psychic distance," which concerns the cultural, linguistic, institutional level and other differences between the home and host countries.[46] In terms of institutional aspects, scholars have found that high regulatory control affects firms negatively in the host countries, thus influencing incoming companies' strategies.[47] Although firms need to deal with the local requirements and cope with these regulations,[48] the unexpected additional costs may offset the benefit of internationalization[49] and may even constitute barriers to entry.[50] Multinationals facing stronger regulatory levels have higher failure rates.[51]

1.2 Entry mode: why do companies choose only a few?

Today, foreign markets are no longer inaccessible or distant, and they often seem inevitable for a company's growth strategy. Given the severe global competition, internationalization is no longer a matter of "*if*," but a matter of "*how*" and "*what*" and "*where*" for companies.[52] The decision to expand abroad has become one of the most important strategic decisions made by companies.[53]

Expansions into foreign markets require decisions on two related but distinct issues.[54] First, a company has to choose an ownership mode: either JV or wholly owned subsidiary (WOS). The investigation of factors that influence the ownership choice is very popular among academics.[55] Second, a company has to choose its entry mode: either via acquisition (buy option) or via greenfield (build option). Here again, many studies have analyzed the factors which influence the entry mode decisions.[56]

These studies typically focused on the internationalization strategies of firms from either particular home countries or entering specific host countries: for example, Japanese firms entering Western Europe,[57] or Japanese firms' outward expansion,[58] or Chinese firms' outward expansion,[59] or Swedish firms' outward expansion,[60] or Japanese firms into the United States,[61] or multinationals into China[62] or MNEs into the United States.[63] These studies are important to understand the internationalization strategies deployed by various companies, and the factors influencing these choices, especially in terms of country-specific advantages or home-country characteristics.

Another variable that studies must address regards the industries in which these multinationals operate. Do the same factors influence internationalization strategies across all industries? Or are they different? After all, companies from different industries usually have their own industry-specific characteristics and different business environments, which affect the key determinants of internationalization.

Introducing the concept of entry strategies

Once a company decides that it should expand abroad, it needs to choose its entry mode from the menu of possible options. The degree of internationalization and the choice of market entry mode are closely linked.[64] The market entry mode must consider the firm's operations, technology, human skills, management and other resources, both in the home country and within the foreign host country.[65] In addition, the entry mode must consider the channels of distribution for the company's sales.

Entry strategies differ by level of control, resource commitment and risk involvement.[66] Control is defined as the ability to influence the systems, methods and solutions. The nature of the company's management is an important variable in entry mode choices, since managers must identify the potential risks and benefits (for example, return on assets) for their firms. The entry mode can increase the profitability and risk, with a low control mode decreasing the resources allocated, but sometimes at the expense of profitability.

Two theoretical approaches often are cited to explain a company's degree of control over its foreign operations:

- The transaction cost approach suggests that a low level of ownership is preferable unless proven otherwise.
- The bargaining power theory states a natural preference for high control unless the government of the host country has greater bargaining power.[67]

Furthermore, the level of control can be divided between full control (WOS for wholly owned subsidiary) and shared control (contracts or JV). The degree or type of control provided by the various ownership modes is a key factor in international expansion strategy.[68]

Entry modes have been extensively researched because they represent fundamental decisions when entering a new market. The entry strategy can refer to a comprehensive plan outlining the objectives, goals, resources and policies that will guide the international operations of a company for a period long enough to achieve sustainable growth in the foreign market.[69] According to this definition, it is also necessary to take into account the selection of a desired product or market, goals and objectives in the target market, the entry mode for that target country, the marketing plan and the control system for monitoring operations. Although different studies come up with different numbers of entry strategies, the following are five main classes, listed in order of increasing control:

- export
- license and franchise
- alliance
- joint ventures
- wholly owned subsidiary

Another study adds contract manufacturing. Although there is much academic debate about types of entry modes, in general, they can be divided into the three simpler

Table 1.2 Principal market entry modes

Exporting modes	Contractual modes	Investment modes	
		Partially owned and controlled	*Wholly owned and controlled*
Direct exporting	Licensing	Joint ventures	Subsidiaries
Agents	Franchising	Partial mergers	Representatives
Distributors	Contract manufacture	and acquisitions	Assembly
E-commerce	Alliances		
E-business	Management service		
Interactive TV	contracts		
Indirect Exporting			
Via domestic			
organizations			
Trading companies			
Export houses			
Piggy backing			

Source: Adopted from Wach 2014

categories: export, contractual and investment entry modes.[70] According to the extent of internalizing or externalizing by the multinational, this classification can also be referred to as export, intermediate and hierarchical modes.[71]

Foreign market entry strategies may be also introduced by four categories: marketing oriented (direct and indirect exporting), contractual, shared owned and controlled as well as wholly owned and fully controlled.[72] These last two entry modes can be considered as investment. Table 1.2[73] summarizes the different types of entry modes under each of the four ownership categories.

Exporting entry mode

Most companies from different industries began initial internationalization via simple exporting modes.[74] Two basic approaches of exporting exist: direct and indirect. Direct exports involve sales to customers located outside the firm's home country. Indirect exports occur when a firm sells its product to a domestic customer (e.g. a domestic distributor handling export markets), which in turn exports the product, possibly even in a modified form. A third form of export covers so-called transfers, which has become more important as multinationals have increased in size. This refers to the selling of goods by a firm in one country to an affiliated firm in another– for example, automobile transmissions from Ford-Mexico to Ford-Europe.

The export entry mode has two main advantages: first, it avoids the often substantial costs of establishing manufacturing operations in the host country; second, it helps a firm progress down the learning curve and discover location economies. Naturally, export also has disadvantages: first, exporting from the firm's home country may not be appropriate if lower-cost locations for manufacturing can be found abroad; the second is that high transportation costs can make exports uneconomical (mainly for bulk products; think of cement which is best produced locally); and third is that tariff or customs barriers can make it uneconomical.

In addition, government policies may influence export decisions. Export promotion policies, export franchising programs and other forms of home-country subsidies encourage the export entry mode. However, host countries may impose tariffs or other non-tariff barriers on imports, thereby discouraging the export entry mode.[75]

Contractual entry modes

Contractual entry modes are long-term relationships between home-country and host-country companies, which involve transfer of technology or human skills. These entry modes include licensing, franchising and other contractual arrangements. Contractual entry modes are used when a firm wants to avoid starting completely new operations in the host market.

Licensing is the entry mode under which the home-country firm (the licensor) sells the right to use its intellectual property (technology, work methods, patents, copyrights, brand names or trademarks) to the host-country firm (the licensee). Numerous international magazines such as *Elle* or *Playboy* are examples of international licenses. The main advantage of licensing is to circumvent import barriers, since there is no physical flow of goods. In addition, licensing helps the home-country firm overcome the high transport costs that export might incur. Licensing also carries lower risk than the investment entry modes. The largest disadvantage of licensing is the licensor's lack of control over the nitty-gritty of the operational plans in the host country. Another disadvantage can be the limited amount of income, since typical licensing contracts last for, say, five to ten years. The risk of creating a locally bred competitor is also high, since the licensee can use the licensor's technology after the contract is finished.[76]

Franchising can be considered as a variation on the licensing theme. Three approaches exist regarding franchising. Approach number one considers franchising as a variation on existing business functional activities and can be studied by applying the models and theories of those functions. Approach number two defines franchising as a unique phenomenon, but its peculiarities can be explained through existing theoretical models. Finally, approach number three considers franchising as a unique phenomenon for entry modes that can only be fully understood though the development or adaptation of models and theories that apply specifically to its practice.[77]

No matter which approach one adheres to, franchising is a specialized form of licensing in which the franchiser not only sells intangible property (normally a trademark) to the franchisee but also insists that the franchisee abide by strict rules in doing business. Think here of McDonald's restaurants or Curves fitness studios. The franchisor is relieved of many of the costs and risks of opening a foreign market on its own, while offering the franchisee the opportunity to build a profitable turnkey operation as quickly as possible.

Other contractual entry modes include, for example, management contracts whereby the home-country firm provides managerial assistance, technical experience or specialized services to a host-country firm for some agreed-upon time in return for a fee. This may be suitable in cases where a government may forbid foreign ownership of firms in certain industries, but lack the technical expertise to manage those firms.

Turnkey projects, defined as contracts by which a firm agrees to fully design, construct and equip a facility and then turn the project over to the purchaser when ready for operation (either for a fixed price, or for payment on a cost-plus basis), are also common contractual agreements in many industrial sectors.

Investment entry modes

All the aforementioned entry modes are "risk-free," in the sense that the home-country company is not investing its own capital to expand abroad. This is internationalization "light," without investing in foreign factors or facilities. As could be expected, a number of firms prefer to enter the international arena by actually owning assets in the host country. Some companies test the international waters via export or contractual arrangements first and then move on to investment-grade entry modes once sufficiently comfortable.

Over the past two decades (1990–2010), FDI has become a major source of capital flows from both developed and developing countries.[78] Multinationals entering a host country via two typical strategies often make these investments: acquisition or greenfield (buy or build).

Acquisition refers to the purchase of an existing local company, while *greenfield* investment is building up a completely new plant.[79] Since these two entry modes represent quite different strategies, they have very distinct consequences in terms of costs, risks and implementation speed.[80]

An acquisition allows a firm to acquire new technological resources,[81] which can substitute for the internal development of technological capabilities;[82] hence, firms with low technological skills are inclined to obtain technology by acquisition of innovative firms.[83] In contrast, firms with strong technological competences tend not to buy existing firms and are thus more likely to enter foreign markets through greenfield investments.[84]

There is also a strong belief that acquisitions allow the investing company to gain access to local networks of suppliers and customers, and thus "purchase" the expertise of the existing workforce.[85] However, acquisitions typically de-motivate the acquired company and increase management costs.[86] Several studies have found that cultural differences increase the probability that acquisitions will fail.[87] For instance, studies have shown that foreign subsidiaries of U.S. companies established by acquisition have a higher rate of failure than those founded by greenfield investment.[88] Therefore, companies choosing the acquisition entry mode need to pay careful attention to post-acquisition management in order to diminish the risks.

Greenfield investment is often used to maximize firm-specific advantages which are embedded in the company[89] and to maintain control over the subsidiary by sending expatriates from headquarters.[90] Greenfield also allows the parent company to hire and train new staff, making it easier to build firm-specific advantages from the outset.[91]

Greenfield investment also offers the flexibility of choosing production facility location, giving the investor those site benefits. However, setting up a new production line invariably takes longer than acquiring an existing plant, making acquisitions the preferred option when opportunity costs are high, such as in high-growth markets.

A *joint venture* (JV) allows ownership while reducing the investment envelope. A JV occurs when two companies (or more) agree to work together and create a jointly owned separate firm to promote a mutual interest. It is considered a flexible mechanism enabling domestic and foreign partners to form a business entity with operations in one or several countries. Thus international joint ventures are intermediate forms of cooperation, somewhere between a simple contractual agreement and a full acquisition.

Usually, the creation of a JV requires a transfer of assets and management know-how. Recently, as a result of economic globalization, the number of international joint ventures is increasing.[92] The main motives to create international joint ventures in the world markets include better resource utilization, legal prerequisite for entry, risk sharing, technology transfer and more. The three primary legal forms that joint ventures take are corporations, partnerships (including limited partnerships) and contractual joint ventures.

A *merger* is basically the amalgamation of separate companies or company divisions. It occurs when combining two or more entities into one, without the creation of a new entity. Mergers in the narrow sense refer merely to a stronger enterprise absorbing a weaker enterprise. Merger activity is likely to lead to economies of scale and a rapid expansion of market share. Further, it allows for decisions to be made more quickly, without having to wait for consensus from another party. In addition, mergers can be used as means to spread risks to various activities and as ways to achieve managerial prestige, access to brands, contracts and networks. Finally, mergers decrease market competition and are therefore best suited to industries where competition is intense. Furthermore, the evaluation of proposed horizontal mergers involves a basic trade-off; thus, mergers may increase market power but may also create efficiencies.[93]

Determinants for entry mode

What makes companies decide to go international? And, more importantly, what factors (or determinants) influence their choice of entry mode?

Some of the clearest research points to three sets of variables:

1   organizational variables consisting of investment size, technology intensity, and foreign experience;
2   cultural variables, including market growth and cultural distance; and
3   transaction cost variables, including firm diversity, product relatedness and uncertainty avoidance.

All three sets show significant correlations to entry mode decisions.[94] The eight most influential factors deserve some further detailed explanations.

Investment size is usually considered relative to the firm's size. The greater the size of the firm, the more extensive its international activities may be. Scholars have found that relative investment size is an important determinant of entry mode choice.[95] For example, a small firm aiming to create a large greenfield venture will be more likely to experience a shortage of financial or managerial resources. An acquisition may not require the same amount of resources; moreover, it may provide new managerial and other resources.

Technology intensity is one of the key factors influencing a firm's entry mode. Companies with higher technology levels prefer greenfield to acquisition as an entry mode, with two reasons offered to explain this.[96] First, transfer technology from the parent company into the acquired firm is difficult due to organizational inertia. Second, it is often hard to reap technological benefits from acquisitions since acquired firms typically have lower technology levels. One study found that technology-intensive Japanese firms prefer greenfield investment since they consider it a more secure way to transfer their capabilities into foreign subsidiaries, with the possibility of molding new management and staff into the culture.[97] A similar study also reported that Japanese investors in the United States showed higher preference for greenfield over acquisition because of the desire to build up their own management systems for technology transfer.[98] Another study showed the positive correlations between R&D (research and development) intensity and greenfield; hence, companies with higher levels of technology were willing to establish new plants using their own competence, while companies with lower levels of technology tended to acquire existing companies to obtain technology.[99] Consequently, acquisition is preferred for companies with lower technology levels since they strive to obtain technology via acquisitions, whereas greenfield is preferred for companies with higher levels of technology because they wish to transfer their technological capabilities with fewer risks.

Foreign experience also has an impact on entry mode decisions. According to one study, the longer a firm's foreign experience, the higher its tendency to acquire.[100] One interpretation is that companies with extensive foreign experience are able to reduce the risk of acquisitions and thus increase the probability of making good acquisitions. Foreign experience helps companies to cope with the local business environment and learn how to communicate and negotiate with the locals. In addition, experience in the host country will increase a firm's ability to assess the true value of local acquisition candidates, thus improving the chance of success. Firms without or with limited experience in the host country would face more obstacles during acquisitions and would therefore be more likely to choose greenfield investments.

Market growth influences both ownership mode and entry mode. In a high-growth market, the new supply created by a greenfield plant can be consumed by the additional market demand, implying there is more space for greenfield in the expanding market.[101] By contrast, a slow-growth or stagnating market will have little room for the new supply from greenfield, which might turn into excess capacity and could lead to predatory competitive price pressure. Hence acquisitions can be preferred in a slow-growth market so as not to increase the additional supply and reduce competitive retaliation.[102]

Market growth also has an impact on acquisition potential. Slow markets may present better opportunities to acquire weaker incumbents struggling with stagnation, and acquisitions then foster market consolidation. On the other hand, in high-growth markets, acquisitions are often the only way to quickly capture some of the action, since greenfield has long lead times (to build new facilities).[103] Ambitious entrepreneurs seeking rapid expansion will favor acquisitions.

Consequently, market growth can be viewed as an inconclusive factor in deciding on acquisition as entry mode: things can go either way, with acquisitions suited to any market. The story is different for greenfield investments, which are preferred in high-growth markets since there is more market demand for the new capacity that will come online.

Cultural distance is one of the factors to be considered for entry mode. The concept of "psychic distance" concerns the cultural, linguistic, institutional level and other differences between home-country and host country.[104] When dealing with acquisition, the acquired firm needs to learn new rules, procedures and organizational cultures, and if the new organization does not match its previous beliefs, its integration will be difficult.[105] Several studies have found that the difficulty in integration due to different corporate cultures often leads to worse performance and the subsequent failure of the acquired subsidiaries.[106] For example, with cultural distance between Japan and the United States being quite big, Japanese investors have avoided acquisitions and preferred greenfield investment in the United States.

To help assess cultural distance, a four-dimensional framework to map national cultures was developed using uncertainty avoidance, individuality, tolerance of power distance and masculinity-femininity.[107] The analysis created ordinal scales for countries for each of these dimensions, based on a standardized factor analysis of questionnaires. Later, in 2010, indulgence was added as a fifth factor to the cultural dimension.

Firm diversity is important since diversified firms have more sophisticated management systems which may provide organizational efficiency when making foreign acquisitions.[108]

Other authors suggest that diversified firms tend to develop broad expertise and, consequently a preference for the acquisition entry mode.[109] Less diversified firms may lack these acquisition and management control skills and therefore tend to invest in greenfield projects.

Product relatedness can be a factor since the entry into a foreign market may be in pursuit of product diversification objectives. If the aim is to transfer knowledge or technologies for creating an existing product, a company will more likely choose greenfield investment. Acquisition may cause competition between products or services, and synergy effects might not be achieved. However if product diversification is the goal, an acquisition may unleash new opportunities if the other firm possesses specific resources or expertise.

Uncertainty avoidance certainly influences entry mode decisions. If the home-country company has a high level of uncertainty avoidance, acquisition will not be the favored entry mode, since it carries risks due to corporate culture differences.[110] For instance, foreign subsidiaries of U.S. firms founded by acquisitions have a higher rate of failure than those founded by greenfield, often stemming from the difficulties in integrating two different organizations.[111] Indeed, the different corporate cultures and different organizational structures present formidable challenges in integrating the acquired firm into the parental system. The difficulty in integration often leads to inferior performance and the subsequent failure of the acquired subsidiaries. As a corollary, one study found that cultures with high uncertainty avoidance attract greenfield investment.[112]

1.3 Ownership mode: why do company choices vary?

Because the ownership mode is a critical parameter in international expansion, companies carefully choose between two alternatives: either partial ownership via a joint venture or full ownership via a wholly owned subsidiary. JV or WOS is one of the most important considerations for companies when they seek to enter foreign markets and has therefore also been thoroughly researched.[113]

Why JV?

Joint ventures consist of new corporate entities with one or more partners, implying that the home-country company possesses only partial ownership of the new company. A wholly owned subsidiary means that the home-country company creates a new host-country subsidiary in which it usually owns 100% of the equity. For picky academics, WOS can be defined as a subsidiary of which the parent company possesses 95% or more of the equity, while JVs can be defined as a subsidiary in which the parent company owns between 5% and 95% of the equity.[114]

Quite obviously, different ownership modes imply different levels of control over the foreign subsidiary. These ownership modes have different implications for the degree of control that a company can exercise over its foreign operation. Since these ownership modes involve resource commitments, the company's initial choice is difficult to modify without considerable loss of time and money. Therefore, the choice of ownership mode is a critical strategic decision and needs to be decided cautiously.

Multinational companies are likely to opt for JVs when the local partners are better qualified to manage local personnel and have established relationships with local suppliers, buyers and institutions.[115] JVs also give access to partner's resources and sharing of assets. JVs facilitate access to resources which are possessed by the partners.

However, JVs can be troubled by the cultural differences with partners and also by difficulties when sharing proprietary assets.[116] Three types of conflicts between JV partners are most common:

1   When the parent company transfers weakly protected proprietary knowledge to the JV subsidiary. The transferred knowledge has to be protected and exclusively used for JV, but sometimes this knowledge leaks out of the JV company.
2   When parent and subsidiary share the same trademark. Intangible assets, such as trademark, are highly important assets and can sometimes be damaged by the negative activities of JV partners.
3   When the JV exports its products back to the parent's home market. In this case, the only winner can be the JV partner.

Although joint ventures always start in the bliss of marital beginnings, they can hit hard times. Conflicts between partners can occur since it is hard to always meet both partners' satisfaction. Therefore, a company forming a JV should be aware of the potential challenges with the partners and try to mitigate those risks in advance.

Why WOS?

A wholly owned subsidiary can help to avoid both the costs of integration of JV and the conflicts over sharing proprietary assets.[117] Moreover, another benefit to the WOS is that the parent company has full control over its foreign subsidiary – namely, the decision-making process of the foreign business unit. However, the greater ownership levels also carry greater risks, both because of the greater financial commitment and also because of the lack of an experienced foreign partner company (as is the case for a JV).[118] Full control carries a high price and entails the commitment of resources, which means there is a trade-off between the control and the costs (and therefore the risks).

One of the key theories that link to the ownership mode is the OLI,[119] which sets up a main framework to explain and examine FDI decisions based on the Ownership, Location and Internalization parameters which characterize a company's international strategy. Ownership advantages in the context of OLI are firm-specific factors such as proprietary resources or managerial capabilities which firms possess. To compete with established host-country firms, home-country firms must possess competitive advantages and skills which can offset the higher cost of doing business abroad. The ownership advantage may derive from different competitive advantages: size, or multinational experience, or the ability to develop differentiated products or talented management, etc.[120]

Another key theory for ownership mode is transaction cost approach, which has been widely applied to analyze FDI.[121] The TCA theory posits that the choice between full and partial ownership depends on the costs and benefits of the ownership level. TCA explains the ownership mode based on the following premise: a low level of ownership is preferable until proven otherwise; this is called the "default" hypothesis.[122] The model then states that a JV will be chosen when the WOS option is relatively costly, whereas WOS will be chosen when it is proven that WOS is more cost efficient than JV.

The basic premise of both the OLI and TCA theories is that the decision on ownership mode is a trade-off between the level of ownership and its costs or risks.[123]

As if two theories did not suffice, the resource-based view (RBV) provides an alternative approach to understanding ownership mode decisions. According to RBV, a firm's value can be evaluated by its own competitive resources, which can be defined as the tangible and intangible assets which are tied to the firm; hence, resources refers not only to natural resources but also capital resources, human resources and intangible resources, etc. The RBV model explains that valuable resources are usually scarce, difficult to reproduce and to substitute, thus firms need to maximize their value through competitive resources.[124] For example, a company which has natural resources may utilize its own resources to cooperate with strategic partners having intangible assets, such as technology. The pair of companies can then productively co-exploit these resources in a new relationship.

Joint ventures are an important way to access resources held by partners. The resource-based view considers alliances and JVs as strategies to access other companies' resources with each partner bringing valuable resources to the table. For a JV to be successful, each partner must have competitive resources to contribute.

Determinants for ownership mode

What makes companies choose between partial or full control? Why do some firms prefer acquisitions and some partnerships? The most popular explanations are grounded in a group of four factors: resource sufficiency, market growth, corruption and the level of regulation.

Resource sufficiency is one of the factors affecting the choice of ownership mode. Especially in resource-intensive industries (e.g. mining or metallurgy), securing natural resources is critical for corporate survival. Companies with higher levels of resource sufficiency are less dependent on resource supply and more independent of their external environment. By contrast, if a company has a lower level of resource sufficiency, it has greater resource dependency and may be vulnerable to external uncertainties. According to the resource dependency theory,[125] control over critical resources gives companies power over relationships with other companies.

However, when companies are unable to get critical resources on their own, they will try to make alliances or joint ventures with partners who have access to the sought-after resources.[126] Such JVs bring competitive advantages to both partners. Local host-country companies are assumed to have better access to local resources, thus companies entering resource-abundant countries prefer JVs with local firms to gain access to those resources.[127]

Market growth can be one of the factors for ownership mode decision. Market potential is one of the location advantages in the OLI theoretical framework. Companies seeking to enter foreign markets favor attractive markets, with attractiveness often characterized by either market potential or growth, both of which have been found to stimulate FDI.[128] In higher-growth countries, investment is expected to provide greater profitability since economies of scale can be achieved quickly and marginal costs drop faster.[129]

In addition, firms tend to invest in countries with large, juicy markets. Empirical studies have revealed the positive relationship between market size and FDI.[130] Consequently, companies often prefer higher ownership levels when investing in host countries with higher market growth and larger size.

Corruption is considered one of the factors influencing ownership choice. Some foreign investors consider corruption morally wrong and stay away from countries with high levels of corruption.[131] This can be explained because corruption disrupts the fair and efficient markets, and a corrupt economy does not provide open and equal market access to all competitors. Competition based on price and quality becomes less important since bribery takes place in secret. Consequently, foreign investors generally try to avoid corrupt host countries since this can increase business inefficiencies as well as distortions in the market. Some developed countries have implemented legal measures against companies that give in to corruption, making business in such countries difficult or illegal, and exposing top management to fines or prison terms.

Research results indicate the negative impact of high levels of non-transparency on FDI. Data from the early 1990s, covering twelve home countries to forty-five host countries, revealed that corruption had significant and negative effects on FDI.[132] Given a choice between a familiar and a less familiar environment in terms of corruption, firms will prefer the former. The concept of "psychic distance" also explains that companies enter foreign markets that are psychologically closer, taking into account the cultural, linguistic and institutional levels between home and host countries.[133]

The level of regulation in the host country also impacts ownership decisions. As could be expected, companies do not like environments with extensive regulatory control: too much red tape is a hindrance to getting business done. When governmental control exceeds an acceptable threshold, it adds management challenges, such as high costs and time wastage, and can even prevent smooth cooperation with local partners.

Extensive regulatory control increases transaction costs, limits firms' strategic options and decreases efficiency, thus reducing the probability of making profitable investments in the host country.[134] However, this does not imply that formal institutional safeguards should not exist in the host country. Scholars have emphasized the important role of formal institutions that provide stability, reduce uncertainty and alleviate information complexity in the business environment.[135] These institutions matter because they write laws and regulations, and proscribe unsuitable corporate behavior. Reasonable levels of regulation provide stable business environments, but beyond an acceptable threshold, the cost of doing business becomes exorbitant, and FDI dries up.

1.4 Internationalization of emerging market firms: what makes the difference?

The clear distinction between companies from emerging and developed markets was made in the 1970s and 1980s, with the rise of literature on so-called Third World multinationals,[136] or, using the current terminology, emerging multinationals. This first wave of interest was mostly concentrated on the so-called south–south operations: those from emerging country to emerging country.[137] The south–north investments (i.e. involving firms from emerging into developed markets) were mostly overlooked, but that has changed dramatically recently.[138] Emerging multinationals are now major players on a global scale, and not a week goes by without a south–north deal being revealed.

Are there differences between multinationals from developed and emerging markets? Although the debate rages, there is proof that pooled statistical treatment is inappropriate.[139] The existing theoretical approaches are also too broad to convincingly explain the internationalization processes of emerging multinationals.[140]

Empirical evidence from several recent studies[141] shows that emerging multinationals started their outbound FDI into developed countries by

- first growing through exports to developed (OECD – Organisation for Economic Co-operation Development) countries, thus acquiring knowledge through partnerships with multinationals from developed economies;

- second, imitating their business models and carrying out domestic mergers and acquisitions; and
- finally, investing abroad in other emerging countries.

Companies from emerging economies start their internationalization process in order to capture resources or critical knowledge, which could be technological know-how, human resources, managerial skills, global brands or R&D capabilities.[142]

Firms with high R&D expenditures expand almost simultaneously into their domestic and international markets, with overseas locations perceived as not simple additions to the home market, but rather as an important component of global presence. Companies with low R&D tend to focus first on their domestic market before internationalization, and they also tend to start with neighboring countries.

One of the commonly accepted viewpoints is that emerging multinationals (EMNEs) are primarily seeking learning opportunities rather than looking for strategic investments.[143] Some empirical studies support this statement. An investigation of Indian pharmaceutical companies uncovered that the main internationalization motive was seeking knowledge and resources by internationalizing their resource base and technology.[144]

In addition to this, EMNEs have other motives, such as escape from somewhat unstable and difficult business environments in their home country, which is referred to as "stability-seeking" or the "system-escape" motivation.[145] Nevertheless, this position is challenged by another viewpoint according to which EMNEs – even from emerging markets with permanent political and economic problems such as Russia – do less "escaping" than "investing" in their image or even country reputation.[146]

Cross-border acquisitions have become a popular way for EMNEs to enter foreign markets. Numerous studies of research institutes and other international organizations provide evidence of the foreign expansion of multinationals from emerging countries.

EMNEs usually skip some of the incremental stages of internationalization and also prefer expeditious M&A transactions over greenfield investments. This is the result of a need for accelerated learning and capability building as well as resource acquisition. It therefore comes as no surprise what Boston Consulting Group found in 2006: the largest 100 firms from emerging markets have internationalized to expand their global footprint. It was also found that the internationalization of these firms resulted not only from exports but also from using other entry modes such as cross-border M&A. In fact, fully 57% of cross-border acquisitions of the EMNE sample from 1985 until 2005 targeted firms in developed countries.[147]

Indian multinationals increased their cross-border acquisitions from 2004 until 2006 by 121%.[148] Even more impressive is the total value of these deals, which exploded twentyfold, from $0.9 billion in 2004 to $21 billion in 2006. India is not alone, with other emerging markets such as China, Brazil, Russia or Malaysia showing similar trends. The total value of Chinese cross-border deals was $12 billion in 2006, a 73% jump over 2005. Among the biggest deals were the $18.2 billion acquisition deal of the Canadian company Inco by the Brazilian mining giant Vale do Rio Doce, the $15.1 billion acquisition of Australian-based Rinker Group by Cemex of Mexico and the $12.5 billion acquisition of Corus Group (United Kingdom) by Tata Steel from India.

Within emerging markets, the role of institutions increases (see Chapter 4). The study of institutional impact across borders complements some of the previously mentioned theories – for example, OLI and TCA.[149] In parallel to the institution-based theory (what are the rules of the game and how to play according to those rules when they are not known and changing?), the co-evolution theoretical research studies how firms co-evolve along with their environment.[150] According to earlier studies,[151] one difference might be the increased uncertainty in emerging markets, which results from environmental changes and institutional transitions. While studies on co-evolution remain rare, research on political strategies suggests that firms operating in developed countries actively try to shape the rules of the game (e.g. by lobbying), whereas emerging multinationals (including some foreign entrants) naturally expect a strong reliance on political capital. Answering the question of "how do these companies accomplish that?" in a non-transparent regulatory and political environment is a great challenge and presents an interesting opportunity for further research.

Amazed by the increased activities and participation of firms from emerging markets in the global economy, scholars have further investigated the phenomenon. One study,[152] for example, investigated the impact of cross-border acquisitions on shareholder value creation. The analysis examined 425 cross-border acquisition deals by Indian firms from 2000 until 2007. The study provides evidence of "positive abnormal returns" for shareholders of the buying firm. Altogether, the conclusion arises that EMNEs use internationalization as a tool to acquire strategic assets from other markets to increase their competitiveness, particularly in times of institutional transitions. Cross-border M&As are a good means to internationalize, as they enable acquiring firms to transform their organization and strategy since they can reconfigure resources and capabilities.[153]

India definitely attracts academic interest. A second study[154] investigated how Indian companies acquire foreign firms to increase value, build new capabilities and learn from their activities abroad. In order to find evidence, the study tested a sample of 175 M&A deals from 2000 to 2006. This study confirms the importance of prior international experience in cross-border acquisitions, particularly when target firms are fully acquired (100% ownership). It further seems that buyers intending to acquire 100% ownership consider industry-specific experience as essential before taking on acquisitions, while this is not the case for joint ventures, where ownership and control is split and shared among all engaged parties.

Within JVs, the division and distribution of resources between subsidiaries allows experience and know-how to be better leveraged; it also diversifies the investment portfolio across different markets. The Indian analysis studied the influence of several variables. Cultural distance and full ownership both have a positive influence on the value of acquisitions. When Indian firms are the buyers, the study found that most deals were conducted in culturally distant countries (developed markets). By contrast to culturally similar countries such as Pakistan or Bangladesh, developed markets offer access, for example, to advanced technologies.

According to a 2014 study,[155] one difference between developed multinationals and EMNEs is in the level of ownership stakes taken. Examining cross-border entry modes, with a specific focus on control and equity levels, the study indicates that developed multinationals, particularly in the high-tech sector, acquire significantly more ownership than EMNEs. The explanation is simple: EMNEs face more uncertainty in high-tech industries and need to be more prudent with this kind of takeover.

When investments involve intellectual property (IP) rights, and are being considered in host countries with large institutional distances (from the home country), companies tend to acquire full, rather than partial, ownership so as to protect their technologies and know-how. This finding holds for both EMNEs and developed multinationals. Companies prefer to shield their know-how through full ownership if the IP protection in the host country is weak, irrespective of the degree of IP protection in the home country.

EMNEs and developed multinationals also have different behaviors regarding market access when investing in host countries with high institutional distance. In such cases, companies from developed countries acquire less control of the target firm, while emerging market firms acquire more control.[156]

Why do EMNEs decide to expand outside their home market? This theme has been extensively researched,[157] and one of the principal findings is that over the last two decades, emerging multinationals have sought to catch up with their developed counterparts. They feel increasing pressure from EMNEs in a highly competitive global environment. Therefore, scholars argue, developed multinationals must beware! It is essential to closely monitor the strategic international activities of EMNEs so as to defend competitive advantages.

As noted previously, motivations for internationalization have been classified extensively. Yet with the increasing importance of south-north FDI, should there be a rethinking of these motives and their classification? Should value-chain considerations be more closely monitored? One 2014 study[158] proposes six categories for foreign investment motivations:

1   end-customer market seeking
2   natural resource seeking
3   downstream and upstream knowledge seeking
4   efficiency seeking
5   global value consolidation seeking
6   geopolitical influence seeking.

Based upon this updated framework, the study indicates that the main reasons for the internationalization of EMNEs are the seeking of end-consumer markets, global value consolidation and additional knowledge.

Emerging markets are often associated with the term *state capitalism*, especially China and Russia. It was even suggested to investigate China's economic growth using comparative and historical studies, since the research based on Western economic frameworks fails to provide clear explanations.[159] A very important variable is the extent to which EMNEs are affiliated with the government or its agencies. The government may exert a strong influence on EMNE expansion abroad, but the impact depends on the degree of the affiliation with the state, the level of state ownership in the EMNE, and on the state's ambitions. Governments have different ways of influencing EMNE expansion, including different institutional pressures: the level of foreign investments, their locations or the target industrial sectors. Yet one can lead the horse to water but one cannot force it to drink. In the end, the extent of internationalization will depend on the company's abilities, resources and competitive advantages.

A very common characteristic of emerging markets is their institutional instability, which can exert a strong influence on EMNE's strategies.[160] Companies have to develop ways to operate under this instability and to quickly adapt to unexpected changes. In order to survive, these companies attempt to control this uncertainty through political give and take. One important source of this instability is unstable rules and regulations, leaving the company to operate in the so-called grey zone. The quality of governance offered by the state varies greatly due to evolving democratic, financial and legal institutions.

In countries with powerful states, managers must kowtow to the state (or the dominant political party) in order to ensure the survival of the company. In cases where company profitability is greatly dependent on political connections, top managers may be sidetracked to focus on political struggles to the detriment of business operations.[161]

On the other hand, strategically important companies may benefit from government protection – for example via artificial entry barriers limiting the intrusion of foreign players on home turf. This may result in higher domestic prices, leading in turn to higher profitability.

China presents somewhat of a unique panorama, with both state-owned EMNEs (e.g. PetroChina) and recent successful private EMNEs (e.g. Legend Computers). Both flavors differ considerably from developed multinationals operating within China, which can be explained by differences in the institutional environment.[162] State-owned multinationals are more fixed asset seeking, as opposed to private multinationals, which are more interested in relational assets. Chinese state-owned MNEs have a better survival rate, and their internationalization motives are not based on economic rationale alone, which sets them apart from privately owned EMNEs. These have different internationalization motives, entry strategies, managerial capabilities and performance potentials.

In Russia, the government also plays an important role in the emergence of Russian MNEs and in outbound FDI from Russia. State-owned enterprises possess a set of advantages (financial capabilities, access to loans from the central bank, administrative support, etc.) that have facilitated their internationalization. At the same time, even in fully or partly privatized enterprises, state influence remains significant, sometimes directly (for example, through residual ownership) and sometimes indirectly.[163] However, government influence varies by industry, being particularly strong in the energy sector and taking only an indirect form in other sectors by incentivizing their development.

In Brazil, the federal government retains much power, and since the 1990s, the role of the state in international business has increased. State-owned companies receive funds and consulting support when planning to internationalize. This support includes participation in international trade fairs, seminars and training programs, or attracting the best students to local universities. In this sense, in order to be successful in Brazil, both domestic and international firms should consider not only local authorities but also the Brazilian federal government as well.[164]

Conclusion

This book adheres to the views that the internationalization strategies of emerging market firms are shaped by institutional, industry and firm-level determinants. Additionally, sector-specific factors influence the appearance of particular strategic patterns, modified according to the resources and capabilities of individual firms. The role of macro institutions in emerging countries is particularly evident in certain industries, where it strongly affects the competitive panorama, technology standards and resources for innovative development, as well as overall growth priorities.[165] In emerging countries, there exist firms whose strategies differ from common patterns. This confirms theoretical assumptions about the co-existence of firm-level determinants as well as direct government influences.

This chapter has opened the debate about the distinctive nature of the geographic expansion of emerging market firms. In this regard, scholars need to differentiate more systematically between existing theoretical approaches and address the variety of these approaches. Managers can also find value here. A better understanding of the complexity of the forces and factors affecting international expansion will provide underpinnings for developing the strategy formulation for their companies. Taking into account the different factors that influence international corporate operations enables planners to work in a more informed context.

References

1 Johanson and Wiedersheim 1975.
2 Reid 1981; Bilkey and Tesar 1977; Johanson and Vahlne 1977.
3 Welch and Luostarinen 1988.
4 Andersen 1993.
5 Elango and Pattnaik 2007.
6 Andersen 1993; Buckley and Casson 1998.
7 Ghanatabadi 2005.
8 Bell 2004.
9 Boddewyn et al. 1986; Katrishen and Scordis 1998.
10 Johanson and Valhne 1990.
11 Majkgård and Sharma 1998.
12 Erramilli 1990; Ekeledo and Sivakumar 1998.
13 Pauwels and Ruyter 2005.
14 Javalgi and Martin 2007.
15 Sanchez-Peinado and Pla-Barber 2006.
16 Erramilli 1990.
17 Cardone-Riportella and Cazorla-Papis' 2001.
18 Wortzel and Vernon-Wortzel 1988.
19 Johanson and Vahlne 1977.
20 Vernon 1966.
21 Aulakh et al. 2000.
22 Ansoff 1989.
23 Brouthers and Brouthers 2000; Buckley and Casson 1981; Dunning 1981, 1988, 1993, 1998; Hennart 1982; Hennart and Park 1993; Kogut and Singh 1988.
24 Czinkota and Ronkainen 2004.
25 Ibid.
26 Bartlett and Ghoshal 1989.
27 Kim 2003.
28 Ghemawat 2001.
29 e.g. Bartlet and Ghoshal 1989.
30 Ansoff 1989.
31 Johanson and Vahlne 1977.
32 Turnbull 1987.
33 Welch and Luostarinen 1988.
34 Buckley and Ghauri 1999.
35 Bartlett and Ghoshal 1989; Buckley and Casson 1981; Dunning 1981, 1988, 1993, 1998; Gatignon and Anderson 1988; Hennart 1982; Luo and Tung 2007; Puig et al. 2014.
36 Dunning 1981, 1988, 1993, 1998.
37 Caves 1971, 1982; Hennart 1982; Kindleberger 1984; Rugman 1982.
38 Buckley and Casson 1981.
39 Chung and Enderwick 2001.
40 Granstrand and Sjolander 1990; Prahalad and Hamel 1990.
41 Buckley and Ghauri 1999.
42 Child and Rodrigues 2005.
43 Luo and Tung 2007.
44 Zaheer 1995.
45 Ahsan and Musteen 2011.
46 Johanson and Vahlne 1977; Johanson and Wiedersheim 1975.
47 Chan et al. 2008; Gaur et al. 2007; Meyer et al. 2009.
48 Levine and Renelt 1992.
49 Arregle et al. 2012.
50 Brouthers and Bamossy 1997.
51 Zaheer and Mosakowski 1997.
52 Mroczek 2014.
53 Goerzen and Beamish 2003; Hitt et al. 1997.
54 Barkema and Vermeulen 1998; Hennart and Park 1993.

55 Agarwal and Ramaswami 1992; Anderson and Gatignon 1986; Hennart 1991.
56 Brouthers and Brouthers 2000; Hennart and Park 1993; Kogut and Singh 1988.
57 Brouthers and Brouthers 2000.
58 Mani et al. 2007.
59 Buckley et al. 2008.
60 Zejan 1990.
61 Hennart and Park 1993.
62 Tse et al. 1997.
63 Kogut and Singh 1988.
64 Anderson and Gatignon 1986; Brouther and Brouther 2000; Gatignon and Anderson 1988; Hennart 1982; Hennart and Park 1993.
65 Hollensen et al. 2011.
66 Chung and Enderwick 2001.
67 Dong et al. 2008.
68 Brookes and Roper 2010.
69 Root 1994.
70 Driscoll and Paliwoda 1997.
71 Hollensen 2001.
72 Lee and Carter 2005.
73 Wach 2014.
74 Johanson and Vahlne 2009.
75 Griffin and Pustay 1995.
76 Root 1994.
77 Hoy and Stanworth 2003.
78 Qui and Wang 2011.
79 Harzing 2002.
80 Lee and Lieberman 2010.
81 Granstrand and Sjolander 1990; Prahalad and Hamel 1990.
82 Wernerfelt 1984.
83 Granstrand and Sjolander 1990; Prahalad and Hamel 1990.
84 Hennart and Park 1993.
85 Caves 1982.
86 Ravenscraft and Scherer 1987.
87 Chatterjee et al. 1992; Datta et al., 1991; Jemison and Sitkin 1986.
88 Delacroix 1993.
89 Hennart and Park 1993.
90 Hofstede 1991.
91 Barkema and Vermeulen 1998.
92 Fan et al. 2012; Dai and Lahiri 2011.
93 Nocke and Whinston 2013.
94 Brouthers and Brouthers 2000.
95 Hennart and Park 1993; Kogut and Singh 1988.
96 Andersson and Svensson 1994; Barkema and Vermeulen 1998; Brouthers and Brouthers 2000.
97 Hennart and Park 1993.
98 Ibid.
99 Kogut and Singh 1988.
100 Andersson and Svensson 1994.
101 Ibid.; Caves and Mehra 1986; Zejan 1990.
102 Brouther and Brouther 2000.
103 Caves and Mehra 1986; Hennart and Park 1993.
104 Johanson and Vahlne 1977; Johanson and Wiedersheim 1975.
105 Barkema and Vermeulen 1998.
106 Caves 1982; Chatterjee et al. 1992; Datta et al. 1991; Jemison and Sitkin 1986.
107 Hofstede 1980.
108 Hennart and Park 1993.
109 Brouthers and Brouthers 2000.
110 Kogut and Singh 1988.
111 Jemison and Sitkin 1986.

112 Brouthers and Brouthers 2000.
113 Panibratov 2009, Agarwal and Ramaswami 1992; Anderson and Gatignon 1986; Dunning 1981, 1988, 1993, 1998.
114 Hennart 1991; Hennart and Park 1993; Makino and Neupert 2000; Mani et al. 2007.
115 Hennart 1988.
116 Johanson and Vahlne 1977; Johanson and Wiedersheim-Paul 1975; Kogut and Singh 1988.
117 Kogut and Singh 1988.
118 Agarwal and Ramaswami 1992.
119 Dunning 1981, 1988, 1993, 1998.
120 Agarwal and Ramaswami 1992; Dunning 1988, 1998.
121 Anderson and Gatignon 1986; Gatignon and Anderson 1988; Hennart 1982; Hennart and Park 1993.
122 Anderson and Gatignon 1986.
123 Agarwal and Ramaswami 1992; Hill et al. 1990; Woodcock et al. 1994.
124 Barney 1991; Peteraf 1993.
125 Pfeffer and Salancik 1978.
126 Hennart and Reddy 1997.
127 Gomes-Casseres 1990.
128 Terpstra and Yu 1988; Weinstein 1977.
129 Agarwal and Ramaswami 1992; Sabi 1988.
130 Davidson 1980; Dunning 1973.
131 Habib and Zurawicki 2002.
132 Ibid.; Drabek and Warren 1999; Wei 2000a.
133 Johanson and Vahlne 1977; Johanson and Wiedersheim 1975.
134 Brouthers and Brouthers 2000; Loree and Guisinger 1995.
135 North 1990; Williamson 2000.
136 e.g., Wells 1983.
137 Lall 1983.
138 Ramamurti 2009; Panibratov 2012.
139 Caves 2007.
140 Chittoor 2009.
141 Balcet and Bruschieri 2010; Gammeltoft et al. 2010.
142 Tsai and Eisingerich 2010.
143 e.g. Narula 2010.
144 Chittoor 2009.
145 Kalotay 2003; Bulatov 1998.
146 Panibratov 2012.
147 Aulakh 2007.
148 Thomson Reuters' SDC Platinum.
149 Peng et al. 2008.
150 Lewin and Volberda 1999.
151 Peng and Zhou 2005.
152 Gubbi et al. 2010.
153 Ibid.
154 Elango and Pattnaik 2007.
155 De Beule et al. 2014.
156 Ibid.
157 Moghaddam et al. 2014; Dunning 1988.
158 Moghaddam et al. 2014.
159 Fligstein and Zhang 2011.
160 Farashahi and Hafsi 2009.
161 Ibid.
162 Liu and Scott-Kennel 2011.
163 Panibratov 2012.
164 Fleury and Fleury 2011.
165 Mihailova and Panibratov 2012.

2 The rise of emerging economies
BRIC and beyond

This chapter provides some historical background for the emerging markets within the BRIC quartet over the recent decades. At the same time, the importance of other developing economies is highlighted and the origins of their economic growth are considered. The inward and the outward investment perspectives for emerging markets and location attractiveness for inward and outward FDI is discussed, both from academic and business viewpoints. Finally, special attention is paid to the Russian market, the least studied, yet promising in terms of growth potential and market transformations.

2.1 Historical background of the emerging economies (EEs)

In the 1970s, there was clear distinction between industrialized countries such as the United States, Western Europe and Japan, and the "less-developed countries" (LDC) that constituted the rest of the world. Those countries were considered risky, but with good profit potential. In the 1980s, the "less-developed" term was deemed politically incorrect and "emerging market" took its place. While global organizations, financial institutions, policy agencies and researchers still do not agree on what constitutes an emerging market, several definitions are worth consideration.

The *Financial Times* provides the following definition of an emerging market: a term that investors use to describe a developing country in which investment would be expected to achieve higher returns but be accompanied by greater risk.[1] In 1988, stock exchange research company MSCI, defined an emerging market as a country that has some characteristics of a developed market but does not meet the standards to be considered developed.[2] An emerging market is defined in terms of the number of quoted companies of a certain size and the proportion of shares available for investors to buy, plus consideration of the market's openness to foreign ownership and capital. According to MSCI, the major characteristics of an emerging market include:

- fast economic growth
- fast urbanization
- young population
- political instability
- infrastructure problems
- currency volatility
- limited equity opportunities
- lower to middle level of per capita income
- weak development of formal institutions
- important role of the state.

The following definition for an emerging market was proposed:

> A society transitioning from a dictatorship to a free-market oriented economy with increasing economic freedom, gradual integration with the global marketplace and with other members of the GEM (Global Emerging Market), an expanding middle class with improving standards of living, social stability and tolerance, as well as increasing cooperation with multilateral institutions.[3]

At the beginning of the 2010s, about fifty countries in the world, representing about 60% of the global population and 45% of the global GDP, could be considered as emerging markets. Table 2.1 summarizes how six renowned international organizations classify various countries considered as emerging markets. The BRIC quartet appears consistently in every index as well as Mexico, Indonesia, the Philippines, South Africa and Turkey.

Table 2.1 Emerging markets according to different sources

Country	IMF (Int'l Monetary Fund)	BRICS+ Next Eleven	FTSE (Financial Time Stock Exchange)	MSCI	S&P (Standard & Poor's)	Dow Jones
Argentina	+					
Bangladesh	+	+	+	+	+	
Brazil	+	+	+	+	+	+
Bulgaria	+					
Chile	+		+	+	+	+
China	+	+	+	+	+	+
Colombia	+		+	+	+	+
Czech Republic			+	+	+	+
Egypt		+	+	+	+	+
Greece				+	+	+
Hungary	+		+	+	+	+
India	+	+	+	+	+	+
Indonesia	+	+	+	+	+	+
Iran		+				
Israel						
Malaysia	+		+	+	+	+
Mauritius						
Mexico	+	+	+	+	+	+
Nigeria		+				
Oman						
Pakistan	+	+	+			
Peru	+		+	+	+	+
Philippines	+	+	+	+	+	+

(*Continued*)

Table 2.1 (Continued)

Country	IMF (Int'l Monetary Fund)	BRICS+ Next Eleven	FTSE (Financial Time Stock Exchange)	MSCI	S&P (Standard & Poor's)	Dow Jones
Poland	+		+	+	+	+
Qatar				+		+
Romania	+					
Russia	+	+	+	+	+	+
Slovenia						
South Africa	+	+	+	+	+	+
South Korea		+		+		
Taiwan			+	+	+	+
Thailand	+		+	+	+	+
Turkey	+	+	+	+	+	+
Ukraine	+					
United Arab Emirates			+	+		+
Venezuela	+					
Vietnam		+				

Today, emerging markets are becoming powerful forces and agents of change in the global landscape.[4] Among the seventeen largest economies by GDP based on PPP (purchasing power parity) valuation in 2015, eight are emerging markets (Figure 2.1).

Trends in FDI flows also demonstrate the growing importance of emerging markets in the global economy. Between 1997 and 2003, emerging market firms engaged in cross-border transactions represented 4% of the value of all global M&A deals. Between 2004 and 2010, this percent increased to 17% of the global total. More than one-third of FDI inflows to emerging markets originate from other emerging markets. According to the United Nations Conference on Trade and Development (UNCTAD), in 2015, emerging markets reached a record for inbound FDI, which reached $741 billion, almost half of total FDI. Asia remains the largest destination for foreign investment. Moreover, emerging economies continue to make up half of the top-ten FDI host economies in 2015 (Figure 2.2).

The World Bank forecasts that the annual value of cross-border M&A transactions undertaken by emerging market firms will double by 2025, while the annual number of cross-border M&A deals is expected to more than triple (from fewer than 2,500 in 2011 to almost 8,000 in 2025). This trend outpaces the underlying GDP growth rates for emerging countries.

2.2 The BRIC quartet of emerging giants

In 2001, Jim O'Neill, chief economist at Goldman Sachs Asset Management, coined the acronym BRIC in the paper "Building Better Global Economic BRICs,"[5] to refer to Brazil, Russia, India and China. Together they represent over 25% of the world's land coverage

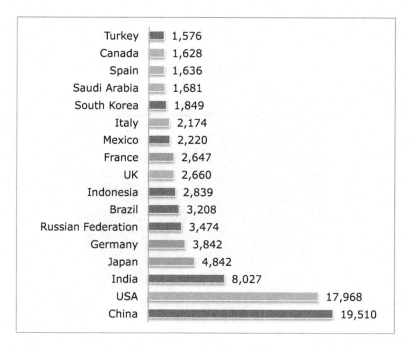

Figure 2.1 The largest economies in 2015

Source: IMF World Forum Outlook, 2015 ("World Economic Outlook Database." International Monetary Fund. April 2016)

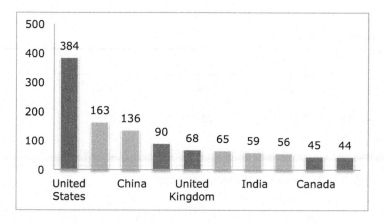

Figure 2.2 Estimated FDI inflows: top-ten host economies in 2015 ($ billions)

Source: Global Investment Trends Monitor, No 22, P.3, UNCTAD, 2015 (http://unctad.org/en/PublicationsLibrary/webdiaeia2016d1_en.pdf)

and 40% of the world's population (Figure 2.3). They were considered to be at similar stages of economic development, and some experts argue that, owing to population size, abundance of resources and speed of progress, in the next decades, they will become more important powers than current global leaders – for example, the G7.[6]

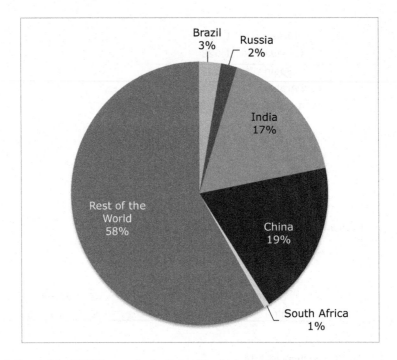

Figure 2.3 Share of the BRICS countries in the world population, 2013

Source: BRICS Joint Statistical Publication 2015, p. 17 (http://www.gks.ru/free_doc/doc_2015/BRICS_ENG.pdf)

Table 2.2 General statistics 2014

Categories	Brazil	Russia	India	China
GDP (PPP), constant, US$ billion	3,113.8	3,402.9	7,044.6	17,188.7
GDP per capita, US$	15,110	23,293	5,439	12,599
GDP growth, annual, %	0.1	0.6	7.3	7.3
Population, total	206,077,898	143,819,569	1,295,291,543	1,364,270,000

Source: The World Bank (http://www.worldbank.org/en/country)

Initially, there was no thought of an alliance, but since 2009, the leaders of the BRIC countries have converged close enough to hold annual summits so as to put common interests on public display.[7] The overarching interest is to convert their economic power into enhanced geopolitical status.

Nowadays these four countries are among the largest and fastest-growing emerging economies. In 2014, the total gross domestic product (GDP) of the BRICS quintet (S stands for South Africa, which joined the group in 2009) reached 30% of the world's GDP, according to IMF statistics.

Brazil

Macro overview

From 2003 to 2013, Brazil experienced a decade of miraculous economic and social progress, lifting over twenty-six million people out of poverty. Inequality was reduced significantly (the Gini Coefficient has fallen 6% in 2013 to 0.54).[8] According to the World Bank, the income of the bottom 40% of the population grew on average 6.1% (in real terms) between 2002 and 2012, compared to overall income growth of 3.5%. Alas, since 2013, the reductions in poverty and inequality have been stagnating.

GDP growth in Brazil has been a dynamic 4.5% annually from 2006 to 2010; however, it has slowed down to 2.1% annually from 2011 to 2014, and disappeared to 0.1% in 2014. Inflation remains high at 6.4% in 2014. See general economic indicators in Table 2.3.

In the recent decades (since the structural reforms of the 1990s), one of the goals for Brazil was the development of an efficient financial system committed to leading the country towards global credit and financial stability.[9] The Brazilian Central Bank has managed the whole system for over twenty years and has also been responsible for controlling the investment framework for foreign capital movement in the country.

Brazil's government introduced a system of tax incentives to encourage investment in the less-developed regions of the country (namely, the Amazon and northeast regions), both for domestic and foreign investors.[10] Even so, the majority of investments remain concentrated in the more industrialized parts of the state.

Brazil's poor-quality infrastructure is notorious. Its rail network is flimsy – the United States with similar land area has a network more than seven times larger – and its roads are in a parlous state of repair, of which only 14% were paved in 2012. This adds costs to doing business, in terms of both money and time. In 2013, the government acted to improve investment in infrastructure and Olympics-related projects should also have some impact.

Reliance on credit-fueled consumption and a lack of investment have led to economic imbalances. Consumer lending in Brazil outpaced that of the other BRICs in 2012 and gross fixed capital formation (18.1% of GDP in 2012) was the lowest of the four economies. A lack of domestic savings makes Brazil dependent on inflows of foreign capital, which at a time of heightened volatility in markets is a clear risk.

For a large economy, Brazil is not a big player in terms of global trade (Table 2.4). In 2012, it ranked as the twenty-second largest exporter globally, far behind Russia, India and China, and accounted for just 7.8% of total BRIC exports. This indicates a lack of global competitiveness, particularly visible in manufacturing.

Lastly, Brazil suffers from a weak currency, just like many emerging markets. Depreciating currencies make exports cheaper and the weaker Real has been a contributing factor

Table 2.3 Brazil. Economic indicators (US$, million)

	2005	2010	2013	2014
GDP, current	882,044	2,143,035	2,243,854	2,199,538
GDP per capita, current US$	4,739	10,978	11,199	10,887
Real GDP growth, y-on-y, %	3.16	7.53	2.49	0.1

Source: UNCTAD 2016 (http://unctadstat.unctad.org/CountryProfile/GeneralProfile/en-GB/076/index.html)

Table 2.4 Brazil. Total merchandise trade (US$, million)

	2005	2010	2013	2014
Merchandise exports	118,529	201,915	242,034	225,101
Merchandise imports	77,628	191,537	250,559	239,150
Merchandise trade balance	40,901	10,378	−8,526	−14,049

Source: UNCTAD 2016 (http://unctadstat.unctad.org/CountryProfile/GeneralProfile/en-GB/076/index.html)

in the acceleration of Brazil's container trade which according to data from Maersk rose by 3.8% in the second quarter of 2013 over the previous quarter. However, a weak currency also fuels inflation by increasing the cost of imports.

Institutional environment

The investment climate in Brazil is traditionally famous for its openness. Foreign capital can freely enter and exit the country, even though a limited number of government-protected sectors exist to safeguard some strategic areas. Foreign companies in Brazil are treated on par with domestic ones, by both government and legal institutions. The Brazilian government seeks to promote new investments and is also willing to provide support to investors seeking advisory services. Tax incentives are generally given at both federal and municipal levels.

According to the EY Business Attractiveness Survey (2012), the top-two business attractions are the huge size of market (for 86.5% of respondents), followed by the solid entrepreneurial culture (71.9%). This implies a favorable business environment and funding support for the companies. On the negative scale, local labor skills were preoccupying for investors.[11] Overall, however, investors have a generally positive view of Brazilian institutions and the political environment, especially in comparison with other emerging economies such as India and Russia.

Access to open financial markets for foreign investors helped to increase overall transparency, since foreign portfolio investors place great importance on information and policy disclosure.[12]

Corruption, fraud and bribery are the most significant issues that Brazilian businesses face nowadays. Transparency International has placed Brazil in sixty-ninth place out of 175 countries in their corruption perception index of 2014.[13] Despite this worrisome statistic, Brazil still manages to host a great deal of foreign investment.

Foreign direct investment

The major international investors in Brazil are companies from the United States, the United Kingdom, Japan, Spain, Germany and China. The main sectors for incoming investment are information and communication technology (ICT) or the industrial sectors (59%), services (27%), retail and consumer products (10%). Barely 4% aims for strategic services such as R&D or education and training.

The Brazilian ICT segment is the world's seventh largest, and the leader in Latin America; it attracted 105 FDI projects in 2011, about 21% of the total number in the country. For 2014, the government is targeting large infrastructure projects including extending broadband access, launching 4G services and 100% telephone coverage in rural areas. These are the key drivers that will push ICT investments forward.

There are a number of industries where multinationals (e.g. Toshiba, IBM, HP, Accenture, Infosys) are already in Brazil via strategic partnerships or acquisitions (e.g. IBM and EBX Group; IBM and Automacao) alongside large foreign players such as Telefónica (Spain), Vivendi (France), Telmex (Mexico) and others.

The manufacturing and retail sectors (accounting for 19% and 10%, respectively, of total FDI projects in the country) are important priorities, given Brazil's policy on increasing middle-class wealth. This has brought multinationals such as Siemens, ArcelorMittal and Doosan (all of them operating mainly through their subsidiaries) into the market. Other companies that have been in Brazil for years plan to continue their market penetration: Nestlé, Danone, Kraft Foods and L'Oréal have recently announced expansion plans in Brazil's retail and consumer products sector.

As in any open economy, Brazilian companies are expanding to other markets. Brazil is home to a vast array of natural resources and is a leading producer of beef, poultry, orange juice, sugar, coffee, soybeans, iron, ore, copper and ethanol. With globalization, capital flows have been easier and investments have increased. In 2013, foreign direct investment into Brazil reached $64 billion, coming primarily from Holland, the United States and Luxemburg.

However, the number of international firms operating in Brazil is below the country's potential because of its poor business environment. Brazil ranks only 130 out of 185 countries in the World Bank's Doing Business, placing it behind China and Russia. A complex tax system and overly bureaucratic processes weaken its business environment. Brazil's FDI flows are presented in Graph 2.1.

Russia

Macro overview

Russia has undergone significant changes since the collapse of the Soviet Union in 1991, moving from a globally isolated, centrally planned economy to a more market-based and

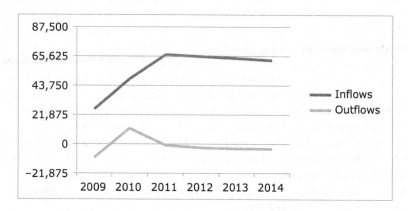

Graph 2.1 Brazil FDI flows

Source: UNCTAD 2016 (http://unctadstat.unctad.org/CountryProfile/GeneralProfile/en-GB/076/index.html)

Table 2.5 Russia. Economic indicators (US$, million)

	2005	*2010*	*2013*	*2014*
GDP, current	764,016	1,524,917	2,096,774	1,865,328
GDP per capita, current US$	5,308	10,618	14,680	13,093
Real GDP growth, y-on-y, %	6.38	4.50	1.32	0.6

Source: UNCTAD 2016 (http://unctadstat.unctad.org/CountryProfile/GeneralProfile/en-GB/643/index.html)

Table 2.6 Russia. Total merchandise trade (US$, million)

	2005	*2010*	*2013*	*2014*
Merchandise exports	243,798	400,630	523,276	497,764
Merchandise imports	125,434	248,634	341,335	308,027
Merchandise trade balance	118,364	151,996	181,941	189,737

Source: UNCTAD 2016 (http://unctadstat.unctad.org/CountryProfile/GeneralProfile/en-GB/643/index.html)

globally integrated economy. Economic reforms in the 1990s privatized most industries, with the energy and defense-related sectors as notable exceptions. Yet the protection of property rights is still weak, and the private sector remains subject to heavy state
interference.

In 2011, Russia became the world's leading oil producer, surpassing Saudi Arabia; Russia
is the second-largest producer of natural gas; Russia holds the world's largest natural gas
reserves, the second-largest coal reserves and the eighth-largest crude oil reserves. Russia is
also a top exporter of metals such as steel and primary aluminium. The general economic
indicators and Russian merchandise trade are presented in Tables 2.5 and 2.6.

Russia's reliance on commodity exports makes it vulnerable to the boom and bust cycles
that follow volatile swings in global prices. Since 2007, the government has embarked
on an ambitious program to reduce this dependency and build up the country's high-
technology sectors, but with few visible results so far. The economy had averaged 7%
growth in the decade following the 1998 Russian financial crisis, resulting in a doubling
of real disposable incomes and the emergence of a middle class.

The Russian economy, however, was one of the hardest hit by the 2008–2009 global
economic crisis, as oil prices plummeted. The foreign credits that Russian banks and firms
relied on also dried up. According to the World Bank, the government's anti-crisis package in 2008–2009 amounted to roughly 6.7% of GDP. The recession bottomed out in
mid-2009 and growth kicked in again as of the third quarter of 2009.

High oil prices buoyed Russian growth in 2011–2012 and helped reduce the recession's
budget deficit. Russia has reduced its unemployment to a record low of 5.5% (2012)[14] and
has capped inflation below double-digit rates. In an attempt to reduce trade barriers for
foreign goods and services and open additional export markets, Russia joined the World
Trade Organization (WTO) in 2012.

In 2015, Russia again fell into recession, with a severe impact on households.[15] A tense
geopolitical context marked by ongoing international sanctions meant the economy

continued to adjust to the 2014 terms-of-trade shock. Low oil & gas prices further underscored Russia's vulnerability to volatile global commodity markets. Although the weak ruble created a price advantage for some industries, encouraging investments in some sectors and a narrow range of exports, it was not sufficient to provoke an overall increase in non-energy exports.

The 2015 economic and geopolitical situation caused private investment to decline drastically, as capital costs rose and consumer demand fell. The erosion of real income increased the poverty rate and the vulnerability of the poorest 40% of the population.[16]

Institutional environment

The role of Russian institutions in terms of the outbound foreign direct investment (OFDI) is influential. For example, there is governmental pressure on companies such as Lukoil to invest more in Kazakhstan rather than in other countries. Russian investments favor the CIS (Commonwealth of Independent States) countries in comparison to the rest of the world due to common history, similar language, geographic proximity and other cultural ties.

However, Russian OFDI to the West is a top priority for many companies that resist strong political and state involvement. Hence Russian foreign policy cannot be considered as the sole determinant of choice for outbound investment. No one can claim, for example, that it is by government writ that the Virgin Islands are an FDI choice, since it is Russian companies who seek tax havens as a way of escaping the system.

Unlike incoming FDI into Russia, which attracts large media attention, Russian OFDI has not attracted attention in terms of the relationship between host country and the Russian investing companies. The biggest portion of Russia's OFDI are investments in natural resources, such as Lukoil's ownership stakes in oilfields in Azerbaijan, Kazakhstan and Uzbekistan, plus refineries and gas stations around Europe and the United States.[17]

However, outbound investments are not only linked "system-escape" motives (to easily accessible tax havens) but also substantially influenced by the opaque Russian business environment. Russian OFDI is often viewed with suspicion and sometimes linked to organized crime and corruption, with the Russian government's involvement. An example of this occurred in 2009 when Russian oil company Surgutneftegaz acquired 21.2% of the Hungarian energy company MOL.[18] This investment was perceived as politically connected since it occurred when Gazprom and the Russian government tried to strengthen their dominance of pipeline network in southeastern Europe via the South Stream gas pipeline, competitor to Nabucco, a Western gas project. Other reasons to suspect the transparency of this deal were the very secretive character of Surgutneftegaz (knowing that the company had no previous OFDI) and that the stake in MOL was acquired at double its market value.[19]

Subsequently, the role of the state-owned multinationals in Russian OFDI is larger than in developed countries. Political aspects are important in Russian OFDI: for instance, the Russian embassies are regular suppliers of crucial information for Russian companies to establish initial contacts with foreign companies. Political support from government institutions is often used to reduce protectionism in countries such as Belarus or Venezuela.[20]

Furthermore, the influence of state institutions in Russian OFDI can be seen through schemes such as "investment-for-debts," enabling some firms to keep high domestic debts because of their international projects. At the same time, this kind of cooperation carries political liabilities, since these companies are tied to Russia's foreign policy and interests.

For instance, the critics say that the biggest factor that influenced Russia's OFDI in Asia were political interests.

All things considered, state support for Russian MNEs is quite weak due to the lack of developed policy instruments. For instance, the Russian export insurance agency that assists multinationals with export credits and OFDI was only established in 2011. Financial support for exports remains in its early stages, and many Russian financial institutions are not rushing in, since they view this as highly risky.

Foreign direct investment

FDI into Russia has very specific characteristics. This specificity is part of the complex relationship that the Russian economy has maintained since the beginning of its transition (over twenty years ago) with international capital transfers. Russia was first marked in the 1990s by the collapse of domestic investment and a massive flight of capital combined with a very low capacity to attract incoming investment from abroad. It was only starting in the 2000s that the tide turned: domestic investment recovered its growth, accompanied by a return of foreign capital inflows; however, this trend reversal was not observed regarding flights of capital, which are still considerable today and primarily motivated by tax evasion. The contrasting developments are not the only paradox when it comes to the Russian economy.

The rapid growth of FDI after the August 1998 market crash was spectacular. From 1992 to 1998, inbound FDI into Russia did not exceed $1.4 billion annually. Thanks to the economic recovery that began in 1999, the FDI valve opened wide, making Russia one of the leading global recipients during the mid-2000s. However, the 2008–2009 crisis dried that fountainhead. Since then growth has resumed but pre-crisis levels have not yet been reclaimed.

On the international level, Russia is favorably positioned. As of the second half of the 2000s, its rank as a destination for FDI considerably improved, placing it in the top-ten worldwide since 2007. Russia also became the leading destination for FDI in Eastern Europe. Unhappily, due to the political tensions with the United States and Europe in 2013–2014 due to the Crimea and Ukraine crises, Russia's FDI flows (both inward and outward) collapsed (see Graph 2.2).

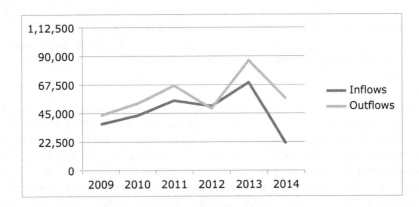

Graph 2.2 Russia FDI flows

Source: UNCTAD 2016 (http://unctadstat.unctad.org/CountryProfile/GeneralProfile/en-GB/643/index.html)

At the same time, Russia has sought to cement economic ties with countries in the former Soviet space through a customs union with Belarus and Kazakhstan, and in the next several years through the creation of a new Russia-led economic zone called the Eurasian Economic Union. Russia has had difficulty attracting foreign direct investment and has experienced large capital outflows in the past several years leading to official programs to improve Russia's international investment climate rankings.

India

Macroeconomic overview

India is the world's fourth-largest economy, with a population of 1.2 billion. Its economic development has been one of the most significant achievements of our times.[21] More than six decades since independence from Britain, India has succeeded its agricultural revolution, transforming the nation from chronic dependence on grain imports into a global net exporter of food. Recent Indian achievements include the doubling of life expectancy, improvements in health conditions, significant increases in literacy levels and the emergence of a strong middle class.

India is known today as the host for impressive pharmaceutical, steel, IT and space technology companies with global reputations. Very soon, India will have the largest and youngest workforce the world has ever seen.[22]

At the same time, India has witnessed the largest rural–urban migration of this century. Over ten million people each year move to cities and towns seeking jobs and opportunities. General economic indicators and Indian total merchandise trade are presented in Tables 2.7 and 2.8.

Table 2.7 India. Economic indicators (US$, million)

	2005	2010	2013	2014
GDP, current	837,499	1,704,795	1,937,797	2,041,085
GDP per capita, current US$	743	1,414	1,548	1,610
Real GDP growth, y-on-y, %	9.28	10.55	5.02	5.40

Source: UNCTAD, General Profile: India, 2016 (http://unctadstat.unctad.org/CountryProfile/GeneralProfile/en-GB/356/index.html)

Table 2.8 India. Total merchandise trade (US$, million)

	2005	2010	2013	2014
Merchandise exports	99,616	226,351	314,848	321,596
Merchandise imports	142,870	350,233	465,397	463,033
Merchandise trade balance	−43,254	−123,881	−150,549	−141,437

Source: UNCTAD 2016 (http://unctadstat.unctad.org/CountryProfile/GeneralProfile/en-GB/356/index.html)

Institutional environment

Although India has achieved significant economic development, institutions have not proceeded apace, forcing many domestic companies to move abroad. For instance, industrial disputes in unionized sectors are still settled by the Industrial Disputes Act of 1947! Also, companies employing more than one hundred people need government permission for layoffs or to cease operation. In addition to this, the time taken to enforce a contract in India is five times longer than in Russia. On average, corporate management spends a whopping 6.7% of their time dealing with different government regulations, taxes and other bureaucratic red tape. The thirty days' delay to obtain an electric connection (compared to seven days for China or four days for South Korea) or excessively longer export clearance times compared to other Asian tigers are examples of this.[23] Even though India has improved its position in the World Bank's Doing Business ranking, it lags severely (rank 155) in terms of starting new businesses. The most challenging task for entrepreneurs is to deal with construction permits (rank 183). Contract enforcement requires up to 1,420 days versus 452 days in Chine, or 307 days in Russia.

Corruption is another important institutional handicap that affects the country's economic development and competitiveness. In fact, 47.5% of Indian companies expect to have to pay bribes or submit to other forms of corruption. Despite the very democratic character of Indian institutions, which encourage legislation via discussion, there are many obstacles resulting from political deadlocks.

The Indian economy does not benefit from the high attractiveness of developed countries or even other emerging markets in Asia. India ranks a lowly 130 in 2016 (World Bank Doing Business),[24] well below Russia (51), China (84) or Brazil (116). Among the key problems for businesspeople in India are weak contract-enforcing institutions, uncompetitive taxation, difficulties in dealing with construction permits and starting new businesses. On the positive side, India does offer easy access to electricity, property guarantees and credit facilities that can stimulate inward investment and helps develop domestic firms and boosts their foreign expansion.

Foreign direct investment

Over the past decades, Indian firms have entered the international merger and acquisitions fray. From 2003 to 2013, India's cumulative OFDI stock exploded thirty-five-fold to reach $241 billion.[25] Since 2004, India's outbound FDI has continuously increased, mostly due to the investment policies enacted that year. The peak point was reached in 2008 when OFDI reached $21 billion. Alas, the past five years have witnessed a decline in the amount of OFDI. In 2013, it was nearly $7.2 billion in value. In 2014, FDI outflow jumped almost sixfold; however, it remains at half the 2007–2008 volume, $9.8 billion.[26] However, the total investment including equity, loans and guarantees issued was around $30 billion. Total Indian FDI (both inward and outward) resumed growth in 2014 (see Graph 2.3).

In 2014, the majority of OFDI was invested in the sector of transport, storage and communication services, accounting for 30.4%. The second-largest sector is manufacturing with 25.9%. Investment in agriculture and mining stood at 16.5%. Activities such as wholesale and retail trade, financial services, insurance and business services and construction captured the rest of the investments.[27]

Informal factors can be influential for Indian outbound investments. There is a noticeable trend among emerging economies, including India, whereby national pride influences

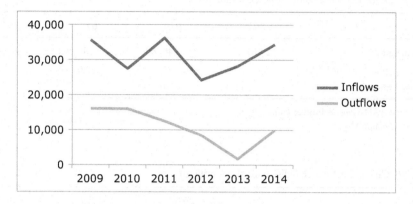

Graph 2.3 India FDI flows

Source: UNCTAD 2016 (http://unctadstat.unctad.org/CountryProfile/GeneralProfile/en-GB/356/index.html)

decision making in irrational ways. For instance, in a bidding war against the Brazilian company CSN, Tata Steel acquired Corus for the tremendously inflated price of $12 billion. In general, informal factors such as culture and customs have been sources for Indian OFDI to become "victim of its own success," due to their inorganic expansion in markets that are not quite familiar.[28]

China

Macro view

Since the market reforms of 1978, China has moved from a centrally planned to a market economy. It experienced enormously rapid economic growth and social development. China's GDP growth averaged about 10% a year during the last decade. This lifted more than five hundred million people out of dire poverty.

Despite such rapid economic development, China remains a developing country, with still very low per capita income compared to advanced economies. Now China is the second country in the world by number of poor people, behind India. See economic indicators in Tables 2.9 and 2.10.

Institutional environment

The specifics of Chinese firms explain the differences in their investment behaviors. The majority of Chinese firms investing overseas are state-owned. Thus their investment strategies may depend on political objectives such as supporting national government foreign policy, or fostering host-country development.[29]

Apart from that, the incentives and opportunities for Chinese firms reflect the different home institutional environment, with a higher level of corruption and weaker stock market regulations. Chinese firms possess competitive advantages in countries with similar institutional settings (for example, in Africa), and this low institutional distance stimulates foreign investment. Chinese firms are experienced in dealing with regulations in opaque

Table 2.9 China. Economic indicators (US$, million)

	2005	2010	2013	2014
GDP, current	2,287,237	5,949,785	9,181,204	10,066,674
GDP per capita, current US$	1,735	4,375	6,626	7,223
Real GDP growth, y-on-y, %	11.3	10.41	7.7	7.4

Source: UNCTAD, General Profile: China, 2016 (http://unctadstat.unctad.org/CountryProfile/GeneralProfile/en-GB/156/index.html)

Table 2.10 China. Total merchandise trade (US$, million)

	2005	2010	2013	2014
Merchandise exports	761,953	1,577,754	2,209,004	2,342,306
Merchandise imports	659,953	1,396,247	1,949,989	1,959,356
Merchandise trade balance	102,000	181,507	259,015	382,950

Source: UNCTAD 2016 (http://unctadstat.unctad.org/CountryProfile/GeneralProfile/en-GB/156/index.html)

business environments.[30] Compared to their developed counterparts, Chinese firms face less risky and costly operations in countries with weak institutions, with the blessing of financial and political backing from the Chinese government. These peculiarities explain why Chinese firms are not risk averse when it comes to investing in host countries with low-quality institutions.[31] Birds of a feather flock together!

Outbound FDI from China to South Asian economies is equally influenced by the macroeconomic and institutional factors, with corruption having an extremely negative impact on Chinese FDI. To attract Chinese investments into South Asia, government policies are predicted to focus on provision of appropriate infrastructure, removal of trade barriers and improvement of institutional climate.[32]

The government plays a strong role in Chinese OFDI by providing incentives to firms that invest abroad. Most of the Chinese firms that are involved in FDI overseas are state owned.[33] The overall success of Chinese firms on the international scene (including Chinese M&A deals) may be explained by state ownership and reforms in the foreign exchange approval system. By introducing supportive policies and reducing restrictions on investments, the government promotes overseas investment through deregulation and liberalization, seeking increased value creation in cross-border M&A.[34] As in other emerging economies, the home government exerts both positive and negative impacts on Chinese companies, providing them with a competitive advantage via official support, yet constraining them via institutional barriers.

Foreign direct investments

China is a relative latecomer to overseas investments. Thirty years ago, the country was a poor agricultural economy of little consequence and negligible capital outflows due to its economic autarky. Today, riding its wave of export-driven growth, it is the largest economy in the world and a top consumer of natural resources such as oil, gas, minerals

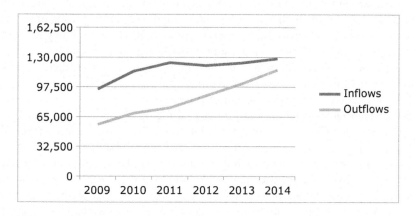

Graph 2.4 China FDI flows

Source: UNCTAD 2016 (http://unctadstat.unctad.org/CountryProfile/GeneralProfile/en-GB/156/index.html)

and timber. With economic growth came the need to secure resources and technologies from abroad. In 1999, the government launched its tenth five-year plan for inward and outward FDI, commonly known as the "Go Out" policy, to promote Chinese investment abroad. The policy expanded to focus on FDI in 2001, and OFDI began to grow (see Graph 2.4).

In 2004, government oversight on OFDI was relaxed and growth became exponential; between 2009 and 2013 alone, China's OFDI flow increased by a staggering 150%.[35] In 2012, China became the third-largest investor in foreign economies, up from sixth place in 2011. In 2013, OFDI amounted to $101 billion, including several mega-deals such as the $15 billion CNOOC-Nexen deal in Canada and the $5 billion Shuanghui-Smithfield deal in the United States, the largest Chinese overseas projects to date in the oil and food industries, respectively.

The scale and scope of China's overseas investments are both growing continuously, with Chinese companies enthusiastically embracing foreign expansion. China is increasing its international presence in all key dimensions of international business: foreign trade, contracted overseas projects, labor service cooperation, FDI, overseas M&A, international financial investments, creation of overseas R&D centers, agricultural cooperation, development of overseas resources and investment in international high-tech ventures.

China's inbound FDI is mainly sourced from other Asian economies. As of 2010, 41% of China's inward foreign direct investment (IFDI) stock was from Hong Kong (China), 7% from Japan, 5% from the Taiwan Province of China, 4% from South Korea and 4% from Singapore. The British Virgin Islands provided 10%, more than the United States and the European Union (EU), each of which supplied 7%; the major sources of European FDI into China came from the United Kingdom and Germany (each with just under 2% of total IFDI). The Cayman Islands supplied about the same proportion, 2%, as the United Kingdom. In 2014, the situation has not changed drastically. The leader of FDI into China remains Hong Kong, accounting for almost 68% of total IFDI stock. Japan in 2014 represented only 3.6% of IFDI, South Korea 3.3%, Singapore about 5%. Other countries never exceed 2% – United States (2%), Germany (1.7%) and the United Kingdom (0.6%). British Virgin Islands supplied 5% of IFDI stock.[36]

A major obstacle to providing an accurate account of the geographic distribution of China's IFDI sources is the high proportion transiting through Hong Kong or through the Caribbean and other tax havens. Matching IFDI and OFDI figures for Hong Kong (China) suggest that much of those flows are passing through from and to China and include an element of round-tripping, though it is also important to note that there is substantial investment from Hong Kong (China) into China's burgeoning property sector and a good part of this is likely to be from Hong Kong tycoons.

IFDI is concentrated in China's eastern coastal regions, especially in Guangdong and Shanghai. Guangdong's attractiveness as an FDI destination in the 1980s was mainly due to its light regulation; relative remoteness from the capital, Beijing (and therefore from central government control); its proximity to the region's largest port, Hong Kong (that was seeking to shed its manufacturing sector); and especially the fact that it contained all but one of the country's special economic zones (SEZs). Shanghai with its strong industrial base and its advantageous location as a major port at the mouth of the Yangtze River also drew large amounts of IFDI. A third major region in the old industrial heartland of northeast coastal China has also developed and is striving to attract FDI. Attempts to boost FDI in China's less-developed interior – namely, Central and West China – are continuing.[37]

An additional growth factor was the long-standing constraint on foreign investment: the only way for foreign companies to enter the Chinese market was via a joint venture with a Chinese company.[38] The fact that relevant legislation existed for a long time and was very comprehensive may have been an advantage for foreign investors.

Criticism of BRIC

Although timely and catchy, the BRIC concept now faces mounting criticism. There is a widespread view that BRIC is nothing more than a neat acronym for the largest emerging economies. Besides this, the four countries have little in common. Indeed, China and India are two manufacturing-based economies, whereas Russia and Brazil are big exporters of natural resources. There are more differences than similarities within the BRIC group.

Moreover, many scholars and experts argue that China is "the muscle of the group."[39] It is the biggest market and as Deutsche Bank Research states: ". . . economically, financially and politically, China overshadows and will continue to overshadow the other BRICs."[40]

Another point of criticism regards the human rights records in the BRIC countries, which impedes these countries from being called emerging and can be a problem in the future. International conflicts either exist or loom between China and Taiwan, Russia and Ukraine, India and Pakistan, which may cause substantial difficulties for economic development. Further risk factors such as civil unrest, unstable political situations, terrorism and more make for unpredictability, and they could have an effect on the development of any country, including BRIC.

Linked to human rights is the development of democracy in the quartet. Although India claims to be the world's biggest democracy since independence (each vote requires 815 million ballots to be printed), Brazil's political past was marred by periods of military rule. Fair elections only resumed in Brazil in 1985. As for Russia and China, the legacy of communism remains strong. Russian elections are held, but are they fair? Overall, this political background does influence investment choices, especially for companies from home countries with strong corporate social responsibility policies.

2.3 Emerging economies: the next wave

Two countries breathing down BRIC's neck are Mexico and South Korea. Mexico takes thirteenth position by nominal GDP, South Korea fifteenth just behind BRIC and G7 economies. The GDP growth of both countries is comparable to BRIC countries at 5% a year. Indonesia and Turkey are very close, using these same indicators. Jim O'Neil, who created the acronym BRIC, came up with the term MIKT to designate Mexico, Indonesia, South Korea and Turkey. The moniker NEXT eleven, also coined by Goldman Sachs, includes a batch of countries that follow the BRICS quintet in terms of GDP: Bangladesh, Egypt, Indonesia, Iran, Mexico, Nigeria, Pakistan, Philippines, Turkey, South Korea and Vietnam.

Mexico

The Mexican economy continued its moderate but steady growth at 2.4% in 2015. Like many emerging countries, Mexico depends on commodity prices and more than others on the neighboring U.S. economy. The slow American growth helps explain Mexico's recent moderate growth (see Table 2.11). Nevertheless, a gradual recovery of economic activity is expected.[41] The expansion of economic activity will be based on growth of private consumption, investment and manufacturing exports (see Table 2.12).

The service sector in Mexico accounts for 62% of total GDP, with the main components being wholesale and retail trade (16% of total GDP), real estate (10%), transport warehousing and communications (7%) and financial services and insurance (6%). The industrial sector represents 18% of GDP with the automotive industry (4% of total GDP) and food (3.8%) being the main drivers. Other important segments include construction, water, gas and electricity distribution – amounting to 8% of national wealth – and mining (about 5%).[42]

The most important export categories are oil and raw materials, representing 14% of total exports in 2011. On the import side, the biggest category is vehicles (10% of imports

Table 2.11 Mexico. Economic indicators (US$, million)

	2005	2010	2013	2014
GDP, current	864,810	1,049,925	1,259,201	1,279,305
GDP per capita, current US$	7,810	8,906	10,293	10,334
Real GDP growth, y-on-y, %	3.08	5.20	1.44	2.1

Source: UNCTAD 2014 (http://unctadstat.unctad.org/CountryProfile/GeneralProfile/en-GB/484/index.html)

Table 2.12 Mexico. Total merchandise trade (US$, million)

	2005	2010	2013	2014
Merchandise exports	214,207	298,305	379,961	397,506
Merchandise imports	228,240	310,205	390,965	411,581
Merchandise trade balance	−14,033	−11,900	−11,005	−14,076

Source: UNCTAD 2014 (http://unctadstat.unctad.org/CountryProfile/GeneralProfile/en-GB/484/index.html)

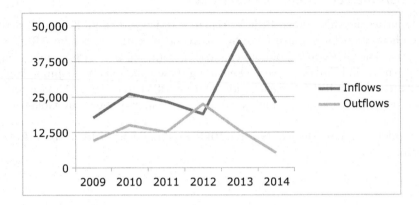

Graph 2.5 Mexico FDI flows

Source: UNCTAD 2014 (http://unctadstat.unctad.org/CountryProfile/GeneralProfile/en-GB/484/index.html)

in 2011).[43] Generally, the most important industrial sectors for Mexico are electricity, automobiles, iron and steel, oil, food and beverages.

Since 2005, Mexico has strengthened its position as an attractive destination for investment (see Graph 2.5). In 2010, Mexico's ranking jumped from nineteenth to eighth position in terms of investment attractiveness, accompanied by a 53% increase in FDI.[44] Foreign companies having established operations in Mexico are raking in billions of dollars in revenues. In turn, this has led to a mounting number of multinationals in Mexico.

Outbound FDI is no new phenomenon for Mexican companies, since they had already tested the American waters, both north and south, during the 1970s. Yet this cross-border expansion ceased with the debt crisis of 1982. OFDI did not restart until the 1990s. The growth of domestic competition and better access to foreign markets enabled Mexican firms to adopt more aggressive strategies in searching for new prospects abroad.

This explains the development of Mexican companies and the reasons for their gradual entry on the international scene. When examining the situation more analytically, one can identify both push and pull factors as motivators for internationalization. Mexican multinationals responded largely to the following push factors:[45]

1   the challenge of unpredictable long-term opportunities in the domestic market, because of problems such as volatile domestic demand;
2   the desire to use their Mexican competitive advantages abroad and thus open up new markets, sometimes by merging their existing export footholds; and
3   the need to adopt more aggressive strategies due to the increased competition following the liberalization of the Mexican economy (in the end of the 1980s), which was accompanied by privatization and deregulation.

The pull factors also include three elements:

1   the geographical proximity of the enormous American market as well as culturally or ethnically close Latin American markets exerted strong attraction;
2   the strategic advantage of forming alliances with sister companies in other markets, and the competitive advantage of transforming domestic brands into global ones by

improving products and logistics and distribution systems; both advantages rendered possible by internationalization; and

3   the impact of policy changes by governments in key markets – namely, the NAFTA free-trade agreement, which gave privileged access to certain markets.

Indonesia

Indonesia is the world's tenth-largest economy (GDP based on purchasing power parity) and the world's fourth most populous nation.[46] As most emerging economies, Indonesia recently experienced a slowdown in its development; however, its growth trajectory is impressive. The gross national income per capita (Atlas method) increased from $560 in 2000 to $3,650 in 2014 (Table 2.13). Poverty reduction programs were very successful, cutting the pool of poor by half since 1999.

Indonesia is implementing a twenty-year development plan, running until 2025. It is divided into four shorter five-year plans, each having different development priorities. The current plan has infrastructure development and the improvement of social assistance programs in education and healthcare as its priorities. Overall, the trade indicators for the economy are positive (Table 2.14), even though the trade balance has dropped into deficit.

The role of the government in market regulation remains quite strong (recall that Indonesia was a dictatorship under Suharto until democracy commenced in 1998), yet it leaves substantial freedom to private enterprise. The government does regulate the activities of foreign investors, mainly by means of legislation. Indonesian law allows foreign companies to establish different types of companies, making practically all types of FDI possible for foreign investors.

Nevertheless, there are some legal restrictions. First foreign companies need permission to perform any business activity in Indonesia (this refers only to FDI and not to non-investing activities such as export). Called Penanaman Modal Asing (PMA), this permission can be obtained from the government's agency Capital Investment Coordinating Board.

Table 2.13 Indonesia. Economic indicators (US$, million)

	2005	2010	2013	2014
GDP, current	285,869	709,191	868,346	848,025
GDP per capita, current US$	1,273	2,947	3,475	3,354
Real GDP growth, y-on-y, %	5.69	6.22	5.78	5.10

Source: UNCTAD, General Profile: Indonesia, 2014 (http://unctadstat.unctad.org/CountryProfile/GeneralProfile/en-GB/360/index.html)

Table 2.14 Indonesia. Total merchandise trade (US$, million)

	2005	2010	2013	2014
Merchandise exports	86,996	158,074	182,552	176,293
Merchandise imports	75,725	135,323	186,629	178,179
Merchandise trade balance	11,271	22,751	−4,077	−1,886

Source: UNCTAD 2014 (http://unctadstat.unctad.org/CountryProfile/GeneralProfile/en-GB/360/index.html)

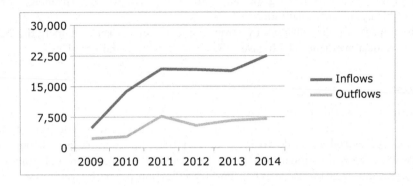

Graph 2.6 Indonesia FDI flows

Source: UNCTAD 2014 (http://unctadstat.unctad.org/CountryProfile/GeneralProfile/en-GB/360/index.html)

Until recently, foreign investors could hold up to 95% of equity in Indonesian companies, meaning 5% at minimum remained in domestic hands. Presidential Decree No. 39
of 2014 loosened things somewhat, with foreigners able to hold up to 100% ownership
in some industries. On the other hand, certain other sectors are capped at between 20%
and 95% for FDI.[47] Moreover, no matter what the proportion of foreign versus domestic
shareholding, after fifteen years of operation, the foreign investor must sell shares to the
domestic residents. This law must be applied at the moment of foundation of the Indonesian FDI-funded company. Government policy gives preference to foreign investors who
focus on the domestic market, as opposed to companies setting up for re-export from an
Indonesian manufacturing base.

Overall, the investment climate is nonetheless considered to be only mildly attractive,
due mainly to difficulties in business operations (high level of bureaucracy, bribery, lack of
transparency, etc.). Nevertheless, given the attractive market size, FDI dynamics are positive
(see Graph 2.6).

The largest inbound investors into Indonesia are Japan, the United Kingdom, Singapore,
Hong Kong, China, Taiwan, the United States, the Netherlands, South Korea, Germany and
Australia. Although the island of Java attracts the bulk of FDI, regions such as Sumatra, Kali-
mantan and Sulawesi are beginning to collect their fair share. Among the inbound investors,
Asian nations make up the bulk of FDI sourcing,[48] which can be explained by their different
perception of country risk compared to companies from Western nations. Another factor is
the cultural proximity of Indonesia, with its large diasporas from other Asian nations.

South Korea

Although South Korea is a high-income country, different sources still relate it to emerging economies. Today, the Republic of Korea is the world's fifteenth-largest economy.
South Korea has shown remarkable success in combining rapid economic growth and significant poverty reduction. Between 1962 and 1994, GDP growth soared at 10% annually,
boosted by annual export increases of 20%. Savings and investments rose to levels above
30% of GDP. In the last two decades, all these indicators maintained positive growth (see
Tables 2.15 and 2.16).

Table 2.15 South Korea. Economic indicators (US$, million)

	2005	*2010*	*2013*	*2014*
GDP, current	898,137	1,094,499	1,304,554	1,415,934
GDP per capita, current US$	19,096	22,588	26,482	28,598
Real GDP growth, y-on-y, %	3.92	6.50	2.97	3.27

Source: UNCTAD, General Profile: South Korea, 2014 (http://unctadstat.unctad.org/CountryProfile/GeneralProfile/en-GB/410/index.html)

Table 2.16 South Korea. Total merchandise trade (US$, million)

	2005	*2010*	*2013*	*2014*
Merchandise exports	284,419	466,384	559,632	572,664
Merchandise imports	261,238	425,212	515,584	525,514
Merchandise trade balance	23,181	41,172	44,048	47,150

Source: UNCTAD 2014 (http://unctadstat.unctad.org/CountryProfile/GeneralProfile/en-GB/410/index.html)

South Korean companies – namely, the traditional Chaebol conglomerates – have established themselves as extremely important multinationals over the past decades. They have been very active in investing abroad. At the first stage of their international expansion, they invested mainly in developed economies. Their size enabled them to seek investment opportunities there. During their next stage of global expansion, they directed investments to developing markets and emerging economies, because of cheaper quality labor and lower production costs.

The most important motives for OFDI from South Korea are cheap workforce, saturated home market, cost advantage abroad and lack of competition.[49] These motivators suggest that the primary target should be emerging economies, quite the opposite of the logic during the early stages of Korean foreign investment. On the other hand, entering developed markets gave them strategic know-how and improved their awareness of the importance of constant innovation and development.

Many South Korean companies, such as Samsung, LG, Hyundai or Kia, are international leaders. Nevertheless, outbound investment is still significantly lower than from other Asian tigers – for example, Singapore. Nonetheless, Korean foreign investment is growing rapidly. In the 2004–2011 period, annual OFDI jumped fourfold, from $5.6 billion to $20 billion per year,[50] even reaching $30 billion in 2012 (see Graph 2.7).

The South Korean government plays an extremely important role for outbound FDI, consistently providing different incentives such as financial help and organizational support. In addition, loans at favorable interest rates are granted to exporters. IT, machinery and transport are the main industries expanding abroad.

Major investment destinations are the United States, China, the Middle East and Africa. In the United States, South Korean firms created more than 32,300 jobs with an average salary of $83,000. Moreover, they invested heavily in R&D in the United States spending more than $372 million on their U.S.-based subsidiaries in 2011.[51]

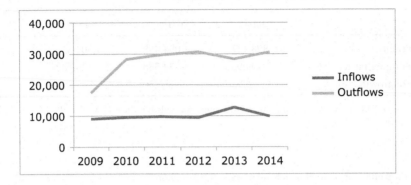

Graph 2.7 South Korea FDI flows

Source: UNCTAD 2014 (http://unctadstat.unctad.org/CountryProfile/GeneralProfile/en-GB/410/index.html)

Table 2.17 Turkey. Economic indicators (US$, million)

	2005	2010	2013	2014
GDP, current	482,986	731,144	822,149	800,998
GDP per capita, current US$	7,130	10,135	10,972	10,562
Real GDP growth, y-on-y, %	8.40	9.16	4.12	2.89

Source: UNCTAD, General Profile: Turkey, 2014 (http://unctadstat.unctad.org/CountryProfile/GeneralProfile/en-GB/792/index.html)

Table 2.18 Turkey. Total merchandise trade (US$, million)

	2005	2010	2013	2014
Merchandise exports	73,476	113,883	151,803	157,617
Merchandise imports	116,774	185,544	251,661	242,177
Merchandise trade balance	−43,298	−71,661	−99,859	−84,560

Source: UNCTAD, General Profile: Turkey, 2014 (http://unctadstat.unctad.org/CountryProfile/GeneralProfile/en-GB/792/index.html)

Turkey

In the last ten years, Turkey has begun to play a prominent role in the world economy by shedding its gritty image and redefining itself as an attractive hub for FDI. With a GDP of $800 billion, Turkey is the seventeenth-largest economy in the world. In less than a decade, its per capita income has nearly tripled and now exceeds $10,500 (Table 2.17). Turkey is a member of the OECD and the G20.[52]

Since 2012, Turkish economic growth has been slowing down, which is reflected in trade activity (Table 2.18). In 2013–2015, geopolitical factors, election-related uncertainties and concerns over the government's handling of corruption allegations weakened business confidence and private demand. In 2014, growth was only 2.9% compared to 4.2% the year before. Turkey has also been vulnerable to changes in investor climate and, like other emerging markets, has experienced significant currency and financial market volatility since 2013.[53]

The main international investors into the country are the Netherlands, Austria, the United States, Belgium, the United Kingdom, France, Luxemburg and Germany. Financial intermediation, manufacturing and construction accounted for 72% of total FDI.

There are many factors at work behind the growth of FDI in Turkey (see Graph 2.8) including the country's location and its young and dynamic population. With these positive attributes, Turkey has seen a massive increase in the number of major international companies choosing to conduct business there. Companies such as Ford Motors, DHL, Coca-Cola, Siemens, Microsoft and Nestlé have all recognized Turkey's potential and therefore set up operations there. DHL, for example, operates over forty offices throughout Turkey, employing over one thousand people and serving 65% of the nation.

American companies provide the majority of FDI in Turkey, with their FDI share increasing from 17.5% in 2007 to 28.4% in 2012. Sectors such as business services, information technology, chemicals, transport and logistics and infrastructure projects have attracted significant American attention.

The majority of FDI into Turkey flows from Europe, North America and the Persian Gulf countries. In 2014, the Netherlands topped the foreign investors list with 17.6% of total IFDI, Germany took the second position with 10.7% and Luxemburg third (7.5%). U.S. investments in 2014 dropped, accounting for 5.3% of total IFDI.[54]

The main recipient sectors in Turkey are manufacturing (33.2% of total), finance and insurance (22%) and information and communication (13.3%). Most Japanese investment focuses on automotive (29.4%) and financial services (17.6%). German investors find appeal in infrastructure, energy, automotive and finance, with the number of German projects in Turkey having grown at an average annual rate of 15.6% since 2007. Germany is also host to a very large community of Turkish immigrants from the German economic miracle of the 1950s and '60s. This diaspora is actively investing in their country of origin.

M&A has been steadily growing in Turkey over the last decades, mainly in the manufacturing and services sectors. The year 2012 witnessed a record number of 259 M&A deals. Given the global backdrop of declining M&A activity, the Turkish success proves

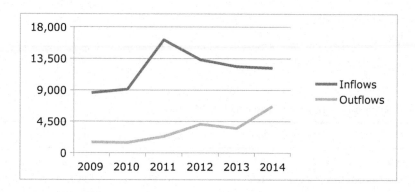

Graph 2.8 Turkey FDI flows

Source: UNCTAD, General Profile: Turkey, 2014 (http://unctadstat.unctad.org/CountryProfile/GeneralProfile/en-GB/792/index.html)

the country's attraction as a major hub for foreign investments, underpinned by the following key factors:

- the improved macroeconomic environment with lower inflation and interest rates, higher-growth and stable financial markets;
- the privatization of state-owned companies gained significant momentum;
- the first successful completion of an IMF program; and
- ongoing negotiations for Turkey's full membership in the EU.

Despite the positive mood surrounding Turkey's potential, there have, nonetheless, been a number of failures. The government's ambitious targets for FDI received a blow when TAQA (the Abu Dhabi national energy company) abandoned its planned $12 billion investment for Turkey's lignite reserves. Turkey also appears to be struggling to attract top technological investment. Despite positive strides in education, Turkey still lacks a skilled and educated workforce. For example, in the higher education and training category, South Korea ranks twenty-second while Turkey languishes in sixty-fifth place. In the innovation and sophistication category, South Korea ranks twentieth and Turkey forty-seventh.

South Africa

South Africa's peaceful political transition was one of the most impressive political achievements of the past century.[55] The supportive global environment and a favorable macroeconomic situation enabled South African GDP to grow at a steady pace up to the global financial crisis of 2008–2009 (Table 2.19).

South Africa is the most attractive African country for investors and for doing business,[56] which makes it a reliable trade partner (Table 2.20). Nowadays, South Africa faces certain challenges such as labor market instability, rising government debt and high current account deficits.

Table 2.19 South Africa. Economic indicators (US$, million)

	2005	2010	2013	2014
GDP, current	257,772	375,348	366,060	349,733
GDP per capita, current US$	5,344	7,295	6,936	6,581
Real GDP growth, y-on-y, %	5.28	3.04	2.21	1.5

Source: UNCTAD, General Profile: South Africa, 2014 (http://unctadstat.unctad.org/CountryProfile/GeneralProfile/en-GB/710/index.html)

Table 2.20 South Africa. Total merchandise trade (US$, million)

	2005	2010	2013	2014
Merchandise exports	51,626	91,347	95,938	91,047
Merchandise imports	62,304	96,835	126,350	121,940
Merchandise trade balance	−10,679	−5,488	−30,412	−30,893

Source: UNCTAD, General Profile: South Africa, 2014 (http://unctadstat.unctad.org/CountryProfile/GeneralProfile/en-GB/710/index.html)

The infrastructure and legislative reforms undertaken by the government played a great role in attracting FDI into South Africa. In particular, the following conditions were provided:

- equal legal conditions for foreign and local investors;
- lifting of state control over the prices of manufactured products;
- no restrictions on private enterprise for foreigners;
- the absence of specific government approvals for investment by foreigners (except for banking and financial activities);
- no minimum capital requirements (except for banking and insurance);
- no restrictions on outflow of profits and dividends (upon exchange control permission); and
- no restrictions on foreign ownership of existing South African companies (excluding banking and finance).

From 2012 to 2013, total inbound FDI almost doubled from $4.5 billion to $8 billion (Graph 2.9), while outbound FDI grew more slowly, from $3 billion to $5.5 billion. Incoming foreign investors are mostly attracted to financial and insurance services, real estate and business services (36% of FDI), mining (31%) and manufacturing (18%). In 2014, OFDI by South African multinationals increased by 4.3% to reach $6.9 billion, making South Africa the largest investor from Africa.

South Africa remains constrained by a number of legislative and political uncertainties that make it less attractive for foreign investors. Recently, the ranking of South Africa plummeted by thirty positions in the World Bank's Doing Business report (from forty-third in 2015 to seventy-third in 2016). In 2014, inward FDI decreased by 31% and amounted to just $5.7 billion.

The unfavorable macroeconomic and political situations caused this significant slowdown. South Africa's economy showed its weakest performance since the global financial crisis. Infrastructure gaps, weak domestic demand and inadequate energy supply led to economic deprivation. Unemployment reached 24% and youth unemployment 49%.

Aside from its tight economic situation, South Africa is seeing political turbulence. Political reforms are not consistent and create uncertainty for investors. Land reform and

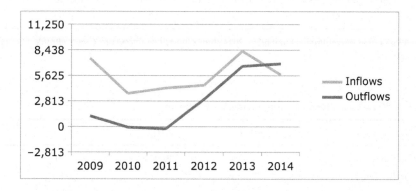

Graph 2.9 South Africa FDI flows

Source: UNCTAD, General Profile: South Africa, 2014 (http://unctadstat.unctad.org/CountryProfile/GeneralProfile/en-GB/710/index.html)

agricultural development policy are also trouble spots. Corruption has also made investors wary, with Transparency International's ranking (at sixty-one in 2015) showing no signs of improvement.

Nevertheless, Chinese and Indian firms continue to be notable investors in Africa in general and in South Africa particularly. For instance, Chinese firms massively invested in South Africa's solar panel industry.

Kazakhstan

Kazakhstan is considered an upper-middle income country. Its GDP per capita exceeded $13,500 in 2013 (Table 2.21), putting it on par with Central European countries (Poland ($13,700, Hungary $13,580, Croatia $13,575). However, with the combined impacts of internal capacity constraints in the oil industry, an unfavorable trade environment and the economic slowdown in Russia, Kazakhstan's economic growth slowed from 6% in 2013 to 4.3% in 2014 (Table 2.22).

Since its independence in 1991, Kazakhstan has succeeded in creating a strong market economy and achieving remarkable results in attracting foreign investment. The total stock of foreign investment in Kazakhstan reached $209.1 billion at the end of 2013. Over 50% ($129.5 billion) of this was FDI, with portfolio and other investments comprising the remaining $79.6 billion. The vast majority of FDI is placed in the oil & gas sector. The biggest investor is the United States (total investment of about $31.4 billion), which has been heavily investing in Kazakhstan's economy since 2005.

Kazakhstan has made efforts to improve its investment climate by abolishing bureaucratic barriers. In 2013, the World Bank ranked the country fifty out of 189 in its Doing Business report. Nevertheless, such steps towards more attractive investment climate cannot overcome corruption and bureaucracy, which remain challenges for foreign investors

Table 2.21 Kazakhstan. Economic indicators (US$, million)

	2005	2010	2013	2014
GDP, current	57,124	148,047	224,415	205,418
GDP per capita, current US$	3,792	9,299	13,650	12,369
Real GDP growth, y-on-y, %	9.7	7.3	6.02	4.3

Source: UNCTAD, General Profile: Kazakhstan, 2014 (http://unctadstat.unctad.org/CountryProfile/GeneralProfile/en-GB/398/index.html)

Table 2.22 Kazakhstan. Total merchandise trade (US$, million)

	2005	2010	2013	2014
Merchandise exports	27,849	59,971	84,700	78,238
Merchandise imports	17,353	31,107	48,806	41,213
Merchandise trade balance	10,496	28,864	35,895	37,025

Source: UNCTAD, General Profile: Kazakhstan, 2014 (http://unctadstat.unctad.org/CountryProfile/GeneralProfile/en-GB/398/index.html)

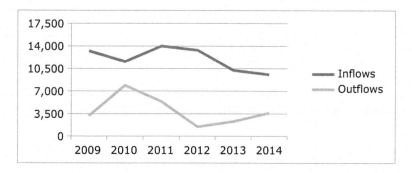

Graph 2.10 Kazakhstan FDI flows

Source: UNCTAD, General Profile: Kazakhstan, 2014 (http://unctadstat.unctad.org/CountryProfile/GeneralProfile/en-GB/398/index.html)

(see Graph 2.10). The underdeveloped manufacturing sector still has trouble attracting FDI, thus requiring further measures.

On May 29, 2014, Kazakhstan, Russia and their customs union partners signed a treaty to create a common economic space called the Eurasian Economic Union (EEU). EEU is expected to further integrate these economies and provide free movement of labor, capital and services within the area. Kazakhstan considers further integration with Russia and Belarus as a chance to attract additional investment by offering expanded market access to those countries.

A new, serious package of incentives for investors was presented to the Parliament in June 2014. Some of these incentives include state compensation for investment costs, corporate income tax exemptions and executing long-term contracts with national companies. All these measures are supposed to make Kazakhstan a much more attractive country in terms of FDI.

Despite all the measures, the government strategy discriminates against foreign investors. So oil multinationals complain that the implementation of the laws is uneven, irregular and non-transparent, especially at the local level. Moreover, some reports claim difficulties in obtaining Kazakh "certificates of origin."

Nigeria

Nigeria is the largest country in Africa with 47% of West Africa's population. It is the biggest oil exporter in Africa, possessing the largest natural gas reserves of the continent. According to the World Bank rankings, Nigeria ranked thirty-sixth out of 47 economies in sub-Saharan Africa, and 169 out of 189 economies globally[57] making it competitive regionally, if not globally. This means that despite its relatively low rank in terms of economic development and critically low GDP per capita (see Table 2.23), Nigeria is among the most competitive in the sub-Saharan region. In 2014, Nigeria outperformed South Africa as the largest African economy, with its GDP (in constant 2011 PPP terms) having reached $1 trillion.

Since 2000, Nigerian economic growth has picked up, with average annual growth of 6.8% over the 2000–2013 period. In spite of the global economic crisis, Nigeria witnessed

Table 2.23 Nigeria. Economic indicators (US$, million)

	2005	2010	2013	2014
GDP, current	180,502	369,062	514,965	566,496
GDP per capita, current US$	1,293	2,311	2,966	3,173
Real GDP growth, y-on-y, %	6.51	7.84	5.39	6.0

Source: UNCTAD, General Profile: Nigeria, 2014 (http://unctadstat.unctad.org/CountryProfile/GeneralProfile/en-GB/566/index.html)

Table 2.24 Nigeria. Total merchandise trade (US$, million)

	2005	2010	2013	2014
Merchandise exports	50,467	8,400	104,000	97,000
Merchandise imports	20,754	44,235	56,000	60,000
Merchandise trade balance	29,713	39,765	48,000	37,000

Source: UNCTAD, General Profile: Nigeria, 2014 (http://unctadstat.unctad.org/CountryProfile/GeneralProfile/en-GB/566/index.html)

strong growth of 7.0% in 2009. Oil accounts for almost 90% of exports and by rough estimation nearly 75% of national consolidated budgetary revenues,[58] which explains the huge positive trade balance for the country (Table 2.24).

Nigeria is one of the consistently fastest-growing emerging economies proving that, on the one hand, it holds promise for international investors, but on the other hand, it suffers many problems with government, social and governance issues.

Nigeria's environment for FDI remains challenging due to weak rule of law, policy instability, political violence and poor infrastructure (including serious deficiencies in power supply currently being addressed by large-scale power privatization). Current legislation allows for 100% foreign ownership of Nigerian firms, except in the oil & gas sector (where private investment remains limited to joint ventures or production sharing agreements) and industries considered crucial to national security (e.g. defense related). The Nigerian government also gives preference to domestic-sourced content in public procurement, including supplies for the important oil & gas sector, as well as for the insurance and banking sectors.

Despite Nigeria's challenging environment for foreign investment, inbound FDI intensity averaged 3.6% of total GDP during the 2007–2012 period (compared to a regional average of 3.2%), driven by oil & gas sector investors, partly due to high energy prices at the time. FDI inflows into the country reached a historical high of $8.7 billion in 2009, although they declined to $7.0 billion in 2012, owing to regulatory uncertainty in the Nigerian oil sector, increasing competition for FDI from economies such as Ghana and the impact of the global economic slowdown of 2011–2012.

Nigeria is one of the top-five FDI host economies in Africa, following South Africa, Congo, Mozambique and Egypt. African FDI inflows have been growing enormously over the course of the last decade: from $1.14 billion in 2001, to almost $9 billion in 2009, but then dropping to $4.6 billion in 2014. Future growth prospects in such markets as Nigeria and Zambia have weakened somewhat as commodity prices fall. Nigeria is the nineteenth-greatest recipient of FDI in the world.

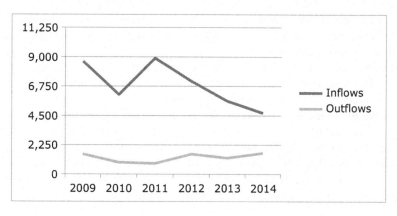

Graph 2.11 Nigeria FDI flows

Source: UNCTAD, General Profile: Nigeria, 2014 (http://unctadstat.unctad.org/CountryProfile/GeneralProfile/en-GB/566/index.html)

Nigeria's most important sources of FDI have traditionally been the home countries of the oil majors. The United States, present in Nigeria's oil sector through Chevron, Texaco and ExxonMobil, had investment stock of $3.4 billion in Nigeria in 2008, the latest figures available. The United Kingdom (Shell Oil's home base) is another key partner, with FDI from the United Kingdom into Nigeria accounting for about 20% of Nigeria's total foreign investment.

As China seeks to expand its trade relationships with Africa, it too is becoming one of Nigeria's most important sources of FDI. Nigeria is China's second-largest trading partner in Africa, after South Africa. China's direct investment stock in Nigeria was reported to be $2.1 billion in 2013. The oil & gas sector receives 75% of China's FDI in Nigeria. Other significant sources of FDI include Italy, Brazil, the Netherlands, France and South Africa.

On the other hand, Nigeria's outbound investments are truly modest (see Graph 2.11). In 2000, OFDI was a piddly $168 million, less than half of the 1990 total of $415 million. However, between 2000 and 2009, the FDI outflows increased continuously. The take-off occurred in 2007. The maximum amount of OFDI was reached in 2009 and 2012 with more than $1.5 billion, which is still disproportionately small compared to the inflows. The official OFDI statistics do not take into account a purportedly massive amount (billions of dollars) in stolen funds from the opaque management of Nigeria national oil company NNPC.[59]

As a relatively undeveloped economy, Nigerian companies focus on home territory first, with many opportunities to invest in profitable, unsaturated sectors. Nigeria is also home to Africa's wealthiest billionaire entrepreneur, Aliko Dangote, whose multinational is active in food, construction and other areas.

2.4 Destinations and motives for OFDI from emerging markets

The level of FDI and its importance change over time and differ by country. Recently, there has been an increase in FDI to developing countries and a more hospitable welcome from governments of host countries. Being dependent on policy barriers, international

FDI flows have been facilitated by the liberalization of investment regimes, which often occurred when governments realized that FDI induced benefits such as technology transfer and capital input. To accelerate FDI inflows, states implemented favorable policies and removed cross-border barriers.

Yet two opposing views on the influence of FDI exist in academic research. One side argues that FDI leads to economic growth and productivity increases, thus contributing to differences in economic development and growth across countries as companies expand opportunities for technology transfer.[60] The opposing side argues that FDI may endanger local capabilities and undercompensate for the extraction of natural resources (oil, minerals and timber, for example) within host countries, or even worse contribute to support for questionable political regimes. To strike a balance, proper FDI policies should stimulate valuable opportunities for firms on both origin and destination sides, with governments simultaneously ensuring protection for local communities.[61]

The role of macroeconomic factors for OFDI from EEs

Outbound FDI from emerging countries has risen significantly since 2005. FDI is one mode for companies to expand internationally. The remarkable growth of emerging economies has attracted the attention of academics and researchers to FDI during the last decade.

Research on FDI determinants distinguishes three groups of causal factors: institutional factors; demand-side factors, such as market size and income distribution; and supply-side factors, such as infrastructure and labor. Another school of thought divides FDI determinants into "push" and "pull" factors; in other words, either home-country attributes that push outbound FDI, or host-country attractions that pull inbound FDI. The main pull factors include large market size, low labor costs, low transaction costs and reduced geographic or cultural distances.[62]

Market size, trade openness and low inflation rates have positive effects on total inward FDI.[63] Greater market potential measured by GDP per capita is also an important factor for FDI flows in East Asia.[64] Countries in South and East Asia invest more readily into countries having higher global economic integration, typically measured by trade openness.[65] On the contrary, trade openness is not a primary factor in increasing FDI inflows into BRICs countries, where sheer market size is the main attraction.[66]

Another pull factor for foreign investors is infrastructure. Even though research findings do differ, they mostly find a positive correlation between FDI in Asia and Latin America and infrastructure.[67] For instance, in Brazil, interest rates, trade openness, economic growth and exchange rates positively affect FDI inflows.[68] According to the opposite opinion, the exchange rate is not significant and its effect may be neutralized by other factors.[69]

Currency movements can also stimulate certain FDI movements. Firms operating in countries with appreciating currencies are most likely to invest in host countries with depreciating currencies. In addition to currency movements, stock market performance indicates that more highly valued firms purchase lower-valued firms. It's also true for the reason that firms from wealthier countries tend to acquire firms from poorer countries because of lower cost of capital in developed markets.[70]

Indicators such as trade flows and GDP per capita reflect efficiency-seeking and market-seeking motives. Trade flows reflect willingness on the part of companies to exploit profit opportunities in the host markets. Trade flows also indicate a higher level of trade openness that also positively affects inward FDI. Growing individual income along with large market size can be an indicator of demand in a particular market attracting FDI. From the given results, market attractiveness for foreign investors depends on macroeconomic growth stability and market's economic openness.[71]

To improve their investment climate, governments tend to implement reforms to lower costs, remove barriers and reduce risks – for example, by establishing investment regimes, special economic zones and tax incentives for foreign investors, and by ratifying international or regional agreements on trade and investment standards.[72] Nevertheless, fiscal incentives cannot compensate for truly unfavorable investment conditions, including institutional barriers, poor infrastructure and macroeconomic factors.[73]

China and India are frequently compared in numerous studies of both outflows and inflows of FDI. The determinants of Russian OFDI have not been as thoroughly researched. Some of the principal academic and statistical findings on outbound investment from the BRIC quartet are synthesized hereafter.

China's outbound FDI

FDI destinations

The recent growth in China's OFDI encouraged scholars to investigate the underlying economic factors. Host-market size, geographic and cultural proximity and host-country natural resource endowments were the main pull factors for drawing Chinese firms outside the Middle Empire.[74] Among the developed economies, the main destinations for Chinese investments are the United States and Australia (see Figure 2.4).

In 2014, FDI outflows from China reached a record high of $116 billion. Remarkably, FDI outflows continue to grow faster than inflows. This trend will continue, particularly in the service and infrastructure-related industries, mainly because of the "One Belt, One Road" strategy (referring to the Silk Road Economic Belt and the 21st Century Maritime Silk Road). The main destination for Chinese OFDI remains Hong Kong (67% of total OFDI in 2014), which does not fully reflect the true final destinations of China's foreign investments. Like many other multinationals, Chinese firms initially invest in tax haven countries or offshore financial centers, such as Hong Kong or the Cayman Islands. The monies then are reinvested to other destinations.

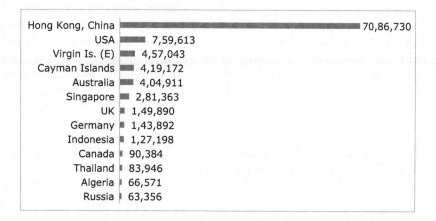

Figure 2.4 Chinese OFDI major destinations. In this chart, figures are $ millions.

Source: China Statistical Yearbook 2014 (http://www.stats.gov.cn/tjsj/ndsj/2014/indexeh.htm)

Chinese OFDI shows interest in countries with weak institutions. Chinese companies have experience in certain institutional environments, and investing in similar environments significantly improves transplantation success rates.[75] While companies from the developed world may find it difficult to operate in markets with excessive bureaucracy, corruption, low transparency and political constraints, Chinese multinationals already have experience with such institutional features.

Cultural and geographic proximity also seem to play a large role in Chinese OFDI. According to China's Ministry of Commerce, the majority (68%) of Chinese OFDI flows into other Asian countries. Only 13% goes to Latin America, 8% to Europe, 4% each to North America and Africa and 3% to Oceania. FDI flows to other Asian countries have increased considerably over the last decade. The establishment of the China-ASEAN Free Trade Area in early 2010 strengthened regional economic cooperation and contributed to the promotion of FDI flows.[76] Furthermore, corridors connecting Asian sub-regions are being established, including the Bangladesh-China-India-Myanmar Economic Corridor and the China-Pakistan Economic Corridor. These initiatives will provide opportunities for economic cooperation and further infrastructure investment. Finally, the establishment of the China (Shanghai) Pilot Free Trade Zone opens up six service industries (finance, transport, commerce and trade, professional services, cultural services and public services) to foreign investors, so China's OFDI is likely to flow even more heavily to other Asian countries (and attract more inbound FDI itself).[77]

Chinese investment in Africa is on the rise as well, having increased from just $1 billion in 2004 to $24.5 billion in 2013.[78] About a third of these investments were in extractive industries, such as mining and oil, while a fifth were in the finance sector. The top African recipient of Chinese FDI is South Africa (22%). Other top recipients include Zimbabwe, Angola, Zambia, Sudan, the DR of Congo and Nigeria.[79] Some recent large projects in the region include China Investment Corporation's (CIC's) purchase of a 25% stake in Shanduka Group in South Africa for $250 million and Temasek's (Singapore's SWF) $1.3 billion purchase of a 20% stake in gas fields in Tanzania. Sinopec plans to invest $20 billion in Africa in the next five years. Investments in Africa and other developing countries are expected to rise in the future as wage competitiveness decreases in China and labor-intensive industries are compelled to relocate.[80]

As regards industries, in 2012, 90% of Chinese outward FDI was invested in six sectors: leasing and business services (33%), finance (18%), mining (14%), wholesale and retail trade (13%), transportation and storage (6%) and manufacturing (6%). However, this distribution may be somewhat distorted. A portion of investments made in leasing and business services (33%) were set up as "investment and asset management subsidiaries" in offshore financial centers, so these investments might have transited elsewhere.[81]

FDI motives

Chinese FDI is motivated by three factors: acquiring advanced technology through M&As, increasing market share and natural resource endowment.[82]

RESOURCE SEEKING

From the perspective of the Chinese government, natural resources are the primary motivator, responsible for huge loans issued for OFDI since 2000s.[83] China's fast economic growth has meant vast amounts of raw materials for its export-driven manufacturing operations.[84] To make matters worse, China has become the second-most voracious energy consumer (after the United States), making the country dependent on oil imports, which is a dependence China seeks to mitigate by securing its own sources.

MARKET SEEKING

Market share gain is the second-largest incentive, representing 15% of state-financed foreign projects. Here Chinese power companies dominate. Chinese firms are driven by market-seeking motives in their internationalization strategy independently of the recipient countries, while other host-country factors vary between high- and low-income countries. FDI determinants and motives of investing firms differ depending on the host-country environment and the industrial sector in which the investor operates. China's OFDI is attracted to the countries that have a high volume of export with China, large market size and rapid economic growth. Chinese firms also account for open economic regimes' strategic assets measured by the ratio of R&D spending to GDP and natural resources in their investment strategies.[85]

TECHNOLOGY SEEKING

OFDI for technology acquisition purposes accounts for only 4% of total OFDI, but this still represents a departure from how other "Asian Miracle" countries operated. China has a sizeable surplus of foreign currencies in an economically depressed global environment, making cheap acquisitions of Western enterprises an enticing option. One disadvantage of this trend is the rising anti-Chinese sentiment in host countries. The U.S. Congress, for example, citing 'national security threats,' has blocked multiple Chinese attempts to purchase American oil, telecoms and appliance companies.[86] As reported by UNCTAD, this type of FDI from China is likely to increase in the future. Given its shale gas reserves, China is seeking to launch joint ventures with American companies in order to access extraction technology. With this goal in mind, Sinochem (China) launched a $1.7 billion venture with Pioneer Natural Resources (United States) in order to acquire a stake in Wolcamp Shale in Texas.

Although market size is one of the OFDI determinants, the most powerful motives for overseas investment remain technology acquisition and natural resources extraction. In the IT sector, favorable conditions in foreign economies and increasing competition in the domestic Chinese market have pushed Chinese firms to seek strategic assets related to R&D, marketing and resources abroad.[87]

To the chagrin of many global players, these priorities indicate that China is not using OFDI for industrial adjustment, or efficiency-seeking purposes. Manufacturing projects from China mainly aim to gain access to technological know-how or new markets rather than to take advantage of cheap labor.[88] China appears to still be able to utilize cheap labor within its own borders in order to maintain a trade advantage.

Host-country institutions also play an important role in Chinese OFDI. Chinese firms do not opt for FDI in the countries with better institutional environments without considering the economic situation in the host country. Hence a combination of economic and institutional factors can be used as a kind of framework for analysis of Chinese OFDI. In the decision-making process of Chinese investors, institutional determinants are often more important than purely economic considerations.[89]

Historical perspective on OFDI

Although China was a late starter (with no inbound FDI at all until 1980, and outbound until 1982, according to UNCTAD), China then rapidly caught up, reaching the $10 billion mark by 1992, after barely twelve years. At the turn of the century, government policy switched from mildly permissive to strongly encouraging. By 2006, Chinese outward FDI stock reached $73 billion, the sixth largest in the developing world. Some of this overseas expansion involved other developing and transition economies. For example, the first group of eight overseas economic and trade cooperation zones included countries in Africa (Nigeria, Mauritius and Zambia), Asia (Mongolia, Pakistan and Thailand) and Eastern Europe (Kazakhstan and Russia). In 2007, China also established a government investment company to manage its $200 billion fund, tapped from huge foreign currency reserves generated from its massive export revenues.

The recent FDI flows from Asia to developed countries are caused by the emergence of China and India as investors, coupled with active M&A activities by investors based in the newly industrialized countries (particularly Singapore). In 2006, Asian investors became a driving force in the M&A boom in Europe. According to the UNCTAD's *World Investment Prospects Survey*, South, East and Southeast Asia were the regions most favored by multinationals for investment, followed by North America and the EU.[90]

China's OFDI stock reached $246 billion by the end of 2009, well over eight times the $28 billion recorded in 2000 and far above the negligible $4 billion of 1990. In recent years, the geographic distribution of China's OFDI has remained stable. The bulk of China's OFDI goes to Asia, accounting for $186 billion (76%) of total OFDI stock in 2009. However, most of that stock (89%) actually went to just one destination: Hong Kong (SAR China).

Hong Kong is often just a transit point for outgoing funds. Examples include Sinopec's acquisition of a 30% stake of Galp Energia (Brazil) in 2011. Sinopec is the largest Chinese oil refiner but the acquisition was made through its Hong Kong subsidiary. Eventually, this $5.2 billion transaction was recorded as OFDI to Hong Kong but not into Brazil.

More recently, much media attention worldwide has focused on Chinese OFDI into Africa, which has risen sharply but still represents a drop in the bucket at less than 4% of the country's global total OFDI in 2009.[91]

With a relatively small exposure to the U.S. subprime crisis in 2008, China was less affected than developed economies. GDP growth slowed somewhat as the country's export markets suffered, but remained strong, supported by an early, large and fast-acting government stimulus package for domestic consumption. With high cash reserves and ample support available from the government, China's multinationals continued their overseas acquisitions. In the end, when global OFDI flows fell by 15% in 2008, Chinese OFDI flows more than doubled. Were it not for the failure of one large deal (the Chinalco-Rio Tinto merger, with an expected value of $19.5 billion), the result would have been an increase in China's total OFDI of 36%.[92]

The rapid rise of Chinese FDI can be largely attributed to the high level of government support, which allows state-controlled banks to lend billions of dollars to companies so as to invest abroad. Moreover, the government exercises a high degree of control over the projects; the companies to which state banks lend are overwhelming state-owned as well, making it easier to dictate how the funds are used.[93] Until 2014, all foreign projects, whether implemented by SOEs or private companies, had to be approved by the Chinese Commission of Commerce, and larger projects (exceeding $300 million for natural resource projects and $100 million for others) required the additional approval of the State Council.[94]

As of 2014, the Chinese Commission of Commerce relaxed the standards, and now only projects above $1 billion in value require approval of the planning commission, NDRC (National Development and Reform Commission), and only those implemented in "sensitive" regions require ministry approval. The level of institutional support has increased over the years. Today, 80%–90% of money used to finance OFDI is obtained from Chinese banks.[95] Even so, private companies are beginning to show greater presence. By the end of 2013, state-owned enterprises originated 55.2% of OFDI, while private-sector firms accounted for 44.8%, up 4.6 percentage points from the previous year.

India's outbound FDI

FDI destinations

Over the decade starting in 2003, India's OFDI stock increased thirty-five-fold to $241 billion in 2013.[96] The appeal of foreign opportunities for Indian capital has not abated, with 2014 seeing a fivefold (486%) jump to $9.8 billion.[97] Nearly 70% of the OFDI stock flowed in the past five years. From 2004 to 2008, Indian multinationals invested $73 billion and more than double that amount ($161 billion) during 2009–2013. Given that India is a low-income country, this explosion in OFDI is noteworthy.

Europe has received the largest share of FDI from India since 2008, followed by Asia, Africa and North America. In Europe, 60% of the investments from India are in the information technology, automotive, manufacturing, financial services and steel sectors. Like other emerging markets, Indian investors actively channel their investments via tax havens or advantageous offshore locales such as Singapore, the British Virgin Islands, Mauritius or the Netherlands (see Figure 2.5). The funds then flow on to the final host countries, although statistics are not available at this level. Within Africa, Mauritius attracted most Indian investments, mainly because of low taxes. Mauritius

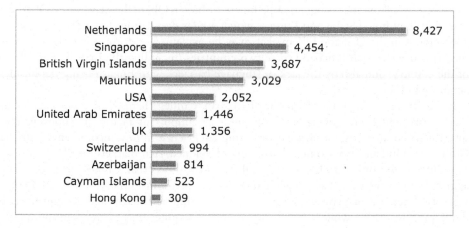

Figure 2.5 Major destinations of Indian OFDI, 2014

Source: Reserve Bank of India 2015 (https://www.rbi.org.in/Scripts/Statistics.aspx)

has signed double tax avoidance treaties with other countries, thus for Indian firms, this country is a departure point to other destinations in Africa or even back to India.[98] After these countries, the United Kingdom and the United States are the top destinations for Indian OFDI.

FDI motives

Despite the scholarly attention devoted to the phenomenon of Indian OFDI, there are no conclusive studies on the determinants of geographic choice. Nonetheless, the research does suggest several possible determinants of Indian outflows.

Overall, Indian multinationals know how to adapt their product and processes to foreign markets. For instance, Tata Motors produces a relatively cheap car, the Nano, for its home market, while simultaneously producing expensive Jaguars for the high-end segment in Europe.

As deregulation of Indian economy took place in the beginning of the 1990s, Indian IT companies experienced a solid growth of international demand, and such IT giants as Tata Consultancy Service, Wipro and Infosys have emerged. Now Indian IT service companies compete with such global players as Accenture and IBM.

Indian multinationals benefit from another ownership advantage: the contribution of know-how and technology from India's well-educated diaspora. One reason for the growing software industry in India is the immigration of many engineers and technicians to Silicon Valley, and second-generation engineers returning to the Motherland. This emigration in fact reduces transaction costs for Indian MNEs expanding into foreign markets, since it provides marketing skills, latest know-how and social capital.

The motives that Indian OFDI has in common correspond to the classic perceptions, of course with certain specifics.

MARKET SEEKING

Indian companies prefer to invest in richer countries.[99] Moreover, these countries as a rule are farther away. Market-related factors dominated in the allocation of Indian OFDI.[100] Besides, physical distance is not an impediment to Indian OFDI: the majority of OFDI was placed in the United States and Europe, which are far destinations for Indian companies. The interest in the U.S. and UK markets may be explained with the relatively short cultural distance between India and these two countries (including the British colonial past of the country) and also by the lack of language barriers, with English being the business language in India.

Indian firms use acquisitions more often than Chinese firms.[101] For both countries, market size and host-country trade openness are important factors in choosing their investment destinations. Given their operating experience in low-income environments, Chinese and Indian firms do not choose only developed, rich markets for FDI. Comparing Chinese and Indian technological multinationals shows that Chinese firms are more aggressive in their targeted assets, while Indian firms prefer investments in less competitive markets. Thus Indian firms exploit existing ownership advantages and acquire firms in developing countries, while Chinese firms tend to acquire strategic assets in more technologically advanced countries.

In the fast-growing countries, Indian firms mostly opt for build rather than buy (i.e. greenfield vs. M&A).[102] However, in some cases, market growth may be irrelevant to decision making for FDI: if large numbers of competitors enter a fast-growth, growth market, success may be compromised.[103] Risk aversion also matters in the decision-making process for Indian companies. The lower the uncertainty in the host country, the more likely a firm will choose an acquisition, when feasible.[104] Acquisitions are often driven by technological benefits. Yet Indian firms operating in technology-intensive sectors also opt for greenfield investments in order to protect their intellectual property.[105]

INSTITUTIONAL MATURITY

The institutional maturity of the destination market (especially regarding government effectiveness and low corruption levels) is an important argument for Indian investors,[106] which is not the case for Chinese companies.[107] It has also been argued that Indian companies choose OFDI in order to distance themselves from potential intervention of the Indian government. Having operations abroad protects Indian multinationals from unwanted meddling by lifting the companies to ambassadors of national pride.

Another key consideration for Indian investing firms is the larger Indian diaspora in the host country, which tends to become an increasingly important motive for MNEs to invest in those countries.[108]

RESOURCE SEEKING

India's OFDI is often led by highly entrepreneurial private firms that have capabilities in design, production, branding and distribution.[109] These firms are innovative at providing products and services of sufficient quality at low prices. Given the scarcity of industrial capacity in relation to India's size, certain strategic state initiatives encouraged public- and private-sector firms to seek natural resources (including energy) abroad in order to facilitate domestic industrial development.[110]

TECHNOLOGY SEEKING

Countries exporting technology are very attractive for India's OFDI. Given that many Indian firms are skilled technologically, such investments further strengthen technological capabilities and protect existing export markets.[111]

Through OFDI, Indian firms predominantly seek new technology and management skills rather than markets.[112] Contrary to most Chinese firms, Indian OFDI heads mostly for high-technology industries rather than resource-based industries. Numerous acquisitions have enabled Indian firms to acquire advanced technologies, brands and market share in foreign markets.

Another important difference with China is that most Indian FDI is made by private firms seeking to acquire intellectual assets and technological know-how, whereas Chinese FDI is mostly undertaken by government-owned firms and driven by resource-seeking motives.

Historical perspective on OFDI

Although Indian outbound FDI pre-dates (1960) the Chinese efforts (1982), India's restrictive OFDI regime limited investments to private company efforts in small, minority joint ventures in developing economies. After 1991, several factors accelerated matters: intense domestic economic competition, the growing global competitiveness of Indian firms and the liberalizations in OFDI and capital market policies. The sectors holding the greatest appeal were IT, pharmaceuticals, telecoms, automotive, metallurgy and services. In many of these sectors, Indian companies have sought to become global leaders.

Three major structural shifts occurred in Indian OFDI since the turn of the century:[113]

- First, the annual OFDI flows multiplied fiftyfold, from $340 million in 2000 to an average of $18 billion in 2007/2008. India has become the world's twenty-first-largest outward investor. Its average annual OFDI flows are now higher than those of many developed market economies.
- Second, manufacturing has displaced services as the principal OFDI driver. It dominated Indian OFDI flows at the turn of the decade, and now its share is growing the fastest. While pharmaceuticals, consumer electronics and automotive accounted for the bulk of manufacturing OFDI in the first half of the decade, the second half has seen a concentration in metallurgy, energy and natural resource investments, as well as increasing activity by consumer goods, including food and beverage.
- Third, over a half of India's total 2002–2009 outbound investments went into developed economies, most of them via M&A deals. In fact, since 2000, Indian firms have tended to use cross-border M&As as the main mode of entry into developed economies.

Using a two-speed tactic – M&A deals versus greenfield – Indian companies systematically acquire leading developed-country firms, thus capturing domain expertise, technological competitiveness, market size and brand recognition. Some of these acquisitions were undertaken to attain global size and status and to build new competitive advantage by combining international technology or know-how with lower-cost Indian labor. Other areas (e.g. telecoms, consumer goods, food, IT, metal and energy) are now also using M&A deals to build market presence.[114]

For entry into emerging markets, Indian multinationals prefer greenfield investments. Energy and mineral security have driven large greenfield investments in developing countries. Whereas Chinese FDI outflows used to be driven by state-owned enterprises and encouraged by proactive government policies, private conglomerates, such as the Tata Group or Bharti Airtel, have made recent Indian investments. As an example, Tata invested $11 billion to acquire Corus Group (United Kingdom and the Netherlands) in early 2007, creating Tata-Corus, the world's fifth-largest steelmaker by revenue.

Russia's FDI

FDI destinations

Russia stands out among emerging countries due to its consistent status as a net exporter and its exceptionally high outward/inward FDI flow ratio.[115] Investment began to flow out of the country as early as the middle of the twentieth century, albeit at low levels. Soviet firms operating abroad, known as "red multinationals,"[116] were very strictly controlled by the government and primarily provided export support abroad.[117]

Outflow volumes began to pick up gradually after the fall of the Soviet Union in the early 1990s. Though the primary focus of Russian enterprises at this time was self-restructuring as opposed to expanding, FDI outflows often exceeded inflows during this period.[118] In the 1990s, OFDI was largely informal and characterized by capital flight. This

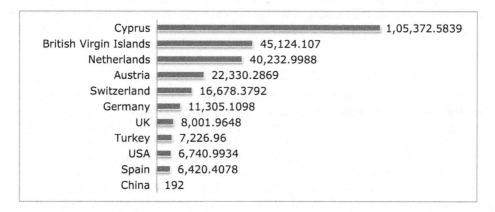

Cyprus — 1,05,372.5839
British Virgin Islands — 45,124.107
Netherlands — 40,232.9988
Austria — 22,330.2869
Switzerland — 16,678.3792
Germany — 11,305.1098
UK — 8,001.9648
Turkey — 7,226.96
USA — 6,740.9934
Spain — 6,420.4078
China — 192

Figure 2.6 Major destinations of Russian OFDI, 2015
Source: Central Bank of Russia 2015 (http://www.cbr.ru/statistics/?PrtId=svs)

exodus was motivated not by any desire to expand abroad, but rather to protect capital from the unstable economy by relocating it in safer places.[119]

Russia actively invests via tax havens, with Cyprus, the British Virgin Islands and the Netherlands accounting for over $190 billion of OFDI flows in 2015 (see Figure 2.6). This recent dramatic switch to offshore destinations can definitely be explained by the worsening economic situation in Russia due to the political tensions in 2013–2015 (Crimea and Ukraine crises).

In 2015, the top-five recipients of Russian FDI, in descending order, were Cyprus, the British Virgin Isles (BVI), the Netherlands, Austria and Switzerland. When disregarding obvious offshore companies and considering true capital investments, the key destinations are advanced economies in Europe and the United States. Many Russian multinationals, however, started their international expansion closer to home, in neighboring CIS countries such as the Ukraine or Kazakhstan.[120] Outflows to this region peaked between 2001 and 2004.

However, recent shifts have occurred in the geographic focus of Russian FDI. Russian companies have been concentrating more and more on other BRIC countries. In 2011, Russian stock in BRIC countries reached $1.1 billion, representing a sharp increase from previous years. According to the UNCTAD, this trend can be explained not by the desire to increase raw material supply, but rather "to expand their control over the value chains of their own natural resources, to build sustainable competitive advantages vis-à-vis other firms, and to strengthen their market positions in key developing countries." Russia has also dipped its toe in African waters. For example, aluminium producer Rusal has operations in Angola, Nigeria and South Africa. Additionally, Russian banks have entered the Dark Continent: Vneshtorgbank, for example, operates in Angola, Namibia, and Côte d'Ivoire.[121] Interest in Africa has been motivated by the desire to access key raw materials as well as gain a foothold in high-potential local markets.

Generally speaking, M&A deals are the most popular investment vehicle chosen by Russian firms, as opposed to greenfield build-ups.[122] Between 2007 and 2011, Russia acquired 476 businesses in Europe and launched only 142 greenfield projects. In 2013 alone, the value of foreign M&As by Russian multinationals increased by over 600% – a figure in large part driven by the acquisition of TNK-BP by oil company Rosneft. This preference for M&As as opposed to creating new facilities corresponds to the desire among Russian businesses for quick returns.[123]

FDI motives

Although a variety of motives help explain Russian OFDI, the dominating incentives are the search for markets and resources. Even so, other determinants such as seeking strategic assets, image building or insurance are also causal factors. Aspirations for better global recognition and improved image abroad have also been considerations for Russian OFDI.[124] In fact, Russian OFDI sets itself apart by the proportion of financial OFDI (as opposed to business expansion OFDI), with both business owners and financial investors wanting to mitigate the economic and political risks in their home market by holding assets offshore (a variety of post-transition "capital flight"). Although the "system-escape" motivation had decreased sharply after 1999, it bounced back during the global crisis.

RESOURCE SEEKING

Before the 2008 economic crisis, the largest outbound deals mainly involved Russian metallurgy and mining firms purchasing assets, mostly in Canada, Italy and the United States. In 2004, Norilsk Nickel acquired a 20% stake (worth $1.2 billion) of South Africa's Gold Fields Ltd., a transaction which made the Russian company the world's fourth-largest gold miner and diversified its operations from existing nickel and palladium production.[125]

Post-crisis, the fastest sector to recover was the oil & gas industry, with some noteworthy OFDI by Russian firms. In 2008–2009, Surgutneftegaz purchased 21% of the shares of Hungarian oil & gas company MOL ($1.8 billion); Lukoil bought 46% of the Lukarco refinery in the Netherlands ($1.65 billion) and acquired 49% of the ERG refinery in Sicily ($1.85 billion), while Rosneft acquired 50% of Ruhr Öl in Germany ($1.6 billion).[126]

The international diversification of the resource base has become vital for large Russian oil & gas companies; a steady supply of inputs at stable prices has become essential to their production processes. Similarly, Russian non-ferrous metal producers such as Rusal, Alrosa and Norilsk Nickel either face the growing cost of mining in Russia, or are unable to increase processing capacity due to lack of raw material reserves. Investing in a continuous supply of natural resources from abroad has become critical for many Russian firms.

MARKET SEEKING

Fewer Russian firms are driven by market-seeking motives, most probably because they are happy with unsaturated domestic demand and do not see any "low-hanging fruit" on the international scene. Telecoms and technology companies are the exceptions, where market- and customer-related motives have motivated OFDI. For instance, VimpelCom registered remarkable investment activity in 2010–2011 by purchasing the Ukrainian Kiyvstar GSM ($5.6 billion) and the Italian WindTelecom SPA ($6.5 billion). Despite expected interest in technologies and know-how, international investments of Russian telecoms was mostly driven by market-seeking motives rather than global technology-seeking motives.

STRATEGIC ASSET SEEKING

A large number of Russian multinationals operate in traditional, resource-intensive industries characterized by mature technologies. However, Russian OFDI in resource-based sectors are also partly driven by technology-access motivations. For example, while acquiring the part of the ISAB refinery in Sicily from ERG in 2008, Lukoil aimed at acquiring specific proprietary assets, including exploration and enhanced oil and recovery technology, as well as modern oil-processing technology.[127] After acquiring 100% of the JV, Lukoil became the sole owner of a €2.35 billion refinery with fully integrated technology capable of producing sixteen-million tons of refined products annually.[128]

Historical perspective on OFDI

Russian capital outflow intensified dramatically in the late 1990s and early 2000s, when the growth rate of OFDI stock surpassed that of other emerging economies such as Brazil and India. This increase can be attributed to several factors: first, the Russian Central Bank began to more accurately record FDI in 2007 (which was likely under-reported before then); second, Russian firms were finally ready to expand after several years of consolidating their competitive advantages on home turf.[129]

Since a good part of the Russian OFDI derives from Russian companies carrying out takeovers abroad, the dynamics of Russian OFDI can be followed using data on cross-border mergers and acquisitions (M&As). In the three-and-a-half year period from January 2005 to June 2008, such M&As exploded more than tenfold compared to 2001–2004, from $5.5 billion to $56.8 billion. Cross-border purchases were mostly in the primary sector (59% of deals from January 1997 to June 2008), followed by manufacturing (23%) and then services (18%), where telecoms dominated.

Russian firms have generally targeted developed-country investments, especially in Europe and North America. Of course, Russian investment has flowed bountifully to neighboring CIS nations – namely, Belarus and Ukraine – followed at a distance by Kazakhstan and Armenia. For some of these countries, Russia is the main source of inward FDI.[130]

As in most countries, the 2008 global financial crisis took its toll on Russian OFDI. From 2007 to 2008, FDI growth still continued, but grew by only about 15% (from $46 billion to $53 billion). In the first quarter of 2009, however, OFDI fell by 15% (from $16 billion to $13 billion) on a year-to-year basis. The data here is open to discussion, since Bank of Russia and Rosstat data differ. Yet the financial crisis has not stopped Russian companies from seeking to expand internationally. The going has been tougher, since commodity prices fluctuated disturbingly and market capitalization shrank. In 2009, there were no signs of the repatriation of Russian financial assets from abroad, notably from international financial centers such as Cyprus, the Netherlands, the British Virgin Islands and Gibraltar, which partly serve as tax havens for Russian firms. These locations still figured prominently in the OFDI flows of Russia in the first quarter of 2009.[131]

Recovery was quick, with over 65% increase between 2009 and 2013.[132] In 2009, Russia became a net outward investor, thanks to stronger commodity prices, a new round of privatization and economic recovery in other large commodity-exporting countries (Kazakhstan and Ukraine). In 2013, the country became the fourth-largest investor in foreign economies – up four places over 2012 – and accounted for 95% of outward invest-ment from all nine CIS-member countries.[133] The value of OFDI flows relative to the GDP of Russia was about 4.1% in 2013.[134]

Today, the state of the Russian economy and FDI is once again changing. Conflicts in the Ukraine have led to a series of sanctions imposed on the Russian Federation by European nations and the United States, and a significantly devalued currency. Plum-meting crude oil prices have dealt a significant blow to the economy, which relies heavily on energy exports. Furthermore, since many Russian multinationals (drivers of OFDI) have close ties to the state, politics play a role in decisions regarding their operations. For example, in late 2014, Gazprom cancelled the South Stream project, a massive oil pipeline to the EU, and incurred massive costs.[135]

Brazil's FDI

FDI destinations

Among Latin American countries, Brazil has shown the most intensive surge in OFDI, representing 40% of the total outward investment in the region. This jump in OFDI is usually justified by the intensification of internal competition, the appreciation of the local currency (Real) and the privatization and deregulation processes happening in the country.

The Brazilian OFDI history can be divided into two periods. From the beginning of the 1990s until 2004, the largest recipients of Brazilian FDI were tax haven countries such as British Virgin Islands, the Bahamas or the Cayman Islands. The share of OFDI to those countries reached 70% of the total. Since 2005, however, Brazilian OFDI has slightly changed direction. By 2010, the share of offshore destinations dropped to 40%. At the same time, the share to Europe increased to 42% and, together with the United States, became the largest recipient of Brazilian OFDI.[136] Nevertheless, in 2014, the share of "real" investments in two main partner economies – Portugal and the United States – remains below that of the single tax haven Cayman Islands (see Figure 2.7).

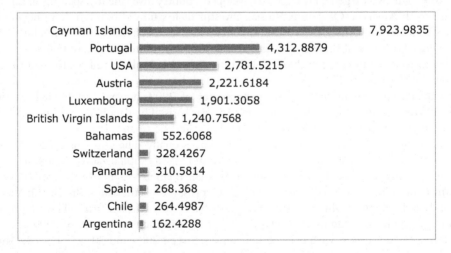

Figure 2.7 Major destinations of Brazilian OFDI, 2014

Source: Brazilian Central Bank 2014 (http://www.bcb.gov.br/?english)

FDI motives

Since 1985, Brazil OFDI has been spearheaded by three main sectors:

- the oil sector, which mainly was looking for sources of oil in different countries to satisfy internal demand;
- construction companies, seeking infrastructure projects abroad to compensate for reduced demand in Brazil; and
- the banking sector, mainly entering foreign markets to satisfy the demand of Brazilian companies operating abroad.

The three segments clearly responded to three types of investment motives: resource seeking, market seeking and strategic asset seeking.

MARKET SEEKING

Here Brazil is no different from other emerging markets. Brazilian investments are attracted to countries with big market potential: the higher the GDP of the host country, the greater the volume of OFDI.[137] Geographical distance also plays an important role, with Latin American countries closer to Brazil receiving greater investment. Suitable institutional environments are a priority for Brazilian firms, as they tend to choose countries with good business climate, political stability and good governance.

EFFICIENCY SEEKING

The increasing cost of doing business in Brazil is another important consideration for international expansion; in some industries, it is cheaper to run production facilities and establish export platforms abroad rather than at home. Although Brazil provides low production costs and flexibility in handling turbulent times (e.g. periods of high inflation), at the same time, Brazil suffers from high labor costs, low incentives for intellectual production, large infrastructure gaps and high taxes.[138] To overcome these disadvantages, Brazilian multinationals have to look for destinations providing better conditions. Examples of Brazilian companies seeking low-cost labor include the equipment manufacturer WEG, and the auto components producer Sabo.

QUALITY OF INSTITUTIONS

Brazilian companies are choosy regarding economic openness and institutional stability when selecting FDI destinations. Since these multinationals are expanding abroad during the earlier stages of Brazilian economic development, specific, often different, determinants are present. By and large, Brazilian firms seek to invest in countries with similar types of domestic environment.[139]

ECONOMIC CONSIDERATIONS

Economic growth and economic freedom of the host country attract FDI from Brazil,[140] with economic factors being even more significant than institutional and political ones in attracting investments.[141] The causal weight of institutional factors appears to be much lower than macroeconomic factors; this explains why economic factors empirically carry more significance for Brazilian OFDI, according to academic research.[142]

Historical perspective on Brazilian OFDI

It is only recently that Brazilian companies started venturing abroad. From 2000 to 2003, outward foreign direct investment (OFDI) averaged only $0.7 billion annually. From 2004 to 2008, this annual average jumped to nearly $14 billion.

In 2007, FDI outflows from Latin America and the Caribbean, excluding offshore financial centers, surged by 125% to $43 billion. The primary sector (agriculture and mining) was the main target of outward FDI, followed by resource-based manufacturing and telecommunications. Brazil is the region's principal FDI source country, with $28 billion in FDI outflows in 2007, the country's highest level ever since the beginning of the twenty-first century and, for the first time, its outflows climbed higher than its inflows.

The $17 billion purchase of Inco (a Canadian nickel producer) by the country's mining company, CVRD, was responsible for a significant share of the increase. It was the largest acquisition ever undertaken by a Latin American company and reflects CVRD's strategy of diversification out of Brazil and iron ore. In addition, a series of other acquisitions and investments by Brazilian companies, such as Itau (banking), Petrobras (oil & gas), Votorantim (cement, pulp and paper, steel and mining), Gerdau (steel), Odebrecht (construction services, petrochemicals) Camargo Corrêa (cement), WEG (motors and generators) and Marcopolo (buses), also contributed to the country's OFDI.[143] Large Brazilian companies are pursuing a strategy of internationalization through FDI.

Despite the financial crisis of 2008, when global FDI inflows fell by roughly 15%, Brazil almost tripled its foreign investments; they exploded from just over $7 billion in 2007 to nearly $21 billion in 2008. Central Bank data puts the current stock of Brazilian OFDI at $104 billion, which is an increase of 89% over 2003.[144]

Much of Brazilian FDI flows to offshore financial centers, which hosted 57% of 2005 Brazilian OFDI stock. The trend over recent years has been for FDI to target developed countries rather than financial centers: their share in Brazil's total OFDI stock jumped from 13% in 2001 to 35% in 2005, while that of developing and transition economies other than financial centers fell from 13% to 8%.[145]

2.5 Institutional determinants for outward FDI from emerging economies

As seen previously, the institutional environment in the destination countries is a critical determinant in deciding on OFDI, and it therefore deserves some detailed attention. Thankfully, existing research on OFDI does go beyond macroeconomic factors and also sheds light on the institutional factors. These rules of the game include both formal and informal rules, as well as constraints that shape business decisions.[146]

The relevance of institutions on attracting FDI was first noticed when research uncovered that economic factors alone could not explain the attractiveness of a country.[147] Indeed institutions play a role in corporate decisions because they facilitate transactions and lower their costs, reducing uncertainty and mitigating risks.[148] Therefore, government agencies, non-profit organizations and local authorities are able to improve attractiveness if they proactively foster institutional efficiency.[149]

Both host-country and home-country institutions are taken into account in corporate FDI decision making. Increasing competition and resource scarcity in the home country, as well as an investment-friendly environment in the host country, will induce firms to internationalize. Conversely, economic growth in the home country and institutional constraints in the host country will lead firms to question overseas expansion.[150]

Taking the home-country perspective, the government can promote OFDI to emerging countries by implementing favorable policies – for example, liberal policies on capital outflows.[151] Yet the governmental position is also related to the level of state ownership in productive assets and certainly can impact on the location and type of outbound investment (e.g. resource or market seeking).[152] Moreover, governments may influence corporate strategic decisions in priority sectors, where investment may receive most-favored treatment.[153]

As for the host-country perspective, the role of economic, institutional and political factors in attracting inbound FDI is almost equally high. Although host-country economic factors have a stronger influence on FDI inflows, the institutional environment measured by rule of law and voice and accountability in the host countries may stimulate FDI inflow, whether from developed or emerging home countries.[154] For example, Brazilian multinationals prefer to invest in countries with good institutional environments, which can be explained by as yet limited global experience and knowledge of foreign markets.[155] Brazilian OFDI is also influenced by the regulatory quality of the host country, its economic performance and cultural distance.[156]

Emerging markets having high corruption levels suffer significant negative impact. Corruption is inherent to an environment with poor legal and regulatory systems that do not function properly. Corruption reduces FDI flows, as it creates barriers and obstacles to foreign investment, increases transaction costs and reduces profits.[157] Yet companies facing corruption issues in their home countries have an advantage in host countries with similar blemishes. Empirical findings indicate higher levels of investment in corrupt-corrupt country pairings than in clean-corrupt pairings, because "clean" multinationals are largely risk averse.[158] Thus the location choice of FDI depends on both home- and host-country corruption indices.

The concept of good governance implies non-corrupt public institutions; an effective, speedy and transparent legal system; political stability; and established governmental policies on international trade. These factors all relate positively to FDI.[159] Thus a government that establishes an effective legal system to control corruption, ensures protection of property and individual rights and enhances political stability creates more fertile ground for incoming FDI. Singapore can be quoted as the extraordinary example, as it attracts far more than its weight in FDI because of its squeaky-clean governance (and low tax rates!). This also explains why the political and economic instability, poor infrastructure and ineffective governance of some other Asian countries, and most African countries, deter much FDI.[160]

Many multinational acquisitions can be explained by the government effectiveness that guarantees the long-term legal protection of company interests.[161] However, government effectiveness does not always attract inward FDI (for example, the case of Latin America), implying that economic conditions and market potential outweigh institutional efficiencies in the region.[162] By other words, the force of the state does also have limits.

Political stability exerts a significant and positive impact on FDI since political risks can imply very high costs to investing firms. For example, in 2007, Bolivia expropriated a Petrobras refinery. Because of the absence of international agreements between Bolivia and Brazil, Petrobras was limited in its options to solve the problem. The Brazilian company's interests were unprotected and ended up sacrificed because of changes in Bolivia's national policy. Another example is BP's failed experience in Russia. TNK-BP was formed in 2003 with the blessings of both Russian president Vladimir Putin and British prime minister Tony Blair. After some years, TNK-BP was accused of insufficient gas production, violating environmental regulations and even espionage. After several years of fighting, the state-owned Russian company Rosneft acquired BP's 50% stake in the TNK-BP joint venture, which turned it into one of the largest listed oil producers. These setbacks justify why politically stable countries receive greater FDI inflows.[163]

The institutional distance between home and host countries is another factor that reduces FDI flows.[164] Countries with developed institutions such as Germany or the United States are less likely to invest in the countries with low-quality institutions, such as Somalia. High institutional distance makes the transfer of management practices and tools from home country to host country complex. This is why companies prefer full acquisitions when their targets are situated in emerging markets characterized by high institutional distance. On the contrary, if the investor wishes to leverage the advantages of operational synergies, it tends to share control with the host company.[165]

One word about a peculiarity of the Chinese market. Even though the Chinese institutional distance is high from just about every country, China is such a large market that foreign investors adapt to the environment in order to remain active.[166] Informal institutional factors are also significant in the OFDI choices of Chinese multinationals. Cultural proximity and common language were found to favorably impact both Chinese and Indian OFDI.[167] And, naturally, even a simple matter such as a common border will stimulate FDI flows between neighboring countries.[168] All these factors comprise informal institutional distance between host and home countries.

2.6 Russia: still solid as BRIC?

What does it mean for a country to be a BRIC? And above all does Russia still qualify? In 2005, Goldman Sachs asked, "How solid are the BRICs?,"[169] and subsequently, in 2013, co-authors Snejina Michailova, Daniel McCarthy and Sheila Puffer (editors of a special issue of the *Critical Perspectives on International Business* journal), asked the question "Russia: As solid as a BRIC?"[170]

Even before the tumble in oil prices (the traditional backbone of Russia's economy), before the devaluation of the ruble in 2014, and before the post-Crimea sanctions, academics were questioning whether Russia was on a similar footing with the strongest emerging markets, and if so, what are the most important distinctions of Russia.

In its 2015 investment report, UNCTAD summed up the effects of the sanctions on the economies of Russia, and of the CIS countries in general. Sanctions were caused by conflict between Russia and Ukraine, and were implemented in March 2014 by the United States, the EU and Japan. Coupled with the strong currency deprivation and other macroeconomic factors, these sanctions affected Russian inward and outward FDI in 2014–2015. The impact on FDI was both direct and indirect. The direct impact can be easily observed by the volume of FDI inflows and outflows in 2014, which fell by a whopping 70% after a decade of steady growth (from $69 to $21 billion in 2014).

The Russian economy suffered from sanctions in three ways: first, massive capital outflows caused a significant depreciation of the ruble and volatility on the foreign exchange markets; second, a limitation on external borrowing as access to international financial markets was restricted for some Russian banks and firms; and third, a drastic reduction of consumption and private investment due to the drop in business and consumer confidence regarding growth prospects.[171]

Natural resources industries were traditionally the most attractive for inbound foreign investments. However, in 2014, FDI in these industries also came to a standstill. Some foreign companies have already started to abandon their Arctic projects. For example, ExxonMobil (United States) had to freeze all ten of its joint ventures with Rosneft in the region. A similar story happened to Shell (United Kingdom + Holland), which suspended its joint project with Gazprom Neft in the Bazhenov area, and for Total (France), which stopped its project with Lukoil.

One of the most visible business impacts of the sanctions was in the automotive industry. In recent years, leading international car manufactures, such as Renault, Volkswagen, Toyota and General Motors, supported by Russian industrial policy, had established production facilities in Russia. In 2014, there was a significant drop in automotive sales in Russia because demand collapsed, and automotive manufacturers had to cut their production. Although Volkswagen simply reduced its production in Kaluga, General Motors announced its complete withdrawal from Russia by December 2015.

The beverage and tobacco industries face similar situations, with large international companies such as Coca-Cola Hellenic, PepsiCo and Carlsberg reassessing their operations in Russia. Coca-Cola Hellenic closed its plant in Nizhny Novgorod, while Carlsberg announced closing two of its ten breweries.

Outbound FDI from Russia also fell victim to the sanctions, dropping by 35% in 2014, from $87 billion in 2013 to $56 billion. Sanctions against state-controlled banks such as VTB, Sberbank and Gazprombank turned into one of the biggest threats to Russian OFDI.

Furthermore, many Russian multinationals that drive OFDI have close ties with the state, with politics invariably playing a role in strategic investment decisions. For example, in late 2014, Gazprom cancelled the South Stream project, a massive oil pipeline to the EU, and incurred massive costs as a result.[172]

The OFDI reductions have also hit neighboring CIS countries, with Russia cutting its CIS outflow almost in half. In the end, the weaker transition economies of Central Asia are experiencing the impact of Western sanctions and suffering since they are closely linked economically to Russia.

Alas, not even Russia's technology has developed a crystal ball. It is difficult to foresee Russia's economic prospects and international position in the short term. Obviously, the switch in economic policy priorities from natural resources to technology will have an impact. Alas, again, despite the manna of high oil prices for almost a decade, instead of investing in technological development and economic diversification, and thus shedding the "Energy Empire" cloak, officials were busy transforming huge oil giant profits into new energy projects and profits (much of which scurried into anonymous offshore havens). Is there a silver lining to the cloud of the dramatic decrease of oil prices and isolation of the Russian economy? It may be the opportunity for the country to re-think its economic policy and build a future on innovation rather than on extraction.

References

1 http://lexicon.ft.com/Term?term=emerging-markets
2 http://www.msci.com/resources/products/indexes/global_equity_indexes/gimi/stdindex/MSCI_Market_Classification_Framework.pdf
3 Kvint 2009.

4   World Bank report *Emerging-Market Multinationals Becoming a Potent Force in Reshaping the Process of Industrial Globalization.*
5   O'Neill 2001.
6   Goldman Sachs 2003.
7   Goldman Sachs 2005.
8   The World Bank.
9   *The Investment Guide to Brazil.* http://arq.apexbrasil.com.br/legado/investmentguidetobrasil2014.pdf
10 U.S. Department of State 2014.
11 Ernst & Young 2012
12 Gaurav 2015
13 Transparency International 2014.
14 Rosstat, 2013
15 The World Bank. Russia overview.
16 Ibid.
17 Hanson 2013.
18 Panibratov and Kalotay 2009.
19 Hanson 2013.
20 Kuznetsov 2011.
21 The World Bank. India's overview.
22 Ibid.
23 Narula and Kodiyat 2013.
24 World Bank "Ease of doing business."
25 Reserve Bank of India. https://www.rbi.org.in
26 http://www.careratings.com/upload/NewsFiles/Studies/Outward%20FDI%20Investment%20by%20India.pdf
27 Ibid.
28 Ibid.
29 Yeung and Liu 2008.
30 Kolstad and Wiig 2012.
31 He and Lyles 2008.
32 Kamal et al. 2014.
33 Berning and Holtbrügge 2012.
34 Du and Boateng 2012; Lu et al. 2010.
35 UNCTAD 2015.
36 China Statistical Yearbook 2015, http://www.stats.gov.cn/tjsj/ndsj/2015/indexeh.htm.
37 http://www.vcc.columbia.edu/files/vale/documents/Profiles_China_IFDI_24_Oct_2012_-_FINAL.pdf
38 Especially before China became a member of the WTO in 2001.
39 Rothkopf, D. What BRIC would be without China . . . Rothkopf.foreignpolicy.com.
40 The Hindu News update service 2009.
41 The World Bank. Mexico's profile.
42 http://www.tradingeconomics.com/mexico/gdp-growth-annual
43 http://atlas.media.mit.edu/profile/country/mex/
44 http://www.ventanamagazine.com/html/articulo.php?ID=287
45 http://gdex.dk/ofdi10/Arturo%20Franco%20-%20OFDI%20The%20case%20of%20Mexico.pdf
46 The World Bank. Indonesia's profile.
47 *Legal Guide to Investment in Indonesia* https://www.allens.com.au/pubs/pdf/Investing-in-Indonesia.pdf
48 http://www3.bkpm.go.id/en/home-investment, Investment Coordinating Board of the Republic of Indonesia BKPM.
49 http://rauli.cbs.dk/index.php/cjas/article/viewFile/2288/2527
50 http://www.ey.com/Publication/vwLUAssets/Beyond_Asia:_South_Korea_Highlights/$FILE/south_korea_Final.pdf
51 http://export.gov/southkorea/build/groups/public/@eg_kr/documents/webcontent/eg_kr_065739.pdf
52 The World Bank.
53 The World Bank. Turkey's profile.

54 Central Bank of Turkey 2014. http://www.tcmb.gov.tr/wps/wcm/connect/tcmb+en/tcmb+en
55 The World Bank.
56 Ernst & Young's 2013a.
57 World Bank 2013.
58 The World Bank.
59 Ross 2014.
60 Kolstad and Wiig 2012.
61 Velde 2006.
62 Aleksynska and Havrylchyk 2013.
63 Jadhav 2012.
64 Quazi 2007.
65 Vogiatzoglou 2007; Hyun and Kim 2010.
66 Vijayakumar et al. 2010.
67 Zhang 2001.
68 Ho et al. 2013.
69 Hyun and Kim 2010.
70 Froot and Stein 1991.
71 Amal et al. 2010.
72 United States agency of international development 2005. https://www.usaid.gov/
73 James 2009.
74 Buckley et al. 2007.
75 Morck et al. 2008.
76 UNCTAD.
77 Ibid.
78 Zhou and Leung 2015.
79 Ibid.
80 UNCTAD.
81 Zhou and Leung 2015.
82 Krkoska and Korniyenko 2008.
83 Sauvant and Nolan 2015.
84 Chang 2014.
85 Zhang and Daly 2011; Amighini et al. 2013.
86 Ibid.
87 Cui and Jiang 2010.
88 Sauvant and Chen 2014.
89 Kang and Jiang 2012.
90 World investment report 2007 by United Nations Conference on Trade and Development (2007, October 16).
91 Davies 2010.
92 Ibid.
93 Irwin and Gallagher 2014.
94 Sauvant and Chen 2014.
95 Zhou and Leung 2015.
96 Reserve Bank of India.
97 UNCTAD.
98 Pradhan 2008.
99 Fung and Garcia-Herrero 2012.
100 Nunnenkamp et al. 2012; Garcia-Herrero and Deorukhkar 2014.
101 De Beule and Duanmu 2012.
102 Larimo 2003.
103 Gomes-Casseres 1990.
104 Mudambi and Navarra 2002.
105 Rienda et al. 2013.
106 Garcia-Herrero and Deorukhkar 2014.
107 Fung and Garcia-Herrero 2012.
108 Nunnenkamp et al. 2012.
109 Govindarajan and Ramamurti 2010.

110 Nagaraj 2006.
111 Garcia-Herrero and Deorukhkar 2014.
112 Pradhan 2011.
113 Satyanand and Raghavendran 2010.
114 Ibid.
115 Driga and Dura 2013.
116 Hamilton 1986.
117 Panibratov 2010.
118 Kalotay and Sulstarova 2010.
119 Panibratov 2010.
120 Kalotay and Sulstarova 2010.
121 UNCTAD.
122 Driga and Dura 2013.
123 Panibratov 2012.
124 Panibratov and Kalotay 2009.
125 Kalotay 2005.
126 Panibratov and Kalotay 2009.
127 Kalotay and Panibratov 2013.
128 http://newsru.com/finance/31dec2013/lukoil.html
129 Kalotay and Sulstarova 2010; Panibratov 2010.
130 Panibratov and Kalotay 2009.
131 Ibid.
132 UNCTAD 2014.
133 Ibid.
134 The World Bank.
135 Lossan, A. 2015. Is Gazprom cutting the Turkish Stream in half? Russia Beyond the Headlines http://rbth.com/business/2015/07/17/is_gazprom_cutting_the_turkish_stream_in_half_47821. html
136 Brazilian Central Bank 2014. http://www.bcb.gov.br/en/
137 Amal and Tomio 2015.
138 Drouvot and Magalhaes 2007.
139 Martins 2012.
140 Bengoa and Sanchez-Robles 2003.
141 Quazi 2007.
142 Amal, Raboch and Tomio 2009.
143 Economic Survey of Latin America and the Caribbean 2007–2008: Macroeconomic policy and volatility. ECLAC 2007. http://www.cepal.org/en/publications/economic-survey-latin-america-and-caribbean-2007-2008-macroeconomic-policy-and
144 Lima and de Barros 2009.
145 World investment report 2007 by United Nations Conference on Trade and Development (2007, October 16).
146 North 1990.
147 Amal et al. 2009.
148 Mudambi and Navarra 2002; North 1990.
149 Bevan and Estrin 2004.
150 Luo and Wang 2012.
151 Goh and Wong 2011.
152 Wang et al. 2012; Peng et al. 2008.
153 Du and Boateng 2015; Panibratov 2012.
154 Malhotra, Russow and Singh 2014.
155 Jadhav 2012.
156 Amal and Tomio 2015.
157 Egger and Winner 2006; Habib and Zurawicki 2002.
158 Cuervo-Cazurra 2006.
159 Mishra and Daly 2007.
160 Mengistu and Adhikary 2011.
161 Deng and Yang 2015; Peng et al. 2008.

162 Amal et al. 2010.
163 Walsh and Yu 2010.
164 Bénassy-Quéré et al. 2007.
165 Contractor et al. 2014.
166 Lu et al. 2010; Hung et al. 2008.
167 Buckley et al. 2007.
168 Cheng and Ma 2008.
169 Goldman Sachs 2005.
170 Michailova, McCarthy and Puffer 2013.
171 World Investment Report 2015.
172 Russia Beyond the Headlines 2015.

3 Sowing knowledge in emerging economies

One of the dramatic disadvantages of emerging market firms is their lack of knowledge of how to operate internationally. Luckily, inward internationalization by foreign multinationals into emerging markets provides local firms with the chance to learn and adopt the practices and strategies of their foreign counterparts.

This chapter will present interesting lessons from global companies with extensive operations in emerging markets. The cases of Royal Dutch Shell, Groupe Casino and Telefónica in Brazil; Volvo, Disney and Google in China; Vodafone and Walmart in India; BP, Caterpillar, DHL and Pfizer in Russia will illustrate and explain how multinationals from advanced economies succeeded (or not) in emerging economies, and what are the most important implications for emerging market firms.

3.1 International companies in Brazil: the cases of Royal Dutch Shell, Groupe Casino and Telefónica

Royal Dutch Shell: being strategic towards Brazil

Company overview

Royal Dutch Shell plc (Shell) is an independent Anglo-Dutch multinational oil & gas corporation headquartered in the Hague, Netherlands, and incorporated in the United Kingdom. The company is engaged in the principal aspects of the oil & gas industry in more than seventy countries[1] and was the fourth-largest company in the world in 2014, in terms of revenue,[2] and one of the sixs oil & gas "supermajors" (which are considered to be BP, Chevron, ExxonMobil, Royal Dutch Shell, Total and ENI, with ConocoPhillips). Although Shell's history dates back to the early nineteenth century, it was officially formed only in 1907, after the merger of Shell Transport & Trading and Royal Dutch Petroleum. Nowadays, its logo is one of the most familiar commercial symbols in the world.

Shell is vertically integrated, operating in three segments:

- upstream, focusing on exploration for new liquids and natural gas reserves and on developing new projects;
- downstream, focusing on turning crude oil into a range of refined products (moved and marketed around the world for domestic, industrial and transport use); and
- corporate, managing upstream activities in North and South America.

Thus Shell is active in every area of the oil & gas industry: exploration and production, refining, distribution and marketing, petrochemicals, power generation and trading.[3] Shell also extracts bitumen from oil sands that is converted into synthetic crude oil.[4]

Shell is one of the world's most valuable companies. For the last twenty-one years, it has been listed on the Fortune 500, which identified its main strengths, weaknesses, opportunities and threats. As for its strengths, it is one of the largest companies in the world, with a highly diversified set of businesses; it operates in a fast-growing segment, liquefied natural gas (LNG) that accounts for the majority of Shell's income. However, the company has seen three straight years of declining revenue and profits due to the 4% decrease of oil & gas production between 2013 and 2014. This fact allowed China's Sinopec to "leapfrog" Shell in terms of annual sales.[5]

During the past years, new opportunities have appeared which the company has been able to capitalize on. First, it pushed forward with new oil & gas projects in countries such as Nigeria, Malaysia and Mexico. Second, it acquired BG Group, which experts claim will make Shell a world leader in LNG production. As for the threats, Shell has pumped billions of dollars into a contentious Alaskan Arctic drilling campaign that has faced major opposition from environmentalists and has prompted concerns over possible spills.[6] Finally, the current volatility in oil prices has put Shell's value at risk.

Since January 2014, Ben van Beurden has been the company's CEO. The company has a primary listing on the London Stock Exchange, secondary listings on Euronext Amsterdam and the New York Stock Exchange and is included in the FTSE 100 Index.

Emerging markets: new opportunities for Shell

In the 1980s, Shell grew through acquisitions and started several challenging offshore exploration projects.[7] It purchased the remaining percent shareholding in Shell Oil in 1985 to consolidate its American operations. Moreover, the 1980s witnessed the increasing development of various offshore exploration projects – new opportunities connected with, for instance, the reopening of Eastern European markets due to the collapse of communist regimes.

During the 1990s, the decade of biomass fuels and gas-to-liquids technology development, Shell developed its LNG business and in the 2000s entered new growth areas in the East. The turn of the century saw Shell begin to move into new growth areas of the world, notably China and Russia (oil & gas projects, including Sakhalin in Russia, and construction of massive petrochemical plants in China to supply the country's rapidly growing consumer market).

There are several major projects under construction in emerging economies, with the notable presence of Shell. There are also few a projects that provide natural gas to the Nigeria LNG plant on Bonny Island and an independent power plant at Gbarain in the Niger Delta. The SSAGS (Southern Swamp Associated Gas Solutions) project in Nigeria is designed to manage natural gas produced along with oil in the Southern Swamp, while the TNP (Trans Niger Pipeline), which is part of the gas liquids evacuation infrastructure, transports around 180,000 barrels of crude oil per day to the Bonny Export Terminal. Additionally, Shell developed a revolutionary floating LNG technology to access offshore gas fields that were otherwise too costly or difficult to develop: the Prelude FLNG project. The company also has a deepwater project in Malikai (Malaysia) as well as several other projects in EEs, including Nigeria, Philippines, Brazil and Russia.

Brazilian energy sector

Brazil is an important regional oil & gas producer and the world's second-largest ethanol fuel producer. It is also the tenth-largest energy consumer in the world and the largest in South America.

In the late 1990s, Brazil's energy sector underwent market liberalization. To establish the legal and regulatory framework, the Petroleum Investment Law was adopted in 1997 with the key objectives of creating governmental agencies responsible for energy policy, the CNPE (National Council for Energy Policy) and the ANP (National Agency of Petroleum, or Natural Gas and Biofuels); increasing competition in the energy market; attracting investments in power generation; and maximizing the use of natural gas. After the law's adoption, the state monopoly of oil & gas exploration was ended, and energy subsidies were reduced. The government, however, retained monopoly control of key energy complexes by administering the price of certain energy products. As a result, energy efficiency (in both residential and industrial sectors) was improved.

Currently, state-owned companies Petroleo Brasileiro S.A. (Petrobras) and Eletrobrás are the major players in Brazil's energy sector. Petrobras (ranked 416 in the Forbes Global 2000 list) is a Brazilian multinational energy corporation headquartered in Rio de Janeiro, and it is one of Shell's major competitors. It is one of the largest companies in the Southern Hemisphere by market capitalization, and even though it ceased to be Brazil's legal oil monopoly after 1997, it remains the Brazilian market leader. Petrobras controls significant oil and energy assets in Africa, North America, South America, Europe and Asia.

Oil production remains on the upswing in Brazil. Between 2010 and 2014, the average daily production of pre-salt level (i.e. offshore) oil grew by a whopping 1,000% from 42,000 to 492,000 BPD. Brazil's offshore production now accounts for 20% of Brazil's oil output and will account for roughly half by 2018 as new wells come online.

At the end of 2015, with the Brazilian economy suffering its worst recession in decades, the State of Rio de Janeiro imposed additional taxes on oil production. Rio de Janeiro is responsible for 67% of crude output and 40% of natural gas. The new flat tax of $0.69 on every barrel produced in the state will mean about $476 million in the state coffers. Among the state's main oil & gas producers are Petroleo Brasileiro, BG Group, Royal Dutch Shell and Portugal's Galp Energia SGPS.

Entering Brazil

Brazil's recent (1980) offshore oil wealth has been a huge driver of FDI. Nearly every major multinational oil firm has a hand in Brazil, with Shell being no exception. The company is considering billions in Brazilian investment in the next years.

SHELL BRASIL PETROLEO

The Rio de Janeiro–based subsidiary of Shell, Shell Brasil Petroleo, is the biggest operator in Brazil after Petrobras. Shell started its operations in Brazil in 1913 and since 1998 has spent more than $7 billion on exploration and production there. In 2015, the company sold its 80% stake in the Bijupirá and Salema fields in the Campos Basin – an offshore operation that started production in 2003 – to local firm HRT Participações em Petroleo.

The company operates various onshore and offshore extraction blocks in the Santos, Espírito Santo and São Francisco basins. Its upstream operations include natural gas and energy generation, oil & gas exploration and production, lubricants and Shell marine (which supplies over 15,000 ships). Its downstream services range from aviation, supply and distribution to retail, with 2,700 points of sale (gas stations).

RAÍZEN JOINT VENTURE WITH COSAN

Raízen, a 50-50 JV formed in February 2010 by Shell and Japanese company Cosan, stands out as one of the most competitive energy companies in the world, and is Brazil's fifth-largest company in terms of revenues. Raízen has nearly forty thousand employees, and its main businesses are in ethanol and sugar production, fuels distribution and cogeneration power.

In the fuels distribution segment, Raízen has a broad presence in Brazil. It has a network of 4,700 fuel stations (under the Shell brand), plus delivery to fifty-four airports and sixty harbor terminals. It annually produces 2 billion liters of ethanol and 4 million tons of sugar and sells 1.5 million mWh of electricity. The company's market value is approximately $15 billion and annual revenues amount to $26 billion. In 2015, Raízen reported revenues of $5.9 billion.[8] As for fuel distribution, Raízen's portfolio includes 5,245 service stations, 910 convenience stores, 60 distribution terminals, 130 million kilometers of distribution trips each year, 58 airports with the company's presence (represents approximately 95% of aviation fuel market demand in Brazil) and 23 billion liters of fuels.

In terms of cogeneration power, Raízen is the leading producer of electricity from sugar cane biomass. The company operates 13 thermoelectric power plants associated with its production units and with total installed capacity of 940 MW. This potential represents annual electricity sales of 2.2 million mWh. This is enough to power a city of five million inhabitants.

Brazil is one of the leading global producers of sugar from sugar cane, and this segment is a significant component of Raízen's business. The company is the leader in sugar production and plays an important role in the region. Moreover, it is becoming the largest sugar exporter, with an annual production of four million tons during the 2011–2012 harvest year. Approximately 70% of the total production was sold to countries such as Russia, China and Indonesia.

Raízen has more than three thousand strategic partners for its sugar cane supply chain, who are responsible for 50% of all raw material processed by the company. It also collaborates with outside institutions renowned for their technical competence and innovative nature, such as Iogen and Codexis. Raízen is notable for its dynamism and innovation in pursuit of sustainable development. As for ethanol production, it represents a significant competitive advantage for Brazil over other countries and contributes to maintaining a cleaner renewable energy mix. Ethyl alcohol, an environmentally friendly fuel, is produced from the fermentation and processing of sugar cane. It attracts substantial financial resources, generates jobs and develops the nation, making it a success story in the production of sustainable energy.

The company exports part of its ethanol production with products including industrial alcohol, neutral alcohol and carburation ethanol. Import and export companies are its principal customers that distribute these products to other countries.

Raízen's integrated logistics drive the efficiencies obtained in its delivery over a vast distribution network. In the B2B segment, the company focuses on efficiency so as to provide savings and sustainability for more than 1,100 clients (among these are cargo and passenger carriers, agribusiness, mining, rail and industrial companies). To this end, Raízen created products aimed at fostering efficient consumption, one of which is Expers, an intelligent system for the management and control of transportation fleets that makes it possible to keep account of fuel purchases and leads to reductions in consumption and CO2 emissions.

THE "PARQUE DAS CONCHAS" PROJECT

Shell has been a leader in deepwater exploration and production for thirty years, and the 2009 Parque das Conchas project off the Brazilian coast is one of the company's most challenging deepwater projects yet. It represents a key milestone in the development and commercialization of Brazil's deepwater oil. Shell is the main operator and has a 50% interest in the project, while Indian company ONGC and Qatar Petroleum International hold 27% and 23%, respectively.

Parque das Conchas is located in the Campos Basin, where the ocean depths reach 1,780 meters. The total area of the basin is 100,000 km², and the reserves are estimated to be 101.53 km³ of natural gas and 1.1 billion m³ of condensate and oil. The heart of the production facility is the floating production and storage (FPSO) vessel, Espirito Santo (built by SBM in Singapore), which has a processing capacity of 100,000 BPD. It was delivered to Brazil in late 2008.

There are three main phases of the project. Phase 1 included the development of three deposits connected to the FPSO vessel via subsea wells and manifolds. It includes nine producing wells and one gas injector well, while the FPSO's design required significant power and heat delivery systems to drive the seabed lift equipment and process the heavy crude oils. The fields came on stream in July 2009, and by July 2013, the project had produced more than seventy million barrels of oil equivalent (BOE). Phase 2 (to tie-in the Argonauta O-North field) came on stream in October 2013 and has an estimated peak production of thirty-five thousand BOE per day. Shell and its partners announced Phase 3 of the project in July of that same year. This part of the project is expected to have a peak production of twenty-eight thousand BOE per day and will include the installation of subsea infrastructure at the Massa and Argonauta O-South fields, which in turn will be connected to the Espírito Santo vessel.

Royal Dutch Shell today: deepwater oil reserves

Despite the drive to cut spending in the face of low oil prices, on 8 April 2015, Shell finally announced it had agreed to buy BG Group for $70 billion, subject to shareholder and regulatory approval (Shell intends to sell parts of its business to pay for the deal). This serious step will make Shell, which currently produces around fifty-two thousand barrels a day, the single largest foreign owner of Brazilian oil with an estimated production of 550,000 BPD by 2020. The deal will also transform Shell into the world's biggest LNG supplier.

The key reason behind Shell's acquisition of BG buy was gaining greater access to Brazil's deep-water oil reserves, which are set to become a key source for meeting growing global demand over the next few decades. Shell only has drilling rights in the so-called Libra Basin, while BG has drilling rights to blocks in Iara, Sapinhoá, Lapa and the Lula (formerly Tupi) plots.

To gain access to the offshore pre-salt oil wells Shell and BG are required by law to partner with Petrobras, which is currently being investigated for orchestrating a decades-long scheme to fraud the government and shareholders out of billions of dollars, with dozens of executives arrested and the bankruptcy of two major construction companies.

Amid the vast corruption scandal, Petrobras is selling assets worth nearly $14 billion. Along with international peers ExxonMobil, Total and BP, Shell has shown interest in Petrobras's producing oilfields as well as operating rights in Brazil's coveted offshore sub-salt basin. According to several sources, Shell has earmarked up to $5 billion for new acquisitions.

According to Shell's top management, Brazil is considered the most exciting area in the world for the oil industry. Shell's long-term goal is to gain a stronger presence in Brazil's deepwater oilfields. Shell has, therefore, announced plans to sell around $30 billion in global assets between 2016 and 2018 to improve its balance sheet and focus on its core deepwater oil and LNG business in Brazil.

Groupe Casino: acquiring another acquirer in Brazil

Company background

Groupe Casino is an international mass retailer headquartered in Saint-Étienne, in central France. It offers high-quality, innovative, attractive private-label products in more than 14,000 stores all around the world and employs over 336,000 employees, accounting for €48.6 billion in revenues and profits of €2.2 billion. Focusing on markets with high potential such as Brazil, Colombia, Thailand and Vietnam, Casino holds leadership positions in these markets (leader in Brazil, Colombia and Vietnam and second rank in Thailand). The chairman and CEO is Jean-Charles Naouri, a French businessman. In 2015, he was ranked number 1,533 and number 35 in the 2015 billionaires list (in the world and France, respectively), with a net worth of $1.2 billion. Besides Casino, Naouri is also a director of Fimalac, a holding company with interests in financial services, luxury hotels and entertainment, and in the Go Sport chain, a sporting goods retailer. In June 2013, he was appointed France's special representative for economic relations with Brazil.

Geoffroy Guichard founded Groupe Casino in 1898. He became the sole proprietor of a grocery store located in the old Casino Lyrique cabaret in Saint-Étienne, which remained the Group's flagship store for many years and is the origin of the group's name.

In its first twenty years, the company opened a number of factories in the Loire region and introduced the concept of private brands and customer loyalty programs (trading stamps for store purchases), and by 1916, it introduced a family allowance fund and a profit-sharing system for staff. In the 1960s, Casino became the first French food retailer to display a sell-by date on its products, a practice that became mandatory in France only in 1984. In 1975, through its expansion into the United States, Casino joined the global fray.

At the beginning of the 2000s, the group began acquiring different retailers: 50% of the variety retailer Monoprix as well as the discount chains Franprix, Leader Price and Cdiscount. By 1992, it had already acquired La Ruche Méridionale before merging with Rallye, a French retailer and Casino's current major shareholder, by giving 30% of its shares.

Therefore, for more than a century now, the Group has expanded and diversified its activities. The main strategy of the company is to move from mass to precision retailing and to be the leader in this field. Aside from its ongoing retail expansion, Groupe Casino grew in other sectors including banking (loans and credit cards) and hospitality/food via Casino Cafeteria and self-service restaurants. As one of the first retailers to introduce private labels to promote its retail brands, the company's brand portfolio covers the major socio-demographic consumer segments: Monoprix stores in the upper range and Casino and Leader Price in the good-value-for-the-money segment.

As for its international ambitions, Casino is currently present in eight countries with 3,539 stores, achieving international sales of €29.2 billion, representing 60% of its total turnover in 2013 (vs. 56% in 2012). The international activities thus represent the bulk of the firm's sales and profits. Casino's geographical choices include countries with high development potential, characterized by young and large populations, strong rates of economic growth and still a low share of organized retail. Thus Casino can build up subsidiaries with a strong local presence. Groupe Casino's focus is currently on the South American and Asian regions: Brazil, Colombia, Argentina, Uruguay, Thailand and Vietnam.

Another aspect of Casino's international expansion is testing the waters for its private-brand labels in countries where it is not yet operating stores – for example, Hong Kong, Singapore and the Philippines. Since 2012, this assertive partnership strategy has given leading local retailers access to Casino and Monoprix products, thus providing additional revenues to Casino and enabling the company to evaluate future growth opportunities.

Brazilian retail market

Nowadays, Brazil is one of Casino's leading markets. The retail industry relies essentially on revenue growth for its profitability, since retail margins are substantially more constrained compared to other industries due to competitive pressures. In 2013, retail represented approximately 5.6% of Brazil's GDP with cumulative revenues of approximately BRL 272 billion.

The Brazilian retail sector is as innovative as retail sectors in the developed world. It is attracting increasing international attention, with global chains waking up to opportunities in Brazil – a country emerging from a long period of economic challenges. The players in the Brazilian retail segment are a mixture of creative chain retailers as well as financiers such as banks who operate retail chains directly. Large Brazilian retailers offer their own credit facilities, with consumer credit being the order of the day for Brazilian retail.[9]

The food sub-segment of the Brazilian retail industry is highly fragmented. Despite consolidation, according to the research firm ABRAS (Brazilian Supermarket Association), in 2014, the revenue of the three-largest food retailers, Pão de Açúcar, Carrefour and Walmart amounted to BRL 140 billion (55% market share) out of a total supermarket revenue of BRL 259 billion.

About Grupo Pão de Açúcar

Casino has been present in Brazil since 1999 via Grupo Pão de Açúcar (GPA, meaning sugar loaf, also the name of the majestic mountain that dominates Rio's bay), a major player in food retailing in Brazil. In 1995, GPA went public on the São Paulo Stock Exchange, raising $112.1 million, and since 1997, it has also listed ADRs (American depositary receipts) on the New York Stock Exchange (raising an additional $172.5 million). With revenues of BRL 64.4 billion in 2013, GPA operates 2,143 stores around the nation, with over 2.7 million m² of sales area, approximately 156,000 staff and 58 distribution centers. Moreover, the largest retailer in Brazil reported a 9.2% organic increase in sales and continued to gain market share over the year.[10]

GPA is the largest international operation of Casino Group. Its business is based on a multi-format structure that allows the company to meet a wide range of consumers' expectations and needs in various regions and diverse economic and social classes with a balance between the following:

- supermarkets (Pão de Açúcar and Extra Supermercado)
- hypermarkets (Extra Hiper)
- electronic products and household appliance stores (Ponto Frio and Casas Bahia)
- proximity stores (Minimercado Extra and Minuto Pão de Açúcar)
- cash-and-carry segments (Assaí)
- gas stations
- drugstores
- e-commerce operations (Extra.com.br, PontoFrio.com, CasasBahia.com.br, Barateiro. com.br, PartiuViagens.com.br and B2B with E-Hub).[11]

GPA covers an extensive portfolio of multi-format banners that it extends with new concepts to meet the needs of the evolving Brazilian customer base. By the end of 2014, GPA enjoyed dominant market positions in São Paulo and Rio de Janeiro, Brazil's two most dynamic cities.

Casino's main competitors are Carrefour (a French retailer, second only to Walmart worldwide, in Brazil since 1975), Walmart Brasil (first entered the market in 1995 through a joint venture with local player Lojas Americanas), Lojas Americanas (founded in 1929 by four Americans; sells clothing, toys, household goods and appliances, chocolates and candies and entertainment), Lojas Renner, CIA Hering (the oldest home-based textile and clothing maker focused on opening stores in tier-two Brazilian cities aimed at the newly emerging middle class who have access to credit), Hypermarcas (maker of pharmaceutical goods and personal hygiene products), Raia Drogasil and Lojas Marisa.

Acquisition process

GPA's history goes back to 1948. In the 1960s and 1970s, it went through a number of significant changes, including the following:

- acquisitions (Sirva-se supermarket chain, Eletroradiobraz chain, Superbom, Peg-pag and Mercantil);
- expansion of the group and foundation of the International Division;
- opening of GPA stores in Portugal, Angola and Spain; and
- inauguration of the first generation of hypermarkets in Brazil.

In the 1990s, GPA started operating with four more formats (Pão de Açúcar, Extra, Super-box and Eletro), all focusing on the Group's core retail food business.

The most important year though was 1999, with the acquisition of the Peralta de Supermercados chain and the link-up with Groupe Casino, which acquired a 24.5% stake in GPA. In 2005, Casino increased its stake to 34%, and the agreement gave Casino an option to buy control of GPA.

Yet, matters took an interesting South American twist when Abilio Diniz, the chairman of GPA, claimed that he had not been notified of the buy-out option. Casino took the first step to take control of the Brazilian retailer. Mr. Diniz said he called a meeting of the Wilkes holding company for June 22 to select a chairman. Casino's chairman and CEO, Jean-Charles Naouri was expected to be named chairman, thus giving him control over Wilkes and, in turn, its main asset, GPA.

In 2011, Diniz teamed up with billionaire banker Andre Esteves[12] to merge GPA with the Brazilian unit of Carrefour. The merger was a move to fend off the agreement that gave control of GPA to Casino, which later described the action as hostile. Casino filed a complaint against its Brazilian partner and denounced the move as illegal and in violation of the 2005 shareholders agreement.[13]

Diniz's proposal to merge with Carrefour was rejected, and Casino increased its stake in the retailer to more than 40%. As of June 2012, Casino Group took full control of GPA.

Market leadership: GPA's strategy

When entering emerging markets, such as Brazil, Casino sought retail chains with strong brand recognition and relationships with local customers, which explains why it decided to operate through GPA. Such a strategy is sustained by retail competitive strengths (brands, exclusive brands, supply chain, global sourcing, partnerships with suppliers and FIC, IT, human capital and sustainability), with ongoing investment to develop the businesses and create value for shareholders, commercial partners and employees. Strategic plans for each business focus on four axes: people and management, innovation and sustainability, growth and operational excellence.[14]

Building on its market leadership, GPA is pursuing its vision of keeping pace with the ever-shifting shopping behavior of consumers in a modern, complex, multicultural society.[15] In order to do so, it offers a range of retail banners with different identities, continuously revitalizes the store concepts and keeps its formats aligned with customer expectations. This commitment has translated into a pioneering approach to segmenting the formats accurately, combined with a strategy of optimizing concepts and processes.[16] For instance, instead of a massive price-cutting campaign, GPA responded to the challenging economy by creating a new premium convenience store concept (Minuto Pão de Açúcar) to address the sophisticated expectations of wealthier customers (e.g. health foods, ready-to-eat). Eventually, GPA gained further market share and improved its margins despite the fall-off in consumer spending.

Another growth driver has been GPA's expansion into multi-channel sales, which include synergies with a galaxy of e-commerce sites on Nova Pontocom, part of the new Cnova e-business.[17] Cnova is a major e-commerce player in Brazil that operates as an e-retailer through its three main B2C sites – extra.com.br, casasbahia.com.br and pontofrio.com – and offers B2B services primarily through Pontofrio Atacado and its eHub.com.br platform. It launched its first marketplace in Brazil in 2013.

Groupe Casino today: further integrating in Latin America

The Latin American market represents nearly half of Groupe Casino's global sales, making it a key strategic element. Unfortunately, due to various macroeconomic factors, the company has been underperforming. The main reasons for this slowdown came from Brazil, which is currently suffering from a major growth slowdown to the point of recession, hindering both sales and also the value of the local currency, the Real. Although these recent downturns are out of Casino's direct control, they exert a direct, negative impact on financials, with the weakening Real wiping out a large chunk of profits.

Casino CEO Jean-Charles Naouri has decided to act on what he can control: strategy. By fostering synergies between Brazil and France, he hopes to bring down costs and to instigate a new managerial culture based on skills transfer and cooperation. Casino recently announced that their Colombian subsidiary Exito will acquire 50% of GPA and 100% of Argentina's Libertad (both being already controlled by Jean-Charles Naouri's firm).[18] Amounting to €1.7 billion, this transaction is expected to help insulate Casino from the recent underperformance in some of the South American countries.

Telefónica: thrash about financials and investments in Brazil

Company background

Telefónica, S.A. is a Spanish integrated telecommunications operator with operations in Europe, Asia, North and South America providing communication, information and entertainment solutions. Its head office is in Madrid, and it operates four business units: Telefónica Europe (operations in Germany, Slovakia, Spain, Ireland, the United Kingdom and the Czech Republic), Telefónica Latinoamérica (Costa Rica, Ecuador, El Salvador, Guatemala, Mexico, Nicaragua, Panama, Peru, Uruguay and Venezuela), Telefónica Digital and Global Resources. The Telefónica Digital business provides digital services, including cloud computing, mobile advertising, mobile to mobile and eHealth. Global Resources offers network and operations, IT, procurement, global solutions, group services and global HR services.[19]

Founded in 1924, Telefónica is now one of the largest telephone operators and mobile network providers in the world. The firm is present in twenty-one countries, employing over 125,000 staff (with an average age of thirty-nine), and consolidated revenues of €35.3 billion for the first nine months of 2015. Telefónica served over 327 million subscribers in September 2014, with more than 251.4 million mobile users, 40 million fixed telephony users, over 21.4 million Internet and data accesses and, finally, 8.2 million pay TV subscribers.[20]

Telefónica is a 100% listed company with more than 1.5 million direct shareholders. Since July 2000, the CEO and chairman of Telefónica is César Alierta Izuel, who guided the company through its significant Latin American expansion. This expansion is why the company holds the worldwide eighth position in the telecoms sector in terms of market capitalization, leads as a European integrated operator and holds the fifteenth position in the Euro Stoxx 50 ranking (September 30, 2012).[21] In May 2015, the company had a market capitalization of $72.3 billion and revenues of $66.8 billion.

Telefónica's customers know the company via high-profile commercial brands, such as Movistar, O2 and Vivo, which provide mobile, landline, Internet and television services to more than three hundred million customers around the world.

Until the 1990s, Telefónica de España, S.A. (Telefónica), a government-controlled public monopoly, operated Spanish telecoms.[22] However, like many of its European and international counterparts, Telefónica was fully privatized in 1997. By 2001, the renamed Telefónica S.A. was the leading telecoms company in the Spanish and Portuguese-speaking regions of the globe, with ten major subsidiary companies including Telefónica de España, Telefónica Latinoamericana, Telefónica Móviles S.A., Terra Lycos S.A., Telefónica Data-Corp S.A., Atento and Admira.

Nowadays, one of Telefónica's major strengths is its infrastructure. In 1926, Telefónica's network was born as an automated telephone center in Madrid, which connected 3.800 kilometers of telephone cables throughout Spain, offering high-quality service to its customers. Telefónica was able to design and build its own network without market pressure, and built a competitive advantage against all potential competitors. This network has been constantly growing and expanding, increasing Telefónica's coverage. Significant investments, mostly via M&A deals, have been made for international expansion, with a strong focus on South America, using different brands. South American investment started in 1990 in Chile and Argentina and then involved the rest of South America, bringing good financial performance up to this day.

Telefónica's network is considered one of the largest in the world; it allows access to a very large portion of the planet and independently sells capacity on such broad networks to other telco companies.[23]

Brazilian telecoms market

The Brazilian telecoms market suffers from split personalities: modern technologies prevail in the center-south portion (LTE, 3G HSPA, DSL ISDB based Digital TV), whereas other regions, particularly the north and northwest, lack even basic analog PSTN telephone lines. The government is currently trying to solve this dichotomy. Total Brazilian investment in fixed and mobile services amounted to BRL 28.8 billion in 2014. The main statistics on households' potential are provided in the Tables 3.1 and 3.2.[24]

Table 3.1[1] Households equipped with telecom-related products in Brazil

Homes with (%)	2013
Television	97.2%
Telephone (fixed or mobile)	92.5%
Radio	75.7%
Computer	48.9%
Computer with Internet access	42.4%
Total of homes (thousands)	65,130

Source: Melchior, Silvia Regina Barbuy – *The International Comparative Legal Guide to: Telecoms, Media & Internet Laws and Regulations 2016* – Brazil Chapter – Published by GLG – Global Legal Group, 9th Edition – UK, 2016

[1] This text first appeared in the Brazil chapter of the *ICLG to: Telecommunications 2016*, published by Global Legal Group (www.iclg.co.uk) and written by Silvia Melchior.

Table 3.2[1] Sector growth sources in Brazil

Sector gross revenue and component (in BRL billions)	2013	2014
Industry	26.7	29.6
STFC (Fixed Telephony)	42.1	40.3
SCM (Fixed Broadband)	27.4	29.1
SMP (Mobile Accesses)	99.9	100.2
SeAC (CTV, DTH, MMDS and Pay TV)	24.9	28.6
SME (Trunking)	6.8	6.3
Total	**227.9**	**234.1**

Source: Melchior, Silvia Regina Barbuy – *The International Comparative Legal Guide to: Telecoms, Media & Internet Laws and Regulations 2016* – Brazil Chapter – Published by GLG – Global Legal Group, 9th Edition – UK, 2016

[1] This text first appeared in the Brazil chapter of the *ICLG to: Telecommunications 2016*, published by Global Legal Group (www.iclg.co.uk) and written by Silvia Melchior.

The Brazilian landline sector is fully open to competition and continues to attract operators. The market is divided between four operators: Telefónica (operating through Telefónica Brasil), América Móvil, Oi and GVT. Telefónica has integrated its landline and mobile services under the brand name Vivo. Its competitor, América Móvil group comprises long-distance incumbent Embratel, mobile operator Claro and cable TV provider Net Serviços. It has started to integrate its landline and mobile services under the brand name Claro that was previously used only for mobile services. Oi (controlled by Brazilian investors and Portugal Telecom) offers landline and mobile services under the Oi brand name. GVT is Brazil's most successful network provider, offering landline services only.

Internet access was launched in Brazil in 1988. Nearly twenty-five years on, in 2010, Brazil ranked ninth worldwide with 13.3 million fixed broadband subscriptions, meaning 6.8% penetration residents. The following year Brazil jumped to fifth[25] rank, with over eighty-nine million Internet users, about 45% of the population. The main Internet service providers in Brazil are Claro Americas, Algar Telecom, Embratel, Global Village Telecom, Intelig Telecom, Internet Group, Net (telecommunications), Oi (telecommunications), Plano Nacional de Banda Larga, Sercomtel, Telefônica Vivo, TIM Brasil, Universo Online, Vivo (telecommunications) and Copel.

Mobile telephony in Brazil began on December 30, 1990, when the Cellular Mobile System began operating in the city of Rio de Janeiro, with a capacity for ten thousand connections. At that time, there were only 667 handsets in the country. Now, according to Anatel (Brazil's Telecommunication National Agency), there are 116 cell phones for every 100 people in Brazil. However, smartphones are still underutilized in Brazil – this is one of the reasons why *Business Week* described how desperately Brazil needs a reform in its mobile sector.

The mobile market is ruled by four companies: Vivo Participações (a Brazilian joint venture between Portugal Telecom and Telefónica), which is the leading wireless company in Brazil; TIM Brasil, controlled by Italian wireless giant TIM; and Claro, controlled by Carlos Slim's America Móvil and Oi, which is the largest landline company in Brazil and at the same time the smallest wireless player of the four.

The 2014 FIFA World Cup held in Brazil provided a stimulus to operators providing new technologies and networks such as LTE and FttP – the Brazilian government helped by legislating tax breaks for new telecom investments in networks that support access to fixed or mobile broadband.[26] The 2016 Olympic Games similarly provided further encouragement from all stakeholders to improve infrastructure (likely to be limited to cities hosting events).

Entering Brazil

Telefónica entered the Brazilian market in 1998 during the restructuring and privatization of Telebrás, by acquiring Telesp, the fixed-phone network of the rich São Paulo state. In the following years, the firm grew by acquiring and merging with several mobile phone operators in the north, northeast, middle and southeast of Brazil. By the end of the 1990s, Telefónica had already invested nearly $10.9 billion in the Latin American region and controlled nearly 40% of its telecommunications. Later, in 2002, Portugal Telecom and Telefónica created a JV to operate in the Brazilian mobile market, and in April 2003, they began their commercial activities and business operations using the brand Vivo.[27]

The year 2010 was for Telefónica in Brazil, which is when it reinforced its presence by increasing its stake in Vivo. In 2012, Telefónica culminated the process of integration and transformation of the company in Brazil, with the launch of Vivo[28] as a national commercial brand for all its services in the country.

The Vivo brand

The CEO and director of Telefónica Brasil is Amos Genish (since May 2015). The company offers its clients a wide range of products: mobile and fixed voice, mobile data, fixed broadband, ultra-fast broadband, pay TV, information technology and digital services. It also operates a retail network with approximately 300 of its own stores and 1,800 other points of sale, where customers can obtain certain services, such as purchasing credit for prepaid phones.[29]

The company's operations consist of local and long distance fixed telephone services; mobile services, including value-added services; data services, including broadband services and mobile data services; pay TV services through the direct-to-home satellite technology, Internet protocol television (IPTV) and cable; and many other services.

Additionally, Vivo sells handsets and hardware accessories in its stores to customers who purchase its services. It sells GSM and other devices, such as handsets, smartphones, broadband USB modems and more.[30]

Telefónica Brasil financials

In May 2015, Telefónica Brasil's Extraordinary Shareholders' Meeting approved the purchase of Global Village Telecom (GVT) from Vivendi. The closing of this transaction, announced in September 2014, places Telefónica Brasil as the Brazilian market's leading integrated operator, both in terms of clients and of revenues, and with a high-value customer profile.

In 2014, Telefónica Brasil significantly reinforced its competitive position in the market. Specifically, in the mobile business, the strategic focus on quality and innovation enabled Telefónica to strengthen its leadership in the higher value segments.[31] At the end of 2014, Telefónica's revenue in Brazil reached €11.2 billion, and the OIBDA stood at €3.5 billion. Revenues in the first quarter of 2015 reached €5.7 billion (+4.6% year-on-year), and the OIBDA stood at €1.8 billion at the end of June (+1.6% y-o-y). At the end of June 2015, Telefónica managed 106.6 million subscribers in Brazil (+4% y-o-y in organic terms). It has been one of the largest private investors in Brazil for almost two decades. In 2014 alone, the investment (just Capex) of Telefónica Brazil totalled €2.9 billion. Capex in the first six months of 2015 reached €961 million.

Weathering the Brazilian recession

The big commodity price downturn of 2015 has had a profound impact on the BRIC quartet, with a particular punch to the Brazilian and Russian economies, both hard hit in their oil earnings. On top of that, Brazil must face its largest corruption scandal in years, with numerous top political figures facing severe turbulence. Recovery will require the country to face its structural problems (both economic and political) with strong resolve.

According to Telefónica's chief operating officer, Jose Maria Alvarez-Pallete, the company's growth in Brazil will probably be strong enough for the telecoms provider to withstand the recession. Pallete remains optimistic, stating that in spite of the economy, the company is improving and will not change its plans.

The deepest economic and political crisis in Brazil in years is expected to cause some damage to Telefónica, especially since the company is still struggling to recover from years of recession in Spain, its main market. Thankfully, in 2015, for the first time in years, the company posted a full quarter of Spanish growth. The current strategy of Telefónica is focused on cutting debt while maintaining a strong dividend policy – a necessity to keep institutional investors on board.

3.2 Western firms in China: the cases of Volvo, Disney and Google

Volvo construction: establishing joint venture in China

Company background

Volvo Group (AB Volvo), founded in 1927, is one of the world's leading manufacturers of heavy-commercial vehicles, diesel engines and other transportation-related products, with strong focuses on safety, quality and environmental care. Volvo also offers a broad range of customized solutions in financing, leasing, insurance and service, as well as transport systems for urban traffic. The company's business units are Volvo Trucks, Mack, Renault Trucks, Volvo Buses, Volvo Construction Equipment, Volvo Penta, Volvo Aero and Volvo Financial Services. It has approximately 100,000 employees and manufacturing plants in 25 countries, yet operates in more than 185 markets.

Volvo Construction Equipment (VCE) is the subsidiary that designs and builds equipment for the construction and other related industries. Having started activity in 1832 in a machine shop in Eskilstuna, Sweden, VCE is the oldest industrial company in the world still active in construction machinery. Its products and services, including global after-sales service and spare-part distribution, are offered in more than 125 countries via either wholly owned or independent dealerships. VCE has production facilities in Sweden, Germany, China, Brazil, Mexico, South Korea, India, Poland and the United States. Its main products are compact excavators (diggers), skid steer loaders and backhoe loaders, but many other types of machinery give VCE a complete product palette. VCE customers operate in various industries such as energy-related industries (oil & gas), heavy infrastructure, road construction and the timber industry.

Chinese construction equipment sector

China has been the world's largest construction market since 2010. There is tremendous, sustained demand for machinery given the myriad different types of construction: buildings, bridges, railways, roads and expressways, airports and so on. With about 405,000 units of machinery in operation, the Chinese market for construction equipment is the world's largest. In fact, China is almost as large as all other countries combined, when measuring the number of units.

During the ten years from 2000 to 2010, sales of construction equipment had an average annual growth rate of 26% every single year, making for a RMB 436 billion market size in 2010. This mouth-watering growth was mainly driven by the large amount of investment in rail and road transport infrastructure as well as real estate construction. The government's RMB 4 trillion economic stimulus plan also helped! Nowadays, there are about 130 companies in China producing and selling construction equipment. The top-ten companies account for about 70% of market share and include Zhonglianzhongke, Zhonggong, Liugong, Xiagong, Xugong and Longgong.

Entry strategy for Chinese market

VCE's entry strategy was a two-phased adventure.

The first phase, which commenced in 2002, was a greenfield investment of $24 million to establish a subsidiary in China in the Pudong district of Shanghai. The money went for the creation of an excavator assembly plant. VCE also made a greenfield investment in its Volvo Technology Center in Jinan, Shandong Province, in 2002.

The second phase of VCE's investment was a so-called brownfield investment in 2007, when the company acquired 70% of Shangdong Lingong Construction Machinery Co. (SDLG), one of the major Chinese construction machinery manufacturers. SDLG was established in 1972 in Linyi City, Shandong Province, and mainly produces loaders, excavators, road rollers, pavers and backhoe loaders. SDLG operates nationwide, with a comprehensive dealer network throughout China.

In September 2006, VCE signed an agreement to make an equity investment of 70% into SLDG, China's fourth-largest producer of wheeled loaders with a market share of around 11% in 2005. VCE appreciated the fact that it could rely on SDLG's existing management, research and manufacturing strengths, while providing investment and technology to grow market share.

Political and legislative issues formed a slight barrier of entry, since VCE needed to obtain the necessary prior regulatory approvals from the Chinese government. In January 2007, VCE received all the approvals for the deal to go through. SLDG knew VCE quite well, since both companies had been cooperating since 2006 in several fields, such as research and development, manufacturing, marketing and brand building. After one year, both companies had integrated their manufacturing, marketing and brand building efforts, which was considered a great achievement by both sides. Volvo had ambitious plans for VCE in China, the core of its entire Asian strategy. In July 2008, SLDG announced its new brand strategy with Volvo.

The two companies decided to maintain both brands in co-existence in China, with Volvo serving the premium customer segment with its established brand, while the Shandong Lingong (SDLG) brand was maintained in the larger segment of entry-level machines, including sixteen different wheeled loaders, backhoe loaders, road rollers and excavators.

In order to better distinguish the price segments of the two product lines, and enhance their image, the companies launched a promotional campaign on CCTV, one of the most popular Chinese television channels. However, advertising followed the established Volvo style, thus emphasizing the relationship between the two brands under one roof. Moreover, both companies emphasize their link throughout the various media campaigns that they run for the two separate brands.

The business of the joint venture today

With the beginning of the joint venture officially starting in January 2007, the first Volvo machinery rolled off SDLG production lines later that year. In 2011 and 2012, VCE and SDLG were the construction equipment leaders in China. They reached a combined market share of 13.7% at the end of 2012, selling a total of 36,455 units. The main focus of the company remains the production of wheel loaders and excavators, which provide the joint firm's leading position. The key competitors include the heavy hitters Caterpillar, Komatsu, LiuGong Machinery, Sany Heavy Industry and Zoomlion.

With Volvo having a long-term view for the China market and for Asia, its 70% stake in SDLG was followed up with specific capital injections for specific projects: $50 million went to expand the production lines in Linyi, $30 million went for the construction of an excavator plant in Shanghai and $30 million was devoted to create the Volvo Technology Center in Jinan. This demonstrates Volvo's commitment and reliance on the Chinese market, and the company's expectation of further developing operations there. Furthermore, VCE announced plans to expand its SDLG product line (and brand) to other markets, including the construction of a manufacturing facility in Brazil. Volvo also promotes the SDLG brand in developed countries via different professional exhibitions.

Walt Disney: cultural adaptation in China

Company background

Walt Disney and Roy Disney created the Walt Disney Company in 1923 in the United States. In recent years, the company has viewed global growth as one of the most crucial tenets of its strategy, with the strong view that long-term growth will rely on the emerging markets of Latin America, Russia, India and China as the most important ones.[32] In general, the company's global outbound strategies have included a mixture of foreign outsourcing, licensing and direct investment.

The company operates five business segments: media networks, parks and resorts, studio entertainment, consumer products and interactive media. This section focuses on the Parks and Resorts division, which includes the famous Disneyland and Disneyworld theme parks. In this business segment, the company uses mainly direct investment as its strategy for foreign expansion. So far, the Walt Disney Company has opened theme parks and resorts in three different countries outside the United States: Tokyo, France and Hong Kong. A fourth resort is being planned in Shanghai.

The magazines *Forbes*, *Fortune* and *Barron's* noted that the Walt Disney Company is one of the world's "most reputable, admired and socially responsible companies." Robert A. Iger, the company's CEO, says, ". . . the long-term strategy of the company is based on creativity, innovative use of technology and global growth."[33] Furthermore, one of the core corporate concepts is the ongoing growth of Disneyland, the theme park. As Walt Disney himself stated, "Disneyland will never be completed. It will continue to grow as long as there is imagination left in the world."[34]

Continuous expansion of Disneyland

TOKYO

The Japanese Disneyland was the first foreign Disney Park to open to the public at Urayasu, just outside of Tokyo, on April 15, 1983. Tokyo was chosen first because Japanese visitors represented a substantial proportion of visitors to the Disney parks in the United States. It was decided that Tokyo Disneyland would be more successful if it resembled the other two American theme parks so popular among Japanese rather than building a completely different park for the Japanese customers.[35] Japanese Oriental Land Company owns and operates Tokyo Disneyland; the company received a license from Disney in return for royalties on sales (10% on admissions and 5% on food and souvenir sales).[36] Disney chose this low-risk option, fearing the risks of going abroad for the first time. Disney, therefore, reneged on any ownership rights. However, the marketing strategy of the company remained the same as for the American theme parks, although some cultural adaptation was carried out.

Tokyo Disneyland is a very successful project, even qualifying as the most successful theme park in the world in the 1990s (it had more visitors than the American Disney parks),[37] and in 2007 it became the world's third most visited theme park with 13.9 million visitors.[38]

PARIS

In 1975, the company management started to think about building a theme park in Europe. Initially, the company considered Britain, Italy, Spain and France, though Britain and Italy were omitted immediately because neither of those countries had a suitably large site available. Deciding between France and Spain, France won and it was decided to build the theme park at Marne-la-Vallée. There were two reasons for this choice: first, the site was relatively close to Paris; second, it had more or less central position in Western Europe. An agreement with the French government was signed in December 1985, including some public investments in the park's infrastructure.

The park finally opened to visitors on April 12, 1992, under the name Euro Disney. Euro Disney SCA, a French company that is 51% owned by the Walt Disney Co., operates the park. For its European venture, Disney wanted a greater share of the park's profits so as not to repeat the "mistake" of Tokyo Disneyland, where the Japanese partner was reaping the bulk of the profits. That's why for Euro Disney, the company kept majority ownership stake and the control of five thousand acres of land.[39]

Alas, attendance forecasts had been too optimistic: the park initially attracted nine million visitors a year rather than the eleven million expected,[40] and hotel occupancy barely breached the 50% level.[41] In addition to the low attendance, there were local protests, as the French were afraid that their culture would be "damaged" by the Disney influence. The situation worsened, and it soon became clear that Euro Disney had too many hotels. Some critics claimed that the number of hotels were unnecessary, as the park was small enough to be seen during a single day. For a period, the company closed hotels during the slack winter months. Another problem was that excessive prices for food and souvenirs prompted visitors to minimize their spending in the theme park. To compound matters, in the summer of 1993, the new Indiana Jones roller-coaster ride collapsed and some visitors were injured.

Therefore, in 1994, the company faced big financial difficulties and was on the verge of bankruptcy. But Disney reached an agreement with its French creditor banks, who agreed to an interest payment moratorium for two years and a three-year postponement for loan repayments. After that, Disney started to adapt to the French culture. For instance, they changed the name of Euro Disney to Disneyland Paris, finally allowed wine to be consumed on the premises and inaugurated new attractions. In 1995, Disneyland Paris finally broke even, and first annual operating profit was announced in November 1995.[42]

Today, Disneyland Paris has overcome local antipathy and now attracts many visitors. Protests, a French national pastime, have died down. In the end, Disneyland Paris turned out to be profitable for France. For instance, 55,000 jobs have been created and $61 billion have been added to the French economy due to additional tourism revenue and taxation.[43]

However, Disneyland Paris still faces financial difficulties. In its twenty-two-year history, the park has rarely turned a profit. The last time this happened was in 2008.[44] The company faces a large debt burden that needed to be repaid to French banks.[45] Among the reasons for the financial difficulties is that the success of Disneyland Tokyo biased management expectations towards optimism: Disneyland Paris took on too much debt and overestimated the spending desires of visitors. For instance, hotels are still under-used, with both French and foreign tourists being mostly day trippers.

HONG KONG

Despite the European fiasco, Disney decided to forge ahead in its international expansion, and in 1999, the company signed an agreement with Hong Kong to build a theme park, which opened in 2005. Several factors influenced Disney's decision. First of all, Hong Kong is quite popular among tourists and according to the WTO, Hong Kong will become the fifth-largest tourist destination by 2020.[46] Besides that, there was strong motivation from Hong Kong authorities to make the deal. Hong Kong lacked entertainment parks, suitable land was available and the project brought both employment and tourism benefits.

In order to enter the Hong Kong market, the Walt Disney Company invested $2.45 billion, while the Hong Kong government invested $22.95 billion. However, the HKSAR (Hong Kong Special Administrative Region) government holds 52% of the shares of the joint venture company (Hong Kong International Theme Park Ltd), whereas Disney holds a minority 48%. The Hong Kong population was much more receptive to the project than the French had been. The same holds true for the Hong Kong authorities who welcomed Disney. Hong Kong chief executive Tung Chee-Wah claimed, "It is an enormous boost for the Hong Kong tourist industry."[47]

Disneyland Hong Kong is located on a 310-acre plot on Lantau Island, a few minutes from the new Hong Kong International Airport. Besides the theme park, Disney decided to construct a Disney-themed resort hotel complex including 1,400 rooms and a retail, dining and entertainment center.

The park is a mix of Eastern and Western cultures, with the usual Magic Kingdom castle, yet performances are in Cantonese, Mandarin and English. Hong Kong Disneyland is the smallest of the worldwide chain. Although the park was opened barely nine years ago, plans are underway to expand it. B. C. Lo, vice president of HK Disneyland public relations quoted the words of Walt Disney: "As long as there is imagination left in the world, Disneyland will never be completed."[48]

SHANGHAI

In 2011, the Walt Disney Company and the Chinese government came to an agreement that Disneyland Shanghai would open to the public at the end of 2015. The new resort will be located in Pudong. Disney will own about 43% of Shanghai Disneyland, while 57% will belong to a holding company formed by a consortium of Chinese companies selected by the government called the Shanghai Shendi (Group) Co.[49] The Walt Disney Company had been waiting more than ten years for the Chinese government to approve the project.[50] A deciding factor for the government was job creation, with Disneyland Shanghai expected to generate tens of thousands of new jobs. According to some estimates, Shanghai Disneyland could also help generate $140 billion in additional GDP.[51]

It was estimated that the theme park alone (without hotels and resort infrastructure) would cost $3.5 billion, by far the largest single foreign investment in China. The theme park will occupy one hundred acres of land, whereas the whole resort (including two theme hotels, a large retail, dining and entertainment venue and other recreation facilities) will necessitate one thousand acres, about the size of the Disneylands in Paris and Tokyo.[52]

Opening the Shanghai resort: new challenge for Disney

The Walt Disney Company had never opened a resort or park in a developing economy with so many institutional differences as in China. Although Hong Kong had strong connections with China, culturally and socio-economically, HK is not like any Chinese province. Expanding beyond the United States, Japan and Europe to Shanghai meant shifting from modernized locations to a more tradition-based Asian culture,[53] which could not be ignored in the case of China.

The two main Chinese holidays are the National Holiday Golden Week around October 1 and the Chinese New Year Golden Week. Thus the traditional Christmas and New Year's Eve or Easter Holiday would be useless in China and need adaptation. Chinese believe in many lucky symbols: the number eight, the representation of fish, bamboo trees and jade stone are believed to bring good luck, and Disneyland Shanghai would need to take this into account, as Chinese are very superstitious.

Tastes also differ widely. To reach its total of over 1,750 restaurants in China, McDonalds had to fight very strong competition from local players as well as KFC, which has succeeded far better. Yet the cultural reasons for this struggle are simple to grasp: Chinese prefer chicken to beef! And Chinese prefer rice to burger buns! Disney had to take that into account and find a way to please Chinese visitors.

The language obstacle is also important: whereas English is well understood in Hong Kong, and some English names can remain, a complete adaptation is necessary in Mainland China.

The design of the "Disney town" also had to be rethought. The Chinese town model (using many interlocking courtyards) is quite widespread. Even in Shanghai, which has become a very modern city of skyscrapers, there are still some neighborhoods built on the Chinese town model, such as the Yu Garden area or the downtown area Qibao.

The Walt Disney Company claims their resorts to be the "happiest places on Earth"; however, the means of achieving that goal are not the same everywhere. Changing environments makes marketing a cross-cultural process and requires that marketers be well versed in national, local and ethnic cultural differences.[54] In particular, developing economies are also generally tradition-based societies in which the way of doing business is different.

Cultural adaptation in Asia

In the Asia-Pacific region, attendance at the top Asian theme parks grew by 5.8% and reached 108.7 million visits in 2012. The leaders in growth were Universal Studios in Japan (14% growth), Hong Kong Disneyland (13.6% growth) and Soncheng Park in Hangzhou (14.2%). Fifteen of the top-twenty parks in the Asia-Pacific region showed a growth in attendance in 2012, with the only declining theme parks being Changzhou Dinosaur Park (−2.9% decline), Happy Valley Beijing (−11%) in China and Dunia Fantasy (−9.8%) in Indonesia.

The leaders in the theme parks industry in the Asia-Pacific region are Tokyo Disneyland, Tokyo Disney Sea, Universal Studios in Japan with eight to fifteen million visitors in 2012 and Ocean Park in Hong Kong and Everland in South Korea with seven to eight million visitors in 2012. The largest concentrations of top Asian theme parks are in China (nine parks) and Japan (five parks).

The cultural adaptation of Disney to Asia factually took place when the company established its park in Hong Kong. First, the company underestimated the number of people coming to Hong Kong Disney Resorts during the main holidays, and Hong Kong Disneyland was created as the smallest of all Disneylands.[55] Furthermore, space in Hong Kong is at a premium, so the founders of Disneyland HK had only limited territory on Lantau Island, which resulted in smaller premises and longer queues.[56] Second, the influence of feng shui on the Chinese way of life was too huge to neglect. The location, the interiors and exteriors of the buildings, all needed be blended with the landscape so as to ensure the proper flow of energy (or chi).[57] Eastern philosophy states that everything should be interconnected, bringing balance between humanity and nature. This explains why the design of the resort faced many difficulties that the company diligently tried to solve.

The five elements of feng shui (water, wood, fire, earth and metal) have been incorporated in every portion of the park. The main entrance gate was rotated twelve degrees to maximize good energy flow, and even the burning ritual was performed after each structure was built. The theme park buildings did not have fourth floors, as the number "four" sounds the same as the word "death" and is considered unlucky. Conversely, the number eight, which signifies prosperity, was used extensively. For example, some rooms are 888 square feet. Even the opening date was chosen according to Chinese numerology: September 12, 2005, at exactly 1:00 p.m. was believed to be the most auspicious time. Other features of Disneyland Hong Kong include the frequent use of the color red, which symbolizes wealth; the absence of clocks, which link to funerals; and appropriate merchandise such as mooncakes for the Chinese Mid-Autumn Festival. Since Hong Kong is officially trilingual (English and both Mandarin and Cantonese), staff were culturally fluent and spoke all three languages.[58]

Burnt by its French experience, the Walt Disney Company made extra efforts to adapt to Chinese local culture, but nonetheless received complaints. Most complaints concerned the size of the park, the long lines, the limited variety of attractions (the park operated only twenty-two out forty attractions) and poor customer service. For the company, the deception was in surprisingly lower than expected attendance. Ticket prices were quickly lowered to boost attendance, additional local merchandise was introduced and new attractions were added.[59]

Although Disneyland Shanghai was expected to open in 2015, the date has already been rescheduled a few times since 2009 (it is currently expected to open in June 2016). Nevertheless, Disneyland expects another success story in Shanghai, having paid close attention to mainland opinions and adjusting as best possible to Chinese exigencies. This first step into the world of emerging economies is extremely important for Disney and might help build a bridge to other important markets such as Brazil or Russia.

Google in China: the trade-off between democracy and censorship

Company history

Since its foundation, Google Inc. has become the major enterprise in the Internet-related products and services sector. Originally, the core business of the company was its web search engine, which the co-founder and CEO Larry Page described as something that "understands exactly what you mean and gives you back exactly what you want." The fast growth led the firm to expand the range of services beyond its core service, including cloud computing, software and advertising technologies; however, the spirit of what Page said remains. Google is estimated to run over one million servers in data centers around the world, process over one billion search requests and about twenty-four petabytes of user-generated data every day.

Google came from a research project created by Larry Page and Sergey Brin when they were computer science grad students at Stanford University. In 1996, they began collaborating on a search engine called BackRub. Then they decided that the BackRub search engine needed a new name and changed it to Google, a play on the word "googol," a mathematical term for the number represented by the numeral one followed by one hundred zeros.[60] The use of the term reflects their mission to organize a seemingly infinite amount of information on the web. In September 1998, Google was incorporated in California.

Google's business model is based on selling advertisements associated with search key-words. To establish its market position, Google acquired many companies, mainly focusing on small venture capital-backed companies (Pyra Labs, which created Blogger; Keyhole; online video site YouTube for $1.65 billion; Applied Semantics; and DoubleClick for $3.1 billion). It also forged partnerships, like that with Yahoo, to become its default search provider; with Universo Online, which makes Google the major search service for millions of Latin Americans; with MySpace, with NASA's Ames Research Center, with Sun Microsystems, with AOL, etc. In 2008, Google developed a partnership with GeoEye to launch a satellite providing Google with high-resolution imagery for Google Earth. Google's international expansion started by establishing offices in Tokyo, then Sydney, Dublin, São Paulo and Mexico City. In 2015, Google owned and operated six data centers across the United States, in Europe (Finland, Belgium, Ireland), in Asia (Singapore and Taiwan) and in South America (Chile).[61]

In order to acquire new start-ups, to form strategic alliances with other big companies and thus maintain its leadership position, Google needed to attract money. Pressure also mounted for Google to pay off its venture investors. So the company decided to go public, with its IPO taking place on August 19, 2004. The S1 form warned potential investors that Google was not just a usual company and that it would always strive for creativity and freedom first. What is more, the form did not include a CEO's name, since that position was open.

Brin and Page always claim their company is different. And their IPO was also different. Unlike the traditional IPOs, they used the Dutch auction in online format, which tends to lower the initial share price. This decision was made to protect their IPO from huge investors and to make it possible for everyone to buy their shares. They also used both A-class and B-class shares so as to retain management by the founders. Google's successful IPO resulted in a $23 billion market capitalization.

Competition with Baidu

China recently hit an important milestone in its Internet development. At the end of 2015, China had 688 million Internet users, more than double the population of the United States.[62]

The Chinese market for Internet services is huge (see Table 3.3), and in 2000, Google started providing its services in the Chinese language. However, Google was not a pioneer

Table 3.3 Internet users in China, 2000–2015

Year	Users	Population	Penetration
2000	22,500,000	1,288,307,100	1.7%
2001	33,700,000	1,288,307,100	2.6%
2002	59,100,000	1,288,307,100	4.6%
2003	69,000,000	1,288,307,100	5.4%
2004	94,000,000	1,288,307,100	7.3%
2005	103,000,000	1,289,664,808	7.9%
2006	137,000,000	1,317,431,495	10.4%
2007	162,000,000	1,317,431,495	12.3%
2008	253,000,000	1,330,044,605	19.0%
2009	384,000,000	1,338,612,968	28.7%
2010	420,000,000	1,330,141,295	31.6%
2015	674,000,000	1,361,512,535	49.5%

Source: Internet Usage Stats and Population Report, China, 2016, http://www.internetworldstats.com/asia/cn.htm

in China. Yahoo was the first major American Internet company to enter the market, introducing a Chinese-language version of its site and opening up an office in Beijing in 1999.[63] But Google's main rival in China was Baidu.

Baidu was incorporated in January 2000 as a Chinese web services company head-quartered in Beijing. Baidu offers many services, including a Chinese-language search engine for websites, audio files and images. Baidu is the number-one search engine in China, controlling 70% of the Chinese search market, according to China Internet watch iResearch (January 2016).

Financially, Baidu took the same road as Google: from venture capital (VC) to initial public offering (IPO). In 2001, the company raised $1.2 million from VC financing and then another $10 million from four VC companies led by Draper Fisher Jurvetson and International Data Group. In 2004, Baidu acquired Hao123.com, a popular Chinese web directory, then ranked twenty-fifth on Alexa.com's global Internet traffic ranking. In March 2005, Baidu began its preparation to go public, and finally in August, it achieved IPO victory in the United States opening at $66 and closing at $120 per share.[64] In 2015, Baidu's market capitalization was $63.67 billion.

Comparing Google and Baidu in Chinese market, several differences in the policy of Google and Baidu became obvious:

- Baidu's market leadership philosophy is premised on localization. Google's strategy is to be spread worldwide.
- Baidu's focus on the Chinese language for its searches is its biggest advantage. Moreover, the company's local connections and home-grown business practices, combined with the strength of its technology, give it an edge over Google.
- Baidu and Google differ in the way they sell advertising to customers. Google distributes a great deal of the company's advertising services through a direct sales structure, whereas Baidu sells ads in China largely through distributors.[65]
- Baidu does not require clients to use credit cards to pay for their advertisements while Google does.

- Baidu offers paid search placement, or the selling of search engine results for particular keywords to the highest bidder, which is not offered by Google.[66]
- Whereas Google has been providing innovative services ranging from Gmail to Google Maps, Baidu remains focused on search services – the service it does best.
- China-based Baidu never had any problems with censorship, while Google suffered from it.

Roadblocks in China

Chinese Internet users were initially able to access google.com in a non-censored version, which was then filtered by the massive Chinese government firewall, slowing the results and making it difficult to compete.

On August 31, 2002, the Chinese government blocked Google to show its displeasure with the company regarding the uncensored search results. However, two weeks later, the service was restored. The next year, the story was repeated: in October 2003, Google in China was blocked again for a short period of time. Government censorship increased over time, making the search engine far slower and less reliable.

In early 2006, there were 350 million mobile phones in use in China. By 2014, this number had exploded to 1.28 billion.[67] Twenty-two percent of all Internet users today live in China; in 2014, their number was 642 million [68] and that number was projected to grow by about 57 million annually. Despite this, Google did not hurry to establish a China-based version of its search engine. Unlike its competitors Yahoo! or Microsoft, Google maintained the U.S.-based version, but with the capability of understanding ideogram-based languages such as Chinese, Japanese and Korean. This strategy enabled Google to gain 25% of the Chinese search market by 2002 and avoid Chinese government censorship completely.

However, the ethical dilemma quickly was unavoidable: should Google self-censor its search results, or not do business in China at all? Google decided that it would be irrational to ignore such an important strategic market (second-largest market with a staggering growth rate), and on January 25, 2006, the company announced the creation of www.google.cn and simultaneously agreed to self-censor its search results.

Wall Street investors estimated the venture as potentially profitable, with the share price rising 3.6% in a single day. Yet, as could be expected, Google was also criticized by media and human rights organizations for abandoning its principles in pursuit of profit.[69] An online poll conducted by the *Financial Times* found 68% of respondents believing that Google was "being evil" in implementing self-censorship. Andrew McLaughlin, an attorney for Google, defended the company's rationale:

> In order to operate in China, we have removed some content from the search results available on Google.cn, in response to local law, regulation, or policy . . . while removing search results is inconsistent with Google's mission, providing no information . . . is more inconsistent with our mission.[70]

So in 2006, Google launched its Chinese-language search engine *google.cn*. Its servers were located in China, and Google's and YouTube's (Google's subdivision) search results were self-censored so that no content objectionable to the Chinese government appeared.[71] Google quickly became popular with white-collar urban professionals who follow Western styles.

After long years of fighting for market share, Google has finally found the suitable market niche, where it has managed to become a leader: the segment of advertising on mobile phone searches. "In mobile-search advertising, queries from users generate related ads, while app-based marketing automatically sends ads to mobile users playing games, viewing videos, or using applications on smartphones and tablet computers."[72]

In 2010, Google announced that it had been the subject of a massive cyber-attack probably originating from the Chinese government.[73] The company claimed that more than thirty company accounts as well as the Gmail accounts of human rights activists on its servers had been hacked. This alleged Chinese government hacking forced Google to withdraw from Mainland China in March 2010.[74] At the same time, Google moved its servers to Hong Kong, which has relatively more freedom than Mainland China. Google proceeded to automatically redirect all search results from Google China (Google.cn) to its unfiltered servers in Google Hong Kong (Google.com.hk). China's government reacted to this step in a tough way: it warned Google to stop the automatic redirection of searches from Mainland China to Hong Kong or risk non-renewal of its business license in China.[75]

Under the strong pressure of human rights organizations, public attitudes and so on, Google finally withdrew from the Chinese continental market in August 2010, switching its Chinese activity to its Hong Kong subsidiary. This has strengthened Baidu, whose stock price rose, reaching a high of $82 in mid-May 2010, more than twice the level it was trading at in January before Google's decision. With Google's withdrawal, Baidu is clearly well positioned to take over an even greater share of the search engine market in China.[76]

3.3 Anglo-American MNEs in India: the cases of Vodafone and Walmart

Vodafone: acquiring Chinese rival to enter India

Company history

Vodafone Group Ltd. is a communications service provider working with more than four hundred million customers and operating in over thirty countries all over the world (Europe, Africa, Middle East and Asia-Pacific markets). Three-quarters of the company's fiscal 2013 revenues came from mobile services. Besides mobile services, Vodafone Group also owns mHealth services (network technologies for healthcare) and Vodafone Foundation (charity).

Vodafone's key worldwide competitors include AT&T (United States), Bharat Sanchar Nigam (India), BT Group (United Kingdom), Deutsche Telekom (Germany), Emirates Telecommunications Company (UAE), France Telecom, Reliance Communications (India), Sprint Nextel (United States), Telecom Italia (Italy) and Telefónica (Spain), among others. With telecoms being one of the hottest growth sectors since the 1980s, Vodafone faces no lack of competition, no matter where it operates.

The head office of the company is in the United Kingdom, and the company employs a total of 101,443 employees. The group recorded revenues of £42.2 billion ($74.1 billion) during the fiscal year ended March 2015 (FY2015; company report).

Vodafone began its history in 1984 as a subsidiary of Racal Electronics. In 1985, it registered its first success: the first cell phone call from London to Newbury using the first mobile network in the United Kingdom. To provide services directly to the public, the company created a new subsidiary, called Vodac, to be the service provider. Vodac existed as part of Racal until 1991, when it was spun off and renamed Vodafone Group.

The company's international expansion was rapid and diversified, which was especially clear in the last two decades. M&A was the preferred tool: multiple acquisitions of European and Asian companies allowed for fast penetration into new and distant markets. Simultaneously, the company was growing through partnerships (including JVs with Microsoft, Nokia, Samsung, Orange, HP, Sun Microsystems, etc.). More recently, the company more focused on markets of the United States, CEE and CIS.

The acquisitions of Azerfon (Azerbaijan) and Borusan Telecom (Turkey) in 2009, Essar Group (in India) and Koc (Turkey) in 2011, Polcomtel (in Poland) in 2013 illustrate Vodafone's interest in emerging markets. That same year, Vodafone made a public takeover offer for Kabel Deutschland Holding. In 2014, Vodafone agreed to acquire Ono (Spain), and two years later, Vodafone created a 50-50 joint venture with Liberty Global, creating a national unified communication provider in the Netherlands.

Overall, it is clear from the brief history of the company's activities that it was extremely active in expanding both abroad and in the United Kingdom. The company used a wide range of tools, such as mergers and acquisitions, joint ventures and other types of contracts. Vodafone group not only provided the companies with mobile and data services but also continuously developed with the help of its innumerable partners.[77]

Indian telecom industry

The roots of the Indian telecom industry go back to 1851, when the British colonial government laid the first operational landlines in Calcutta. After India's independence in 1947, all foreign telecoms companies were nationalized and merged into a single government monopoly. Liberalization of the Indian telecommunication sector started in 1981, when French company Alcatel CIT and state-owned Telecom Company merged. Indian Prime Minister Indira Gandhi signed the contract. Yet it was still a long way to the full liberalization of telecoms in India, which started in 1995 when foreign companies were allowed to form joint ventures. Since 2000, the allowable stake for foreigners was lifted to 74%. In 2002, the government decided to cut its stake of 53% to 26% in VSNL (the largest telecom company), which is now called Tata Communication after the Tata Group completely acquired VSNL.

India's telecoms sector has undergone revolution since 2000, with a tremendous spurt in customer growth. Nowadays, India represents the third largest worldwide telecoms market (after the United States and China), and the second largest among the emerging economies, after China. It is the fastest-growing market in the world and is one of India's key GDP growth drivers. Given the ongoing investments into infrastructure expansion, the country is projected to witness even higher Internet, broadband and mobile subscriber penetrations in the future.[78]

Telecom deals are considered horizontal mergers, as both buyer and seller belong to the same industry, chasing competitive benefits through deal-making. Furthermore, such transactions result in cutting operational costs of both parties (economies of scale) and achieving a greater market share with an aim for market control.

The Indian M&A Trend Report (2013) indicates (see Table 3.4) that the telecoms sector occupied the fifth place in terms of deal volume in 2013.[79]

Although telecoms deals are fewer than in other sectors (e.g. chemicals), they tend to be of far higher value, given the astonishing profitability of telecoms operators. Overall,

Table 3.4 M&A deals in India

Industry	Q1 – Q3 2013			Q1 – Q3 2012			Change	
	Value ($m)	Market share (%)	Deal count	Value ($m)	Market share (%)	Deal count	Value (%)	Deal count
Consumer	3,954.4	23.3	17	973.6	3.2	21	306.1	−4
Construction	3,821.8	22.5	11	584.5	1.9	14	553.9	−3
Chemicals	2,229.7	13.1	52	3,147.7	10.4	48	−29.2	4
Pharmaceuticals	1,844.1	10.9	24	902.4	3	19	104.4	5
Telecommunications	1,573.8	9.3	4	791.8	2.6	2	98.8	2
Total	13,423.8		108	6,400		104		

Source: Publication by Transactions Advisory Services Practice for EY in India (http://www.ey.com/Publication/vwLUAssets/EY-transaction-real-estate-advisory-services/$FILE/EY-transaction-real-estate-advisory-services.pdf)

Indian telecom sector revenues grew by 13.4% in 2012. The IMF forecasts that revenue will expand at an annual rate of 5.7%.

In addition to the general liquidity of the Indian M&A sector, foreign telecoms investors are attracted by several industry-specific factors in India:

- globally, the fastest-growing telecoms market in terms of subscriber base;
- telecoms companies are attracted to the low costs of software programming in India, an important cost component given the frequent technological updates;
- the recent development of new telecoms technologies by Indian firms has sparked the interest of foreign companies in terms of joint ventures or acquisitions;
- February 2014 regulatory changes by the Ministry of Telecoms, allowing up to 50% combined market share post-acquisition. For deals exceeding 50% market share, a one-year reduction allowance period;[80]
- Indian's authorities have also opened doors for multinational telecommunication companies by making the complete ownership in incumbent firms possible, which was previously capped at 74%; and
- rating agency Fitch expects the Indian telecom market to reach a consolidation phase, with larger operators acquiring smaller competitors.

However, one can always expect surprises when doing M&A deals in India. For instance, a January 2014 law requires buyers of Indian mobile phone companies to pay a fee to the government, in addition to the acquiring sum. This might deter future deals.[81]

Acquisition of Hutchison by Vodafone

On May 8, 2007, Vodafone Group (United Kingdom) completed the purchase of a controlling stake in Hutchison Essar (India) through a deal with the Hong Kong–based Hutchison Telecommunication International Ltd. (HTIL). This was seen as a great opportunity for the English company (while based in the Netherlands) to grow in emerging markets, since Hutchison Essar was India's fourth-largest mobile operator at the time. Vodafone bought a 52% stake for $11.1 billion from Hutchison Telecom International, making it the biggest deal ever in Indian telecoms. The final deal price was discounted to $10.9 billion, after eliminating the stake of HEL, which had a 29.2 million subscriber base in thirteen out of India's twenty-eight circles. India's telecom regulators have divided the country up into a number of regions called Telecom Circles or Telecom Service Areas. These regions are broken down into four groups: metro circles, A, B and C circles. The metro circles are the most dense population centers such as Delhi, Kolkata and Mumbai.

Before submitting its bid, there were many issues confronting Vodafone in order to close the deal. First of all, Essar submitted an $11 billion bid and, as the operational partner, had a right of first refusal. Second, there were regulatory issues.

The shareholder agreement was signed on March 22, 2007, giving Vodafone a controlling 52% stake, Essar 33% and minority shareholders, such as Asim Ghosh, Infrastructure Development Finance Company and Analjit Singh together, the remaining 15% stake in the company.[82] Hutchison International had several reasons to sell its stake:

- First, it needed cash in order to fund business expansion in Europe.
- Second, urban markets in India were already becoming saturated. Future expansion in rural areas might lead to falling average revenue per user.
- Third, the deal enabled Hutchison to become one of Asia's best-capitalized companies.[83]

Therefore, selling its lucrative Indian subsidiary was a useful step in its own expansion plans.[84]

Since Vodafone wished to introduce its global brand to India, the shareholders agreed to replace the existing "Hutch" brand with "Vodafone." Another goal was to bring 3G service to rural areas, thus expanding geographic coverage and increasing the customer base to include the rural masses. Thereafter, the plan was to launch inexpensive cell phones in the Indian market under the Vodafone brand. Leveraging Vodafone's global power in supplying millions of low-cost handsets from across the world to India was the key factor here.[85]

This was not Vodafone's first attempt to enter the Indian market via acquisition; it had previously tried to expand its stake in Bharti. However, Bharti was traditional, tightly held, family-run business and it refused to share control with an outside organization.[86] It was only after this failure that Vodafone turned to Hutchison in order to crack into the Indian market. Although critics lamented that Vodafone overpaid for its stake in Hutchison Essar, the deal helped Vodafone to expand into emerging markets at a time when saturation was hitting its core European markets.

Undeniably, the deal benefitted the average Indian. Competition increased in the market, providing customers with a wider range of services, in more outlets and at better prices. The Indian telecoms market as a whole benefitted from Vodafone's international expertise.

Roots of the problems: relationships with the government

When in 2007, Vodafone purchased the majority stake in the Indian operations of Hutchison Essar (JV of Hong Kong–based Hutchison and Indian Essar) it did not pay any taxes.[87] When considering the $11.2 billion amount of the deal,[88] the taxes could have amounted to as much as $1.8 billion.[89] However, since the a deal was structured between two foreign entities (Vodafone of the United Kingdom and Hutchison of Hong Kong), under the existing laws at the time, Vodafone was not liable to pay any tax to the Indian government. When, five years later, in 2012 (the Indian judicial system is notoriously slow!), the case was brought to court, Vodafone initiated litigation. The Indian Supreme Court confirmed that no laws were broken, and the company indeed did not have to pay taxes.

Astonishingly, the Ministry of Finance, nonetheless, managed to modify legislation afterwards to force Vodafone to pay $2 billion in taxes, leading of course to a series of subsequent lawsuits.

Aside from the court case regarding the retroactive tax liabilities, Vodafone also claims the government desires to charge transfer-pricing taxes for the various Indian call centers that handle customer service for worldwide Vodafone group companies. All in all, it seems clear that the Indian government was trying to charge taxes on one event twice.[90] To help protect its commercial interest and operations, Vodafone requested that the UN Commission of International Trade Law intervene. As a sort of arbitrator extraordinaire, this Commission helps both parties to ensure the legitimacy of their claims and then facilitates a peaceful legal solution.

India accused Vodafone of sabotaging the negotiations,[91] claiming that Vodafone tried to combine two tax disputes (Hutchison Essar transaction and transfer pricing), of "being inflexible" and of using inappropriate foreign investment protection legislation.[92]

Although initially targeted at Vodafone, this particular case also affected other global giants such as AT&T or brewer SAB Miller.[93] The impact to the Indian image in attracting international inbound FDI is hard to estimate. The risk of sudden changes in legislation, taxation or government policies is certainly one of the external factors that multinational companies take into account when deciding where to invest. Countries that change predictably (or do not change at all!) are obviously more attractive, since they offer lower risk. One thing is flexible legislation, but retroactive policy changes – such as the one in India – is heresy for business, since it makes it possible for the government to claim virtually anything, breaking all previous agreements and reviewing all existing rules.

Alas, the Indian government has a track record of unpredictable behavior towards mobile operators. Another earthquake took place in 2012 when the government "recalled" 122 licenses[94] that it had previously auctioned to mobile operators, meaning that the companies had to bid again to repurchase the licenses. Fortunately, Vodafone did not struggle here as much as other companies. However, the implication is that foreign companies in India can never be 100% sure of sustainable performance.

No mistakes made

The deal of acquiring Indian venture of Hong Kong–based Hutchison was extremely beneficial for the company. The company gave Vodafone access to a fastest-growing telecom market, and it was expected that vast expertise of the company would help bring the market share in India to 20% from 16% in just a year.[95]

What makes the case interesting is that Vodafone actually did nothing wrong. It adequately assessed the benefits of the deal, conducted a very successful roll-out, ensured efficient cultural cooperation and managed to smooth the differences between companies. Moreover, the company performed most of the steps, presented in Chapter 1, which discusses strategies to decrease the risk exposure in the telecoms industry and more generally in emerging markets. Nonetheless, the merger faced very profound challenges due to institutional reasons.

Vodafone underestimated the legal pressures that it was poised to face after entering the market. The company created a legal team to facilitate the market entry, but this team concentrated on industry-related risks and focused on choosing between various forms of expansion (e.g. joint venture vs. M&A deal) rather than assessing the systemic risks linked to the Indian regulatory environment. Although there were significant risks that strict regulatory authorities might harm company expansion, these were correctly assessed, and the company was largely successful in mitigating them.

Walmart: challenging traditions in India

Company history

Wal-Mart Stores, Inc. (now branded as Walmart), is an American multinational retail corporation (and a classical example of a multinational) that runs chains of large discount department stores and warehouse stores. The company is the largest retailer in the world and the world's largest public corporation.[96]

Walmart's operations are organized into three divisions: Walmart Stores United States, Sam's Club (which offers bulk items to customers who purchase warehouse memberships), and Walmart International. The company does business in nine different retail formats: supercenters, food and drugs, general merchandise stores, bodegas (small markets), cash-and-carry stores, membership warehouse clubs, apparel stores, soft discount stores and restaurants.

Over the last decade, Walmart grew sales by approximately 7% on an average annual rate. In 2015, Walmart worldwide achieved revenues of $482.2 billion, a more than 2% increase over the previous year.[97]

Founded in 1962 in Arkansas, Walmart rose from a regional to national giant in the late 1980s and early 1990s, and the company opened its first international store in Mexico City in 1991. Walmart has pursued globalization aggressively ever since. In 1993, just 1% of all Walmart stores were located outside the United States, but by 1998, that had grown to 18%. Between 1995 and 1998, 5% of the company's growth in sales and 4% of its growth in profits came from international operations. Mike Duke, the retail giant's president and chief executive, stated in 2012, "Today, we do more business outside the United States than we did in all of Walmart when I joined in 1995."[98] In 2013, Walmart's international sales were $141 billion, or 29% of total sales, a 3% increase over 2014.[99]

As of January 2014, Walmart's international operations include 6,337 stores (operating under fifty-five different names) in twenty-six countries outside the United States, with more than 796,000 associates (staff). In the United States, the company operates under the Walmart name, in Mexico as Walmart de México y Centroamérica, in the United Kingdom as Asda and in Japan as Seiyu. According to the company website, Walmart International is currently the fastest-growing part of the business.

International expansion of Walmart was conducted through three primary entry strategies:

- acquisitions (Argentina, Brazil, Canada, and the United Kingdom – the company now has wholly owned operations there)
- joint ventures (China, India)
- several majority-owned subsidiaries (Walmex in Mexico and Central American Retail Holding Company (CARHCO), consisting of more than 360 supermarkets and other stores in Guatemala, El Salvador, Honduras, Nicaragua, and Costa Rica)

As it can be seen from the list of countries where Walmart operates, the company has not focused on any particular region and covers both developed and emerging markets including Africa. During the first five years of its globalization (1991 to 1995), Walmart concentrated heavily on establishing a presence in the Americas: Mexico, Brazil, Argentina and Canada.

Walmart's main reason for expanding internationally was market seeking: the company needed to show increases in both sales and profits to satisfy capital market expectations. Given the necessity for growth, Walmart could not afford to restrict its operations to the United States for three main reasons:[100] most of the domestic markets were saturated, the United States accounts for just over 4% of the world's population and emerging markets, with their lower levels of disposable income, offered huge platforms for growth in discount retailing.

Other positive external factors were the rapid expansion of information technology, increasing cultural homogenization and lowered trade barriers; other companies had already capitalized on them, so Walmart had no choice but to pursue globalization aggressively to meet this competition. The company needed to grow in order to survive, and the international arena was the only one in which significant growth was possible.

Walmart's investments outside North America have had mixed results: its operations in the United Kingdom, South America and China are highly successful, whereas ventures in Germany, South Korea, India and Russia were unsuccessful. As an example of failure, India presents revealing insights.

Indian retail market

India's growth took place across all economic sectors, but formal retail showed especially high growth, since Indian consumers had long been accustomed to informal, small-scale retail operations. The retail market in India accounts for about 15% of GDP.[101] Retail market in India is famous globally as a result of its volume and growth. It plays a momentous role in India's economy and leads the growth of country to the increased trend. The success of India's economy through a factor like retail market can be seen from the Table 3.5.

One key feature of the Indian market is the revolution in shopping in India, marked by drastic changes in consumer behavior and shopping formats. Modern retailing has made its appearance in the form of bustling shopping centers, multi-storied malls and huge urban complexes that offer shopping, entertainment and food all under one roof.

Table 3.5 India – macroeconomic details

Indicator	Unit	2010	2011	2012	2013
GDP, PPP (per capita)	USD	3,453.82	3,777.92	4,103.79	4,434.57
GDP, PPP (per capita growth)	%	12.013	9.38	8.62	8.06
Gross disposable income per household, USD	USD	5,295.26	6,151.04	6,867.1	7,627.55
Gross disposable income per household, USD (growth)	%	16.37	16.37	11.64	11.07
Rural population as % of total population	%	70.20	70.20	69.75	69.53
Urban population as % of total population	%	29.79	29.79	30.24	30.46

Source: World Bank Data 2015 (http://data.worldbank.org)

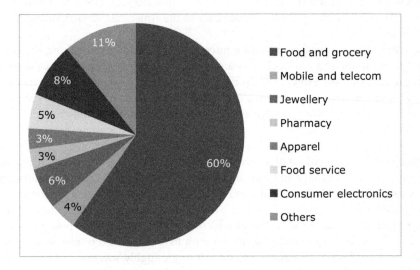

Figure 3.1 Breakdown of the Indian retail market by segment

Source: India Retail Report 2013, Deloitte (http://rasci.in/downloads/2013/Indian_Retail_Market_Opening.pdf)

The vast middle class and almost untapped retail industry are the key attractive forces for global retail giants wanting to enter the Indian retail segment (Figure 3.1). Indian retail is expected to grow 25% annually. The Indian retail industry is expected to reach $750 to $850 billion by 2015. Food and grocery is the largest category within the retail sector with 60% share followed by apparel and mobile segment.

Like all retail markets, India has its own specificities, which foreign entrants must heed. First of all, Indian consumers demand access to products and services that delight and excite them, are of good quality and provide value of money. Second, GDP per capita levels in India are growing, meaning higher disposable income. This means consumers are experimenting with brands, trying new products and so forth. Third, consumption patterns are changing. During the period of heavy-handed state economic diktat, the focus of Indian consumers was on saving. The recent economic boom and the evolving retail market are ensuring that consumers spend more money across categories.

What went wrong in India?

In 2007, Walmart and Bharti Enterprises established a joint venture, Bharti Walmart Private Limited, for wholesale cash-and-carry and back-end supply chain management operations in India. A typical wholesale cash-and-carry store is a massive facility that sells a wide range of fruits and vegetables, groceries and staples, stationery, footwear, clothing, consumer durables and other general merchandise items.

Since Indian retail law does not allow multi-brand foreign retailers to sell directly to consumers, Walmart had no choice but to enter via a joint venture.

Bharti Walmart jointly built twenty superstores, located in major cities such as Amritsar, Zirakpur, Jalandhar, Kota, Bhopal, Ludhiana, Rajpur, Indore, Vijayawada, Agra, Meerut, Lucknow and Jammu. Walmart tried to target the northern regions of India for its cash-and-carry business. It opened its first store in Amritsar in May 2009.

Walmart's long-term strategy in India was to open its retail stores nationwide. The government's decision to allow 51% of FDI in multi-brand retail encouraged Walmart to invest in the front-end retail segment. This company, as a foreign brand, had various strategies to promote its place in Indian market. For instances, it took part in charitable events (and contributed close to $245 million to charities annually) and marketed itself as a community-based institute. In addition, it offered affordable health plans starting from $23.[102]

On the location dimension, its absolute size makes India an attractive country for Walmart, but one with limitations that need to be managed effectively for success. India's population is over a billion, although a large percentage of the population is poor; the middle class has been estimated to include 300 million people, more than the total U.S. population. This is an immense advantage for Walmart strategy, as there is a large population in the segment it typically serves.

Although large in size, the diversity and heterogeneity of the Indian market makes it tremendously complex. Religion, language, dialect, value systems, food habits, economic buying power, clothing selection, fabric, tradition and access to transportation are all attributes that clearly add complexity to the market; there are sub-markets within markets in India. While the Indian middle class customer is a value-conscious shopper, she is very hard to please. This is best expressed by the customer's mindset of "wanting a world-class product at Indian prices." So Walmart's traditional business model, offering the lowest prices, might not gain traction in India without substantial modifications.[103]

Segmenting the market was a key to success: how could Walmart develop localized merchandise and efficiently source its product range (seventy-five thousand items sold in a typical supercenter)?[104] In case of supply chain strategy, Walmart's plan was to bring its global supply chain capabilities and expertise to India while customizing them to the unique requirements of the Indian market.

Yet daily operational problems occurred, coupled with the institutional and cultural constraints. One such issue was that the Indian government required retailers to source 30% of stock from small suppliers, quite a task for Walmart, which was used to massive ordering. Another problem was the ongoing American investigation of fraud in Mexico, Brazil, China and India. In India, the investigation centered on whether a loan made by Walmart to Bharti broke foreign investment rules, although both parties denied any wrongdoing.[105]

Real estate issues proved another prickly issue in India, especially given the notoriously slow permit processing times. In September 2011, Walmart had approached a real estate developer with an eye towards building a wholesale store. Within three months, they had signed a contract saying the developer would build and then lease a building for a wholesale store on a four-acre plot.[106] The developer told Walmart it would take up to nine months to get the permits needed to begin construction and one additional year to build the store, meaning almost two years before the store could open. Yet Walmart insisted the store be ready within twelve months. Eager to start earning rent and recouping his investment, the developer started construction soon after, even though all required permits were not in hand. In December 2011, the developer received a notice from a municipal agency ordering a halt to construction because of the missing permits. In February 2012, the government sealed the site.[107]

All in all, in October 2013, Walmart and Bharti announced they were ending their retail partnership, with the U.S. giant saying India's foreign investment rules were partly to blame for the split. Walmart explained its decision to split from Bharti was based on external and internal factors, including the new FDI policy.[108] In reality, the group had been frustrated by the government's new conditions for FDI, the internal bribery probe and the faltering relationship with Bharti, owner of India's top mobile phone operator. To finalize its exit, Walmart bought out Bharti's shares, taking full control of only twenty cash-and-carry stores in India. After that, Walmart kept its India plans on hold.[109]

Walmart's entry strategy (via JV) was compulsory due to protectionist restrictions. Yet one advantage of the JV was that the costs and risks were shared, giving a certain degree of control while limiting the risk exposure. The second advantage was that Walmart gained quick access to knowledge about the host-country environment (India). A third benefit was that the JV was more politically acceptable in India.

One of Walmart's common operating choices is to place its shopping centers away from city centers. This strategy was ill suited to India given the low ratio of Indians owning cars. In turn, this drastically reduced the number of buyers flocking to the huge discount retail centers. Although consumers appreciated the low pricing of the wholesale shop, they found it too far removed from the city and not worth the extra effort every week.

Another strategy of Walmart's is to have everything under one roof, from farm produce to do-it-yourself plumbing kits, or even refrigerators. In this manner, via impulse purchasing, a customer who comes to buy one item ends up buying more. Indians were not (yet) accustomed to this behavior and did not accept buying groceries and other items at the same time, or under the same roof.

In some cities, Indian consumers preferred local retailers (kirana) to Walmart. A kirana store owner generally knows every customer and maintains a personal rapport. Local retailers also offer home delivery and consumer credit – services that Walmart could not match.

Another non-transferable consumer habit was buying to stock at home. Walmart customers in developed countries purchase some goods to last them a month or even more, buying at wholesale prices. But Indians are neither comfortable eating canned foods, nor eating non-fresh groceries (meat, fish, vegetables), meaning drastic sales drops for Walmart Bharti.

Although Walmart brought its global supply chain capabilities and expertise to India, it confronted underdeveloped physical infrastructure and a lack of modern tracking technology, which placed significant limitations on efficiency.

To conclude, the entry strategy of Walmart was appropriate, but the joint venture's market penetration strategies were not successful. It could not develop a suitable strategy against well-established local retailers and well-entrenched consumer habits. It faced increasing pressure from local civil rights groups and traditional shop owners. Moreover, misunderstanding the culture and living style of Indians was another reason for Walmart's failure in India.

Lastly, the partner company could not lead Walmart managers to any alternative success plan or strategy for the Indian market. Even though India as an emerging market had high potential, the company could not find its fit in the market.

3.4 Foreigners in Russia: the cases of DHL, Accor and TNK-BP

DHL: combining promotion and investment in Russia

Company background

Three budding entrepreneurs, Adrian Dalsey, Larry Hillblom and Robert Lynn, founded DHL in San Francisco in 1969. The initials of their last names became the company's name. DHL has continued to expand at a phenomenal rate. Today, it stands tall as the global market leader of the international express and logistics industry. DHL now belongs to Deutsche Post, the German postal giant. The group generated revenue of more than €56.6 billion in 2014.[110]

Back in 1969, DHL began its adventure by shipping newspapers by airplane from San Francisco to Honolulu. Years passed and the DHL network grew ever larger, gradually reaching out to new customers in many countries around the world. As the market developed and became more complex, DHL adjusted to meet the changing needs of its customers.

Today, DHL's international network links more than 220 countries and territories worldwide. DHL also offers unparalleled expertise in express, air and ocean freight, overland transport, contract logistics solutions and international mail services.

From 1969 until today, the company's approach and dedication has remained the same, with the delivery of excellent customer service being key to success. Never complacent, DHL has become a brand acknowledged for personal commitment, proactive solutions and local strength. At the heart of its success are its employees who focus on the customers' needs and provide individually customized solutions.

Why Russia?

The most important reason why DHL decided to enter the Russian market in 1984 is that the demand for transport services has grown considerably over the last decades (with an average annual growth rate of 16%) and the future expectation is that demand for transport will keep up, due to the expected growth of trade between Russia and the world.

Another attractive feature of the Russian market is the lack of domestic competition and the limited experience in efficient logistics. Many Russian logistics companies have high storage and operating costs, and experts believe that these costs will increase over time.[111] Moreover, since the traditional Russian logistics service providers focus mainly on storage and transportation, there is an opportunity for value-added services such as assembly services, packaging and the use of Internet-based services. While some Russian-based logistics companies started to offer such value-added services, they were not able to comply with the increasing demand for such services due to a lack of know-how and experience. This spelled a window of opportunity for DHL. Furthermore, DHL believed it could use its experience and mass to offer better delivery speeds, while keeping costs reasonable.

A final reason that speaks in favor of the Russian logistics market is that is has governmental support, with the Russian government wanting to expand the market to diversify the economy. The sector was seen as an important driver for national economic growth. Large investments were expected to expand existing logistics centers as well as build new warehouses. An example of this is the investment of hundreds of millions of euros to develop a series of logistics terminals in the Moscow area.

Strategy in Russia

Established in 1984, DHL Russia progressively expanded to serve over five hundred towns and cities across Russia, with a network of over 130 stations, representing 99% of the total population. DHL Russia operates a fleet of over 550 commercial vehicles. But Russia has not been the only focus of DHL Russia, as it created enhanced connections to Europe.

In line with the company's global door-to-door principle, Russian packages and freight are picked up from the sender to be delivered directly to the receiver. Back when the company was founded, this principle transformed the industry and significantly influenced the logistics business worldwide.

DHL first opened its office in Moscow shortly after the first area, including the largest cities in different regions of Russia such as St. Petersburg (northwest), Novosibirsk (Siberia), Vladivostok (far east) and Togliatti (south), was covered. DHL's roll-out was fast and today it has branches in more than 120 cities and towns from Kaliningrad to Vladivostok.

DHL works in two segments: domestic and international express delivery. The company set up a network of scheduled ground transport links between the major cities (Moscow, St. Petersburg, Samara, Ekaterinburg and others). Besides, DHL can provide daily air links between Russia and Europe: six times per week from Moscow to the Leipzig hub and five times per week from St. Petersburg to Helsinki.

DHL's Russian success is largely due to the innovative service level provided, which is supported by the necessary, very large investments in the market. This commitment to investing in order to provide the same service level as elsewhere enabled DHL to become the only express carrier offering overnight service between Europe and Russia, as well as one of the most extensive express delivery networks in Russia with over 150 offices offering pickup and delivery to over 600 cities in the Russian Federation, and it has set up a network of seven freight-handling terminals in the country's largest cities in order to do so.

Another key factor in the company's Russian success was the advertising campaign promoting the company simultaneously in Russian and CIS cities. Furthermore, the campaign was customized at the regional level, making it even closer to local customer needs. This approach, quite unique for Russia at that time, helped the brand to grow rapidly during the 1990s. Subsequently, the DHL brand rapidly became recognizable and familiar to Russians, with brand awareness exceeding 90% in the Russian Federation today.[112]

Main competitors

FedEx started operating in Russia in 1991, seven years after DHL, and features a strong brand image in the country and all over the world. In 2011, the company was named the eighth best-admired company globally by *Fortune* magazine.[113] FedEx provides transportation, e-commerce and business services. The company offers integrated business applications through its operating companies. The company's subsidiary, Federal Express Corporation (FedEx Express), is the world's largest express transportation company. FedEx operates throughout the United States as well as in 220 countries worldwide.

FedEx operates an integrated global network, including 52,886 drop-off locations, (including 4,974 U.S. post offices), 1,057 operations facilities (warehouses), with 676 in the United States and 381 outside the United States. On average every day, FedEx handles approximately 3.5 million packages and 11 million pounds of freight, which are shipped using 684 aircraft and approximately 43,000 motorized vehicles. The FedEx Express segment also includes FedEx Trade Networks, which provides international trade services, specialized customs brokerage, global cargo distribution and trade facilitation solutions. FedEx Trade Networks operates through 120 offices in 95 service locations throughout North America and in Asia, Europe, the Middle East and Latin America.[114]

TNT Express N.V. is an international express services company with headquarters in Hoofddorp, Holland, founded in 1946. The company has fully owned operations in sixty-five countries and delivers documents, parcels and pieces of freight to over two hundred countries. TNT employs 83,235 people.

TNT Express in Russia has been operating since 1989 through contractors. In 1993, the first office was opened in Moscow. The company is primarily engaged in the shipment of goods and documents from customer to customer by road, rail, water and air. Shipments are either delivered the same day, the next day or on a specified day, as specified by the customer and depending on the nature of the delivery. In addition to shipping and delivery, TNT offers auxiliary services, such as storage, special courier services for pharmaceutical industries, handling of import and export formalities and a range of industry solutions, among other things.

TNT's network is concentrated in Europe and Asia, but the group is expanding its operations worldwide, including the Middle East and South America. The company has 58,722 employees in 61 countries, 54 cargo planes flying more than 700 trips weekly and 72 European logistics hubs.

United Parcel Service (UPS) is one of the largest package delivery companies in the world, a leader in the U.S. less-than-truckload industry and a global leader in supply chain management operations.

UPS was registered in Russia in 1993.[115] The company's diversified product portfolio and extensive operational network enable it to serve a broad range of customers across major international markets and provides it the benefit of economies of scale. However, government regulations could put pressure on the company and impact its cost structure. UPS has a strong brand image. For instance, in 2011, the annual BrandZ Top 100 survey ranked UPS brand number one among logistics brands with a value of $35.7 billion and an overall ranking of seventeen on the top-one hundred list.[116] Moreover, UPS was named in 2011 as number thirty in the Fortune's World's Most Admired Companies.[117] UPS provides its full range of services in Russia: domestic delivery, international delivery and freight services.

EMS Russian Post is the Russian link in the worldwide chain of global express mail services operated by each national postal monopoly. This network provides express services within Russia and abroad, although not necessarily overnight service to all countries. EMS Russian Post is within the top-five Russian express service providers and had low rates as its main competitive advantage. This is possible since the service uses existing postal infrastructure, thus avoiding costly investment.

EMS Russian Post holds the leadership position in the segment of express shipments of light cargo (less than thirty kgs). In 2013, Russian Post revenues were RUB 24 billion ($755 million). EMS contributed RUB 3 billion ($95,125) 3% higher than in 2012.[118] Stable prices are a strong competitive advantage for the company, with tariffs for express services unchanged since 2004.[119]

Marketing strategy of DHL in Russia

When entering new markets DHL offers one of three pricing options: frequency discount, monthly handling fee or loaded half kilo. Frequency discounts enable customers to decrease their final price up to 35%, depending on the number of parcels shipped during the month. The monthly handling fee is charged to customers who want to be included on DHL's regular monthly pickup routes. Lastly, the loaded half-kilo price scheme functions like a frequency discount, except that the discount is based on total weight shipped during a particular month (rather than the total number of shipments). The company also offers a special price to companies that opt exclusively for DHL for all their express shipping needs.

In order to succeed in Russia, DHL needed to develop an effective marketing campaign that would connect with potential customers. Research by AC Nielsen pointed to Russia becoming the largest European consumer market by 2025. The promise for DHL lay in the rise in demand for logistics and express delivery services. Despite the massive challenge of insufficient infrastructure, DHL could not afford to miss out on the Russian market, which would help connect global activities and enabled the company to stay competitive on a long-term basis. Yet DHL knew it had to adapt its campaign to specific Russian cultural characteristics. Only such an approach could result in widespread brand acceptance by Russian customers.[120]

DHL was no newcomer to the Russian sphere of influence. Even back in the 1990s, shortly after the collapse of Soviet Union, DHL started promotion in both CIS countries and Russia. The main hurdle was the general lack about knowledge of DHL services. The advertising campaign, therefore, stressed introducing the actual express delivery service itself. But the real uniqueness of this marketing campaign lay in its regional development. It was designed specifically for the Russian-speaking nations so as to address their similar cultural aspects and perceptions.

One key component of DHL's campaign was direct mail. According to TNS Infratest, Russia is among few nations where direct mail (dialog marketing) is very young and therefore still provides outstanding response rates. In comparison with Europe, only 34% of Russian consumers receive direct mails at least once a week, whereas in Europe the figure is twice as high (68%). Furthermore, direct mail still elicits interest in Russia, with over half of Russian consumers actually reading the messages. This provides direct mail (the fastest-growing marketing segment in Russia) with great potential and advantages over the mass-market advertising methods. Since Russian consumers tend to respond and appreciate direct mail only when they can see some value added, DHL developed complex targeted mailings that included samples, coupons or gift certificates.

In addition, DHL Global Mail obtained a license to provide postal services in Russia, one of the biggest mail markets in the world. In order to operate effectively, DHL cooperates with Russian Post. DHL set up a new entity to operate in Russia and CIS countries and, using a database of Russian-speaking companies and communities around the world, it provided customers entering Russia with direct marketing support to easily reach their target groups.

The extensive marketing campaign paid off smartly. The campaign included mass media (press, television, radio and Internet) as well as flyers, mailshots and outdoor billboards. The Russian website explained the standard services offered and published articles from the Russian press about recent achievements and struggles. Thanks to the intensive marketing push in Russia, the Russian expression for "overnight delivery" is simply the name DHL, and brand awareness exceeds 90%.

Investment of DHL in the Russian market

Since 1984, Deutsche Post DHL made substantial inbound FDI investments into the Russian Federation in order to establish its operations. These investments were mainly in the infrastructure sector, of critical importance to the company's operations. At the start of 2002, DHL announced that it would invest into the development of the northwest part of Russia. This desire to invest in this area reflected DHL's business success, with a doubling of revenue from this area for 2001 compared to the previous year.[121] Moreover, the country manager for DHL Russia stated that each year 10% of the company's Russian profit was reinvested locally.

In 2005, Deutsche Post DHL announced its intention to invest $50 million in the Russian market because its fast growth and the low market penetration of top competitors (the sole world market wherein the "big four" DHL, UPS, FedEx and TNT possessed below 50% share) promised great expansion opportunities.[122] The bulk of this investment – the first large investment of any of the "big four" in the Russian market – financed the construction of a modern logistics infrastructure in Russia – namely, more than ten new customs terminals, logistics centers and warehouses for both international and domestic shipments.[123] This $50 million investment alone amounted to as much as the company had invested cumulatively since 1984 and showed that DHL Russia's focus was educating personnel and purchasing equipment making acquisitions before expanding big by themselves.[124] The main benefit of such large investments was to place DHL Russia beyond the reach of local competitors who mostly unable to afford outlays on their scale.

The conclusion on the strategy of DHL in Russia is that DHL wanted to offer a new and innovative service to the Russian market by combining the different sectors of the industry and thereby providing a service that was unknown of before. The success of the company and its position as a market leader in its industry are the result of focusing and investing heavily in bringing new and innovative services and products to the market and by improving the familiarity of the brand. The strategy of DHL of investing heavily on its own distinctive product and market recognition have made the company the biggest express logistics company of Russia and the only one-stop shop in the industry.

Accor: meeting customers' expectations in Russia

Company background

Accor Group is a French hotel group created in 1967. It operates in ninety-two countries with more than 3,700 hotels having 480,000 rooms and operating under the brands Hotel F1, Ibis Budget, Ibis Styles, Ibis, Adagio, Adagio Access, Mercure, Novotel, Grand Mercure, Pullman, MGallery and Sofitel. It is the European leader and ranked sixth worldwide in 2013.[125] With the hotel industry being very fragmented and national, most of Accor's competitors remain focused on their domestic markets, while Accor has concentrated on an expansion strategy.

In order to capitalize on geographic proximity, market control, moderate competition and the travel patterns of its French customers, for many years Accor's geographical expansion was focused and limited to Europe. In 1972, the group opened hotels in francophone neighboring countries (Belgium and Switzerland), with obvious options because of strong trade links with France. At the very beginning, the internationalization of Accor was not so dominant, whereas now it is considered a pillar of the company's strategic objectives illustrated by its slogan: "Open new frontiers in hospitality." Between 1976 and 1979, some operations in Africa, the Middle East and South America confirmed the company's interest in the BRIC areas.[126]

In 2003, the Accor Group made an additional move, with its annual report stating how important the BRIC countries have become for geographic expansion: "By the 2020 horizon, global tourism is expected to make its sharpest increase in emerging markets such as China, India or Russia. For Accor, these new markets show considerable development potential."[127] For 2015, the group set the BRIC area as a strategic priority, with the corporate objective that the company would become one of the top-three hotel groups worldwide.

Competitive pressure

In 2014, Accor's market share in Russia was 14% of retail value, in second place after Carlson Rezidor (28%), but ahead of InterContinental Hotels (13%), Marriott International (11%), Hilton Worldwide (6%) and others.[128]

Hilton Hotel is the most ambitious for their developments. All these operators plan to develop their chains in Russia for several reasons. First, the developing countries represent the best market opportunities for hotel chains moreover Russia will host the World Football Championship 2018 and other world events, thereby hotel operators will be intent on opening new hotels in the host cities. Consequently, Russia is viewed as a growth engine by Accor with a global economic expansion the previous years and a real GDP growth higher than the world average. Furthermore, The CIS and Russia have not been penetrated strongly by the main hotel brands. Around 54% of existing hotel rooms is concentrated in the two Russia major cities, St. Petersburg and Moscow. At the horizon of 2017, 32,000 creation rooms are planned.[129] Till recently, Russia was mainly viewed as a business tourism country that could explain the strong concentration of hotels in the two largest business centers of Russia. Nevertheless, some world events (APEC and Shanghai Cooperation Organization summits, the winter Olympic Games in Sochi, the football World Cup 2022) lead some hotel operators to implement their businesses in other large Russian cities.

Overall, twenty international hotel operators work in Russia. Among these twenty actors, five major actors distinguish from the others with 71% of market share (Rezidor Hotel Group, InterContinental Hotels, Marriott and Accor, which reached 13% of market share at the end of 2013).

Increasing its footprint in Russia

The Accor Group has been operating in Russian market since 1992 when it launched its business in Moscow and St. Petersburg. After the collapse of Soviet Union in 1991, Accor quickly realized the opportunities of the vast, and vastly underdeveloped, Russian market. With its economic and political borders disappearing, the new post-Soviet Russia was like a gargantuan pot of honey for Western European investors.

The very first project launched by Accor in Russia was the construction of the Novotel Sheremetievo Airport hotel near Moscow. Even today, this deluxe hotel remains one of the most popular places to stay for Russian and foreign businessmen due to its convenient location near the international airport, and thus allowing guest to avoid the horrendous Moscow traffic. In 2011, the hotel could boast of a 99% occupancy rate for its 493 rooms.[130]

In 2001, the Accor Group established a subsidiary, Russian Management Hotel Company LLC (RMHC or Accor Russia CIS) to develop and operate its hotel properties across all brands in Russia and other CIS countries. The main functions of RMHC consisted of

- making hotel management contracts;
- facilitating the design, construction and equipment of all the properties in the area, in compliance with worldwide Accor standards;
- providing resources to establish and maintain the international Accor standards (including staff coaching, loyalty programs, link to the international reservation system); and
- promoting contacts of Accor Russian hotels with foreign partners.

Based in Moscow, RMHC spreads the group's management and business practices from other markets and shares its expertise all over the world. Today, the company is acknowledged as a leading hotel chain operator, with several prestigious Russian awards to its credit: the "Golden Brick" prize for Commercial Real Estate, the Federal Award for hotel development and the individual "Leadership Award" attributed to the Russia managing director Alexis Delaroff in 2013.

Within Russia, in 2015, Accor operated a total of thirty-one hotels with some five thousand rooms, the most popular brand being *Pullman* (one property), *Ibis* (ten properties), *Novotel* (five), *Mercure* (ten) and *Adagio* (one).[131] These properties have spread beyond Moscow and St. Petersburg to include such Russian cities as Yekaterinburg, Kazan, Nizhny Novgorod, Yaroslavl, Sochi, Omsk, Samara and Kaliningrad.

In 2010, the company announced new strategic plans for accelerating its presence in Russia and the CIS, with top management considering Russia a focus market in the East European zone. The strategic goals were to open at least fifty new hotels (meaning over ten thousand rooms) in the area by 2020, concentrating mainly on large cities. According to Accor CEO Yann Caillere,

> Russia and the CIS are key regions for our group's dynamic expansion. Thanks to our strong brand portfolio, from luxury to budget, our powerful distribution system and our operational excellence, we are ideally positioned to seize the opportunities of this booming market.[132]

Accor has developed a relatively new hotel segment for the market: modern, comfortable hotels at reasonable prices. The international competitors don't cover this segment, making it possible for Accor to occupy the niche. In developed markets, such as Western Europe, Accor's main rival in the budget segment is *Holiday Inn Express*, but this company is not yet present in Russia. In the absence of severe competition, Accor is trying to capture the economy segment and make Russian consumers as loyal as possible.

What accounts for Accor's success after barely a few decades in Russia? Its main source of competitive advantage is its focus on the mid-scale and budget segments with its *Ibis* brand, catering to the newly formed middle class. *Ibis's* cost-effective offering satisfies the growing demand in this socio-economic category. Yet Accor's portfolio has not neglected the upscale Russian and tourist; here the *Novotel* upscale brand has strong positions in Moscow and St. Petersburg, offering luxury, splendid service and high quality.

In support of its expansion plans, Accor opened in 2012 the first hotel under the *Mercure* brand targeted at business and leisure travelers, *Mercure* Arbat Moscow, with a total capacity of 109 rooms. This brand introduces a new approach for emerging market tourists with expectations of high quality. Within the next years, more *Mercure* hotels are expected to open in Lipetsk, Kemerovo, Tyumen, Rostov-on-Don and Koprino.

In 2012, the famous Russian resort center of Rosa Khutor (near Sochi) signed an agreement with RMHC to build an Accor hotel under the *Mercure* brand. The choice of *Mercure* was not fortuitous: it was already familiar to tourists in the alpine resorts of France, Switzerland and Germany. Rosa Khutor was fast becoming a major venue for ski competitions: European Ski Cup in 2011, World Cup stage in 2012 and, finally, downhill ski events during the Sochi Winter Olympic Games in February 2014. In addition to the *Mercure* four-star hotel, Accor also built a five-star upscale *Pullman* hotel in the Olympic Center, with views of the Black Sea, Sochi's long coastline and the mountainous Caucasus skyline. Both hotels also have conference halls for up to eight hundred guests.[133]

The 2014 Winter Olympic Games held in Sochi played an important role in hotel development in Russia. Many renowned hotel chains invested heavily in modern infrastructure in Sochi, with Accor being no exception. Eric Laporte, Accor director of operations for South Russia, reckoned that for a long time "Sochi has been underserved by major hotel brands."[134]

During the summer of 2013, Accor opened the *Novotel* Moscow city hotel in partnership with Tashir holdings, one of the largest real estate developers in Russia. The overall investment made by the two parties is estimated at about €160 million. This project is Accor's fifth hotel in Moscow and currently is the only hotel operating in Moscow City – a newly created international business center.

In 2014, the company made a long-term agreement with another big Russian real estate agent, Patero Development to manage a large hotel complex in the city center near the Kievsky railway station. Accor plans three hotels with a total capacity of seven hundred rooms: *Novotel* Kievskaya, *Ibis* Kievskaya and *Adagio* Kievskaya, with openings originally planned for 2015 and then postponed to 2016. "The opening of this combo in Moscow will add much-needed modern inventory to Russia's capital city. Moscow serves as a gateway to the country for business travelers, and we are committed to offering our customers more choice of consistently high-quality accommodation in the region," explained Alexis Delaroff, Accor CEO in Russia and CIS.[135]

As for regional markets, the Accor Group is strengthening its presence in the Western part of the country. Kaliningrad plays an important part here, with its strategic key position on the Russian political and economic landscapes. In 2013, Accor opened its *Ibis* Kaliningrad Center, the third project in its ongoing collaboration with Turkish company Akfen Real Estate Investment Trust.[136]

All the Russian hotels within the Accor Group provide the "15-minute guarantee," meaning that any guest problem (whether room conditions, meals or other services) will be solved within fifteen minutes, or the particular service is provided free of charge. This rule maintains a uniform high-quality service worldwide, ensuring guests that they receive the same care in Paris as well as in Samara.

To sum up, during 2013, Accor Group broadened its Russian network by nine hotels; in 2014, it was planning to open five properties and ten in 2015. By 2016, the plan was to reach a supply of fifty hotels across Russia.

Overall prospects

Investment in hotels in Russia has grown significantly in the last decade. The low overall room supply, economic growth, improvement of business climate and the increase of business and tourism travel are key factors that have driven these new investments (see Table 3.6). Russia remains one of the most attractive markets for hotel companies in the world. The global hospitality industry kept growing during 2013–2014 (overall revenue per room growth of 4.5%), and the industry continues to gain momentum even in the face of accelerating geopolitical instability.[137] Despite this instability, international hotel operators plan to open new hotels in Russian and CIS with respective additional capacities of 7,400 and 4,700 rooms.[138]

Accor has ambitious plans, with forecasts that by 2017 the company expects to increase its market share, probably reaching 22%.[139] According to an analysis by consulting firm Ernst & Young, by 2017, Accor will operate sixty-seven hotels, versus forty-four operated by current market leader Rezidor, giving Accor a 22% share in room supply for international brands, in comparison with 13% today share.[140]

Table 3.6 International hotels operations in Russia in 2013 and forecast by 2017

Operator	Existing (October 2013)		Future (by 2017)		Total amount by 2017 (existing + future)	
	Hotels	Rooms	Hotels	Rooms	Hotels	Rooms
The Rezidor Hotel Group	22	6,871	22	4,659	44	11,530
Accor	16	3,311	51	9,337	67	12,648
InterContinental Hotels Group	14	3,900	9	2,537	23	6,437
Marriott International	14	3,494	11	2,517	25	6,011
Hilton Worldwide	5	868	21	4,127	26	4,995

Source: Hotel operators data, EY (http://ru.investinrussia.com/data/files/sectors/0_EY-International-hotel-brands-2014-analytics.pdf)

In 2015, Accor revealed four new hotel projects (Moscow, Cheboksary, Tyumen and Voronezh), with an additional four hotels planned for 2015–2016 (two in Krasnoyarsk, Moscow region, Krasnodar).

The Table 3.6 below illustrates how hyper-active the Russian market is, with a planned doubling of capacity for the top five international chains, from 18,445 to 41,580 rooms in four years (+125%). According to this data, Accor will become the major actor on the Russian market in 2017 overtaking its main competitor, Rezidor Hotel Group.

Accor runs its hotels mainly through management agreement and franchise in Russia. By the end of the year 2016, Accor will definitely be the top operator in this region. It's the fastest-growing international operator in CIS and Russia. In order to maintain the fast pace of development, Accor has affirmed its expansion objectives. Its goals through 2016 are to open 30,000 rooms a year on franchise and management contacts and get 5,000 additional rooms per year through acquisition.

BP: Buy-sell in Russia

Company background

The history of British Petroleum (BP) goes back to 1908, when William Knox D'Arcy, who was granted an exploration concession by the Iranian Shah in 1901 and discovered the first commercially significant oilfield in the Middle East.[141] The Anglo-Persian Oil Company (APOC), predecessor of BP, was founded to exploit the oilfield. In 1935, APOC was renamed the Anglo-Iranian Oil Company (AIOC), and then in 1954 it was renamed British Petroleum Company (BP).

During the next decades after the official BP brand establishment, the company expanded its operations to other regions, exploiting oil and natural gas fields in such countries and regions as Canada, Africa, South and Central America, Europe, Alaska and New Guinea.[142]

After it became the first European firm to explore oilfields of Iran and the Middle East, BP confirmed its reputation as a pioneering company, distinguishing itself as the first company in sub-Saharan Africa (Nigeria, 1956), in Alaska (1959)[143] and in the British North Sea (1965) – a particularly important feat given the backdrop of volatility in the Middle East during the 1970s.

BP currently operates in more than eighty countries in Europe, North and South America, Asia and Oceania and Africa. The main oil & gas fields for the company are in the North Sea (Andrew oilfield, ETAP complex, Everest gas field), Norway (Ula oilfield, Walhall oilfield), Gulf of Mexico deepwater (Atlantis oilfield, Thunder horse oilfield), Alaska (Prudhoe Bay field), Caspian region (Shahdeniz gas field), Angola (Plutonio oilfield) and Austrolasia (Angel gas field, North Rankin field, Goodwyn gas field).[144]

The total proven commercial reserves of BP as of December 2015 were 17,180 million barrels of oil equivalent (BOE, which is a unit of energy based on the approximate energy released by burning one barrel of crude oil). The company produces around 3.3 million barrels of oil equivalent per day and has around 17,200 retail sites.[145]

BP has acquired several ethanol plants in Brazil and PTA chemical production plants in China. Alternative energy is expected to be the fastest-growing energy sector over the next twenty years, with global biofuels production projected to more than triple. These strategic acquisitions underline BP's commitment to building substantial businesses in both growing economies and growing market segments, as well as continuing its expansion in Brazil and China through investments.

What drives investments in Russia's oil & gas?

Advantages that ensure the attractiveness of investments in the oil & gas industry in Russia are as follows: Russia has a strong resource base.

After the collapse of the Soviet Union (USSR) large foreign companies finally had the possibility of entering the Russian market, characterized by its huge resource base, its proximity to markets with growing demand in Asia and Europe, its competitive operating costs and the government's prioritization of projects in oil & gas. Needless to say, BP was among the first to knock on the Russian door. Oil companies are on permanent lookout for the next deposit, since ever-increasing demand means new wells need to come online permanently. Entering the Russian market with its newly commissioned deposits might help with this problem. High expectations were also laid on offshore fields (the Caspian, the Black Sea and the Arctic Region) that had not yet been fully explored.

Operations in Russia

In early 1990s, BP started operations in Azerbaijan.[146] The jump from there into the Russian neighbor was then only a question of time, patience and skill. BP's operations in the Russian market can be divided into two main branches:

- The first branch is the 2003 joint venture with TNK for oil production, transportation and refinery.
- The second branch concerns other, non-TNK related activities that BP carries out in Russia. There are four segments of these activities: marine fuel (Baltic Petroleum, 1993), air fuel (Air BP, 1990), lubricants (Setra Lubricants, 1998) and retail trading (IST group, 1991).[147]

However, since 2003, BP's main operations in Russia are housed in the joint venture TNK-BP, which quickly became the fourth-largest company in the Russian oil & gas sector.

In fact, even though multiple BP products have been present in Russia since 1990s, the launch of the TNK-BP joint venture is considered BP's real attempt to invest in Russia.

Joint venture in Russia

The main strategic decision in the BP internationalization process was the creation of TNK-BP, the joint venture between British Petroleum and the AAR consortium (AAR stands for "Access Industries," "Alfa Group" and "Renova"), owned by a group of Russian billionaires. BP and AAR each own 50% of TNK-BP International Limited, which in turn owns 95% of TNK-BP Holding, with the remaining 5% traded on public markets.[148]

The deal was announced as the largest investment project to that date in Russian history.[149] The company held licenses to a number of lucrative oilfields, located in Siberia and the Volga-Ural region. When BP formed an alliance with the AAR consortium in 2003, it secured the support of a powerful and unique private corporate partner for its upstream operations in Russia. AAR seemed to stand out amongst other domestic corporate groups for several reasons:[150]

- AAR's internal corporate composition was unlike any other in Russia.
- AAR was one of the very few Russian corporate groups with control over a highly lucrative oil asset: Tyumen Oil Company (TNK in short).
- The billionaires' consortium had traditionally enjoyed excellent communications channels with the Kremlin, while never challenging those in power.
- Top corporate executives from AAR (Alfa-Bank in particular) had often moved up to high positions within the Russian government.
- By linking with BP, AAR's goal was to develop a JV company operating along Western standards.

Its highly diversified portfolio and its international nature not only set AAR apart from other Russian investment groups but, moreover, secured its operations and assets from state intervention. BP and AAR seemed to be attractive partners, each bringing its own set of values and assets to the joint venture.

Therefore, AAR appears to possess not only a strong entrepreneurial drive, a good grasp of the Russian political and economic system and Western ways of doing business (including the use of Western contracts) but also enjoyed excellent communication channels with the government.[151] The Russian government recognized AAR's unique role in the oil sector and granted TNK-BP the unique status of being the sole joint venture in which the foreign partner was allowed a stake larger than 49%.

In 2010, TNK-BP (excluding its 50% share in Slavneft) produced on average 1.74 million barrels per day of oil equivalent and was among the top-ten energy companies in the world.[152]

Approaching Gazprom

According to the shareholder agreement, the partners could not leave the joint venture until the beginning of 2008 (after a five-year hiatus period). However, the tension between AAR and BP was increasing, with AAR exerting pressure on BP. The official version states that the major shareholders could not agree on the company's future development, including international expansion. AAR accused BP of preventing TNK-BP's international development since it contravened BP interests.[153]

As a result, BP started exploring its options, in particular the possibility of replacing AAR with Gazprom in the TNK-BP venture in 2007. Why this shift? Apart from the political decline of the Russian oligarchs, there were other important reasons driving BP into Gazprom's arms.[154] Foremost, since 2006, Gazprom was responsible for all natural gas exports,[155] including the Kovykta field, one of the most important TNK-BP assets and one of the globe's best natural gas fields.[156] The deposit is located close to the hungry Asian gas markets and holds more than an estimated two trillion cubic meters of natural gas. So any successful commercial development of the field and its exports to Asia was impossible without Gazprom's involvement. At first, BP considered an option to sell a 63% stake of the project directly to Gazprom, but the deal stalled, and BP decided to look for a potential replacement of AAR with Gazprom.

Surely Gazprom wished to obtain a controlling stake in TNK-BP, which would have made Gazprom a major player in the Russian oil sector. Yet this scenario would not have been supported by Russian Prime Minister Vladimir Putin. Moreover, Deputy Prime Minister Igor Sechin (Rosneft's chairman at that time) objected to the transformation of the TNK-BP venture into a Gazprom-BP partnership because any Gazprom oil acquisitions would undermine the existing dominance of Rosneft in the Russian oil sector.

Most importantly, the Gazprom-BP deal would have undermined the existing status quo between Gazprom and Rosneft as state energy champions, each with their own energy turf: gas and oil, respectively. Furthermore, a possible Gazprom-BP partnership might cause disaffection among independent gas producers and oilmen in Russia, and lead to the increase of the state share in Russian oil production above 50%, which in turn might affect the country's investment climate.[157]

Last but not least, AAR was not interested in selling its share in the joint venture to Gazprom, since it has always hinted that TNK-BP was a long-term investment.

Corporate clash

Fierce confrontation between AAR and BP to develop its Russian joint venture coincided with the alleged negotiations between BP and Gazprom to replace the oligarchs. However, the possibility of Gazprom's participation in the joint venture was not the primary cause of the clash between AAR and BP; it derived from certain corporate governance issues and broader strategic divergences between partners regarding national and international expansion.

It seems natural that BP would want to increase its presence in Russia and the CIS, since Russia is a key non-OPEC oil producer and the largest exporter of natural gas in the world. In addition, Russia is blessed by geology, with one of the highest hydrocarbon potentials in the world.[158]

However, from the point of view of AAR, BP appeared not only to have the upper hand in managing TNK-BP but also seemed to treat the JV merely as its Russian subsidiary, focusing on projects within the former Soviet Union. AAR, on the other hand, wanted TNK-BP to become a global player by expanding its operations outside of Russia, to the Middle East, North Africa, Latin America, Asia and Europe. The brightest examples of this divergence of interests was connected with Venezuelan, Iraqi and Lithuanian expansion opportunities. BP blocked all three of these initiatives due to political issues in Venezuela and Iraq and overpriced assets in Lithuania.

One can understand that this reluctance to see TNK-BP expand abroad was associated with BP's fear of seeing its Russian joint venture turn into a new global competitor. Moreover, BP's apparent resistance to TNK-BP's international expansion was perceived in Russia as running against national interests on the global stage. Taking into consideration these factors, BP was unlikely to receive Kremlin support in its growing conflict with AAR.[159]

Another stumbling block in the relationship between AAR and BP was the composition of the TNK-BP board, in which BP had five representatives and AAR had only four. Plus the joint venture's CEO, Robert Dudley, was suspected of extending greater preference to BP than to AAR.[160] Russian shareholders were also skeptical of the practice of bringing in temporary BP expatriates on expensive assignments, without necessarily needing them. BP countered that the managerial, technical and financial expertise of its staff was of great benefit to TNK-BP.

The growing conflict between AAR and BP even hindered normal company operations. In 2008, AAR allegedly facilitated tax, visa and work permit investigations into BP personnel by Russian regulatory agencies. In April 2008, TNK-BP had tax claims for 2004–2005 in the amount of six billion rubles. In late February, TNK-BP held seizure of documents in the criminal case against Sidanco Oil Company. In March, the TNK-BP offices were searched under investigation in the case of industrial espionage.[161] As a result, Robert Dudley fled Russia in July 2008 and even tried to run TNK-BP from abroad.

The conflict was settled after Dudley resigned and a new shareholding agreement was signed, giving both AAR and BP four board representatives each, with three additional independent directors. Moreover, the parties agreed to start the expansion beyond Russia and Ukraine and appointed an independent CEO.[162]

However, the peace between BP and AAR did not last long: after a few years, in 2011, BP and Rosneft decided to create a strategic partnership for the joint development of hydrocarbons in the Arctic. Another indicator of the impossibility of reconciliation was the departure of the first independent directors in 2011.[163]

Considering Rosneft and Arctic region

In the beginning of 2011, Rosneft and BP announced their intention to establish a global strategic alliance. The companies even planned to go so far as to exchange shares (9.53% of Rosneft's for 5% of BP's) and established a joint venture in the Arctic Region. Prime Minister Vladimir Putin and President Dmitry Medvedev approved the transaction, and the deal was declared as "the agreement of the year."[164]

But the AAR consortium announced that BP had violated its shareholder agreement, according to which TNK-BP held the exclusive partner role in Russia. According to AAR, BP could have dealt with Rosneft only after discussing the details with the TNK-BP board of directors and obtaining approval. Since BP did not comply with these conditions, a court upheld AAR's claim to suspend the transaction.[165]

Thereafter, one of BP's options was to buy out AAR's share of the joint venture. BP offered AAR $27 billion, but AAR estimated its stake at $40 billion, which BP simply could not afford.[166] Another option was for Rosneft to purchase the AAR stake, but Rosneft was only interested in a partnership with BP, since TNK-BP lacked the experience and technology for the complex Arctic project. Another issue was that Rosneft could not afford to purchase the AAR stake in the JV since Rosneft was already carrying $23 billion in debt, which constituted 36% of Rosneft's 2010 annual revenue. For international oil & gas companies, the acceptable debt-to-revenue ratio ranges from 10% to15%.[167]

Even in collaboration with BP, it was still questionable whether Rosneft could, or needed to, buy out the stake. First, AAR did not seem to be interested in selling their shares. Second, by then Rosneft had already received attractive offers from ExxonMobil, Shell, Chevron and other companies.[168] All the other options to solve the problem led to the direct or indirect involvement of AAR, which was undesirable both for BP and Rosneft.

The end of TNK-BP

In October 2012, BP's board of directors unanimously agreed to sell its TNK-BP share to Rosneft. Five months later, Rosneft announced the completion of the acquisition of 100% of TNK-BP. Rosneft paid $16.65 billion and 12.84% of its own shares to BP and $27.73 billion to AAR. Thus the monetary part of both transactions equals $44.38 billion. As a result, BP became the second-largest Rosneft shareholder, holding 19.75% of Rosneft stock.[169] BP took two seats on the Rosneft board, including one offered to Dudley, who served as chief executive of TNK-BP until 2008.[170] In turn, the acquisition of TNK-BP will give Rosneft about half of Russia's energy sector and make it the world's largest publicly traded oil group.[171]

Rosneft chief executive Igor Sechin "invited" BP to join exploration projects with his invigorated company: "The pot is so enormous that we would welcome BP at one of our larger projects," he said. "We already know what they would prefer to develop and in the near future we will find the one."[172] Carl-Henric Svanberg, BP chairman, said his company would be able to "leverage our unique expertise to create value for BP and our shareholders, for Rosneft and for Russia."[173] Therefore, BP is not going to abandon Russia.

The sale of TNK-BP shares by BP, announced in 2012 after a series of conflicts with the AAR partners, took place in March 2013.[174] The full acquisition of TNK-BP by government-controlled Rosneft became the largest deal in Russian history and one of the largest cash acquisitions in the world.[175]

Although BP received a hefty portfolio of Rosneft shares after the deal (about 20% in total, given the additional 12.84% from the deal), the sale of the joint venture implied radical changes of BP corporate strategy in Russia. The deal also increased the overall government share in Russia's oil sector, the world's largest by output, to more than 50%. This has drawn criticism from some analysts and managers of non-state enterprises who fear it would hinder competition and production growth.[176]

Consequences for the parties

The case of AAR and BP joint venture was, for a while, a showcase of successful partnership between international investors and large Russian business.[177] Therefore, the Russian government was unwilling to interfere in the relationship between the partners. The detachment of this powerful overseer let the internal TNK-BP conflicts fester and become infected, to the point of non-resolution. Virtually the entire history of TNK-BP became associated with problems and conflicts – namely, because of the lack of a shared vision for expansion. Nevertheless, BP showed persistence, spending ten years trying to manage the situation in Russia.

BP invested $8 billion in cash, shares and assets when it formed TNK-BP[178] and received a total of $19 billion in dividends over the 2003–2012 decade.[179] TNK-BP accounted for approximately 30% of BP's global output,[180] 27% of its reserves[181] and about 10% of its profits on average.[182] Moreover, according to some specialists, BP's 50% stake in a Russian oil producer is now considered an anomaly. If BP were investing today, it would hardly get more than 25% of the business.[183] BP considered this joint venture as a company that would stay in Russia and that would give them access to Russia's oil reserves.

However, AAR had a different vision regarding TNK-BP's future. The Russian partners had a more ambitious view of the company, in conflict with BP's (self-)interests. Therefore, the partners blocked each other's propositions, exerted pressure on each other and in fact paralyzed the growth of TNK-BP.

To sum up, despite the fact that TNK-BP represented one of BP's prime corporate assets that generated stable cash flows, BP preferred to sell its share in the joint venture to bet on a bigger horse, while also risking its future in Russia.

References

1 http://markets.ft.com/research/Markets/Tearsheets/Business-profile?s=RDSA:LSE
2 https://www.google.com/finance?q=NYSE:RDS.A&fstype=ii&ei=zbBdU5C-L8TVqQGPRg
3 http://markets.ft.com/research/Markets/Tearsheets/Business-profile?s=RDSA:LSE
4 Ibid.
5 http://fortune.com/global500/royal-dutch-shell-3/
6 Ibid.
7 http://www.shell.com/about-us/who-we-are/1980s-to-the-new-millennium.html
8 http://ethanolproducer.com/articles/11958/raizen-reports-increased-net-revenue-in-quarterly-report
9 http://www.investinbrazil.biz/industry/retail-market/retail-market-industry-brazil
10 http://www.groupe-casino.fr/en/the-group/message-from-jean-charles-naouri/
11 http://www.gpari.com.br/grupopaodeacucar/web/mobile/conteudo_mobile.asp?idioma=1&tipo=29948&conta=44
12 CEO of Banco BTG Pactual SA.
13 http://www.bloomberg.com/news/articles/2012-05-14/casino-to-become-sole-controller-of-brazil-s-pao-de-acucar
14 http://www.gpari.com.br/conteudo_en.asp?idioma=1&conta=44&tipo=29950
15 http://www.groupe-casino.fr/en/wp-content/uploads/sites/2/2015/05/Annual-Report-Groupe-Casino-2014_EN.pdf
16 Ibid.
17 http://www.groupe-casino.fr/en/wp-content/uploads/sites/2/2015/05/RA-2014-GB.pdf
18 http://www.examiner.com/article/ceo-jean-charles-naouri-is-shaking-up-casino-group-s-latam-strategy-and-strength
19 http://www.forbes.com/companies/telefonica/
20 http://www.telefonica.com/en/about_telefonica/html/in_brief/magnitudes.shtml
21 http://repositorio.ucp.pt/bitstream/10400.14/14525/1/Evidence%20of%20a%20glocal%20marketing%20strategy-%20a%20case%20study%20in%20the%20Brazilian%20telecommunication%20market.pdf
22 http://www.fundinguniverse.com/company-histories/telef%C3%B3nica-s-a-history/
23 *An Analysis of the European Telecommunications Strategic Environment: How Can Strategic Actions Be Defined to Adapt to the New Scenario? A Telefónica Case Study.* https://www.politesi.polimi.it/bitstream/10589/80703/1/2013_07_Albini.pdf
24 http://www.teleco.com.br/en/en_estatis.asp
25 https://en.wikipedia.org/wiki/List_of_countries_by_number_of_Internet_users
26 http://www.budde.com.au/Research/Brazil-Telecom-Market-Trends-Key-Statistics-and-Regulatory-Overview.html?r=51#sthash.hu7a2M92.dpuf
27 https://www.telefonica.com/en/web/about_telefonica/geographic_spread/brazil
28 Vivo is the largest telecommunications company in Brazil, headquartered in São Paulo.
29 http://www.reuters.com/finance/stocks/companyProfile?symbol=VIV
30 Ibid.
31 Ibid.
32 Official site Disney. http://thewaltdisneycompany.com/about-disney

33 Annual Report 2013 Disney. http://thewaltdisneycompany.com/sites/default/files/reports/10k-wrap-2013.pdf
34 Ibid.
35 The History of DisneyLand Paris. http://www.solarius.com/dvp/dlp/dlp-history.htm
36 Raz 2000.
37 Ibid.
38 The Japan Times 2016.
39 Gumbel 2012.
40 The History of DisneyLand Paris. http://www.solarius.com/dvp/dlp/dlp-history.htm
41 Gumbel 2012.
42 The History of DisneyLand Paris. http://www.solarius.com/dvp/dlp/dlp-history.htm
43 Gumbel 2012.
44 The *Guardian*. http://www.theguardian.com/film/2014/oct/06/disneyland-paris-asks-billion-euro-emergency-rescue
45 Gumbel 2012.
46 Behan 2004.
47 Juan 2007.
48 Ibid.
49 'China approves Disney theme park in Shanghai' 2009.
50 Chog 2009.
51 Li 2009.
52 'China approves Disney theme park in Shanghai' 2009.
53 Socio-cultural problems faced by Disney Walt in overseas markets, 18 May 2011. http://scholarly-articles-research.blogspot.ru/2011/05/socio-cultural-problems-faced-by-disney.html
54 Tian 2009.
55 Fung and Lee 2009.
56 Moran and Keane 2013.
57 Holson 2005.
58 Kweh 2010.
59 Yung 2014.
60 Google Inc. History. http://www.google.com/about/company/history/
61 Ibid.
62 Lee 2016.
63 http://www.nytimes.com/2006/04/23/magazine/23google.html?pagewanted=all&_r=1&
64 Cheng 2005.
65 Linda, Sau-ling LAI, In search of excellence – Google vs Baidu. http://www.waset.org/journals/waset/v60/v60-208.pdf
66 'Baidu gains more search market share in Q3' 2010.
67 http://www.statista.com/statistics/278204/china-mobile-users-by-month
68 http://www.internetlivestats.com/internet-users/
69 Review 2007.
70 Langberg 2006.
71 Eco, Kumar and Yao 2011.
72 Thompson 2006.
73 Vascellaro, Dean and Gorman 2011.
74 Helft and Barboza 2010.
75 Eco, Kumar and Yao 2011.
76 Wells 2010.
77 Vodafone Group Ltd.: company profile [Electronic resource]. http://360.datamonitor.com/
78 Verma and Sharma 2014.
79 India M&A trend report: Q1 – Q3 2013 (2013); merger market; http://www.mergermarket.com/pdf/IndiaTrendReportQ1-Q32013.pdf.
80 Business Standard 2014.
81 Krishna 2014.
82 Parker 2007.
83 Pandey, Sharma, Saboo (PGDIE, NITIE) and Narayana Rao 2007
84 Chowdhury 2014.

85 Blitz and Barber 2013.
86 'Behind the deal: Vodafone takes over Hutchison Whampoa's Indian Unit' [Electronic resource] 2007.
87 India offers to negotiate settlement in Vodafone tax case, *Wall Street Journal*. http://online.wsj.com/news/articles/SB10001424127887324063304578525083219173760
88 Vodafone seeks arbitration in India tax dispute, *Wall Street Journal*. http://online.wsj.com/news/articles/SB10001424052702303880604579402832593095924
89 Vodafone blames India for collapse of $2 billion tax dispute talks. *Reuters*. http://www.reuters.com/article/2014/02/19/us-vodafone-india-tax-idUSBREA1I1JQ20140219
90 Ibid.
91 http://www.madhyam.org.in/vodafones-tax-dispute-which-way-are-we-headed/
92 Vodafone seeks arbitration in India tax dispute. *Wall Street Journal*. http://online.wsj.com/news/articles/SB10001424052702303880604579402832593095924
93 Ibid.
94 'Vodafone applies to buy out India partners for $1.7 billion' 2013.
95 'Behind the deal: Vodafone takes over Hutchison Whampoa's India unit' 2007.
96 CNN Money Fortune Global 500 2015.
97 Walmart Annual Report 2015. http://s2.q4cdn.com/056532643/files/doc_financials/2015/annual/2015-annual-report.pdf
98 Daniel 2010.
99 Walmart Annual Report 2015.
100 Govindarajan and Gupta 1999.
101 Dikshit 2011.
102 Wohl 2012.
103 Halepete et al. 2008.
104 Ibid.
105 Loeb 2013.
106 Bahree 2013.
107 Ibid.
108 'US giant Walmart quits India after venture ends' 2013.
109 http://www.bloomberg.com/news/articles/2014-10-23/wal-mart-struggles-to-crack-retail-market-in-india
110 Walmart Annual Report 2014.
111 Balbutskaya 2014
112 Super-Brands.Ru.2016. http://www.super-brands.ru/archdocs/DHL_en.pdf
113 *CNN Money* 2011.
114 Datamonitor, FedEx Corporation, Apr. 2011.
115 Spark database profile.
116 Datamonitor, United Parcel Service, Inc. Jun. 2011.
117 *CNN Money* 2011.
118 EMS Russian Post. Annual report 2013.
119 Russian Post. Annual report 2009.
120 http://www.dhl.com/en/mail/mail_essentials/dm_guide/studies_and_expert_information/publications/russia.html
121 Axel Gietz, Corporate-affairs director of DHL Worldwide, 2002.
122 Frank-Eaves Underer, General Director of DHL in the CIS, 2005.
123 http://expert.ru/expert/2005/39/39ex-news341_7272/
124 Ibid.
125 Accor official website: http://www.accor.com/en/brands/brand-portfolio.html
126 Xerfi700doc, Accor (étude de groupe) 2012.
127 Accor 2004 Annual report.
128 http://www.ey.com/Publication/vwLUAssets/EY-International-hotel-brands-reviews-2015-ENG/$FILE/EY-International-hotel-brands-reviews-2015-ENG.pdf
129 Ernst & Young report: International hotel chains in Russia, www.investinrussia.ru/data/files/.../EY-International-hotel-brands-2014-analytics.pdf (2014).
130 Interview of Alexis Delaroff. Official site of Interfax. http://www.interfax.ru/tourism/tourisminf.asp?id=193062&sec=1467

131 http://www.accorhotels-group.com/en/group/accorhotels-worldwide/europe/russia.html
132 Accor celebrates the opening of its 18th hotels in Russia and CIS, the Novotel Moscow city. Press release from July 9th 2013. http://www.accor.com/fileadmin/user_upload/Contenus_Accor/Presse/Pressreleases/2013/EN/20130709_pr_novotel_moscow_city_and_expansion_in_russia_cis.pdf
133 Ibid.
134 Accor adds to Sochi's growing "Hotel row." Sochi magazine. http://sochimagazine.com/accor-hotels-add-to-sochis-growing-hotel-row/
135 'Expansion of Accor in Moscow with the signing of 3 hotels that will add 700 rooms to the Group's portfolio' 2013.
136 Akfen REIT. http://www.akfen.com.tr/en/yatirimlar/gayrimenkul/
137 Global hospitality insights. Top thoughts for 2015. http://www.ey.com/Publication/vwLUAssets/ey-global-hospitality-insights-2015/$FILE/ey-global-hospitality-insights-2015.pdf
138 http://www.hotelier.pro/news/item/978-jllnew/978-jllnew
139 KPMG: International hotel operators in Russia, https://home.kpmg.com/ru/en/home/media/press-releases/2015/01/hotel-operators-russia-cis-2015.html (October 2012).
140 International hotel brands in Russia. EY official site. http://www.ey.com/Publication/vwLUAssets/EY-International-Hotel-Brands-in-Russia-2014/$FILE/EY-International-Hotel-Brands-in-Russia-2014.pdf
141 Business: The company file: From Anglo-Persian Oil to BP Amoco. *BBC News*. http://news.bbc.co.uk/2/hi/business/149259.stm
142 Business: The company file: From Anglo-Persian Oil to BP Amoco. *BBC News*. http://news.bbc.co.uk/2/hi/business/149259.stm
143 'Timeline: Alaska pipeline chronology' 2006.
144 Britannica Online Encyclopedia, BP plc. http://www.britannica.com/EBchecked/topic/80326/BP-PLC
145 BP website.
146 BP, BP in Azerbaijan, http://www.bp.com/sectiongenericarticle.do?categoryId=430&contentId=2000578
147 BP, About BP in Russia, What we do. http://www.bp.com/subsection.do?categoryId=9009641&contentId=7018401
148 TNK-BP, About the company brief. http://www.tnk-bp.com/en/company/company/
149 ВР, Энергетическая компания, Lenta.ru. http://lenta.ru/lib/14172583/#68
150 BP, Russian billionaires, and the Kremlin: A power triangle that never was, *Oxford Energy Comment*. http://www.oxfordenergy.org/wpcms/wp-content/uploads/2011/11/BP-Russian-billionaires-and-the-Kremlin.pdf
151 Ibid.
152 TNK-BP, About the company brief. http://www.tnk-bp.com/en/company/company/
153 http://ria.ru/spravka/20080530/108877833.html
154 BP, Russian billionaires, and the Kremlin: A power triangle that never was, *Oxford Energy Comment*. http://www.oxfordenergy.org/wpcms/wp-content/uploads/2011/11/BP-Russian-billionaires-and-the-Kremlin.pdf
155 Госдума приняла законопроект, предоставляющий "Газпрому" эксклюзивное право на экспорт газа. ИА «Финмаркет». http://www.finmarket.ru/z/nws/news.asp?id=504872&hot=504874
156 Mason 2011.
157 BP, Russian billionaires, and the Kremlin: A power triangle that never was, *Oxford Energy Comment*. http://www.oxfordenergy.org/wpcms/wp-content/uploads/2011/11/BP-Russian-billionaires-and-the-Kremlin.pdf
158 Preliminary geospatial analysis of arctic ocean hydrocarbon resources, *US Department of Energy*. http://www.pnl.gov/main/publications/external/technical_reports/PNNL-17922.pdf
159 BP, Russian billionaires, and the Kremlin: A power triangle that never was, *Oxford Energy Comment*. http://www.oxfordenergy.org/wpcms/wp-content/uploads/2011/11/BP-Russian-billionaires-and-the-Kremlin.pdf
160 Rosneft's acquisition of TNK-BP, *Russian-American Business*. http://russianamericanbusiness.org/web_CURRENT/articles/1271/1/Rosneft%92s-acquisition-of-TNK-BP
161 Газпром хочет купить ТНК-ВР, ЗАО. «ВЗГЛЯД.РУ».http://vz.ru/economy/2008/4/24/162533.html

162 TNK-BP chief departs, ending management dispute, *Chron.* http://www.chron.com/business/energy/article/TNK-BP-chief-departs-ending-management-dispute-1758425.php

163 Роснефть + ТНК-ВР: Как я провел десять лет, *Interfax.* http://www.interfax.by/article/100169

164 «Сделка года» между «Роснефтью» и ВР сорвалась, ЗАО Бизнес Ньюс Медиа. http://www.vedomosti.ru/companies/news/1269483/stokgolmskij_arbitrazh_razreshil_obmen_akciyami_bp_i

165 Ibid.

166 Почему "Роснефть" отказалась продолжать переговоры с ВР?, *BBC.* http://www.bbc.co.uk/russian/business/2011/05/110517_bp_rosneft_reasons.shtml

167 BP, Russian billionaires, and the Kremlin: A power triangle that never was, *Oxford Energy Comment.* http://www.oxfordenergy.org/wpcms/wp-content/uploads/2011/11/BP-Russian-billionaires-and-the-Kremlin.pdf

168 Почему "Роснефть" отказалась продолжать переговоры с ВР?, *BBC.* http://www.bbc.co.uk/russian/business/2011/05/110517_bp_rosneft_reasons.shtml

169 «Роснефть» провозгласила себя крупнейшей в мире публичной нефтегазовой компанией, ЗАО Бизнес Ньюс Медиа. http://www.vedomosti.ru/companies/news/10295091/rosneft_kupila_tnkvr

170 'Rosneft pays out in historic TNK-BP deal completion' 2013.

171 BP sells TNK-BP stake to Russia's Rosneft, *BBC.* http://www.bbc.co.uk/news/business-20030610

172 Rosneft pays out in historic TNK-BP deal completion, *The Reuters.* http://www.reuters.com/article/2013/03/21/us-rosneft-tnkbp-deal-idUSBRE92K0IZ20130321

173 'Rosneft completes TNK-BP takeover paving way for BP to return cash to shareholders' 2015.

174 «Роснефть» купила ТНК-ВР точно в срок, РБК, 22 March 2013. http://rbcdaily.ru/tek/562949986333912

175 «Роснефть», Чистая победа, The official site of Rosneft company. http://www.rosneft.ru/news/news_about/18032013.html

176 'Rosneft pays out in historic TNK-BP deal completion' 2013.

177 BP, Russian billionaires, and the Kremlin: A power triangle that never was, *Oxford Energy Comment.* http://www.oxfordenergy.org/wpcms/wp-content/uploads/2011/11/BP-Russian-billionaires-and-the-Kremlin.pdf

178 'Rosneft completes acquisition of TNK-BP' 2013.

179 BP announces $8 billion share buyback, *TheNewsTribune.com.* http://www.thenewstribune.com/2013/03/22/2525078/bp-announces-8-billion-share-buyback.html

180 Зачем «Роснефти» выкупать долю британцев в ТНК-ВР?, *Forbes.* http://www.forbes.ru/sobytiya/84540-zachem-rosnefti-vykupat-dolyu-britantsev-v-tnk-bp

181 Ibid.

182 The Economist. Russia: A negotiated peace at TNK-BP?

183 Ibid.

Part II

The changing view of international strategy

4 Theoretical explanation of internationalization

Traditionally, internationalization has been viewed as the process whereby companies increase their involvement in international markets, although there is no agreed-upon definition of internationalization. There are three groups of internationalization theories that strive to explain why companies become involved in international activities:[1]

- First is the *evolution (or stage) model* of internationalization – i.e. whereby internationalization is presented as a gradual, incremental process.
- Second is the *conditional model* of internationalization – i.e. a model that postulates certain conditions and actions that companies should take in case these conditions occur. These models are formulated in accordance with the formula: "If . . . then . . ."
- Third is the *action-oriented model* that focuses attention on the process of interaction between economic agents.

The main idea of the *evolution* or *stage model* of internationalization is that a company goes through a series of successive stages in its international expansion. Internationalization is seen as a sequential, arranged process that is similar for all businesses.

According to the *conditional models*, the company is exposed to a turbulent and generally unfavorable environment. The goal of the company's management is to achieve the best balance between the environment (opportunities and threats) and firm (strengths and weaknesses). With this in mind, there are three main components of conditional models:

- environmental factors – i.e. the model of the environment in which the firm operates
- opportunities, or alternatives available to the firm
- decision-making criteria – i.e. the criteria used by managers to make decisions (e.g. maximization of profit, market share, control, reducing risks)

Action-oriented models are based on three fundamentally different ways of organizing economic activity: hierarchy, market and network. The company, as the basic element of any economy, is usually characterized by a *hierarchy*, which means that company resources are distributed in accordance with the decisions of managers. In a market economy it is the function of the companies, driven by the forces of competition, to try to get access to limited resources.

Finally, for the *action-oriented models*, individual producers are linked in a *network* of relationships, or what can be called an industrial system of companies engaged in the production, distribution and sale of products. According to this network view, internationalization

is seen as the development of a company by establishing relationships with foreign partners, which can be done through the following avenues:

- international expansion – i.e. a fixed position with respect to the foreign partners in
  the network, with which the company has no connections
- international market penetration – i.e. the development of positions in foreign networks with which the company has already established a relationship
- international integration – i.e. to enhance the coordination between the positions of
  the company in various foreign networks

Since the 1930s, theoretical foundations for internationalization and explanations of the
international strategy choice were based upon strong economic perspectives, with transaction cost approach, resource-based view or organizational theory. John Commons, an
American institutional economist from Ohio, first introduced the idea that transactions
form "the basis of economic thinking."[2] Later, many academics, including prominent
scholars such as Coase[3] and Williamson,[4] further studied and developed the concept of
transactions.

Roland Coase[5] used the term *transaction cost* when proposing a theoretical framework
to predict (1) when firms will perform certain tasks and (2) when certain economic tasks
will be performed in a market. Later Coase also came up with the term *cost of market transactions* when he further discussed the transaction cost concept.[6] However, the argument
for transaction cost became popular and widely known through Oliver Williamson's[7]
outstanding paper on transaction cost economics, for which he received the 2009 Nobel
Economic Prize.

Another stream of research on the internationalization is based upon John Dunning's
eclectic paradigm.[8] One of the core concepts of Dunning's theory is *internalization,* which
is based, in turn, on the transaction cost theory. Buckley and Casson developed internationalization theory.[9] The theory puts a focus on intermediate product markets and its
imperfections that generate monopolistic advantages of firms and implies that external
transactions take place if their costs are lower than internal costs. Dunning argued that
internalization theory is important when explaining foreign direct investment flows and
thus used parts of the theory in his *eclectic* paradigm.

The two pillars that explain firms' motives to internationalize – *resource seeking* and *market seeking* – have been widely referenced and debated in the past. In reality, these terms
may be also referred to as horizontal and vertical integration, respectively. Early studies
conclude that market-seeking motives arise to avoid transportation costs as well as to overcome tariffs.[10] Scholars agree that for multinationals, one of the most crucial decisions is
whether to serve foreign markets by export or by setting up production facilities abroad.[11]
The resource-seeking motives aim to relocate parts of the value chain to take advantage
of lower production costs and/or to gain access to local resources.[12] This has also been
referred to and further developed as the *knowledge capital model*.[13]

In discussions on this theme, other authors suggested developing more complex models
that would investigate the internationalization strategies with more than just the twin
resource and market causes.[14] Although the horizontal and vertical integration perspective is narrower and more focused on cost considerations, substantial similarities exist here
with Dunning's differentiation of *market-* versus *resource-seeking* motives.

In more recent studies, scholars moved the research focus towards *organizational learning*
and the *resource-based view (RBV)*.[15] Both concepts result from investigating the drivers of

organizational performance. Many studies have found evidence supporting the argument of the RBV, which states that the extent to which a particular firm possesses strategic resources is in positive correlation with the company's performance.[16]

Since 2000, the focus in the field of internationalization has moved again. Numerous recent studies[17] have investigated factors such as quality of institutions or cultural distance as key determinants of internationalization and FDI strategies. Many theoretical frameworks are based upon institutional and socio-cultural theories, reflecting a shift away from the previous misbalance, where economic and financial aspects dominated in internationalization studies. This tunnel vision, it was felt, did not provide sufficiently comprehensive information on the complexity of international strategies.

4.1 The resource-based view of internationalization

In order to analyze how a sustainable competitive advantage can be reached, the resource-based view (RBV) is an important theoretical approach in research on international business.[18] The basic assumption of the RBV is that a company's strategic competitive advantage is generated based on its internal resources. Ideally, these should be rare, valuable, non-substitutable and inimitable[19] so that a well-managed company can exploit these assets to generate competitive advantage(s).[20] Furthermore, it is crucial that these resources be non-reproducible by competitors.[21]

The resource-based theory of competitive advantage emerged in the early 1980s and is applicable to multinationals as well as to their subsidiaries. Early studies already suggest the importance of intangible resources for the creation of sustained competitive advantage (SCA). For example, organizational culture was listed among the intangible factors that can yield competitive advantage.[22] Academics also carefully investigated the strategic factor market and concluded that not only the product side but also the resource side matters. They showed that firms seek positions in terms of resources that are difficult or impossible to copy by competitors; they also studied the impact that resources have on profitability as well as on different elements of the strategy such as the first-mover advantage, M&A and sequential entry.[23]

A fundamental work in the RBV theory was that of Jay Barney in 1991.[24] He investigated and discussed SCA from the resource-based perspective and claimed that the nature of a company's resources and their distribution between firms are necessary conditions for SCA to exist. In particular, resources should be heterogeneously (unequally) distributed among firms and not be mobile for SCA to flourish. Barney even goes so far as to propose an evaluation model for resources in terms of their ability to generate SCA: for this purpose, resources of the firm should be valuable, rare, imperfectly imitable and not substitutable.

Further studies, emphasizing the importance of capabilities for SCA creation, revealed more complex variables, such as the differences between capabilities (defined as "the socially complex routines that determine the efficiency with which firms physically transform inputs into outputs"[25]) and resources.

It is important to highlight the growing interest for intangible resources within the RBV research. While intangible resources were studied from the very early stages of the development of the resource-based theory,[26] it was only in the 2000s that intangible resources started garnering intense interest. The understanding arose that a greater degree of resource intangibility would lead to improved SCA for a company.[27]

The resource-based view of the firm is one of the most consistent and coherent theories that one can apply when studying emerging markets and their multinationals. Moreover, the RBV directly shapes the conceptualization of political factors for firms' internationalization, which are referred to as particular cases of the resources and capabilities. Thus the main theories and arguments existing within the resource-based view of the firm can be applicable to side studies related to internationalization.

The nature of the strategic factors acquired by a company during its international investments was argued to be critical for its resource side and hence also for competitive advantages.[28]

Although the RBV is strongly present in research on international business,[29] its applicability as a theoretical framework is not fully accepted.[30] One of the RBV shortcomings is that an advantage based on a company's home-country resources may not necessarily carry over to host countries.[31] This means that resource-based advantages may disappear when entering new markets. With all countries being different, certain resources may even generate a disadvantage in a host country, even though they were the source of SCA in another. That is why country-specific contextual differences – and their impact resource-based advantages – must be considered by companies in order to make better internationalization decisions (both in terms of entry mode and post-entry strategy).[32]

Equally important is finding the right balance between creating resource-based advantages and their costs. In order to deal with foreign institutions, it is often unavoidable for companies to incur additional costs and management time. One possible way to face this international issue successfully is to adjust a company's organizational structure according to its environment – for example, via wholly owned foreign structures or by creating partnerships through international joint ventures.[33]

To sum up, in the context of internationalization of EMFs and outward FDI from emerging economies, the resource-based view approach is incomplete without involving institutional studies.

4.2 The rising dominance of institutional perspective

The place of institutions in international business studies

Since 2000, an entire innovative body of academic research having an institution-based view has emerged in the literature on international business. One of the first and most popular works that focuses on institutions is the best-seller *Institutions and Organizations* by Richard Scott.[34] Later, Scott published articles with an institutional perspective – namely, with a specific focus on Chinese enterprises.[35] Other popular works include articles by Mike Peng, including his early works "Towards an Institution-Based View of Business Strategy" and "An Institution-Based View of International Business Strategy: A Focus on Emerging Economies."[36] His more recent works emphasize different aspects of institutional impacts on internationalization and again in their majority use China as the national context.[37]

There is clear recognition of the research heritage left by Douglas North and his works on institutions[38] that are traditionally referred to while investigating the international strategy. Based on North's theories, at the macro level (or country level), scholars have developed a contemporary understanding of institutions.[39] North defines institutions as *formal rules* (laws, regulations, economic rules, etc.) and *informal rules* (standards of behavior, traditions, sets of widely accepted rules, etc.). An institutional framework can only be seen as complete when both formal and informal institutions are taken into consideration.

Later, Scott further refined North's definition of the institutions by introducing a frame-work based upon three pillars:[40]

1   The *regulatory pillar* (includes the existing rules and laws).
2   The *cognitive pillar* (includes shared social behavior that is widely accepted as well as the perception of what can be taken for granted or what is considered typical).
3   The *normative pillar* (includes believes and social values, as well as norms that decide what is right and appropriate for a member of a specific society).

This framework provides a basis to analyze the institutional profile of a specific country.[41] However, no matter how a country's institutional profile is established, the thinking remains the same: the institutional profiles of host and home countries affect internation-alization choices.

On the destination side, when firms internationalize they face the host-country institu-tions. These institutions result from the regulatory, cognitive and normative frameworks of host environments and may have a strong impact the company's external and internal practices and standards.[42] Host-country institutions either impede or facilitate the transfer of corporate practices or strategies of the parent company to its foreign antenna.[43] This impact on multinationals led scholars to develop the new terms *liability of foreignness*[44] and *liability of multinationality*,[45] respectively (more on these concepts in Chapter 11).

On the origin side, the constellation of home-country institutions may also impact a firm's internationalization process.[46] For instance, stable and liberal polices encourage cross-border investments, while discretionary policies that fluctuate with different elec-torates will lead to the contrary.[47] In line with Scott, other scholars provide evidence that specific features of the home-country institutions shape the strategies of Chinese multi-nationals, which the Chinese government formally and informally enforces. In the case of China, state support for the internationalization of Chinese multinationals (e.g. Sinopec, Huawei) is becoming the standard.[48]

Scholars have coined the new term *institutional dualism* to reflect the importance of the vector of both home- and host-country institutions.[49] Some of the research seeks to under-stand how the institutional dualism shapes upstream decision making on the choice of host countries.[50] Other research focuses on the likelihood that a cross-border acquisition will be successful.[51] Some scholars argue that the likelihood of a successful Chinese cross-border acquisition is lower in cases when the host country has low institutional quality.[52]

Macro-level and sectoral impacts on firms' internationalization

The success or failure of a company's internationalization is determined by various fac-tors at different levels. In this book, as well in our other works,[53] we propose a multi-level approach considering factors from three key levels.

•   At the country level, international strategy is determined by the quality of the host-country institutions and the cultural distance between home and host economies.
•   At the industry level, international strategy depends on the strict institutional con-straints or incentives that determine value creation by firms.
•   At the firm level, not only firm size and revenue but also intangibles such as political connections or managerial expertise bring success to companies, or make them depart markets after incurring losses.

The logic followed in this book is macro-level institutions influence industrial development, industrial progress (also subject of institutional pressures) defines company parameters and company strategies (influenced by institutions as well) add value to the national economy and indirectly shape political stability, which are both pillars of the macro environment. This consequence of developments, such as a Moebius strip, shows different faces of the same process.

The influence of *macro-level factors* is the departing point of the institutional impacts of firms' internationalization. These institutional forces are understood as the set of formal rules and informal constraints that govern economic activity in the country.[54] Such rules shape the standards of technology, resource endowments and innovation patterns. The institutional factors define the pace and level of sectoral development in the country and its comparative technological advantages.

Political factors have a particularly powerful influence on the internationalization process of emerging market firms. Examples of these factors are the various government decisions providing a special support to strategically important industries and the development of competition policies affecting the monopolistic nature of competition in industry.[55] Hence a degree of state participation in the industries and firms development represents another important country-bound factor of the institutional influence.

The country institutions are closely interrelated with the promotion of industrial progress. Patterns of restructuring are institutionally determined and vary across industries according to the market demand, finance and technological requirements. The literature on national systems of innovation in emerging markets demonstrates the strong role of macro-institutional factors in determining the basic features of technology accumulation, technical change and diffusion of innovation during the transition period.[56] Inward and outward FDI policies are also sector specific and developed to assist the domestic industrial development. Overall, industry characteristics that shape firms' international strategies are strongly affected by the macro-level institutions.

Two important dimensions for formal and informal institutions are corruption and culture, consequently – both are widely discussed in the literature.

Corruption is often regarded as a tax for the foreign firm,[57] and scholars argue that the biggest challenge for MNEs is not even the actual costs of doing business, but rather the estimation of cultural costs that the firm needs to consider owing to the uncertainty resulting from corrupt conditions.[58] Corrupt conditions include bribes to government officials but also transaction costs due to poor contract enforcement.[59] Information asymmetry while seeking relevant knowledge of the market and of rules of the game that are hidden from foreign firms, as well as problems in gaining legitimacy due to low transparency, are recognized as additional corruption-related cost drivers.[60] Scholars who studied the influence of corruption on internationalization mostly concluded that the corrupt conditions in the host country creates significant costs for the foreign firm and consequently has a negative impact on FDI inflows to a host country, a phenomenon called the "grabbing hand" of corruption.[61] However, another stream of studies suggests that corruption can also act as the "helping hand,"[62] where scholars argue that bribing mechanisms can facilitate transactions and speed up processes, which supports internationalization and FDI.

Various characteristics of institutional quality are often positively and even strongly tied with each other.[63] Therefore, when dealing with formal institutions, it is essential for MNE to take into account additional governance-related factors, such as business freedom and investment freedom that explain the quality of formal institutions in general.[64] The traditional perspective is that MNEs from emerging economies face competitive disadvantages in the global business environment compared to those firms from developed markets.[65] This is supported by internationalization theories that focus on latecomers. It is argued that these latecomers from emerging markets act more aggressive and engage in risk taking in order to catch up with firms from developed markets.[66] In the case of many emerging MNEs, this aggressive and risk-taking behavior in developed markets where business freedom and investment freedom are high leads to a greater variety of firms' results – some obtain great success due to this strategy and some withdraw from operations.

Cultural distance between host and home countries, as the key informal institutional determinant, plays a critical role in the success or failure of international strategy. Cultural distance has an influence on (1) the learning and synergy stimulus, (2) the potential competency and knowledge transfer and (3) the transaction costs resulting from intercultural contact and geographic diversification.[67] Therefore, a MNE's ability to generate value by capitalizing on assets of distant cultures depends on its capacity to overcome this distance.

The larger the cultural distance between two countries, the more management styles and practices as well as corporate values tend to differ.[68] These differences lead to cultural shocks and conflicts that result from ambiguity. Therefore, a lower cultural distance between host and home markets has a positive influence on the value of the shared intangible assets between parties within joint ventures or mergers. In particular, employees with similar values facilitate learning, interaction and resource exchanges. By contrast, a high level of cultural distance results in higher transaction costs during geographic expansion, which can further hinder the transfer of competencies through national borders and thus reduce the value of going abroad.

Overall, the agreement exists that a low level of cultural distance attracts more FDI and thus has a positive impact on the internationalization process.

Sector-level determinants are strongly influenced by institutional factors on sector-specific determinants through setting the standards and provision of the resources and incentive structures. The industrial sectors represent structured organizational fields defined according to the level and the type of technology, resource endowments, competition type and relationship with the government authorities. Sectoral studies show that such factors as an access to markets, technology and finance differentiate firms' operations in various industries.[69] Within sectors, the types of technologies promote particular ways of industry organization, the nature of innovations, dynamics of networks and regulative frameworks.

National security is sometimes argued to be an additional motive for internationalization of EMFs.[70] Countries not only implement rules and laws to regulate competition but also to protect industries that are sensitive to national security or sovereignty, such as energy, military or telecoms. This makes national security both macro- and sector-related factors for firms' internationalization. Taking this into account, financial or economic relations alone certainly cannot describe the success or failure of OFDI. Due to perceived threats of national security and other political concerns, a host government can hinder an investing firm from completing certain deals in the name of national security or to protect certain firms from competition.[71]

Industries that are of high political interest to the home government and where inward FDI might therefore face resistance are referred to as *sensitive industries*.[72] This goes in line with academics studying Russian firms and using Russia as a context, which proves that industries matter and suggests that future research should include industries.[73] For example, if a Russian bank acquires another financial organization abroad, it faces strict regulations in the host country owing to the nature of the banking industry being considered as very sensitive.[74]

To summarize, sectoral differences not only define specific patterns of corporate behavior (including in foreign markets) but also provide a context for homogeneous internationalization strategies, implying an impact on the international strategy choices for firms in that sector. Overall, industry-specific characteristics such as access to markets, capital and infrastructure requirements play an important role in the shaping of international strategies of EMFs.

Firm-level determinants: from organizational to institutional perspective

In strategy, literature based on organizational perspective, firm-level determinants such as internal systems and processes, characteristics of owners and CEOs, management and leadership styles, types of corporate ownership and company performance affect firms' choices with regard to their strategic alternatives.[75]

Various emerging market studies have recently examined the influence of specific firm-level factors on EMFs. Such resources as personal, inter-firm and external networks,[76] common language with international partners[77] and ethnic identity[78] were found to assist EMFs in overcoming the liability of foreignness that they face when operating in the markets of Western Europe or the United States. Ownership structure was argued to influence strategic orientations of EMFs and to affect their internationalization.[79] Successful EMNEs also have distinctive capabilities such as the ability to operate in weak institutional environments[80] and to treat global competition as an opportunity to build missing capabilities.[81] Also, these firms have an adaptive capability to transform key resources into positive performance outcomes.[82]

In addition to the internal organizational factors that were presented earlier, there are also institutional factors affecting the international strategy choice at the firm level. In the scope of macro-level institutions, the connectedness to the governments is often highlighted as the critical factor for EMFs' international development.[83] Home governments might impose direct restrictions or incentives on firms' activities; an example of such influence is the intervention into operations of national leaders, even in those industries where the majority of companies are independent in their development and even in firms without state ownership.[84]

There are other institutional forces of a sociological nature directly influencing firms' behavior. With the reference to coercive, mimetic and normative pressures that institutional environment imposes on firms to appear legitimate and conform to prevailing norms, scholars find that these pressures affect the foreign market entry mode choice by EMFs as a means to appear legitimate in the host countries.[85] Another example is managerial professional background which represents one of the influencing factors resulting in a certain degree of conformity in firms' behavior. In emerging economies this pressure is particularly evident when there is a pressure to avoid a "Soviet-style" management and to adopt a market-based style to appear competitive in new economic realities.[86]

In sum, the concordance among scholars exist that firm-specific resources and capabilities affect the extent of internationalization and success of the international strategies. Nevertheless, the EE context means some companies deviate from the initially predicted strategic choices. There are also specific macro- and micro-level institutional forces directly affecting firms' strategies, which can both either promote their unique behavior (sometimes in contrast to theoretical predictions) or push to conform to the general patterns suggested in the literature.

All three levels of institutional influences are, in fact, reflective of those interactions (or direct transactions) that the firm undertakes while doing business (including abroad). In case of an international move, these transactions become much more complicated and their results unpredictable. This is why it makes sense to focus in the next section on two interrelated approaches – TCA and OLI.

4.3 From transaction cost approach to eclectic paradigm

Transaction cost approach

One of the most widespread theories to explain the effect of market imperfections on corporate strategy and the multinational firms' choice of different entry modes and post-entry strategies is the transaction cost theory, often referred as transaction cost approach (TCA). This theory postulates that market failure is a driving factor for internalizing activities that previously had been external to the firm (a strategy also known as vertical integration). This also provides ways to reduce risks by integrating economic activities.

In the context of international business, the importance of TCA increases. Failures in the domestic market make firms more interested in seeking opportunities abroad. In addition, in the case of large multinationals and their foreign projects, acquisition is often interpreted scholarly as a way to decrease host-market imperfections, or improve links between the home and host markets.

At the basis of the TCA lies a simple choice: a company can either outsource certain activities or integrate them into its own value chain. This is the "make or buy" decision,[87] which becomes even more critical at the international level. According to the TCA, the question of whether an important external activity should be integrated or not depends on the specificity of such factors as investment required, frequency and costs of interaction between the firm and the supplier, amount of uncertainty and eventual opportunity to the supplier (due for instance to economies of scale).[88,89]

This contemporary TCA is based on the early works of Ronald Coase. He stated that if vertical integration was a generically sound strategy, then surely all companies would be vertically integrated and, if companies were able to organize production efficiently, then surely all production would be undertaken by just one big company.[90] Coase made these observations in his 1937 groundbreaking article entitled "The Nature of the Firm," in which he developed a theory to explain the existence of companies and their vertical structure.[91] The aim of the theory was to explain why companies exist and the importance of the price mechanism in determining their growth.

Coase states,

> A point must be reached where the costs of organizing an extra transaction within the firm are equal to the costs involved in carrying out the transaction in the open market, or, to the costs of organizing by another entrepreneur.[92]

At such a stage, the company would cease to grow, otherwise all production would be carried out by one big company. This theory is applied to vertical integration to explain its existence and determine when it becomes uneconomical for a company to further integrate. According to this theory, a company may continue to integrate if the cost of organizing the production of a previously bought-in product is less than the transaction cost. Generally, this means that a company will continue to integrate vertically and monopolize an industry if it can at the same time maintain efficiency (efficiency in this context meaning keeping the cost of organizing production below transaction cost).

The motivations for vertical integration are widely explained by Oliver Williamson, one of the most renowned researchers on the topic, who treats vertical integration as the result of market failure.[93] Williamson, however, developed further his theory and illustrated other issues which are related to why a company may become integrated, which he claims to be incentives for integration. These all come under market failure considerations and the most important are monopolistic supply, contractual incompleteness problems, price discrimination and entry barriers and the difficulty in obtaining relevant information.

The limitation of Williamson's theory is that it applies mostly to production stages of firm activity. Parts of his theory may not be applicable to other stages of the value chain. The works of both Coase and Williamson form the basis for many other theories, with TCA used and enhanced by many other scholars.[94] The principal difficulty in applying TCA is to accurately estimate transaction costs, since short-term and long-term costs are different, and the full cost consequences of integration decisions are extremely difficult to forecast. Otherwise, many recent studies on international business refer to factors such as the corruption perception index (CPI) or the rule of law, which enable planners to estimate the transaction costs to be faced when investing abroad.

Eclectic paradigm

John Dunning[95] elaborated another theory to explain why firms turn to geographic expansion: the *eclectic paradigm* (or *OLI)*. Why eclectic? Possibly because the theory is quite broad and derives its ideas from a broad and diverse range of sources. This theory identifies three aspects that influence and determine a firm's internationalization decisions:

- O stands for *ownership advantage*;
- L stands for *location advantage*; and
- I stands for *internalization advantage*.

Dunning adopted a reductionist approach wherein three distinct types of advantages were used as "envelope concepts to explain multinational activities."[96]

The *ownership advantage* is explained by Dunning as the competitive advantage of holding greater technology and capital, with the capability of combining these assets with those of a foreign partner. Intangible assets, such as technological or marketing knowledge or superior managerial capabilities, can compensate for the liability of foreignness, allowing firms to successfully compete with indigenous firms and other multinationals.[97]

The *location advantage* represents the comparative cost advantage of country-specific inputs (e.g. materials, labor, natural resources or technology), or the cost of trade barriers between countries. These particular advantages are not only country specific but also tied down to location – that is, they are internationally immobile.[98] A firm will choose a location advantage when establishing facilities in another market that gives easy access to resources or assets. In this case, the firm will set up production or research facilities in the more favorable foreign market.[99]

The *internalization advantage* can be gained by a company when incorporating heretofore external assets and knowledge into its internal processes and thereby hindering competitors.[100] Factually, this is a transaction attribute that applies in the case when the firm prefers to exploit its ownership advantages internally rather than by outsourcing, licensing or collaborating with a local partner. This type of advantage minimizes transaction costs associated with the inter-firm transfer of proprietary knowledge and capabilities.[101]

According to scholars who supported and extended OLI, internalization can be efficient only when management understands and correctly analyzes the market in which the internalization is to take place.[102] The advantages of in-house production can, however, be reduced by the additional costs of maintaining internalization. External market imperfections result in greater advantages from internalization, and this internalization is a result of one or more of four factors: industry, nation, region and firm-specific factors.

Let us return to the eclectic nature of the paradigm for a moment. What are some of the theory's sources? For the ownership advantages, the references to resource-based view (RBV) include firm-specific factors such as proprietary resources or managerial capabilities.[103] To compete with local firms, foreign entrants must have competitive advantages and skills which can offset the higher cost of doing business in host countries. The ownership advantage is reflected by company size, multinational experience and ability to develop differentiated products,[104] which refers to organizational theory.

The institutional theoretical framework are part of the eclectic bouquet when it comes to location advantages. The accessibility to markets or resources is critical for companies seeking to enter foreign markets. These multinationals favor more attractive markets, often characterized by market growth or potential, both considered important determinants for foreign investment.[105] In some countries with high market growth, investment is expected to provide a greater profitability, implying that parent companies seek to possess higher equity levels.

The last flower in the eclectic bouquet comes from the transaction cost approach (TCA): internalization advantages come from sharing assets and reducing transaction costs.[106] This internalization decision is based on the cost difference between

a) sharing the assets and skills with a host-country firm; and
b) integrating these resources within the firm.

The main proposition of the eclectic paradigm is that an international firm has to have not only particular advantages (O, L, or I) over local firms but must also possess a combination of these advantages before engaging in international production.

The eclectic paradigm is regarded as one of the most important contributions in international business theory. Within a few decades, it reached the top of the international strategy literature and is constantly discussed and developed.

Over time, Dunning emphasized the role of locational choice for foreign investments. In relation to OLI is the concept of firm-specific advantages (FSA) and country-specific advantages (CSA) that factually refers to ownership advantages (the O in OLI) and location advantages (the L in OLI), respectively. For firms that expand abroad, an important portion of the country-specific advantage reflects home-country features such as macroeconomic situation, country image or domestic government policies. CSA can be very strong for companies from emerging economies – namely, advantages such as low cost of labor or monopolistic power.[107]

A number of arguments have been leveled at this approach[108] – namely, because emerging multinationals do not have enough power and do not fulfill the required conditions. It is argued that emerging multinationals are driven to internationalize not by host-country location advantages, but rather by home-country location disadvantages. They are trying to escape the unstable environments of their domestic markets.[109] In addition, it is claimed that emerging multinationals have a different perspective regarding resources acquired via internalization.[110] Rather than adopting the OLI approach, these emerging market companies rely on linkage, leverage and learning (3L) of international resources.[111]

This criticism, together with empirical evidence, has led Dunning to acknowledge the limitations of the ownership advantages for emerging multinationals.[112] He argued that these firms internationalize using a two-stage model: first, they invest in developed countries in order to gain access or to augment their ownership advantages rather than just exploit them. Then, in the second stage, they follow the logic of the OLI paradigm.

The investment development path

It was recognized by Dunning[113] that modifications in a country's economic development result in changes in a firm's OLI advantages and therefore its internationalization choices. The *investment development path* (IDP) theory was therefore included in an extended eclectic paradigm; it is another flower in the bouquet, so to speak. The IDP concept explains the changes in a country's inward and outward FDI position as a result of the country's economic development.[114] The IDP identifies five stages in a country's development.

The first stage refers to a country's pre-industrialization phase, when inward and outward FDI are virtually non-existent.[115] Location advantages are only linked to natural resources, which are sufficient to induce FDI – namely, in strategically important industries such as oil & gas or mining – that attract investors even to poor institutional and economic environments. The only FDI available is targeted at labor-intensive production facilities creating consumer products.[116] There are no ownership advantages, due to the protected and limited domestic market, coupled with the disadvantages of a recently developing economy.

The second stage involves increasing inward FDI but limited outward FDI. International companies begin establishing local production units to take advantage of the growing domestic market, both in purchasing power and even size.[117] Government efforts towards providing better infrastructure, transport, education and healthcare systems result in increasing location advantages. Any outbound FDI targets either new resources or markets.[118]

The third stage displays reduced inward FDI and increased outward FDI, with most outward investment going towards countries that are lower on the IDP.[119] Living standards and customer expectations rise and the country moves towards economic maturity. Internationalization through greenfield ventures or M&A is done for the purpose of attaining efficiency and strategic asset attainment. Ownership advantages move from natural resources to managerial competency.[120]

During stage four, outward FDI grows faster than inward FDI. Domestic companies begin competing in international markets and production tends towards capital-intensive manufacturing due to the low cost of capital as opposed to higher cost of labor. Location advantages shift from natural to created assets. Internationalization through FDI is more prominent than exports, as companies increase internalization to maintain ownership advantages.[121] Countries in the fourth stage are known as being in a post-industrial economy with predominant service sector, greater research and development for new production methods, new products and investments are made more for efficiency and asset growth through entry modes such as M&A deals and strategic alliances.[122]

The fifth stage is an advanced version of the fourth stage, characterized by similar behavior and causes for internationalization. Examples of fifth stage countries are Sweden, the United States and Japan. Inward FDI into these Stage 5 countries comes from lower IDP countries seeking new knowledge and markets, or from Stage 4 and 5 countries in search of efficiency.[123] Increased internationalization leads to a more interlinked world with fading physical boundaries and greater strategic investments in assets. Mergers, acquisitions and strategic alliances are methods sought to improve ownership advantages. Stage 5 countries progressively become more similar as they strive to improve their ownership advantages through these transactions.[124]

Applying the eclectic paradigm to emerging markets

As scholars recognize the power of the OLI framework, research is taking hold on its applicability to emerging markets and their multinationals. With emerging markets spawning a growing number of multinationals and volume of outbound FDI, Dunning's eclectic paradigm[125] has been declared "the most straightforward articulation of the firm's strategic motivation to become a multinational."[126] Over the years, the eclectic paradigm's O, L and I advantages have also become conditions justifying the appearance of emerging multinationals.[127]

In fact, the ownership advantage does not necessarily originate in the company's home country. Rather, the company may acquire and augment it from the host country abroad.[128] In 1993, Dunning attempted to address the tension between the notion of asset exploitation and asset hunting (both motivations for international expansion) by recognizing that firms can go abroad to exploit or to acquire ownership advantages.[129] As emerging multinationals typically suffer from latecomer disadvantages, they actively invest abroad and often use cross-border acquisitions for quick access to global brands, technologies and markets.

In the last revision of the OLI concept,[130] the eclectic paradigm was broadened to include institutional theory, building on the research of North.[131] This co-evolutionary viewpoint[132] explains the internationalization motives of emerging multinationals, where the institutional distance between home and host countries is no longer an obstacle to expansion, but on the contrary, a motive.

While many emerging multinationals expand abroad by capitalizing on home-country advantages,[133] these advantages have different origins. For example, China and India benefit from relatively cheap labor, while Russia has natural resource (oil & gas) and country-specific advantages and Brazil exploits its mineral advantages.[134] However, CSAs cannot fully explain the emergence of select Russian multinationals, since those advantages are available to all Russian firms, yet only a small fraction engage in cross-border expansion.

This shortcoming was predicted in the latest development of the eclectic paradigm.[135] In addition to the traditional, asset-related ownership advantage (referred to as *Oa*), a new institutional ownership advantage was introduced (referred to as *Oi*).

The institutional ownership advantage Oi "incorporates firm-specific norms and values guiding decision making, as well as an imprint of the institutional environment of the home-country."[136] One specific Oi advantage plays a profound role in the activities of emerging multinationals when the home-country government has direct ownership.[137] Firms with government ownership may have privileged access to resources, unlike firms without government ownership.[138] Furthermore, the government typically provides financial aid to avoid bankruptcy, so firms with higher government stakes can better withstand risks and uncertainties in foreign host countries. Firms with lesser or no government ownership do not have this protection.[139] This government protection and involvement in turn enhances the bargaining position of emerging multinationals when negotiating with foreign partners.[140] In sensitive industries, the government involvement may not necessarily be direct (through ownership) but could be indirect – for example, through company participation by state officials, or by the provision of government contracts or by granting political recourse, which may be critical for international success.[141]

4.4 From Uppsala model to network perspective

Original Uppsala model: step by step

Developed in late 1970s by Jan Johanson and Jan-Erik Vahlne, the Uppsala model was a result of studies on internationalization carried out in 1975. Like our previous theoretical frameworks, the Uppsala model attempts to explain what process lead companies to expand abroad. The Uppsala model questions the common assumption that people are rational and that they make decisions after comparing the costs and benefits of different options. Uppsala explains that this rationality does not play a role in the decision of internationalizing to a particular market. Instead, most firms internationalize slowly and with caution, choosing their first international destination to be one that is similar to the home market in terms of cultural behavior, language and business practices. A study of the companies in the model put forth the phenomenon of sudden and unplanned export to a market.[142] Uppsala further explained that internationalization is a step-by-step learning process for each company, which results from sudden demand from foreign markets, as opposed to a deliberate choice or decision to expand to a particular market.[143]

The Uppsala model relies heavily on the concept of market knowledge: the more a company learns from early internationalization stages, the easier the following step will be. In addition, good market knowledge implies understanding the prospects and risks of further market involvement. Also important to the Uppsala model is the notion of market commitment. A company expanding abroad will need to decide which assets to dedicate to the overseas market and which amount of FDI it should ante up, based on experience from earlier operations.

Market knowledge

Market knowledge can be of two types: objective knowledge, which is taught knowledge passed on through books and word of mouth, and experiential knowledge, which is knowledge gained through experience.[144] Market knowledge is instrumental in the selection of a new foreign market. The best way to gain in-depth market knowledge is by experience. Progressive market expansion and a step-by-step approach are the best ways to gain experience and expand profitably.[145] Experiential knowledge needs to be learned and is a continuous process.[146] This knowledge is not easily transferrable from one person to another. Obtaining experiential knowledge by hiring people who have the relevant experience is one method of quick market knowledge attainment. However, hiring outsiders exposes companies to the threat of "misfits" incorrectly attuned into organizational processes and goals. While this limitation holds true for marketing and management activities, product knowledge can be obtained through experienced outside sources.[147]

Market commitment

Market commitment is measured by two parameters: a) the amount of resources invested in a particular market and b) the immobility of resources suited only for the chosen market. For example, if a company has invested heavily, but in a "liquid" market, then the market commitment is not high. However, resources such as staff with experience in the selected market imply a high market commitment, since moving such talent to another market would be costly.[148]

Commitment decisions have to do with the decision of either increasing or decreasing a company's resource investment in a market. This decision is taken on the basis of the risks and opportunities that the market provides, the decision is a result of two factors: the amount of market knowledge the company possesses and the present commitment that the company has made. Most companies continue to increase their market commitment until the risk limit, which marks the point where it becomes too risky for them to increase commitment. It is common practice to attempt to decrease market risks by learning more about the market and specializing the services and even products to gain greater customer satisfaction and a bigger customer base.[149]

Current business activities

The current commitment that the company has within a market determines the business activities that are carried out. For new companies, it is necessary to repeat these activities regularly until an effect is noticed on the market. Only through current business activities can a company gain experiential knowledge about a market. In cases where the product being offered is novel or complex, the company may face a greater risk due to lack of knowledge about the market and its opportunities.[150]

Companies increase their market commitment by exploiting market opportunities and positive economic environmental factors and implementing activities to reduce market risks. This increases market knowledge, which improves scenarios for future decisions. This completes the decision-making process of the Uppsala model. Greater market knowledge means greater understanding of market risks and more informed decision about the extent of investment. Accurate risk assessment leads to greater investment.[151]

The studied cases of the model bring forth a better understanding of the internationalization process. Most internationalization decisions begin as a result of an agent's initiation into export. This is then followed by the establishment of a sales office. As market knowledge and commitment grows, local production is also set up.[152]

Uppsala 2.0: reducing distance via networks

Johanson and Vahlne announced in 2009 that their original Uppsala model needed to be updated to suit the current business environment, especially given the additional empirical knowledge.[153] According to the 1977 theory, customers and suppliers are independent factors, which is not true in today's scenario. Interdependent relationships create the current interconnected network of the business world, in which suppliers and customers are an inherent part, and internationalization is now viewed as a firm's attempt to strengthen its position in this network. Factors such as physical distance are no longer as important for entry mode choice, while factors such as business relationships have gained in importance.[154] Market knowledge and market commitment are now developed through business networks and relationships, which is proprietary information unavailable to outsiders.

The revised model also led to revised terminology. *Market knowledge* now encompasses multiple variables including opportunities, needs, relationships, capabilities and strategies, thereby recognizing their roles as drivers of internationalization. Based on the understanding that internationalization can be defined as improving a firm's network position, *market commitment* is now called *network position*, which also includes variables such as trust, knowledge and commitment. The importance given to each of these sub-variables decides the level of success of the internationalization.

Change has been introduced and it includes *relationships*, which can be described as the commitment to relationships within a network and can be concerned with increasing or decreasing the relationship commitment in a market. Any market commitment decision is clearly visible by its investment size, mode of entry and dependence level.[155] Another factor of change is *learning, creating and trust building*. The earlier model explained *current activities* as the cause for knowledge, commitment and trust, but *knowledge* has now been replaced by *learning*. Learning is one step ahead of the knowledge gained through *experience*. The attractiveness of the available opportunities defines how well a firm learns, creates knowledge and builds trust.[156]

According to Uppsala 2.0, why do firms want to expand abroad? The motive is either to find new business through the network, or to accompany a partner across borders to maintain or strengthen an existing relationship. The chosen market or partner will be based on the attractiveness of the market or the potential partner's position in the network. While physical distance is not necessarily a factor here, it will matter in a situation where a firm does not have a strong partner. In such a case, a firm will choose either a market with attractive options for growth of its network, or an agent who can introduce the firm into a strong network to expand. However, short physical distance will not be the only determinant.[157] Internationalization can be a result of the desire to use the network to gain knowledge about a foreign market opportunity or to take advantage of the trust between partners.[158]

The revised model does not discriminate between large and small firms. However, any advantage that larger firms may have – for example, early awareness of an international deal – is the result of experiential knowledge as opposed to a difference in size itself. These large firms also have the advantage of already existing networks and knowledge of new markets, which may also be the cause for the fast growth of international companies.[159]

To generalize, the model was developed using empirical data from Swedish firms. The key statements of the Uppsala model are firms develop their activities abroad over time and in an incremental fashion, based on their knowledge development; this development is explained by the concept of psychic distance, with firms expanding first into markets which were psychically close and thereafter into more distant markets as knowledge developed.[160]

The model was praised by some but also heavily criticized by others.

On the positive side, the Uppsala model does explain how Russian resource-based companies expanded abroad, first starting with export activities and later acquiring foreign assets and establishing subsidiaries.[161] For critics, Uppsala is less and less correlated with empirical evidence from contemporary business evidence, in particular that the stages model is not appropriate for emerging and transitional countries.[162] Another research stream argues that the international strategy of BRIC multinationals contradicts Uppsala, with these firms sometimes starting their internationalization with aggressive acquisitions, thus skipping intermediate stages.[163]

Conclusion: seeking new theories to fit the new multinational game

Traditional theories conclude that emerging multinationals, whether expanding to developed or emerging markets, face intense competition from developed multinationals that traditionally possess advantages, such as technological know-how, deep financial pockets or innovative manufacturing operations. Despite these handicaps, some emerging multinationals have expanded internationally and have demonstrated outstanding results, even outperforming their developed rivals.

This induced scholars to ask several important questions regarding emerging multinationals:

- Where do their competitive advantages originate?
- What is their motivation to go abroad?
- What constraints do they face in their internationalization? How do they deal with them?
- How are they able to compete with multinationals from developed countries?

To find answers to these questions, academics challenged the existing theories, proposing new concepts such as the springboard perspective or the transformation of competitive disadvantages into advantages for emerging multinationals (discussed in Chapter 6).

Overall, the existing theories attempt to explain not just what international strategy is but also discuss obstacles related to corporate internationalization and offer solutions to overcome these hurdles. In the early literature, economic barriers were considered the most important obstacles, whereas later research uncovered new difficulties such as institutional and cultural barriers.

Researchers distinguish between internal and external barriers for internationalization. Internal barriers derive from a company's available resources and approach to internationalization. A lack of knowledge, either experiential knowledge or market specific knowledge, is common during initial geographic expansion and can only be remedied by operational presence on the ground.[164] Inadequate resources or lack of commitment to foreign markets are other important risks.[165]

External obstacles to internationalization arise from either foreign or domestic barriers. A sort of fence consisting of economic, institutional and cultural barriers surrounds each national market.[166] The most discussed in the literature are economic barriers such as direct and indirect trade barriers. Governments also play a role, either via protectionism for domestic business, or by lack of assistance for outbound expanders. Both can block the internationalization of a company.

Socio-cultural barriers between target country and the home country can be seen through the terms of psychic distance, or in terms of cultural distance.[167] The nature of infrastructure and other environmental factors in host countries can also greatly influence the implementation of a company's expansion plans.[168]

As business become increasingly international, and as companies from emerging and developing countries make their mark in the business arena, scholars are busy developing and refining new theories to fit the changing panorama.

References

1 Johanson and Vahlne 1990.
2 Commons 1931.
3 Coase 1937, 1960.
4 Williamson 1989.
5 Coase 1937.
6 Coase 1960.
7 Williamson 1989.
8 Dunning 1981, 1993.

9   Buckley and Casson 1976.
10 Markusen 1984.
11 Horstmann 1992; Brainard 1997; Markusen and Venables 1998.
12 Helpman 1984.
13 Markusen and Maskus 2002.
14 Yeaple 2003; Grossman, Helpman and Szeidl 2006.
15 Barkema and Vermeulen 1998.
16 Crook, Ketchen, Combs and Todd 2008.
17 Nadolska and Barkema 2007; Peng, Wang and Jinag 2008; Dikova, Rao Sahib and van Witteloostuijn 2010; King, Dalton, Daily and Covin 2004.
18 Peng 2001.
19 Barney 1991.
20 Brouthers, Brouthers and Werner 2008.
21 Barney 1991.
22 Barney 1986b.
23 Wernerfelt 1984.
24 Barney 1991.
25 Collis 1994.
26 Barney 1986b.
27 Villalonga 2004.
28 Barney 1986a.
29 Peng 2001.
30 Barney 1991.
31 Brouthers, Brouthers and Werner 2008.
32 Ibid.
33 Ibid.
34 Scott 1995.
35 Scott 2002.
36 Peng 2002; Peng, Wang and Jiang 2008.
37 Young, Tsai, Wang, Liu and Ahlstrom 2014; Du and Boateng 2015; Sun, Peng, Lee and Tan 2015.
38 North 1990, 1994, 2005.
39 Dunning and Lundan 2008a.
40 Scott 1995.
41 Zhang, Zhou and Ebbers 2011.
42 Kostova and Zaheer 1999.
43 Kostova and Roth 2002.
44 Zaheer 1995.
45 Sethi and Judge 2009.
46 Buckley, Clegg, Cross, Liu, Voss and Zheng 2007.
47 Zhang, Zhou and Ebbers 2011.
48 Warner, Hong and Xu 2004.
49 Kostova and Roth 2002.
50 Xu and Shenkar 2002.
51 Dikova, Rao Sahib and van Witteloostuijn 2010.
52 Zhang, Zhou and Ebbers 2011.
53 Mihailova and Panibratov 2012.
54 North 1990.
55 Panibratov 2015.
56 Radosevic and Sadowski 2004.
57 Mauro 1995; Voyer and Beamish 2004.
58 Wei 2000a.
59 Fisman 2001.
60 Javorcik and Wei 2009.
61 Mauro 1995; Petrou and Thanos 2014.
62 Wheeler and Mody 1992; Egger and Winner 2005.
63 Shleifer and Vishny 1993.
64 Weitzel and Berns 2006.

65 Luo, Xue and Han 2010.
66 Luo and Tung 2007; Luo and Rui 2009.
67 Stahl and Voigt 2008.
68 Morosini, Shane and Singh 1998.
69 Yin and Shanley 2008.
70 Zhang, Zhou and Ebbers 2011.
71 Toth 2008.
72 Zhang, Zhou and Ebbers 2011.
73 Mihailova and Panibratov 2012; Annushkina and Colonel 2013.
74 Panibratov and Verbá 2011.
75 Hitt and Tyler 1991; Romanelli and Tushman 1986.
76 Kotabe, Jiang and Murray 2010; Musteen, Francis and Datta 2010; Thomas, Eden, Hitt and Miller 2007.
77 Latukha 2015.
78 Miller, Thomas, Eden and Hitt 2008.
79 Bhaumik, Driffield and Pal 2010.
80 Del Sol and Kogan 2007.
81 Bonaglia, Goldstein and Mathews 2007.
82 Lu, Zhou, Bruton and Li 2010.
83 Luo, Xue and Han 2010.
84 Panibratov 2012.
85 Ang and Michailova 2008; Demirbag, Tatoglu and Glaister 2009; Deng 2009.
86 Mihailova and Panibratov 2012.
87 Beverelli and Mahlstein 2011; Williamson 1985.
88 Williamson 2008.
89 Argyres 1995.
90 Coase 1937.
91 Ibid.
92 Ibid.
93 Williamson 1971.
94 Casson 1984; Klein, Crawford and Alchian 1978; Caves and Bradburd 1988.
95 Dunning 2001.
96 Verbeke and Yuan 2010; Dunning 2000.
97 Hymer 1976; Zaheer 1995.
98 Hashai and Buckley 2014.
99 Dunning 2001; Dunning and Lundan 2008a.
100 Dunning 2001; Dunning and Lundan 2008b.
101 Buckley and Casson 1976; Rugman 1981.
102 Buckley and Casson 2009.
103 Barney 1991.
104 Agarwal and Ramaswami 1992; Dunning 1988.
105 Terpstra and Yu 1988; Weinstein 1977.
106 Safarian 2003.
107 Andreff 2003.
108 e.g. Svetlicic 2003.
109 Svetlicic 2003; Cuervo-Cazurra 2007.
110 Mathews 2006.
111 Ibid.
112 Dunning 2006.
113 Dunning 2001.
114 Dunning and Narula 1996.
115 Dunning 2001.
116 Dunning and Lundan 2008b.
117 Narula and Dunning 2010.
118 Dunning and Lundan 2008a.
119 Dunning and Narula 1996.
120 Dunning and Lundan 2008b.

121 Dunning and Narula 1996.
122 Dunning and Lundan 2008b.
123 Ibid.; Dunning and Narula 1996.
124 Dunning 2009.
125 Dunning 1977, 1981, 1993, 1998.
126 Hashai and Buckley 2014.
127 Ibid. 2014.
128 Buckley and Hashai 2009.
129 Eden and Dai 2010.
130 Dunning and Lundan 2008b.
131 North 1990.
132 Cantwell, Dunning and Lundan 2010.
133 Rugman 2009.
134 Hennart 2012.
135 Dunning and Lundan 2008a.
136 Eden and Dai 2010.
137 Cuervo-Cazurra and Genc 2008; Le and O'Brien 2010; Ramaswamy, Li and Veliyath 2002.
138 Pan, Teng, Supapol, Lu, Huang and Wang 2014.
139 Cui and Jiang 2012; Morck et al., 2008.
140 Xia, Ma, Lu and Yiu 2014.
141 Panibratov 2012.
142 Johanson and Vahlne 2009.
143 Johanson and Vahlne 1977.
144 Penrose 1966.
145 Johanson and Vahlne 1977.
146 Penrose 1966.
147 Johanson and Vahlne 1977.
148 Ibid.
149 Ibid.
150 Ibid.
151 Ibid.
152 Ibid.
153 Johanson and Vahlne 2009.
154 Ibid.
155 Ibid.
156 Ibid.
157 Ibid.
158 Larson 1992.
159 Johanson and Vahlne 2009.
160 Johanson and Vahlne 1977.
161 Kalotay 2008.
162 Svetlicic 2003.
163 Cuervo-Cazurra 2006, 2008; Ramamurti, 2009.
164 Johanson and Vahlne 2009.
165 Dunning 1998.
166 Johanson and Vahlne 2009.
167 Hofstede 1991.
168 Hollensen 2001.

5 Dynamic perspective on internationalization

This chapter presents the dynamics of corporate international expansion. Let us use the example of a train to illustrate this dynamic. When a train departs, it slowly picks up speed. It progressively accelerates and, in the case of a high-speed bullet train, it can go almost as fast as a small aircraft. A proper locomotive (or traction system) will enable the train to pull into its destination fast and on schedule. Naturally, the quality of the fuel is important. Using this example, a company departs on its international journey with export activities. Arrival is associated with foreign direct investment, the ultimate stage of a company's internationalization. As for the fuel, M&A transactions can provide the train with high speed, whereas joint ventures will make it express. Yet the journey does not depend on the fuel alone. The track and ballast must be of good quality, just as for successful deals, companies sometimes need to maintain political connections and always need to heed cultural differences.

Internationalization always starts as an export activity, which is not only predicted by the Uppsala school but also demonstrated in reality by the majority of companies having international activities. While almost all firms place a first toe in the international waters by exporting their products or services, only a portion remain active exporters, with the rest switching from export to other forms of operations such as international joint ventures (JVs), acquisitions or greenfield operations (starting from scratch).

After cutting their teeth on export, companies may move through several stages of internationalization to finally face the FDI option (there exists no more intense a mode of internationalization). Even so, FDI may differ in its nature: greenfield investment is selected by firms in no hurry for market penetration and focused on the careful establishment of their foreign operations. Acquisitions are the mode of choice for companies seeking fast and mostly reliable entry, often in an attempt to catch up with rivals, yet sometimes also as a reaction to economic or political changes in the environment.

Firms that actively invest abroad are known as multinational enterprises (or MNEs), and these firms are an inherent part of FDI-related activities, both in home and host countries. In their domestic markets, MNEs generate capital and accumulate other resources, such as technology, talent or political backup, which facilitate their international expansion. MNEs may also be targets for acquisition by foreign MNEs from abroad. In the host countries where they operate, the roles of MNEs are just as diverse: they are investors, acquirers, rivals, rules of the game changers and policy influencers.

Finally, the dynamism of the internationalization process in general, and of MNEs in particular, depends largely on the technology that plays an increasingly critical role in international strategy. This, in turn, results in alternative ways to "turbo" internationalization, as witnessed by service industries, "born global" firms and high-tech companies.

5.1 Export strategy: point of departure

Export and company growth

International diversification strategy plays an important role for both large and small firms since it represents a significant process for acquiring economies of scope and scale, as well as expanding one's customer base.[1] Yet, like smoking, it may prove hazardous to a company's health. International expansion is risky and may cause complications. Going abroad requires that firms acquire specific knowledge or cognition about foreign markets, yet this supports corporate development by providing international bearings. However, firms that limit themselves to export activities will also face growth constraints in the long run.

The trade theories developed by David Ricardo and later developed as mathematical model by Eli Heckscher and Bertil Ohlin (known as H-O model) purely investigate the phenomena of goods and services exchanges between countries without regard for the impact of companies on trade.[2] However, more recent models constructed with the use of Dixit-Stiglitz monopolistic competition framework do take companies into account and try to explain the vast volumes of trade among countries with firm-level factors of production.[3] From this perspective, an important assumption is made: in terms of technology and productivity, companies belonging to the same industry are rather symmetric.[4] Symmetric means homogeneous, or just similar. Most importantly, this means that if a company is able to find export markets, it will exploit these and absorb export and trade costs in the process.

However, research since 2000 has shown that exporting firms are highly asymmetric. Firms are actually heterogeneous in terms of their productivity levels, but they co-exist in an industry because each firm faces initial uncertainty concerning its productivity.[5] Although export is costly, it offers a way for companies to go abroad just after gaining knowledge regarding its productivity.

As a rule, just a limited number of companies in each specific industry engage in export, and they do not represent a random sample. Exporting companies are, as a rule, larger and more productive than companies that operate only domestically. This productivity advantage of exporting companies facilitates the amortization of fixed investments (e.g. new distribution network establishment, market research or product modification costs).

The initial empirical research[6] which addressed the problems of size, productivity and international activity of companies stated that in general, exporting companies are larger and more efficient and that such companies follow the principle of self-selection. Using a sample of approximately sixty thousand American companies between 1984 and 1992, research showed that even if only small firms are considered, exporting companies are 50% to 60% bigger than their non-exporting counterparts; moreover, their total employment and total shipments are twice as large, and labor productivity is 24% higher. In addition, the research identified differences in labor structure, with more non-production employees in exporting firms and a significant positive difference in terms of wages for all employees.

In other studies, the factors influencing a company's decision to export were identified as productivity levels, the value of fixed investments for exporting and the magnitude of variable costs.[7] Different combinations of these factors define the framework that establish productivity thresholds for different options. Should the company produce and operate only in its domestic market? Or should it commence export to international markets or even invest abroad? Most studies have shown that productivity governs the firm's performance regardless of the company's decision to export or not. Only the most productive firms engage in foreign activities; moreover, foreign direct investments become viable options to the most productive international firms.[8]

Even though research supports the positive correlation between company size and productivity, evidence exists that this is not always the rule. Although larger companies more easily overcome high export barriers, some companies grow and increase their productivity due to their export engagement. This phenomenon is denoted in literature as the "learning-by-exporting" effect, and research suggests several causes. The virtuous circle linking an exporting company, its international competitors and its consumers brings benefits: a better understanding of processes, cost reductions and opportunities for quality improvements or innovations.[9] Companies that export their goods or services to international markets (especially to large and significant markets) take advantage of spillovers from more sophisticated markets – a trickle-down effect, if you wish.

Three components of the external environment are particularly pertinent to export activities:[10]

- *Market turbulence* refers to the level of insecurity in the external environment, obliging companies to adapt strategies in order to keep abreast of changing customer needs. For example, mobile telephony clearly illustrates a turbulent market. With competition so intense, none of the competitors is ready to mount a serious challenge. There are thousands of tariffs and mobile phone handsets, and there is little brand loyalty, with customers choosing the best hardware and service deals and good prices. Another example is the travel industry, where environmental, political and economic issues can cause turbulence. The Russian travel industry experienced serious turbulence in 2015 after an aircraft crash in Egypt, conflict with Turkey and the currency devaluation.
- *Technological turbulence* refers to the high rates of technological change in manufacturing of products, or any technology intrinsic to the product itself. For instance, shorter product life cycles as a result of technological turbulence can make it more difficult for producers and retailers to maintain targeted customer service levels. One example is the quick boom and unexpectedly quick saturation of the video game market.
- *Environmental turbulence* represents the competitive and institutional situation surrounding the export-oriented enterprise. Examples here include changes in tax regulations or when the home country shifts political or trade alliances.

In most research, the spotlight is set on environmental turbulence, as it affects export activities. Some authors find a positive relationship between the level of competitive intensity of a market and the level of company performance.[11]

Exporting firms enjoy the benefits of scale economies, cost advantages and possibly rapid increases in profits. These firms become more competitive by increasing their efficiency and more innovative given their exposure to new, sometimes tough, local competitors. Once a company starts to export, it needs to stay on the ball, improving its performance in order to stay competitive.[12]

Performance, self-selection, learning by exporting

Many empirical and theoretical studies have investigated the relationship between a company's export orientation and its productivity growth. One key topic of research was self-selection among companies: when a firm chooses of its own free will to start exporting, does that have an impact or a correlation on its performance?[13] Though most research supports the finding that exporting firms are on average more efficient than non-exporting companies, there is scant agreement on the causes. In particular, does an initial positive difference in productivity lead companies to become exporters, or vice-versa: did productivity increase as a consequence of the add-on exports? Then it dawned on researchers that this relationship can in fact be binary. This revelation caused modifications in the econometric models used in research. Self-selection was included as a control variable, which otherwise would exaggerate the impact of learning by exporting.

Although most research agrees upon the effect of self-selection, some evidence has been found to support the learning-by-exporting phenomena. For example, if a company is more productive in the first, pre-export, period, it is more likely to start exporting in a second period, which in turn facilitates further increases in productivity. A virtuous circle, so to speak. Moreover, research points out that company ownership plays an important role: domestically controlled companies can learn more from international markets than those under foreign ownership.[14]

The impact of the export strategy on a firm's productivity is often studied by examining the decision making on whether and how to enter foreign markets.[15] The most important firm-level factors for this decision are firm productivity, industry-fixed costs, size of market, human capital available and technology/R&D intensity.

One study investigated 3,500 Swedish manufacturing firms for a period of almost twenty years. Sweden was chosen because of its high trade orientation, with trade revenues accounting for about 60% of GDP and 85% of all companies being active exporters. The study concluded that trade participation helped increase the competitiveness of exporting companies to such an extent that they drove competing companies which operated on the domestic market out of the industry.[16] The majority of exporters are comparatively young and very productive companies, and are able to replace older and less productive firms which do not export. Another finding of this study is that the majority of non-exporting companies originated in industries where export involved high transportation costs.

In all these studies, there was clear evidence that exporting firms do have a significantly higher productivity growth, with export activities having a positive effect on productivity, growth and overall performance.

Export and corruption

Research on export activities is often linked with corruption studies, which can be explained by the fact that both practices appeared centuries ago. The role of corruption on the growth of export-oriented companies was covered only partially in research. Usually the discussion is in the context of research covering the influence of corruption on FDI and trade balances for specific countries.[17] Moreover, this phenomenon was mostly considered at a macro level – i.e. the level of influence of corruption on export performance of particular countries or its economic growth.

However, if we consider the institutional side of the business environment, if a host country experiences high levels of corruption (as is the case for many emerging markets), then research conclusions are not as homogeneous.

Past research has mostly considered the influence of corruption on company performance at the country level. Corruption has been perceived as detrimental to both FDI and human capital inflows and therefore is an obstacle to economic growth.[18] In the particular case of Russia, given the recent collapse of the former communist bloc (less than three decades ago), not much research has been done in this sphere from a company perspective. There are especially significant gaps in the study of the influence of corruption on export-oriented companies. So far, the main focus of researchers has been on other issues, such as the negative impact of "unofficial payments" on corporate growth.[19]

Corruption raises the cost of trade, and firms switch from export to IJV or FDI in an attempt to avoid it. Surprisingly, corruption does not disappear but simply changes forms, and in many cases, it becomes stronger and more costly. This issue will be addressed in later chapters of this book, with the particular reference to emerging markets and their multinationals.

5.2 Foreign direct investments: arrival station

The level of FDI and its importance have been changing over time and differ across nations. Recently there has been an increase in FDI to emerging markets and more favorable host-country government policies so as to attract inbound FDI. Being dependent on policy barriers, FDI flows have been facilitated by the liberalization of FDI regimes. As governments realized the benefits of FDI, such as technology and capital input, they started promoting FDI flows by implementing favorable policies, removing barriers and establishing special economic zones.

Two opposite views on the influence of FDI exist within research. From the host-country perspective, FDI does have positive appeal: it leads to economic growth, increases in productivity and, therefore, contributes to differences in economic development and growth across countries, as the companies may expand opportunities for technology transfer.[20] On the other hand, FDI may endanger local capabilities and undercompensate the use of natural resources of the host countries, or even contribute support to questionable regimes in host countries. Thus FDI represents valuable opportunities for firms from both developing and developed economies, while governments need to establish policies that promote the suitable foreign investment while simultaneously protecting local communities.[21]

In recent decades, outbound FDI from emerging markets was redirected from developed countries (Europe and Americas) to other emerging markets (with a strong interest in the BRIC countries). The expansion into BRIC countries can only be partially explained by the desire of multinationals to strengthen their positions in rapidly developing countries. There are many other motives behind this trend, which require additional explanations.

FDI in the context of internationalization theory

Multiple studies show that macroeconomic and institutional environments determine FDI location choices, with home and host countries affecting FDI patterns. Several theories are specifically relevant in explaining this phenomenon.

According to the investment development path theory,[22] both outward and inward FDI depend on the level of economic development. This path is divided into five development stages, during which firm-specific and location-specific advantages change. A country will also refocus from inward to outward FDI (refer to Chapter 4 for details).

Dunning's IDP paradigm states that FDI depends on the level of economic development, reflected by the country's GDP, or GDP per capita, as well as the country's net outward investment.[23] Companies undergo structural changes as a natural consequence of a country's development, which affects FDI inflows and outflows, which in turn impacts national economic structure. Thus there is a dynamic interaction between the two.[24]

Economic development, location and ownership advantages characterize the firm and attract FDI.[25] Inward FDI increases location and ownership advantages of firms and, thus, favors outward FDI. The development factors of the home country have an impact on

FDI levels, proven by many studies on both developed and developing countries.[26] High levels of economic development are, in turn, associated with the ownership advantages of investing firms, meaning for them availability of capital and know-how that push companies to invest abroad. Technology endowments also encourage firms to go to foreign markets with FDI to exploit their competitive advantage, thus emerging market firms are likely to possess lower-level technology and have an advantage on similar markets.[27] Overall, the greater the competitive advantage of investing firms compared to those of the host country, the more they are likely to increase their foreign investment portfolios; firms prefer to engage in FDI instead of licensing or franchising if the benefits of internalizing foreign markets will be greater.[28]

Various theories (agency cost, transaction cost, modern property rights, information asymmetry) state that firms prefer to engage in investment activities in countries with favorable business environments and good property rights protection that minimize costs of doing business.[29] For instance, transaction cost theory suggests that economic regulations affect the investment climate of a country by decreasing or increasing risks and thus influencing FDI flows. Good governance is able to create favorable investment climates for foreign investors,[30] while well-enforced rules and regulations in addition to stable government policies foster capital flows.[31]

Political risk is one of the institutional factors that affects investing companies in the early stages of FDI activities in a new location.[32] Politically unstable countries are likely to have high levels of corruption, weak property rights protection, burdensome regulations and high barriers to inward investment.[33] Such conditions increase the level of uncertainty in these countries and mean higher transaction costs.

Political economy theory posits that government and businesses are interconnected. Governments create regulations and laws, while businesses try to shape governmental policies.[34] In order to promote OFDI, governments liberalize economic conditions and diminish economic barriers to encourage the flow of resources, capital and knowledge. In such conditions, firms benefit more from global value chains, acquire strategic, organizational and technological advantages that are transferred to the local level and enhance national competitiveness.

According to the resource-based view, firms expand to foreign markets by exploiting valuable resources, such as technology, scientific knowledge and brands. By deploying resources in several markets, firms diversify risks and achieve economies of scale and scope. The various approaches to outward FDI such as asset seeking and resource exploitation are based on the resource-based view.[35]

The strategic intent perspective posits that firms internationalize to attain specific goals such as exploiting their ownership advantages, acquiring strategic assets and improving their overall performance. At the same time, firms aim to avoid institutional constraints in home and host countries. Thus FDI decisions are made rationally for strategic purposes.[36]

How well theories developed in the context of developed markets transfer to emerging markets is under question. There does seem to be consensus that institutional theory provides a better grounding to explain the outbound investments made by emerging multinationals, in contrast to well-established theories such as RBV or OLI.[37]

Macroeconomic factors for FDI

Most research on the causes (or determinants) of FDI distinguishes three groups of factors: institutional factors; demand–side factors, such as market size and income distribution; and supply-side factors, such as infrastructure and labor. Another reference frame depicts FDI factors as either "push" or "pull." Home-country attributes that encourage outward FDI are "push," whereas host-country attributes that attract inward FDI are "pull." The main host–country factors refer to large market size, low labor costs, low transaction costs and low geographic and cultural distance, many of which are applicable to emerging markets.[38]

As could be expected, China draws the bulk of the studies on FDI in emerging markets, yet scholars have also investigated other developing economies. Studies on Latin American countries focus on determinants for inward FDI flows, more than outward flows. For inward FDI into these countries, economic growth and economic freedom of the host country are important motivators.[39] Similarly, in Asian markets, economic factors are more significant than institutional and political ones as FDI determinants.[40] The significance of real GDP and GDP per capita as indicators of market appeal demonstrate the market-seeking motives of BRIC multinationals in expanding abroad.

As for India, its main charms for inbound FDI are its market size, trade openness and low inflation rate.[41] Greater market wealth, as measured by GDP per capita is an important factor for FDI flows in East Asia.[42] Countries of South and East Asia invest more in the economies that have a higher integration level in the global economy that is proxied by trade openness.[43] Although some controversy remains, most studies agree that good infrastructure development correlates positively with FDI in Asia and Latin America.[44]

What attracts FDI to Brazil? Low interest rates, trade openness, economic growth and exchange rate positively affect FDI inflows,[45] although the impact of the exchange rate is questionable, and other factors may neutralize its effect.[46]

Based on empirical results, conclusions about the motives and projections of investing firms have been established. Trade flows, inflation rate and GDP per capita are not only important determinants but also reflect the efficiency-seeking and market-seeking motives of foreign investment by multinationals. The link between trade flows and FDI flows imply that multinationals export the output from their subsidiaries established in host countries. Further indicators of FDI attractiveness include growing individual income along with large market size. High trade flows also mean a higher level of trade openness, which positively affects inward FDI. Thus, overall, market attractiveness for foreign investors depends on a savvy portfolio mix including macroeconomic growth, stability and economic openness.[47]

Institutional determinants for FDI

The existing literature focuses not only on macroeconomic determinants for outward FDI from emerging economies but also evaluates institutional factors. The relevance of institutions for competitiveness of a recipient country was noticed when the researchers observed that economic factors alone could not explain the attractiveness of a country for foreign investment. Along with macroeconomic conditions, institutions impact investment strategy of the companies by facilitating transactions and lowering their costs, thus reducing uncertainty and mitigating risks.[48] From the source-country perspective, the home government is able to promote outward FDI in emerging countries by an implementation of favorable policies such as liberal policy on capital outflows.[49] Therefore, government agencies, non-profit organizations and local authorities are able to improve market efficiency.[50]

The role of the government in corporate internationalization is related to the level of state ownership. Government involvement has an impact on the level, location and type of investment (resource seeking or market seeking).[51] Moreover, governments may influence company decisions to expand by fostering investment in strategically important sectors.[52]

The role of institutions in creating favorable investment environments is really huge. Foreign investors have much less knowledge and skills to successfully operate in a host country and thus established institutions, well-developed legal systems and low corruption levels imply lower risks. Most studies in this field found positive associations of institutional stability with FDI flows.[53]

The more focused view on BRIC economies showed that, while economic factors have a stronger influence on FDI inflows, outward FDI from BRIC countries is more influenced by the institutional environment in the host countries.[54] For example, Brazilian multinationals are mainly influenced by the regulatory quality of the host country, economic performance and cultural distance,[55] and prefer to invest in countries with good institutional environments to a higher extent than Asian firms, which can be explained by the limited global experience and knowledge about foreign markets.[56]

Emerging economies have a relatively high level of corruption, which significantly affects FDI. Corruption is inherent to the environment with poor legal and regulatory systems that do not function properly. Corruption reduces FDI flows, as it creates barriers and obstacles to foreign investment, increases transactional costs of investment and reduces profits.[57] Naturally, companies facing corruption issues in the countries of origin have an advantage in the host countries with high corruption levels. Firms with corruptive environments at home country do better to invest in the economies with similar conditions, because the firms that lack such experience will most probably be risk averse.[58] Thus location choice of FDI depends on both home- and host-country corruption indexes.

The concept of good governance implies non-corrupt public institutions, effective and transparent legal systems, political stability and governmental policies on international trade. Scholars argue that not all governance factors are equally important and highlight the role of government stability, corruption, bureaucratic quality and law and order in attracting FDI.[59] The government that establishes an effective legal system to control corruption, ensures property and individual rights protection and enhances political stability is able to attract more FDI in the country.

This explains, for example, why some of the Asian countries do not attract much FDI; this is due to political and economic instability, poor infrastructure and ineffective governance.[60] Inward FDI in Latin America suffers from the government ineffectiveness, but still increases, which might signify that economic conditions and market potential outweigh institutional inefficiencies in the region.[61]

Political stability was proved to be one of the critical arguments for inward FDI, because political risks imply high costs to foreign MNEs. For this reason, politically stable countries receive greater volumes of foreign investments. Besides, political stability induces the establishment of a favorable investment climate and thus increases inward FDI, which is evidenced by factually all EEs.

The factor reducing FDI flows is institutional distance that reflects the differences in quality of institutions between home and host countries.[62] Economies with developed institutions such as EU countries or the United States are less likely to invest in the countries with low-quality institutions. High institutional distance makes the transfer of management practices and tools from the home to the host country complex. Companies prefer full acquisitions when their targets are situated in emerging economies characterized by high institutional distance. To the contrary, if the company is willing to leverage advantages of synergies, it tends to share control with the local company.[63]

Table 5.1 FDI factors listed in the existing studies

	Host-country factors	Home-country factors	Distance
Macroeconomic	Market size Transaction costs Labor Trade openness Bilateral trade	Real GDP GDP per capita GDP growth Trade openness Bilateral trade	Geographic distance Cultural distance Institutional distance
Institutional	Rule of law Corruption Government effectiveness Infrastructure Political stability Regulatory quality	Rule of law Corruption Government effectiveness Infrastructure Political stability Regulatory quality + Taxation State ownership Capital incentives	

Legal institutions, bureaucracy and corruption have been proved to play an important role in FDI inflows independent of GDP per capita. Governments of developing countries must be encouraged to improve the quality of institutions and thus lower institutional distance in order to receive more FDI.[64]

Governments impact FDI decisions of companies through taxation policy, legal framework and bureaucratic efficiency. Compliance with government regulations implies costs to the companies that are also taken into account by the managers when making FDI decisions. An effective and transparent legal system enhances property rights and attracts more FDI.[65] Developing countries attract less investment due to weak institutions providing poor protection of property rights and lack of reliable judicial and legal systems.[66]

The papers studying the effects of institutional environment and its components argue that institutions are important determinants for outward and inward FDI in EEs. Nevertheless, there are important and paradoxical extensions that have already been discussed in the previous chapter and will be supported with companies' cases in the subsequent chapters. Overall, the scholars use similar factors to assess their influence on inward and outward FDI of emerging and developed economies (see Table 5.1), but their findings differ to a great extent depending on the region, industry and firms.

5.3 MNEs and M&As: the locomotive and the engine

However, in the end, no matter how much discussion is given regarding countries and their charms, in the end, all international business boils down to one key actor: the multinational enterprise. Although academics disagree in defining exactly what an MNE is, there are no significant differences: any corporation that is registered and operates in more than one country at a time is an MNE.[67] Our MNE may be diversely called multinational corporation, multinational enterprise, multinational company, transnational company or transnational corporation.

The history of the theoretical works in the field of international business strategy can be divided into three main periods.[68] The first period includes studies that focus on the macroeconomic level and do not address company-specific issues. This includes every-thing before 1960[69] as well as some studies published soon after that date.[70]

The second period started in 1960 with Hymer's PhD thesis: "The International Opera-tions of National Firms: A Study of Direct Foreign Investment."[71] Thereafter, studies changed their focus from country level to firm level.[72] Overall, most theoretical work concerning the firm level and the creation of the firm-specific advantages internationally were produced during this period.

The third period started in the 1980s and continues to this day. A switch of attention towards the subsidiary level characterizes this period.[73] Another important tendency of studies in the last decade is the regional orientation. Scholars increasingly focus their attention on the interaction of MNE subsidiaries with the countries in which they oper-ate, often taking a region-specific view (e.g. Eastern Europe).[74]

An important function of multinationals is that they are the most powerful and often the only vehicle for FDI. MNEs bring FDI into economies that require better develop-ment through money inflows from other countries and also transfer capital abroad out of economies where excessive capital is seeking profitable employ.

Decades ago, firms could choose freely between the two main entry modes: acquisition or greenfield. Both were viable options. Yet greenfield was often the preferred choice, since it allowed firms to choose their exact operating parameters: location, people, orga-nization of facilities and brand name. Second, the authorities in host countries were more interested in new investments and jobs, and hence provided MNEs with assistance and incentives. More recently, the room for greenfield investments has been squeezed. Setting up production facilities in too many locations makes no sense; competitors have grown stronger, or multinationals have started facing third-rate location portfolio options, per-haps left best untouched. Given these diminishing greenfield returns, the only option for MNEs that are still interested in international growth is to acquire what they cannot build. Besides, acquisitions do have their advantages, as mentioned previously.

Acquisition is, in a general sense, an act of becoming the owner of a certain property. Economically, an acquisition is the purchase of a company, either fully or partially.[75] Usu-ally this is done by purchasing a firm's shares. Generally speaking, acquisitions occur to improve the "present, short-term or long-term financial position of one or both compa-nies or to provide a strategic advantage to one or both companies involved."[76] The same holds true for mergers. The biggest difference in a merger lies in the equality of its part-ners, with both parties having agreed in advance. One could speak of a union. Mergers are mostly neglected in this book.

Scholars distinguish between two types of acquisitions.[77] The first is *acquisition of total assets,* which refers to the case where a company buys the total assets of another company. This form was very popular during the 1980s when companies acquired assets in order to then pare off individual business units and them separately at a higher profit. The most common strategic reasons to acquire a company include to purchase a direct competitor in order to consolidate the market, to gain in size and therefore use any forms of synergies or financial benefits or to acquire vital partners in the companies supply chain (supplier, distributor).

In contrast to the total asset acquisition, the *product line or business unit acquisition* is used to obtain a single product line or business unit. In this case, the company is more interested in a special new technology/product or wishes to widen its existing product range. Such transactions often occur when a company doesn't have the time to develop the technology internally (through internal or organic growth).[78]

Features of acquisitions

Acquisitions should be compared with other entry modes based on three criteria: cost of entry, risk of entry and speed of entry.[79]

An acquisition usually carries various *costs* such as a significant financial premium, transaction costs caused by information asymmetry and expenses for the integration of the acquired firm. The buyer has to take a seller's firm-specific assets into account, especially when the deal includes much tacit knowledge. Such knowledge may be difficult for staff of the buyer to access and integrate and may thus require additional resources[80] leading to unexpected secondary costs. For its part, the seller may need to unlearn old routines and overcome cultural differences.[81] An acquisition, therefore, often bears higher costs than internal development. Furthermore, scholars suggest that joint ventures are the preferred market entry strategy when big cultural differences exist between the buyer and seller companies.[82] This can be explained mainly by the high adaptation costs of an acquisition.

In addition to costs, acquisitions bear a certain *risk*. Because a large financial outlay (in the form of a lump sum) is made in advance without the certainty of success, acquisitions are generally riskier than internal development involving numerous smaller investments over a longer period of time. Furthermore, if the seller is not carefully analyzed (process of due diligence), information asymmetries may cause the buyer to overpay for the assets or, worse yet, to buy a lemon.[83] Acquisitions do provide one certain benefit over internally grown projects: the buyer is acquiring a functioning business.[84]

The *speed* with which a company wishes to enter a new market is also a decisive criterion in choosing an entry mode. Researchers agree that acquisitions take very little time, once the pool of potential companies has been evaluated.[85]

In sum, an acquisition is a suitable measure when a change of company structure is required and time is limited. It allows a firm to acquire new resources in the form of knowledge or products, or to become active in completely new markets within a short time span. However, the potential risks and costs of an acquisition should not be underestimated. The corporate road is littered with the carcasses of acquisitions gone awry, with the skeletons of unfortunate ex-CEOs still at the wheel. This explains why many firms opt for acquisitions of companies with whom they have worked before so that a friendly takeover may happen.

As for companies with a strong R&D focus, they tend to first grow internally, since they initially develop their technologies in-house and succeed in the market via their superior technology.[86] This is especially true for acquisitions in emerging markets such as Russia, since local firms cannot usually compete on the same technology level as firms from industrial countries. Furthermore, it is often difficult to establish a given technology within the seller, because of organizational inertia.[87]

Practical aspects of deal-making

Deal-making is one of the most glamourous aspects of business. For the short period of the deal – whether merger of equals or acquisition of a "weaker" company – the top managements for both buying and selling a company are in the spotlight. The transactions are usually broken down into mergers and acquisitions, which is why the art of the deal is coined M&A. Before analyzing cross-border M&A deals and their subsequent integration process, it is important to understand the motivation for the deal. What justification does a buying company have to go out and risk its future with a deal? This fundamental issue affects the procedure and the results of the deal.

M&A transactions have often been broken down into *scale deals* (those involving companies in the same business area) and *scope deals* (involving new business segments or markets).[88] M&A deals also vary according to the motives of the buyer:[89]

- *Exploitation* deals increase company value, with a low-risk level.
- *Exploration* deals open new opportunities and potential for value creation, at a medium risk level.
- *Preservation* deals help to control competitors – average value added.
- *Survival* deals help companies to retain their current position – low value added.

The biggest risk for a deal-making company is to treat all deals alike. A study – based on a quantitative assessment of 175 mergers across industries and regions taken from A. T. Kearney's global Merger Endgame database of six hundred thousand companies – identified seven types of M&A deals:[90]

- *Volume extension*: horizontal integration aiming at increasing the market share and achieving economies of scale.
- *Regional extension*: horizontal integration aiming at entering new markets and leveraging geographical advantages.
- *Product extension*: horizontal integration aiming at increasing the portfolio, cross-selling products and services.
- *Competency extension*: partial horizontal integration of companies that generally were not competitors and where the deal target is one part of a buyer's value chain (often marketing, distribution or R&D). The buyer gains access to the seller's key know-how and technologies so as to strengthen core competencies and increase customer value.
- *Forward extension*: vertical integration aiming at new market segments, channels and customers.
- *Backward extension*: vertical integration aiming at suppliers and strategic resources.
- *Business extension*: merger between different types of businesses aiming at entering new markets, diversifying business, mitigating risks, exploring new opportunities and capturing synergies.

One critical consideration of M&A is post-deal integration. Table 5.2 provides a synthetic overview of some of key success factors for transactions, depending on the deal motivation for the buyer and the characteristics of the seller.

Acquisitions are complex phenomenon, not only because they may involve huge investments but also because they require massive organizational efforts due to the involvement of different management and operational teams, as well as different corporate cultures. This means it is mission critical to define and clearly state the motives and goals of the deals in order to articulate the appropriate strategy and then deploy the right tools to reap the hoped-for results.

Acquiring across borders is not duty-free shopping . . .

Market-seeking M&As

Large markets are like honey pots. They attract M&A deals since they offer economies of scale in production and distribution of goods and services in the host country.[91] What's more, they may provide consolidation economies that can reduce the costs for all producers

Table 5.2 Critical considerations for M&A transactions[92]

Acquisition motives	Size and type of acquired business			
	Small single-unit firm	Functional	Divisionalized	Conglomerate
Increase market share in a limited product/ market domain	Integrate physical assets, production and marketing functions	Integrate product lines and functional areas	Integrate only the relevant division	
Reduce competition	Integrate procedural aspects	Emphasize procedural and socio-cultural integration		
Impulse purchase	Examine fit between strategy and acquired firm characteristics and do selective integration			
Buying technology	Integrate physical assets, especially technological systems	Employ comprehensive integration of the procedural, physical and socio-cultural aspects	Integrate physical assets and procedures of the division that possess the technology	
Rapid growth		Integrate physical assets and procedures	Restrict integration to monitor financial performance of divisions	Do not integrate beyond legal requirements
Exploit multiple synergies	Integrate comprehensively	Integrate comprehensively: emphasize functional area integration	Selectively integrate divisions that have synergy with the firm	Focus on financial synergies

Source: Shrivastava 1986

in that market.[93] As market size increases, so do opportunities for the efficient utilization of resources and for exploitation of economies of scale and scope.[94]

For multinationals, cross-border M&As are a double whammy: they can be an efficient way to gain more power and control over new markets, and they can reduce dependence on home markets.[95] Larger markets are typically associated with the ability of multinationals to develop firm-specific advantages through local acquisitions.[96] Furthermore, acquired companies in larger markets can be exploited to export to smaller regional markets. By concentrating production in one host-country location, the buyer can simultaneously gain economies of scale and minimize transportation costs.[97]

Based on this, expansion into neighboring markets makes good sense. Telecoms illustrate this well. South African telecoms operator MTN expands in the neighboring African countries, and Russian MTS concentrates on the CIS countries. In their international strategy, both prefer to regionalize rather than globalize.

Resource-seeking M&As

Emerging multinationals engage in resource-seeking deals in order to satisfy increased demand for their products both domestically and overseas.[98] For large energy companies from emerging markets, for example, the international diversification of the resource base has become vital. This provides an essential factor for the production processes: a steady supply of raw materials (inputs) at stable prices. Hence the numerous M&A transactions targeting host-country natural resources. For example, Rusal operates in Guinea to mine bauxite, whereas Alrosa (Russian diamond empire) aims at exploring South Africa since it already operates in Angola.

Deals that have resource-seeking motives are important drivers of foreign investment since firms rely on resource availability for ongoing activity.[99] Firms thus resort to cross-border M&As in order to cope with environmental uncertainty and absorb more (or cheaper) resources.[100] Such deals are simple and frequently successful since they match the resources of the seller with the needs of the buyer.[101] As can be expected, resource-rich host countries are the preferred investment location by both developed and emerging multinationals.

Strategic asset-seeking M&As

Some transactions are after "non-kickable" assets. They seek to capture knowledge in order to develop new advantages or to upgrade existing ones. Indeed, information-intensive industries contain both tacit and codified knowledge as their main competitive advantages, replacing physical assets as the key resources.[102] Knowledge-seeking deals may satisfy a desire to gain quick access to technological innovations, advanced marketing and management know-how through acquisitions. Past studies suggest that both patent-protected technologies (high-tech or pharma sectors, for example) and managerial know-how are major motivations for multinationals to engage in cross-border M&As.[103] Many have resorted to aggressive acquisitions in order to access novel product technology, established brand names and distribution networks abroad. Examples include the acquisition of Volvo by Geely and of Rover by Tata Motors. Both firms acquired technology and brand names which gave them fast penetration into the heart of the automotive industry.

By contrast, a significant number of emerging multinationals from BRIC countries operate in traditional, resource-intensive industries characterized by mature technologies. However, cross-border deals by these firms in resource-intensive sectors are also partly driven by technology-access motivations, where they aim at acquiring advanced technology, including exploration and enhanced oil and recovery technology, as well as modern oil-processing technology.[104]

Efficiency-seeking M&As

Efficiency-seeking investment is driven by the motivation to spread activities in a company's value chain across different geographies in order to exploit differences in the availability and the cost of production factors.[105] For example, a financial or consultancy services company with labor-intensive back-office operations might choose to acquire a lower-cost, yet skilled, offshoring operation in an emerging market. Such deals aim at producing intermediate or final goods in the cheapest locations, primarily for export to third markets.[106] Essentially, this corporate decision is about how best to configure its international portfolio of activities in accordance with the comparative advantages of each location[107] and in order to maximize efficiency and reduce costs. Thus this type of foreign investment is said to be efficiency seeking when the firm can gain from the common governance of geographically dispersed activities in the presence of economies of scale and scope.

Typically, labor-cost differentials are considered a key determinant of efficiency-seeking FDI.[108] However, the spread of activity geographically involves a great deal of coordination and knowledge transfer, hence cost reductions via cheaper labor start making sense for higher-cost emerging countries, such as Russia or South Korea. For example, a Russian manufacturing firm can quite easily find opportunities to lower its operating costs via cheaper labor. A Chinese or Indonesian multinational will find this more difficult.

Other motivating factors

There are plenty of motives for a company to expand its foreign operations through M&A transactions: decreasing transaction costs; gaining a monopolistic position; acquiring R&D; gaining power and some personal motives; getting access to resources, knowledge and capabilities; and gaining efficiency, economies of scale, tax benefits, etc.[109] A deal may also help a company to fulfill its strategic plan: diversifying, defending current market share and position, improving the company's innovative activities by gaining new knowledge and resources, accelerating time to market and expanding to new product or geographic segments are just a few of the strategic goals that an acquisition may help achieve.

Companies that grow by doing deals expose themselves to the risk of not gaining the necessary insights into the true success or failure factors. If the acquisitions prove themselves successful, they can provide numerous benefits such as increased market share, renewed core capabilities and access to capital or other resources at lower costs. On the other hand, failure can significantly harm a company's position, performance and internal atmosphere.

Why do certain M&A transactions succeed and others fail? None of the academic research has assessed all the crucial factors at play. Many studies emphasize one particular aspect of deal-making, with human resource issues being a key area of research.[110] Since top managers (and other people) play the most important roles in the negotiations that influence the final outcome, these studies focus on the people and their knowledge. In other words, a buyer should pay significant attention and do thorough research on the seller's internal environment and HR policies in order to be successful. Further studies underline that a buyer with previous transaction experience will have greater chances at renewed success, not only in the M&A process but also in post-acquisition performance.[111] Prior deal experience, or hiring managers with such experience, tends to ensure better performance not only in the short term but also in the long run. The hypothesis here is that deal-making is considered a difficult and expensive strategy. Huge investments and many other resources are required, implying that the costs of failure are quite high. Managers who have previous deals under their belts are better at predicting potential problems and devising better solutions.

The fit between the two or more companies participating in the deal is also key to success, according to scholars. When two companies start negotiating as buyer-seller, they should assess both internal factors (such as corporate culture, HR approaches, internal procedures, knowledge) and external ones (market conditions, competition, access to suppliers, customers and resources, etc.). The chances for a successful outcome will be much higher if there is compatibility on these issues between the two companies and their environments. In the future, the buyer may then face fewer problems and conflicts.

Since many different aspects of M&A are equally important, the majority of research highlights the fact that all research is highly interconnected and complementary. One of the key measures of M&A success is to understand whether the deal enabled the company to build competitive advantage, or if something went wrong and it did not succeed in gaining this advantage. Furthermore, such competitive advantage gains should not only be in the short term but also for the long run.

During crisis periods, the approach to M&A deals may change. Buyers may be satisfied with short-term gains and sellers more desperate to close a deal in order to survive (the so-called fire sale). Buyers can acquire companies at lower valuations and then build the businesses up from a quite low level. Even so, most sellers are not stupid! When negotiating their terms for a deal, they still consider long-term strategic perspectives.

How do things change in the cross-border context? Not necessarily much, with one study showing that assessing internal factors (e.g. resources, capabilities and competencies) as the key determinant in gaining competitive advantage in cross-border expansion.[112] This means that a multinational should first evaluate its resources and then decide whether an M&A transaction is the right choice as an entry mode. Examples of such resources include company knowledge, expertise, experience, networks, financial capabilities and much more.

Nevertheless, the rapidly changing business environment in most industries makes it difficult to build sustainable competitive advantages in the long run. Doing a one-time deal does not guarantee steady-state survival. A successful cross-border buyer will need to fit its home-country internal capabilities, competences and resources to the needs and characteristics of the host-country internal environment. This is critical considering the international nature of cross-border M&A and all the more so in more highly volatile emerging markets.[113]

M&A risks and opportunities

Different studies distinguish various risks and opportunities that may lead to positive or negative synergy creation. Successful deals face two types of potential risks.[114] The first is the *means of payment* risk. Deals with all-cash payment are considered to have better results than all-equity or combined payment deals. Second, *fraction of managerial ownership* in the buyer firm is important. If managers don't own shares of the firm, they are less motivated to produce good results and less interested in integrating the acquired company.

The impact of an *industry specification* on M&A is another important consideration. After evaluating the results of thirty thousand M&A deals conducted across different industries, scholars founded similarities among deals industry by industry. Therefore, they concluded that the specific industry should also be taken into account when planning a transaction.[115] For instance, across all regions that local deals dominated the automotive M&A landscape, only 8%–10% of deals within this industry are cross borders.[116]

Another comprehensive analysis of forty-five thousand different metrics connected with post-merger integration identified the thirty-five factors that potentially influence the integration process the most. These factors were divided into four risk categories: synergy, structure, people and project risks.[117] Naturally, cross-border deals need to also consider the different social, cultural and political issues at play.

5.4 Intangible strategies: fueling the process

The internationalization process is traditionally considered as a sequence of steps starting from "easy" or "light" forms (trade/export) to more complicated or "heavy" forms (acquisitions or greenfields). This perspective reflects the natural evolution of companies over time, as both internationalization and firm size increase.

Alas, if only it were so simple! That would be without taking into account the twenty-first century profusion of companies that go international at warp speed: service companies, often of lesser scale, that forge ahead faster since they have large networks and do not need to confront the headaches of products and fixed assets. In this subsection, three additional perspectives on internationalization are provided: service firms, companies "born global" and partnerships.

Internationalization of service companies

Some researchers argue that the theories developed to explain the internationalization of manufacturing sectors are equally applicable to the service branches,[118] while other scholars have questioned this assumption.[119] Do hard services (e.g. electricity maintenance or water supply), with their decoupled production and consumption, and soft services (e.g. consultancy or security), for which production and consumption occur simultaneously, differ in their internationalization processes?[120] Hard services can be internationalized in the manner of manufacturing industries; soft services cannot. Hence soft services should logically follow different strategies.[121] Hard services must be physically close to customers (imagine car dealerships or elevators installations), which is not true for soft services (programmers or lawyers can serve their clients by email or phone).

Soft services firms face export difficulties because this requires a separation of producer and consumer,[122] and therefore they are limited to the choice between contractual relationship, licensing, franchising and foreign direct investment (joint venture or wholly owned subsidiary). Some of these strategies require substantial resources and managerial commitment, and do not allow the company to benefit from the experience accumulated through a more gradual approach.[123]

Scholars have identified three modes of service export:[124] 1) supplying the service from operations based in the home country to customers located abroad (Internet companies and media – for example, CNN in Russia), 2) supplying the service from operations based in the host country to indigenous customers (telecoms – e.g. MTS in India), and 3) foreign customers receive services in the home country of the service provider (tourism and entertainment parks – e.g. Disneyland in the United States).

The resource-based view (RBV, see Chapter 4) has emerged as a framework in examining suitable competitive advantage in the areas of service marketing and management,[125] pointing out that the degree of control needed over the business influences the choice of entry decision. Control determines risks, success of strategic goals, the degree of intangibility of services and the ultimate performance of the company.

Important elements in the framework for service firms' internationalization are company-level resources; management characteristics; firm characteristics, including competitive and international advantages; degree of involvement/risk; and, finally, host-country factors.[126] Firm-level resources, management and firm characteristics allow the company to generate unique competitive and international advantages, which can then generate returns. Company-related resources and characteristics lead to the strategy choice given the consideration by host-country factors, which also affect the decision on entry mode.

Cultural distance does not significantly influence the choice of entry mode made by service firms.[127] Nevertheless, a negative relationship between international experience and the choice of higher control when operating abroad is partially supported by earlier studies' results. Service firms tended to use more integrated (higher control) entry modes the larger the size of the foreign market and the greater the unavailability of host-country suitable partners and the firm's corporate policy on keeping control of operations.[128] These firms tend to use less integrated (lower-control) strategies the greater the restriction on foreign ownership, the firm's aversion to environmental risk, the desire to be rapidly established and the constraints on internal resources.

The fact that service companies from EEs are capable of growth and internationalization has tended to be ignored.[129] Service firms from EEs are increasing their efforts to integrate into the global economy, and they have already started exporting abroad. Scholars have suggested several drivers behind the considerable growth of the service sector in recent decades in the economies of both industrialized and developing countries: intense competition in domestic markets, profit margin pressure and the opportunity to develop business in foreign markets.[130]

The established viewpoint is that the international expansion of companies from emerging markets is primarily accomplished by production at home and exporting goods to foreign markets.[131] These companies follow both the internationalization[132] and international product life-cycle[133] models. They first go overseas through exporting and then when market knowledge is obtained, they commit in the form of more investment-oriented strategies. The majority of EMFs are still in the early stages of the internationalization process, whereby exporting is dominant.[134] The exception is the high-tech companies which internationalize "virtually" without having the need to invest or export.

Born global

History

In the beginning of the 1990s, a new concept was introduced because of the emergence of a new type of multinational: the "born global" company.[135] Companies of this new type started appearing in developed economies (United States, Australia, Japan, Denmark, etc.), but born global companies can be found in developing countries as well by now. Internet firms illustrate this phenomenon, with companies such as Alibaba, Google or Facebook being present worldwide immediately.

Although definitions of born global companies vary, one could generalize as follows: a born global company is an SME (small-to-medium enterprise) that goes international shortly after the company's establishment (typically defined as two to three years by most researchers) and that has two basic features: a niche market orientation and a need for international scale to reach success.[136] At the same time, some companies, even in the natural resource sectors, could be qualified as born global, with the example of Inter RAO UES (see Chapter 12), established by the Russian energy holding to export electricity production.

Even though the born global concept dates back to 1993, it is still considered to be relatively new and understudied. The concept of born global was introduced in 1993, although some academics hinted at its conceptual existence before then. Why? Some companies were showing deviations from the traditional, gradual internationalization patterns. The growing presence of homogenous outlets on a global scale facilitated turbo internationalization, so to speak. Did this spell the end of the Uppsala model, with its slow geographic expansion and relatively slow acquiring of foreign market knowledge? Indeed the new breed of born global companies was going global fast, as a core part of their development strategy and using the home-country market only for testing and initial set-up.

Features of born global company

At the core of the born global species is the notion that it requires international scale quickly. What does this mean? Usually, it refers to one of two things: either the home country is insufficient for reaching breakeven, or it is too small for the company's true development. This is often described as "the company addresses the global market as its target market." So the core determinants of a born global company are global market insight and company size.

There are several other features that characterize born global companies:

- The extensive use of personal and business networks in international development – namely, for many of the companies engaged in technology-intensive industries (even though technology was often not proprietary and available to others).[137]
- The involvement of the entrepreneurial skills of the CEO or founder. In this sense, the management role was addressed as a primary growth driver, also mentioning product customization and international marketing application.[138] The role of the company founder is also widely considered as a critical explanation, with prior international experience (academic or professional) and commitment to international development being key traits.[139] In the case of born global SMEs, the entrepreneurial role is very important due to high responsibility and risk.[140]
- The strong presence of intangible assets.
- One important implication from research is that niche markets with easier international trade were seen as fertile soil for the emergence of born global companies – a basic distinction between born global companies and traditional international ventures.[141]
- Brand development has also been pointed out as a determinant that facilitates the internationalization process (think Starbucks).[142] Some Finland-based, born global companies suggest specific features connected to branding activities that affect born global performance in their international development.[143]

The born global theory is largely based on the *non-availability approach* developed by Kravis, which is based on Heckshner–Ohlin model and could be treated as an extension of the latter. According to this theory, there are two basic reasons for international trade: technological progress and product differentiation. Technological progress implies difference between production costs in different countries. This difference is made of different factors – for example, of resources availability – though technological advance is the key factor in this sense.[144] The Heckshner–Ohlin model, therefore, infers that specific countries and companies from that country, given their level of technology development, will tend to produce a certain type of good.

The *technology gap concept* by Posner, which described the introduction of new goods to a market in the international perspective, is also important to the born global fans. A country that launches a new product (as a result of research and entrepreneurial activities inside the country) has an advantage vis-à-vis other countries due to their inability to produce the same good.[145] The time period until local production can start is called imitation lag, and it consists of several parts. First is the demand lag: the time between the introduction of the product in the innovating country and awareness about the innovation among potential foreign customers. Second is the foreign reaction lag: the time before companies in the importing countries start considering this as a potential competitive threat. Then there is the domestic reaction lag: the time required for all companies in the importing country to understand the competition. Finally, there is the learning period: the time required for the local companies to learn to produce the item and begin selling it.

This theory is hardly useful in its minutiae, but it is important as a framework to understand foreign reactions in international markets. At the same time, it brings imitation to mind, which is especially important in specific industries where the speed of foreign reactions is very fast.

Applicability to BRIC countries

Much recent research has focused on born global companies originating from emerging economies. One primary insight here is the connection between customer orientation and key development drivers for born global companies. In a sample of Indian born global firms[146] confirmed by Brazilian research,[147] a relationship between financial performance and knowledge intensity, customer orientation and entrepreneurial culture was found.

Born global firms have one distinctive feature: their rapid internationalization.[148] However, they may be following the sequential internationalization of the Uppsala model, but at turbo speed. Born global firms prefer one dominant internationalization path rather than expanding geographic scope or diversifying foreign operations.[149]

Born global firms from emerging markets pursue their internationalization through non-systematically planned actions. What's more, these firms are more likely to be born regional than born global.[150] Strategic alliances and networking activities which assist firms with critical resources and knowledge, as well as institutional and government support, are among the critical success factors.

One good example of a born global industry from emerging markets is Chinese wind turbine manufacturing. It sprouted from nowhere in the mid-2000s to reach world leadership by 2009.[151] The growth of wind turbine manufacturing in China is attributed not only to the development of Chinese domestic market, but more significantly to its expansion into foreign markets.

Partnership: the "light" version of internationalization?

In recent decades, a great number of works have analyzed partnerships in the international environment.[152] Most of these studies argue that partnerships are recommended for large firms[153] as well as for small- and medium-sized firms.[154] Partnerships in international markets are necessary mainly because individual players may not have all the assets required for overseas expansion such as country-specific knowledge.[155] Various empirical studies[156] have supported the argument for partnerships. Examples of strategic partnership are Xerox and EDS IT outsourcing, or Marriott Hotel and Tyson's Corner.

Partnerships are defined in various ways by different sources. A strategic partnership is defined as a management approach used by two or more organizations which share a commitment to achieve a common goal by combining their resources and coordinating their activities.[157] A partnership may or may not involve equity investments. It denotes strategic or/and operational coordination, joint research and development, technology exchanges, co-marketing, etc. A business partnership is usually seen as a type of entity in which partners share in the profits or losses of the business. Key features of a partnership in a business context are most often associated with the collaborative relationship in which the main features are joint work toward shared objectives through a mutually agreed division of labor, advantages for all parties who are involved, management by ownership which leads to the rising sustainability for all partners and an increasing reputation of all parties involved due to the reliance on each other's needs.[158]

Partnerships in an internationalization context are often referred to multi-organizational collaborations, which are, in turn, defined as cooperative, interorganizational relationships that are negotiated in an ongoing communicative process. This term encompasses various forms of cooperation, such as alliances, associations, consortia, joint ventures, networks and roundtables.[159] More generally, a multi-organizational collaboration is seen as a situation in which people from different companies or organizations collaborate across organizational boundaries towards some positive end and which takes the form of alliances, joint ventures, networks, contacting and outsourcing, joint working and so on.[160] It is therefore often project based.

As partnerships can be traditionally identified as collaboration agreements and relationships between two or more companies are set up to reach a number of coherent aims participating in a deal while remaining independent outside this deal,[161] from an international operations perspective, partnership-based strategy includes joint ventures, licensing and joint distribution networks.[162]

Sometimes alliances are the only way to expand geographically when political or legal barriers exist. As an example, in the case of airlines, different alliances are a common way of expanding abroad because direct investments are immense and transactions can become legal nightmares given national security concerns. For instance, the airspace above specific countries or special itineraries may be off-limits for foreign operators, while an alliance gives firms the opportunity to sell tickets on partner company flights[163] and thus overcome legal barriers to increase market share.

The traditional literature indicates that many firms nowadays have a strong need for partnerships to gain access to external resources.[164] Much discussion is dedicated to the analysis of partnership by SMEs. Since smaller firms generally suffer from resource constraints in overseas markets, partnerships render international expansion possible.[165] They can be used by SMEs to build innovative capabilities and technological competence; to overcome weaknesses, such as poor financial position or low levels of expertise in production, marketing and management;[166] and to access alternative methods of serving customers.[167]

Analyzing partnerships in the area of science and technology, scholars insist that in this area, public/private collaboration is highly valuable, with different participants jointly contributing either financial, research, human or infrastructure resources.[168] As such, many of these partnerships focus on innovations and are more than a simple contract mechanism.

High-technology firms have demonstrated the value of relationships in boosting international growth[169] and competitive advantage, implying that partnering relationships between firms are influential throughout the internationalization process. In one specific case, a software firm's strategic partner enabled it to offer a more complete solution to customers and provide localization or other development assistance. Though partnering is seen as an integral part of the international entry mode palette,[170] limited research exists that examines the partnering activities of high-tech companies. Partnerships are quite complicated to monitor, but they make cross-border operations both easier and more reliable in terms of local support, knowledge of the market and business relations in the region, which are hard to gain through solo penetration.

Yet partnerships are no panacea, starting with the difficulty in finding appropriate and reliable partners. Then partnerships can be hard to manage, since they are a delicate balancing act: the partners involved want their financial independence, yet wish to acquiring benefits from the partners. Furthermore, since no joint business unit is established, each partner can have different objectives, regardless of the other partners' interests. This means paying attention to the actions of all partners and can require company resources. Furthermore, a partnership may make a company vulnerable. Sharing parts of production processes, unique resources or expertise and disclosing internal information can lead to leaks. This information can be exploited either by partner companies (e.g. to improve their market presence and to compete with the "injured" company) or by third parties who might have gained this information by chance. These security issues are considerable, and it is difficult to strike a balance in what information to provide to partners. The openness is an equilibrium somewhere between the necessity to gain profits from the partnership and not too much so as to let competition profit from it.

Despite the managerial complexity of the partnership, it is definitely useful for establishing a presence in foreign markets, gaining inner knowledge and getting the most out of specific resources without over-stretching the corporate budget or capabilities.

Conclusion

To conclude, these three concepts – service firms' internationalization, born global and partnerships – open additional horizons in understanding why and how firms internationalize in contrast to more traditional viewpoints and what can be an alternative international strategy that might help a company obtain markets and customers abroad without having strong financial or institutional support.

In reality, there are many more intangibles that explain why firms internationalize, what makes them successful (or not) in foreign markets and how they develop their competitive advantages during expansion abroad. Some of these explanations (such as governmental involvement, image improvement and political connections) will be presented in Chapter 11. Knowledge and culture-related actions will be discussed in Chapter 12.

References

1 Lu and Beamish 2001.
2 Schumpeter 1954.
3 Dixit and Stiglitz 1977.
4 Dixit and Stiglitz 1977.
5 Melitz 2003.
6 Bernard and Jensen 1999.
7 Helpman, Melitz and Yeaple 2004.
8 Ibid.
9 Greenaway and Kneller 2004.
10 Kaleka and Berthon 2006.
11 Powers and Loyka 2010.
12 Bernard and Jensen 1999.
13 Ibid.
14 Baldwin and Gu 2003.
15 Greenaway and Kneller 2004.
16 Greenaway, Gullstrand and Kneller 2005.
17 Barassi and Zhou 2012.
18 Mauro 1995; Lambsdorff 2007.

19 Tanzi and Davoodi 2001; Damania, Fredriksson and Mani 2004; Fisman and Svensson 2007.
20 Kolstad and Wiig 2012.
21 Te Velde and Bezemer 2006.
22 Dunning 2001; Dunning and Narula 1996.
23 Dunning 1988.
24 Buckley and Casson 1998.
25 Stoian and Filippaios 2008; Stoian 2013.
26 Bellak 2001; Andreff 2002.
27 Salehizadeh 2007.
28 Dunning 2000.
29 Akerlof 1970; Williamson 1971; Jensen and Meckling 1976.
30 Globerman and Shapiro 2002.
31 La Porta, Lopez-de-Silanes, Shleifer, and Vishny 1999.
32 Demirbag et al. 2007.
33 Brouthers and Brouthers 2000.
34 Quer, Claver and Rienda 2011.
35 Wang, Hong, Kafouros and Boateng 2012.
36 Rui and Yip 2008.
37 Berning and Holtbrügge 2012.
38 Aleksynska and Havrylchyk 2013.
39 Bengoa and Sanchez-Robles 2003.
40 Quazi 2007.
41 Jadhav 2012.
42 Quazi 2007.
43 Vogiatzoglou 2007; Hyun and Kim 2010.
44 Zhang and Daly 2011.
45 Ho et al. 2013.
46 Hyun and Kim 2010.
47 Amal and Tomio 2015.
48 North 1990; Mudambi and Navarra 2002.
49 Goh and Wong 2011.
50 Bevan and Estrin 2004.
51 Wang, Hong, Kafouros and Boateng 2012; Peng et al. 2008.
52 Du and Boateng 2015.
53 Wei 2000; Alfaro et al. 2005; Aizenman and Spiegel 2006.
54 Malhotra, Russow and Singh 2014.
55 Amal and Tomio 2015.
56 Jadhav 2012.
57 Egger and Winner 2005; Habib and Zurawicki 2001.
58 Cuervo-Cazurra, 2008.
59 Mishra and Daly 2007.
60 Mengistu and Adhikary 2011.
61 Amal et al. 2010.
62 Bénassy-Quéré et al. 2007.
63 Contractor et al. 2014.
64 Brada, Drabek and Perez 2012.
65 Globerman and Shapiro 2002.
66 Seyoum 2009.
67 Encyclopaedia Britannica.
68 Rugman, Verbeke and Nguyen 2011.
69 Dunning 1958.
70 Vernon 1966.
71 Hymer 1976.
72 Kindelberger 1969; Caves 1971; Dunning 1977; Johanson and Vahlne 1977; Rugman 1981; Zaheer 1995.
73 Hamel and Prahalad 1983; Birkinshaw 1996, 1997; Rugman and Verbeke 2001.
74 Manea and Pearce 2006; Rugman and Verbeke 2008.

75　Halibozek and Kovacich 2005.
76　Ibid.
77　Ibid.
78　Lee and Lieberman 2010.
79　Ibid.
80　Cheng 2006.
81　Barkema and Vermeulen 1998.
82　Hennart and Reddy 1997.
83　Akerlof 1970.
84　Lee and Lieberman 2010.
85　Ibid.
86　Barkema and Vermeulen 1998.
87　Ibid.
88　Rouse and Frame 2009
89　Angwin 2007.
90　Rothenbuecher, Schrottke and Niewiem 2008.
91　Kyrkilis and Pantelidis 2003; Tolentino 2010.
92　Shrivastava 1986.
93　Dunning 2009.
94　UNCTAD 1998.
95　Pfeffer and Salancik 2003.
96　Di Giovanni 2005; Nicholson and Salaber 2013.
97　De Beule and Duanmu 2012.
98　Ibid.
99　Deng and Yang 2015.
100　Pfeffer and Salancik 2003.
101　Haleblian, Devers, McNamara, Carpenter and Davison 2009.
102　Nachum and Zaheer 2005.
103　Rabbiossi, Stefano and Bertoni 2012; Jullens 2013.
104　Kalotay and Panibratov 2013.
105　Nachum and Zaheer 2005.
106　Dunning 1993.
107　Zaheer and Marakhan 2001.
108　Schneider and Frey 1985; Wheeler and Mody 1992; London and Ross 1995; Summary and Summary 1995.
109　Boeh and Beamish 2007.
110　Daniel 2001; Latukha and Panibratov 2015.
111　Vasilaki and O'Regan 2008.
112　Prahalad and Hamel 1990.
113　Sarala and Vaara 2010.
114　Goergen and Renneboog 2003.
115　Kröger, Von Zeisel 2004.
116　http://www.pwc.com/gx/en/automotive/publications/assets/pwc-auto-manda-insights-2014.pdf
117　Gerds and Strottmann 2010.
118　Boddewyn, Soehl and Picard 1986.
119　Johanson and Vahlne 1990.
120　Majkgård and Sharma 1998.
121　Erramilli 1990; Ekeledo and Sivakumar 1998.
122　Erramilli 1990.
123　Carman and Lengeard 1980.
124　Aharoni 1999.
125　Javalgi and Martin 2007.
126　Ibid.
127　Sanchez-Peinado and Pla-Barber 2006.
128　Erramilli 1990.
129　Pauwels and Ruyter 2005.
130　Cardone-Riportella and Cazorla-Papis 2001.

131 Wortzel and Vernon-Wortzel 1988.
132 Johanson and Vahlne 1977.
133 Vernon 1966.
134 Aulakh, Kotabe and Teegen 2000.
135 Cavusgil and Knight 2009.
136 Rennie 1993.
137 Ganitsky 1989.
138 Oviatt and McDougall 1994.
139 Andersson and Victor 2003.
140 Shirokova and Tsukanova 2013.
141 Knight and Cavusgil 1996.
142 Gabrielsson and Manek Kirpalani 2004.
143 Knight, Madsen and Servais 2004.
144 Gandolfo 1998.
145 Vernon 1966.
146 Kim, Basu, Naidu and Cavusgil 2011.
147 Dib, da Rocha and da Silva 2010.
148 Hashai and Almor 2004.
149 Hashai 2011.
150 Kiss et al. 2012.
151 Lewis 2011.
152 Stuart 2000; Phan, Styles and Patterson 2005; Brouthers and Hennart 2007.
153 Hill 2001.
154 Lu and Beamish 2001.
155 Johanson and Vahlne 1977.
156 Burgers, Hill and Kim 1993; Shan, Walker and Kogut 1994.
157 Bennett and Jayes 1995.
158 Axelrod 2004.
159 Lawrence, Hardy and Phillips 2002.
160 Huxham and Vangen 2005.
161 Phan, Styles and Patterson 2005.
162 Lee and Gongming 2008.
163 Kraats 2000.
164 Lu and Beamish 2001.
165 Coviello and Munro 1997; Harris and Wheeler 2005.
166 Jarratt 1998.
167 Elmuti and Kathawala 2001.
168 Cervantes 1998.
169 Coviello and Munro 1997.
170 Kanter 1994.

6 Can competitive advantage cross borders?

Competitive advantage is an important theoretical argument in the analysis of company strategy and a critical factor in explaining company successes and failures. Companies strive to outcompete their rivals by seeking advantages that are most beneficial in their particular business environment. The stronger the company's competitive advantage, the greater the chances it has to expand successfully in foreign markets. There is a hitch however! Who guarantees that a domestic competitive advantage will provide the same benefits in foreign markets where the business environment may differ radically from the home market?

In this chapter, the ambiguous role and meaning of competitive advantage (CA) for emerging multinationals (EMNEs) is discussed. According to established theories, emerging multinationals are at a disadvantage vis-à-vis advanced market firms. On the other hand, these disadvantages may work to the benefit of emerging multinationals when expanding into other developing markets. This implies that the concept of CA differs from what was suggested by scholars a few decades ago. This also provides emerging multinationals more efficient entry and competition in many international marketplaces.

6.1 Environmental effects on investing firms

FDI is regularly mentioned in tandem with the loosely defined investment climate described as "the institutional policy and regulatory environment in which firms operate."[1] Other academics mention the entrepreneurial climate: ". . . the result of many factors, including the minimization of rules and regulations, tax incentives, and training and counseling services for new businesses."[2] These two definitions (and many others) seek to capture the Holy Grail: what combination of factors makes a country attractive to investment from abroad?

Investment climate is routinely viewed to be the main (and sometimes the only) FDI determinant. However, FDI allocation lies beyond investment climate alone – namely, since investors from different countries estimate investment climates differently. Also, FDI-related decisions are made at the company level, where complex concepts such as investment climate may be of little relevance. At the same time, while companies do not take investment climate per se into account, factors included in the complex indicator do affect corporate decisions regarding foreign investments.

Environmental factors behind the growth of FDI in EEs

FDI is "one of the most stable forms of capital inflows to emerging markets . . . even during the emerging market crises of the mid-to-late 1990s, foreign direct investment did not flee emerging markets."[3] This notion is upheld by the FDI data provided in the previous section. Researchers cite several potential explanations for the development of FDI flows. For example, FDI depends on macroeconomic stability.[4] It means that global flows are stable in the long run but each company is choosy about where to direct its investments.

Many scholars consider the quality of institutions as a key FDI driver, especially relevant for emerging countries. Many scholars refer to corruption as a strong FDI barrier,[5] which acts like a tax, thus lowering investor interest in the country. Government support for local companies (indicating protection from foreign competition) is another factor hindering FDI from entering emerging countries.[6] In many developing economies, competition conditions improved as a result of economic crises, which diminished the state's ability to protect local firms. One opinion exists that crises may lead to a reduction in corruption and therefore ultimately lead to lower FDI barriers.[7] This assumption can be validated by taking a look at the growth of FDI inflows to Russia after 1998 and 2009. However, one needs to consider that this is not the only (and certainly not the most important) factor that was responsible for the post-crisis growth of FDI inflows.

Another perspective holds that national boundaries create transaction costs: "Within a country, implicit contracts are often embedded in social networks which provide sanctions against opportunistic behavior."[8] Additionally, transaction costs arise from the difference in regulation and the way of doing business, both formal and informal. Moreover, unification of institutions across countries (a process that takes place in Russia in the form of road maps) may not always be desirable:

> Differences in national institutions serve a real and useful purpose. They are rooted in national preferences, sustain social compacts, and allow developing nations to find their way out of poverty. Eliminating this diversity might not be beneficial even if it were possible.[9]

Furthermore, additional factors affecting FDI flows may include international tax regimes. For example, the British Virgin and Cayman Islands rank highly for FDI outflows because they create favorable conditions for hosting capital and reinvesting it elsewhere. FDI and trade flows are inversely correlated with distance (the so-called gravity model). This means that investors prefer larger economies that are also located geographically closer to their home countries. Finally, previously accumulated foreign direct investment (FDI stock) may attract further investment, somewhat like a herding instinct. Therefore, FDI stock may also play a significant role in explaining further FDI growth.

Investment climate: inward FDI view

Potential FDI determinants can be classified into three categories by relation to the government policy model. First, there are endogenous factors that can be directly affected by government actions in the short run. These factors depend on specific economic policies – for example, the burden of government regulation on business, the corporate tax rates, the minimum time required to set up a company or the speed to export goods. The type of existing political system relates to the group of exogenous factors, while the actual governance applied by it is an endogenous factor.

Second, FDI is affected by exogenous factors upon which governments have no short-term control. These factors include the corruption index, the quality of local infrastructure and growth of GDP per capita. Although these parameters cannot be controlled in the short term, governments can certainly affect them in the long run.

Third, there are factors relating to the global economic environment that are outside the government's control, whether in the long or the short terms. Among these factors are major economic shocks such as the recent recession or drops in commodity prices.

While the first two groups of parameters are addressed in the present work, it is virtually impossible to do the same for this third group of parameters. However, it is still possible to take them into account indirectly by introducing dummy variables for the advanced/non-advanced types of economies and geographical regions, and also by using fixed effects in the panel analysis to capture the year-by-year changes in the macroeconomic conditions.

To qualify a country's investment climate, the complex indicator tries to capture all endogenous and exogenous factors in a single number and may include the following endogenous factors:

- quality of governance
- tax revenue
- total tax rate
- cost of starting a business
- property rights
- burden of government regulation
- time required to start a business
- time required to export
- impact of rules on FDI
- employment flexibility.

Exogenous factors typically include the following:

- GDP
- local competition
- openness to trade
- balanced budget
- inflation
- quality of overall infrastructure
- cluster development
- quality of local suppliers
- technology transfer
- reliance of professional management
- corruption
- entrepreneurial activity
- education.

Three different classifications of investment climate determinants are provided below: Buckley and Casson (Table 6.1), Dunning (Table 6.2) and more recent studies (Table 6.3).

Country-specific factors affecting outward investments

For multinationals seeking to invest abroad, an understanding of host-country environments helps to shape the investment strategy. Yet this evaluation is often complicated due

Table 6.1 Multi-determinants of FDI (multi-level view)[10]

Industry-specific factors	Region-specific factors	Nation-specific factors	Firm-specific factors
Product type Market structure Economies of scale	Distance Cultural differences	Political factors Financial factors	Management skills

Source: Adapted from Buckley and Casson 1976

Table 6.2 Determinants of FDI (OLI or Dunning view)[11]

Ownership advantages	Location advantages	Internalization advantages
Company production process: patents, technical knowledge, management skills, reputation	Host-market advantages: access to protected market, favorable taxes, lower production and transportation costs, lower risk, favorable structure of competition	Lowering transaction costs, minimizing technology imitation, maintaining firm reputation via effective management and quality control

Source: Adapted from Dunning and Lundan, 2008a (p. 101–102)

Table 6.3 Determinants of FDI (push-pull view)[12]

Push factors	Pull factors		Locational factors
Home policy direction (examples: "Go Global" policy implemented by Chinese government) State ownership BIT (bilateral investments treaties)	Host formal institutions	Host informal institutions	**Market size:** GDP, GDP per capita, GDP growth **Resources:** ore and metal export, gas and oil export **Strategic assets:** annually applied patents **Trade dependence:** trade volume

Source: Adapted from Buckley, Pei, Qing, Surender and Pan 2015 Buckley, P., Yu, P., Liu, Q., Munjal, S. and Tai, P. *Institution and Location Strategies of Multinationals Corporations from Emerging Economies: Evidence from China Cross-border Merger and Acquisitions.* Conference proceeding, AIB UK and Ireland Chapter.

to the political shifts and policy changes that accompany elections. The state launches initiatives and regulates business environment but can send contradictory messages. Moreover, some of the factors can be controlled in the short run (for example, tax rates), while others can only be manipulated in the long run (for example, overall quality of infrastructure) (Table 6.4).

6.2 International perspective for competitive advantage

Theoretical interpretation of competitive advantage

Michael Porter initially introduced the term *competitive advantage* in his 1990 book *Competitive Advantage* and defined it as a strategic advantage that enables a company to

Table 6.4 How country-specific characteristics affect FDI[13]

Type of FDI*	Reasons for the company to invest	Important factors for the company	Corresponding factors on the country level
Horizontal	• Reduce production costs by exploiting low operating expenses in the target country • Further growth of the product market	1 Presence of skilled labor	• Average length of workforce education • Length of advanced education (secondary, tertiary)
		2 Overall cost of local labor	• Average level of wages • Ability to lay off
		3 Ability to export produced goods back to home or target market	• Country's openness to trade • Time to export goods
Vertical	• Reduce transaction costs • Access local market of the target country	1 Ability to either import production components or buy them from local suppliers	• Country's openness to trade • Quality of local suppliers • Level of cluster development
		2 Sophisticated local market possessing purchasing power	• GDP per capita • GDP per capita growth • Sophistication of marketing
		3 Limited competition on the local market	• Intensity of local competition
Both horizontal and vertical	• Combination of reasons for horizontal and vertical FDI	1 High quality of infrastructure	• Quality of overall infrastructure
		2 Reasonable level of financial burden of operating in the target country	• Total corporate tax rate • Overall level of taxes collected by the state • Financial burden imposed by regulations • Corruption index
		3 Effective legal system	• Level of property rights protection • Quality of governance • Speed of judicial system
		4 Presence of competent management to avoid agency problems	• Reliability and quality of professional management
		5 Government support for new businesses	• Cost of starting a business • Time required to start a business • Entrepreneurial activity in the target country
		6 Healthy macroeconomic situation in the target country	• Level of inflation • Budget balance • GDP • GDP per capita growth

Source: Adapted from Faeth 2009

* Some country-level factors can be controlled by the state, at least to a certain extent, which, in turn, may affect companies' decisions to invest in a particular country.

outperform competitors in its industry.[14] This advantage strengthens the position of the firm in its competitive environment. In other words, this is something that a company has, while its competitors do not; something that the company can do and others cannot; and something that the firm does better than its competitors.[15]

CA was also defined as the ability to perform better than competitors in a particular market, which is achieved by the corresponding use of resources and capabilities. Since superior performance under high competitive pressure remains a crucial topic of business research, many definitions of CA co-exist. One of the other classical interpretations of possessing CA means "implementing a value-creating strategy not simultaneously being implemented" by rivals.[16] In addition, for a firm, CA means that it gets a constantly higher profit over rival firms or has a corresponding potential.[17]

Competitive advantage is interpreted according to several different views.

The *industrial organization view* highlights the importance of structural forces in the industry, the competitive environment and the resulting impact on CA. The logic here is that industry can be clearly characterized by average profitability, which in turn determines the profitability of the firms. Within any given industry, companies must exert continuous efforts to capture and retain advantageous positions.

Consequently, the strategic analysis is based on the identification and evaluation of external forces, thus implying external focus. Therefore, since all companies within a particular industry are influenced by the same set of factors, the ultimate goal of any firm is to achieve advantageous differences with respect to competitors (e.g. low pricing, better service, different positioning). It is worth mentioning that CA depends on company positioning, which, in combination with industry factors, influences corporate profits. In a high-opportunity market, a well-positioned company will reap higher-than-average profits. On the other hand, a company operating in the presence of negative forces and in a weak competitive position will not achieve desirable profitability levels.

The *guerrilla view* emphasizes the fleeting nature of CA due to the unstable environment that experiences continuous change. Since country-specific factors, combined with evolving technological edge, are not constant, sustainable CA cannot exist in a static manner. Therefore, being a market leader requires rapid and frequently repeated strategic adaptations and course corrections. Reconfiguring company assets and strategy implementation will help overcome competitors and maintain market share in the long term.[18]

The *resource-based view* (RBV) is probably the most widely used in order to describe formation of competitive advantage. According to the RBV, the firm is a unique combination of assets and capabilities in a very broad sense. Since the company's actual market experience can also be considered valuable, each competing firm has a virtually unique combination of resources. These resources and capabilities determine the effectiveness and efficiency of operations, and those that are critical to the company can turn into sustainable CA and therefore achieve desired profitability. Resources in this case can take the shape of financial, physical, human, intangible, structural and cultural assets used by organizations to develop, manufacture and deliver its products or services to customers.[19]

Not all resources are born equal. Some do drive competitiveness, so the following logic was offered to better identify which resources may generate competitive advantages:[20]

1   Resources are considered valuable if they add value that can be measured. Such resources can help leverage external inputs (e.g. innovative practices or marketing initiatives) so as to increase sales or offset negative influences. Flexibility is paramount: the value of specific resources can be brought into question when external factors change, also reflecting the guerrilla view.

2   The extent to which a particular resource is rare on the market can undoubtedly create a sustainable CA. However, again, beware of short-lived advantages: once brought

to market, a rare resource quickly becomes desired by competitors, who will do their utmost to obtain or replicate it.

3   If the resources cannot be imitated by rivals, stable revenues will result. However, given the current stages of technology, business and information development, there are few possibilities to make an asset inimitable, and this feature consequently has little durability in the long term, especially in knowledge-intensive industries. There are at least two general methods of imitation: substitution and full duplication. In this light, intangibles, including reputation, trust and culture are generally more sustainable in the short term.

The ability to mold such resources into CA requires an organization to have the necessary structure, internal regulations and policies, as well as business processes. Without fulfilling these conditions, possessing CA would not result in their correct exploitation and would not drive further profitability. In other words, the winning strategy means that the different resources directly controlled by the company enables it to offer competitive products at competitive prices.

As we can see, the *industrial organization view* focuses on the external environment, competitive landscape and competitive positioning; *RBV* concentrates on the internal characteristics of the firm and on the ways to exploit it in a sustainable and value-adding manner; and, finally, the *guerrilla view* treats the environment as chaos and considers long-term strategy as an evolving suite of short-term strategic actions.

The competitive advantage of one firm over others is temporal and exists only in the short-term period.[21] Such advantage is called the "disequilibrium phenomena," which occurs with change that comes from either internal or external sources (see Table 6.1).

Changes in the external environment create new possibilities for profits. In order to earn these, companies need to first identify and then exploit the emerging business opportunities – a capability that was initially called entrepreneurship.[22] Using this concept, the speed of a company's reaction to new opportunities is key to its success on the market.

In order to respond to changes in the business environment, companies require both information to identify opportunities and flexibility to adapt the firm's capabilities to external shifts. Given the time lag between the moment when change occurs and the moment when this change is identified by market researchers or industry analysts, companies need to "keep their antennae out." To achieve such constant awareness, relationships with other actors on supply chain are valuable.

On the other hand, CA can also originate from internal change, which comes from innovations.[23] Innovation is especially important for industries with a homogeneous set of incumbents. Innovative firms can decrease the pressure of price competition, which – all other things being equal – should drive profits to zero. In such a setting, the creativity of rivals can have more disrupting impact than their ability to quickly imitate resources. Although innovation typically refers to either product or process innovation, *strategic innovation* underlines changes in the business model that result in a strongly increased performance.[24]

Strategic innovation is not static in nature and, depending on each specific industry, can have plenty of followers. Therefore, top management buy-in and full support is necessary for a company to engage in a continuous process of strategic innovation.

In synthesis, industries that are dynamic, and whose companies possess more heterogeneous resources and capabilities, have larger potential for shifting competitive advantages.

How sustainable is competitive advantage?

A company lives with a permanent spear of Damocles over its head: how sustainable is its competitive advantage in its home turf and also how useful is this CA when entering unknown foreign environments?[25] In order to sustain its current advantages and, hopefully, develop new future ones, a company needs certain protective barriers (or isolating mechanisms[26]) against imitation.

The process of imitation occurs in several stages. During a first stage, the company identifies specific advantages held by a competitor. Thereafter, the company evaluates the possible benefits of replicating the advantage and determines to what extent new business opportunities would outweigh the required investment. In the final stage, the company then proceeds to acquire the specific assets needed to match its rival.[27]

One sure-fire isolating mechanism is to prevent rivals from knowing about your outstanding performance by keeping it secret. Avoidance of disclosure is simpler for privately held firms. Publicly held firms may have a more difficult time, but they can always consolidate divisional results to hide the exact source of exceptional profit due to CA.

A second solution is for firms to implement either preemption or deterrence instruments to reduce imitation opportunities. While preemption assumes occupation of certain segments or market niches and is frequently associated with restricting access with multiple patents, deterrence broadly means threat and can take different forms, such as (temporary) price dumping.

Another obstacle to imitation? Causal ambiguity. When it is not perfectly clear what specific facet of CA accounts for the major portion of additional profit (e.g. was it a product innovation or better financing options?), competitors may hesitate to invest in projects with uncertain outcomes.

If in the end a company feels it has properly identified the necessary resources for the missing CA, the imitation process can proceed in either of two ways. The first way is to develop the resources internally. Yet even if the expected profit covers the required investments, in-house development can take significant time; in turbulent industries, the resulting assets can become useless by the time they are developed. This may justify path two: acquiring the necessary assets from external parties. In this case, depending on the degree to which the resources are transferable, high transaction costs will probably occur (Table 6.2).

If a company has the benefit of first-mover advantage over its competitors, this can offer additional protection from imitation. Perhaps the most obvious examples of first-mover protection are patents and copyrights. Yet the first-mover advantage presents various other advantages for its owners:

- establishing control over limited resources;
- the ability to reinvest initial profits to develop assets faster than followers; and
- achieving and exploiting advantageous relationships with stakeholders.

Since a perfectly efficient competitive world exists only in the minds of economists, the vast majority of goods or services worldwide present significant opportunities for developing competitive advantages. Since companies are endowed with highly differentiated resources and capabilities, there are many ways to avoid direct rivalry and to decrease price pressure. When all the barriers to imitation are set up and imitation is hardly possible (for example, in the pharmaceutical sector), competitors can always rely on substitution.

You can't afford the $30,000 Harley-Davidson motorcycle? Settle for a $15,000 Japanese pseudo-chopper instead!

The factors that either simplify or complicate imitation change across industries. In certain cases, the specifics of a particular industry can create additional barriers. For example, in the high-tech industries, information complexity prevents rivals from fully diagnosing competitive advantages of the leader. In addition, as far as resource advantages frequently bear cumulative character, acquisition of such resources can be problematic.

Internationalization perspective for CA

To conquer foreign markets, firms are even more aggressive in leveraging their competitive advantages. This becomes especially obvious in the cases of mega deals (transactions over the value of $1 billion) that indicate the global ambitions of EMNEs, when these firms leapfrog onto the global scene. Russian multinationals are very illustrative in this regard – for example, with Norilsk Nickel's $1.2 billion acquisition of Gold Fields (South Africa) in 2004 and the $6.3 billion acquisition of Lion Ore (Canada) in 2007, or Lukoil's $2 billion acquisition of an ERG oil refinery (Italy) in 2008.[28] More recent examples include the Sberbank takeover of DenizBank (Turkey) in 2012 for $3.6 billion, Polymetal's acquisition of Atlynalmas Gold (Kazakhstan) for $1.1 billion and Yamal Razvitie's purchase of a 60% stake in Arctic Russia BV from Italian ENI Spa for $3 billion, both in 2014.

Country-specific advantages (CSA) are unique for each country and can come from resource endowments (Brazil and Russia are good examples), qualitative and quantitative labor force characteristics (China and India), country brand (India for IT and Russia for gas) and political, economic, social and technological factors. Multinationals create strategic opportunities through interactions of country-specific advantages and firm-specific advantages.[29]

However, this approach ignores firms that may have assets that create specific disadvantages at home yet may transform into advantages abroad.[30] Such resources can affect value creation in the new environment. Through learning or knowledge acquisition, firms can turn firm-specific or country-specific disadvantages into advantages.

Advantages and disadvantages can evolve over time not only due to competitive pressure and internal policies but also due to host-country institutions. From this point of view, institutions can be defined by sets of rules, both formal and informal, together with their enforcing arrangements.

Take the example of corruption in BRIC countries, without pointing any specific fingers. Corruption is the product of government policy. Although corruption may disadvantage local firms when operating domestically, when they go abroad into other BRIC countries, emerging multinationals will have an advantage over their developed cousins. They will feel more comfortable when communicating and dealing with local firms.

Firm-specific advantages (FSA) are "firm-level factors that confer competitive advantage"; they are "unique, proprietary capabilities, built upon product or process technology, marketing or distribution skills."[31] These advantages are created through the internalization of assets, which are under the firm's control.

Analysis of interaction between FSA, industry and institutions showed that choices are usually interrelated with advantages and limitations of constraints posed by institutions. This means that such factors can constitute country-specific advantages and country-specific disadvantages. Further, in developed countries, institutions create CSA if they enforce effective market mechanisms.[32] On the other hand, in emerging markets, they create country-specific disadvantages if they cannot guarantee an effective market. It was found as well that in emerging countries, informal institutions are significant.

The theoretical and empirical analyses of CSA and FSA became an important and inherent part of international competitiveness studies. Based on this distinction, scholars suggest classifying multinationals according to their ability to access and exploit CSA in knowledge and resources, stating that FSA then determines the marketability of company products and services. These differences between CSA and FSA allowed for a better understanding of emerging market firms and, in particular, multinationals.

Among major competitive advantages specific to particular firms are size, managerial skills, financial capabilities,[33] relationships and business networks among firms,[34] R&D and marketing capabilities.[35] In addition, entrepreneurship is also an important firm-specific asset, as it can create dynamic capabilities and identify opportunities via effective cooperation or negotiations with external parties.

Given the rising importance of emerging markets, a more sophisticated perspective on competitive advantage is needed in order to evaluate how emerging multinationals can leverage advantages that are affected by both country-specific advantages and disadvantages. Such factors include competitiveness and regulatory frameworks that influence operations in emerging markets: the home country's overall economic competitiveness probably influences development of competitive advantages of its local firms, including marketing, production technology, physical capital and managerial capabilities. Clearly, this approach has strong explanatory power, as it is consistent with the fundamentals of the competitive advantage theory.[36]

Building CA as a part of international strategy

How can a multinational decide whether a given foreign environment will be supportive or detrimental to its home-country competitive advantage? Different frameworks were created to investigate the impact of the external environmental impact, including political, economic, social and technological factors analysis.[37] These factors can either threaten or welcome a multinational. If the firm is able to properly analyze and evaluate these factors, it should be able to respond by adapting to this host-country environment. At the same time, the firm is influenced by the bargaining power of suppliers, customers, the threat of new entrants and substitutes.[38] Considered together, these form the host-country microenvironment.

There are not only risks – quite obviously, or else multinationals would not exist – since smart firms can effectively exploit environmental opportunities and may even respond to home-country threats via strategic choices to achieve superior performance abroad.

With the reference to the international strategy, the nature of CA on each market depends on whether firms implement global or localization strategies.[39] Global strategy implies one common strategy for all markets, as if they were one homogenous market, whereas localization refers to extensive adaptation and adjustments to each foreign market. Firms that implement a common (or standard) global strategy perceive internationalization not as a strategic opportunity but rather as a necessity due to competitive pressure. Yet the standardization of operations, the integration of activities and the alignment across subsidiaries usually results in multiple cross-border synergies that improve the value-creation process through creating CAs as follows:[40]

- Aligning market positions enables firm to successfully deal with foreign customers, which leads to a globally coordinated product or service offering. This also enables multinationals to effectively take on local competitors by focusing on a specific market segment and not spreading its resources too widely.

- Integrating activities leads to a more efficient value-creation process and strengthens the company's competitive advantage in each market. A company can leverage scale economies if it pools costly activities in one or several locations. These economies are achieved by integrating R&D, procurement and production. Firm can also benefit from location advantages in countries that have more favorable investment climates and better industry regulations.

- Leveraging resources by reallocating existing resources across countries (including domestic and international markets), or by cloning resource configurations that fit each market. This potentially leads to the re-configuration of the global corporate value chain – a pre-condition for creating or improving international competition.

On the other hand, companies do well to avoid over-standardization when necessary. One size does not always fit all! Companies should fine-tune to particular country requirements by providing adequate response to locally changing environments. McDonald's offers beer in Germany and strictly no beef in cow-sacred India! This calls then for both adaptability and responsiveness, which should not be treated as equal. While adaptation can be reactive, responsiveness shows proactive thinking. An insensitive firm that ignores these dimensions and relies on the same FSA for each market will probably lose its lead to more nimble competitors.

With communication and logistics between locations being easier and cheaper, global convergence is taking hold. The fast spread and replication of new products and services, as well as management practices, is the norm. It used to take one year or more for Hollywood hits to reach foreign screens. Now movie releases are quasi-simultaneous across the globe. This global homogenization has gradually erased many country differences. Long-term strategic thinking emphasizes the increased importance of global coordination activities instead of the proliferation of diversity.[41]

Thus a global approach to internationalization reduces investments and decreases operational costs, while marketing activities adopt a one-size-fits-all tactic, which in turn introduces worldwide scale economies. Such centralization and coordination, described as a "centralized hub"[42] is recognized as more effective and efficient than the previous model: the federation of self-controlled foreign subsidiaries.

Not everyone agrees that homogenization is the right tactic. Host-country business environments are the product of historical evolution based on cultural foundations, with resulting values and norms having a stable character. For example, political and legal systems in most countries are extremely diverse. Multinationals need to adapt, sometimes even within different regions of the same country, not only in emerging markets such as Brazil or Russia but also in large developed economies such as the United States, where regional power shifts have accompanied political decentralization.

So international managers must once again tread the delicate balance between homogenization and localization. Although some political trends, technologies and social behavior may have become unified across borders, deep cultural differences and constraints do require adaptation capabilities. This is what makes some companies great at internationalization and makes others fail.

Yet in the end, good localization helps firms to form new competencies and innovative capabilities that result in competitive advantage. Therefore, global and local elements of the strategy should not be mutually exclusive but balanced within one company in order to create sustainable CA in new markets.

6.3 Advantages and disadvantages of emerging market firms

Traditional theories conclude that emerging multinationals (EMNEs), whether expanding into developed or emerging markets, face intense competition from their developed brethren. These developed multinationals traditionally possess advantages, such as technological know-hows, substantial financial resources and innovative manufacturing processes, which may be difficult to replicate. Nonetheless, some emerging multinationals have demonstrated outstanding results, and some even outperform their more developed rivals. They sometimes even overtake their developed rivals in other developed markets. This prompted scholars to question their assumptions regarding internationalization strategy.

Where do EMNEs competitive advantages originate?

Though is generally accepted that emerging multinationals operate with a disadvantage, these latecomers to international expansion do reap certain advantages. Over recent years, there has been an increasing amount of research conducted in this field, partly due to the increased interest for emerging markets.[43]

Emerging multinationals are able to transform market difficulties to their advantage largely thanks to their familiarity with more complex institutional settings and their expertise in managing in such environments.[44] Basically, EMNEs are better adapted to other developing markets in terms of understanding and managing client needs, production facilities and distribution networks.[45] EMNEs are also more efficient in the challenging institutional environment – namely, flawed operating mechanisms, inefficient judicial systems, frequently changing regulations and heavy bribery and bureaucracy.[46] In contrast, developed multinationals often encounter difficulties with poorly developed infrastructure and market mechanisms, along with markets offering low protection of intellectual property rights.[47]

Studies show that emerging multinationals prove flexible in adapting to dynamic demand and supply changes; they find the right markets to operate and make profits. On the demand side, EMNEs are scalable to make a profit. EMNEs operating in large home countries (e.g. Brazil, India, Kazakhstan or Nigeria) can tap into welcome economies of scope, which can trigger exports, the first step in internationalization.[48] On the supply side, emerging economies – with the helping hand of big brother government – often create vertically competitive industries, or clusters, by concentrating interconnected companies, specialized suppliers, associated universities and research institutions.[49] In addition, although EMNEs usually suffer from lower technological capability, some are able to generate disruptive innovations, or re-combinations of technologies suitable for developing markets.[50]

Perhaps one of the most useful frameworks for understanding EMNE competitive advantages suggests the following five EMNE strongpoints:[51]

- *Product adaptation:* emerging multinationals are competitive in developed countries because they adapt the products to local needs, particularly by making it affordable and easy to maintain products.
- *Product and operation excellence:* EMNEs can have enhanced production efficiency and process excellence by utilizing more labor and less capital, reducing overhead costs and leveraging their latecomer advantage.

- *Privileged access to resources and markets:* A handful of EMNEs, especially state-owned enterprises (SOEs), are able to access home-country resources – namely, cheap capital with priority access.
- *Adversity advantage:* EMNEs are capable of operating efficiently in the difficult environment of other emerging markets.
- *Traditional intangible assets:* certain EMNEs do have advanced technologies and strong brands, and are able to roll-out their brand internationally.

What motivates emerging multinationals to go abroad?

Emerging multinationals start to go abroad for different motives. Research has pointed to numerous theories to understand the motives for the internationalization of EMNEs: FDI and portfolio investment theory,[52] firm-specific competitive advantages theory,[53] risk diversification[54] and the eclectic paradigm,[55] just to name a few.

MNEs, whether from emerging or developed markets, are basically seen as seekers of various things: natural resources, new markets, improved efficiency, strategic assets or new capabilities.[56] Some multinationals are motivated by escape investment, in order to avoid restrictive legislation and policies imposed by government. Preferential financial and non-financial treatment offered by home and/or host governments can also motivate some companies.[57] Some MNEs are motivated by complex, extrinsic factors[58] such as climate change (power generating firms), epidemics (pharma companies) or political instability in overseas regions (military firms).

In an attempt to fit all these motivating factors into a single coherent framework, scholars defined four categories of motivators: firm-level, industry-level, transaction-specific and institutional contexts.[59]

Firm-level considerations include firm size, firm type and ownership, resource and capabilities, network ties, export intensity, international orientation and experience and managerial influence. Assuming that the goal of emerging multinationals is to strengthen the competitive advantages of their enterprises, their behavior principally depends on these firm-level factors. Take the example of Chinese telecoms equipment manufacturer ZTE, which operates in more than 160 countries (see Chapter 8). Its successful internationalization is based on its low product prices, two, three or even sometimes four times lower than those of Western rivals. The secret behind these prices was inexpensive labor and easy access to financing since it is state-owned.

Industry-level factors include industry structure, industry sectors, industrial policy and industrial competition. The industrial factors do not differ significantly between regions, which means that EMNEs can be analyzed in the same way as developed multinationals. Haier, the largest Chinese manufacturer of household appliance in the so-called white-goods industry, provides a telling example. Haier was forced overseas in order to save its market position in the fragmented and regionalized industry. In the United States, the five largest firms hold almost 99% of the market. In Europe, it is about 60%. Due to differences in customer preferences and standards, brand loyalty and high transportation costs, few global players offer a large product range in a number of foreign markets. Others are strong regional or niche players. Yet the Chinese market was largely closed for foreign firms, enabling Haier to grow in a protected environment. Once ready to expand abroad, Haier's international strategy consisted of acquiring companies with good facilities, good quality and good distribution channels, yet they suffered from poor management. By purchasing eighteen such firms, Haier obtained the necessary technologies and resources to compete with established industry giants, such as Electrolux or Whirlpool.[60]

Transaction-specific antecedents include project importance, high- versus low-profile investments and market seeking versus strategic asset seeking. Compared to the two previous levels, transaction-specific drivers are more related to short-term and issue-specific influences. Brazilian company Vale (see Chapter 7) operates in mining, smelting and logistics, among other areas. From the beginning of its international expansion, Vale has focused on greenfield projects – namely, in promising mineral deposits that could lead to sustained organic growth. As a result, Vale is currently most internationalized in its mineral exploration projects.[61]

Institutional context is mostly related to home-country institutional factors – for example, the role of government. In China, the central planning system has implications in propelling the internationalization process of Chinese multinationals – namely, in strategic areas such as oil & gas or mining. The government, therefore, has a different impact for SOEs and for private companies. The Indian government is also highly involved in its domestic market, which can significantly influence foreign inbound investment. The case of Russian multinationals and their internationalization will be covered in greater detail in section 6.4.

The so-called *springboard perspective* adds another hypothesis: it argues that emerging multinationals use cross-border expansion as a springboard to exploit their competitive advantages. By acquiring critical resources from abroad, they "compete more effectively against their global rivals at home and abroad, and reduce their vulnerability to institutional and market constraints at home."[62] The springboard view highlights the two features of the related activities:

• Their recurring character – for example, a first foreign transaction might overcome the emerging multinationals' disadvantage in brand awareness and international reputation (e.g. Geely buys Volvo), while a second acquisition of a foreign logistics or distribution company may rectify its deficiency in accessing foreign customers (e.g. acquisition of Grupo Pão de Açúcar by Groupe Casino; see Chapter 3).
• Their reciprocal character, when host-country activities are strongly integrated back into home-country activities (for example Alfa-Bank establishing its Cyprus-based Alfa Capital Holdings; see Chapter 10).

What explains the springboard behavior? Some argue that it allows emerging multinationals to overcome their latecomer disadvantage via a series of aggressive, risk-taking measures by proactively acquiring critical assets to compensate for their competitive disadvantages.[63]

The springboard theory also states that when it comes to competing with strong rivals from advanced economies, emerging multinationals often use the *coopetition approach*. This approach posits that one of the smartest ways to compete is to establish connections and partnerships with competitors. This is important not only for emerging multinationals (in terms of transferring modern practices to emerging marketing) but also for developed multinationals. These latter need to shift their perception about emerging multinationals from "weak competitors" to "smart and gaining competitive power." The springboard theory encourages cooperation among multinationals: choose a benchmark company, which will serve as a tutor to gain experience, and then successfully compete with other players in the market.

What puts EMNEs at a disadvantage in their internationalization?

Organizational studies provide several explanations for the possible constraints firms meet when they internationalize. However, the phenomenon that emerging market firms are able to expand to new markets and successfully compete with developed market firms is relatively new. Therefore, no theoretical framework yet exists that can fully explain the internationalization process of emerging multinationals. Some existing theories comment on the disadvantages of emerging MNEs, and hence these theories provide some grounding.

The *product life-cycle theory* suggests that firms in developing economies produce goods at lower cost compared to firms from developed economies. Why? Because products manufactured in emerging economies are low-end standardized or commoditized products, while products originating from developed economies are high-end and new. Therefore, firms in developed economies can charge higher prices and thus reap higher margins. As the new high-end products mature, they become standardized, and firms can reduce costs by moving production to emerging economies and then export the products back to developed markets. For firms originating in emerging economies; however, internationalization implies higher costs than in their home markets, and they more frequently set up distribution channels rather than establishing production facilities. Since emerging market companies have lower margins, increasing the value of their products becomes the most important challenge when internationalizing.[64]

The *Uppsala model* suggests that companies face barriers constituted by the psychological distance between their home markets and foreign markets. This psychological distance is due to differences in language, education, business practices, culture and religion. The model predicts that businesses first expand to markets within shorter psychological distance and then gradually expand to more distant markets after gaining knowledge.[65]

The *economic distance approach* argues that the distance between home and host country depends mostly on the difference in economic development between the two countries. Furthermore, the approach argues that economic distance can explain the success of specific forms of FDI.[66] The economic distance stems from differences in technological capability and differences in factor costs.[67] MNEs have the opportunity to exploit the resources that exist in a country when they invest in a less-developed market compared to the home market. However, when a company invests in a market that is more developed than the home market, it faces the prospect of resource exploration.[68]

The *institutional distance concept* explains FDI country choices by examining the differences in institutions in the home and host country. Scholars argue that this distance is determined by distances on the regulative, normative and cognitive dimensions of institutions and that these dimensions impact the launch of foreign investment, entry mode and performance.[69]

Emerging multinationals: no big difference in fact

One simple viewpoint is that emerging multinationals are just like any ordinary company, and they find their competitive advantages in similar ways. The argument to support this position is that there are no subjective prejudices against emerging multinationals and these companies are just ordinary market players.[70] Bountiful evidence supports that Americans and Europeans fly Embraer planes just as readily as they fly Airbus or Boeing aircraft, or that Europeans heat their homes with Gazprom gas just as readily as with Libyan crude.

However, a strong prejudice still exists that EMNEs face more hurdles in developed markets than developed multinationals in emerging markets. Is there truly a stigma of *being from an emerging market?* While the majority of literature does agree on this conclusion, the studies fail to verify which factors might lead to higher discrimination against emerging multinationals.[71]

With emerging multinationals being a heterogeneous bunch, even within one country, the consensus is that they are engaged in fair competition based on the quality of product, price or other objective criteria. Prejudice of the "they are from an emerging market" kind seems outlandish. The most illustrative example is that the "Made in China" handicap is no longer valid. But in order to be competitive, emerging multinationals need to have at least comparable levels of market knowledge, access to resources or reliable financial backup. If facing these handicaps, emerging multinationals would constantly lag behind their developed rivals and hence will always be followers and second-class firms.

Many scholars claim that the way emerging multinationals compete with their developed cousins is connected to the internationalization models.[72] Empirical evidence from emerging markets emphasizes the contradictory features of two concepts.

The *stages model* basically assumes that internationalization of firms happens in a gradual and orderly manner, with firms starting their export activities only after domestic expansion. This model also states that during internationalization, it is fundamental to accumulate experience in order to extend the corporate knowledge about host markets.

Yet many EMNEs skip some of the internationalization steps and apply more risky strategies without passing through all the stages. For EMNEs, the use of domestic networks is a bridgehead in order to expand abroad. Some EMNEs compete with developed counterparts by building strong relationships with customers, suppliers and even governments well in advance of investing abroad.

So without doubt the *springboard perspective* is the more suited theory describing how emerging multinationals expand globally, and why they are often comparable to their rivals from developed economies.

6.4 How Russian multinationals have gone abroad

To illustrate the theoretical framework provided in the previous pages, let us examine how Russian companies – long constrained within Soviet-era borders – have gone international.

The internationalization strategy of emerging multinationals is affected by multiple determinants: industry-level and firm-level factors, as well the institutional environment. Industry-level determinants are important: they provide specific understanding of internationalization strategies, which, in turn, help to comprehend the diversity and to obtain the comparative insights of these firms across various national contexts. Indeed, firms in a particular sector experience similar resource, technology and institutional constraints and incentives, as well as the need for infrastructure. Given this set of constraints and incentives, firms adopt strategies based on their own resources and capabilities, and deal with micro-level pressures originating from the external environment.

The mixed role of institutions is both an obstacle and an additional perspective for understanding and illustrating the different levels and types of institutional impact from firm and country levels. The importance of integrating macro- and micro-institutions has been emphasized in other recent studies[73] that allowed for integrating various institutionally based CAs into one theoretical framework.

Based on the previous studies, it is important to know how and why multiple-level forces result in various international strategies within a single country environment. Normally, the patterns of strategic choice are defined at the industry level and their further transformations depend on the firm-specific characteristics. This allows for a more detailed look at a strategy across contexts.

In the literature on EMNEs, little is said about their international strategies' patterns, especially when attempting to investigate a non-Chinese context. For the example of Russian MNEs, in this section, I will look beyond the institutional features of EMNEs' international expansion and apply industry-level characteristics to these firms' strategy. This section is broadly based on the research that I conducted together with Irina Mihailova and that was devoted to the international strategy of Russian firms.[74]

Industry-specific factors of CA

Russian multinationals display certain common traits in their internationalization strategies, and these are often common to the industrial segment in which they are active. That is why the sector-by-sector analysis of industry-level determinants that influence the geographic expansion patterns of these firms is useful.

In the *oil & gas* industry, natural resources are the key assets which determine the competitiveness of firms. Due to resource scarcity, the nature of competition is oligopolistic: only a few large companies exist. Given the strategic nature of oil & gas, a high degree of state involvement occurs. This represents one of the most distinctive features of this industry. The Russian government maintains stakes in almost all companies, either via direct shareholding, by influencing company boards, by setting regulations or by providing the drilling and operating licenses. This is, undoubtedly, the strongest institutional factor that affects the industry players. Capital requirements are very highly due to the complex, diversified and expensive infrastructure for exploration, production, refining and transportation of the output(s). The technical side of this industry is sophisticated and the role of technology is also high.

For *metallurgy*, just as for the oil & gas industry, competitiveness depends on access to natural resources such as different types of ore as well as cheap energy. Infrastructure and technology requirements are high, meaning the choice of location is critical. Although the number of players in the industry is relatively small, the intensity of competition is high, and state influence is lower than in the oil & gas industry. The market itself is highly stable due to the peaceful co-existence of several oligopolies, who are quite equally treated by the government.

The *banking* sector retains the legacy of the Soviet-era lack of competition: there are few major players with large scales of operations and large market shares. However, the competition among these few players has grown, leading to their rise in interest for easier foreign markets. The technology used in the banking sector is neither as sophisticated as that in the IT sector, nor as expensive as in the oil & gas sector. Also, banking operations do not require large and capital-intensive infrastructure. The Russian government plays regulatory and supervisory roles in both domestic and foreign operations since state interests arise in financing foreign deals.

The *telecommunications* market is oligopolistic, shared amongst the few players having purchased licenses during government auctions. Infrastructure expenditures are very high, and companies compete for both technical and managerial innovations which can lead to increased market share. Telecoms companies are bound to relatively high investments in R&D and technological development, with customers expecting better and better performance and a greater number of services. Yet domestic telecoms firms have largely invested via the backward transfer of existing Western technologies into Russia. The government involvement is mostly moderate.

In the *automotive industry*, capital and infrastructure requirements are high. Firms need to continuously undertake R&D activity to stay competitive, which forces them to cooperate domestically and internationally. This sector was one of the first which witnessed a large amount of inward FDI from multinationals such as Ford, Nissan, Renault, Toyota, Volkswagen and others. The role of the government is controversial in this sector: on the one hand, it provides foreign firms with incentives to invest into the domestic market, which undermines the development of a home-grown industry; on the other hand, there are also attempts to attract foreign investors and to motivate them to transfer technological knowledge through the establishment of various types of cooperative ventures with Russian companies.

Two examples clearly illustrate the interest of Russian companies in capturing technology and absorbing knowledge from foreign investors: the joint venture between AvtoVaz and General Motors to produce the Chevrolet Niva model and the alliance of Renault-Nissan with AvtoVaz.

In the *construction industry*, both capital requirements as well as infrastructure needs are limited, and R&D intensity is relatively low. Domestic competition is fierce, and many Russian construction firms seek foreign contracts to secure their home operations. The Russian government is not directly involved, neither in the domestic nor the foreign operations of companies. Despite the low government profile, institutional factors have an impact – namely, via the standards and norms that regulate construction.

The typical Russian *information technology (IT) sector* player is a privately owned small company. Domestically, such firms may benefit from government contracts to service state organizations. While in certain cases R&D expenditures can be very high, no substantial financing is required in this sector. Human capital and innovation represent the cornerstones for success. Competition is intense, which pushes firms towards cooperative behavior for specific projects. The government is not involved in direct regulation, with the exception of companies taking part in state programs (primarily R&D and innovation related). One of the serious problems in the high-tech sector in Russia is the lack of macro-level institutions influencing the activities of Russian companies – for example, weak property rights regulation, which undermines their competitive development.

The analysis of Russian multinational internationalization can be differentiated according to two key dimensions: (1) the *role of the state* and (2) *capital and infrastructure* requirements (see Table 6.2). The first group (oil & gas industry) is characterized by high state influence and capital and infrastructure requirements. The second group (banking sector) is under high state influence, but has relatively low capital and infrastructure needs. The third group (metallurgy, telecoms and automotive) is not exposed to direct state influence, but has large capital and infrastructure requirements. The last group (IT and construction) lives in bliss: neither state influence, nor excessive capital and infrastructure requirements.

The question now is whether these groups display similar patterns in their international expansion.

Internationalization patterns of Russian multinationals

The analysis of how Russian firms have crossed borders shows that there are clear patterns of international strategies pursued by companies in each of the four categories in Table 6.2.

Group 1: oil & gas

The pattern of international expansion depends on the industry's characteristics in a rather straightforward manner. Characterized by scarce oil & gas reserves, there simply is little space for establishing new businesses via greenfield investments (from scratch). The expansion takes place primarily through brownfield investment when the company builds facilities based on existing assets or facilities with the aim of transferring Russian firms' assets abroad in order to further expand distribution networks and, in return, to gain technologies, know-how and sales revenues. Via acquisitions (which is a sort of brownfield strategy), joint ventures and cooperation agreements, Russian oil & gas companies exploit existing frameworks when doing business internationally.

Group 2: banking

The process of going international usually begins by setting up a representative office which evaluates the market potential and decides on a suitable larger-scale entry mode and schedule. Foreign expansion is either customer following (potential target markets for existing bank customers) or market seeking (expanding the markets as a growth incentive). Most of the foreign operations of Russian banks have been initiated by subsidiaries located around the world. Once the decision to expand internationally is made, the preferred entry mode for Russian banks is by acquiring an existing bank.

Group 3: metallurgy, telecoms and automotive

Here, internationalization has focused on less-developed economies, with takeovers being the tactic to access these countries' markets and infrastructure. Indeed, transactions have proven the fastest and most efficient way for Russian firms in these sectors, given the high capital and specialized infrastructure requirements.

The state plays an important double role in this sector's cross-border expansion. First, the government supports and often promotes these foreign acquisitions as a tool for the diversification of nationally strategic assets. Second, the state benefits from the increase of influence over these foreign economies via these deals. Thus the growth across national borders is led by economic considerations by both firms and the state. Several companies noted that the government role in internationalization is huge. Human resources and R&D are also of importance in motivating the choice of acquisition targets.

Group 4: IT and construction

In these more fragmented segments, there is no clear pattern for the modes of operation which vary greatly across countries. However, companies here adopt a similar logic: they pursue opportunities to expand into new (emerging) markets, often by following existing clients or by exploring partnerships to strengthen their capabilities. Mostly mid-sized, these firms occupy specific niches where they can grow, exploiting their existing competitive capabilities.

Overall, across all four groups, despite the existence of patterns indicating the presence of common logic in the internationalization strategies, the empirical evidence shows companies that deviate in their strategies due to their specific characteristics. Let us examine these in further detail.

How do firm-specific advantages affect internationalization?

As we can see from the Table 6.5, in the *oil & gas*, group the exception to the rule is Lukoil. While other companies in the group (Gazprom and Rosneft) are state-owned and influence competition towards an inefficient position, Lukoil operates in the manner of a profit-seeking company. Its core activities, the downstream refining and marketing, are subject to less state control than the upstream exploration and production activities of other players and are open to greater competition, which also explains the greater attention to operational efficiency and profit margins. What makes Lukoil an outlier is its stronger focus on profitability due to the lesser dependence on the state.

In the *banking* group, Alfa-Bank, established as part of a business holding, is the black sheep. Even though this bank enjoys strong support from the government, its international

Table 6.5 Patterns of internationalization strategies

		Technology and capital intensive	
		Yes	No
State control	High	**#1 Oil & gas** Strict state control over operations of the companies. High capital requirements due to the complications and extent of infrastructure. Alliances and IJVs are preferred: provide integration opportunities in the global industry. Significant initial investments in joint projects help overcome high entry barriers linked to expensive infrastructure and technologies. Political motives often dominate economic ones. Aggressive expansion strategies accompanied by large-scale acquisitions.	**#2 Banking** Close government supervision of banking activities. Low capex for infrastructure (property, computing equipment). Capital requirements for growth can be relatively high. Initial foreign entry via representative offices, which act as first market explorations. Then progression to acquisitions if the market is deemed valuable. Economic motives dominate, despite the real government role in ownership of many banks.
	Low	**#3 Metals, telecoms, automotive** No direct government control over operations in these sectors. Capital and infrastructure requirements are high. International expansion mostly via acquisitions. Transactions often the only possible form of entry mode due to the high requirements of infrastructure and the lack of space for greenfield investments. Moderate state role. Companies are independent and possess large capital. Independent choice of attractive target host countries.	**#4 IT, construction** No state involvement in these sectors. Except as work provider for tenders. Capital can be minimal to allow company growth. Partnerships most common form of both entry strategy and post-entry operational set-up. Relatively low financial risks in international expansions, which are project based: either following the market or the client. Some IJVs help strengthen innovative capacities and R&D capabilities. Almost no political motives for international growth. Herd instinct: often follow other large firms in their international expansion and less dynamic.

Source: Adapted from Mihailova and Panibratov 2012

expansion is to a larger extent driven by profit- and market-seeking motives than is the case for other Russian banks. Alfa–Bank was the first Russian bank with substantial non-state capital.

In the *metallurgy, telecoms and automotive* group, Severstal (metallurgy) deserves notice. While most of the firms in metallurgy are focusing on the acquisition of emerging market companies, especially in geographies holding raw materials reserves for their business (backward internationalization), Severstal has aggressively undertaken risky forward acquisitions in developed countries (in the EU and the United States, in particular), which allowed the company to gain closer access to customers and to overcome the trade barriers, tariffs and duties.

In the *IT and construction* group, Sitronics (IT) runs counter to the norm, with its close cooperation with the Russian government. This ensures support for its successful development. This cooperation funnels R&D activities from other large, state-controlled companies to Sitronics, which is crucial for competitiveness in the IT industry. Some argue that Sitronics's unique position is explained by its proximity to the government, and by servicing government-related contracts and projects.

Conclusion

The international strategies of Russian multinationals are shaped by institutional, industry-level and firm-level factors. Sector-specific determinants – namely, the level of government control and the level of capital required – affect the type of cross-border strategy chosen by most multinationals. Institutions strongly affect competitive rules, technology standards and resources for innovative development, as well as growth priorities.

Industry-specific factors are strongly affected by macro-level institutions and to a large degree pre-establish certain patterns for corporate growth strategies. This has important implications for research since it provides a better understanding of the reasons different national contexts originate different internationalization strategies for domestic MNEs. Indeed, scholars aiming to understand the distinctive nature of EMNE strategies should incorporate industry-level factors and compare the strategies within or across different industries rather than within or across various national contexts, be it emerging economies or developed countries. These findings support the premises of the "external control" perspective from the strategy research and encourage the development of more "fine-grained" approaches to better understand the nature of EMNE internationalization strategies.

Empirical research validates the argument that firm-specific resources and capabilities can justify deviation in behavior from patterns pre-defined by industry-specific factors. The existence of firms whose strategies differ from the common pattern is in line with our theoretical assumption about the role of firm-level determinants as well as direct relationships with government. This deviation may either be in terms of structural differences of strategy elements or in the scale of the internationalization implementation. For example, firm-specific determinants can influence the number of foreign markets chosen for expansion, the speed of expansion or the performance outcomes of the internationalization.

References

1 Dollar, Hallward-Driemeier and Mengistae 2006.
2 Wilkinson 2006.

3 Calomiris 2005.
4 Ito and Krueger 2001.
5 Wei 2000b; Wei and Wu 2002.
6 Krugman 2000.
7 Kaminsky and Schumukler 2002.
8 Rodrik 2005.
9 Ibid.
10 Buckley and Casson 1976.
11 Dunning 1977, 1979.
12 Buckley et al. 2015.
13 Faeth 2009.
14 Porter 1985.
15 Coulter 2009.
16 Barney 2001.
17 Grant 2010.
18 Coulter 2009.
19 Barney 2001.
20 Coulter 2009.
21 Grant 2010.
22 Rumelt 1987.
23 Grant 2010.
24 Hamel 2003.
25 Kumar, Jones, Venkatesan and Leone 2011; Rugman, Oh and Lim 2012.
26 Rumelt 1987.
27 Grant 2010.
28 Kalotay and Panibratov 2013.
29 Rugman et al. 2012.
30 Cuervo-Cazurra and Un 2005.
31 Rugman et al. 2012.
32 Meyer et al. 2009.
33 Rugman et al. 2012.
34 Johansson and Vahlne 2009.
35 Buckley and Casson 2010.
36 Porter 1985.
37 Thompson and Strickland 1999.
38 Porter 1985.
39 De Wit and Meyer 2010.
40 Ibid.
41 Ibid.
42 Bartlett and Ghoshal 1995.
43 Hoskisson et al. 2013.
44 Cuervo-Cazurra and Genc 2008.
45 Lall 1983.
46 Ghemawat and Khanna 1998; Khanna and Palepu 1997.
47 Prahalad and Lieberthal 1998.
48 Krugman 1979.
49 Porter 1990.
50 Cantwell and Barnard 2008.
51 Ramamurti 2009.
52 Hymer 1976.
53 Buckley and Casson 1976.
54 Rugman 1979.
55 Dunning 1980.
56 Dunning and Lundan 2008a.
57 Luo and Tung 2007.
58 van Tulder 2015.
59 Deng 2012.

60 Duysters et al. 2007.
61 Fleury and Fleury 2009.
62 Luo and Tung 2007.
63 Ibid.
64 Vernon 1966.
65 Johanson and Vahlne 1977.
66 Tsang and Yip 2007.
67 Ghemawat 2001.
68 Tsang and Yip 2007.
69 Xu and Shenkar 2002.
70 Held and Berg 2015.
71 Ibid.
72 Kuada and Sorensen 2013.
73 Dunning and Lundan 2008b.
74 Mihailova and Panibratov 2012.

Part III

Internationalization from emerging markets

7 International strategies of Brazilian multinationals

This chapter will analyze the process of Brazilian integration in the world economy and discuss Brazilian companies' perspectives on internationalization. Particular attention will be paid to outward investments from Brazil, with regional and sector-specific views from multinationals having expanded abroad.

The chapter will present two cases on Brazilian multinationals: Embraer and Vale, with their contrasting strategies, where one company selectively targets international markets and the second expands over continents.

7.1 Globalization of Brazil and international investments of Brazilian firms

Internationalization of economy: recent trends

Brazil can be referred to as an agricultural powerhouse, dominating the coffee, orange juice and sugar markets. At the same time, manufacturing makes up almost 14% of GDP, and Brazil's service sector accounts for approximately two-thirds of GDP.[1] With the Brazilian government having launched a four-year investment program in infrastructure, energy and social development, alongside the major global events such as the soccer cup FIFA 2014 and the Olympic Games 2016 in Rio de Janeiro, the landscape for investment opportunities is fertile.

Proven mineral resources are extensive. The large iron ore and manganese reserves are important sources of industrial raw materials for local processing and for export earnings. Deposits of nickel, tin, chromite, bauxite, beryllium, copper, lead, tungsten, zinc, gold and other minerals are also exploited. High-quality, coking-grade coal required in the steel industry is in short supply. Brazil is also one of the world's largest producers of hydroelectric power, which provides about 90% of the nation's electricity. The country also actively develops a network of commercial nuclear reactors, with plans to expand energy supply nationwide.[2]

The services sector (including hospitality, retail sales, financial services, IT BPO and personal services) represents 67.5% of Brazil's GDP and employs around 66% of the country's workforce. The mining, aerospace and agricultural sectors all rely on a buoyant finance sector in order to fund future projects.[3]

Brazil has an export-oriented economy, with 46% of total exports being raw materials and 38% manufactured goods. According to the Economic Complexity Index, Brazil ranks as the twenty-second-largest exporter worldwide. The country exports soybeans and related soy products (11% of total exports), transport equipment and components

(10%), oil and oil products (8%), meat (4%) and iron ore (15%). The main export partners are China (19% of total exports), the United States (13%), Argentina (7%), the Netherlands (5%), Germany and Japan (3% each).[4]

Brazil's global perspective resulted from economic transformation in the 1990s, when most of the economic reforms were implemented and new patterns of national competitiveness were established. These reforms also created the conditions in the domestic market necessary for the internationalization of Brazilian firms. The general framework of the reforms was based on three fundamental instruments: Plano Real, economic openness and regional integration.[5] The so-called Plano Real is now regarded as one of the most important and successful strategies in Brazilian history for controlling inflation, reducing the degree of external vulnerability and creating the economic and political conditions needed for long-term stability. The macroeconomic changes created the conditions for a positive investment climate and, therefore, for the increased competitiveness of the Brazilian economy.

The second part of the plan was a systematic program to facilitate the liberalization of foreign trade and external financial flows. These changes provided new opportunities for economic growth, but they also exposed the country to strong competition and new challenges. The third reform was a stabilization plan to foster regional economic integration. The creation of the Mercosur trading area contributed significantly to the increase of trade among its five member countries (and six associate countries) and stimulated new external investments. During this period, Brazil went on to establish a basis for the expansion of business investment projects of its multinationals. By benefitting companies through the elimination or reduction of tariff barriers, Mercosur contributed to the international expansion of Brazilian companies. This international expansion was not only limited to export increase but also manifested itself in a very gradual path via the establishment of sales and production subsidiaries.[6]

Brazilian firms were late entrants into the global market, which can be explained by several reasons. First, there was the lack of strategic advantages due to macroeconomic impediments: high interest rates, exchange volatility, lack of long-term financing resources. Also, why go abroad when the possibility existed of operating in the large and protected domestic market? Additionally, Brazilian firms tend to have vertically integrated business models, which are difficult to duplicate abroad. Finally, they could be characterized as suffering from a lack of global outlook due to drastic cultural differences, great physical distance and even a sense of being inferior to Americans and Europeans – i.e. the liability of origin (see Chapter 11).[7]

However, recent factors have led to a change in the mindset of the local enterprises: economic, fiscal and institutional stabilization; the wave of globalization; and overvalued currency from 2007 to 2012, which is beneficial for FDI, just to name a few. What is more, many Brazilian firms can no longer settle for only operating in the domestic market, either because of market saturation at home or due to fierce international competitors entering Brazil.

Many Brazilian multinationals went abroad as a hedge against Brazilian country risk. One example is Odebrecht Engineering, a Brazilian construction company that found itself too dependent on state infrastructure projects for its own taste. An Odebrecht executive pointed out, "Our main motivation in this process [of internationalization] was . . . the need to diversify into new market segments in order to reduce the volatility risk in the Brazilian market at the time."[8] The availability of long-term financing from the Brazilian Development Bank led to a major acquisition spree abroad during the 2010s.[9]

Interestingly enough, the common pattern for internationalization of the Brazilian firms was expansion into Latin American markets first and then a shift into more distant worldwide markets.

Many Brazilian companies went abroad in search of new technology. For Brazilian steel companies – for example, acquisitions (the preferred mode of market entry) enabled them to learn new processes and diversify product lines.[10]

Several Brazilian companies expanded overseas to follow customers. Firms from service industries (e.g. business software supplier Totvs) can internationalize to serve their clients abroad and thus establish foreign operations.[11] Another example is Stefanini, a Brazilian training and system maintenance company that started its internationalization process as a reaction to one of their client's opening a subsidiary abroad in the early 2000s.

Brazilian foreign assets are mostly held by the country's biggest multinationals: Itausa (holding company), Vale (mining), Odebrecht (engineering and construction), Petrobras (oil & gas), Gerdau (steel), Votarantim (conglomerate), JBS (food) and Embraer (aerospace and defense).[12]

Brazilian multinationals are often seen as companies with modest track records when it comes to internationalization. Some authors claim that among the reasons are the large size of the domestic market and the availability of natural resources, meaning little incentive to expand activities abroad.[13]

The biggest Brazilian companies concentrate a big share of resources, including financial ones. Thus, in 2012, the ten largest Brazilian companies held 40% of the revenue of the largest one hundred Brazilian firms. As a benchmark, this share is usually just 25% worldwide.[14]

In 2015, the Forbes 2000 top public companies included ten Brazilian firms. Among these, three are financial institutions (Itau Holding, Banco do Brasil, Banco Bradesco), two are from the extractive sector (Petrobras and Vale), two are a food processing companies (JBS and BRF) and one is a retailer (Companhia Brasileira de Distribuicao). This ventilation echoes Brazil's role as a regional financial center, a natural resource powerhouse, a large-scale food exporter and a booming domestic consumer market.

Table 7.1 Brazilian companies among the world's biggest public companies

Rank	Company	Industry	Sales	Profits	Assets	Market value
42	Itau Unibanco Holding	Regional banks	76.6	9.2	424	63.7
61	Banco Bradesco	Regional banks	66.7	6.5	403.1	51.4
133	Banco do Brasil	Regional banks	68.8	5	482.9	23.6
413	Vale	Iron and steal	37.5	0.41	116. 4	29
416	Petrobras	Oil & gas operations	143.7	7.5	298.7	44.4
453	JBS	Food processing	51.2	0.87	31.2	14.7
681	BRF	Food processing	13.2	0.95	14.2	18.2
776	Itausa	Conglomerates	2.1	3.4	18.3	21.2
806	Companhia Brasileira de Distribuicao	Food retail	27.8	0.54	17.1	8.5

Note: All financial figures in $ billions for 2015

Source: *Forbes* (http://www.forbes.com/global2000/list/)

According to another source,[15] Brazil's most internationalized company is the food processing company JBS-Friboi, followed by Gerdau, the largest steel producer in Latin America and the software company Stefanini IT Solutions.

OFDI and MNEs: Geography and strategy

Comparing Brazil to other emerging markets, outbound FDI is still small. From 2010 to 2013, the net outward investment from Brazil amounted to only $4.2 billion, which is far below the performance of other emerging countries such as India ($38 billion), South Africa ($8.2 billion), Turkey ($10.9 billion) and others.[16] Several factors explain this underperformance. First, historic protectionism of Brazil's trade and industrial policies remains strong, and the taxation of the profits of Brazilian multinationals is high. However, this fact did not impede hundreds Brazilian companies from taking their business abroad. Some Brazilian multinationals already operate in more than a dozen countries, with a predilection for other South American countries. In fact, 52% of Brazilian multinationals surveyed by Fundação Dom Cabral in 2014 indicated South America as the preferred destination for their first foreign subsidiary. North America came in second, with 33.3%.[17]

This explains the geographic density of Brazilian OFDI: in 2009, the Americas received 70% of Brazilian OFDI moneys, while Europe captured 29% and the remainder settled for a measly 1%.[18] In 2010, the United States hosted over 15% of Brazilian OFDI and Austria was the biggest recipient in Europe, hosting almost 20% of Brazilian OFDI.[19]

According to Brazilian researchers, the main drivers of foreign investment for Brazilian multinationals are market-seeking motives, home-market instability avoidance and better intellectual property protection abroad. For example, to gain stronger IP protection, Brazilian companies often register their trademarks and patents in the United States, Germany and the Netherlands. These countries, plus Canada and the United Kingdom, also attract Brazilian R&D investments.[20]

Brazil-Russia investment relations

Russia and Brazil are both extremely rich in natural resources. Russia has vast oil & gas reserves, and Brazil is rich in soybeans and iron ore. It comes as no surprise that these resources determine the areas of Russian-Brazilian investments.

The most important deals between the two countries include

- the Memorandum of Understanding between Gazprom and Petrobras, both oil & Gas giants;
- the joint venture between Mir Steel UK (subsidiary of Russian metallurgy giant Mechel) and Brazilian iron producer Usina Siderurgica do Para; and
- the acquisition by Severstal (another Russian steel giant) of 25% in Brazil's SPG Mineracao iron ore exploration firm.

In February 2007, Gazprom and Petrobras signed an agreement to cooperate in hydrocarbon exploration, production, transmission and marketing. Special attention was paid to the development of offshore deposits as well as novel technologies and LNG production. Significant investments are connected to this deal.

In 2010, Gazprom opened a representative office in Rio de Janeiro. The aim here was to use Brazil as a stepping stone for other South American countries. The office was conceived to provide information and analysis support for regional projects and to help coordinate Gazprom subsidiaries in Latin America.[21]

Another Russian premiere was the $800 million joint venture between Brazilian iron producer Usina Siderurgica do Para and Russian steelmaker and coal producer OAO Mechel (owned by Russian billionaire Igor Zyuzin).[22] The planned investment in this project is a staggering $5 billion for the construction of a metallurgical complex in Bakar (Pará State), composed of a steel mill, coke storage facility and harbor.

The JV between Mir Steel UK and Usipar aimed to establish a new holding company RAM (Russian and Monteiro), with 75% of equity belonging to Russia and 25% to Brazil, and a new plant having a capacity of 2.5 million tons of steel by 2015. Unfortunately, the crisis in Russia postponed these grandiose plans.

Russian steel giant Severstal made another investment in steel production, albeit smaller, in May 2011. It acquired 25% in Brazil's SPG Mineracao iron ore exploration firm for $49 million.

> Severstal considers the project to be highly promising, with preliminary estimated reserves at 0.5–1.5 billion tons of ore and an approximate content of iron at 40% to 45%. Potential production is estimated at 10 to 20 million tons of iron ore concentrate.[23]

7.2 Targeting markets selectively: case of Embraer

Company overview

Embraer is a large Brazilian multinational company operating in the extremely competitive aircraft industry. Founded in 1969 as a government-owned entity, Embraer produces commercial, military and executive aircraft. The company was sold off in 1997 during the Brazilian privatization wave. Embraer started out by producing and selling the Bandeirante, a turboprop aircraft intended for both civilian and military use, with a fifteen to twenty-one passenger capacity.[24] Thereafter, a large number of governmental orders arrived to deliver defense aircraft to suit Brazilian needs. At this stage, Embraer relied on licensing agreements in order to acquire lacking technologies – namely, from the Italian company Aermacchi. Other notable developments during Embraer's beginnings in Brazil included a high-performance glider and an agricultural crop duster. So the diversification in terms of product range was very high.

At the end of the 1970s, joint programs with Aeritalia (now Alenia) and Aermacchi, both Italian manufacturers, enabled Embraer to gain new technologies, which in turn enabled the production of new commercial aircraft. Since then, the huge success achieved by these planes, as well as the subsequent confirmation of Embraer's presence in both the executive jet segment as well as expansion into aeronautical services, have justified its take-off in foreign markets. With customers worldwide and important partners in the international arena in all stages of its supply chain, Embraer is now a major Brazilian exporter, with a rich portfolio of products and services in four business units: commercial aviation, executive aviation, defense and security and systems.

In 2000, Embraer went public with its first public placement (IPO) to accumulate new funds for further business development. Embraer's stated strategy is, on the one hand, to consolidate its presence as one of the main global players in the aeronautical and defense and security markets; moreover, it intends to extend beyond the development of existing technologies. Large projects in new industries are taken on in order to penetrate new product and geographical markets. Currently in development stage is a new military air-craft expected to set new standards in tactical airlift capability. The focus of the company thus remains on innovation and technological enhancement.

In 2014, Embraer's revenues totaled 14,935.9m reals ($6.3 billion), up 10% over its 2013 results (13,635.8m reals). Growth in revenue was attributed to several factors, including the favorable exchange rate fluctuation (devaluation of the real vis-à-vis the dollar), which boosted income in reals – namely, for the defense and security divisions, which witnessed 32% growth. For 2014, Embraer's gross margin was 19.8%, a 2.9% drop in comparison to 2013. This was caused by a shift in the production mix of the commercial aviation divi-sion: greater deliveries of the E175 aircraft, which is less expensive than its larger brothers, the E190 and E195. Additionally, the sales volume of large executive aviation aircraft also dropped, substituted by smaller, less expensive models.

In 2014, Embraer's three main business units saw overall annual revenues increase by 9.5%. The biggest growth came from the defense and security division, with a 32% increase to 3.43 billion reals. The commercial and executive aviation divisions achieved more moderate revenue rises: 4% and 5%, respectively (to 7.48 and 3.85 billion reals). Other activities generated revenues of 184.2 million reals (Figure 7.1).

Embraer operates subsidiaries on every continent, including countries such as China, France, Ireland, the Netherlands, Portugal, Singapore, the United Arab Emirates, the United Kingdom and the United States. North America remains the largest source of revenue, accounting for almost half of the company total (48%; see Figure 7.1). The second biggest market is the domestic Brazilian market, which supplies 21% of total revenue, about the same level as 2013. Due to the aftermath of financial crisis, the European market's revenue

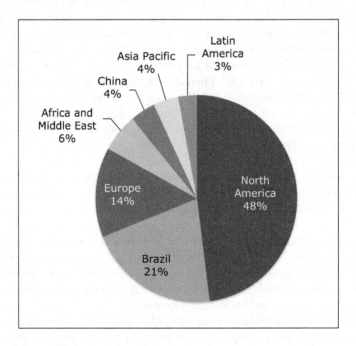

Figure 7.1 Breakdown of Embraer revenues by region

Source: Embraer website (http://www.embraer.com/en-us/conhecaembraer/embraernumeros/pages/home.aspx)

continued to decline, falling to 14%. The revenue generated in Latin America, China and Asia Pacific fell to 3%, 4% and 4%, respectively, while Africa and the Middle East rose to 6% of the total. Embraer's export sales totaled $3.81 billion in 2013, making the company Brazil's seventh-largest exporter and a substantial pillar of foreign trade.

Embraer has a one-track mind, focused on innovation. Innovations introduced during the first half of the 2010s accounted for 46% of net revenues in 2014. The company introduced a whopping 20,062 innovations in 2014 – a remarkable indicator of success in implementing this strategy for innovation.

Competitive environment

Embraer faces tough competition from established players such as Boeing and Airbus, who together accounted for 65% of global aircraft sales in 2012. Embraer must also contend with newer players such as Mitsubishi Regional Jet and the recent Chinese entry, COMAC. Competition is somewhat reduced by relatively high entry barriers and exit costs. However, this oligopolistic market boils with internal rivalry for cheap resources spread internationally, the skilled labor force and reliable partners. Dependence on suppliers is one of the obstacles in increasing profit margins. The industry can be, therefore, considered as highly competitive and unattractive for newcomers, despite its profitability.

Embraer is focused on lowering costs and thus earning high profits and exploiting economies of scope. It builds better products, which creates value both for the company and its customers. Embraer does its utmost to reduce customers' after-sales service requirements, which has helped build the brand name and create satisfied (repeat) customers. The company applies economies of scope by using similar technologies in creating different product ranges. This reduces design costs and allows greater investment in R&D.

To satisfy customer needs and preferences, Embraer invests heavily in R&D – namely, to comply with global standards and regulations. Although more costly, this increases aircraft reliability and customer satisfaction. By increasing head space, luggage and legroom in its aircraft, Embraer has better client satisfaction rates than its competitors.

Embraer benefits from cheaper yet highly skilled labor because of the rapidly developing educational system in Brazil, the availability of local raw materials, the low manufacturing costs of an emerging country, a strong brand name backed by more than fifty years of history and the stable domestic demand. In addition, the company has a strong supply chain as well as a distribution and sales network including post-sales support and customer care.

Embraer moved some of its manufacturing facilities abroad in order to diversify its portfolio, acquire innovative know-how and managerial practices. This also enables the company to position its products slightly differently, depending on the production facility. Balancing the constant trade-off between innovation and additional costs, Embraer, nonetheless, manages to create products differentiated from its competitors – a restless and aggressive crowd.

Aircraft manufacturing has many specificities, creating obstacles for new entrants, so the emergence of new competitors is difficult nowadays. First of all, fixed costs are very high. Entrants hesitate to enter the market since the payback period can be very long before profits start to accumulate. There is also an outright risk of never recuperating one's investment since aircraft sales are big-ticket items with extremely picky customers (namely, airlines and leasing companies).

The competitive environment will remain largely the same, yet Embraer has the potential to challenge the quasi-duopoly of developed-country multinationals. Embraer has accumulated the capacity to compete head–on in the commercial aviation segment and is now doing so.

Embraer's investments

Embraer started its foreign investments relatively early, nine years after its creation. In its early stages, Embraer signed a manufacturing cooperation agreement with the U.S. aircraft manufacturer Piper. The aim was to carry out production of an import substitution model. In 1979, the company made its first greenfield investment, entering the U.S. market via a wholly owned subsidiary. This first American office provided technical support to new customers. Then, in 1981, the company opened its Fort Lauderdale facility, including offices for corporate headquarters, marketing staff for commercial aircraft and equipment for jets. Embraer then took off internationally with a mixed portfolio of

• further subsidiaries abroad (Australia, China, France, Great Britain, Ireland, the Netherlands, Portugal, Spain, Singapore, Switzerland and Uruguay);
• acquisitions of existing aircraft engineering companies (e.g. the merger with the Neiva company in 1980; the acquisition of Celsius Aerotech in Nashville in 2002);
• joint ventures in 1983 with aircraft-building companies worldwide (e.g. service agreement with Atlantic Southeast Airlines) and in 1999 with Liebherr Group;
• partnerships in 1983 with the Chinese government to develop the China-Brazil Earth Resource Satellite and in 1999 with the European Aeronautic Defense and Space (EADS) company; and
• agreements for combined deliveries of military and commercial airliners for the further sales in third-party countries (purchasing agreement with Jet Airways of India in 2002 and with LOT Polish airlines in 2004, etc.).

Embraer intensively invests into R&D and runs two research centers for this purpose. Its foreign center (Embraer Engineering and Technology Center) was established in 2013 in Melbourne (Florida, United States) creating about two hundred new jobs. The company is proud of its American activities and appreciates the acknowledgment by local authorities of its employment efforts.[25] Additionally, the United States seems like a brilliant source of further investment opportunities for Embraer in the developed world. In 2013, Embraer invested a total of about $580 million, of which $100 million was for research, $300 million for product development and $180 million for capital expenditures.[26]

Entering the United States

Although they have long-established trade relations, Brazil and the United States continue developing new initiatives. In March 2011, the two nations signed the Agreement on Trade and Economic Cooperation, which enhances cooperation and collaboration on trade and investment. The agreement immediately expanded direct trade and investment opportunities, and is intended to foster innovation, trade facilitation and FDI.[27] The U.S. goods trade surplus with Brazil was $11.6 billion in 2012 – an increase of $413 million over 2011. Both U.S. goods exports and imports have risen, and Brazil represented the seventh-largest export market and the fifteenth-largest import market for the United States in 2012. Brazil's FDI into the United States totaled $5 billion in 2011. Although

Brazil-owned companies totaled $1.3 billion in U.S. sales, this was still only about one-tenth of what U.S. companies sold in Brazil.[28]

In 2005, Embraer announced the expansion of its maintenance operations in Nashville, Tennessee, to meet growing demand for full-service aircraft maintenance in the United States. Already in 2006, Embraer opened its 7,250 m² hangar at Nashville International Airport, providing 165 full-time jobs, as well as aircraft maintenance and repairs for its growing customer fleet in North America. In the same year, three new service centers were inaugurated in Florida, Arizona and Connecticut. Yet it was only in 2008 that Embraer started construction of its first assembly plant in the United States in Florida, which was completed in 2011 at a cost of $48 million.[29]

In 2012, the development of the new Embraer Engineering and Technology Center USA began and opened two years later. The investment was $24 million. Embraer employs 1,300 people in the United States out of its headquarters in Fort Lauderdale. The company manufactures executive jets on Florida's Space Coast, assembles military planes in Jacksonville and plans further development of its high-tech research center in Florida – namely, by employing former NASA engineers.

The close relationships between Brazil and the United States enabled Embraer, one of the biggest aircraft manufacturers in the world, to set up its North American branch without fighting trade restrictions. Nevertheless, the company was careful in choosing where exactly to invest. Florida was selected because of its favorable business climate, skilled labor force, the excellent prospects for greenfield investment and the similar way of executing the construction processes (building facilities) – requirements that are not necessarily filled by other states, which often have different legislation.

To sum up, Embraer entered the U.S. market with both FDI and partnerships. The company did not face any significant problems and did not suffer any severe trade barriers. After signing the Agreement on Trade and Economic relations, the expansion of the Brazilian company into the United States was even smoother because of the nature of the agreement – it was a sound foundation for a future development of trade and investment relationships with American continent firms. Overall Embraer has invested around $1 billion in its U.S. operations since 1979.[30]

Opportunities in China

Although China has been one of Brazil's biggest export markets over the past decade, and it replaced the United States as principal partner in 2012, the two countries have seen difficult situations over the past years. At first, the Chinese government imposed barriers on manufactured imports from Brazil, while Asian companies were simultaneously aggressively pursuing market share in Brazil through cheap exports. Given the danger to local Brazilian producers, retaliatory tariffs and taxes were imposed, especially on Chinese vehicles. Given the tit-for-tat behavior, trade suffered. For example, Embraer was not granted access to the Chinese market for almost a decade, until 2000, when China's Sichuan Airlines signed an agreement to buy Embraer's ERJ145 jets.[31,32]

In 2012, the two emerging giants finally signed trade agreements to boost their exchange of goods and services. In seeking new growth opportunities, the two countries decided to collaborate, opening the potential of both markets. This pact was expected to continue loosening investment regulations in the mining, aviation and infrastructure sectors, helping companies from both countries to expand. The Brazilian government clarified its intention to "tap China's growing local market by boosting manufactured goods exports and creating joint ventures with the Asian giant."[33]

Embraer was no exception to this rule and could finally invest in the Chinese market. Yet the ten-year entry lag meant that Chinese manufacturers had already started producing regional jets. As a result, Embraer focused on business aircraft, opening a JV with Harbin Aircraft Ltd. to produce planes locally – a crucial step in order to increase productivity, cut costs and generate profits.

Harbin-Embraer joint venture

In 2002, Embraer decided to enter a strategic JV with the Chinese state-owned company Harbin Aircraft. The declared goal was to produce the ERJ145 model (regional jets that would serve Chinese customers on regional feeder routes), marking its first facility outside Brazil for regional jet assembly. In China, the number of state-owned companies was dropping as the government trimmed off loss-making SOEs, and therefore the volume of inward FDI into China was increasing. Chinese companies were seeking JV partners based on long-term goals: technological and managerial capabilities, as well as intangible assets. Embraer's stable background and earlier privatization meant it made a good fit for the Chinese.

Both Embraer and Harbin Aircraft are government-backed, and therefore the JV was also expected to reflect the policies of China and Brazil. In 2002, the ERJ145 took off, securing Embraer an impressive market share of 78% of China's regional aviation market.[34] About 70% of China's domestic market consists of low- and medium-demand daily routes that carry twenty-five to three hundred passengers each way, but Chinese domestic air travel is expected to explode. The number of regional airports has grown from 111 in 2005 to 163 in 2013, while the number of passengers flying regional routes has grown 120% over the past years.[35]

In June 2010, in light of its increasing customer base, Embraer set up its first wholly owned subsidiary in Beijing: Embraer China Aircraft Technical Services (ECA Ltd.) focusing on after-sale support. Given its growing customer base with solid orders for executive and regional jets in Asia, Embraer announced in March 2015 that by 2023 China would likely account for half of its forecast business jet sales, a number well beyond eight hundred units. For the successor of the Legacy 600 business jet, Embraer uses the same premises where it builds the ERJ 145. This underlines that the JV has become an ongoing business engagement between two equal partners.

Guan Dongyuan, president of Embraer China, confirmed that the company remains confident that China will eventually ease duties on imported aircraft components.[36] However, the extra 8% import duty on components does make profit and value creation more difficult. Even though the tax may eventually be abandoned, the production of aircraft in China may continue to be subject to various obstacles. For Embraer, one of these is the lack of competent personnel to operate the aircraft and meet the needs of business aviation. Embraer tackled this problem by collaborating with regulatory authorities and market leaders in training.

In terms of market development, it is expected that the Chinese government sooner or later will open up further to foreign investors. Therefore, the successful opening of ECA Ltd. in Beijing can be considered a milestone that will likely grant Embraer a sustained competitive advantage in the Chinese aircraft market.

Outcomes in China

Embraer is an emerging multinational, but also a mature and sophisticated company. This is why the company relies on carefully selected partnerships. The collaboration with Harbin Aircraft is a perfect example. The rising demand for domestic air travel in China meant a solid underpinning for increased demand for jets. Partnering with Harbin Aircraft, which is owned by the national Aviation Industry Corporation of China (AVIC), enabled Embraer to partake in the unsaturated Chinese market, with huge potential demand.

Embraer also successfully identified related niches (training of airport staff and flight personnel), which otherwise would have been beyond the company's reach. This proactive behavior can be considered market building. Nevertheless, it makes sense that Embraer did not vertically integrate into the air travel business itself, especially since FDI into China is still subject to many obstacles (e.g. the import tax on plane parts). Embraer assembles its aircraft in China by importing different plane components. For example, the 170/190 regional jet family is developed through partnerships with sixteen risk-sharing partners and twenty-two main suppliers. Embraer does the design and the aircraft development, including manufacturing of the fuselage, wing assembly and final aircraft integration. Other companies such as Kawasaki Heavy Industries from Japan, Sonaca of Belgium, Latecoere of France and Gamesa of Spain are responsible for other structural sections of the aircraft. General Electric supplies engines and nacelles. The assembly line in Harbin pays 22% tax on parts imports, which makes building jets in China more expensive than elsewhere.[37]

FDI in France[38]

Another important international market for Embraer is France. France has had a positive trend of FDI inflows in the country over the past years. Although globally these money flows slowed down in advanced economies, the country has always registered an excellent amount of foreign investment. Ever since 2008, according to the OECD, it has been among the top-ten FDI magnets.[39] The former economy minister Christine Lagarde described 2010 as a "record-breaking year." Furthermore, in 2013, France was in among the top-five FDI inflow recipients in Europe, grabbing the lead over Germany, the engine of the EU economy.

On the other hand, the French government has also been described as protectionist in some matters. For example, Italian companies were fended off when trying to acquire a majority stake in EDF, the leading French energy giant. Furthermore, the French government has published a list of eleven strategic industrial sectors that are closely monitored and protected from foreign takeover. Thus there are some concerns that France retains Gaullist economic traits. Another drawback is the country's inflexible labor market.

However, several characteristics do make France attractive: the large domestic market and its small francophone satellites (Belgium and Switzerland), reliable infrastructure, the highly educated workforce and low-cost energy. Such advantages convinced companies such as Embraer to choose France, often using the country as a springboard for further EU expansion.

Embraer has been operating in France since 1982, more or less, through sales representatives. The company established its Embraer Aviation International headquarters in Paris in 1983. Embraer started full-scale investment in France in 2008 by building a wholly owned service center at the Le Bourget airport outside Paris. Seven years later, after good growth performance, Embraer Executive Jets announced expansion plans at the facility. The new 4,000 m² (43,000 square feet) service center is twice as large as the previous facility. The president and CEO of Embraer Executive Jets commented that Le Bourget is not only its main hub for business aviation in Europe but also "the base of our support operations in the region and plays a key role in our expansion strategy."[40]

France was chosen because of the quality of its workforce. Besides the Paris region and particularly the closeness to Roissy-Charles de Gaulle Airport, the company considered it a strategic location. France's central geographic position within Europe was also an important factor, as was the proximity to North Africa, another promising market for Embraer.[41]

Supply chain management

The supply chain connects all the stages of a manufacturing company's value chain. In the case of aircraft manufacturers, it has enormous complexity and requires special management attention. An aircraft is a combination of a large number of different components which effectively interact with one another. Consequently, gathering the whole supply chain inside a single company is an impossible task and would impose a huge risk on the company.

Instead, every modern aircraft producer – just like every auto manufacturer – creates and manages a network of suppliers, while typically retaining some key manufacturing components internally. Such networks include a variety of suppliers from all over the world who dispatch products ranging from complex electronics to raw materials.

Embraer's supply chain consists of two blocks. The first domestic block is located in Brazil. Its role is the extraction, processing and supply of the raw materials required by Embraer. The second block is international and supplies the company with system components and certain raw materials as well. For example, the design for the Embraer 170 was done in the United Kingdom, engines come from General Electric (United States), high-quality fuselage aluminium is supplied from Germany and solid rivets are made in France.

The company pays close attention to a group of critical suppliers. These companies are labelled "high risk" due to the threat to the entire assembly process in the case of either supply delays or contract breaking. Embraer constantly conducts specific evaluations and audits to predict, evaluate and reduce these risks. It also makes considerable effort to reduce the number of critical suppliers.

The company also runs an Embraer Entrepreneurial Excellence program for both domestic and international suppliers, which is aimed to train suppliers' personnel and improve their business processes.

Another important aspect of Embraer's supply chain is its relational governance. This means that the supplier-contractor relationship is based on a mutual reliance, grounded on reputation, cultural-social-spatial proximity, family and ethnic connections and other parameters. Since this type of governance implies extensive sharing of knowledge and information, it requires thorough selection of suppliers and tight control over specifications and high-value activities. It also means that suppliers receive incentives to complete orders on time, so they often show initiative and therefore enjoy increased contractual freedom. Such linkages between partners are complicated to build and require important amounts of time, meaning it is hard to reconfigure the supply chain quickly.

Although this approach might seem typical for socially minded Brazilians, it is actually implemented by all major aircraft producers in the world. However, there is a case of a radical change of the governance paradigm by industry co-leader Boeing. Quite recently, Boeing began development and production of its 787 Dreamliner. It is a jumbo jet that pushes technological limits by introducing a new carbon-based fuselage in place of traditional aluminium -alloy based materials. This project had increased complexity, which meant that Boeing's supply chain experienced a shock. There was a question of if the chain would manage to cope with such a complicated task, and it did not. This forced Boeing to forfeit the relational type and switch to hierarchical. The hierarchical relationship implies vertical integration with tight managerial control over leading suppliers.

Boeing's early plans for the inaugural 787 flight were scheduled for August 2007. After five delay announcements, the test flight was finally conducted in December 2009. Many airlines claimed to seek compensation for the delays.[42]

The same story has happened with the double-decker Airbus A380. Airbus announced a first delay in June 2005, followed by a second announcement in June 2006. This caused a 26% drop in the share price of the Airbus parent EADS. In 2009, only ten aircraft could be delivered out of the eighteen promised.

Although Embraer's reputation was not tarred by similar delays, its Legacy 500 was postponed from 2013 to 2014. More recently, in 2015, Embraer delayed the delivery of its first twin-engine KC-390s to the Brazilian Air Force for two years. The initial plan had called for delivery by 2016, but the devaluation of the Brazilian real and government spending cuts postponed matters to 2018.[43]

As internationalization and globalization increase, the supply chains of the leading aircraft producers are definitely subject to change in the near future. Given the growing complexity of aircraft, it is inevitable that supply chain risks will rise, forcing companies to regularly revise their chains. As the world's third-largest aircraft manufacturer, Embraer is no exception and is already planning supply chain innovations to compete with the leaders.

Since the proximity to the customer is not significant for aircraft manufacturers, geographic investment choices depend more on benefits such as business conditions (e.g. legislation, tax incentives, cheap or highly qualified labor force) and closer vicinity to suppliers. The latter is crucial in the case of the supply chain, since it allows for better control over suppliers, greater options in searching for suppliers and lead time reduction.

This shows in Embraer's FDI strategy. The company has already established main facilities in Europe (France and Portugal) and in the United States. It also created JVs with Portuguese and Chinese aerospace producers. Portugal serves as a convenient base for Embraer's European operations due to such factors as shared culture and language, educated and relatively cheap labor force. China is Embraer's important customer and worldwide production center at the same time, which means favorable foreign investments policy and high efficiency of supply chain.

Another particular feature of Embraer's supply chain is its reflective stance for key decision points. Haste makes waste seems to be the cautious thinking at Embraer. This is what sets Embraer apart from its competitors. When Boeing starts aircraft production it knows exactly what model and configuration are being built, for which client. For Embraer, its many products (mostly regional jets) pass through several decision points during production. At production kick-off, management chooses the product family (for regional jets, families 170 and 190, which vary in terms of size mainly). After six to eight months of production, the particular platform (model) is then chosen. For example, the 170 family can become either model 170 or 175 at this stage. After another two to four months, the aircraft is then customized with the seating layout, interior design, external paint and other client-customized features. This method grants Embraer greater flexibility in production, thus reducing contractual and supply chain risks: a time window exists to change the particular model of the aircraft while in production.

Staying away from Airbus and Boeing territory is key to Embraer's commercial-aircraft strategy as the company looks to grow. "The fact that defense can grow to be a solid business and business aviation to be another important pillar is embedded in our decision not to try to engage in larger commercial aircraft," says President/CEO Frederico Fleury Curado. "Diversification is a need for us. I don't see either being larger than commercial aircraft, at least on the visible horizon, but they can be important enough."[44]

Contemporary global challenges make Embraer carefully develop its supply chain, which is, in fact, not so difficult – the company just has to continue doing what it does now. First, approaching markets where the most important suppliers are present. Proximity to them means decreased lead times, increased range of partners available and, therefore, reduced risks and costs. Second, tightening control over suppliers, especially in the most complex projects due to the right effort-risk balance and ability to accumulate experience for future transformation. Third, implementing a cultural change, which is the key not only for supply chain but also for the whole international strategy of the company. Finally, developing postponement strategies further, which supports product customization and strategy flexibility.

Predicting the future of Embraer

Embraer is now ranked number three in aircraft manufacturing and certainly has the necessary technological expertise. Their M&A activities included the acquisition of a former JV with Liebherr (aerospace system and component manufacturer) and currently holding 65% in OGMA (major Portuguese aviation manufacturer, offering services like maintenance, repair and overhaul of civilian and military aircraft).[45]

Another new market for Embraer is India, which is one of the juiciest markets in the world. The business environment in India is usually very highly rated by companies having local experience. Among the important Indian features are the existence of a well-developed local supplier network, numerous industrial clusters and the fast development of scientific institutions and R&D centers. India is particularly highly ranked regarding the availability of scientists and engineers with a good command of English. These factors contribute to good assessments in terms of access to modern technology and innovation capabilities.[46]

All this encouraged Embraer to enter India to a greater extent, especially after the 2014 order by Indian carrier Air Costa of fifty E-Jets E2 with an option on fifty more. With this order, the total E-Jets E2 orders reached two hundred planes with two hundred options since the launch of the E2 program.

Both the United States and India are strategic markets for Embraer and highly important for the company. The difference is that the U.S. market is highly competitive but also highly profitable because of the high average income per capita of consumers and the large overall market size. Embraer also benefits from a good reputation in the United States. However labor costs are very high. Embraer has built a successful U.S. presence due to the country's proximity. Expanding into the United States has been a means for Embraer to increase its efficiency. Although India is more distant, and the margins are lower there, this is compensated by the huge market growth potential.

7.3 Spreading operations globally: case of Vale

Company overview

Vale was founded in 1942 under the name Companhia Vale do Rio Doce (also known as CVRD prior to 2007) in Itabira, about 545 kilometers from Rio de Janeiro. It used to be majority-owned by the Brazilian government. The company has been very success-ful from its very beginnings, with Vale accounting for 80% of overall Brazilian iron ore export barely seven years after its creation. In 1974, CVRD became the largest worldwide exporter of iron ore – a title that it still holds today.[47]

Vale is the leader in the production and export of iron ore and the largest manufacturer of nickel. Vale, Rio Tinto and BHP Billiton are the top iron ore producers and exporters in the world. In 2013, the three main players covered over 58% of the global seaborne iron ore market. Vale has about 26% market share, substantially more than its main competi-tors. Vale exported 311 million tons of iron ore from Brazil versus 209 million tons for Rio Tinto and 186 million tons for BHP. In 1982, the company diversified out of iron and nickel by producing aluminium in Rio de Janeiro.

Geographically, Vale first expanded within Brazil, moving from the southeast into the northeast, central west and northern regions of Brazil in order to diversify its mineral product portfolio and logistics services. In 1997, Vale was partially privatized, with the National Steel Company acquiring 41.73%. Many politicians were opposed to the priva-tization, which did not go smoothly. However, the company remained publicly traded on both the BOVESPA and NYSE exchanges.[48] After its privatization, Vale turned its main focus on the mining business and accelerated its internationalization, especially after dis-posing of its Cenibra wood pulp business for $760.5 million.[49]

With a mission "to be the number one global natural resources company in creating long term value, through excellence and passion for people and the planet," Vale is present in over thirty countries, on five continents, with headquarters in Rio de Janeiro and with total revenues of $37.5 billion in 2014.[50] In 2014, Vale employed 766,531 staff.[51] During its seventy years of existence, the company has extracted over five billion tons of iron ore, enough for a forest of 375,000 Eiffel Towers! Aside from being the largest producer of iron ore and nickel in the world, Vale also operates hydroelectric plants and a network of railroads, ships and ports, making it the largest logistics operator in Brazil.

As if that was not enough, Vale also produces manganese, copper, bauxite, potash and cobalt. Vale does both the extractive mining and then the higher value-added metallurgy (i.e. transformation of ore into metals such as copper or cobalt). The mining process is extremely capital consuming, which is not only the case of Vale but also of other emerg-ing MNEs in extractive industries. For instance, Indonesian metallurgy company Krakatau Steel has invested $600 million for the blast furnace complex, which is being built on sixty hectares in the company's industrial compound in Cilegon, Banten.[52] Billions of dollars can be spent easily to develop one large mining project.

Background for internationalization

Over time, Vale became a large multinational, with diversified activities in mining and metallurgy, and of course a huge logistics operator. On its path to global renown, Vale went through every stage of the internationalization process: it started with simple export, then sales and marketing subsidiaries, then establishing JVs, and finally setting up produc-tion facilities in mining (on its own) and metallurgy (via JVs with steel companies). Its intense foreign expansion relied on a combination of market and non-market tactics, often reaching goals via political and social leverage.

Because it deals with natural resources that are part of non-renewable country assets, the mining industry is highly regulated. Government, and therefore politics, plays a significant role. In this industry, non-market strategies are imperative to gain competitive advantage both in the home and host country.[53] In fact, a prior president of Brazil (Getulio Vargas) established Vale in 1942. The company started as a state-owned operation. Vale's internationalization process dates back to when Vargas created the National Bank for Economic and Social Development (BNDES) to finance Brazilian companies in their expansion abroad. Consequently, BNDES became Vale's main shareholder.

Using BNDES funds, Vale started massive exporting in 1970, thanks to its constantly growing iron ore production.[54] With revenue gradually increasing from both national and international sources, Vale started diversifying by acquisitions and international JVs and then extended its product portfolio into aluminium, manganese, phosphates (for fertilizers) and other resources.

Vale starts in China

Vale first tested the Chinese waters in 1973, when it sold its first shipload of iron ore to China. In 1994, the company decided to further expand its partnership by establishing an office in China. This strategic step was meant to provide better market intelligence and assess additional activities in China. Vale then developed a series of mutually beneficial JVs with China's largest steel producer, Baosteel. Nowadays, Vale generates 40% of its revenue from China via numerous JVs in the country.[55]

Through a joint venture, Vale operates two coal mines in Henan Province. Vale owns a 25% stake, the other stakes belonging to Youngmei, Baosteel and other minority stakeholders. In 2008, Vale launched another joint venture with Halswell and the Yueyufeng Zhuhai Plant. The iron ore pellet facility is located in Guangdong Province as part of the Yueyufeng steel-making complex, which provides port facilities for receiving pellet feed produced at Vale's mines in Brazil.

In 2011, Vale started a joint venture with Anyang Plant in Henan province. The plant can produce up to 1.2 million metric tons of iron ore pellets annually. Vale has a 25% stake.

In partnership with two Chinese companies, Vale also owns a metallurgical coke plant in Shandong province. The Yanzhou plant produces metallurgical coke, methanol, tar oil and benzene.

Another of Vale's projects in China is the Dalian Refinery, a nickel refinery in Liaoning Province. Vale operates it through joint venture, possessing 98.3%. The partner here is Ningbo Sunhu Chemicals. For all these Chinese JVs, the business logic is that Brazil provides raw materials that are then processed in China for local use or re-export.

Increasing footprint

The pace of growth dampened in the 1980s and 1990s because of the Brazilian "lost decade," when the Latin American financial crisis hit, and several countries accumulated too much foreign debt, forcing debt payment rescheduling. Given the lack of capital to invest abroad, Vale chose export as its main foreign entry mode, until its 1997 privatization. Until privatization, Vale had been a national company, with its main focus being its domestic market. After privatization, Vale revised its portfolio (namely, investments in non-core activities in Brazil) and decided to expand its global footprint by increasing FDI and JVs, with the aim of becoming a leading international mining company.[56] Vale's intense expansion strategy was so successful that it became the world's largest metal and mining company based on 2014 revenues.[57]

Vale also has a long history with the United States, going back to the early 1950s when Vale started exporting iron ore, as well as 80% of its iron production. Today Vale has a commercial office in New Jersey and a stake in California Steel Industries.[58]

Although Vale's bread and butter activities remain exploration and exploitation, the company does not forget R&D, which traditionally receives a generous budget. Driven by its diversification strategy and R&D innovations, the company takes the risk of being proactive. Within the African continent, rich in terms of resources and cheap labor, Vale has often benefitted from first-mover advantage.

Between 2003 and 2007, Vale successfully managed to increase its worldwide footprint, which declined, however, after 2007. The volume of foreign disinvestment (withdrawals) started increasing due to a changing corporate strategy under newly appointed CEO Murilo Ferreira, refocusing on the Brazilian market for exporting iron ore and narrowing foreign investments as of 2012.

Vale's worldwide portfolio

Because Vale has a very diverse portfolio of international ventures, the company chooses different approaches for different markets. When making its choice, Vale's checklist includes transaction costs, potential benefits of the market under consideration and the strategic importance of the market overall. During the very intense expansion spurt between 2002 and 2008, the main focus was on less-developed countries rich in resources and cheap in labor. However these markets also present many obstacles – namely, political instability and corruption. Vale responded to these persistent "non-market" pressures by investing into the potential countries to overcome entry barriers. Further discussion of this comes at the end of this chapter.

Across the geographies where it operates, Vale deploys a variety of strategic approaches tailored to specific market needs and opportunities. One cannot talk of a "one-size-fits-all" situation, especially since Vale's investments vary radically, depending on whether it is investing a simple sales offices, in logistics infrastructure (e.g. ports, rail links for ore export), in mining deposits (e.g. open sky vs. subterranean) or in metallurgy transformation facilities (smelters, etc.).

American ventures: In Argentina, South America's second-largest country with forty million inhabitants, apart from having a sales office in Buenos Aires, Vale also operates a 100%-owned port called Vale Logistics Argentina, which connects South America to the Asian-European markets. Vale invested massively in the country, in railway renovation and construction. However, its ongoing project, Ria Colorado, to develop a potash mine was suspended in 2013 due to misalignments in equity shareholdings.

In Peru, in 2002, Vale established a JV with Mitsui and Mosaic (Vale's stake is 40%) to operate the Bajover mine with its huge phosphate rock reserves. The JV also includes a concentration plant with a port and employs more than 1,800 people. In Chile, Vale conducts mineral exploration projects, coordinating matters from its Santiago office.

As for North America, Vale's operations focus on Canada. In 2006, Vale acquired, for nearly $20 billion, 100% of nickel producer Inco Ltd,[59] one of two of Canada's largest mining companies, where it employs 1,500 staff. Canada played a key role for Vale during the height of its international expansion, with three major projects going on simultaneously (Sudbury Basin, Thompson and Voisey's Bay). Canada has also been a showcase for Vale's environment-friendly strategy, with a $1 billion budget to reduce polluting emissions, one of the largest programs in all of Canada.

European ventures: In Europe, Vale's first stop was Salzburg (Austria) where in 2005, it established Vale International Holdings GmbH, responsible for all its African, South American, Asian, European and Middle Eastern subsidiaries. In 2006, Vale invested around SFr 50 million on its Swiss sales office to support its extensive commodity trading and sales activities (iron ore, nickel, copper and coal).

African ventures: Every self-respecting mining company has a foothold in Africa, and Vale is no exception. In fact, the company operates in four different African countries. Guinea is both the diamond in its African crown and the thorn in its foot (more on that in the next section). Guinea holds one of those mining miracles that makes the extractive industry believe in higher powers: the Simadou iron ore vein, one of the best undeveloped deposits in the world. In 2006, Vale acquired 51% of the license from Israeli wildcatter Barry Steinmetz (BSG Resources). Despite its large investments in the country, Vale had

Table 7.2 Synopsis of Vale's international activities

Country	Project	Activities	Since	Type	Vale's stake
Australia	Isaac Plains I-II	Metallurgy & thermal coal	2017	JV with Sumitomo	50%
Australia	Carborough Downs	Metallurgy & thermal coal	2007	JV	85%
Australia	Integra Coal	Metallurgy & thermal coal	2007	JV	61.2%
Australia	Belvedere	Developing an underground coal mine	2007	Wholly owned	100%
India		Sales office			
Indonesia	Larona Hydroelectric	Hydroelectric power	1979	Wholly owned	100%
Indonesia	Balambano Hydroelectric	Hydroelectric power	1979	Wholly owned	100%
Indonesia	Karebbe Hydroelectric	Hydroelectric power	2011	Wholly owned	100%
Indonesia	Vale Indonesia Tbk	Nickel	2006	Wholly owned	100%
Indonesia	Sorowako Complex	Nickel	2016	JV	59.3%
Japan	Matsusaka Refinery	Refinery	1955	JV	87.2%
Malaysia	Teluk Rubiah Maritime Terminal	Logistics	2014	Wholly owned	100%
Oman	Sohar Complex	Iron ore	2011	JV	70%
Taiwan	Taiwan Nickel	Nickel	2006	JV	49.9%
South Korea	Korea Niquel Corporation	Nickel	1989	JV	25%
Singapore		Sales office	2007		
China	Zhuhai Plant	Iron ore pellet plant	2008	JV	25%
China	Refinery	Nickel	2008	JV	98.3%

Source: Vale website (www.vale.com)

to suspend its activities in 2014 due to a complex politico-legal wrangle with the Guinean government and Australian rival Rio Tinto.

Moving to more stable markets, in Malawi, Vale embarked on a 50-50 coal joint venture with Japanese company Mitsui. Vale gained a foothold in Mozambique in 2008 when it successfully obtained the rights to develop the Moatize mine through its second 50-50 JV with Mitsui. The company also conducts a structured environment program by investing in water and air quality campaigns and waste treatments. In Zambia, Vale has operated since 2010 through a 50-50 JV with African Rainbow Minerals to produce copper.

Asian ventures: Asia and Oceania add yet another arrow to Vale's quiver – namely, in coal production (for coking coal for metallurgy and thermal coal for energy production). To this avail, since 2007, Vale has chosen to establish JVs with local companies. Part of its strategy here is also to invest in "non-market tools" – namely, better relationships with local authorities. For instance, Vale invested more than $2.5 million in a geo-microbiology knowledge center in Australia. In Malaysia, the company launched an advanced environment protection program in a nature preserve. Similarly, in Oman on the Indian Ocean, Vale poured $50 million into technologies to reduce the environmental impact of the Sohar Industrial Complex.[60]

FDI strategy

After the privatization, Vale became more focused on the mining business. The company's business strategy has been evolving during the past decade to a strategy of maintaining a leadership position in the global iron ore market and to grow through world-class assets while maintaining low-cost structure and well-established and disciplined management. Vale's business strategy has been dedicated in enhancing their competitiveness through continuous investments in railroads within their global distribution network. In fact, the quality of the railroads is crucial for Vale competitiveness in the global market. Therefore, investments in railway assets have been a primary concern of the company in order to meet the needs of their iron ore business. In this context, Vale's commercial strategy is to build an efficient global distribution network. Thus Vale invests in floating transfer stations (FTS) in Philippines, in a distribution center in Oman and in the development of a distribution center in Malaysia. In order to strengthen its position and future expansion in Mozambique, Vale is currently investing in the railroad capacity by renewing the existing railway network or building new one in Nacala-a-Velha.[61]

Vale's program of foreign investments has been very extensive for the past decade. The company has completed the construction of a hydrometallurgical facility in Long Harbour in 2013 in Labrador, Canada. This refinery has an estimated capacity of 50,000 tpy of finished nickel, copper and cobalt co-product streams. Another project is the construction of a nickel-copper mine, Totten, in Sudbury in Ontario, Canada, with the nominal capacity of 8,000 tpy nickel and 10,000 tpy of copper.[62] Other investments by Vale in 2014 were the expansion of the Burcutu plant, the part of the company's Southeastern System, and the Teluk Rubiah Distribution Center in Malaysia. The latter one is a maritime terminal with a private jetty and depth to receive vessels with a capacity of 400,000 DWT. One of Vale's largest projects is the Nacala Corridor, railway and port infrastructure development in Mozambique, connecting Nacala-a-Velha maritime terminal with Moatize.[63]

During internationalization, Vale tried to diversify and become independent of the national market, which led to aggressive exploration and investments in the less-developed markets in Africa and Asia, and the company has focused on acquisitions. Vale invested in a Mozambique (2003) mining project and acquired companies for potassium in Argentina (2004) and phosphate in Peru (2005). Furthermore, Vale acquired the Canadian company INCO in 2006, which enabled Vale to include nickel in their core business also. In Australia, Vale acquired AMCI Holdings, which enabled Vale to enter not only the Australian market, but also the Chinese market. Vale made various investments in Angola, South Africa, Chile, Gabon, Guinea, Mongolia and Mozambique, which made the company one of the major players in the mining industry in the world.[64]

Vale experienced many barriers to their future expansion and outward FDI imposed by the Brazilian government, which is one of the main stakeholders of the company. In order to avoid such influence, Agnelli, the CEO of Vale, tried to convince the government to sell their shares of the company, which eventually will enable the company to properly implement its expansion strategies and to properly direct their investments. Therefore, while exploitation was the core activity for growth, the Brazilian government insisted on neglecting technological innovations and focusing on the steel manufacturing. Such imposed barriers come from particular political disputes that hamper the growth of the company.[65]

Problems related to expansion

Mining is not for the faint of heart. Commodity prices fluctuate wildly, and companies in this segment need good, strong guts and quick reactions. Vale is no exception to the rule: it has needed to adapt its operations and cost structure to the economic trends. For example, during the global financial crisis in 2008, which impacted Chinese demand for metals and minerals. This pressure from China resulted in a 45% drop in prices. How did Vale react? It entered into maritime shipping, thus gaining in competitiveness by including sea transport costs in its pricing schemes! Vale re-assessed the global potential for minerals and metals, and refocused on less-developed markets instead of the developed economies that were suffering from Lehman Brothers blues. It is not by chance that in the past decade, Vale decided to direct its investments into Asia and Africa.[66]

Although the bottom line is the company's prime preoccupation, it is not to the detriment of corporate social responsibility – namely, better compliance with local regulations, controls and procedures in the countries where Vale operates. The regulations for exploring land areas and exploiting deposits are very different by country. Vale, therefore, faces very different challenges in each foreign market, thus forcing the company to adapt each time to local conditions. The first step in this adaptation process is integrating with the regional communities where the operations take place. For instance, in Mozambique, Vale had to adapt to local traditions, where local villagers believe that their land links them to their ancestors. Vale had to perform various rituals with local leaders before starting its mining activities. Another cultural twist came from the strong relationship of Mozambicans with nature, especially with a giant tree called the baobab, considered to be sacred. Many local employees asked Vale to disburse their salaries under a baobab tree.[67]

Peruvian local communities proved to be another challenge for Vale in adapting business practices to local community demands. Vale held fifty meetings with town and village representatives, during which the project was fully explained. Furthermore, by establishing various agreements with universities and other training centers, Vale defined the socio-economic demands of the locals and then invested in the appropriate social projects.[68] In the end, that is how Vale finally received local approval for the project.

Obviously, a company with such a wide international footprint cannot always be consistent in its strategy, especially given the variety and diversity of its labor force. Vale did encounter difficulties in educating its workers, especially staff from Africa and from smaller Asian countries. Disregard for labor laws was sometimes fostered by employees ready to work overtime when the company pays. Serious mining accidents started occurring more frequently, resulting in injuries and even deaths. Unfortunately, this is the case of the whole mining industry and not only of a given company.

Corruption issues

In January 2012, Vale won a prize that it would have preferred not to win since it goes to companies whose activities infringe human rights, or destroy nature or are involved in corrupt deals. Greenpeace and the Berne Declaration awarded their Public Eye Award to Vale as the worst company of the year.[69] Ouch.

The main accusation regarded Vale's double standard. In developed countries, such as Australia and Canada, Vale behaved as a good, clean company, with no participation in questionable transactions. Alas, in countries with less-developed standards of transparency or lower moral standards for business, Vale seemed to accept corrupt practices.

Yet the straw that broke the camel's back was in Vale's own backyard, in the Amazon rainforest state of Para, for the construction of the Belo Monte dam. Not only could Vale's construction destroy the pristine nature of that Amazonian area, but there were also local aboriginal tribes living in there. More damning yet, Vale started construction with just a partial license in hand, causing a public uproar. Brazilian laws stipulate that it is illegal to issue partial project licenses, but even more so to start work therewith. The partial license for Belo Monte was issued by the IBAMA (the Brazilian Institute of Environment and Renewable Natural Resources), perceived in Brazil as the administrative arm of the Ministry of the Environment. Speculation abounded that corruption must have greased the wheels of the machinery in granting the partial license. In February of 2011, a lawsuit was initiated, which some claim was the biggest public hearing Brazil has ever had.

In December 2014, Vale had to contend with a legal bombshell when Australian mining giant Rio Tinto accused Vale and billionaire Barry Steinmetz of illegally acquiring the rights for the Simandou iron ore deposit in Guinea.[70]

The project is located in the southeast of Guinea. The partners include the Republic of Guinea (7.5%), Rio Tinto (46.57%), Aluminium Corporation of China ("Chinalco") (41.3%) and the International Finance Corporation ("IFC") (4.625%), which is a member of the World Bank Group.[71] The project is the largest combined iron ore mine and infrastructure project ever developed in Africa, with the potential to transform the Guinean economy and transport infrastructure.

As of 2012, with over US$3 billion already committed to the project,[72] Rio Tinto started pouring investments in the mine, expecting that Simandou would generate massive future cash flows. Vale smelled the opportunity and put out feelers to see if Rio Tinto would sell. Pretending interest, Vale was in fact obtaining confidential operational information elaborated by Rio Tinto on Simandou expansion strategies.[73]

Then suddenly it became publicly known that Rio Tinto no longer possessed the rights to Simandou. Claims flew that Vale, along with Barry Steinmetz, had corrupted Guinean government officials to misappropriate Rio Tinto's rights. Given such public accusations, and after several changes in government, Guinea decided to conduct a special investigation which proved the Rio Tinto version of facts. As could be expected given the high stakes – both financial and for reputations – Vale and Steinmetz immediately appealed the verdict. After long judicial proceedings, Vale managed to overturn the charges and was declared innocent.

Hero or villain?

As a huge multinational that has successfully managed to spread its wings over many continents, Vale earns kudos for great strategic thinking. The company is very flexible; it knows how to adapt to new environments and circumstances, and skillfully selects the right entry strategy for each particular market. The fact that Vale successfully operates in countries that scare the pants off other multinationals shows the company's mettle. Vale's cultural policy remains homogenous, with its strong people orientation, meaning no particular adjustments are needed. Vale actively uses all entry modes – joint ventures, M&A transactions and greenfield investments – and chooses them based on location and target country rules.

Vale is a very ambitious corporation that is constantly seeking ways to expand its business and to make it more efficient. Even though Vale has at times come under suspicion concerning corruption issues, the company has so far always managed to come out clean.

References

1 Euromonitor: Brazil Country Profile.
2 www.ipardes.gov.br/anuario_2005/2infraestrutura/qdo2_1_1.xls
3 http://www.forexnews.com/blog/2013/03/14/brazilian-economy/#sthash.iBZvLdEG.dpuf
4 http://www.tradingeconomics.com/brazil/exports
5 Cristini and Amal 2006.
6 https://www.cairn.info/revue-management-2015–1-page-78.htm
7 Carneiro and Brenes 2014.
8 Wheatley 2010.
9 Carneiro and Brenes 2014.
10 Wheatley 2010.
11 Ibid.
12 Campanario, Stal and da Silva 2012.
13 Casanova and Kassum 2013.
14 Ibid.
15 Transnationality Ranking of Brazilian Companies 2012. http://www.fdc.org.br/pt/Documents/2012/ranking_transnacionais_brasileiras2012.pdf
16 Da Motta Veiga 2014.
17 Ibid.
18 Campanario, Stal and da Silva 2012.
19 UNCTAD World Investment Report 2011.
20 Sheng and Carrera Júnior 2016.
21 Gazprom opens a representative office in Rio de Janeiro. http://www.gazprom.com/press/news/2011/november/article122451/
22 https://www.vedomosti.ru/business/news/2016/03/09/632890-zyuzin
23 'Trade with Brazil gains momentum' 2011.
24 Embraer 2015.
25 http://www.fditracker.com/2012/03/embraer-from-brazil-to-establish-r.html
26 http://web.b.ebscohost.com.ezproxy.gsom.spbu.ru:2048/ehost/detail?vid=4&sid=a401eadc-339b-40fc-aa0d-cdb9b0749d16%40sessionmgr113&hid=120&bdata=Jmxhbmc9cnUmc2l0ZT1laG9zdC1saXZl#db=bwh&AN=B4Z3030174036
27 http://www.ustr.gov/countries-regions/americas/brazil
28 http://www.fditracker.com/2012/11/brazil-based-embraer-breaks-ground-on.html

29 Mann 2014.
30 Ibid.
31 http://articles.chicagotribune.com/2012–06–21/business/sns-rt-us-brazil-china-mantegabre85l01u-20120621_1_brazilian-president-dilma-rousseff-china-brazilian-market
32 Ibid.
33 Ibid.
34 Embraer website.
35 http://www.globaltimes.cn/content/951031.shtml
36 Waldron 2015.
37 http://europe.chinadaily.com.cn/business/2015–06/13/content_20992755.htm
38 http://dealbook.nytimes.com/2011/03/28/france-sees-surge-in-foreign-investments/?_php=true&_type=blogs&_r=0
39 http://www.oecd.org/daf/inv/investment-policy/FDI-in-Figures-Feb-2014.pdf
40 http://www.embraer.com/en-us/imprensaeventos/press-releases/noticias/pages/embraer-aviacao-executiva-anuncia-novo-centro-de-servicos-na-franca.aspx.
41 Foreign investors: France remains on course. France in Canada. French Embassy in Ottawa. http://www.ambafrance-ca.org/Foreign-investors-France-remains
42 http://profit.ndtv.com/news/corporates/article-govt-approves-air-india-compensation-package-for-dreamliner-delay-308387
43 http://www.ainonline.com/aviation-news/defense/2015–07–30/embraer-delays-deliveries-kc-390-airlifter-two-years
44 http://aviationweek.com/awin/new-e-jet-family-versus-smaller-cseries
45 Doors promises new investment Embraer in Portugal http://bestportugueseeconomy.blogspot.ru/2015/04/doors-promises-new-investment-embraer.html
46 The Global Competitiveness Report.
47 Vale History, www.vale.com
48 www.vale.com
49 http://www.prnewswire.com/news-releases/cvrd-concludes-the-sale-of-cenibra-72035497.html
50 http://www.vale.com/EN/aboutvale/mission/Pages/default.aspx
51 Vale Annual Report 2014.
52 Smith 2013.
53 http://lexicon.ft.com/Term?term=non_market-strategy
54 Vale Nossa Historia 2012.
55 http://www.vale.com/EN/aboutvale/news/pages/vale-na-china.aspx
56 Rodrigues and Dieleman 2014.
57 http://www.mining-technology.com/features/featuremining-giants – the-top-ten-richest-mining-companies-4203262/
58 http://www.vale.com/brasil/EN/aboutvale/across-world/Pages/default.aspx
59 Austen 2006.
60 Vale across the world 2016.
61 Vale Annual Report 2013, p.18.
62 Ibid., p.20.
63 Ibid., p.21.
64 Rodrigues and Dieleman 2014.
65 Ibid.
66 Ibid.
67 Vale History Book 2012.
68 Ibid.
69 Public Eye Nominations 2012.
70 Kiernan 2014.
71 Rio Tinto 2014.
72 Rio Tinto 2012.
73 Kiernan 2014.

8 International strategies of Chinese multinationals

This chapter presents the integration of Chinese multinationals in the global economy, including the role of the domestic market role for internationalization of Chinese firms. Greater attention is paid to outbound investment from China, with the industry and regional analysis of outward investments from China. Two specific multinational companies will be covered: Geely and ZTE. Both companies have strengthened their international standing via knowledge and technology development. Yet auto manufacturer Geely operates via intensive joint ventures and deal transactions, while ZTE has expanded more gradually, relying more on greenfield development than on takeover. Understanding the strategies of these multinationals is easier when justifying it using some of the theories discussed in earlier chapters.

8.1 Globalization of China and international investments of Chinese firms

Internationalization of economy: recent trends

China has the world's second-largest economy in terms of nominal GDP, totaling approximately $10.4 trillion. On a purchasing power parity basis (PPP), China's economy is the world's largest, with a 2014 PPP GDP of $18 billion.[1] On a per capita basis, the story is somewhat different given the massive Chinese population: the GDP per capita was only $13,224 in 2014, leaving China in the middle of the pack, behind more than eighty wealthier countries.[2]

Nowadays, China is a socialist republic ruled by a single party, the Chinese Communist Party (CCP). There are twenty-two provinces, and four municipalities directly under central government control, as well as five autonomous regions. The total population of the country is about 1.38 billion people (2015 estimate), spread over the country's 9.6 million km².

Since its founding in 1949, the People's Republic of China has been a Soviet-style, centrally planned economy governed by the communist party. After Mao's death in 1976 and the subsequent end of the Cultural Revolution, new Chinese leadership under Deng Xiaoping started to gradually reform the economy and move towards a more market-oriented mixed economy, yet ruthlessly preserving one-party rule. Inefficient state-owned enterprises were restructured, farmland was privatized and foreign trade became a major priority.

Since launching reform and opening up the country, China has experienced sustained economic growth, with many Chinese firms gradually increasing their international exposure and activities. Expanding internationally so as to increase revenues, capture greater resources and acquire advanced management experience has become a common undertaking of many Chinese firms. State-owned enterprises (SOEs) still dominate China's economy, accounting for 46% of industrial output. SOEs produce over 50% of China's goods and services, and employ over half of the nation's labor force.[3] Naturally, in some sectors, state enterprises remain the major players in China. In the tobacco, electric power generation and oil extraction sectors, for example, state companies account for over 90% of output. But in many other industries, from general-purpose machinery to paper and plastics, the state share is less than 15%. As for services, state companies still dominate telecoms, financial services and transportation, but more than four-fifths of retailers, accounting for about half of retail sales, are privately controlled.[4]

Despite the size of the SOEs, China's private sector has expanded rapidly and experienced healthy development in recent years. The status and economic contribution of private enterprises received official recognition in the ninth National People's Congress held in March 1999. By the end of 2014, there were 15.5 million privately held enterprises (compared to 1.76 million in 2000).[5]

Being a member of the WTO, China reached a total international trade value of $4.16 trillion in 2013, $2.21 trillion of which were exports. China is the largest exporter of industrial goods. The output includes such industrial products as steel, coal, electricity, cement, fertilizer and woven cotton fabrics.

In 2014, exports of machinery, electrical and electronic products grew by 3.7%, exports of garment grew by 5.2% and footwear increased by 10.8%. In 2015, exports of electrical and electronic products grew by 0.1% (in US$ terms), exports of garment and footwear dropped by 6.4% and 4.8%, respectively.

Over the 2010 to 2014 period, the fastest-growing Chinese export items were as follows:[6]

1 gems, precious metals, coins: up by 403.8% since 2010 ($63.2 billion)
2 collector's items, art, antiques: up by 320.6% ($675,029,000)
3 cocoa: up by 123.8% ($475,789,000)
4 feathers, artificial flowers, hair: up by 114.9% ($6,538,741,000)
5 aircraft, spacecraft: up by 113.8% ($2,704,470,000)
6 furskins and artificial fur: up by 109.0% ($4,154,986,000)
7 gums, resins: up by 102.1% ($1,305,992,000)
8 zinc: up by 100.1% ($572,821,000)
9 live trees and plants: up by 99.4% ($409,937,000)
10 ceramic products: up by 98.9% ($22,075,606,000).

The on the other side, the fastest-growing Chinese imports were as follows:

1 collector items, art, antiques: up by 2,281% (US$613,452,000)
2 cereals: up by 311.3% ($6,174,666,000)
3 gems, precious metals, coins: up by 286.3% ($41,899,468,000)
4 umbrellas, walking-sticks: up by 257.9% ($22,063,000)
5 dairy, eggs, honey: up by 224.4% ($6,487,117,000)
6 live animals: up by 210.2% ($835,042,000)
7 tobacco: up by 164.7% ($2,092,762,000)
8 meat: up by 162.5% ($5,841,175,000)
9 knit or crochet clothing: up by 152.6% ($2,067,015,000)
10 clothing (not knit or crochet): up by 150.6% ($3,559,110,000).

Table 8.1 The world's biggest public companies. China

Rank	Company	Industry	Sales	Profits	Assets	Market value
1	ICBC	Banking	166.8	44.8	3,322	278.3
2	China Construction Bank	Banking	130.5	37	2,698	212.9
3	Agricultural bank of China	Banking	129.2	29.1	2,574.8	189.9
4	Bank of China	Banking	120.3	27.5	2,458.3	199.1
8	PetroChina	Oil & gas operations	333.4	17.4	387.7	334.6
20	China Mobile	Telecoms	104.1	17.7	209	271.5
24	Sinopec	Oil & gas	427.6	7.7	233.9	121
32	Ping An Insurance Group	Insurance	75.3	6.4	645.7	113.8
37	China Life Insurance	Insurance	71.4	5.2	362.1	160.5

Note: All financials in $ billions, 2015

Source: *Forbes* (http://www.forbes.com/global2000/list/)

Worldwide, China is the undisputed trading leader. In 2015, China's total external trade reached $4.3 billion. Even so, in 2015, exports and imports dropped by 2.8% and 14.1% (in dollar terms), respectively, resulting in a trade surplus of $594.5 billion.[7] In 2014, China's top-ten export markets were the United States, Hong Kong, Japan, South Korea, Germany, the Netherlands, Vietnam, the United Kingdom, India and Russia. China's total exports with these ten economies together accounted for about 59% of total exports.

In line with the overall internationalization of the national economy, Chinese multi-national continue their impressive rise and expansion. China (both mainland and Hong Kong) added more entrants than any other country in the annual Forbes list of the world's two thousand largest firms. For the first time, China surpassed its historical rival Japan to become the second-ranked country, with 232 companies on the Forbes list, a fivefold jump from 2003.

While a major portion of China's largest companies remain state-owned, private firms are gaining share (Table 8.1), in part thanks to a heated IPO market both at home and over-seas. For example, in 2014, e-commerce giant Alibaba debuted on Forbes position 269 after launching the world's largest IPO in history. Other notable newcomers include Dalian Wanda Commercial Properties, owned by China's richest man Wang Jianlin, and Lens Technologies, which turned its founder Zhou Qunfei into the world's richest self-made woman.[8]

OFDI and MNEs: geography and strategy

Three main factors motivate Chinese multinationals to invest abroad: acquiring advanced technology through transactions (M&A deals), increasing market share and natural resource endowment.[9] For the Chinese government, natural resources are the primary motivator, accountable for 81% of the loans issued for OFDI since 2002.[10] As a growing energy consumer, second only to the United States, China is currently dependent on oil imports – a dependence the country would like to mitigate by securing its own sources. Market share gain is the second-largest reason for foreign investment, representing 15% of state-financed projects. Here Chinese power companies dominate. Technology acquisition is the grounds for only 4% of total OFDI. Yet this is still a departure from how other "Asian Miracle" countries operate.

China possesses sizeable foreign currency reserves. Given the economically depressed global environment, a cheap acquisition of Western enterprises has become an enticing option. One drawback to this approach is the anti-Chinese sentiment generated in host countries. The American Congress, for example, citing "national security threats," has blocked multiple Chinese attempts to purchase American oil, telecoms and appliance companies.[11] The rich American shale gas resources have been a strong motivator for China to launch JVs with American companies in order to access extraction technology. With this goal in mind, Sinochem (China) launched a $1.7 billion venture with Pioneer Natural Resources (United States) in order to acquire a stake in Wolcamp Shale in Texas.

These different Chinese interests indicate not just use of OFDI for "industrial adjustment" or "efficiency-seeking" investment opportunities. Manufacturing projects from China mainly aim to gain access to technological know-how or new markets rather than to take advantage of cheap labor.[12] China still holds its cheap labor advantage, which it uses within its own borders on its eastern coast in order to maintain its export advantage.

Besides their preference for countries with similar (relatively weak) institutions, Chinese multinationals also place weight on cultural and geographic proximity.[13] According to China's Ministry of Commerce, the majority (68%) of Chinese outbound FDI flows into other Asian countries. Next in queue are Latin America (13%), Europe (8%), North America and Africa (4% each) and, finally, 3% to Australia. FDI flows to other Asian countries have increased considerably over the last decade. The establishment of the China-ASEAN free-trade area in early 2010 strengthened regional economic cooperation and contributed to the promotion of two-way FDI flows.[14] Furthermore, corridors connecting South Asia and East and Southeast Asia are being established, including the Bangladesh-China-India-Myanmar Economic Corridor and the China-Pakistan Economic Corridor. These initiatives provide opportunities for economic cooperation and further infrastructure investment. Finally, the establishment of the China Pilot Free Trade Zone in Shanghai opens up six service industries (finance, transport, commerce and trade, professional services, cultural services and public services) to foreign investors, so China's FDI is likely to flow even more heavily to other Asian countries.[15]

Other, more distant destinations for Chinese OFDI are also on the rise, as in the case of Africa where investment from China increased from just $1 billion in 2004 to $24.5 billion in 2013.[16] About a third of these investments were in the extractive industries – namely, mining and oil – while another fifth were in the finance sector. The top African recipient of Chinese FDI is South Africa (22%). Other recipients include Zimbabwe, Angola, Zambia, Sudan, Congo-Kinshasa and Nigeria.[17] Some recent large projects in the region include the purchase by the China Investment Corporation of a 25% stake in Shanduka Group in South Africa for $250 million and Sinopec's $2.4 billion deal in Angola for rich offshore deepwater prospecting blocks. Overall, investments in Africa and other less-developed regions are expected to rise in the future as wage competitiveness decreases in China and companies in labor-intensive industries are compelled to relocate.[18]

Regarding the breakdown in 2012 by industry of outbound FDI, 90% of investment focused on six sectors: leasing and business services (33%), finance (18%), mining (14%), wholesale and retail trade (13%), transportation and storage (6%) and manufacturing (6%). However, this distribution may be somewhat distorted. A portion of the investments in leasing and business services were to establish investment and asset management subsidiaries in offshore financial centers. These funds probably were then redirected to unspecified value-producing activities.[19]

China-Russia investment relations

China is one of Russia's main trading partners. In 2012, the volume of trade between the two countries reached a historical high point, at $87.5 billion. However, in 2015, this volume dropped by 29.3% to $50 billion.[20] This drop can be attributed to the slowing of economic growth in both countries; the sharpening geopolitical situation, including Western sanctions and consequent drop of oil prices; and the erosion of purchasing power in Russia in general. Russia nonetheless ranked as the fifteenth-largest Chinese trade partner.

Cooperation between the two countries has historically relied on lending as opposed to FDI. The vast majority (91.5%) of Chinese direct investment in the area has been concentrated instead in Kazakhstan.[21] Although smaller, Chinese investments are more diverse in Russia than in Kazakhstan, where they focus almost exclusively on energy. In 2014, the number of cooperation agreements between Russia and China grew dramatically, indicating a brighter future for direct investment.

Chinese investments in Russia are concentrated in Siberia, the Russian Far East (with the vast majority located close to the Chinese border) and in metropolises such as Moscow and St. Petersburg. Consistent with their overall internationalization motives, the primary driver for OFDI in Russia is resource seeking. Prominent industries have included energy (natural gas and oil), forestry and retail.

Forestry

As the largest timber importer in the world, one of China's key focuses is in forestry. One-quarter of the world's timber reserves are located in Russia, the majority of which is in Siberia. Nonetheless, most Chinese projects in this industry have been small scale, consisting of sawmills close to the border to process logs for low-value basic imports.[22] The lack of formal investment is perhaps due to the large level of illegal activity in this sector: the Chinese-Russian timber trade is fraught with both illegal harvesting and illegal exports.

In 2007, the Russian government introduced a number of policies meant to spur investment, including tax incentives for new projects, and saw a subsequent increase in foreign and domestic investment, including from China, although the projects remained relatively small.[23] In 2013, the Russia-Chinese Investment Group acquired a 42% stake in Russian Forest Products to support the company in developing higher margin wood processing, in part through the construction of a center for deep-wood processing.[24]

Oil & gas

Chinese oil-related investments into Russia were relatively slow to develop despite the proximity of the countries. Until 1995, China imported no crude oil at all from Russia. In the last decade, there have been several large investments in infrastructure in order to expand gas and oil trade between the two countries. The most significant of these projects was the East Siberian–Pacific Ocean pipeline, which was built to supply the Asian-Pacific markets with Russian crude oil. Following this deal, investment in the industry began to increase. In 2006, CNPC bought a $500 million stake in Rosneft, while Sinopec purchased a 96.9% stake in Udmurtneft for $3.5 billion from TNK-BP International. The latter acquisition, which was channeled through the British Virgin Islands, demonstrates how many Chinese investments in Russia do not appear in the FDI statistics due to the fiscal optimization channeling.[25] In 2013, CNPC acquired a 20% stake in Yamal-SPG.[26]

The recent crisis in Russia has spurred a new wave of Chinese investment in the energy sector. In 2014, China struck two large energy deals with Russian enterprises: the first was $400 billion deal between Gazprom and CNPC, and the second was the sale of a 10% stake in Rosneft's Siberian unit to CNPC in order to refinance debt, which Rosneft was unable to pay due to depressed oil prices.

Automotive

Unlike European car companies, in the car-hungry Russian market, Chinese companies pursue a cost leadership strategy and therefore pose the greatest competitive threat to domestic producers.[27] Russian standards for emissions and safety are lower than in more developed countries, allowing Chinese models to be sold directly in the Russian market without many adaptations. Many companies, such as Lifan, have chosen a simple export strategy; however, Chery dared to take the first-mover advantage and was the first Chinese brand to enter Russia in 2005. First Russia's Avtotor started assembling the car, but in 2008, another company, Taganrogsky Avtomobilny Zavod, took over the assembly of the Chery A5 sedan, using complete-knocked-down kits from China. The Chery Fora in Russia was renamed the Vortex Estina. A year after its establishment in Moscow, Chery Automobile Rus began to sell cars, reaching sales of twelve thousand units in the first six months. Two years later, in 2007, Chery had a brief partnership with Kaliningrad plant Avtotor. Russia tried to promote automotive joint ventures by offering either duty-free or low duties on component imports, but failed in most cases, as with Chery and Avtotor, to honor the incentive.

Other companies have been slow to invest directly. Great Wall Motors invested RMB3.2 billion ($454 million) to build a plant in the Tula Oblast region in order to reduce costs and relieve competitive pressure. Chengfeng Motors has considered a similar shift in production, but still the plans did not come true. As Western companies such as GM leave the Russian market, there is potential for Chinese companies to utilize their competitive advantages and direct investment to gain additional market share.

To sum up, OFDI from China to Russia has been minimal over the years, but this may be poised to change. Amid political tensions, the Russian government is increasingly prepared to offer incentives to Chinese companies to invest in various industries, and indeed several deals have already been inked. China could greatly benefit from the positive relationship with the government, their understanding of the weak institutions in Russia compared to competitors, the vast resource pool and the growth potential.

8.2 Capturing knowledge: case of Geely

Company overview

Geely Automobile Holdings (Geely), formerly known as Guorun Holdings, is an investment holding company that manufactures automobiles through its subsidiaries. It is also engaged in the research, production, marketing and sales of sedans and related automobile components in China. The company operates primarily in Hong Kong and China. It is headquartered in Hangzhou and employs more than eighteen thousand people. Geely's fast development means that the company is among China's top-five-hundred companies since 2007 and a top-ten auto manufacturer since 2008.[28] Geely is recognized as one of the most innovative enterprises in China[29] and "Complete Vehicle Export Base in China."

Geely was founded in 1986 as a refrigerator manufacturer, using money borrowed from family. Its founder, Li Shufu, transformed the company into a motorcycle maker in 1994 by acquiring a bankrupt state-owned firm.[30] Then, in 1997, Geely started to make small vans. In 2002, car production began.

In 2003, Geely and Guorun Holdings Ltd, its partner in the Hong Kong Special Administrative Region, agreed to two deals to form new joint ventures. In the same year, the company set up an auto parts subsidiary in Taizhou of the Zhejiang province. Later in the same year, the company acquired another asset under Zhejiang Geely Holding.

In 2004, Guorun was renamed Geely. In the following year, the company started trial production of small family sedans at the Luqiao plant of Taizhou, Zhejiang. In 2006, the company set up 46.8%-owned JV with Geely Holding Limited through transferring the production facilities in Linhai and Luqiao from Zhejiang Geely to the two new associates Zhejiang Kingkong Automobile Company Limited and Zhejiang Ruhoo Automobile Company. In the same year, Geely established its 51%-owned Shanghai LTI Automobile Components company to produce the localized TX4 model, mostly used as taxicabs in the United Kingdom.

Further in 2006, the company, through its subsidiary Geely International Corporation, signed an agreement with the Rolf Group of Russia to import and sell Geely sedans in the Russian market. In the same year, Geely formed a wholly owned subsidiary, Zhejiang Kingkong Auto Parts R&D Company Limited.

From 2005 to 2012, Geely's annual sales volume increased fourfold due to the company's technological competitive advantage and the rapid expansion of its sales network. The company has organized its operations in two divisions: automobiles and components, and gearboxes. The first division manufactures and sells cars, automobile parts and related components (excluding gearboxes). The company produces automobiles under three customer brands:

- GL Eagle, known as an entry-level brand, the line includes GL Eagle Panda;
- Emgrand, launched in 2009 as a medium to high-end luxury brand; and
- Englon, launched in 2010 as replacement of Shanghai Maple brand, including the former Maple Huapu hatchback, and the Maple Hysoul M206 aimed at female consumers. Englon also includes the TX4 taxicab.

Geely also manufactures and develops engine platforms, self-developed engines, automatic and manual transmissions. In 2009, Geely acquired one of the world's largest automatic transmission company Australian DSI. After that, Geely launched the project of localization of DSI transmission gearbox and three factories to produce DSI transmissions in China were set up in Hunan Province, Shandong Province and Chongqing. The platform produces a diversity of products that can be fitted onto different car models. It is planned that DSI automatic gearboxes will match with all Geely car models.

The company operates nine manufacturing plants throughout China, having a total annual production capacity of approximately 625,000 units (vehicles, engines and gearboxes). The company sells its ten major models under three product brands (GL Eagle, Emgrand and Englon) via a dealership network of some 1000 outlets in China, including 400 exclusive dealerships, as well as 581 4S dealers.[31] Geely also exports its vehicles to thirty-seven countries through thirty-seven exclusive sales agents, operating forty-three sales and service outlets, mainly in Egypt, Uruguay, Russia, Ethiopia, Ukraine, Iraq, Sri Lanka, Indonesia and Belarus.

Preconditions for internationalization

The 1978 economic reforms helped the Chinese automobile industry take off. Before 2000, the Chinese automotive market underwent severe structural changes. China's membership in the WTO (December 2001) led to increases in both auto exports and imports. Motorization really began in 2002, and the country enjoyed a rapidly expanding market: new car sales increased by one million units annually. This progress was largely due to the independent Chinese automobile manufacturers, referring to companies manufacturing complete cars using independent management systems and independent brands, along with Chinese capital. They also sought to make cars using their own research and development. Among these manufacturers, Geely and Chery can be ranked as leaders, followed by Brilliance Auto, BYD Auto, Hafei Automobile, JAC Motors Chongqing, Lifan Automobile, Great Wall Motor and Yutong Bus. Whereas private manufacturers concentrated on passenger vehicles, state-owned manufacturers focused on commercial vehicles (trucks, buses).

Suddenly, in 2004, the Chinese market cooled drastically as the market reached saturation. As a result, independent manufactures started to seek new markets and paid serious attention to exports. This shock woke up the Chinese automobile industry, which started a wave of massive exports. Yet it was no easy feat for Chinese companies to develop successful foreign expansion strategies, especially for the private firms.

These efforts gave some stability to the industry, and since foreign manufacturers were focused on the Chinese market, Chinese automakers could seek solace in developing markets – for example, in Southeast Asia or Africa. Exports from independent manufacturers drastically increased.

International strategy

As opposed to Brazilian and Russian carmakers, Chinese companies were fast on their feet: they caught up quickly and produced indigenous cars during a first stage and proceeded to international expansion shortly thereafter.[32] Geely chose to position its efforts on the low-end segment, using technology to achieve low production costs and therefore low prices. Thus international growth was driven by asset-seeking acquisitions in the global market.[33]

Export activity

Geely started exporting in 2003 and currently sells its cars in about forty countries. Given Geely's relative youth in the auto sector, it faces strong competition from long-established European, American and somewhat younger Asian manufacturers (Japan and South Korea). The company therefore decided to focus its international expansion strategy on developing countries – namely, in the Middle East and Eastern Europe, as well as Central and South America. In 2012, some of its most important export destinations in terms of sales volume are Ukraine, Russia, Saudi Arabia and Iraq.

It was as of 2012 that the company's export boom started. Export volume increased from 6,677 units in the first half of 2012 to 10,308 units in the second half of the year. In

2013, Geely exported over 120,000 cars. Russia was Geely's largest overseas market, with annual sales of around thirty thousand vehicles.[34] Around ten thousand cars were sold in Egypt and Saudi Arabia.[35]

In addition to direct exports of finished vehicles from China, Geely also assembles some models through joint ventures or contract manufacturing agreements with local partners in Egypt, Uruguay, Russia, Ethiopia, Ukraine, Iraq, Sri Lanka, Indonesia and Belarus. More than half of Geely's overseas sales are assembled in the localized plants. For instance, in 2012, Geely set up assembly in Egypt to produce its Emgrand EC7 model. After six months, its local dealerships were selling one thousand vehicles per month, reaching the top-ten rank locally.

Developing countries in the Eastern Europe, Central and South America and the Middle East remain the most important export markets. Egypt, Russia, Belarus, Saudi Arabia, Iran and Uruguay together accounted for almost 80% of the total export in 2014. At the end of 2014, Geely exported to 35 countries through 38 exclusive sales agents and 476 sales and service outlets in these countries. In 2014, Geely sold a total of 417,851 units of vehicle, 24% less than in 2013. Foreign sales suffered even more: they accounted for 14.3% of total sales, but dropped 49.8% (see Figure 8.1).[36] The cause? Sharp declines in vehicle sales in key foreign markets such as Russia. Despite this, Geely keeps improving its competitive advantages and achieving impressive market shares in most of its major export markets.[37]

In 2014, Geely started a major restructuring of its sales and marketing system, aiming to improve product quality and service. By 2016, the company expected that its three brands (GL Eagle, Emgrand and Englon) to be consolidated under the single Geely brand. Yet production diversification continued unabated – namely, to face the challenge of electric or hybrid innovations. In 2015, the company set up Xin Dayang Electric Vehicles as a 50-50 joint venture engaged in the production of car parts and engines, electric vehicles and the provision of related after-sales services in China.

The focus of the Group's export business strategy in 2013 was localization of production in major export markets. Assembly of the Geely Panda and the EC7 models started in its plant in Uruguay in early 2013, whereas the assembly of the SC7 model in another joint venture plant in Belarus also started in February 2013. The company started sales of its first SUV, the GX7, in major export markets in 2013.

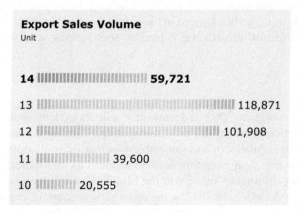

Figure 8.1 Geely export sales volume 2010–2014

Source: Geely Annual Report 2014 (http://www.geelyauto.com.hk/core/files/financial/en/2014–02.pdf)

The BelGee joint venture in Belarus was set up in 2013 with Geely holding 35.6%, the majority 54.8% stake belonging to Belarusian Autoworks (BelAz), and 9.6% to Soyuza-vtoteknologii (SOYUZ). The JV started producing the Geely SL in 2013, but the plant's capacity is gradually increasing to reach 120,000 units to accommodate assembly of additional models (GX7, SC5 and Panda CROSS).

The Uruguay joint venture in cooperation with local partner Nordex started assembling the Geely LC and Emgrand 7 models for sales in the Central and Southern American market as of 2014. To reduce its exposure to financial risk and currency devaluations, Geely aims to increase the proportion of its costs in local currencies to engage in local business activities.

Joining new assets

In February 2014, Geely acquired Emerald Automotive, a British manufacturer of electric and hybrid minivans. Geely's goal was to expand its opportunities for next generation urban taxis, including hybrid or electric vehicles. Geely committed to invest $200 million in Emerald over the 2014–2019 period.

Just one year earlier, in 2013, Geely had placed its first toe in the taxicab segment by acquiring Manganese Bronze, the well-known manufacturer of the roomy black London taxi's, for GBP 11 million ($17.5 million). Geely had taken a first shareholding in the company in 2006 but sales dropped, losses accumulated and bankruptcy had to be initiated. Part of the problem was that rivals Daimler and Nissan entered the taxicab market niche, taking the profitability away. For Geely, this acquisition was a new opportunity to enter the European market and to expand the process of the production of next generation of cars.

The Chinese government's ambition was to increase the number of hybrid and electric cars to five hundred thousand by 2015 and to five million by 2020. To support this surge, the construction of urban charging stations forged ahead, reaching one thousand units by the end of 2014.

At the end of 2013, Geely announced its intention of setting up assembly facilities in Cuba. Geely was preparing to start the project using SKD (semi knocked down) assembly. SKD is core to Geely's international strategy, with a goal of setting up fifteen assembly facilities abroad by 2015. Cuba is one of the most attractive markets for Geely in Latin America and the Caribbean.

Geely's internationalization strategy consisted of three steps. The first was to sell cars in developing countries in the Middle East, Northern Africa and South America so as to become familiar with the overseas markets and to lay a foundation for its development in international markets. The second step was to export cars to Eastern European countries and Russia. Here Geely went further and opened several CKD (completely knocked down) assembly plants in the region.

Developed markets (Europe and North America) will constitute the third step for Geely, yet this challenge is expected to be monumental. Zhang Lin, Geely's vice president for exports, mentioned in 2012 that Geely will continue to focus on emerging markets for exports. He also explained that the company will remain careful about entering European or the North American markets over the next four or five years due to the lack of the clear understanding of these markets' product planning.[38]

The lack of technology and know-how, the scarcity of management skills and knowledge and the limited ability to satisfy local requirements and regulations (environmental in particular) significantly restrict Geely's entry into developed markets. China also faces an image obstacle: in developed markets, "Made in China" still often means "cheap and poor quality."

For its international expansion, Geely has been using both "greenfield" joint ventures and acquisitions, but prefers acquisitions. Geely is building a portfolio of brands and technical capabilities, and a capability to integrate foreign know-how into its business: a skill set that will be increasingly important in a hyper-competitive global automotive industry.

In 2009, Geely acquired the Australian company Drivetrain Systems International (DSI), the world's second-largest gearbox manufacturer and automatic transmission supplier. This was a major step forward for Geely, since about 80% of all vehicles sold in China use automatic transmissions, unlike most international markets that rely heavily on manual systems.

In 2013, Geely established a JV with American Detroit Electric to co-develop pure electric vehicles for the Chinese market. The sales of the first electric models started in 2014 under the Emgrand nameplate.

The big leap: acquiring Volvo

Undeniably, one of Geely's biggest leaps into the international scene, and one which finally gave it true worldwide exposure, was the acquisition in 2010 of the automotive division of Swedish Volvo. At the time, not only was it the largest overseas acquisition by a Chinese company ($1.5 billion), but it also attracted a lot of attention in the media. The acquisition of the Swedish giant with so much history in the world vehicle market by a young, small and relatively unknown Chinese company became an outstanding event.

Although there were certainly opportunistic reasons for Geely's acquisition – Ford's cry for help was the siren song – most often four strong rationales are evoked as justification: access to Volvo's technology, Volvo's brand, Volvo's market share and the fast-growing Chinese auto sector. With the United States and Europe representing almost two-thirds of Volvo sales (18% and 43%, respectively), the acquisition would provide Geely with fast access to those markets.

Acquisition process

The financial crisis of 2007–2009 triggered a global economic recession and caused the large U.S. auto industry to suffer huge losses due to the abrupt drop in spending. While two of the "big three" auto manufacturers (Chrysler and GM) announced bankruptcy plans, Ford opted instead to sell one of its subsidiaries, Swedish Volvo Cars. The buyer? The little-known Chinese company Geely, specializing in low-quality and low-cost cars. Li Shufu, founder of Geely Group, claimed that this deal was akin to "a world famous movie star marrying a peasant in China." Apart from the difficulty of getting anyone at Volvo – or Geely – to take the proposal seriously, the deal would be complex, additionally so because it would be international.

It took three years for the peasant to seduce the diva. In 2007, Li Shufu sent a first letter to the U.S. headquarters of Ford, Volvo's owner, expressing interest in purchasing Volvo. The letter was ignored. Early in 2008, Li Shufu met a senior Ford executive at the Detroit auto show. Ford was courteous but appeared unimpressed by Geely's small size. During the Detroit auto show in 2009, Li Shufu visited Ford once again. This time, a very senior executive promised that Geely would be notified promptly if the U.S. carmaker decided to sell Volvo. In April 2009, Ford shared operational and financial data on Volvo with Geely, providing valuable insight for moving ahead with the deal.

Li Shufu set up an acquisition team. He retained Rothschild, an investment bank with experience in acquisitions, to help in negotiating the deal. Geely also submitted a report to China's National Development and Reform Commission, which oversees economic and social policymaking, restating the importance of the Volvo deal for the Chinese auto industry. Geely was confident it could turn loss-making Volvo into a profitable company. Geely reassured Ford and Volvo that production would stay in Sweden and Belgium; it promised to respect Volvo's culture of safety and efficiency; it had to reassure Ford that it could, as the maker of cheap cars, take on a premium brand.

Although the acquisition agreement between Geely and Volvo was more or less ready at the end of 2009, negotiations on intellectual property rights lasted almost until late July 2010. The marathon negotiations came to an end on August 2, 2010, when Ford and Geely signed a final agreement. The length of the acquisition process was not just due to the prestige issue of a small Chinese low-cost company acquiring a world-famous luxury brand, but it was also linked to international regulations issues and the IP details.

The final deal amounted to $1.5 billion, significantly lower than the $2.5 billion initially sought by Ford. Geely invested RMB 4.1 billion ($600 million) via Beijing Geely Kaisheng International Investment Co., a company established in September 2009. Two government-backed organizations also provided financing: Daqing State Owned Assets Co. invested RMB 3 million and Shanghai Jiaerwo Co., a newly established company by the Shanghai Jiading District Government, Shanghai Municipality, provided RMB 1 billion.

The three companies provided $1.1 billion. The remaining financing was from China Construction Bank (London) and Ford, with $200 million each.

After the deal

Chairman Li Shufu became the head of the board of Volvo Cars, which also included Hans-Olov Olsson, the Swedish carmaker's former CEO. Oskarsson replaced Stuart Rowley as interim chief financial officer of Volvo Cars.

Even though the deal turned out to be successful and profitable for both parties, the companies faced a number of challenges on their way to fruitful cooperation. Geely and Volvo differed in some very important aspects: from sales and profitability, to political regime and cultural differences. Experts pointed out three major challenges in the marriage: corporate culture, cost structure and management by finance.

The successful acquisition of Volvo Cars was the result of extensive research beforehand and the favorable conjunction of external and internal factors. Geely's top management team started preparing itself for an international acquisition in 2002. The deal was completed in 2010. Moreover, Ford's financial situation pushed it to sell Volvo. Geely has stressed that it is giving its Swedish subsidiary the liberty to operate as a stand-alone company. This acquisition was a two-way street. In one direction, Geely took control of Volvo through its massive investment. In the other direction, new Volvo established or expanded its operations in China (R&D, manufacturing and dealership development).

Since the acquisition, Geely's sales have been rising (see Table 8.2), though not as fast as planned. The company missed its 2011 sales goal due to a slowdown in the Chinese auto market over the course of the previous year. Chinese car sellers and the U.S. dollar crisis, along with difficulties obtaining credit,[39] explain the terrible results in 2014; however,

Table 8.2 Volvo and Geely unit sales before and after the deal

	Volvo sales	% change	Geely sales	% change
2008	374,297		204,205	
2009	334,808	−10.6	326,710	60.0
2010	373,525	11.6	415,286	27.1
2011	449,255	20.3	421,385	1.5
2012	421,951	−6.1	491,444	16.6
2013	427,840	1.4	549,600	11.8
2014	465,866	8.9	358,130	−34.8

Source: Company websites (http://global.geely.com, http://www.volvo.com)

others are of the opinion that the poor marketing and sales system were the cause of the firm's poor performance.

Prospects

Both Geely and Volvo seem to have accomplished most of the goals they set before the acquisition. The annual reports since 2012 show substantial sales and revenue growth in all markets. The companies also claim to have developed various synergies, in spite of their differences. Volvo can be thankful for the following contributions from Geely: C-segment platform development, small engine development, component sourcing in China and the sale of the P2 platform technology to Geely.[40]

There are no visible obstacles that would stop the marriage from working efficiently. With the Chinese car market growing rapidly – it has already passed the U.S. market in unit volume – the prospects seem rosy for the alliance.

Geely goes to Russia

When Russia shook off its communist cloak in the 1990s, it was a country of battered, simple cars. After the currency crisis of 1998, the Russian economy regained its footing, with both economic growth and per capita wealth on the rise. The sustained economic growth meant growing demand for automobiles. Since the majority of cars in the country were in dire need of replacement, new car sales as well as used cars from Western Europe made rapid progress, assisted by growing personal incomes. The Russian market became one of the most promising targets for global car manufacturers (see Table 8.3). Furthermore, the increase in gasoline prices in the 2000s changed behaviors: instead of relying on old gas guzzlers or small cars, the Russian upper and middle class started actively buying new cars, not only Russian brands but also foreign.

The Russian market, with its pent-up demand, recovered quickly from the economic crisis of 2008. By 2011, car sales exceeded their 2008 level, reaching $65 billion. In 2012, growth slowed to 15.4%, still very high, yet much lower than the two previous years.[41] In 2014, due to the hard economic situation, the lack of foreign currency and geopolitical instability, auto sales in Russia dropped by 16% in dollar value. Certainly, part of the cause was the 22% explosion in average new vehicle prices in 2015. In 2015, the slump

Table 8.3 Foreign automakers entry into the Russian market

Entry year	Manufacturer	Russian strategy
1995	Daewoo Nexia, Daewoo Espero	Partnership (Doninvest)
1998	Renault	Partnership (Autoframos)
2002	Ford	Greenfield project
2004, 2006	Kia Motors, Chery Automobile	Partnership (Autotor)
2007	Toyota	Greenfield project
2007	Volkswagen	Greenfield project
2008	General Motors (Opel, Chevrolet)	Greenfield project
2009	Nissan	Greenfield project
2010	Hyundai	Greenfield project
2010	Peugeot Citroen, Mitsubishi	Greenfield project

Source: Company corporate websites

worsened, with a 45% decrease.[42] Nevertheless, Russia was ranked fifth among European countries for new vehicle sales.

The Russian market leader in 2015 was Lada (18.7% market share), followed by Kia (11.2%), Hyundai (10.2%), Renault (8.1%), Toyota and Nissan (with 6.9 and 6.8%, respectively).[43] The key players all operate production facilities in Russia. Those selling via imports had significantly lower market shares. In 2015, Russian car factories churned out 1.2 million vehicles, a 27% drop compared to 2014.

In terms of manufacturing cost structures, the top players in the market are on an equal footing, yet AutoVAZ (maker of the Lada brand) still possesses the low-cost advantage. International competitors rely not so much on cost competition, but concentrate on differentiation.[44] Before the ruble crisis of 2014–2015, the Russian automotive market was forecast to reach saturation, with price competition becoming more intense.

Penetration of Chinese car maker into Russia

What attracted the private manufacturers to Russia? Powerful firms with wide-ranging personal connections in both countries emerged. The first person to successfully enter the Russian market was a Chinese diplomat stationed in Russia, Zhu Jingcheng. After a first project involving the export of Chinese telecoms technology to Russia, he received a proposal to work on exporting Chinese cars.

In 2004, his efforts led to the creation of Siberian Automobile Export (SAE), a company specialized in automobile exports, with the ZX pickup truck becoming the first Chinese vehicle exported to Russia. SAE enabled deeper interactions between Russian and Chinese automakers and provided support to other related businesses. Furthermore, both sides sensed the opportunity for a deal. Due to Zhu Jingcheng's government and business connections, SAE could easily penetrate the Russian market and the Chinese as well. Other factors which boosted the cooperation were the familiarity with the Russian culture, business traditions and customs and the high number of Chinese employees proficient in Russian.

However, when exporting its first ZX pickups to Russia, SAE faced its first difficulties related to model certification. Russia implements the multinational agreement (Uniform

Technical Prescriptions for Vehicles) from the UN Economic Commission for Europe approved in 1958. Alas, Chinese manufacturers did not adhere to the UTPV agreement, so the Chinese auto inspection certificates were refused. The Russian side insisted that tests be carried out by the Russian National Automobile Standards Certification Centre, proof of remaining doubts about the quality of Chinese vehicles. This loomed as a serious obstacle since the pickup trucks had to be specially tested and the officially translated approvals cost a mint and substantial time, possibly up to eighteen months.

Geely enters Russia

Geely was not the first Chinese car manufacturer to enter the Russian market. In 2004, Great Wall Motors started to export its models to Russia in cooperation with IRITO, a distribution company that later obtained exclusive rights for Great Wall vehicles. One year later, Chery launched a car assembly plant with Avtotor in the Kaliningrad region. Chery managed to comply with all legal requirements and received state approval to launch so-called CKD assembling (assembly from completely knocked down car kits). Smaller Geely was a bit late, jumping onto the Russian bandwagon in 2006–2007.

Geely made a conscious decision to enter the Russian market after many other Chinese manufacturers. The company wanted to offer the Russian consumers the proper cars to meet their demands by emphasizing modern design, better manufacturing quality and safety than many Russian models. Geely knew that it not only had to improve the perception of Chinese cars in Russia but also identify its specific market niche.

Manufacturing

In 2006, Geely established a joint venture with the AMUR (Automobiles and Motors of the Urals) auto assembly plant in the Sverdlovsk Region. The contract assumed the assembly of up to thirty thousand Geely cars annually in SKD mode (semi knocked down – i.e. using fewer parts than CKD assembly) and a switch to CKD within eighteen months, as well as full localization of production within two to three years.[45] The total investment for the project amounted to approximately $70 million.[46] According to the contract, Geely planned to sell up to $1.5 billion worth of cars in Russia over five years.[47] In June 2007, the first Geely Otaka sedans rolled off the assembly line.[48] Although 2007 production had been slotted at 17,000 vehicles, the actual production was only 4,225 vehicles.[49] The plan to move to full-blown production and localization was never realized.

In 2008, two key events shifted Geely's position in the Russian market. First, the company failed to obtain the CKD-production mode permit from the Ministry of Economic Development. The two relevant ministries did not permit the production of Chinese cars in Russia. One of the reasons was the protectionist position of the Russian government vis-à-vis AvtoVAZ, the national car manufacturer.[50] Geely's cars not only targeted the same market segment, but were offered at approximately the same price and quality level. Furthermore, the localization of production and the implementation of CKD-production mode would have lowered the costs of Geely's cars manufactured in Russia. This posed a potential threat to AvtoVAZ, since Geely, as well as other Chinese manufacturers, could easily have become key competitors in Russia.

By 2009, Geely had almost doubled its sales volume to 7,600 units, making it the number-one brand among Chinese automakers. The company wanted to proceed to the next investment step by shifting to CKD-production mode. Yet this required government

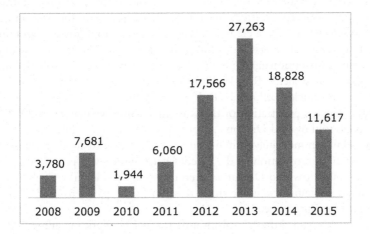

Graph 8.1 Geely's new passenger cars sales volume in Russia, 2008–2012[51]

Source: Association of European Business (http://www.aebrus.ru/en/media/press-releases/sales-of-cars-and-light-commercial-vehicles.php)

permission, and the government had other priorities: saving local manufacturers. In November 2008, a temporary car components import duty was introduced by the government, amounting to 15% of the customs value of imports of spare parts and components (and a minimum tariff of €5,000 per truck). Alternatively, import duties on complete cars was set at 30% of customs value.[52]

As a result, imported components saw their prices skyrocket. AMUR could no longer import the quantity of spare parts needed to produce its contractually obligated volumes, and the volume of cars assembled dropped. Later, the production of Geely cars was even temporarily halted. However, with the temporary duties becoming permanent in 2009, Geely decided not to prolong its contract with AMUR, suspending production in Sverdlovsk (see Graph 8.1).

This failure, however, did not prevent Geely from further attempts to establish its production in Russia. At the end of 2009, Geely launched its own local production in test mode. This time the cars were manufactured at the Derways plant, a privately owned automaker located in Cherkessk, about 1,494 kilometers east of Moscow.[53] In January 2010, the first Geely MK vehicles, Geely Emgrand, were produced in CKD mode. In August 2011, the production of the Geely MK Cross was launched, and nine months later, the production of the Geely Emgrand began. Both the MK Cross and the Emerald met the EURO 4 standard.[54] Thus Geely Company not only managed to set up production of its cars in Russia, but the company also extended the range of models available to Russian customers. As can be seen in Graph 8.1, the number of new Geely cars sold in Russia has been increasing steadily starting from 2010. This trend can also partly be explained by Geely's distribution strategy.

Distribution

For its distribution in Russia, Geely partnered with the largest local car dealerships instead of building its own distribution network from the scratch. In November 2006, agreements were signed with IncomeAvto Holding, the third-largest Russian car seller (2.3% market share), and IncomeAvto became the exclusive Geely distributor in Russia.[55] However, IncomeAvto was never able to effectively introduce the car brand on the Russian market. The company was also involved in a credit scandal that later led to insolvency and finally bankruptcy. With contractual obligations unfulfilled, Geely started seeking a new distributor.

For its second distribution agreement (Q3 2007), Geely turned to Rolf Holding, another major Russian auto dealer.[56] Rolf Holding established a subsidiary called Red Dragon, offering Chinese vehicles exclusively. Rolf was to build an independent network of dealers to support Geely's penetration of the Russian automotive market in 2007.[57] The first Chinese models sold by Red Dragon appeared on the market in July 2008.[58] To hedge its bets, Geely did not immediately switch from one distributor to another. Until 2009, IncomeAvto continued distribution of the Geely Otaka, which was produced at the AMUR assembly plant, whereas Red Dragon offered two other models: the Geely FC2 and FC3. Red Dragon also obtained exclusive rights to sell original spare parts and to provide after-sales service and maintenance.

Rolf's expertise enabled the constitution of a dealer network including 102 dealerships in 2008,[59] a number that grew to 130 one year later.[60] However, at the end of 2010, Rolf announced plans to cease distribution of Geely vehicles. The Group's Geely segment revenue dropped from 1,717 ml RUR in 2009 to 543 ml RUR in 2010. Rolf's Red Dragon subsidiary was liquidated soon afterwards.

In May 2011, Geely inaugurated its wholly owned subsidiary Geely Motors Rus.[61]

Planning next steps

Geely's production in Cherkessk, though quite successful, is associated with relatively high transportation costs, since new car sales are predominantly in the central and northwestern Federal Districts. Furthermore, since Geely's target markets are not fully saturated, Geely opted to establish BelGee, a joint venture with BelAz, a Belorussian company. With an initial production capacity of ten thousand units per annum, the JV started the production of the Geely SL model (SC7) in 2013. Now BelGee also produces Geely Emgrand X7 and Geely LC-CROSS. The shareholders of the JV included BelAz (50%) and Geely Holdings (32.5%), with the other shares in free float.[62] In 2011, a new assembly plant in Borisov required total investment of about $250 million and provided employment to about 3,500 local staff.[63] The first Belarus-produced Geely SC7 sedans rolled off the lines in 2012. Manufacturing in Belarus proved to be less costly than in Russia. In fact, Geely exported part of its Borisov production to Russia, with the first cars reaching Russian dealerships in 2013.[64] Although Geely wanted to establish full operations in Belarus, the economic downturn of 2013–2014 delayed the construction of the plant, with the opening postponed to 2016.[65] Thus Geely strengthened its presence in the Russian market by both producing cars locally, but also by importing vehicles from neighboring, friendly (and import-tariff-free) CIS countries.

Prospects globally and in Russia

Utilizing global consolidation strategy gives Chinese companies such as Geely an opportunity to combine country-specific advantages such as access to low-cost labor and capital (supported by Chinese government or financial institutions) with firm-specific advantages (world-known brand, technologies, know-how, distribution network and managerial skills) of well-established companies such as Volvo.

Russia is mainly aspiring to boost its own industry. None of the Chinese companies was interested in maintaining the local Russian interest and, without demonstrating this interest, they were seen as grey market contributors. Thus Russian government introduced more strict policy to avoid the grey market and to get rid of Chinese cars. As a result, the most promising projects were interrupted (such as Chery Automobile's partnership with Avtotor, or Geely's project that aimed to expand into Russia and export completed cars in partnership with Rolf and Lifan automobile.[66]

For the Chinese companies, it is not an easy task to penetrate the Russian markets. Nowadays, they concentrate more on CIS countries, mainly the Ukraine. Yet, with Chinese automotive industry growing, Geely has great opportunities of expanding their automobiles globally including advanced and emerging economies. Geely may use the national or regional economic downturns to its own advantage and seek additional assets that would benefit their strategy. For Geely, becoming a global brand occurred after overcoming serious challenges. In other countries, such as Russia, the route may be much shorter.

One problem remained unsolved. In Russia, Geely was a late entrant, lagging behind European, U.S.-based and even other Chinese car manufacturers. At the outset, in 2006, Geely chose an all-out frontal attack strategy, with the hope of gaining large Russian market share via a large investment in 2006–2011. When this failed, Geely opted for a more targeted tactic, using the CIS countries as launching pads (Belarus in 2011), and focusing on its SC7model.

Thanks to the 2010 customs union between Russia, Belarus and Kazakhstan, customs registration procedures were simplified. Thus vehicles produced in Belarus or Kazakhstan are not subject to import duties, making it attractive to produce vehicles in Belarus for re-sale into Russia.

Conclusion

Overall, in its internationalization, Geely follows a very diverse approach. The company acquires aggressively when it needs to immediately acquire the knowledge to be able to get to the heart of the world's automotive industry, which was the case in acquiring the Volvo brand. The company is wise enough to copy others' technologies and designs rather than investing in their own brand-new models. Copying famous Bavarian cars makes sense: these models are not yet fully outdated and are in demand in many countries, especially in EEs. Why not use this as an opportunity to copy-paste and then sell? Finally, the company targets strategic markets from neighboring locations: this is cheaper and safer. Why not?

8.3 Cultivating knowledge: case of ZTE

Company overview

ZTE Corporation is a Chinese multinational telecoms equipment and systems company. ZTE operates via three business units:

- carrier networks (network infrastructure belonging to a telecoms service provider) – 54% of revenues
- terminals – 29% of revenues
- telecommunications – 17% of revenues

The company is listed on both the Hong Kong and Shenzhen stock exchanges. ZTE's main products are wireless, exchange, optical transmission, mobile phones and telecoms software. ZTE primarily sells products under its own brand, although it is also an original equipment manufacturer (OEM), meaning that it manufactures "generic" equipment that other companies re-sell.

ZTE, initially founded as Zhongxing Semiconductor Co., Ltd in 1985, is a telecommunications equipment company headquartered in Shenzhen, China. In 1995, ZTE became the first Chinese telecoms equipment provider to attain a ISO9001 quality standard certificate and since then has embarked on a multi-product R&D strategy across the wireless switching, transmission, access, videoconferencing and power supply systems' domains. In 1997, the company was listed on the Shenzhen Stock Exchange, and in 1999, ZTE established its first overseas office in Islamabad, Pakistan.[67] Since then, ZTE has only grown and reached new milestones in not only its home market but also worldwide. In 2003, ZTE set international expansion as its strategic emphasis, more than doubling its international marketing staff. By 2008, ZTE had become a truly global firm with sales in 140 countries across five continents.

Among other things, ZTE designs and then manufactures mobile phone handsets. This equipment is classified into families according to the transmission technology used: first CDMA, next GSM and then LTE (4G LTE). In 2009, about 20% of all GSM hardware sold throughout the world was ZTE branded;[68] in 2011, ZTE held around 7% of the key LTE patents. That same year, the first smartphone with dual GPS/Glonass navigation was launched by ZTE. Nowadays, ZTE supplies its equipment to the United Kingdom's Vodafone, Canadian Telus, Australia's Telstra, France Telecom and others.

Intense focus on R&D and breaking global entry barriers through stakeholder collaborations and patent protection have spelt success for ZTE in more than seventy international markets. Traditionally, ZTE has offered mid-range devices, which have slimmer margins compared to high-end devices. In 2013, ZTE was the fifth-largest company in the global mobile phone equipment market after global giants such as Apple, Samsung and LG. It is the third most popular phone maker in the United States and is also the fastest-growing vendor, with a year-on-year growth of 85.7% in Q1, 2013.

What is intriguing about ZTE's story is the fact that it started out as a humble business in 1985. By 2000, it had explored various international markets, and within a decade, its revenues from foreign operations accounted for 60% of total revenue, exceeding Chinese revenues for the first time in 2007.

Telecoms technology is a field of rapid and dynamic growth, and ZTE has not only kept abreast of the latest developments but has also pioneered some innovations and introduced entire countries to cutting-edge technology. Despite ZTE's commercial success globally, there are questions of how much ZTE as a brand has made an impact in user's minds. Because the company operates through collaborations with telecoms operators and well-known brands in different countries, ZTE is often an unfamiliar name. This paradox makes it all the more interesting and challenging to understand the firm's internationalization strategy and how it created a stronghold in global markets, as well as evaluate its ventures and document learnings from its successes and failures.

Internationalization of ZTE: step by step

Thirty years after its foundation, ZTE refers to itself as "born to be international."[69] Its internationalization strategy can be considered to have started in 1995. Over the past

Table 8.4 ZTE's internationalization from 2001 to 2004

	2001	2002	2003	2004	2004 growth
Revenue	9.4	10.8	17.1	22.7	33%
Domestic revenue	9.0	9.6	15.1	17.8	18%
International revenue	0.4	1.2	2.0	4.9	150%
% of international business	4%	11%	11%	22%	88%

Note: All figures in RMB billion

Source: ZTE Annual reports 2004, 2005

twenty years, ZTE has gathered vast global expertise and is dedicated to remaining a leading provider of telecoms equipment and network solutions. With operations in 160 countries and 18 global R&D centers, the company has realized its vision.

ZTE's internationalization process can be divided into three distinct phases. During each step, the company has had a different market focus and therefore followed different strategies.

Step 1: exploring developing markets (1995–2004)

During its first ten years of geographic expansion, ZTE explored developing countries and made significant breakthroughs. The company took its first step toward globalization in 1995 by setting up branches in Indonesia. As Table 8.4 reveals, as of 2001, the revenue generated from international markets increased as a percentage of total revenue from 4% in 2001 to 22% in 2004. Thus non-Chinese sales gradually became the lion's share of ZTE's business and the area of main growth.

During this exploratory period, the entry strategy consisted mostly of export. Yet by 2004, ZTE was comfortable enough to localize some non-productive functions: marketing, human resources and finance. In fact, ZTE also went public on the Hang Seng stock market that same year. Relationships with Brazil, India, Indonesia, Pakistan and Russia were also established in that fruitful year. Thus, by phase one, ZTE had established a solid international presence, becoming a respected player in both technology, product positioning, marketing and even its financing capacity. For select foreign markets, ZTE chooses to establish its own subsidiaries, alliances or R&D units – for example, in San Diego, Dallas and Seoul.

Step 2: exploring developed markets (2005–2009)

With its three main strategic development axes being mobile telephony, 3G services and international expansion, ZTE declared 2005 its "internationalization year." ZTE intensified its efforts on foreign markets and restructured its operational assets, enterprise culture and management in order to render the company international inside and out. One main shift included the transfer of the international management headquarters outside China to Singapore. Fourteen overseas areas were defined and manage over seventy target markets.

ZTE also decided it was strong enough to take on developed markets. Starting from Europe, ZTE signed strategic contracts to build business partnerships with local telecoms companies such as Portugal Telecom and France Telecom. Furthermore, ZTE established fifteen agents in various European countries to provide localized market consulting, technology support and service centers.

Step 3: comprehensive market expansion (since 2010)

The internationalization of ZTE became comprehensive from 2010. With respect to the global telecommunications market, the company has provided innovative technology and product solutions to telecommunications service providers and government and corporate customers in more than 160 countries and regions.

ZTE operates international subsidiaries in Indonesia, Australia, Europe and the Americas. ZTE entered the Australian market in 2005, and four years later, ZTE Australia Ltd was supplying large customers such as telecoms operators Telstra and Optus. ZTE's European base is in Dusseldorf, Germany, with 60% of personnel recruited locally.[70] In Brazil, ZTE has offices in São Paulo, Rio de Janeiro and Brasilia, serving the country market with mobile devices and network solutions. ZTE operates R&D centers in the United States, South Korea, Sweden, Austria, India and Pakistan.

The development of the overseas business since 2013, especially in the U.S. and European markets, has contributed significantly to getting the company out of the trough. As shown in the Table 8.5, ZTE's revenue from the United States, Europe and Oceania accounted for 23.7% of the total in 2011, but this share rose to 27.7% in 2014. Gross margin in these regions climbed to 24.5% in 2014 from 18.8% in 2011.

Overall, ZTE's internationalization followed three stages, first in developing markets (Stage 1), next onto developed markets (Stage 2) and then more aggressive in Stage 3. After learning from its experience, the company knew when to take risks – namely, in order to acquire knowledge quickly. ZTE was differentiating between capital-intensive tasks and softer expansion methods. The role of these soft approaches (including knowledge, R&D, marketing and HR) was extremely important for internationalization, which is covered further in the following few sections.

Table 8.5 Breakdown of ZTE revenue by region, 2011–2014

Revenues	2011	2012	2013	2014
China	45.80%	47.00%	47.40%	49.80%
Asia (excluding China)	18.10%	19.10%	18.40%	14.90%
Africa	12.40%	9.30%	7.80%	7.60%
Europe, America and Oceania	23.70%	24.70%	26.40%	27.70%
Gross margin	2011	2012	2013	2014
China	33.50%	26.60%	33.30%	34.70%
Asia (excluding China)	25.90%	20.50%	24.60%	31.40%
Africa	46.70%	29.60%	25.80%	36.80%
Europe, America and Oceania	18.80%	19.30%	26.80%	24.50%

Source: ZTE Annual reports 2012, 2013, 2014, 2015

Three dimensions of knowledge: developing, training and disseminating

The internationalization of telecoms manufacturers such as ZTE involves different steps in their value chain. In the pre-production phase, R&D functions are critical since they enable the development of the new equipment and the software that runs it. In the production phase, highly mechanized, capital-intensive manufacturing is typically done in China and neighboring countries that have qualified labor at reasonable salaries. The post-production phase includes marketing, sales and service, and is focused on all the customers that may be reachable, including domestic and foreign markets.

Research and development strategy

While ZTE's initial internationalization steps involved mostly post-production phases – namely, marketing and sales – the company has been considered aggressive and active in its foreign R&D activities. With more than 10% of annual revenue being invested in global R&D, ZTE has established twenty state-of-the-art R&D centers in the China, France, India and employs over thirty thousand research professionals. As well as ZTE subsidiaries have innovation departments, many of them devoted to ensuring good localization of the product palette to national needs.[71]

The company's R&D centers serve three main objectives. First off, as a player in this technology-intensive industry, ZTE must fight for technological leadership by innovating before its competitors. The survival of the company is at stake, and the R&D centers are the innovative muscles of the company. Second, state-of-the-art R&D attracts global top talent, especially critical in the fastest-moving developed markets, where non-innovative hardware makers litter the roadside (e.g. Motorola, Nokia, Alcatel). Third, R&D is critical for developing new product generations. Even in the 2G and 3G areas, where ZTE had no first entry advantage, developing innovative applications for customers can increase market share.

ZTE's bet on R&D paid back in good measure. By 2011, ZTE had become the number-one patent applicant in the world, according to the PCT (Patent Cooperation Treaty) ranking, indicating its strong capacity to innovate.[72]

HR strategy

ZTE quickly understood that going international did not only mean selling its gear abroad but also included the human resource area. Starting in 2006, the company made substantial efforts to localize its staff. Taking the United States as an example, 80% of local employees are American, after seventeen years of American presence.[73]

The localization of human resources required further efforts in developing markets. In the case of Ethiopia, ZTE signed a $1.5 billion cooperation contract in 2006, to build the national telecom network. The market penetration of mobile telephony increased from 1.5% to 7% within one year. Yet the lack of local IT talent crimped local development. To overcome this hurdle, ZTE leveraged its global resources to design and implement training materials and courses, and set up teaching teams, thus providing free telecom training for local technicians. Its targets were college students and engineers in related industries. From 2007 to date, with local government support, ZTE has established seven telecoms labs in Ethiopia, provided training for more than one thousand telecom engineers to date.[74]

The company has established overseas training centers in many countries, providing training to more than 130,000 people from more than 100 countries. This localized human resources strategy not only provides support for market development but also benefits local adaptation and industry development as a whole by helping to understand market needs via trainees.

Branding and marketing strategy

As a hardware manufacturer, ZTE found it difficult to enter developed markets. After all, these markets already sourced their manufacturing in China or in neighboring countries. Although ZTE did benefit from a cost leader position, the company also sought differentiation via branding activities.

In the United States, ZTE is actively involved in local communities – namely, via its sponsorship of the Houston Rockets basketball team. Communication with fans is both via online and offline channels. Other branding activities involve the organization of local sports activities and other corporate social responsibility events. These efforts seek to make ZTE part of the local communities, since the company focuses on mobile phones for individual customers. These efforts have made ZTE a brand with 17% market recognition, the fourth most popular largest mobile handset supplier in the United States.

ZTE has geographically segmented its markets into the China, Asia Pacific, Europe, CIS, North America, Latin America and Middle East Africa regions. It has created a strong foothold in more than seventy international markets through its strategy of tying up with existing mobile operators (i.e. with unbranded handsets) rather than branding its own products. Also, ZTE has always targeted the mass market and mid-tier segments, being a cost leader rather than a differentiator. In 2014, the company took the decision to move away from the low end and to seek a brighter, more profitable future in mid-tier and premium handsets. Initially, the company suffered, losing market share in China, but it has now rebounded, reaping the rewards of its long-term bet, with 65% of sales coming from outside of China.

ZTE has successfully captured share in major markets and yet, until recently, was hardly a well-known brand. Consumer awareness was low – if not non-existent – in part because the company had deliberately wanted to mask its Chinese roots when "Made in China" was synonymous with cheap and low quality. However, ZTE has grown out of its peasant roots and is all set to reveal itself to the world – for example, the firm recently launched the Axon-ZTE's premium brand in America, which was developed to suit American tastes and exigencies.

The company has identified the United States and some top European and Asian countries as its core target markets for the near future, with the goal of being in the top-three league in all countries. This will require an aggressive branding push. To quote Zeng Zuezhong, CEO of ZTE's terminal business, "We are investing heavily to expand our brand recognition, collaborating with internet players like Baidu and Google, localizing our offering, and shifting from a B2B strategy to a B2C strategy."[75]

This changing approach is clearly visible in the way ZTE has been adapting not only its communication but also its products to the different markets. And the marketing departments are not complaining about the ever-increased budgets over the past few years.

In early 2015, ZTE became the fourth-largest smartphone manufacturer in the United States, after Samsung, Apple and LG. ZTE has worked hard over the past few years to "Americanize" its organization and has poured staff and development resources into its

U.S. operations. In the words of Lixin Cheng, CEO of the American operation, "We really localized our effort. I plugged into this market, and I was able to convince headquarters to listen to me and trust me." As an example of the localization effort, ZTE has sponsored three NBA teams. It began in 2014 with sponsorship of the Houston Rockets, then added the New York Knicks and the Golden State Warriors in 2015, who went on to win their first championship in forty years.

As for the Southeast Asian region, ZTE increased its marketing budget by 50% to a record $20 million in 2015. In a press release, ZTE Mobile Devices CEO Jacky Zhang explained that Thailand is ZTE's second most important market in Southeast Asia after Indonesia. ZTE already claimed 10% share of the Southeast Asian mid-to-high-end smartphone markets in 2014. According to the *Bangkok Post*, ZTE is targeting sales of 2.5 million smartphones in Thailand in 2015, more than double the 1.1 million sold in 2014. This would represent a market share of 15%–18%, making ZTE Thailand's fourth-largest smartphone vendor.[76]

Partnership in Russia

In 2015, ZTE and Yota (a Russian telecoms company that also produces electronics) agreed on a partnership. Yota's best known, yet contested, product is the Yotaphone, featuring two screens, one of which is made using ebook technology. The phone is not very popular in Russia due to its disputable functionality and high price tag. The high price was necessary since production was carried out by Hi-P, a company famous for its cooperation with Motorola and BlackBerry. Saddled with such high production costs, Yota needed a quick solution, especially after several cases of misunderstanding with Hi-P.

When ZTE learned of this quandary, it immediately offered its production capacities to Yota. In September 2015, the companies signed a deal, which may seem more alike Yota's internationalization, but in fact helps ZTE in its recent entry in the Russian market.

ZTE is known for seeking foreign targets having either know-how, patents or technologies. For its part, Yota is quite famous for possessing new technologies so in advance that they have not even been implemented in its own products. For ZTE, the Yota "cry for help" represents an opportunity to not only gain marginal profit from its production capacities but also an opportunity to acquire technology, to gain knowledge about the Russian market and to plan further expansion of its own smartphones, cheaper and slightly more efficient than the Yota handsets.

This deal was also a departure from ZTE's normal mode, without acquisition of a local player, but rather an alliance or partnership. Time will show whether the deal will outlive its opportunistic roots and become a true cooperation of technologically well-endowed telecoms competitors.

Back to theory

To sum up, ZTE started its internationalization by relying on well-established partners having better access to consumers: mobile operators. Later on, after capturing sizeable share in foreign markets and gaining knowledge from its multiple endeavors, LTE commenced its serious efforts to create a popular and respected consumer brand. This is reflected in its launching products to suit geographies (Axon in the United States), its effort to localize its communications and its year-on-year increasing spend on advertising and promotion, not only in absolute terms but also as a fraction of total expenditures.

In the case of ZTE, the Uppsala model fits quite nicely: geographic expansion was not radical but in stages after absorbing knowledge and learning from experience. In fact, the first steps of the international expansion fit the model perfectly: the first steps were in countries close both geographically and culturally. The distance was minimized. At least that is the superficial view; the deeper rationale was slightly different. One of those reasons was the need for resources and strategic assets, such as patents, technologies, talented human resources and distribution channels. This first stage was quite swift since ZTE really needed such resources for its stability and in order to gain competitive advantages for further expansion. ZTE partnered with competitors (mobile operators) in order to capture those resources, although later in the game it was to ZTE's advantage to reclaim its independence.

For ZTE, market breakthroughs have happened in both developing and developed countries. The market development path has been very caution, just as the Uppsala pattern predicts.

For research and development, ZTE has followed a more aggressive path. In part, this is simply because telecoms is innovation intensive, and keeping up with innovations made by others will not provide the firm a leadership position. Technology development stirs the competitive cauldron, making it possible for newcomers to beat established players. ZTE's management made the bet that heavy investment in R&D could turn the company into an international industry leader.

Overcoming multiple challenges, ZTE has always been considered a strong player for IT solutions and a reliable partner. That was demonstrated with Yota Russia, a partnership with the innovation-driven Russian company that brought ZTE not only additional revenues but, more importantly, in-depth knowledge about Russian market needs and recent Yota technologies.

ZTE also made a drastic shift in its market strategy as a result of its progressive and successful international expansion: it moved from an anonymous B2B operator (hidden behind mobile operators) to a B2C company selling its branded handsets to customers directly. That transmogrification required guts, since substantial marketing budgets had to be invested in the hope of convincing picky consumers that ZTE meant quality and technological reliability, and not the old "Made in China" stigma. What is important now is to develop and successfully implement the efficient post-entry strategy in foreign markets.

References

1 World Bank.
2 International Monetary Fund, World Economic Outlook Database, October 2015.
3 Economic Structure of China 2013.
4 http://www.bloombergview.com/articles/2014–10–14/private-companies-are-driving-china-s-growth
5 Economic and Trade Information on China 2015.
6 http://www.worldstopexports.com/fastest-growing-chinese-export-products/
7 Economic and Trade Information on China 2015.
8 http://www.forbes.com/sites/liyanchen/2015/05/06/2015-global-2000-the-largest-companies-in-china/#7f951c911188
9 Krkoska and Korniyenko 2008.
10 Kamal et al. 2014.
11 Ibid.
12 Sauvant and Chen 2014.
13 Morck et al. 2008.
14 UNCTAD 2014.

15 UNCTAD 2014.
16 Zhou and Leung 2015.
17 Ibid.
18 UNCTAD 2014.
19 Zhou and Leung 2015.
20 Ministry of Economic Development of the Russian Federation 2014.
21 Eurasian Development Bank 2014, http://eabr.org/e/
22 Simeone 2013.
23 Ibid
24 Russia-China Investment Fund 2013.
25 Krkoska and Korniyenko 2008.
26 Eurasian Development Bank 2014.
27 Krkoska and Korniyenko 2008.
28 Geely website, http://global.geely.com/
29 "Innovative Enterprise of China" – award, information from the website, http://global.geely.com/geely_overview.php
30 http://www.economist.com/node/16750095?story_id=16750095&CFID=152275665&CFTOKEN=56924159
31 Automotive franchise business model, including vehicle sales, spare parts, service and survey.
32 Richet and Ruet 2008.
33 Balcet et al. 2012.
34 Shanghai Geely Meijiafeng International Trade Co Ltd.
35 http://www.chinatoday.com.cn/english/economy/2014–02/07/content_594542_3.htm
36 Geely Annual Report 2014. http://www.geelyauto.com.hk/core/files/financial/en/2014-02.pdf
37 Ibid.
38 'Geely speeds up overseas expansion, considering building plants in Brazil, India and Iran' 2012.
39 Zheng and Murphy 2015.
40 Volvo 2012 annual report.
41 MarketLine Industry Profile: Automotive manufacturing in Russia. Datamonitor, August 2013.
42 PWC 2015.
43 Ernst & Young 2013b.
44 An overview of the Russian and CIS automotive industry in Russia and CIS, 2013.
45 https://www.autostat.ru/articles/24878/
46 http://www.rbcdaily.ru/industry/562949979053261
47 'China to flood Russia with its low-quality cars over 5 years' 2007.
48 http://www.apiural.ru/news/economy/30895/?print
49 http://www.vedomosti.ru/newspaper/articles/2007/08/31/dilery-veryat-v-kitajcev
50 Krkoska and Korniyenko 2008.
51 AEB Press Releases.
52 http://www.tsouz.ru/news/Documents/auto29–03–13.pdf
53 Rolf Group Annual Report 2007.
54 Derways: Production of Geely cars, Official Derways Web site, http://derways.ru/?id=20
55 http://www.finmarket.ru/news/586396
56 http://www.rbc.ru/
57 Rolf Group Company Profile, 8 January 2013, MarketLine, p.5.
58 Rolf Group Annual Report 2007.
59 Rolf Group Annual Report 2008.
60 Rolf Group Annual Report 2009.
61 Geely Moors Rus: About the company Official Web page, Available at: http://www.geely-motors.com/o-kompanii
62 http://www.n1.by/news/2012/05/30/324191.html
63 http://www.autostat.ru/news/view/12620
64 Ibid.
65 http://eng.belta.by/economics/view/construction-of-belgee-factory-in-belarus-discussed-86632–2015/
66 Jansson 2008.
67 History – ZTE Corporation (History – ZTE Corporation), wwwen.zte.com

68 http://www.reuters.com/article/idUSHKG24779620091118
69 ZTE 2015. http://www.zte.com.cn/global
70 http://wwwen.zte.com.cn/en/press_center/news/200811/t20081118_160172.html
71 Fang Li 2010.
72 Kang 2014.
73 An interview with Lixin Cheng. 2016.
74 Niu and Liu 2016.
75 Segan 2015.
76 Bushell-Embling 2015.

9 International strategies of Indian multinationals

India presents a very different internationalization portrait from China – namely, because services (in particular IT and outsourcing or offshoring services) represent a substantial portion of Indian outbound FDI. In this chapter, we examine Indian integration in the global marketplace and elaborate on the role of the Indian domestic market for the global expansion of MNEs from India. After analyzing the sectoral and geographic distribution of Indian OFDI, empirical evidence from Tata Motors and Wipro, multinationals with highly developed manufacturing and service capabilities, will be used as case studies. Both companies will be considered in the context of "old" views and "fresh" insights.

9.1 Globalization of India and international investments of Indian firms

Internationalization of economy: recent trends

For India (as for other BRIC countries), the 2005–2014 period was marred by significant economic slowdown. Countries that had traditionally attracted significant FDI lost their competitive advantage as they faced numerous social, technical, financial and structural problems. Many Indian funds changed their investment policies and shifted investments to developed economies such as the United States. As a result, exchange rates came under pressure, and high priority projects and fundamental research programs for the modernization of the economy or improved social policies faced funding shortcomings. Nonetheless, several of India's competitive advantages remain strong, including the huge domestic market potential, low labor costs and stable and independent macroeconomic policy.

After Narendra Modi took office in 2014, India's economic growth increased. GDP growth in 2014 reached 7.2%, and 7.5% growth was predicted for 2015–2016. Other positive trends included the exchange rate stabilization, reduction of the balance of payments deficit and decreasing inflation rate.[1]

Agriculture plays a crucial role in India's economy. Over 58% of the rural households depend on agriculture for their livelihood. Along with fisheries and forestry, agriculture is one of the largest contributors to domestic GDP. India is the largest producer, consumer and exporter of spices and spice products. It ranks third globally in farm and agriculture output, with agricultural products representing 10% of national exports.

Multiple factors have facilitated recent growth in the agriculture sector including growth in household income and consumption, expansion of food processing activities and the increase in agricultural exports. Rising private participation in Indian agriculture, the growth of organic farming and the use of information technology are some of the key trends in modern Indian agro-processing.

India has a diversified financial sector, which is also witnessing rapid expansion. The sector's main participants are commercial banks, insurance companies, non-banking financial companies, co-operatives, pension funds, mutual funds and other smaller financial entities. Commercial banks remain the key actors, accounting for more than 60% of the total assets held by the financial system.

Thanks to a relatively strong educational system, and the national use of English as the main language of business, India's services sector has made rapid strides since 2000 to emerge as the largest and one of the fastest-growing sectors of the economy. It covers a wide variety of activities including trade, hotel and restaurants; transport, storage and communications; financing, insurance, real estate, business services, community, social and personal services; and services associated with construction. The services sector is not only the dominant sector in India's GDP – accounting for 52% of GDP in 2014 – but also attracts significant foreign investment flows, contributes significantly to exports and provides massive employment.

India accounts for 1.44% of world exports and 2.12% of world imports for merchandise trade and 3.34% of exports and 3.31% of imports for commercial services trade. In 2014, India was ranked eighth in terms of commercial services exports.[2] India's major trading partner countries are the United States (14%), the United Arab Emirates (11%) and China (5%). India also exports to Europe, with its largest partners being Germany and the United Kingdom (2% each).[3]

The globalization of the Indian economy passed through several stages.[4] The first, from 1992 to 1995, the so-called automatic route, limited overseas investments but allowed cash remittances, which in turn opened a variety of internationalization options for Indian firms, from export to OFDI.

The second period of India transformation happened between 1995 and 2000, when the "fast track route" was instituted. It raised the outbound investment limit from US$2 to US$4 million yet maintained the remittance limit at $0.5 million. The system became clearer when legislative decisions were transferred from the Ministry of Trade to the Reserve Bank of India. Since then, outward investments had to be justified by commercial interest and also the country's interests. For outflows beyond $4 million, investments have to be approved by a special committee including representatives of the Ministries of Finance, Foreign Affairs and Commerce. But up to this limit and typically up to $15 million, it is the Ministry of Finance alone that approves outbound investments, upon review of a special committee. OFDI was usually approved if global depository notes were used to raise the funds. Further liberalization occurred at the end of 1999, when the Foreign Exchange Management Act was voted in, thus decriminalizing remittance offenses.

From 2000 to the present date, the OFDI ceiling has been raised to $100 million and further 200% (in 2005) and 400% (in 2007).[5] When the Indian authorities opened the investment gates, inbound FDI rapidly flowed into India, but it took several years for Indian investors to find the courage or the resources to go abroad. A key facilitator was when the Reserve Bank of India opened its single-window system, enabling Indian companies to invest abroad in a simple way.

Today, Indian investors understand the interest in investing abroad – namely, via financial havens such as Singapore (which accounts for 3% of Indian exports), which centralize their global investment portfolios.

India has emerged as one of the strongest deal-makers worldwide – namely, in terms of cross-border acquisitions.[6] M&A activity increased in 2014 with deals amounting to

Table 9.1 Indian companies ranked among the world's largest

Rank	Company	Industry	Sales	Profits	Assets	Market value
142	Reliance Industries	Oil & gas	71.7	3.7	76.6	42.9
152	State Bank of India	Banking	40.8	2.3	400.6	33
183	Oil & Natural Gas	Oil & gas	28.7	4.4	59.3	43.7
263	Tata Motors	Automotive	42.3	2.7	37.4	28.8
283	ICICI Bank	Banking	14.2	1.9	124.8	30
349	Indian Oil	Oil & gas	74.3	1.2	44.7	14.6
376	HDFC Bank	Banking	8.4	1.4	84.3	41.6
431	NTPC	Power	12.9	1.9	35.4	20.2
485	HDFC	Banking, finance	6.8	1.4	51.9	33.7
485	Tata Consultancy Services	IT	15.1	3.5	11.0	80.3

Note: All financial figures in $ billions

Source: *Forbes* (http://www.forbes.com/global2000/list/)

$38.1 billion, compared to $28.2 billion in 2013 and $35.4 billion in 2012. Telecom was the dominant sector for M&A, with 40% of the total transaction value. In 2015, private equity investments increased 86% to $1.43 billion.

Ten Indian firms made the 2015 Forbes list of the world's biggest public companies. Among of these were three oil & gas operators (Reliance Industries, Oil & Natural Gas and Indian Oil), three financial organizations (State Bank of India, ICICI Bank, and HDFC Bank) and two service firms (HDFC and Tata Consultancy Services). In fact, only three of the top-ten Indian multinationals operate in natural resources, while the remaining seven are in manufacturing or services (Table 9.1).

OFDI and MNEs: geography and strategy

Since the year 2000, India's multinationals have been hard at work expanding internationally. As a consequence, India's OFDI stock has grown seventy-five-fold from $1.7 billion in 2000 to $129.6 billion in 2014.[7] Indian companies are not that interested in other emerging markets; their preference is for richer economies, with low barriers and openness to trade. Nevertheless, Asia and Africa are also important destinations.

While Europe quenches technology- and market-seeking needs, Asia and Africa are strategic choices for the future as resource providers and also as emerging markets with potential customers.

Offshore centers with favorable tax treatment are usual transit points for Indian OFDI (the three favorite being Singapore, Mauritius and the Netherlands) on their way to the final destination.

Historical connections such as the presence of a diaspora are one of the determinants in the choice of location for India's investments. This partly explains the high FDI intensity in Kenya, Gabon or the United Arab Emirates.[8]

In 2014, the bulk of OFDI flowed into sectors such as transport, storage and communication services, accounting for 30.4% of the total. The second-largest sector is manufacturing, with 25.87%. Investment in the primary sector (agriculture and mining) stood at 16.5%. Activities like wholesale, retail trade, financial, insurance and business services, construction and community received the rest of the investments.

Indian multinationals diverge from common patterns. Their competitive advantage cannot be pigeonholed as either strictly technological or cost based. A large number of Indian multinationals are services based, primarily IT-enabled services, which internationalization literature covers less. While the initial globalization project of Indian IT firms was often related to low value-added outsourcing tasks (e.g. data entry or customer service), the Indian IT industry is progressively shifting to higher value-added KPO services (knowledge process outsourcing – e.g. including software programming, legal services, engineering studies). Furthermore, many Indian firms that compete from a low-cost position in manufacturing do so in traditionally R&D-intensive industries; consider, for instance, Tata in car manufacturing, Dr Reddy's in pharmaceuticals or Wipro in IT. A pertinent question is thus whether Indian multinationals represent a new breed of companies that build their competitive advantage in novel ways: firms that derive their advantage from service rather than technological innovations and manufacturing enterprises that straddle a low-cost and medium technology position.[9]

Since about 2005, Indian companies have relied increasingly on transactions for market entry. The volume of M&A deals grew fivefold (486%) during that period, reaching a volume of $9.8 billion in 2014.[10] The highest growth spurts have occurred since 2010. Indian acquisitions cover a range of industries. We cite a few examples below:

- In the oil & gas field, ONGC Videsh Limited (OVL) has grown by acquiring foreign assets and has around twenty projects overseas. In 2003, OVL acquired 25% of Talisman Energy (Canada). In 2012, OVL engaged in deepwater drilling in Cuba together with Statoil (Norway) and Repsol (Spain) and acquired ConocoPhillips's 8.4% stake in the Kashagan oilfield in Kazakhstan. In 2014, OVL and Oil India expanded to Mozambique by acquiring 10% of Videocon Group. OVL also operates subsidiaries in Latin America (Brazil, Colombia, Cuba, Venezuela), in Africa (Libya, Nigeria, Sudan, Mozambique) and also in Russia, Syria, Iraq, Kazakhstan, Vietnam and Myanmar.
- Tata Steel, the most internationally diversified steel producer with operations in almost thirty countries and a commercial presence in fifty markets, follows the same strategy. The company completed the largest acquisition in Indian history in 2006 when it acquired steel producer Corus.
- Tata Global Beverages started in 1962 as a JV between Indian and UK-based tea companies, and now successfully operates in global markets. Today it is the world's second-largest tea company with a brand presence in more than forty countries across Asia, Europe, North America and Australia. Its international expansion relies on acquisitions of local companies as well as alliances with global partners such as Starbucks.

Indian multinationals are very quick on their feet and appear well prepared to adapt to changing global environments. They integrate themselves into partnerships, both domestically and abroad. They diversify operations and geographies, and this helps them to spread revenue risks. Even less diversified firms spread production and sales in several regions, which adds regional synergy to their expansion.

It is important to underline the role of informal or nationalistic determinants (*or motivating factors*), which are quite influential for Indian OFDI. One recent example was the acquisition by Tata Steel of the British-Dutch metallurgy giant Corus in a bidding war against Brazilian Companhia Siderurgica Nacional (CSN), which ended with a tremendously inflated price of $12 billion. In general, motivators such as pride, culture and customs have caused Indian OFDI to become a "victim of its own success." Inorganic expansion in markets that are perhaps less familiar carries higher risks.[11]

India-Russia investments relations

Over many decades, India and Russia have enjoyed a warm cooperative relationship, with both countries having shared outdated socialist central planning for a long period and common geopolitical threats (China and the United States). Both countries have enhanced their economic cooperation through bilateral trade and mutual FDI. The bilateral trade of the two countries amounted to $9.5 billion in 2014, of which $3.2 billion came from Indian exports and $6.3 billion from Russian exports. In terms of outward FDI, India has invested about $7 billion in Russia, while Russian investment in India amounted to $3 billion.[12]

Indian exports to Russia were mainly products such as tobacco, coffee, manufactured goods, pharmaceuticals, iron, steel and apparel. India's imports from Russia include military equipment, fertilizers, diamonds, steel and nuclear power equipment.

The cumulative investments of India in Russia for the past decade amounted to $8 billion in projects such as the Imperial Energy Tomsk, Volzhsky Abrasive Works Volgograd, Sakhalin and Commercial Indo Bank. While the Russian investments in India totaled $4 billion in projects such as Kamaz Vectra, Shyam Sistema Telecom Ltd, Sberbank and VTB.[13]

Various government initiatives – namely, economic forums – facilitate not only government-to-business investments but also business-to-business investments. Both countries have also established banking links by opening representative branches and offices. Russian banks such as Sberbank, Vnesheconombank, Gazprombank, VTB and Promsvyazbank have opened Indian branch offices, while the Indian Commercial Bank and ICICI have started offering services in Russia. Another area of priority cooperation and investment is hydrocarbons, with Indian companies actively investing in energy projects in Russia. One such instance is ONGC Videsh, which has a 20% stake in the Sakhalin I field, and has also acquired Imperial Energy in Tomsk. Other sectors witnessing large deals between Russia and India are pharmaceuticals, IT, trade in rough diamonds and construction.[14]

9.2 Acquiring to sell: case of Tata Motors

Company overview

Tata Motors Limited (Tata hereafter) is India's largest automobile company. It is the leader in commercial vehicles in each segment and among the top in passenger vehicles with products in the compact, midsize car and utility vehicle segments. It is also the world's fifth-largest truck manufacturer and fourth-largest bus manufacturer.

Tata classifies its products in four categories:

1 passenger cars (family cars with maximum seating for five people): Tata Micro Nano, Tata Indica and others
2 utility vehicles: Safari DiCOR, Sumo Gold, Xenon XT and others
3 light commercial vehicles (to carry cargo): Ace (maximum 1 ton), RX Pickup (1 to 1.5 tons) and Ultra Range 407 (2.25 to 7.5 tons)
4 medium- and heavy-commercial vehicles: vans and light trucks (Winger, Venture), minibuses and coaches (Divo, Habit, Intea)

Via subsidiaries, Tata is also engaged in engineering and automotive solutions, manufacturing of automotive components, supply chain activities, vehicle financing, machine tools and factory automation solutions.[15] It is one of the top-fifteen emerging markets companies in terms of R&D expenditures.[16]

From 1954, when its first vehicle rolled off the assembly line, up until 2013, over eight million Tata vehicles have been set loose on the Indian roads. The company's manufacturing plants are spread across India: Jamshedpur (Jharkhand in the east), Pune (Maharashtra in the west), Lucknow (Uttar Pradesh in the north), Pantnagar (Uttarakhand), Sanand (Gujarat) and Dharwad (Karnataka). Tata is the market leader for commercial vehicles and in second position for passenger vehicles. It is also the world's fifth-largest medium and heavy truck manufacturer and the fourth-largest heavy bus manufacturer.

An active exporter since 1961, Tata is one of the most globalized firms with operations in more than 180 countries including developed economies (such as the United States, the United Kingdom, Italy, Spain), emerging markets (including Brazil, China, and South Africa) and frontier countries (Pakistan, Bangladesh). Tata has manufacturing facilities in the United Kingdom, South Korea, Thailand, South Africa and Indonesia.[17]

The company's commercial and passenger vehicles are already being marketed in countries in Europe, Africa, the Middle East, Southeast Asia, South Asia, South America, Australia, CIS and Russia. It has franchisee/joint venture assembly operations in Bangladesh, Ukraine and Senegal.

The company employs over sixty thousand people around the globe.[18]

Tata cars, buses and trucks are sold in 182 countries in Europe, Africa, the Middle East, South Asia, and Southeast Asia and Australia. Through subsidiaries and associate companies, Tata has international operations in the United Kingdom, South Korea, Thailand, Spain, South Africa and Indonesia. Among its subsidiaries is Jaguar Land Rover, acquired in 2008.

Tata's consolidated revenues in 2014–2015 were $42 billion. It is the leader in each of the commercial vehicle segments and also leads in different segments of passenger vehicles, such as compact and midsize cars as well as utility vehicles. Tata was ranked 287th in the Fortune Global 500 ranking in 2014. The company's dealership, sales and services network includes over 6,600 points around the world.

The Indian automotive industry has grown very quickly in the past decades thanks to market liberalization, changes in automotive production legislation and increasing consumer wealth. Indian engineers have adapted production and vehicle designs to the specific market needs. In emerging markets, demand focuses on simple, reliable and cheap products, and Tata fits the mold. In particular, Tata innovated with the world's least expensive car, the Nano, priced at around $2,400. Although the Nano's sales are disappointing, it nonetheless encourages the company to push for innovation in "frugal engineering" and to pursue potential markets worldwide for its products.[19]

First international steps

Tata's international operations started in 1961, with the export of its first truck to Sri Lanka. However, for the next forty years, international operations were random and insignificant. The situation changed after Tata's successful domestic expansion. In 2001, acting CEO Ratan Tata renewed the company's international business strategy, deciding to make the company global. This meant true international growth instead of simply exporting production from India.[20]

In 2001, the success of the Indica passenger car, hatchback model led to the first consignment of 160 cars shipped to Malta. The same year, Tata signed a JV with Daimler Chrysler in order to expand its market share to the United States.[21] In 2002, after two hundred thousand Indica cars are rolled out and five hundred thousand passenger vehicles rolled out, Tata signed a product agreement with the UK-based MG Rover to produce the CityRover, signing a five-year contract with MG Rover to supply one hundred thousand CityRovers.[22]

Tata started to expand horizontally in neighboring countries with similar cultural distance and business environment. Tata focused on a dozen countries with market conditions similar to India's.[23] Among those countries were South Korea (Daewoo acquisition), Thailand (JV with Thonburi Automotive Plant), South Africa (export operations) and Argentina (in alliance with Fiat). In the first decade of the twenty-first century, the company linked the majority of its international investments with India. At the same time, more distant and less similar locations also were targeted.

Tata's coffers started filling, thanks to the success of its Indica model. So in 2004, Tata took over the South Korean company Daewoo Commercial Vehicle for $102 million in an effort to give their brand more international exposure. Tata cooperated with Daewoo to develop trucks such as the Novus and World Truck models, and also jointly produced buses (GloBus and StarBus). Tata also floated shares on the U.S. stock market that year.

In 2005, Tata acquired a 21% stake in Hispano Carrocera, a Spanish bus manufacturer. Tata raised its stake to 100% in November 2009 and then renamed the company. Tata and Brazilian bus manufacturer Marcopolo announced a JV to manufacture fully built buses in 2006. The plant was located in Dharward, India. With 2005 being a busy year, Tata also announced three additional cooperation agreements with the Fiat Group of Italy to produce both Fiat and Tata cars and Fiat powertrains. The six-year sales and distribution JV between the two companies ended in May 2012, at which point Fiat sold the designs for its popular Punto model to Tata for Indian development.

In 2007, Tata and Thonburi Automotive Assembly Plant announced the formation of a JV in Thailand to manufacture, assemble and market pickup trucks. In 2008, Tata signed the definitive agreement with Ford to purchase Jaguar and Land Rover. Tata introduced the new Super Milo range of buses the same year. In 2009, Tata launched its Nano model as well as premium luxury vehicles (Jaguar XF, XFR and XKR and Land Rover Discovery 3). In 2011, Tata unveiled an assembly plant in South Africa, and Land Rover inaugurated a new car assembly plant in Pune, India.[24]

Tata's choice of foreign markets uses two main determinants: good GDP growth rates and high consumer purchasing power. To the extent possible, Tata also opts for markets with similar norms and values to India's. For example, in terms of consumer behavior and distribution networks, South Africa was identified as one of the best markets. Starting with export to this country, Tata continued developing its operations, thereby opening an assembly plant in 2009.

In its deal-making (acquisitions or JVs), Tata selects firms that have well-known brands, good reputations, and perform relatively well, which generally yields good results.[25] After the 2008 takeover of Jaguar and Land Rover, Tata marketed them in India as luxury car brands by Tata. This acquisition was extremely successful, not only in the UK market but also in India and China.[26] The mixture of high technology from the United Kingdom and affordable labor cost and materials from India have given Tata a stronger competitive advantage in the global automotive market. By 2009, some 70% of Tata's revenues came from foreign operations.[27]

Tata was not the only Indian car maker with an international strategy. Maruti Udyog, another Indian automotive firm, started collaboration with Japanese car maker Suzuki, which also invested in India. However, Maruti also benefitted from government financial support to update its technology. Car manufacturing is capital intensive, so local governments may provide financial support to local firms to either acquire businesses or to update technology from advanced markets. Many family-owned automotive component suppliers in India also bought foreign expertise to help improve their competitive position,[28] an example that Russia and some other emerging markets could also follow.

It can be instructive to examine parallel expansion situations for the same company, particularly when the company comes from a BRIC member country. For Tata, very different strategies were adopted for China versus the United Kingdom. An examination of these two cases will help explain the different strategic considerations.

Tata's strategy in China

China is one of the largest markets for the automotive industry (see the case on Geely, page 239), and India is a major car exporter.[29] Both countries are developing at a very fast pace. Furthermore, the automotive industry in both countries started at the same point a few decades ago, with outdated technology sprouting from transition economies. Despite these similarities, the Indian and Chinese automotive industries are very different.

In China, almost all automotive companies (including small and medium sized) have JVs with automotive giants from developed markets such as BMW, GM or Audi, following the Chinese investment law for the auto industry.[30] The goal here is to quickly obtain high technology from developed markets. India also opened its auto sector to FDI, yet without imposing the same restrictions as China. It appears that India learned more from its collaboration with foreign counterparts than China did and possesses more up-to-date technology.

Tata entered the Chinese market in 2008, substantially later than other big global auto companies. Given that the Chinese market is very competitive (all major automakers view China as a key strategic market and therefore invest heavily in China), Tata faced severe competition.[31] Thankfully for Tata, many Chinese are getting vastly rich, and the top-end luxury segment has space. Jaguar Land Rover (JLR), as the only luxury brand presented by Tata in China, received very successful sales in China. In 2011 alone, sales of JLR vehicles in China jumped about 80%. Tata chose luxury cars for its Chinese entry because Chinese consumers appreciate both the quality and the design of European cars. Also, the Chinese government takes a better view of high-technology, high-quality products launched by foreign investors.

Given the success of its Jaguar brand in China, Tata proceeded to build a local assembly plant. In this regard, Tata was subject, like other manufacturers, to Chinese legislation,[32] which required that it constitute a 50-50 joint venture with a Chinese partner. Tata chose Chery for this purpose. Yet other restrictions also applied: increasing the R&D level of technology within a certain time frame, producing economic and environmentally friendly cars and more. Such constraints also implied additional expenditures. Tata, therefore, had many considerations in assessing its investment into China.

Another automotive project of Tata Group in China

Given China's importance in the global auto market, Tata also considered building a R&D center for high-quality products to serve the needs of small-size and fuel-efficient cars. Tata made sizeable efforts to find the right partnerships with local suppliers.[33]

With this vision, Nanjing Tata AutoComp Systems (NTACS) was incorporated in 2007 as a wholly foreign-owned enterprise within Tata AutoComp Systems.[34] NTACS manufactures automotive parts, specifically plastic injection-molded components and sub-assemblies used in the interiors and exteriors of automobiles. This includes interior parts such as air vents and grab handles, as well as external components such as cowl grilles and dashboard panels. Sourcing from China enabled Tata to support its customer needs by increasing locally sourced components in their vehicles, while also catering to their vehicle platforms in Europe and the United States.[35]

NTACS's main challenge arose from the unique business culture in China, which demands a deep understanding of local protocols and modes of operation, and the setting up of business systems that are in tune with global best practices. A second challenge, and this confronts most foreign operations in China, pertains to training local people. Indian managers generally have a low opinion of postings in China, as compared to the United States and Europe.

Tata faced cultural and language barriers in China that far exceeded those of its other international ventures.[36] First, Indian and Chinese managers are quite different. Indian managers are more open in expressing their ideas and talk more than their Chinese colleagues. On the other hand, Chinese managers are more "pragmatic and disciplined, and sometimes very aggressive when setting business targets."[37] For Tata, there was a steep learning curve in order to comprehend Chinese culture, consumer behavior and market trends, and to compete in a market with ever-tightening regulations for clean and energy-efficient cars.

The lack of knowledge of the Chinese language and culture means that experienced Indian professionals are reluctant to accept long-term assignments in China. Additionally, especially in the smaller Chinese cities, there was the challenge of finding employees with working knowledge of English.

Tata's strategy in the United Kingdom

UK automotive manufacturing dates back at the end of the nineteenth century. In the 1950s, it was the world's second-largest manufacturer behind the United States and the largest exporter.[38] Since then it has fallen drastically, claiming only ninth position in terms of new vehicle registrations, with China and the United States leading.[39]

Almost every major brand has manufacturing operations in the United Kingdom (partly to satisfy the need to build right-hand steering vehicles), and customers pay attention to quality and price features. Typical segments are middle class to premium. British-built cars are exported mostly to the EU, with Russia and the United States as the second most popular destinations (in 2011).[40] In 2010, vehicle exports amounted to GBP 29 billion, with 78% of produced vehicles being exported.[41]

In 2014, the United Kingdom produced more than 1.5 million cars, its largest output since 2007, making the United Kingdom the fourteenth-largest car producer in the world and the fourth largest in Europe. In 2012, there were thirty-one manufacturing sites located in the United Kingdom. The largest car manufacturers in 2013 in terms of volume were Nissan (Japan), Land Rover (India), Mini/BMW (Germany), Honda and Toyota (Japan).[42]

The industry is subject to a number of rules and regulations. First there are both international and national safety standards which need to be met, along with end-of-life recycling requirements which cause cost pressure for UK operators. Engine emissions are subject to evolving standards, currently Euro 6 levels. The industry is also committed to reducing CO_2 emissions in the manufacturing process. EU, the United Kingdom and other international regulations apply.

Understandably, from Tata's viewpoint, the Indian and British markets seem different economically, technologically and culturally, implying costly investments to gain initial market knowledge. This helps explain why Tata entered the affluent UK market in 2002 via a manufacturing and supply agreement with MG Rover Group (Land Rover). Tata modified the model according to specifications, using its own Indica model for part of the design, and the CityRover was sold under Rover's trademark. Distribution was done through Land Rover's network.[43] Struggling with quality problems and keeping up with the market standards, the CityRover received poor reviews and sold poorly. Nonetheless, in the end, Tata gained precious Western market experience, which would come in handy later on.

Auto manufacturing in Europe requires strong technical knowledge. This explains the 2015 establishment of Tata European Technical Center (with activities in R&D and engineering) close to Warwick University in Coventry, which employed 250 people. The center's aim was to add to the company's existing yet limited knowledge and undertake third-party work for other automotive companies or public institutions. To date, Tata has invested more than GBP 85 million in the R&D center–related projects.[44,45]

Yet 2007 marked the turning point for Tata in the United Kingdom when it acquired the struggling Jaguar Land Rover division from Ford for $3 billion. Ford was in bad shape at that time. In 2006, it had recorded losses of $12.7 billion, including $318 million in losses at Jaguar Land Rover. Tata was also struggling with rising material costs, making the investment even riskier.[46,47] Yet this is a story with a happy ending, since, under Tata's wing, Jaguar Land Rover turned a profit of £2.61 billion in 2015, up 4.5% on the previous year, showing how the table turned.

In 2007, more than 90% of Tata's revenues came from domestic Indian sales, and as the financial crisis hit hard in Europe and the United States but not India, this was the perfect opportunity to invest. The investment introduced Tata to the premium and luxury segments, a world away from its core low cost, low end of the market. Long-term benefits for Tata included component sourcing, low-cost engineering and design services (three production plants and two advanced design centers).[48] The acquisition more than doubled Tata's overall revenues and quadrupled its revenues from passenger vehicles. Furthermore, the deal shifted the revenue streams away from Asia and towards Europe and helped launch the Tata Nano.[49]

Tata made substantial efforts to bring the Nano to Europe in 2011. The car was unique in terms of manufacturing, fuel consumption, looks and pricing; however, it was plagued by rising costs, some related to satisfying European regulatory needs. The Nano was launched in the United Kingdom in 2011, and as with its first adventure with CityRover in 2002, the Nano did not meet its expectations. Perhaps some of the blame lay with the higher-than-expected price tag: GBP 4,000 instead of the planned GBP 1,500.[50]

Encouraged by the emerging British eco-car market, and hoping for first-mover advantage, Tata then decided in 2011 to produce the Indica Vista EV, an electric car, at Coventry, with a roll-out planned for 2012. This enabled Tata to use some of the production facilities and knowledge from the Jaguar Land Rover deal as well as R&D and engineering from the European Technical Centre.[51,52]

In order to boost the electric car sales, Tata secured a deal whereby the UK government subsidized 25% of the purchase price up to GBP 5,000, thus easing the sticker shock in the short run.[53] Alas, in 2012, Tata announced it was halting production because of slow market growth and high production costs at least until 2014, without having released a single car.[54] In 2011, only 940 electric cars were sold throughout Britain, of which only twenty-five came from Tata, putting a damper on growth. Moreover, Tata expressed concern about the poor network of electric charging stations.

The United Kingdom example shows that Tata still does not have knowledge, products or capabilities to compete with the top players of the developed markets. Thus it needs to expand or modify its product range along with its resource base and match its offering with the requirements of the high-end brands. On the other hand, it may be able to acquire the appropriate knowledge or products outside, as it did with Jaguar Land Rover and turned them to powerful weapons by relocating them to their best global position for capturing new markets.

Adapting to local markets

Tata succeeded in acquiring an international brand (Jaguar) and then expanding it into emerging markets. Yet launching a greenfield brand in developed markets is far more complex.

As a first step, Tata's marketing strategy is very conscious about which car might correspond to which specific customer need. This approach allows the company to fit each region more suitably, if local tastes have been properly assessed. Although the company releases regular innovations in existing models, there always remains one strategic difference: Tata is designing for Indian (and Asian) exigencies and not with the high-speed standards of engineering excellence of global players.

This explains why the Indica and Indigo models have sluggish performance in terms of speed and acceleration, but offer the fuel efficiency, maintainability and spaciousness that are key factors given the household budgets and road and traffic conditions in India.[55] There is no point designing a car that can run at one hundred miles per hour when the most that emerging markets roads can handle is seventy miles an hour.

Tata defeated its rivals in India and in other markets by seizing opportunities well ahead of the competition. Furthermore, in India, Tata can first secure a customer base through pre-bookings for not-yet-released models and then start manufacturing – a successful tactic to gain customer loyalty in several foreign markets.[56]

The suppliers of Tata are largely Indian-based, meaning many of them do not have the competencies to accompany the global expansion of the company. Facing this challenge, Tata must relocate local managers or engineers for its global expansion. Indian expatriates run many foreign operations.

Tata runs a tight ship so it can offer low prices to Indian customers. Suppliers have very little bargaining power in the lean supply chain that Tata has set up. Tata faces certain barriers to its entry and adaptation in many markets (e.g. tightening emissions norms), but gradually works on the innovative solutions without damaging its local Indian cost advantages too heavily. The ill-fated Nano launch in the United Kingdom showed the company's ability to adapt to local conditions (stringent emissions and safety norms in Europe), yet also proved that local tastes are the toughest variable to understand.

Stung by the Nano flop, Tata's new strategy when going international is to develop dedicated manufacturing facilities, marketing teams and sales teams in order to meet local customer needs. The strategy is to develop self-contained operations in a narrow band of selected countries, evaluating locations on the basis of market opportunities and labor skills.[57]

Joint ventures play a significant role in entering and understanding new geographic markets. This approach allows Tata Motors to diversify its risks by working with companies that already possess experience in the area. Such collaborations also give Tata's international image a boost, since it remains mostly known as the leader in India.

Thanks to its acquired Land Rover and Jaguar brands, Tata had an opportunity to enter the premium segment, in which case it will develop a new strategy or improve the existing one in order to face new customers' needs and thereby improve its position on the global market as well as creating brand loyalty.

9.3 Acquiring to learn: case of Wipro

Company overview

Wipro Group is a large Indian conglomerate that operates via multiple separate corporate entities, all wholly owned. This case study focuses on the largest of the business units, Wipro Technologies. The group's other main subsidiaries include Wipro Consumer Care & Lighting, Wipro GE Medical Systems Limited and Wipro Infrastructure Engineering. Wipro also has a hardware business unit called Wipro Infotech that sells notebooks, desktop computers and storage devices, primarily to government departments and public sector undertakings in India.

Wipro Technologies is a global IT, consulting and outsourcing company serving clients in around 175 cities across 6 continents.[58] The company operates through two key IT segments: services and products, offering a comprehensive range of software solutions, IT consulting, business process outsourcing (BPO), cloud mobility, analytics services and solutions and R&D services to its clients.[59]

Wipro Technologies offers services including embedded systems, enterprise applications, networking, telecoms solutions and web-based applications to a multitude of business sectors (banking, insurance, industry, etc.). The company operates in the following four broad areas:

IT services: Wipro IT services serves the information technology needs of the entire business value chain. It offers services ranging from business intelligence, service-oriented architecture, enterprise applications (CRM, ERP, SCM), and quality consulting to different industries such as automotive electronics, finance, medical devices and many more.

Product engineering services (PES): Wipro is one of the largest independent providers of R&D services in the world. Wipro's "extended engineering" model aims to leverage R&D investment and access new knowledge and experience across the globe, people and technical infrastructure. The PES unit operates fourteen Centres of Excellence in domains such as grid computing, wireless network devices, automotive infotainment and gaming and animation.

Technology infrastructure services (TIS): TIS provides global remote infrastructure services such as infrastructure consulting, system integration, data center management, IT help desk services, IT infrastructure security services, remote management and telecom infrastructure services for customers across the globe. TIS established the world's first Global Command Centre (GCC) in 2002 to provide remote monitoring and management services based on customer-specific service level agreements (SLAs) to manage customers' IT infrastructure.

Business process outsourcing (BPO): Wipro's BPO service offerings include business process re-engineering, integrating technology with BPO and knowledge services. Wipro emerged as one of the largest BPO providers when it acquired Spectramind in 2002. In 2008, it had over nineteen thousand people operating out of nine different locations globally. It delivered process specific solutions in areas like finance & accounting, human resources, loyalty and knowledge services. Its customers are in various industries including banking, insurance, travel, telecoms and healthcare.

Since 2010, Wipro Technologies has achieved huge growth in terms of employees, market share and revenues. Whereas in 2003, Wipro was primarily considered a low-cost provider of routine software programming services,[60] today it has grown to a competitive and innovative global player. Being India's third largest and among the world's top five IT companies in terms of market capitalization, gives an idea of the importance of Wipro.

The company's business strategy within the last decade has been focused on becoming a true global technology powerhouse.[61] Calling their mission the "intensity to win," Wipro strongly aims to be the best.[62]

The company's growth has been significant since the beginning of the century: from 40,000 employees in 2005, to over 175,000 employees currently working in approximately 100 countries.[63] Wipro's revenues have increased dramatically every year since the early 1990s. Company's revenues was approximately $6.9 billion (INR 374.3 billion) in 2013, an increase of 0.7% over 2012. In FY2014/15 (ended March 31, 2015), the company posted revenues of $7.6 billion.[64] The company is headquartered in Karnataka, India and operates across North America, Europe, Latin America and Asia.

The company's customer base is wide and includes dozens of the world's leading companies, across diverse industries. The banking, financial services and insurance sector is the largest vertical, contributing 26.2% of Wipro revenues in FY2015. Among the other client sectors served: manufacturing and high-tech (18.2%); energy, natural resources and utilities (16.2%); retail, consumer goods, transportation and government (14.1%); global media and telecoms (13.9%); and healthcare, life sciences and services (11.4%).[65] Further none of the clients account for more than 10% of the company's IT product or service revenues.[66]

The company's clients are spread all over the world. However, the company depends heavily on mature markets such as the United States and the Europe for the bulk of its revenues. Thus, in FY2014, Wipro generated 73.4% of its revenue from the United States and Europe, while India accounted for only 10.6% and the rest of the world for 16%. Moreover, for its IT services branch, Wipro is even more Western dependent, with 49% of revenue from the United States and 30% from Europe. Although Wipro generates revenues from a diversified service portfolio, its geographic revenue base remains concentrated. Any disruptions in the economic or political conditions in these regions could significantly impact the demand for the company's services and its revenues and profitability.[67]

Rooted in vegetables

Wipro was founded in 1945 as Western Indian Vegetable Products by M. H. Hasham Premji and began operations with an oil mill and a hydrogenated cooking oil-processing plant, before going public in 1947 for roughly $30,000.[68] Over the years, Wipro diversified into several unrelated businesses, including soaps, wax, tin containers for packaging and crushing. Gaining financial strength, the company further diversified into IT and healthcare equipment, two growing sectors for India. Wipro diversified into computers in the mid-1970s almost as soon as India's computer industry sprouted roots.[69]

Yet the IT era for the company truly began in 1980, when Wipro set up its IT business in Bangalore under the Ashok Narasimhan brand, and dealing mostly in hardware, not software services. In the early 1980s, the company began assembling Canon, Cisco Systems, Epson, HP and Sun products, selling through its network of dealers.[70] Wipro also started to manufacture its own branded hardware in 1985, aiming to reinforce its image of outstanding quality positioned more upscale than many competitors with cheaper products.

In the 1980s, Wipro produced microprocessor-based minicomputers under its own brand and sold them through its dealer network. In the 1990s, after a series of Indian government reforms led to increased foreign investments in India and the transformation of the country in a leading global IT hub, Wipro reinforced its production assembly for international firms such as Apple, Canon, Cisco, Sun and other well-known Western brands. Moreover, while providing a range of IT services, including hardware design, networking and communications and operating system support, the company also diversified into other businesses.[71] For instance, in 1992, Wipro set up a lighting business that offered a variety of lighting solutions for domestic, commercial, industrial and pharmaceutical lab environments. In 1999, Wipro forayed into residential Internet services market through a JV with Royal Dutch Telecom, aiming to conquer the Indian market.

By 1998, Bangalore had become one of the most important IT centers in India, its equivalent of Silicon Valley, with about 250 high-tech firms based there. At this time, Wipro was the second-largest software exporter in India, with the software and hardware divisions bringing in about 60% of company sales and 75% of profits. Naturally, Wipro became a key figure of this Bangalore cluster. However, it was not cost efficient enough to produce its own computers, thus limiting itself to the assembly and sale of established Western brands.

International strategy

In the first decade of the twenty-first century, Wipro has been trying to spread even wider globally, via acquisitions, JVs and the creation of solutions offices. This globalization strategy was driven by the following logic:

- traditionally Wipro is far from customers, yet that enables the firm to keep Indian costs low and also to work on projects at night when customers are asleep (thanks to time zone differences);
- at the same time, proximity to customers overseas makes sense when choosing countries which are not too costly for operations;
- technology and knowledge in host countries can create a flow of skills and innovations specific to those markets; and
- when put together, this allows for better and faster customer service.

This client-centric strategy plays a very important role in the company's success. For Wipro, the strong relationship to its customers is mission critical, with client communications being vital in maintaining high service quality and competitive advantage.[72]

Wipro even went so far as to introduce a metric to include customer demands and wishes in its development of software and technology, in order to "win together to create synergy."[73] Customers are strongly regarded as business partners who take part in product development so as to fully meet expectations and needs. Wipro wishes to help customers save money, find new revenue streams and become more efficient. This win-win relationship with partners generates trust and means Wipro can become a core part of the customer's business.[74]

If the quality of customer relations is critical, the quality of solutions offered is just as important. To do so, Wipro seeks to form alliances with technology leaders abroad, with a target of capturing at least 80% market share.[75] The idea is that by combining Wipro's IT expertise with the partners' specific sector knowledge, the two companies can build on mutual strengths, create new value, widen their product and service range so as to both grow.

Finally, about one-third of the total revenues come from R&D outsourcing, which provides access to high-technology innovations and progress.[76] Altogether, this formed a new company message, "applied innovation," replacing the prior cost saving and process orientation to position it differently from other Indian IT companies and to become competitive in the U.S. market.

It must be mentioned that another Indian IT giant, Tata Consultancy Services, laid the groundwork for international expansion from which other firms benefitted.

Making Wipro into a brand

With Wipro Technologies already well established in the United States, Europe and Japan, and possessing the required know-how, top management felt the time had come for the company to have a strong brand name. This would also help reduce the price differential with respect to developed competitors, hopefully from the current 49% to about 20%. This proved difficult in a very competitive market. IT services always struggle for comparative advantage and market recognition. Software coding and programming are considered generic services (commodities) since they cannot be appreciated by most end users. In 2007, in the United States, brand awareness for Wipro was only 50%, compared to 100% recognition for IBM or Accenture.[77]

The company set its mind to developing tactics to develop awareness so as to differentiate itself from competitors. One natural option was to emphasize its strong drive for innovation. To support this idea, Wipro's innovation council allowed every employee to contribute her ideas and innovations, and even obtain funding for three years for interesting or promising concepts.

International roll-out

The first important step in Wipro's internationalization was the decentralization away from India towards other countries; the reason for this was, as the company's CEO said, "With 145,000 people[78] you can't run anything centrally. It's a losing battle. If all decisions have to come back to India, you can't react quickly enough in front of the customer."[79]

During this period of time (1980s–1990s), the company began to shift its focus towards healthcare, data and telecoms and enterprise resource planning. These operations targeted mainly the American market. A crucial stepping stone was the Wipro GE Medical Systems joint venture formed in 1989 with General Electric for the manufacture, sale and service of diagnostic and imaging products. The JV has also an OEM sourcing arrangement with Elpro International, for locally made X-ray products. In 1990, the JV became a subsidiary of Wipro. This JV helped the company to diversify further and tap into a new customer segment.

When entering untouched markets in Europe (e.g. Cologne in 2007), local solution centers and offices were established as bridgeheads, employing skilled local staff instead of bringing Indian workers to the country. In this manner, software development and solution services were processed locally: by locals for locals, providing a higher amount of interaction with customers as well as the possibility to respond immediately to specific customer demands.

Certainly, Wipro's success in India can be attributed to its control over its full value chain, including R&D, product processing, business and technology solutions, delivery, as well as consulting. Extending this model to global markets was a no-brainer. Furthermore, the company's reputation as having deep technology expertise and industry-specific experience helped to gain customers.[80]

Crossing the Atlantic

In the beginning of the twenty-first century, the company made the first physical step towards the American market by moving its software headquarters to Santa Clara, California. At that time, Wipro's client base primarily consisted of American companies, and the growing demand for IT services meant ever-increasing demand. Moreover, the company also listed its stock on the New York Stock Exchange in 2000. There were several reasons for this choice: to gain local USD currency for Western acquisitions, to attract talent by offering dollar-denominated stock options, to strengthen the brand by giving it financial credibility and awareness among financial analysts and to force discipline on the organization by imposing quarterly performance targets.[81]

To increase its recognition in the U.S. market, Wipro has been relying on a deal-based strategy. In 2002, its first international acquisition was a company called AMS for $26 million. Five years later, in 2007, Wipro acquired Infocrossing, a provider of IT infrastructure management, enterprise application and BPO services, for $700 million.[82] This gave Wipro a bigger footprint in the United States, plus greater recognition and market share. It was Wipro's largest acquisition and considered a risky move into the U.S. market. Another important move in the same year was the formation of a strategic alliance with Cisco Systems, connecting Cisco's industry-leading networking hardware (servers) with Wipro's IT abilities – namely, software for infrastructure and managed services.

In the following years, Wipro acquired further IT companies, such as the global oil & gas IT practice of SAIC (Science Applications International Corporation) in 2011 for $150 million,[83] which was an important contribution to the company's vertical (i.e. industry-specific) product range.

Thanks to these deals, the United States quickly became Wipro's largest geographical market. In 2013, American revenues accounted for 45.8% of total company revenues ($3.2 billion) – an increase of 16.4% over the previous year.[84]

M&A and partnerships as the cornerstone for expansion

Transactions have become the centerpiece of Wipro's growth strategy in developed markets. Following a so-called string-of-pearls strategy, the company has acquired more than thirty companies worldwide. Following this strategy of inorganic growth in advanced markets, Wipro was seeking innovation and knowledge transfer rather than just sales growth. The company has always been most interested in partners that could add value, in order to extend the value chain.

Although aggressive in its M&A strategy, Wipro was doing acquisitions judiciously and keeping them small.[85] This approach proved judicious, since many analyses have shown that most big-ticket acquisitions fail to pay off for shareholders. The worldwide economic slowdown in 2001 and 2002 did reduce the pace of growth for the entire tech industry, and Wipro's buying habit as well.

From 2002 to 2006, Wipro made a series of small acquisitions to get a foothold in the IT consulting sector in the United States.[86] One of the most important acquisitions was Nerve Wire Inc., a boutique financial services firm, with about ninety consultants, in Newton, Massachusetts. The purpose was to gain expertise in consulting to the financial sector. By 2006, Wipro had organized itself into more than a dozen verticals, including finance, telecoms, manufacturing, retailing, etc.

Europe was also an active arena for Wipro, with acquisitions that included NewLogic (Austria) in 2005 for $56 million and Enabler (Portugal) in 2006 for $52 million. In 2006, the company also acquired mPower (American payment system solutions with R&D in China) for $28 million, cMango (American technology developer) for $20 million, Quantech Global (American engineering design and analysis services firm) for $10 million, Saraware (Finnish wireless design services firm) for €25 million euro and Hydrauto (Swedish provider of hydraulic components) for $31 million.

The main idea behind the series of these small strategic deals was to add expertise and intellectual property, open new markets or enhance service lines and strengthen company's tech infrastructure services capabilities. In 2007, the company expanded operations in Canada, Germany, France, Eastern Europe, the Middle East and China.

Apart from two sound acquisitions of Infocrossing and SAIC in the United States, in 2009, the company acquired Citi Technology Services, the India-based captive provider of IT services and solutions,[87] the Yardley business in Asia, Middle East, Australia and certain African markets for $45.5 million from the UK-based Lornamead Group.[88] Yet since 2007, Wipro has been more focused on partnerships and strategic alliances than on acquisitions. Alliances with strong Western partners such as Microsoft and Cisco facilitate profitable co-innovation projects. The main goal of such partnerships is to offer customers a choice of best-of-breed products and technologies. Some of the Wipro partners in different areas include Microsoft, Oracle, SAP, Telefónica, Google, Nokia Siemens Networks and Tele2. With these firms, Wipro develops and implements Internet strategies, develops industry and customer solutions, explores market opportunities in other industries, supports databases, works with semiconductors and develops R&D partnerships.

Beyond developed markets . . .

Although Wipro focused mostly on Western markets in its early years of internationalization, the company did establish small solutions offices to serve emerging markets such as China (2004) and the Philippines (2008). Unlike its approach in developed markets, the aim here is to produce at low cost, without any larger growth ambitions so far.

Although in no hurry to enter emerging markets, Wipro's interest has been aroused as IT demand grows there. Markets in Africa, Asia Pacific and Latin America have become much bigger today and are developing at high speed with rising technology demand, whereas Western markets are closer to saturation, although still showing sustained demand for IT. To stay close to its customers, existing and future ones, Wipro aims to continue its policy of opening local offices in emerging host countries, just as it did in Europe ten years ago.

Future prospects

Wipro's amazing growth can be attributed to several causes. First, India, and particularly its IT industry, succeeded in generating talented programmers and engineers. Second, instead of competing in the field of software production against such giants as Microsoft or Oracle, Wipro tapped the market of IT consulting. Thus software producers who potentially could have been Wipro rivals became Wipro clients.

Wipro has already created a broad client base worldwide and continues growing rapidly even while keeping a low-risk profile. This approach includes the infrastructure to facilitate communication and collaboration between the company's far-flung outposts. The company has strengthened its image, notoriety and grown significantly via diverse transactions. Wipro has sealed several deals with large global corporations and at the same time increased its local presence, thus strengthening its position in the IT service sector. Careful to avoid over-dependence on the massive USA market, Wipro also built up its European business.

Wipro's future growth strategy focuses on three main targets: strategic innovation, conquering emerging markets and the green policy.

Innovation is foremost, since it has never been more vital to stay innovative in order to stay strong given the fierce current competition. The IT market is renowned as being ruthless in its continuous development and innovation. The company that does not pay close attention can be outdated in a flash. Innovation is in the form of new products and services, but also in business practices.

Going green has also become an important part of Wipro's strategy. Given the global concern about planetary welfare and ecological sustainability, Wipro wishes to be an active part of the green community. This is not only a marketing message for customers but also a means of cutting costs, with eco-efficiency helping to reduce costs.[89] With data centers being huge power consumers, IT companies play a large role in terms of greenhouse gas emissions. Wipro's aim is to minimize its carbon footprint by reducing their data center sizes, which will be both more eco-friendly and cut costs. This strategy will be implemented by increasing cloud computing to decrease the number of servers and to virtualize most of the remaining ones to reduce the amount of data. On top of that, old servers and computers will be replaced by more energy-efficient and eco-friendly models.

Emerging markets are the third strategic pillar. On top of inherent market attractiveness, emerging host countries offer low-cost labor, coupled with a growing availability of skilled staff, as well as developing infrastructure. Combined these pull factors justify Wipro's plans to expand further into these emerging markets.

The future of Wipro looks bright; the plans for innovation seem promising. By taking part in the green business wave, the company adheres to current business ethics, thus gaining trust and reputation. Its plan to expand further into developing economies leaves space for expansion, growth and further company prosperity.

References

1 'A chance to fly. India has a rare opportunity to become the world's most dynamic big economy,' The *Economist*. 21–27.02.2015. P.9.
2 India profile, World Trade Organization, http://stat.wto.org/CountryProfile/WSDBCountryPFView.aspx?Language=E&Country=IN
3 The Atlas of Economic complexity 2016.
4 Munjal, Buckley, Enderwick and Forsans 2014.
5 Ibid.
6 India in business Ministry of External Affairs, Govt. of India, http://indiainbusiness.nic.in/newdesign/index.php?param=advantage/163
7 UNCTAD 2015.
8 Ibid.
9 http://unctad.org/en/publicationslibrary/ier2013_en.pdf

10 UNCTAD 2015.
11 Narula and Kodiyat 2014.
12 Indian Embassy 2015, http://www.indianembassy.ru/
13 Ibid.
14 Ibid.
15 http://www.tatamotors.com/about-us/company-profile.php
16 http://www.oecd.org/sti/inno/oecd-inclusive-innovation.pdf
17 http://www.tatamotors.ru/company/overview.aspx
18 http://www.forbes.com/companies/tata-motors/
19 Ramsinghani 2012.
20 Salvan 2011.
21 Management Discussion and Analysis by Tata Motors (2012), http://tatamotors.com/investors/
    financials/67-ar-html/pdf/Management_Discussion_and_Analysis.pdf
22 http://profit.ndtv.com/stock/tata-motors-ltd_tatamotors/reports
23 Patibandla 2009.
24 http://articles.economictimes.indiatimes.com/2006–09–07/news/27436717_1_tata-ace-ace-
    mini-truck-passenger-vehicle
25 KPMG http://www.kpmg.de/docs/Eastern_Germany_as_a_Location_for_Indian_Direct_Investment_
    022008.pdf
26 Xinhua 2012.
27 Salvan 2011.
28 Stucchi 2012.
29 Amighini 2012.
30 Ibid.
31 'China story' 2011.
32 Guo, Wei, Li and Wang 2000.
33 Annual Report 2011–12, www.tatamotors.com. P.9.
34 'China story' 2011.
35 Ibid.
36 Ibid.
37 Ibid.
38 http://www.smmt.co.uk/downloads/SMMT%20KPMG%20UK%20Automotive%20Exec%20
    Summary.zip
39 http://www.bis.gov.uk/files/file51139.pdf
40 SMMT 2012.
41 http://www.bis.gov.uk/files/file51139.pdf
42 SMMT 2015.
43 http://www.tata.com/innovation/articles/inside.aspx?artid=NXJRb+NnnZ0=
44 http://www.eurekamagazine.co.uk/design-engineering-news/tata-motors-adds-100-jobs-at-
    uk-rd-facility/32653/
45 http://www.aronline.co.uk/blogs/news/tata-motors-uk-production-gives-vista-ev-a-headstart-on-
    nissan-leaf/
46 *Business Strategy Review*. 2010. The Tata Way.
47 The economist intelligence unit. Country monitor, 3 September 2007.
48 Salvan 2011.
49 http://www.tata.com/innovation/articles/inside.aspx?artid=NXJRb+NnnZ0=
50 Autoexpress.co.uk. 2011, Car Reviews: Tata-Nano, http://www.autoexpress.co.uk/car-reviews/
    17794/tata-nano
51 Autocar.co.uk. 2011. Tata Boosts UK Presence, http://www.autocar.co.uk/car-news/industry/
    tata-boosts-uk-presence
52 Automotive manufacturing solutions. 2011. Tata starts UK production of EV model.
53 Ibid.
54 'Tata Motors ready to pull plug on UK launch' 2010.
55 http://www.tatamotors.com/investors/annualreports-pdf/Annual-Report-2012–2013.pdf
56 http://www.tuacoecdmneguidelines.org/companydetails2.asp?organisationID=23141
57 http://www.slideshare.net/kpmg/kpmg-auto-exec-survey-2013
58 About Wipro. – Wipro Limited, 2016. – http://www.wipro.com/about-Wipro/

59 About Wipro. – Wipro Limited, 2014. –http://www.wipro.com.
60 Hamm.
61 Wipro's new strategy: Outsource locally' 2014.
62 About Wipro. – Wipro Limited, 2014. http://www.wipro.com.
63 Ibid.
64 About Wipro. – Wipro Limited, 2016. – http://www.wipro.com/about-Wipro/
65 http://www.wipro.com/documents/investors/pdf-files/Wipro-Investor-Presentation-Q4-FY15.pdf
66 MarketLine. Wipro company profile, www.marketline.com viewed 22 may 2015.
67 Ibid.
68 Wipro Limited. – HighBeam, Inc., 2014. http://www.encyclopedia.com
69 Ibid.
70 About Wipro. – Wipro Limited, 2014. http://www.wipro.com
71 Wipro Limited. – HighBeam, Inc., 2014. http://www.encyclopedia.com
72 We are sticking to a long-term strategy, says Wipro CEO Acquisitions. Business Line, 2014. http://www.thehindubusinessline.com
73 About Wipro. – Wipro Limited, 2014. http://www.wipro.com
74 'Wipro's CFO Suresh Senapathy on current changes' 2014.
75 'Wipro is now decentralising like crazy' 2014.
76 Indian Outsourcer Wipro's Strategy: Innovation Push, Global Hiring, Acquisitions. CXO Media Inc, 1994–2014. http://www.cio.com
77 Ibid.
78 It was said when the company had 30 thousand people less than nowadays.
79 'Wipro is now decentralising like crazy' 2014.
80 About Wipro. – Wipro Limited, 2014. http://www.wipro.com
81 Wipro own data.
82 Wipro to acquire US services provider Infocrossing. InfoWorld, 1994–2014, http://www.infoworld.com
83 Wipro to acquire SAIC's global oil and gas information technology services business 2014.
84 Growth Strategies for 2012 and Beyond 2014.
85 Hamm.
86 Ibid.
87 'Citi completes sale of Citigroup Technology Services Ltd.' India 2014.
88 Wipro Limited. – HighBeam, Inc., 2014. http://www.encyclopedia.com.
89 Growth Strategies for 2012 and Beyond. Wipro Limited, 2014. http://www.wipro.com

10 International strategies of Russian multinationals

This chapter, like preceding ones, will commence with an analysis of Russia's entry onto the global scene, and proceed with a discussion of the home market role in the internationalization of Russian enterprises. Thereafter the analysis of outbound investment (OFDI) will be presented, with the sectoral and regional analysis of investment flows from Russia.

One difference in this chapter is that it will review three firms (cases studies) instead of the usual two, as in previous chapters. There are two reasons for this. The first is that usually, Russian multinationals are traditionally associated with three large industries: oil & gas, metallurgy and banking; it makes sense to illustrate each in this chapter. The second reason is that Russian multinationals show a variety of strategies and approaches, even when operating in similar industries. Even the two extractive firms in this chapter display very different strategies.

The case studies will present three main internationalization approaches of Russian firms: high reliance on aggressive acquisitions (the case of Severstal), more sustainable investment in own manufacturing facilities (Gazprom Neft) and following clients' needs into international markets (Alfa–Bank). This chapter will explain how and why Russian firms internationalize, what their motives for expansion are and what the origins of their advantages are. An important outcome of this chapter is the lessons from understudied but very important investors from emerging world.

10.1 Globalization of Russia and international investments of Russian firms

Internationalization of economy: recent trends

Russia ranks as the tenth-largest economy in the world, with 2014 GDP of $1.86 trillion.[1] GDP per capita (on a PPP basis) has almost tripled since 1999 and is the highest among the BRIC quartet. The Russian economy had been expected to grow to $3.9 trillion by 2017, according to former IMF forecasts. Less sanguine now, the World Bank expects Russia to face a long journey to recovery. While the conditions that pushed Russia's economy into recession may be gradually abating, the World Bank's current baseline scenario anticipates a further contraction of 1.9% in 2016, before growth resumes at a modest rate of 1.1% in 2017.[2]

Russia's domestic market remains one of the largest in the world, ranking eighth out of 148 countries. Russia is also the world leader in commodities production. In addition to major commodities such as oil, gas and metals, it possesses the world's largest reserves of timber, fresh water, agricultural land, etc.

The Russian government is committed to increasing its economic competitiveness and making Russia a more attractive investment destination. With a personal income tax rate of 13% for residents, a corporate tax rate of 20% and a VAT rate of 18%, Russia has one of the most generous tax regimes in the world, not including offshore tax havens. FDI into Russia exceeded $69 billion in 2013,[3] which places Russia fourth in the global FDI inflow ranking, after China (including Hong Kong), the United States and Canada.

The year 2015 inflicted a shock on the Russian economy, with FDI patterns once again changing. Conflicts in Crimea and the Ukraine have led to a series of sanctions imposed on the Russian Federation by European nations and the United States, and a significantly devalued currency. Plummeting petroleum prices have also taken their toll on the oil-dependent economy. The related geopolitical uncertainty could have some dire consequences for Russian companies investing abroad. Banks in developed countries, upon which many companies rely, may be unwilling to extend lines of credit as the perceived riskiness increases (UNCTAD). Furthermore, many drivers of Russian OFDI have close ties to the state, meaning that politics invariably plays a role in investment decisions. For example, in late 2014, Gazprom cancelled the South Stream project, a massive oil pipeline to the EU, incurring massive costs as a result.[4]

With access to Western capital markets drying up, Russian multinationals will likely rely increasingly on Eastern allies, changing the geographic dynamics of OFDI profoundly. Gazprom was planning the Turkish Stream pipeline which could allow natural gas to flow via Turkey thus bypassing Ukraine, where the contested gas transit contract expires in 2019. Unfortunately, the November 2015 downing of a Russian military jet by the Turkish military near the Syrian border immediately flared into geopolitical tension between the countries. In December 2015, the project was annulled by presidential order.

Greece, amid its own economic catastrophe, has recently emerged as a surprising ally, and is preparing to sign a $5 billion gas contract with Russia. Yet another problem lurks here, that of the large Syrian migrant population in Greece, and the increased country risk associated with the Hellenic Republic. Gazprom, Edison (Italy) and DEPA (Greece) nonetheless signed an agreement to study Russian gas supply to Greece and then to Italy, under the Adriatic Sea, as an alternative to the South Stream or Turkish Stream pipelines.

Russia today is considered as one of leading nations for protectionist policies. In 2013, the trading block including Russia, Belarus and Kazakhstan was responsible for 33% of worldwide protectionism,[5] with 43.4% of the protectionist policies devoted to bailouts and direct subsidies for local companies and 15.5% constituting tariff measures.[6]

Russia has regular trade surpluses primarily due to exports of commodities such as oil and natural gas (57% of total exports), nickel, palladium, iron and chemical products. Other top exports include cars, military equipment and timber. Russia's main trading partners are China (7% of total exports) and Germany (also 7%).

Contrary to the preconceived idea that Russian foreign trade is only natural resources, software exports have jumped from $120 million in 2000 to $6 billion in 2014.[7] Since the year 2000, the IT market has been growing by 30%–40% per annum. The engine of the growth is offshore programming, where Russian coders do work for clients in developed markets. Currently, Russia controls 3% of the offshore software development market and is the third leading country (after India and China) among software exporters. A number of factors support the development of Russian IT, including government support.

Table 10.1 Russian companies among the largest public companies

Rank	Company	Industry	Sales	Profits	Assets	Market value
27	Gazprom	Oil & gas	158	24.1	356	62.5
59	Rosneft	Oil & gas	129	9	150	51.1
109	Lukoil	Oil & gas	121.4	4.7	111.8	43.5
124	Sberbank	Banking	58.1	7.6	420	26.9
209	Surgutneftegas	Oil & gas	26.6	8.8	74.6	24.2
555	Transneft	Oil & gas	22	4.1	56.8	3.6
576	Norilsk Nickel	Mining, metals	11.9	1.9	13.1	29.2
615	VTB bank	Banking	28.4	0.11	203.2	14.6
701	Magnit	Retail	19.8	1.2	6.1	20.4
710	Tatneft	Oil & gas	12.3	2.4	12.2	12.1

Note: All financial figures in $ billions for 2015

Source: *Forbes* (http://www.forbes.com/global2000/list/)

The position of Russia as one of the leading emerging economies in terms of outbound FDI is supported by dozens of Russian multinationals in various industries, many of which are present in the Forbes Global ranking (see Table 10.1).

As the table shows, six of ten largest Russian firms operate in the oil & gas segment, and one operates in metallurgy, confirming the established view that the top Russian multinationals are mostly in the extractive industries.

OFDI and MNEs: geography and strategy

The number of Soviet companies operating abroad started to increase after the Second World War, and particularly after the 1960s economic reforms. Nevertheless, the outbound investment of Soviet firms was relatively modest, since few Soviet companies operated abroad.[8] Soviet subsidiaries operated in around thirty-five countries to promote exports of the national goods, and some of these firms provided Soviet enterprises with business services, such as transportation, insurance and banking services.

These "red multinationals" were mostly active in the COMECON economic area, comprising the countries of the former Eastern Bloc, along with a number of communist brother states elsewhere in the world. Given the absence of business legislation, and lack of finance and management knowledge, it was mostly socialist ideology that kept the red multinationals in business.[9] The operations of Soviet subsidiaries abroad were not motivated by economic logic but rather driven by political ambitions linked to the East-West rivalry. Most of the red multinationals had their headquarters in Moscow, which explains why, after the collapse of the USSR, the overwhelming majority of their foreign subsidiaries were either integrated into the new Russian mother company, or sold off to local investors in each country where they had operated.[10]

Outbound investment (OFDI) from Russia began to intensify dramatically in the late 1990s and early 2000s. After 2005, the volume of Russian investment outflows was one of the highest in the world, while it ceased in 2014–2015 due to geopolitical and macroeconomic reasons. In 2013, Russia appeared to be one of the leading investors abroad with over $95 billion OFDI. In fact, Russian companies were so anxious to catch up with other multinationals that the growth rate of OFDI outstripped that of other emerging economies such as Brazil and India. This increase can also be attributed to two other factors: first, the Bank of Russia began to record FDI in a more accurate manner (likely under-reported before) and second, Russian companies were ready to expand after several years of progressively developing their competitive advantages within Russia.[11]

As in most countries, Russian OFDI decreased in the wake of 2008 global financial crisis. Nonetheless, foreign investments were quick to recover: Russia's OFDI flow increased by over 65% between 2009 and 2013. Between 2008 and 2012, and in line with the general trend, when FDI stocks held between the EU and the BRIC countries doubled, Russian FDI positions in the EU increased by 155%.[12]

In 2013, the country became the fourth-largest investor in foreign economies and accounted for 95% of OFDI from CIS countries.[13] The value of OFDI flows relative to Russian GDP was about 4.1% in 2013.[14]

Russian multinationals with foreign investments display several common traits: monopolistic (or oligopolistic) position in Russia, leading position in the sector, sufficient export revenues to finance operations abroad and the willingness to be active on a global scale.[15] Russian multinationals typically begin their international expansion in other CIS countries such as Ukraine or Kazakhstan.[16] Outflows to this region peaked between 2001 and 2004.

However, there have been recent shifts in the geographic focus of Russian investments. It is the other BRICS countries that arouse the envy of Russian companies. In 2011, Russian stock in the BRICS countries reached $1.1 billion,[17] representing a sharp increase from previous years. This trend can be explained not only by the desire to increase the efficiency of raw material supply. Indeed, Russian multinationals wanted to establish control globally over the value chains of their own businesses and secure natural resources under their operations so as to build competitive advantages. Lastly, these companies wanted to strengthen themselves in important overseas markets including other developing countries. Russia has also dipped a toe in African waters. For example, aluminium producer Rusal has initiated operations in Angola, Guinea, Nigeria and South Africa. Russian banks have followed suit with Vneshtorgbank opening the first majority foreign-owned bank in Angola as well as operations in Namibia and Côte d'Ivoire. Russian Renaissance Capital acquired 25% of Ecobank, a Togo-based bank with operations in thirty-six African nations.[18] Interest in Africa has been motivated by the desire to access key raw materials as well as tap into local markets which are expected to grow substantially.

In 2013, the top-ten recipients of Russian FDI, ranked in order, were Cyprus, the Netherlands, the BVI, Switzerland, Luxembourg, the United Kingdom, the United States, Jersey, Germany, and Gibraltar. Eliminating obvious offshore tax havens to consider real capital investments, the key hosts are advanced economies in Europe and the United States.

The extensive reliance on offshore tax havens for OFDI led the Russian government to complain of the institutional damage caused, and to vote a January 1, 2015, law that instituted an anti-offshoring tax regimen. The next few years may see some capital return to Russia.

Russian investment in the remaining part of BRIC

Russian investments in other EEs are varied, both in terms of their distribution by industry and the strategies of the multinationals at play. In this section, the milestones and trends will be highlighted.

Brazil

Both Russia and Brazil are extremely rich in natural resources. Russia has extensive oil & gas reserves and Brazil is rich in hydrocarbons and iron ore. In reality, these resources determine the area of Russian investments in Brazil. The main deals made by Russian companies were

- the 2007 memorandum of understanding that was signed between Gazprom and Brazilian oil & gas giant Petrobras;
- the establishment of a joint venture between Mir Steel UK (subsidiary of the Russian metallurgy company Mechel) and Brazilian iron producer Usina Siderurgica do Para; and
- the acquisition by Severstal of a 25% stake in Brazil's SPG Mineracao iron ore exploration firm.

The discovery of rich hydrocarbon deposits in Brazil (namely, deep offshore) and the high-growth rates of Brazilian natural gas consumption provided the groundwork for Gazprom's effective entry into Brazil. In February 2007, the company signed a Memorandum of Understanding with Petrobras that stipulates mutually beneficial cooperation in the hydrocarbon exploration, production, transmission and marketing sectors. Special attention was paid to the cooperation in offshore fields development as well as novel technologies and LNG production.

In 2010, Gazprom opened a representative office in Rio de Janeiro to assist in the expanding Gazprom's Latin American presence beyond Brazil. As a far-flung strategic antenna, this Rio office was to provide information and analysis support for the projects being planned and implemented in the region, and to help coordinate efforts of other Gazprom subsidiaries in Latin America.[19]

Another headline-grabbing project was Mechel's investment in the Brazilian steel industry through its $800 million joint venture with iron producer Usina Siderurgica do Para. Russian billionaire Igor Zyuzin (owner of Russian steelmaker and coal producer Mechel) made the investment.

The volume of planned investment in this project was $5 billion including the construction of a metallurgical complex in the town of Bakar (State of Pará), including the steel mill, coke storage facilities and a harbor. Also in metallurgy, Mir Steel UK (controlled by Igor Zyuzin) and Usipar signed a joint venture to establish RAM (Russian and Monteiro), a new company with 75% of equity belonging to Mir Steel. The new rolling mill should produce 2.5 million tons of steel, starting in 2015. However, in 2011, plans for new steelworks projects with Russia were postponed due to unfavorable market conditions in the global steel sector.[20]

Through this deal, Mechel would be able to supply coal from its Bluestone company, located in the United States (RAM will be the closest to those deposits), since Brazil possesses cheap iron ore but no coal.[21]

Russia's steel giant, Severstal, made another investment in steel production in May 2011. It acquired 25% of Brazil's SPG Mineracao iron ore exploration firm for $49 million. Severstal was considering the project to be highly promising, with preliminary estimated reserves at around 1 billion tons of high-density ore, at approximately 40%–45% richness. The production volume was estimated at ten to twenty million tons of iron ore concentrate.[22]

In 2013, Russia's third largest oil producer TNK-BP gained approval from Brazil's petroleum regulator to conclude a $1 billion deal with HRT Participações em Petroleo SA to explore for oil. TNK-BP acquired a 45% stake in an oil & gas production project in the Solimoes River basin (Amazonas State). Initially, the value of the contract was set at $1 billion, yet over a ten-year period it could rise to $5 billion, depending on the size of the reserves found.

Another interesting joint venture that has been the subject of discussion since 2011, is that between the Rosoboronexport (part of the Rostec State Corporation) and a Brazilian company, for the manufacture of soft-skinned police vehicles. Russia has already exported military equipment including helicopters, police vehicles, and more.

When Brazilian company Odebrecht visited Moscow in 2012, three companies (Rosoboronexport, Vertolety Rossii (Russian helicopter manufacturer) and Odedrecht Defensa e Technologia) signed a memorandum of understanding setting out the framework for a joint venture in Brazil to assemble Russian helicopters (first the Mi-171-line, then a service center for the Mi-35M) and to develop Brazil's air defense system.

The forthcoming discussions will focus on the form of cooperation: licensed production facilities, joint R&D projects, the development of new models of weapons and military equipment, including for delivery to third countries. As Sergey Ladygin, deputy general director of Rosoboronexport, explained,

> We have a huge potential for further enhancing cooperation with Brazil. Today, we are laying the foundation of not just separate, even major projects, but the broadest industrial, scientific and technological cooperation, which will positively impact both interstate relationship and the economies of both countries.[23]

In 2016, a new contract to supply the Pantsir air missile system to Brazil should be signed. The negotiations on this contract started back in 2012, but Brazilian economic problems forced budget cuts, and the contract was postponed, yet it remains on the agenda to this day.

Given that Russia has been exporting finished military products to Brazil for a long time, the next step in internationalization might include local production and development in Brazil.[24]

As Brazil and Russia get to know each other better as business partners, the relationship has gradually developed. Although many of the deals are in the steel and extractive industries, where investment amounts are usually seven digits or more, some of the deals are also made by relatively small high-tech companies and seek to exploit the potential of Russian home country R&D. One such illustrative case is the KGK company which entered the Brazilian market with its GPS tracking systems.[25]

Nevertheless, not all projects are going successfully, Rosoboronexport is still discussing the future extension of collaboration and deal with Usipar was postponed for several years due to problems in the industry. Up to now, military cooperation remains at the level of simple exports of ready-made Russian military products.

India

Over the 2009–2014 period, Russian exports to India were relatively stable, on a level of $6.3 billion in 2010 and 2014, and a peak of $8 billion in 2012. The bilateral trade between the two countries amounted to $9.51 billion in 2014, of which $6.34 billion were Russian exports.

FDI from Russia into India was another story, with far bigger swings: from a meager $2 million in 2009, to a peak of $597 million in 2010, then a drop to $17 million in 2011, another jump to $275 million in 2012 and a plunge to $1 million in 2013 – a real roller-coaster ride![26] The cumulative Russian OFDI stock in India in 2000–2014 amounted $3 billion.[27]

Russia established banking links in India, with Sberbank, Vnesheconombank, Gazprombank, VTB and Promsvyazbank taking leading roles by opening branches. The other priority areas of mutual cooperation and investment are the areas of hydrocarbons, pharmaceuticals, IT, rough diamonds and various construction projects. These sectors are where the majority of "big deals" were concluded.[28] Some of the most significant Russian investments in India, totaling $4 billion, were projects by companies such as Kamaz Vectra, Shyam Sistema Telecom Ltd, Sberbank and VTB.[29]

An important initiative to launch cooperation projects in the oil & gas field was made by Gazprom International that signed a strategic cooperation agreement with the Indian company Gas Authority of India Ltd. and a Memorandum of Understanding with ONGC Videsh (the overseas investment arm of top Indian oil explorer Oil and Natural Gas Corp.). Gazprom is also collaborating with Reliance Industries for a joint venture in the Indian gas sector. Gazprom is considering increasing its LNG supplies to India to five million metric tons/year by 2020.[30]

Rosneft, the Russian state-owned oil company, also does business with India to strengthen its Asian position. In July 2015, Rosneft acquired up to 49% of an Essar Oil refinery and will supply one hundred million tons of crude oil to the Essar Group over ten years. In addition, the groups signed a preliminary agreement for Rosneft to acquire a minority equity stake in the Vadinar refinery, India's second largest, in the state of Gujarat.[31]

In 2014, Russia's largest power generating company, RusHydro, signed a joint cooperation declaration (JCD) to design the second phase of the 3.8 GW Upper Siang hydropower project – one of the largest hydroelectric plants in Asia and the largest one in India. RusHydro International AG and RusHydro International India Private Limited, a Russian-Indian JV, will design the project.[32] The total cost is estimated at $16 billion. This deal came on the sidelines of Vladimir Putin's visit to New Delhi.[33] The Indian government regards the facility as a high-priority national project, given the spotty power supply situation in India (brownouts and blackouts).[34]

Non-natural resource Russian firms are also active in India. In May 2010, Sberbank of Russia OJSC was granted a license for banking operations in New Delhi, the objective being to create a springboard into the India market.[35] Rosatom was contracted to build twelve nuclear reactors by 2035 in India, including two new units at the Kudankulam Nuclear Power Plant. Russia's satellite navigation system Glonass created a $100 million joint venture to manufacture navigation systems in India.[36]

China

From 2012 to 2014, Russia's foreign trade with China averaged around $88 billion per year. In 2015, trading between two countries dropped by 29.3% to $50 billion,[37] due to economic slow-downs in both countries, the fall in oil & gas prices (which constitute almost 70% of Russian exports to China) and the erosion of purchasing power in Russia which crimped Russian demand for Chinese goods. Nevertheless, Russia maintained its position as fifteenth-largest Chinese trade partner. Even so, Russia's share of the Chinese exports is rather small: 2.15% of total, 2.24% of exports and 2.03% of imports.[38]

Russian investments in China are very modest. The first outbound investment from Russia into China took place in 2005, and by 2007, a measly $54 million had been invested in total, which accounted for about 1.2% of the total Russian OFDI stock. By 2014, the numbers did not look any better, with Russian OFDI stock in China at only $195 million, or 0.05% of total OFDI stock.[39]

The number of Russian investment projects in China in 2013 reached 2,500[40] including the activity of small and medium-sized firms. Very often OFDI from Russia enters China via Hong Kong, or through other offshore zones. The low level of Russian FDI in China can be explained by two factors. First, the use of offshore transit countries (the BVI and Hong Kong) obfuscates the true origin of investments. Second, Chinese companies prefer establishing fully owned companies with the minimum statutory capital of around $400, which are likely to require significantly higher financing later on.[41] These projects, while nominally small, are likely worth far more in reality.

The Russian projects in China follow the general patterns of Russian investments elsewhere. First of all, large state-controlled or state-related companies account for most greenfield and brownfield projects in China. Here, the most significant projects include

- in 2005–2008, the acquisition of two aluminium smelters in China by UC Rusal, the world's largest aluminium producer;
- in 2008, a joint venture between Chinalco and Aricom, for the construction of a titanium sponge factory in China, with Aricom investment of $207 million and controlling 65% of the JV;[42] and
- in 2010, the Vostok Petrochemicals joint venture between Rosneft (49%) and CNPC (51%) to build an oil refining facility in Tianjin, China.

Apart from these big-scale projects, several smaller ones, each worth less than $30 million, have been undertaken in the last two decades. They cover a variety of industries ranging from construction and electronic appliances, to trade and furniture. The absence of any systematic or big-scale investment in particular industries apart from energy and metallurgy proves that private Russian investors prefer other markets, while large state-related or state-owned companies are slowly expanding into China.

Russian investment in other emerging economies

Three destinations for Russian economic activity (including export and FDI) that are less developed than trade relations between Russia and Europe or China, are Latin America, Sub-Saharan Africa and the CIS countries. From these three regions, we will take five countries and present the picture of Russian business interests in these economies.

Argentina

The investment volumes between Russia and Argentina are increasing from year to year, with accumulated Argentinian investment in Russia of $14.8 million, and Russian investments in Argentina of $12.9 million. The trade turnover in 2013 was $2.5 billion, including exports from Argentina of $809 million, and exports from Russia of $1.7 billion,[43] most of which (83%) is diesel oil, since Argentina requires energy resources.[44]

An additional support to investment activities was provided by cooperation between Russian banks such as Gazprombank and Russia's Agricultural bank, and Ministry of

Economy of Argentina.[45] Interbank transactions facilitate investments cooperation for several reasons. First, they show the good example of how firms can build synergy. Second, it becomes easier for firms to accumulate additional funding. Third, such transactions prove the reliability of the partners. If they do occur, investors are more willing to take risk and internationalize despite the unstable economic performance of both countries.

Russia's investment projects in Argentina are at different stages of development:

1   State Corporation Rosatom is negotiating for the construction of nuclear power plants. Project details are not revealed and have been negotiated since 2011.
2   Power Machines and Holding Inter are involved in the construction of thermal power plants with the share of 50% after winning the tender by offering the most balanced projects which cost less than $4.9 billion.
3   Russian Railways are involved, via a JV, in the reconstruction of the railway line to San Martin and long-term improvement of road conditions since 2004.[46] However, Argentina nationalized all railways in March 2015 and denied access to any private firm. The reason for this decision was the assumption that state is much more efficient than the private sector. It was based on the past observations of successful nationalizations of such industries as water and electricity supply, nationally owned airlines and oil company YPT. A major setback for Russian Railways is the absence of compensation on projects which were launched but not yet completed, even though the government is interested in electrifying railways and receiving high-quality railroad equipment, which are the main issues of the investments made by Russian Railways. Russian Railways denied several projects in Argentina as they deemed to be to time and money consuming despite the fact that they had the opportunity to increase its presence in the region. This was the bi-oceanic logistic channel Aconcagua, which includes building of the railway and tunnel from Argentina to Chile. Investments in the total amount of $10 billion were required taking into consideration that modern technologies were to be applied.

The main strategic goals of Russian Railways are to act independently providing Argentina with highly innovative and original equipment, creation of image as reliable partner and building strong relations with the government. It is involved not only in big projects, which it is able to choose, but also in everyday activities. This implies investments which are constantly increasing since 2004. From this time, they own here an office, where both representatives of Russia and Argentina work. It accounts for the supervision on the implementation of project and interaction with local authorities.

4   Institute Orgenergostroi – the construction of thermal power plants using biofuel. The investment amounts have not been disclosed. Both countries are seeking alternative energy sources, since both economies depend on natural resources.
5   Kamaz – organization of the assembly production of trucks in Argentina.[47] Vehicles are to be localized to suit the climate and soils and also reflect consumer demand. Production facilities are installed locally since both import fees and transportation costs are high and might make for non-competitive pricing. Since these vehicles have already good reputations in Argentina, so there are limited risks of failure. Kamaz already operates subsidiaries in Chile, Venezuela, Nicaragua and Panama and is also interested in product diversification into public transport.
6   Lukoil – exploration and production of hydrocarbons. Cooperation involves supply of fuel oil and diesel fuel for Enarsa, also in cooperation with Repsol, and using the

infrastructure of Pobater. In 2008 Lukoil acquired 30% of Repsol, leader in exploration and production of oil & gas extraction, transportation, storage, processing and trade in Argentina and other Latin American countries. Pobater owns oil storage depots and refineries located in the Buenos Aires region. If an interaction is limited only to agency operations in the oil trade, it is unlikely that the margin from this activity will exceed 7–8%. So JV and FDI in this case can lead to substantial increase in productivity. Significant synergy of the participation of Lukoil in these operations can be gained as this company lacks own refineries in the region.[48] Lukoil will try to develop cooperation with Enarsa in exploration and production in 2016, and most likely offshore: the participation of the company in mining projects in Argentina is mandatory. It is the only company in oil industry which can be considered as profit seeking. It puts the major emphasis on internationalization of not core activities and this special strategy leads to high profit margins.

Overall, the modest investment relations between the two countries is somewhat compensated by their rapid development, so that we can hope for closer investment cooperation between the two countries in the near future.

Chile

For the time being, Russian investment into Chile amounts to only $1.3 million.[49] Nevertheless, two countries have been working on improvement of economic relationships. Recent events have also boosted trade volumes.

The total trade between Chile and Russia amounted to $743 million in 2013.[50] Chile exports accounted for $694 million, while Russian exports were only $49 million. It brings Chile to fifty-one place in Russian import list. Russia itself is ranked in top-five greatest Chile trade partners.

Russia exports mostly chemical industry goods and minerals. Machinery, equipment, FMCG, agricultural goods, metals and other products represent an insignificant share of Chile imports from Russia. By contrast, Chile exports mostly food and agricultural goods into Russia (95.9%). Food imports have expanded greatly during 2014, thanks to the European ban on exports to Russia. Chile has filled the void.

As was already mentioned, the volume of Russian investment in Chile is quite small. Nevertheless, experts underline the importance of economic cooperation. Several joint business projects have been launched. For example, public corporation Power Machines supplied hydroelectric power station Nuble with electro-mechanical equipment. Another Russian manufacturer Energomashexport Corporation supplied the hydropower plants San Pedro and Rucatayo with similar machinery. Some further projects are being initiated by Russian Ministry of Economic Development – for example, with a huge Chilean commerce and industrial group Errazuriz. Another project involved the construction of an experimental wave farm (electric power plant). In 2011, Russian corporation RusHydro started working on the project. Other Russian public company United Heavy Machinery Plant has signed an agent agreement with Chilean MAEN Ltd. The company supplies heading and mining equipment. Two countries have strong interest in global positioning and navigation industry. Corporation Russian Navigation Technologies is engaged in joint projects with Chilean – Russian radio navigation company Radio Naval. They established a pilot project to equip Chilean ships with navigation systems.[51]

Several forthcoming large investment projects could prove very attractive for Russian enterprises. A huge tender for power plant construction is to be announced in 2015. The plant should use solar energy and produce 100 megawatt of energy (capacity could be extended to 200 megawatt). The project costs approximately $200 million. The Power Machines corporation should start turnkey project for construction and supply of machinery hall for power plant La Mina. Other Russian company SPbEC Mining (in cooperation with German Becker Mining Systems) is interested in providing complete turnkey solutions for Chile.[52]

From this overview, we can derive that Russian enterprises are mostly interested in the development of energy infrastructure, mining, defense and telecommunication.

To sum up, though investment flow from Russia to Chile is very limited, governments of both countries are highly interested in its expansion. Russia and Chile traditionally had good relations regarding trade exchanges. The recent sanctions imposed by the EU and United States against Russia are shaping new relations between Latin America and Russia. In reply to those sanctions, Russia favors trade exchanges with Latin America. In the recent interview, the head of Chilean Ministry of Foreign Affairs claimed that Chile, due to its favorable investment climate, is a very attractive destination for Russian FDI, not only as a separate country but also as a key to the whole Latin American market. Recently, the director of the country's International Economic Relations office Andrès Rebolledo declared that his country sees the Russian embargo as an opportunity for Chile.[53]

Russia FDI in sub-Saharan Africa

Russia is also investing in emerging economies in African continent, even though it is not as active in the region as China or Brazil. Nevertheless, it maintains many intensive relations developed during the Soviet period. Over thirty Russian companies are present and involved in African natural resource development projects, mostly in Angola, Guinea, Nigeria, South Africa and Namibia.[54]

The major sectors in which Russian companies operate are mineral resources, energy, infrastructure, telecommunications, fishing, education, health, tourism and defense.

This expansion reached $20 billion[55] in 2008, but it remains of marginal dimensions compared to other regions of developing countries; in effect, in 2010, Africa captured only 1.8%[56] of the overall Russian FDI flow to developing countries.

Considering the cross-border M&A acquisitions, the principal entry mode for Russian MNEs, during the period 2000–2008 the EU attracted the majority of deals, with the United Kingdom as the principal recipient; in fact, it hosted 33.5% of overall M&As in the period 2005–2008. In Africa, the country with the most M&A operations is Nigeria, but even so it captured only 0.5% of the Russian worldwide transactions.[57]

One of the major operation in the sub-Saharan African area was the 2007 acquisition by Norilsk Nickel, the Russian largest diversified mining and metallurgical company and the Botswana company Tati Nickel. The operation had a value of $2.5 billion[58] and Norilsk gained 85% stake in Tati, obtaining the control of the Phoenix open-pit mine that contained 27 million tons of ore and of an ore processing plant capable of processing five million tons per year.[59]

Another important acquisition was the 2010 deal by Lukoil, the Russian oil giant, in Côte d'Ivoire and Ghana, that allowed the company to acquire 56.66% stake in Ghana's Cape Three Points Deep Water for $900 million and the control of 10,500 km^2 deepwater blocks that allow the company to develop a project that was expected to yield up to six billion barrels of oil & gas.[60]

Rusal, the world's largest aluminium company, acquired the majority stake in Alscon, a Nigerian aluminium smelter company for $250 million in 2008.[61] "Nigeria is one of the few locations in the world that can provide low-cost energy required for aluminium production," claimed Rusal's director for international and special projects, Alexander Livshits.[62]

The activity of Rusal in Nigeria has been important to maximize its competitive advantage on the world market because it allowed the company to access to a supply of low-cost energy for the aluminium production, especially hydro energy, while worldwide high oil prices and a shortage of oil refining capacity drove up the production costs for both alumina refineries and the cost of petroleum coke for aluminium smelters.

Other Russian companies with operations in sub-Saharan Africa are Alrosa, Gazprom, Severstal-Gold, Gammachim, Vnesheconombank and VTB bank which are involved in some large-scale investment projects in the area.[63]

South Africa

Russian exports to South Africa are varied. The most important export component are chemical products for $36 billion, a sign of modernization of this country. Russia also exports some other metals for $16 billion. The third main part of export comes from machinery with $13 billion. Among the other export categories are cereals, wood, iron and steel and fertilizer.

Good relations between two countries have encouraged Pretoria to examine the eventuality of buying Russian nuclear technology for energy production, while Russia is willing to import more meat and agricultural products from South Africa, since the EU's embargo. But the nuclear plants are not welcomed by opposition parties and by a local NGO (Earthlife Africa). Politicians fear about the lack of transparency, potential bribes and the profitability of such project. The NGO considers this investment as a huge menace for local people and the environment. To convince the population to support this project, the government argues that will be a huge driver for the economic growth, because it will increase the power supply. In fact, this plan forecasts 9.6 GW of new nuclear capacity by 2030, and the value of this deal is yet unknown. This deal is considered as a deal between countries rather than between companies.

After suffering from the low price of platinum, Russia and South Africa are setting up a new OPEC-like producer's alliance. In fact, since they possess 80% of platinum group reserves (South Africa produces 73% of the world's platinum reserves and Russia produces 47% of global palladium reserves), a new agreement could allow them to control the platinum market by adjusting the production or setting up some embargos in a growing market since it is used a lot to limit car pollution. One of their main actions would be to counter over supply of platinum through tax and incentives or without creating a real cartel. Since platinum is in higher demand for production, as an alternative currency (such as gold) or as an investment, the control of 80% of the total production by this alliance would allow South African production to become more profitable and to provide a good solution in case of financial crisis, since its price should grow rapidly. Between 2008 and 2011, its price increased by more than twofold, from $800 to $1,900 per ounce.

Even if this situation seems to be beneficial for both countries, we see that Russia is increasing its exports year after year; when it imports less and less from South Africa, then the balance of payment becomes even more in favor of the African country. (From 2004 to 2012, the Russian investments fell from $1.221 billion to $0.140 billion, when African investments in Russia increased from nothing in 2004 to $3.4 billion in 2012.) This new agreement should reduce this gap and both countries will benefit from it.

Russia has chosen to write off debts of $20 billion from African countries (South Africa included). Moreover, the Russian government has made trading between BRICS a major focus of its foreign policy. The intention of Vladimir Putin and Jacob Zuma to improve relation is clear, as we have seen Jacob Zuma avoiding the vote against the Russian foreign policy concerning Ukraine, in the United Nations. This economic and political cooperation can help to build a long-term successful cooperation.

Overall, Russian firms locate into African countries since they identify a legislative and political environment favorable to Russian companies, thanks to local government economic policy objectives. By doing business in those countries they have benefitted from facilitations, low-cost labor force, low-cost energy supplies and direct control of assets (location advantages).

Ultimately Russian companies expanded their presence in sub-Saharan Africa especially by taking full control of the subsidiaries, because those external markets were imperfect, characterized by high transaction costs and high level of risk and uncertainty (internalization advantages).

Kazakhstan

Among CIS countries, Kazakhstan is the major trade partner of Russia. In the beginning of 2013, the volume of investments between these two countries reached $15.3 billion. The most attractive industries in Russia are oil & gas and construction, so a lot of investments from Kazakhstan go in this direction. As regards Russian FDI in Kazakhstan, they are mostly oil & gas, manufacturing, transport and construction. This is reflected in the following projects.

The Caspian pipeline consortium (CPC) is the most challenging project that connects Western Kazakhstan crude oilfields with Russian terminals located on the Black Sea coast. The current capacity is planned to be expanded to 67 million tons per year by building ten additional oil-pumping stations and reservoirs. The joint shareholders are Russia with 31% (Transneft 24%, CPC Company 7%) and Kazakhstan with 20.75% (KazMunaiGaz 19%, Kazakhstan Pipeline Ventures LLC 1.75%). Total volume of investment in these countries in 2013 was $1.37 billion.

The main interest of Russian companies in Kazakhstan lies in the field of fossil fuels. The following projects are the main FDI participants and projects:

1　Lukoil and KazMunaiGaz partner project on hydrocarbon deposits of Khvalinskoe.
2　Lukoil project on hydrocarbon deposits of geological field Centralnaya.
3　Joint project of Rosneft and KazMunaiGaz on hydrocarbon deposits of geological field Kurmangazi.
4　Joint exploration by Rosneft and KazMunaiGaz of fossil fuels in the block of Tube-Karagan and Atashskaya.
5　Rosneft participation in exploration of Adaiskii field.
6　Lukoil participation in exploration of Karachaganak and Tengiz oil deposit.

As regards the mining and energy sectors, the following projects are noteworthy:

1　Partner project on uranium mining on Zarechnoe deposit; the uranium will be transferred to Russia.

2   Partner project on uranium mining on Budenovskoe deposit. Russian–Kazakh enterprise that will extract uranium, enrich it and then establish supply chain to Russian, Kazakh and third–world markets.
3   Russian–Kazakh company Nuclear Stations that will possess nuclear reactors of the third generation.
4   Development and expansion of Akimbastuzskaya GRES-2 by building additional power blocks.
5   Rusal project on improvement and modernization of coil extraction at Bagatir Kamir.
6   Rusal project of building an aluminium factory with the minimum capacity of five hundred thousand ton of crude aluminium in Pavlodarskaya oblast.

The volume of accumulated investments in Kazakh economy rose on 1.6% in 2014 and was about $6 billion. By this indicator, Russia is only seventh in rank of foreign investors in Kazakhstan.[64] Although, the data presented by Bank of Kazakhstan often diverge with real situation. Such a divergence is explained by significant role of offshores and foreign jurisdictions in structuring investment flows. It is a notable peculiarity that among the biggest investors is BVI and Cayman Islands. Eurasian Development Bank estimates the volume of Russian FDI in Kazakhstan as $9.3 billion at the beginning of 2014.[65]

The majority of Russian business activity in Kazakhstan is in the extractive sector. Since economic integration in the free-trade zone, they are more diversified: agro–industrial complex (22%), construction (23%), transport and logistics (30%), hotels (16%) and other.[66]

Four years of Custom Union's existing (for 2014) has not lead to significant changes in investment flows between Russia and Kazakhstan. The volume and structure of mutual investments still does not match the claimed level of integration in post-Soviet area. One should note that according to united custom territory there is no custom dues and restrictions that leads to increasing role of export trade between countries of Custom Union. The fact, in turn, decreases FDI's gains. It seems that creation of Eurasian Union in medium-term perspective cannot dramatically change the situation.

On May 29, 2014, Kazakhstan, Russia and the other customs union partners signed a treaty to create a common economic space called Eurasian Economic Union. This union is expected to further integrate their economies and provide free movement of labor force, capital and services on their common territory. Kazakhstan considers further integration with Russia and Belarus as a chance to make Kazakhstan more attractive for FDI by expanding market access to those countries. A new law with a serious package of incentives for investors was presented to the Parliament in June 2014. Some these incentives include state compensation of investment costs, corporate income tax exemptions and executing long-term contracts with national companies. All these measures are supposed to make Kazakhstan a much more attractive country in terms of FDI.

The variety of Russia's interests in foreign investments and related modes of foreign operations is partly illustrated in the earlier section. The company cases presented in the following sections provides a more in-depth, managerial view.

10.2 Catching the fish and throwing it back: case of Severstal

Company overview

Severstal is a vertically integrated Russian group of companies specializing in steel production, and its related mining activities. It was initially established as a state-run steel mill meant to exploit iron ore and coal deposits discovered in the 1930s and supply the north-western region of Russia with iron for its economic growth. In 1940, the USSR Council of People's Commissars approved the Decree on the Organization of a Metallurgical Base in the northwest of the USSR, which authorized the construction of a metallurgic plant in Cherepovets. Postponed for several years due to World War II, construction did not begin until the 1950s. The steel rolling mill was finally inaugurated in 1951. Yet the birthday of the company is considered to be August 24, 1955, when operations at the Cherepovets Metallurgic Plant began and the plant produced its first steel. By the 1960s, the plant became a full cycle integrated iron and steel works.

Due to the plant's large volume of production and the complexity of the production process, the Cherepovets Metallurgic Plant was restructured by the USSR in the 1980s into the State Enterprise Cherepovets Steel Mill. In September 1993, in accordance with a presidential decree, the mill was privatized and registered by the Cherepovets Mayor's Office as "Severstal."

Since its incorporation in 1993, Severstal has expanded considerably. In 2002, the company became the Severstal Group, reflecting its expansion into mining, coking and other secondary endeavors.[67] The company has two main divisions: Severstal Resources and Severstal Steel.

Severstal Resources, formed through various acquisitions over the past decade, supplies the majority of iron ore and coal needed for Severstal Steel's operations. Additionally, it sells to external customers. It comprises two iron ore integrated works (Karelian Pellet and Olkon), coal companies throughout northwestern Russia, a Liberian iron ore exploration project (Severstal Liberia Iron Ore), and a research institute (SPb Giproshakht). According to the most recent annual report, in 2013, the company sold a total of 15.1 million tons of iron ore, and 10.1 million tons of coal. Vladimir Larin has been CEO of this division since 2010.

Severstal Steel is among the top steel producers in Russia, providing high value-added flat steel-products, such as galvanized sheet and pipes. Alexander Grubman heads the division. It consists of six divisions: steel, metal ware, pipes, trading, services and scrap procurement.

Additionally, Severstal owns several non-related businesses, including an airline, Severstal Air, and a professional ice hockey club, the *Severstal Cherepovets*.

In 2003, the company became the first Russian steel company to expand internationally when the company bought industrial and mining assets in the United States. Today, they own industrial facilities in Russia, the Ukraine and Europe, as well as key mining assets in Russia and Liberia. The company also expanded into the gold industry in 2007 with the establishment of Nordgold. However, the gold segment was separated after only four years, following a change in Severstal's business strategy, and split off from the GDR listings on the London Stock Exchange.

Severstal faces three major competitors in the steel market: Novolipetskiy (NLMK), Magnitogorsky Kombinat and Evraz. The relationship between the Big Four can be described as oligopolistic; there are four distinct regions for steel in Russia, each occupied by one company, with virtually no overlap. Severstal dominates the sector.

The company is listed on the Moscow Exchange (MICEX), and its stocks have been traded on the London Exchange (LSE) since 2006. With over 61,000 employees, Severstal is among the top-twenty-five steel producers in the world.[68] In 2013, the Boston Consulting Group included Severstal on their list of the top 100 companies from rapidly developing economies, a list which included only six Russian companies, in all.

In 2014, the company reported revenues of $8.3 billion, down from $9.4 billion in 2013. Net income in 2014 was a loss of $1.6 billion, compared with a net profit of $89 million the previous year. The huge net loss was in large part attributable to currency losses.

Severstal's owner is Aleksey Mordashov, who holds 82.37% of the company's shares. Mordashov has repeatedly stated that he is prepared to reduce his stake in the company to below 50% in order to close a deal that would move the company upward in the global rankings. For example, in 2006, he offered 89.6% of Severstal for 25% of Arcelor.[69] This deal would have created the largest steel company in the world. However, it eventually fell through, and no other similar mega-deal has presented itself, but it indicates Mordashov's level of commitment to Severstal's success.

Internationalization

Like all Russian steel companies, Severstal's first exposure to international business was via exports, which constituted a large portion of their total business. In 1999, nearly 60% of total sales were exports, with key markets being Turkey, the United States, Taiwan, South Korea and Germany.[70] Of these exports, 40% were sold directly to end users, i.e., without going through sales representatives or wholesalers. This first entry mode is consistent with the classical stages of internationalization, in which a company tests the international waters through low-risk entry modes. Even though Severstal lacked such advantages as international experience, strong brand, stable cash flows, technology, or a stable domestic environment – typically needed to invest abroad – it was able to use its cost advantage gained from cheap labor and its favorable position close to European markets so as to be a competitive exporter. The company established Severstallat in Latvia 1992 to provide forwarding services on exported products. Later, three more such companies were established in Poland, Belarus and the Ukraine. In 2014, these subsidiaries were renamed Severstal Distribution, forming a common network with one set of standards.

The year 2003 represented a dramatic change for Severstal's strategy. The company acquired Rouge Steel that year, an integrated steel-making facility based in Michigan, United States, for $260 million, and later it renamed Severstal Dearborn. Severstal began making other acquisitions of mining assets, plants, and even diversified into the gold sector over the next few years. In 2008, it became a rabid buyer, making seven acquisitions in just one year: Sparrow Point based in Maryland, United States; African Iron Ore Group Ltd (West Africa); PBS Coals (Pennsylvania, United States); Balazhal (Kazakhstan); Esmark Incorporated (West Virginia, United States); WCI (Ohio, United States); and a 53% stake in High River Gold (Burkina Faso). The aggressive acquisitions period was short-lived. In 2011, the company gradually sold off some of its foreign assets, leaving only operations in Russia, Liberia, Belarus, Latvia, the Ukraine and Italy as of 2015.

Severstal North America (United States)

The 2003 acquisition of Rouge Steel (later Severstal Dearborn) was only the first of many projects that Severstal's North American (SNA) division launched. In 2005, Severstal started their only greenfield project, a 1.5 million-ton-per-year capacity mini-mill in Columbus, Mississippi, known as SeverCorr (later renamed Severstal Columbus). The North American division began to expand rapidly after this; in 2007 and 2008, SNA acquired the Sparrows Point plant in Baltimore, WSI, a high-quality flat steel producer, and Esmark, another flat producer, for a total of around $2.5 billion. Severstal then acquired 71% of its first American mining operation, PBS Coals, for $1.3 billion in 2008. PBS covered roughly half of SNA's coal needs, creating a fairly self-contained production cycle for Severstal in the United States.

SNA also established a number of joint ventures, which had two main aims: to ensure self-sufficiency in raw materials, and to expand manufacturing of value-added products. SNA's resource-seeking JV was Mountain State Carbon LLC, a 50-50 project with Renco Group, which provided 60% of Severstal Dearborn's coke. Several joint ventures extended the value chain and included Double Eagle Steel Coating Company, a 50-50 venture with United States Steel Corporation to produce galvanized sheet; Spartan Steel Coating LLC, a project with Worthington Steel of Michigan, also to produce galvanized sheet; and Mississippi Steel Processing LLC, a JV with Merlo Holdings Inc and Layhill Ventures LLC to process heavy gauge.

By 2008, SNA was the fourth-largest steel producer in the United States, employing over two thousand people. Partially as a result of the subsidiary's success, the proportion of Severstal's output which was exported declined drastically. Whereas 42% of the company's sales were exports in 2003, by 2007, this dropped to only 28.6%.[71]

In June 2014, Severstal sold both U.S. plants to Steel Dynamics Inc. and AK Holding Corp. for $2.33 billion, thereby exiting the U.S. market. At this point, it had already sold off its other assets, including PBS Coals. The decision to dismantle Severstal North American has been attributed in part to increasing political tensions between the Russian Federation and the United States over the crisis in the Ukraine. While Severstal has not been targeted by sanctions, as of 2014, OAO Bank Rossiya was, and Severstal CEO Aleksey Mordashov controls 6% of the bank.[72] Furthermore, since the global financial crisis of 2008, the U.S. steel industry has suffered from depressed prices due to excess capacity.

What is striking about Severstal's first acquisition is that the majority of Russian companies start their internationalization by investing in surrounding CIS countries before moving on to more advanced economies. The close geographical and culture proximity of the Russian Federation to other CIS nations make this a logical progression.

Severstal leapfrogged – both in advanced and developing markets – by moving directly from its low-risk export activities to a high-risk wholly owned subsidiary.

Severstal entered the U.S. market with two handicaps. Its production technology was inferior to that of its American competitors, and its low production costs due to cheap labor were not transferable to the United States. Nonetheless, Severstal had considerable cash flows, which allowed the company to finance acquisitions. By establishing relatively autonomous facilities in the United States, Severstal could bypass protectionist measures such as import quotas and tariffs and sell directly into the American market. Additionally, direct investment in the United States reduced the number of intermediaries needed in transactions, and eliminated currency exchange risks.

For Severstal, the motives for coming to the United States were twofold: to gain access to the large American auto industry (a market-seeking motive) and to gain access to value-adding technology (strategic asset seeking). Severstal's exposure to the United States also generated a shift in the company culture, from a relatively controlled Soviet style to a more Western style. The "Achieve More Together" initiative, launched in 2010, focused on transparency and teamwork. The company also begun to produce galvanized sheet steel – a technology it accessed in the United States.

Nordgold (Kazakhstan)

In 2007, Severstal established Nordgold and initiated its expansion into gold mining via the gradual acquisition of Celtic Resources, the owner of the Suzdal and Zherek mines in Kazakhstan. By January 2008, Severstal was full owner. In 2008, the company acquired

Semgeo, owner of the Bazkhal mine (also in Kazakhstan), and in 2008 bought a 53.8% controlling stake of High River Gold, owner of various mines in Russia and Burkina Faso.[73] In 2010, Severstal initiated the acquisition of Crew Gold, owner of the Lefa mine in Guinea. By 2011, the full acquisition was completed, and Severstal also increased its stake in High River Gold to 75.1%. About $124 million per year was spent on exploration activity.

In 2010 and 2011, productivity and revenues of Nordgold increased sizably. The company's annual revenue grew from $754 million in 2010 to $1,182 million in 2011, and gold production increased from 589 Koz to 754 Koz in the same period. Growth was attributed to increased productivity in the African mines; the Burkina Faso project was projected to contribute significantly to productivity. Cash flows also were growing at a healthy rate; in 2011, operating cash flow had increased 59.6% over the previous year to $397.6 million. Healthy cash flow was considered vital in order to pursue the company's expansion strategy.

In November 2011, Severstal announced the spin-off of Nordgold through a share exchange offer. The separation was fully complete by March 2012. According to the company, this was the first case of a Russian company implementing a cost-neutral exchange of shares between two companies. On its first day of trading, the market capitalization of Nordgold was $2.8 billion, twice its start-up costs. Mordashov remains the majority shareholder of Nordgold, with 88.9% ownership of the authorized capital. The company has continued to operate successfully, increasing its gold production by 7% in 2014.[74]

Severstal stated in its 2012 annual report that the decision to sell its Nordgold division reflected a strategic change for the company. They claimed that they wanted to focus on their core business and maintain their position as a leading, fully integrated steel and steel-related mining company.[75]

In 2006, gold prices were beginning to rise. This trend continued throughout Severstal's expansion in the gold industry, but prices became volatile in 2011, which coincided with Severstal's decision to divest. Judging by gold prices alone, this appears to have been a good time to separate, as prices have steadily dropped since mid-2012. Overall, the motivation for this project seemed to be increasing shareholder value by taking advantage of desirable market conditions. And it certainly made Aleksey Mordoshov a very wealthy man!

Other acquisitions

In 2006, Severstal became the majority shareholder the bankrupt Lucchini Group, a top European steel company. The division included two steel plants and several JVs in Italy, four plants and a research center in France and a Western European distribution network. Severstal assumed full ownership by 2010, but the enterprise was not profitable. Lucchini was declared insolvent in 2012 and placed under special administration. Redaelli is another of Severstal's Italian subsidiaries; a steel-wire ropes manufacturer which Severstal acquired in 2008 and still owns today.

In 2006, Severstal made two further acquisitions: Carrington Wire (United Kingdom) and Dneprometiz (Ukraine), both wire and metal ware producers. The acquisitions were made to strengthen Severstal's position in the metal ware market. Carrington Wire was closed in 2010 due to a contraction in the steel-wire market. Following the closure of the plant, Severstal allegedly failed to meet pension obligations of £20 million, prompting an investigation by the British Pension Regulator. The investigation was terminated when Severstal agreed to pay an £8.5 million settlement.

The project that attracted much attention of the business community was the failed merger of Arcelor and Severstal in 2006. This merger would have resulted in the largest steel company in the world, which could have exploited the country- and firm-specific advantages of both a Russian and a European steel company. Instead, Arcelor merged with another emerging market company, Indian steel firm Mittal, and formed the global leader, ArcelorMittal.

Overall, Severstal's motives for investing in Europe are quite similar to its American ones: better access to European consumers, and to the valuable technological and managerial know-how of EU target companies. Severstal established a services center in Latvia before making acquisitions farther west.

The acquisition of Ukrainian Dneprometiz represents a more traditional investment for a Russian firm. As with Kazakhstan (perhaps even more so), Ukraine is geographically and culturally close to Russia, with weak institutions. Until the Ukraine crisis in 2014, Russian-Ukrainian political ties were extremely close, with Russia holding significant bargaining power in the relationship as a provider of heavily discounted energy resources. These factors all made Ukraine an attractive place for Russian investment. There was often an efficiency-seeking component in Ukrainian deals, with wages lower in the country.

Mining projects

In 2008, Severstal signed a mineral development agreement with the government of Liberia for a 61.5% interest in the Putu Range project, a 13-kilometers-long, iron-rich ridge, 130 kilometers inland from the deepwater shoreline of eastern Liberia. The development agreement runs for 25 years from September 2010. In 2012, Severstal acquired the remaining 38.5% interest from Afferro Mining. In 2015, the company announced that it was looking for a partner for the project, as it was not in a position to develop the project alone. They cited unfavorable market conditions: iron ore prices decreased dramatically, and the Ebola outbreak, though quickly contained, critically affected the Liberian economy.[76]

In 2012, Severstal acquired 25% of the Ampara iron ore deposit in Brazil, but withdrew in 2013 due to unfavorable market conditions.

As of 2013, Severstal had a 33.2% stake in International Mineral Beneficiation Services (South Africa). Together with IMBS, Severstal planned to launch the first commercial full-size 50-ktpa iron ore reduction unit in 2014 at the Palabora copper deposit in South Africa.

Severstal hosting in Russia

Severstal was also active in greeting foreign companies into Russia – namely, via joint ventures, and more specifically for the production of automotive components requiring substantial steel content, such as chassis or body parts.

In 2010, the Spanish firm Gestamp established a joint venture with Severstal to produce body stamping products for five of Volkswagen Group's car models for the automotive and electrical industries in the Kaluga region – namely, the large Volkswagen assembly plant. The JV was to inaugurate an extra production line with an annual capacity of 72,000 tons of automotive body parts.

At the beginning of 2014, Severstal launched a new steel service center in joint venture with Japanese giant Mitsui: Severstal-SMC-Vsevolozhsk, which started commercial deliveries to customers in the automotive sector shortly thereafter. Blank parts produced on this line will be delivered on JV with Gestamp for the production of stamped car body parts. The end users of the goods supposed to be machine-building companies as Ford, Nissan and Toyota. The JV's clients include automotive manufacturers, equipment producers, air conditioning system producers and others.

Conclusion

A general observation about Severstal's internationalization is that it was perhaps too aggressive. The company instigated a large number of projects since 2005 and ended many of them, often after only a few years. The company simultaneously pursued a resource-seeking strategy (in Africa and Kazakhstan) and a market/strategic asset/capability-seeking strategy (in the EU and the United States). While the former was well justified, motivations behind the latter remain somewhat vague, especially since the Severstal strategy in developed countries seems to have backfired. The company was unable to withstand challenging market conditions, a fact which is most likely attributable to their relatively poor ownership advantages compared to the developed markets players. That is not to say that there was nothing gained from these projects, especially in regards to expansion into Western markets; the company has likely acquired valuable experience, technology, and knowledge.

The recent currency crisis has also given Severstal an increased cost advantage on the export market, so the company will probably use this to its advantage while continuing its expansion, both domestically and internationally. Meanwhile, the company has stated that its current strategy is to concentrate on cost reduction in order to generate strong cash flows, which it could then potentially invest in value-adding technology and future foreign projects.

The whole steel industry faces major challenges today. First of all, the export market is shaky due to poor macroeconomic conditions and overcapacity. Many developed countries, such as the United States, have protectionist policies in place, including quotas on Russian steel. However, since Russia was admitted to the WTO in 2012, these limitations have gradually diminished. Alas, taking their stead are new geopolitical risks due to the Ukraine conflict and subsequent sanctions. While the activities of steel manufacturers have not been targeted directly, sanctions have limited the ability to access lines of credit and refinance debt.[77] As a result of these challenges, production and profitability have been in slight decline over the past few years. In light of this, the Russian government has indicated its readiness to again support the industry through these difficult times.

On the other hand, the steel industry could benefit from the ongoing crisis. The significant decline of the ruble has lowered costs and made Russian steel very attractive on the export market.[78]

10.3 Acquisitions on the sly: case of Gazprom Neft

Company overview

JSC Gazprom Neft is one of 280 subsidiaries belonging to Gazprom group. Gazprom Neft is a vertically integrated oil company dealing with oil & gas exploration and production, refining and production and sale of petroleum products. The company refines near 80% of the crude oil it produces, one of the highest ratios of all Russian companies in the sector. Today, Gazprom Neft is the third-largest company in Russia by refining volume and fourth by production.[79]

Gazprom deals with natural gas, Gasprom Neft with oil; they are not rivals. With leading positions in oil production and refining activities in Russia and operational presence in more than fifty foreign countries, Gazprom Neft is an apt example of a company from an emerging (transitional) country that became international.

The company started in 1995 under the name Sibneft (Siberian Oil Company) under Russian government ownership. Soon after privatization was allowed, private investors purchased 49% of Sibneft. The company was expanding rapidly due to its resource base, efficient refining operations, and professional management.

In 2005, Gazprom Group acquired a controlling stake (75.68%) in Sibneft, which was majority-owned (74%) by the government. Sibneft was promptly rebaptized Joint Stock Company Gazprom Neft. Currently, Gazprom owns 95.68% of the company's shares, while the remaining 4.32% are publicly traded (20% of shares originally owned by the Italian oil & gas company ENI were also acquired by Gazprom).

Gazprom Neft is a major player on the Russian oil & gas market, producing and distributing a wide range of products to different industries, both in Russia and abroad. It is the third-largest oil company in Russia by refining volume and fourth largest in terms of production.[80]

The company has 1.44 billion tons of proven hydrocarbon reserves, placing it in the top-twenty global producers of crude oil. In 2014, production volumes increased by 4.19% over the previous year. Revenues, EBITDA and net profit advanced by 2.84%, 4.22% and 1.39% respectively.[81]

Gazprom Neft operates in the most significant oil & gas producing regions of Russia and refines approximately 80% of all the oil it produces with its main refineries located in the Omsk, Moscow and Yaroslavl regions (oblasts), and in Serbia. Apart from exports, the company operates a vast network of retail outlets in Russia and abroad, including 1,750 filling stations in Russia, the CIS and Europe.

Building its position domestically . . .

Gazprom Neft Group consists of more than seventy production, refining and sales subsidiaries in Russia and other countries. Its business structure includes production, oilfield, refining, sales of petroleum products, lubricants, exports, aircraft refueling, and ship bunkering. The company's consumer products include: auto gasoline (particularly, a premium class fuel G-drive), auto diesel fuel, natural gas fuel, lubricants (motor oils "G-Energy' and "Gazpromneft"). Products for businesses include: fuel cards, ship fuel, ship oil, aircraft fuel, asphaltic materials, furnace oil, gas condensate, methane and petrochemicals.

The company is interested in developing internationally with plans in place to ensure that at least 10% of its overall oil production takes place outside of Russia. Gazprom Neft focuses on the Middle East, West Africa, the Balkans, Latin America and North Africa. It also focuses on refining operations in Europe and South-East Asia.[82]

The company's main retail sales objective is to maximize sales though its own distribution channels for all petroleum products. This process may involve franchising to increase the company's commercial presence in key customer markets. In 2025, the company targets to capture 30% of the market for aviation fuel, bunkering (ships) and bitumen materials.[83]

On the Russian market, most of the Gazprom Neft's crude oil is produced by its subsidiaries, such as OJSC Gazprom NeftNoyabrskneftegaz, LLC Gazprom Neft-Khantos, LLC

Gazprom Neft-East and CJSC Gazprom Neft Orenburg. The main regions of operations are: Yamal-Nenets Autonomous District, KhantyMansiysk Autonomous District, as well as the Omsk, Tomsk, Tyumen, Orenburg, and Irkutsk regions.

The company's key greenfield projects in Russia are SeverEnergia (JV with Rosneft) and Messoyakha (JV with Novatek). The company, together with its subsidiaries, holds the exploration and production rights for seventy licensed areas across eight regions of the Russian Federation and on the shelf of the Pechora Sea.

Gazprom Neft is also a party to a number of production sharing agreements and hydrocarbon exploration and production projects. For example, in a JV with TNK-BP, the company is developing the West-Messoyakha and East-Messoyakha sites.

In 2012, the company established Gazprom Gazomotornoye Toplivo, a company designed to promote ecologically safe natural gas combustion engines, which has reached agreements with leading Russian auto and transport companies such as AvtoVAZ and Russian Railways.[84]

Among Gazprom Neft's current deposits under exploration are: Novy Port, Messoyakha, Prirazlomnoye, Chona, Dolginskoye and SeverEnergia projects.

. . . And developing international projects

Gazprom Neft is motivated to enter international markets by two main determinants: acquiring new outlets for its products, and gaining knowledge and experience that can be applied to domestic production. Yet as a company with extensive government ownership, political imperatives weigh heavily in the choice of international options.

Gazprom Neft is represented in many countries, including Serbia, Iraq, Venezuela, and the CIS (see Table 10.2).[85] In 2006, the company established its subsidiary Gazprom Neft Asia, as a vehicle to enter the Central Asia retail market and sell petroleum products in Kyrgyzstan, Tajikistan, and Kazakhstan.

Table 10.2 International operations of Gazprom Neft

Country	Operations
Angola	Geological prospecting and mining
Belarus	Retail wholesale
Bulgaria	Retail wholesale
Bosnia and Herzegovina	Retail wholesale
Estonia	Marine bunkering
Hungary	Geological prospecting and mining, retail wholesale
Italy	Refining, oil production
Kazakhstan	Retail wholesale
Kyrgyzstan	Aero refueling, retail wholesale
Romania	Geological prospecting and mining, marine bunkering, retail wholesale
Serbia	Geological prospecting and mining, refining, oil production, bitumen materials, retail wholesale
Tajikistan	Retail wholesale
Venezuela	Geological prospecting and mining

Source: Gazprom Neft website (http://www.gazprom-neft.ru)

In its strategic approach, Gazprom Neft mostly chooses

- brownfield investments;
- acquiring already existing entities, such as oil refineries; or
- establishing JVs with foreign oil & gas companies to cooperate in prospecting for and then producing oil.

Acquisition of Naftna Industrija Srbije (NIS) in Serbia

Serbian multinational oil & gas company NIS is Gazprom Neft's largest foreign asset. In 2008 it acquired a controlling share of the company and now owns 56.15% of its share capital.[86] Gazprom Neft paid €400 million, with contract obligations to invest at least €500 million to modernize NIS business by 2012.

NIS is one of the largest energy companies in Eastern Europe whose major activities include exploration, production and refining, sales and distribution of a wide range of petroleum products. In Serbia, NIS has two refining centers with total annual capacity of 7.3 million tons: Pancevo and Novi Sad. It controls 78% of the total domestic petroleum products market and distributes its goods through a network of over 480 gas stations and oil storage facilities.

The company has three oil & gas production units and operates 70 production permits for oil across Serbia, Angola, Bosnia and Herzegovina, Hungary and Romania and one production unit for the preparation and transportation of oil & gas. It also opened representative offices in Russia, Turkmenistan, Angola, Bulgaria, Hungary, Bosnia and Herzegovina, and Croatia. NIS has fifty-three oil & gas fields in Serbia, and 650 oil wells and ninety-five gas wells currently being exploited.[87]

Gazprom Neft maintains tight control over its Serbian subsidiary. Moreover, both the chairman (head of the company's board) and the CEO are Russian.[88] The oil products that are distributed by NIS are sold under its name since it has already gained trust in Serbia and neighboring countries. However, NIS is also developing Gazprom Neft's premium brand of fuel for introduction in Serbia.

Although acquired as a turnkey business unit, NIS did require substantial infrastructure improvements, which Gazprom Neft financed. The goal was to enable production of high-quality oil products.

For Gazprom Neft, it was a strategically important acquisition. It could provide not only instant entrance on the Serbian market but also an opportunity for a far broader expansion, via NIS connections, into neighboring country markets. Among the main international partners of NIS, and by extension of Gazprom Neft, are

In Hungary

- Falcon, a Canadian company specializing in prospecting and mining
- RAG, a European gas storage operator, specializing in prospecting and mining in Austria, Germany, Hungary and Poland

In Romania

- East West Petroleum, a Canadian company focusing on conventional crude oil sources
- Moesia Oil & gas, an Irish company doing prospecting and mining in Eastern Europe
- Zeta Petroleum, a British company specializing in oil prospecting in Romania and Eastern Europe

In Bosnia and Herzegovina

*   Jadran-Naftagas, a joint venture with NeftegasInCor[89]

Acquisition of the Bari (Italy) refinery

Another example of Gazprom Neft's strategy is the 2009 acquisition from Chevron Global Energy of its oil and lubricant production plant in Bari, in Italy's southern heel.

According to Gazprom Neft Executive Board Chairman Alexander Dyukov, this acquisition corresponded with the strategy of development of the company's business in the field of oils and lubricants production (especially its "G-Energy" oil). It enabled Gazprom Neft to acquire a production site in Europe, as well as up-to-date technologies and a stable marketing structure.[90] G-Energy oil is developed for the latest models of European, United States and Japanese cars, and fits the requirements of world's leading auto manufacturers. G-Energy service centers have already launched in Russia, Armenia, Georgia, Belarus and Kazakhstan. The Gazprom Neft strategy is to develop its technological leadership on the Russian market, by investing in innovative technologies and lubricants quality.

The capacity of the facility is up to 30,000 tons of oils and 6 tons of lubricants annually. It was decided to rename the Chevron Italia S.p.A. to Gazpromneft Italia S.p.A. LLC Gazprom Neft – Lubricants is an operational administrator of the facility. Products manufactured at the facility are sold both in Italian and Russian markets.

Operation of the Badra oilfield in Iraq

Badra Oilfield development and production service contract with the government of Iraq was signed in 2010 after a tender initiated by the Iraqi government. The tender was won by a consortium of international companies, with Gazprom Neft in the lead (30% of stakes). The partners included Kogas of Korea (22.5%), Petronas of Malaysia (15%), TRAO of Turkey (7.5%) and OEC of Iraq representing the Iraqi government (25%).

The Badra field development was planned as a twenty-year development with a possible five-year extension. The estimated investment in the project amounts to $2 billion. The agreement stipulates investors will be reimbursed for costs incurred and paid a 5.5% bonus per barrel of oil produced.[91]

The Badra Oilfield holds an estimated 3 billion barrels of reserves, with maximum oil production expected to total about 170,000 barrels per day. In March 2014, the oilfield was connected to the export pipeline system of Iraq, and in August, the commercial production and shipments initiated. In 2015, Gazprom Neft announced the doubling of oil production to 28,000 barrels per day. Despite this promising result, Gazprom Neft faced difficulties, and had to postpone the start date due to "the failure on the part of certain contractors to fulfill their contractual obligations and certain issues related to the safety and security of employees and property."[92] Moreover, Gazprom increased its cost estimated for Badra from the initial $2 billion to $3 billion.

Among the challenges for the Russian company may have been the territory of the field which is considered difficult in terms of geological structure. In addition, in order to begin development of the field, proper infrastructure needed to be in place, so additional investments had to be incurred.

Acquisition of marine bunkering companies in Romania and Estonia

Apart from developing its production and refinery business operations, Gazprom Neft is also increasing its international presence in such business sector as marine bunkering. This refers to the action of supplying a ship with bunker, the name given to the heavy fuel that is used to operate ships.

In 2007 Gazprom Neft established Gazpromneft Marine Bunker (GMB), as subsidiary to provide year-round supplies of marine fuel and oil for ships. With a share of 21% on the Russian bunkering market at the end of 2015, the company now operates in fifteen sea and nine river ports. These are to ships what gas stations are to cars. One small difference: when a large ship fills its tanks, the bill comes out to about $700,000![93]

In March 2013, GMB acquired its first foreign asset, Marine Bunker Balkan S.A. from a Romanian company, Unicom Holding.[94] This decision was driven by the company's objective to become a significant player on the international bunker fuel market, to achieve a 27% share of the Russian marine fuel market, to develop its own terminal network and to increase its own fleet by 2025. By acquiring this asset, GMB was aiming to learn about the European markets, and strengthen its positions in the Romanian Black Sea ports of Mangalia and Midia. After the acquisition, the company expected the annual bunker fuel sales to exceed 100,000 tons.

Later, in August 2013, GMB acquired another bunkering company, Baltic Marine Bunker AS, from Estonian company NT Marine AS. The assets of this second bunkering company include a bunkering tanker with a total deadweight of 2,786 tons handling both dark and light types of marine fuel.[95]

Acquisition of bitumen plant in Kazakhstan

Another strategic deal of Gazprom Neft was the acquisition, at the beginning of 2013, of Bitumen Plant LLP, a company manufacturing bitumen for road construction and roofing in Southern Kazakhstan. The production facility with an annual capacity of 280,000 tons is one of the leading producers of bitumen in Kazakhstan. This step was important for the Russian company for three reasons. First, the new facility was fully equipped and linked, including blowing towers, feedstock storage unit, rail links, and truck and rail loading platforms. Second, one of its key competitive advantages is its close proximity to the transit route between Eastern Russia and Western China. Third, the demand for bitumen is growing steadily, and this is expected to guarantee the company additional supply opportunities. Overall, the acquisition of Bitumen Plant LLP will not only cover 20% of Kazakhstan's bitumen demand, but will strengthen its Central Asian position.[96]

Further plans in Vietnam and behind

Gazprom Neft's next step? Look in Vietnam's direction. In April 2015, a number of agreements with Vietnam Oil & gas Group (PetroVietnam) were signed. These agreements were intended to extend the collaboration activity between the parties and focus on two main projects.

The first project concerns joint oil & gas exploration production and development activities on the Pechora Sea shelf.[97] The second outlines key provisions of Gazprom Neft's partial acquisition of the Dung Quat refinery from Binh Son Refining and Petrochemical Company. The Russian company plans to buy a 49% stake and then to modernize the refinery to reach an annual capacity of 8.5 million tons versus existing 6.5 million tons. Gazprom Neft also plans to improve operational processes at the plant, allowing it to produce Euro-5 standard motor fuels.

Conclusion

Although Gazprom Neft started operations in the Siberian "gulag," it never felt constrained by the Arctic tundra. On the contrary, with abundant cash flows from its operations, it quickly set its dual international strategy.

First, it recognized quickly that having the government as owner meant playing by certain rules. Some strategic decisions might be made based not only on economic reasoning but also on the government's political motives. Yet government backing also meant the availability of deep pockets, in case of international difficulty.

Second, the company places its strategic focus on diversification, of both its international destinations and its business lines. In particular, Gazprom Neft extended not only its core activity (oil production) but also stretched into subsidiary businesses such as marine bunkering and downstream lubricants.

Lastly, given the limited development of the domestic technologies as well as the legal limitations for the foreign incoming investment into the Russian oil & gas sector, Gazprom Neft seeks not only geographic expansion but also the acquisition of state-of-the-art knowledge and know-how to be implemented in its business.

10.4 Serving customers in a way the state cannot: case of Alfa-Bank

Company overview

Established in 1990, Alfa-Bank is the largest privately owned Russian bank.[98] It is part of Alfa Group Consortium, which has interests in commercial and investment banking and asset management, insurance, retail trade, oil & gas, telecoms, media and more.[99]

As the heart and the wallet of the group, Alfa-Bank operates in all sectors of retail and wholesale banking, including corporate and retail lending, deposits, investment banking, foreign exchange operations, payment and account services and many other financial services both for individuals and for corporations.

Alfa-Bank was founded in 1990 as a limited liability partnership. It quickly obtained its license for banking operations in 1991 from the Bank of Russia and gradually extended its operations by obtaining licenses for additional activities and memberships in financial "supply chain" services, such as the Moscow Interbank Currency Exchange, MasterCard/Europay or Visa International in the early 1990s. In 1998, Alfa-Bank restructured from a limited liability company to an open joint stock company. The ownership of the bank is shared mainly by few individuals, with co-founder Mikhail Fridman (the second-wealthiest person in Russia according to Forbes) being the dominant owner and the leading decision maker.

Alfa-Bank's activity is divided in six main business divisions: corporate banking, investment banking, retail banking, customers' services, treasury and e-business, which are supported by a series of operational activities. Headquartered in Moscow, Alfa-Bank employed around twenty-five thousand employees in seven countries in 2014.

In 2003, Alfa-Bank established a record in high-growth profits and since has enjoyed great increases in its profits, with an almost five times increase from 2003 to 2014.

Benefiting from these profitable results, the bank expanded rapidly both in Russia and abroad, with assets growing almost tenfold over the decade.[100] Alfa-Bank operates more than 800 agencies in Russia and abroad, handling a total of 160,000 corporate clients and 11.4 million retail clients.[101] In 2014, Alfa-Bank had operating income before reserves of $2.6 billion, with total assets of $31.5 billion.

In 2014, *The Banker* magazine ranked it fourth-largest Russian bank (236th worldwide), after Sberbank (43rd), VTB Bank (80th) and Gazprombank (169th). The bank has been distinguished with various awards, including Best Russian Bank or Best IT Bank in Russia by various media including *EuroMoney*, *Global Finance* or *C-news*.

The bank aims to maintain its status as the leading private bank in Russia by focusing on four strategic principles: client focus, attention to modern technologies, high operational efficiency and cautious risk management.

Even though major ratings agencies such as Fitch, Moody and S&P have given Alfa-Bank negative outlooks, this mainly reflects the difficult Russian macroeconomic prospects as well as constraints on financial organizations from economic sanctions. Alfa-Bank is nonetheless recognized for its strong financial performance and its leading position in the private sector.[102] Despite the recent negative economic indicators, Alfa-Bank retains its lead as the top private bank by total assets, total equity, customer accounts and quality of loan portfolio in Russia.

Internationalization begins

Alfa-Bank first began its internationalization in 1994 in Kazakhstan but truly began to look at emerging markets as great opportunities in 2000 when it acquired 76% of Kiev Investment Bank, followed by a merger with Alfa Capital Ukraine, its existing Ukrainian operation. Alfa-Bank Ukraine was fully registered in 2001, opening the door to a series of further expansion initiatives.

Particularly active in Russia and Ukraine, ranking among the top ten banks in both countries,[103] Alfa-Bank also operates branches in Kazakhstan and Belarus, as well as a subsidiary in the Netherlands, Amsterdam Trade Bank N.V. Finally, Alfa-Bank also operates in the United Kingdom via Alfa Capital Markets and in the United States with Alforma Capital Markets Inc., which both operate as financial subsidiaries.[104]

Internationalization in the CIS

One of the most important regions for Alfa-Bank's international expansion is the CIS, where the bank has been present since 1994 and has subsidiaries in three nations: Belarus, Kazakhstan, and the Ukraine.

Alfa-Bank Ukraine

Alfa-Bank Ukraine is one of the largest and most reliable commercial banks in Ukraine based on capital indicators. It is one of the ten largest banks in the country, according to the Ukraine central bank's ranking. The bank offers convenient modern banking services for clients in all segments, from private parties to huge corporations, by being one of the leaders in new technologies implementation. Headquartered in Kiev, the bank operates 107 departments and branches nationwide. As of December 31, 2014 Alfa-Bank Ukraine served more than 11,000 corporate and 1 million private clients, with more than 4,500 staff.

Alfa-Bank strategy in Ukraine is to grow at the market level by developing a full-service banking model, retail landing and ensuring operation efficiency. Alfa-Bank Ukraine's story starts on a smaller scale, with Vito bank (Commerce Bank for Customer Assistance), established in November 1992 in Kiev and reorganized as Kievinvestbank in 1995. Several year later, the Alfa Group started buying shares in Kievinvestbank. By March 2000, Alfa Group held 75% of the bank, and by the end of the year merged Kievinvestbank with Alfa Capital Ukraine, the other Ukrainian asset of Alfa Group. Post merger, the bank was renamed Alfa-Bank Ukraine and after a series of additional stock issues the bank became one of top ten Ukrainian banks.

Alfa-Bank Ukraine had been partially owned by Alfa-Bank Russia before 2006, when the share of Russian subsidiary were sold to ABH Ukraine Limited (currently 100% owner of Alfa-Bank Ukraine), a subsidiary of ABHH located in Cyprus offshore zone. ABH Holding S.A. (ABHH) is a private investment company with head office in Luxembourg, investing in financial groups in SIC countries and Europe. ABHH's subsidiaries are Alfa-Bank Ukraine, Alfa-Bank Russia, Alfa-Bank Belarus, Alfa-Bank Kazakhstan and Amsterdam Trade Bank. This ownership structure allows a Russian bank to overcome a legal hurdle: to get a direct permission from the Russian Central Bank to establish a foreign subsidiary.[105] This is how Alfa-Bank acquired banks in Ukraine and Belarus through its Cyprus holding company. In 2009, Alfa-Bank Ukraine underwent reorganization and became a public joint stock company. Since then, the bank has been developing management and enhancing the quality of its services. Alfa-Bank Ukraine is one of the top ten banks in Ukraine.

For its next Ukrainian acquisition, in April 2014, Alfa-Bank Ukraine targeted the Ukrainian subsidiary of Bank of Cyprus Group, 99.77% of which it acquired. The value of the deal was €202.5 million, including the debt portfolio.[106]

After 18 months of ingestion, Alfa-Bank Ukraine was ready for its next quarry: in August 2015, the planned acquisition of Ukrsocbank, the Ukrainian subsidiary of UniCredit Group, was announced. The deal should be completed in 2016. However, there is already a lot of publicity, and two financial giants – UniCredit and Alfa Group – have already seemed to come to an agreement. Alexander Lukanov, the president of Alfa-Bank Ukraine claimed that the announced merger is not accidental.[107] For more than two years the group was preparing the deal by accumulating shares of an Italian subsidiary. They also referred to the long-lasting cooperation and negotiations with UniCredit. After the merger, Alfa-Bank Ukraine would control the aggregate assets of 85.6 billion grivnas (around $32 billion), making it the fourth-largest Ukrainian bank.

The aggressive expansion plans by Alfa-Bank into the Ukrainian market is evident. The fact that Alfa-Bank was one of the main candidates for acquiring the Raiffeisen bank subsidiary Bank Aval in 2013 supports this point. In the current economic situation, Alfa-Bank Ukraine tries to gain the greater market share in redistribution process after many European players have left the country.

Alfa-Bank Belarus

As was the case for Ukraine, Alfa-Bank developed its Belarussian presence by a string of acquisitions, starting in 2008. In June 2008, Alfa-Bank (via its Luxembourg holding ABHH) acquired a controlling stake in Mezhtorgbank, one of the leading Belarus banks at the time. Four years later, in November 2012, Alfa-Bank (Belarus) bought Belrosbank, which is the eleventh-largest Belarus bank in terms of its retail credit portfolio. Alfa-Bank

Russia and ABH Belarus Limited, a wholly owned subsidiary of ABHH, jointly own Belrosbank.

The acquisition of Belrosbank from Rosbank, a subsidiary of the French Société Générale Group, fit into Alfa-Bank's international strategy. The local objective in Belarus is to strengthen Alfa-Bank's presence in corporate and retail banking. As a result of this merger, Alfa-Bank Belarus's assets and client portfolio have doubled, while the number of offices trebled. This enabled Alfa-Bank to implement better systems and operations, thus competing more efficiently with other Belarus banks. This merger gave Alfa-Bank the opportunity to establish an expansion plan for Belarus, and for CIS countries in general.

In 2015, Alfa-Bank Russia initiated a six-month syndicated loan for Alfa-Bank Belarus amounting to $30 million and €4 million, with a six-month optional extension. Mostly Russian financial institutions participated in the underwriting. The deal was possible because of the long cooperation between the banks, and the high credit ranking of the debtor.

According to 2014 results, Alfa-Bank Belarus serves more than 116,000 private clients, with a branch office network that includes forty agencies in Belarus, including the head office in Minsk. The bank figures among the top ten Belarussian banks, based on assets.

Alfa-Bank Kazakhstan

Alfa-Bank Kazakhstan was established in 1994, is one of the most dynamic banks in Kazakhstan, with the head office located in Almaty, and a number of agencies in more than ten cities throughout the country. Alfa-Bank Kazakhstan offers both commercial and retail banking services. In 2014, the bank served 187,980 private clients.[108] Since 1994, the ownership structure has not changed, with the final owner being ABHH, based in Luxembourg.

Different scenarios for the CIS region

Based on recent developments, the three countries currently present quite different scenarios: Ukraine has distanced itself greatly from Russia since Alfa-Bank's entry in 2000_, while Belarus and Kazakhstan in some ways have moved closer. However, even the latter two have lately shown more autonomy, not accepting every dictate issued from Moscow, This willingness to assert themselves might not have been that prominent, had Russia not been in economic crisis, and thus unable to provide boosting to their economies. This was not the case when Alfa-Bank first expanded into Belarus and Kazakhstan.

Belarus and Ukraine are both geographic neighbors of Russia's, and both part of the Slavic language and ethnic groups. Ties between the three countries are historically strong. Kazakhstan is a bit further removed from Russia in both language and culture, even though many Kazakhs also speak Russian. However, the institutional background is similar and both nations share a long common history. The Kazakh economy also mirrors Russia's, both being resource-based, with oil being the dominant Kazakh economic driver.

Alfa-Bank entered Kazakhstan relatively early on, and with a unique approach compared to its other international forays. The company entered that market in the early 1990s via greenfield investment, whereas the bulk of its internationalization was in the 2000s via M&A deals. But at the time, 1994, the banking market in Kazakhstan, as well as in Russia, was still very new and just recently reformed to allow foreign investment. Although market entrance was easier, the menu of possible acquisitions was neither large nor very appetizing.

The greenfield Kazakhstan investment has yielded a small harvest: the bank has captured less than 2% of the overall market,[109] not much to show for over twenty years of activity. Part of this may be due to the heavier focus on corporate clients, to the detriment of the retail segment, which is the focus in Belarus and Ukraine. Yet Alfa–Bank has not given up: it plans to strengthen its position through product diversification, better service quality and expansion to other cities.

Regarding Ukraine and Belarus, Alfa–Bank entered and then expanded by buying existing banks. This strategy gave Alfa–Bank an immediate foothold and platform for expansion, based on human and material assets in place: employees with deep country knowledge, and the established networks of bank branches to interact with customers. In line with many large international banks takeover strategy, Alfa–Bank also acquired minor and weaker players in the market.

Ukraine and Belarus were targeted in the early 2000s, significantly later than in Kazakhstan. However, Alfa–Bank entered the markets at a time when many Russian multinationals were starting their initial international expansion, and it can be argued that Alfa–Bank followed its customers to a certain extent.

Operations in developed countries

Alfa–Bank is present in three of the most important financial developed markets: the United States, the United Kingdom and the Netherlands.

Alforma Capital Markets (United States)

In April 2001, Alfa–Bank Russia acquired 100% of Compass Financial Corporation (United States), and renamed it Alfa Capital Markets Inc. Therefore, Alfa–Bank has established its presence in the United States with a brownfield investment.

Alforma Capital Markets is an Alfa–Bank branch office in New York. It was established in 2001 as an investment subsidiary of Alfa–Bank. Before 2008, the company was known as Alfa Capital Markets (United States) and was then renamed. The subsidiary is oriented on servicing institutional investors and hedge funds in the United States, Canada and Latin America. It provides brokerage and investment services to U.S. institutional clients who wish to invest in Russia and CIS.

In September 2015, Alfa–Bank representatives announced sale of Alforma Capital Markets to BCS Financial Group. This decision was based on several consecutive years of losses by the U.S. representative office. Alfa–Bank first mentioned an intent to liquidate the subsidiary in the beginning of the year. However, because of bureaucracy, selling Alforma Capital Markets is preferable to liquidation. The deal is forecast to be closed by the end of 2015 if financial regulation authorities give their consent.[110]

Alfa Capital Markets (London)

Alfa Capital Markets was founded in 2000 and is an international investment banking affiliate of Alfa–Bank, located in London. The main purpose of Alfa Capital Markets is to provide Russian and Ukrainian companies with a source to raise capital outside of Russia. Alfa Capital Markets is a member of the London Stock Exchange. Therefore, it also allows a large pool of non-Russian investors to access companies in the CIS. Alfa Capital Markets performs brokerage and investment services. The main strength of this financial institution is its close connections with Alfa-Bank, and its expertise and knowledge about the CIS markets. Alfa Capital Markets is fully owned by Alfa Capital Holdings, based in Cyprus.

Amsterdam Trade Bank N.V. (Holland)

Amsterdam Trade Bank N.V. (ATB) was registered in October, 1994 in Amsterdam as a subsidiary of Russian SBS-AGRO Bank. Since 2001, it is 100% owned by Alfa-Bank. It operates with a universal bank license, issued by the Dutch Central Bank. Alfa-Bank Russia acquired the bank outright in March, 2001, with the intent to make it a leading financial instrument between CIS and EU countries. The purpose of the acquisition was, first, to serve Russian clients in Europe, and second, to support trade and partnerships between Russian and EU firms. To do so, ATB's focus is on commercial credit, structural trade finance and treasury operations. ATB offers both client-oriented and general services in export-import and project financing, investment and international payment areas. ATB also has representative offices in Moscow and Almaty and employs around 150 people.

The motives behind U.S. and UK strategy

In the early 2000s, Russia experienced a huge internationalization wave, with many Russian firms deciding to expand into foreign markets, or initiating large-scale investments. To raise funds, these companies needed to access to foreign capital markets. Alfa-Bank recognized this need and decided to offer its existing clients access to foreign capital. By acquiring trade banks in the United States and United Kingdom, they were granted permission to operate on the two largest stock exchanges. The representative office in London was given all licenses necessary for securities and futures operations regulation by the Financial Services Authority. Alfa Securities became the first Russian financial institution to be granted the FSA license, after the Russian currency crisis of 1998. The U.S. branch of Alfa-Bank was given the NASD license, meaning it could offer brokerage and dealer services, thus significantly diversifying company operations.

Alfa-Bank was cautiously realistic in approaching the hyper-developed UK and U.S. markets. Both are saturated with top quality banks fighting for market share. This explains why Alfa-Bank took a niche strategy, avoiding the development of a network of retail agencies, as it had done in the neighboring CIS countries. Alfa-Bank's s connections, expertise and knowledge of the CIS markets did provide it with one significant competitive advantage.

Another motive for Alfa-Bank's Western foray was to host the capital flight of Russian firms at the end of 1990s. In 2001, when Alfa-Bank's established its Anglo-Saxon antennae, the ruble crisis of 1998 was fresh in memories. Many Russian firms and wealthy individuals were moving assets abroad, particularly to stable developed countries, in order to reduce their exposure to Russian economic and political fluctuations. Risk mitigation is hardly an uncommon motive for foreign expansion, particularly in the banking industry. However, since Alfa-Bank already had tax options available via its Cyprus and Dutch locations, accommodating capital flight was not likely the primary impetus for its expansion to the United Kingdom and United States.

The Netherlands

The Netherlands and Europe are highly regulated markets in which Alfa-Bank could have created its own subsidiaries. However, the bank adopted a more aggressive strategy by buying a relatively small and weak player and investing heavily in it. At that time (2001), Amsterdam Trade Bank (ATB) was barely seven years old. So it represented an affordable expense, but mostly a convenient stepping stone since accredited by the Dutch Central Bank, and full member of Interpay Netherlands, therefore entitled to issue individual and corporate debit cards. ATB was also part of S.W.I.F.T, TARGET and BGC,[111] the Dutch clearing system allowing transactions to be made easily in the whole Euro zone with the introduction of the new European currency in 2002. The takeover thus allowed Alfa-Bank to obtain a quicker access to the market by exploiting all these accreditations, but also gave access to expert insight on the European market. In 2003, ATB became an active retail bank in the Netherlands, and then in 2006, it expanded to Germany and Austria.

Contrary to other Alfa-Bank subsidiaries, ATB kept its original name after being acquired. Reputation plays a key role in banking. Since ATB is the only subsidiary operating in retail banking in a non-CIS country, the decision to keep the ATB name might have reflected the fact that customers might have feared banking with a Russian financial institution.

In August 2015, Alfa-Bank Russia announced the transfer of ATB ownership directly to its Luxembourg holding ABHH. This would allow Alfa-Bank Russia to set €230 million free, and to make the financial support procedure easier.

Through its Dutch subsidiary, Alfa-Bank became the only Russian bank to wholly own a bank in the EU. As more and more Russian businesses expanded into Europe, Alfa-Bank's "follow the client" model acted as a bridge in providing financial services to customers between European and CIS countries.

Alfa Capital Holdings (Cyprus) Ltd

Alfa Capital Holdings Limited is a fully established investment company located in Cyprus. The company is wholly owned by ABH Financial Limited, Alfa-Bank's subsidiary in Luxembourg. It provides financial services to institutional investors – namely, access to Russian and CIS firms – and the opportunity for companies to raise funds on stock markets.

Cyprus is a well-known offshore zone and tax haven for many corporations, in particular emerging multinationals. Before the 2013 crisis, Cypriot banks possessed assets several times higher than Cypriot GDP. The country was also a favorite gathering point for Russian capital, flowing in from various sources. The very low corporate tax rate of 4.25% and intergovernmental agreements for double-taxation avoidance helps explain why many Russian banks and other institutions rapidly established subsidiaries there from 1993 to 1995.[112] Offshore companies and non-residents are also not subject to currency controls or restrictions.

In the 1990s, Cyprus's banking system expanded rapidly. Cyprus became a winning location because of the growing number of banks, updated financial regulations, expanding branch office network, efficient correspondence and transaction system with global banks and the sophisticated financial and legal infrastructure for clients.

Russian multinationals often use their Cyprus subsidiaries when acquiring foreign firms, using their home-country bank to service the deal. This allows Russian banks to overcome pesky legal hurdles – namely, the legal requirement to obtain central bank permission for founding foreign subsidiaries or representative offices. Alfa-Bank was no exception: it used Alfa Capital Holdings in Cyprus to acquire banks in Ukraine and Belarus.[113]

Zuno (Austria)

In September 2015, ABHH announced the acquisition of Austrian online bank Zuno from Raiffeisen Bank International. Zuno has around 250,000 customers, deposits of €720 million and a debt portfolio of €55 million. Based in Vienna but actually operating in the ex-Czechoslovakia, Zuno employs around 190 people. The deal was expected to be closed in the first half of 2016.

This acquisition gives Alfa-Bank immediate access to two previously unexploited markets: Slovakia and the Czech Republic. Moreover, operating under Austrian license, Zuno can expand by simple notification process into any European country, including other fast-growing Eastern European countries.

While Alfa-Bank already offers its own online and mobile services, Zuno operates only in this sector and possesses a superior IT platform. By acquiring Zuno, Alfa-Bank gains access to this technological know-how, which it can use to improve its own services and security.

Marginal costs associated with each new client in direct banking is close to zero, meaning that developing this segment could be highly profitable for Alfa-Bank in the future, if it proceeds cautiously. Customers must feel that their banking platform is reliable, secure, easy to navigate, and transparent. Any slip-ups on these counts can cause irreversible damage to the bank's reputation, and operations. By acquiring Zuno, Alfa-Bank reduced its learning curve for digital banking and increased its chances of quick success.

Conclusion

To conclude, Alfa-Bank's primary entry mode into foreign markets has been via the acquisition of majority-owned or wholly owned subsidiaries in both the CIS and Western markets. This is not only in line with the nature of the banking industry that makes less risky entry modes implausible, but also reflects the common tendency of emerging multinationals to go for full control due to need for immediate resource access and, potentially, to an aversion for sharing power.

The bank's strategy was three-pronged. It entered the CIS countries (geographically and culturally close) in order to expand its retail operations. In addition, the liability of foreignness was more limited than in more distant countries. On these markets, Alfa-Bank was able to exploit its comfort in less stable institutional environments so as to gain commercial success in countries. What's more, the healthy market growth offered ample expansion opportunities.

Simultaneously, Alfa-Bank expanded into Western markets for the purpose of accessing financial resources and industry know-how, in order to improve its domestic position. It never went on to develop its retail banking activities in these markets, avoiding challenges such as the liability of foreignness, the lack of ownership advantages, and the presence of saturated markets. The exception here is the Netherlands; in this context, Alfa-Bank both had access to foreign capital and success in the commercial banking segment. It is important to note that it never rebranded the bank to reflect Russian ownership, and this was probably not a coincidence. The recent acquisition of Zuno seems to also have a dual motive of market and asset seeking, and only time will tell which aspect will be of more value.

Finally, through its strategic ownership and holding structure, Alfa-Bank has used its expansion into the Netherlands and Cyprus for tax advantages.

Active internationally since 1994, Alfa-Bank has been aggressive in the more familiar CIS areas, and more cautious in developed Western markets. With over twenty years of experience under its belt, Alfa-Bank may now consider riskier ventures in the future.

References

1 World Bank 2015.
2 http://www.worldbank.org/en/country/russia/overview
3 UNCTAD 2015.
4 Russia Beyond the Headlines 2015. http://rbth.com/business/2015/07/17/is_gazprom_cutting_the_turkish_stream_in_half_47821.html
5 Miles 2013.
6 'Russia leads the world in protectionist trade measures, study says' 2014.
7 12th Annual Survey of Russian software export, 2015.
8 Liuhto and Majuri 2014.
9 Hamilton 1986.
10 Liuhto and Majuri 2014.
11 Kalotay and Sulstarova 2010; Panibratov 2010.
12 'Foreign direct investment between the European Union and BRIC' 2014.
13 UNCTAD 2014.
14 World Bank 2015.
15 Vahtra and Liuhto 2005.
16 Kalotay and Sulstarova 2010.
17 The rise of BRICS FDI and Africa 2013, http://unctad.org/en/pages/newsdetails.aspx?OriginalVersionID=436.
18 Ibid.
19 Gazprom opens a representative office in Rio de Janeiro. http://www.gazprom.com/press/news/2011/november/article122451/
20 http://www.worldal.com/news/russia/2011-07-15/131072626335948.shtml
21 "Мечел" вплавляется на бразильский рынок http://www.kommersant.ru/doc/1492282
22 'Trade with Brazil gains momentum' 2011.
23 Rosoboronexport Will Discuss Technology Partnership with Brazil at LAAD. 2015. http://rostec.ru/en/media/pressrelease/4516309
24 Ibid.
25 Latukha et al. 2011.
26 http://www.ved.gov.ru/exportcountries/in/in_ru_relations/in_ru_trade/
27 Indian Embassy. 2015. http://indianembassy.ru/index.php?option=com_content&view=article&id=705&Itemid=705&lang=en
28 Ibid.
29 Ibid.
30 http://www.zargaz.ru/en/operations/country/india
31 Hille, and Crabtree 2015.
32 RusHydro. http://www.eng.rushydro.ru/press/news/90400.html
33 'Arunachal, RusHydro seal hydropower deal' 2014.
34 RusHydro. http://www.eng.rushydro.ru/press/news/90400.html
35 http://data.sberbank.ru/en/about/global_business/branches/india_en/?base=beta
36 http://tass.ru/en/economy/766435
37 Ministry of Economic Development of the Russian Federation 2014.
38 China Statistical Yearbook 2014. http://www.stats.gov.cn/tjsj/ndsj/2014/indexeh.htm
39 China Statistical Yearbook 2013, 2014, Central Bank of Russia 2015.
40 Ministry of Economic Development of the Russian Federation 2014.
41 Krkoska and Korniyenko 2008.
42 Chinalco Sets up JV with Aricom. http://english.caijing.com.cn/2008-09-22/110029960.html
43 Webpage of external economic information of Ministry of Economic Development of Russian Federation. Портал внешнеэкономической информации Министерства экономического развития Российской Федерации. http://www.ved.gov.ru

44 World Development Indicators Database. http://databank.worldbank.org/ddp/home.do?Step=12& id=4&CNO=2
45 Ministry of Economic Development of the Russian Federation 2015.
46 Russian Railways. http://rzd.ru/
47 "Камаз" может разместить в Аргентине сборочное СП. 2014. *Vedomosti*, 13 December. https:// www.vedomosti.ru/auto/news/2014/12/13/kamaz-mozhet-razmestit-v-argentine-sborochnoe-sp
48 Lukoil. http://www.lukoil.ru/
49 Russian Federation Federal State Statistic Service. http://www.cbr.ru/
50 Ibid.
51 Polpred.com. November 2011. № 467601. http://polpred.com/?ns=1&ns_id=467601
52 National Coordination Center for Economic Relations Development with Asian – Pacific Region Countries. http://aprcenter.ru/component/k2/item/103-obzor-ekonomiki-chili.html
53 'Russian food embargo an opportunity for Latin America' 2014.
54 Cross-border M&A database, UNCTAD.
55 Annual Report 2011, African Development Bank Group.
56 Ibid.
57 UNCTAD Statistics.
58 Annual Report 2011, African Development Bank Group.
59 Annual report 2011, Norlisk Nickel.
60 *Russian Today* news publication reported December 14, 2011.
61 Annual Report 2011, African Development Bank Group.
62 The Moscow Times, Russia, Thursday, March 2, 2006.
63 Annual Report 2011, African Development Bank Group.
64 National Bank of Kazakhstan.
65 Center of Integrational Researches of Eurasian Development Bank.
66 National Bank of Kazakhstan.
67 Conner and Milford 2008.
68 World Steel Association 2014.
69 Fortescue 2013.
70 Severstal. Annual Reports. 2000–2013. http://www.severstal.com/eng/ir/results_and_reports/ annual_reports/index.phtml
71 Fortescue 2013.
72 Bloomberg 2014.
73 http://www.nordgold.com/about/history/
74 Prime 2015.
75 Severstal Annual Report 2012.
76 *Mining Weekly* 2015.
77 Infomine 2014. http://www.infomine.com/
78 Weak Russian Ruble Pushes Severstal's Q1 Margin to Record High 2015.
79 http://www.gazprom-neft.com/company/at-a-glance/
80 Gazprom Neft at a glance. http://www.gazprom-neft.com/company/at-a-glance/
81 Gazprom Neft Annual Report 2014.
82 The 2025 Development Strategy for OJSC Gazprom Neft.
83 Ibid.
84 http://www.gazprom.ru/about/subsidiaries/list-items/611153/
85 http://www.gazprom-neft.com/company/map/
86 Serbia signs strategic energy deal with Russia 2008.
87 http://www.nis.eu/en/about-us/company-information/nis-in-numbers
88 NIS Annual Report 2013.
89 Ibid.
90 http://www.gazprom-neft.com/press-center/news/2707/
91 http://www.gazprom.com/about/production/projects/deposits/iraq/
92 http://www.iraq-businessnews.com/2013/11/23/gazprom-delays-oilfield-launch/
93 Estimate for Queeen Mary at 4,381 metric tons of fuel at $160/ton
94 Company Overview of Gazpromneft Marine Bunker Balkan SA. http://www.bloomberg.com/ research/stocks/private/snapshot.asp?privcapid=212818177
95 http://www.gazprom-neft.com/press-center/news/1095398/

 96 http://www.gazprom-neft.com/press-center/news/997300/
 97 http://www.gazprom-neft.com/press-center/news/1106772/
 98 Business Monitor International 2014.
 99 Alfa-Group 2015.
100 Alfa-Bank 2015.
101 Alfa-Bank 2014.
102 Standard and Poor's 2014.
103 *The Banker* 2015.
104 Alfa-Bank 2015.
105 Abalkina 2014.
106 http://en.interfax.com.ua/news/economic/262359.html
107 "Alfa Bank" and "Ukrsotsbank" form the third largest bank merger in Ukraine. http://ukrainian-crisis.net/news/12772
108 Alfa-Bank Kazakhstan 2014.
109 Ibid.
110 Vedimosti 2015.
111 Amsterdam Trade Bank 2001.
112 Banki-delo.ru.
113 Abalkina 2014.

Part IV

What shapes the strategy of emerging multinationals

11 Non-market strategy perspective

This chapter presents non-market perspectives regarding international business in emerging economies. Among the non-market factors are institutional impacts, in particular referring to government influences. Another factor is the concept of liability of foreignness, which loosely refers to the fact that an entering multinational is perceived as being from abroad. This has an impact on the real cost of doing business abroad. How do emerging market firms minimize these liabilities? Finally, we examine the role of political affiliation in the competitiveness of emerging multinationals.

11.1 From market-based to non-market viewpoint

Most established theories argue that multinationals build their expansion strategies based on market considerations, or more broadly on economic considerations, while institutional factors play an important but still secondary role. Yet for BRIC multinationals, the institutional factors play an important role in understanding possible expansion paths, and a variety of non-market dimensions influence outbound investments.

Before analyzing non-market (or institutional) determinants, it may be useful to review four of the principal market factors.

Host-country GDP

What makes a multinational want to expand into a specific host country? GDP and GDP per capita, although quite sweeping indicators, are measures of the absolute market size and market attractiveness of a host country. As such, they can be viewed as proxies to explain the market-seeking motivations for the internationalization of multinationals.[1] Host country market size is a significant determinant and has a positive impact on FDI flow: as market size increases, opportunities for profitable investment grow. Market size is usually considered one of the major determinants for foreign investments, and explains the string of international investments in production facilities and distribution networks by multinationals.

Natural resource endowments of host country

Prior research has also widely considered resource-seeking investments by multinationals. Emerging multinationals are no exception, with recent trends in outward investment by BRIC companies demonstrating that OFDI is often strongly motivated by the need to satisfy growing demand for primary resources, especially via investments in less-developed

countries.[2] For other countries – Russia being an illustrative case – resource-seeking investment motives are strong in the mining and metallurgical industries, which face a triad of
threats: trade barriers imposed by other countries, growing production costs in the home
country and a need to diversify their resource base.[3] The resource endowment of the host
country often influences investments from emerging multinationals.

Geographic distance

Emerging multinationals with market-seeking motivations serve geographically proxi-
mate locations via simple export, and more distant markets through FDI.[4] As distance
increases, resulting in the growth of transaction costs,[5] there is a question mark: which
strategy best fits this situation? In other words, it might just so happen that a company will
decide against FDI, and revert to a choice between export and JV. However, the recent
trends in the internationalization of emerging multinationals (again, based on examples
from China and Russia) show that the majority of FDI flows into nearby countries.

Home-country GDP

The home-country environment, including GDP size and growth rate, is often perceived
as an extension of the ownership advantage of domestic multinationals and, therefore, as an
important determinant of OFDI flows from that home country.[6] In emerging economies,
the largest shares of total OFDI are perceived to be carried out by the flagship multinationals that contribute the most to the GDP growth.

Apart from such macroeconomic indices (or factors), the influence of non-market factors (institutional development including regulations, culture, and governance) on the
geographic expansion of emerging companies is becoming increasingly relevant in the
analysis of emerging economies and their corporate titans.

Institutional indicators

The institutional and governance frameworks are argued to be important determinants of
FDI, especially in case of emerging economies.[7] Poor legal protection leads to increasing
costs of business operations, decreasing FDI motivation, while poor institutions result in
underdeveloped infrastructure, which negatively influences FDI inflows into host countries. There is also empirical evidence that poor corruption indices strongly and negatively
influence FDI.[8]

However, a number of studies on OFDI from emerging economies have concluded that
emerging multinationals possess a competitive advantage in countries with poor institutions. For example, the higher level of corruption in China renders Chinese multinationals more familiar with operations in opaque business environments, where bribery may
abound.[9] A similar situation may be observed with Russian firms, especially those that
serve their domestic clients with good reputation abroad.

Regulatory distance

Regulatory quality encapsulates such aspects as price control, tax policy, anti-monopoly
policy, lack of protectionism, competition, subsidies and many other government policies
that affect business. Good regulatory policy captures the ability of the government to

formulate and implement sound policies and regulations that permit and promote private sector development. Regulatory distance characterizes the difference between the home-country and host-country political systems. It is measured by the difference in the values of the Political Instability Index for the two countries.[10] Most often, the quality of governmental regulations positively influences FDI, although this may not be true for countries with similarly low institutional indicators. Birds of a feather flock together!

Cultural distance

Since informal institutions influence the rules of the investment game,[11] in emerging economies informal institutions often substitute for formal ones because of underdevelopment.[12] Therefore for emerging multinationals similar cultural environments plays an important role in choosing the OFDI destinations.

Involvement of the state

The role of the state in OFDI is traditionally explained through either direct state ownership[13] or via organizational linkages, such as politicians serving as board members or on the top management team.[14] As for personal relationships – such as the relations of CEOs with parliament members or even the head of state – they are hidden and irregular, in literature as well as in real life. Yet, these 'political' relationships or ties are considered as an efficient tool that provides better access to decision makers, and better bargaining or lobbying skills.[15] Emerging economies, and the BRIC quartet in particular, are fertile soil in which to study the role of the state in the process of international investments of domestic firms, with Russia arguably being the most controversial case.[16] This informal government role affects outbound FDI from emerging markets at least to the same extent as the more formal macroeconomic determinants.

11.2 Government involvement in the international strategy

Government and international business

It comes as no surprise that government policies influence business, its operations and its entry modes, via various laws, regulations, trade barriers, etc. Moreover, specific government actions can directly discourage or prevent the growth of international business. To protect local businesses from foreign competition, governments may establish trade barriers: actions or policies that make it difficult to trade across borders. Governments that establish such trade barriers are enforcing protectionism, the government policy of protecting domestic industries from foreign competition.[17] Policies and politics play a key role in the decisions of emerging market firms to invest overseas, as well as in the modalities and locations of their expansion.

Sometimes government encourages business to go international, by promoting actions to directly develop and promote international business, for example by providing export counseling and training, export insurance, export subsidies and tax credits. Governments view exporting as an effective way to create jobs and foster economic prosperity. Governments encourage incoming business through a number of techniques: free-trade or special economic zones, granting most-favored-nation status, establishing free-trade agreements, providing export insurance to exporters to guarantee against foreign commercial and political risks, providing free or subsidized export marketing assistance to exporters to help research foreign markets promote their products overseas and find foreign buyers, providing tax incentives for foreign companies to invest and to locate manufacturing plants in their countries or reducing or eliminating trade barriers such as tariffs, import licenses and quotas.

One of the most effective and proven ways to promote international business, is for governments to create free-trade zones in their countries. These designed areas, usually around a seaport or airport, allow tenant companies (investors) to import products duty-free to be stored for re-export, or assembled in local manufacturing. Products that are re-exported from the zone incur no import duties. Perhaps the best-known free-trade zone is the Shenzhen area near Hong Kong, which acted as the motor for China's test of free-market private enterprise and grew from a fishing village into a massive industrial hub.

A government can also encourage international trade by granting most-favored-nation (MFN) status to other countries. This status allows a country to export into the granting country under the lowest customs duty rates, whereas imports from non-MFN countries are charged higher duties.

In addition, countries may choose to establish bilateral free-trade agreements with one another. Such agreements eliminate duties and trade barriers on products traded between the signatory countries.

Another trading zone is a common market, which helps to promote trade among its members. In such markets the member countries agree to eliminate duties and other trade barriers, allowing companies to invest freely in each member country (and sometimes even allowing workers to move freely across borders, as is the case in the twenty-eight-member EU). A common market also imposes homogenous external duties on products being imported from non-member states.

In many countries, the central and local governments play an active role in economic matters. Savvy firms are usually aware of government priorities and preferences, and often take advantage of such policies. State support provides firms from developing countries with privileged access to certain inputs, preferential financing, subsidies and other support. As an example gas contract between Russian Gazprom and Chinese CNPC – both sides agreed to offer tax preferences for the companies. China also supports its manufacturers of solar panels through concessional lending.

Governments pay particular attention to their domestic industrial titans, and to strategic industries that they see as deserving priority for industrial development (for example oil & gas in Saudi Arabia or aircraft manufacturer Airbus in Europe). Why? First because large firms are better endowed to manage international expansion and its complex processes, and achieve global competitiveness. Second because large companies also wield economic and political power. Lastly, and referring to the Dunning theory (Chapter 4), the government itself is an ownership-specific advantage for national firms.[18]

Furthermore, state ownership can also limit the agency problem: with government representative(s) on board, it is easy to monitor management activities.[19] Furthermore, the government's extended foreign network can obtain information from various sources, and can facilitate access to different channels of financing.[20] Hence, in many cases, government-linked companies (companies that have a primary commercial objective and in which the government has a direct stake)[21] can be successful and obtain fast and impressive results.[22]

Within internationalization the roles of home and host governments are equally significant and add an element of complexity, being divided on political and economic dimensions. The dual role of the state – controlling and regulating of the private sector, and enacting appropriate economic policy – is very important for the economic performance of these countries.[23]

Government policies to support corporate development differ between developed and developing countries. This is often due to differences in business sophistication, culture and the level of industrialization. Differences between home- and host-country environments causing a liability of foreignness (see section 11.2) are based on three factors: exchange risk of operating in a foreign market, discrimination by local authorities against foreign entrants, and unfamiliarity with the host-country market.[24]

Government, OFDI and emerging multinationals

Going abroad is no piece of cake. Internationalization means a great deal of complexity and uncertainty because of the major procedural hurdles to overcome.[25] For example, cross-border acquisitions have to comply with both home- and host-market regulations, such as antitrust laws and M&A procedures, supervised by government authorities – namely, regulatory agencies.

Government policies affect foreign investments through laws and regulations, but also via supportive measures, for example access to financing and favorable conditions from host-country governments seeking to boost specific industries (e.g. business process outsourcing in India).[26] Another example is the strategic government support for privileged access to raw materials: here low-cost capital and subsidies help emerging multinationals as they internationalize.[27]

Institutional theory has defined the role of the home-country government as a key rule-maker, the guarantor of a rule-abiding framework that provides the stability and continuity on which long-term investments are made.[28] Rule-abiding refers to the proper control, governance and direction of social entities that are subject to guidance or regulations conforming to certain principles, rules and norms. Continuity is considered as the state of being uninterrupted in sequence, succession, essence or idea. Continuity can refer to a condition of national politics and economy, evolving without significant interruptions.[29]

Furthermore, the role of the government in institutional development is likely to depend on the specific institutional arrangements in place and on the strength of the government as a rule-maker. In many emerging economies institutional changes are government-driven.[30] Governments can even define the regulations and motivate investment activities (inbound or outbound) via targeted financial support for specific projects.[31]

Emerging multinationals face weak institutional contexts at both national and local levels, which places them at a disadvantage on the global stage.[32] This means that home-country governments in emerging markets must establish country-level policies to facilitate OFDI. Yet considerable regional differences exist within the BRIC economies.[33] Since China is the most prominent example of the outbound investment boom, most academic research covers Chinese examples. Other emerging economies have seen less evidence of international expansion of domestic firms.

The Chinese government is strongly proactive in exploring important outbound FDI projects. State-owned enterprises (SOEs) are the means to this end, and this trend has grown over the past decades.[34] The Chinese government has to approve any outbound FDI, to verify that it complies with national policies.

This active home-country intervention in the geographic expansion of Chinese companies, and behind China's OFDI, is considered as both positive and negative.[35] The state's role was restrictive in 1980s, and then supportive since the end of 1990s. The government has used a series of policy tools such as low-interest financing, favorable exchange rates, reduced taxation and subsidized insurance for expatriates to facilitate OFDI. The negative role was played is due to the destination of OFDI mostly into tax havens such as Hong Kong, resulting in the capital round-tripping, with consequent investing back to China as by foreign investors, which was advantageous in terms of taxation and other concessions at home. Therefore, the negative role of the government was in its discrimination of domestic companies, especially non-state-owned firms.

Government policies had direct and indirect effects on the OFDI destination choices made by Chinese firms.[36] Generally, the institutional environment is considered an important determinant of OFDI. Although supportive policies and the improved institutional framework are seen as positively influencing Chinese corporate geographic expansion, policies do sometimes have negative consequences. For example, China's restrictive policy that prevented FDI but promoted international joint ventures led to the delay of substantial projects requiring foreign investor participation. Another restrictive policy applied toward outbound expansion of Chinese firms so as to have them invest domestically instead. Hence, the significance of government actions, rules and regulations, in providing a steady and supportive institutional setting for OFDI.[37]

For Chinese firms the major institutional factors that boosted internationalization have been the government's active industrial policy and China's admission into the WTO in 2001. The industrial policy focused on fostering inbound FDI so that state-controlled enterprises received foreign capital, technology, management systems and other benefits through licensing agreements, joint ventures and other strategic alliances with Western firms. Via such alliances and contracts, Chinese SOEs were able to acquire up-to-date technologies, market knowledge, international contacts, networks and foreign capital and thus prepare their own international expansion.[38]

BRIC governments have different influences on OFDI dynamics. At one end of the spectrum is heavy-handed China, where foreign expansion is impossible without state approval (even the WTO recently tried to convince China to facilitate geographic expansion of its companies!). At the other end of the spectrum one finds Brazil, where an ineffective government has never implemented an efficient OFDI policy, yet domestic companies foray abroad much more easily. The better Brazilian dynamic is partly explained by the activity of the business-like export promotion agency (APEX), which helps national firms to develop their capabilities and accumulate resources for international expansion. Another crutch in support is from new financing programs offered by Brazilian Development Bank (BNDES) providing better access to foreign markets.

The government of Brazil has adopted a strategy to support industries that are already highly competitive internationally, but with lower potential for the domestic economy. The Brazilian government and BNDES took advantage of their oligopolistic supply of industrial credit in the Brazilian domestic market to increase their shareholder position in some of the largest Brazilian multinationals. Moreover, BNDES directly injected money into companies to support internationalization via overseas acquisitions, and to finance the expansion of technology-intensive companies.[39]

Between 2007 and 2010, the government rolled out its Production Development Policy, an industrial policy with specific goals for OFDI support, targeted to industries where Brazil already possessed competitive leadership: aeronautics, oil & gas, petrochemicals, mining, steel, paper & pulp, and meat. In some of Brazilian multinationals, by acquiring shares, the government had the ability to influence board composition and operational decisions.[40]

BNDES activities ceased in 2011 when Brazilian growth slowed down dramatically. A new policy called Bigger Brazil was launched. Its purpose was to support OFDI not only in already-competitive industries but also involve companies aiming to obtain foreign technologies or access to new markets. However, this policy did not involve any further instruments, and no actions were implemented to enforce this new OFDI promotion strategy.[41]

The environmental uncertainties in Turkey, including the national economic policy, influenced the competitiveness and therefore the internationalization process of Turkish firms.[42] Turkish business groups in their global expansion were not as successful as some international competitors such as Samsung, Tata and Haier were. The first reason being several periods of economic and political turbulence, and the uncertainty in which the firms have evolved; the second is the over-diversification of family-owned conglomerates and the over-protection that they enjoyed from government policies.

All the aforementioned examples show that in case the government is over-protective of the national companies and competition, a situation can arise where emerging multinationals lack the knowledge and capabilities to operate successfully on the international scene. However, when home-country governments accept and encourage foreign competition, the national companies adapt in order to survive, and thereafter are better equipped for international operations of their own.

The government and Russian MNEs: the case of energy firms

The production of energy, be it oil, natural gas, coal or other natural underground resources, has always split countries as regards the extent of government intervention. Most developed economies, such as the United States, Japan or France, regard this as an area for private sector investment, with the government role being limited to taxation issues. For other countries, such as Saudi Arabia, Venezuela or Norway, these are sovereign resources that state-owned companies are to exploit and develop. In Russia, the pendulum has swung both directions. With the Russian government moving to recapture the oil and metallurgy assets lost to oligarch hands in the 1990s, the state role in the industry has increased.[43]

Government rules and directives govern the sector, from commercial activities of oil companies to major new projects. Joint ventures with foreign oil companies or mergers must be submitted to Russian federal authorities prior to execution.[44] During the Yeltsin presidency of the 1990s, a small minority of powerful people close to the president, both private and government officials were the main decision makers in Russia; this period was referred to as "oligarchic capitalism."[45] In contrast, Vladimir Putin's economic policies, especially after his re-election in 2004, are described as state-managed or network capitalism.[46] The more recent definition – Putin's "sistema" – implies a mixture of formal and informal rules: a mixture of clear laws and regulations on one side, and the sometimes murky networks and connections on the other.[47]

The Russian government has a direct control over strategic sectors, as a part of government strategy of maximizing the role that oil & gas MNEs play in the country's foreign policy. The government interest in other industries is also growing: firms in around forty sectors were targeted for nationalization through transformation in SOEs.[48]

Even privately owned Russian oil companies tend to act in line with Russian foreign policy in order to avoid unnecessary problems inside the country and gain political favor.[49] Many private companies experienced government intrusion, including Gazprom, Rosneft,

VTB bank and Alrosa.[50] One blaring example of direct state interference in the energy sector was the 2007 nationalization of Yukos, where the Russian government decided it would not allow the natural resource sector to become dominated by foreign capital and took over the company.[51]

Yukos company management had previously decided, without consulting the government, to sell some of its shares to foreign corporations, most notably Chevron (Texaco) and ExxonMobil. This could potentially lead to significantly lower state influence in some big energy projects, such as East Siberian pipeline. After the arrest of Yukos CEO Mikhail Khodorkovsky, the core assets of Yukos, including its main production unit Yuganskneftegas in Nefteyugansk (Khanty-Mansiysk Autonomous Okrug), were sold by the state in order to repay tax debt to a Baikal finance group in a closed auction, which than re-sold Yuganskneftegas to Rosneft, the state-owned oil company. This was an exception rather than example of how Russian government managed to get controlling stake in one of the multinationals in a strategic sector. At the same time, this exceptional government interference served as a lesson to other oligarchs with controlling stakes in energy companies; they became much more cooperative in selling shares to the government, thus giving the government controlling influence over the strategic sector.[52]

Nowadays, the two most powerful oil companies directly connected to the state are Gazprom and Rosneft. Gazprom's internationalization directly reflects Russian government policy and interests. The government is Gazprom's ultimate controlling party, with an interest above 50%, in terms of direct and indirect ownership. Thus, in 2014, the government owned 38.37% of Gazprom, with a further 11.86% owned by government-controlled entities.[53] This explains the government's huge influence on company operations in Russia and abroad. Furthermore, public economic and social policies directly affect the company's financial position, operational results and cash flows. Furthermore, after the privatization in 1992, the government imposed that the company guarantee an uninterrupted supply of natural gas to its Russian customers, at government-controlled prices.

Rosneft follows the same mold as Gazprom, with its international projects also relating to Russian political ambitions and foreign trade policy priorities. Moreover, Rosneft and Gazprom are usually part of the government's foreign affairs retinue. Commonly, when Russia meets representatives of other governments to sign agreements or discuss cooperation, a business delegation accompanies the state officials. Thus, Rosneft often acts as Russian "ambassador of oil & gas" to the countries of strategic interest. For example, Rosneft is active in Kazakhstan, where it develops the Aday field, together with Chinese company Sinopec. Along with other Russian oil companies, Rosneft invested in Venezuela. Rosneft also operates in "socialist" Algeria, an area in the commercial and political interests of both the company and the Russian state. Another example of an investment with political undertones is the East Siberia-Pacific Ocean (ESPO) pipeline, the first stage of which was launched in December 2009. The idea behind this project was to show to Europe that Russia has alternative markets into which it can sell oil and natural gas.

Overall, the role of government in the oil & gas sector is very high, given government ownership and fear of potential interference. Strategic decisions depend on government policy. There is an effective state control of the sector. The government exerts major influence on the industry, since the entire industry depends on political decisions. Energy investments in China reflect the political power play. Because of the economic sanctions imposed by the West, China has become Russia's main international partner in many sectors, including oil & gas. Russian firms with state ownership (including Gazprom and Rosneft) dominate the scene, and have become the main investors into China. Yet privately held Lukoil was not able to join the China bandwagon, and does not operate widely in China.

There are also disadvantages to the visible government links: sometimes Russian companies are perceived as undesired partners because of the political baggage, one notable case being Lukoil's failures to acquire refineries in Poland and Lithuania.[54] Other transactions made by Russian multinationals also showed government pressures, whether Russian and foreign. One such example was the acquisition by Surgutneftegas of a 21.2% stake in the Hungarian company MOL. Why this sudden interest in the small Hungarian market on the part of a very conservative and strictly Russia-focused company? Russian government influence, and the desire to give Surgutneftegas some international prestige. On the other hand, the Hungarian government responded strongly, by reducing Surgutneftegas shareholder rights.[55]

Government interference in the energy sector progressively raised concerns that limitations on domestic private producers as well as foreign investors might harm the sector in the long run. Indeed, a lack of investment in the development of new oil & gas fields and in infrastructure or technology upgrades did hurt industry productivity. In order to avoid any further declines in production or transportation systems, experts predicted that the Russian government would encourage foreign investors by creating a stable business environment. To do so, the government needs to change the current legislation which favors SOEs.[56] This is problematic since state-owned firms can be more closely controlled, and hence easier to manipulate.

The world economic crisis of 2008 provided state-owned and state-supported EMNEs with a great opportunity to invest abroad, with low and even distress prices in many developed countries.[57] Russian oil & gas companies were not hit hard by the crisis and their future is often predicted to be much brighter than of companies from other sectors.[58] In addition, two of the three largest investment projects in the oil & gas sector gave even greater power to Russian multinationals.[59]

The consequences of the 2014–2015 commodity price crisis (crude oil dropped from $110 to $40 per barrel) are not clear yet. On the one hand, oil profits declined. On the other, the national economy recognized the limits of an energy-based "imperialism." Since barrel prices cannot be regulated or influenced by the state, only two options are open: transformation or resignation.

The role of the Russian government in other strategic sectors, e.g. metallurgy or banking, is less prominent. The metallurgy industry of the Russian Federation is also under the strict government control. The basic difference is that the major companies (Evraz, Norilsk Nickel and Rusal) are privately owned, and there is no formal government ownership in the companies. But since the government considers natural resources (including metals) as state assets, the government exerts behind-the-scenes pressure and influence on company shareholders and owners.

In the banking sector, most of the largest Russian banks are state-owned (VTB and Sberbank), and others are sometimes linked to the excess liquidities of resource giants (e.g. Gazprombank). These banks benefit from government contracts and deposits. Expanding abroad through subsidiaries requires a ministerial license, illustrating once again the role of the state in banking internationalization. In the case of Gazprombank, it is clear that SOEs expect government backup and financial support in their commercial activities. However, in most foreign countries, there are strict rules and regulations regarding the banking sector. Russian state-owned banks therefore have to comply with both sets of complicated rules and regulations. For these banks, geographic expansion is a very sensitive area. In the end, state-owned banks, despite all their cushy benefits, have difficulty expanding abroad precisely because they are state-owned.

The Russian banking system is headed by the Central Bank of Russia, which prints money, supports Russia's currency reserves, implements the foreign exchange control legislation, and regulates and supervises Russian banks and other credit institutions. The central bank also keeps budgetary accounts and accounts of state agencies and authorities, runs the national settlement system and conducts banking transactions. Given these extensive powers, and its ownership of controlling stakes in Sberbank, and, until recently, VTB bank, it is difficult for Russian banks to expand internationally unless the government gives approval. In turn, Sberbank and VTB have a high influence on Russian government and their CEOs are among Russian policy strategists.

11.3 Overcoming the liability of foreignness

The liability of foreignness (LOF) concept refers to the additional costs that multinationals face, compared to local competitors, when operating abroad. The term was initially coined[60] to separate purely economic costs of doing business abroad (CDBA) from more tacit and social costs.[61] The CDBA costs can be easily quantified and hence have been researched more in-depth under transaction-cost theory, whereas the more qualitative ones received additional attention from academics and researchers later on.[62]

Multinationals acquire good business chromosomes. They possess specific advantages that stem from their international character, including larger asset bases, learning capabilities, possibilities to reap economies of scale and scope across borders, experience and mode advantages, which can all contribute to their foreign subsidiaries.[63] These qualities may be viewed as factors that help diminish LOF impacts. However, these multinational advantages are only apparent when being compared to purely domestic firms in the host country. The advantages disappear when comparing to host-country multinationals, or to subsidiaries of other foreign companies.[64]

Theoretical research has been concentrating on aspects such as source identification and classification,[65] whereas practical research focuses mostly on the strategic implications of LOF, such as market entry strategies[66] and the internationalization process.[67] As usual, there is relatively little research of LOF in the context of emerging markets, even though the competitiveness of emerging multinationals is a very hot topic (indeed, only five out of twenty-seven scientific studies, reviewed a few years ago, specifically concentrated on issues connected with LOF with respect to EMFs).[68]

Drivers and effects of LOF

"Indigenous firms have better access to relevant market information, are more deeply embedded in the national environment, and do not face any foreign exchange risks," explains professor Stephen Hymer in his 1976 seminal study of international corporate expansion.[69] All foreign newcomers to a host-country will be automatically at a disadvantage compared to local, established competitors. Initially, the foreignness liability was seen in terms of the cost of setting up a new subsidiary, implying that these disadvantages were akin to national barriers to entry, but more in terms of lack of knowledge and acquisition costs. Thus in his dissertation Hymer viewed them as a fixed, one-time investment, to be incurred by a multinational when setting up a subsidiary, which can be easily done.

This concept remained underdeveloped until Srilata Zaheer's well-known publication in 1995, which brought about significant discussion, regarding the definition of LOF itself:

> The costs of doing business abroad that result in a competitive disadvantage for an MNC sub-unit . . . broadly defined as all additional costs a firm operating in a market overseas incurs, that a local firm would not incur.[70]

Fifteen years later, LOF was specified as

> additional costs a company might experience while operating abroad, as compared to local firms, due to the spatial distance between the firm's home-country headquarters and a host country operation and their unfamiliarity and lack of legitimacy in a host-country market.[71]

Over two decades, various scholars concentrated on different aspects of the foreignness liability, including the definition and classification of the different liabilities and their sources.[72] Constructive academic thought was given to possible strategies on overcoming the liabilities, and achieve competitive advantage while operating in foreign markets.[73]

The corporate learning curve is an important factor in overcoming the LOF handicap. After a certain period, companies learn the local specifics and adjust to them, thus reducing the costs of their international operations; the level of a firm's legitimacy and acceptance by the host-country ecosystem also grows over time.[74]

In an attempt to compare the performance of firms in order to assess the extent of the LOF handicap,[75] different categories of companies were considered. Traditionally, the comparison was between local firms and the incoming multinational. Then academics started focusing on domestic multinationals. Comparing domestic multinationals to incoming multinationals was considering one method of measuring the host-country LOFs.[76]

Drivers of LOF

Why are there additional costs for doing business abroad? Why does it cost more for a Milan-based company to do business in close-by Switzerland than in Rome, many hundreds of kilometers more distant? Various factors have an impact on the liability of foreignness and their significance in the internationalization process varies greatly, depending on the industry, and the level of development of the home- and host countries.[77] On the one hand, there exist industry-specific LOFs that have diverse impacts on companies. On the other hand, other LOFs are linked to developed versus emerging market characteristics.[78]

Finally, the LOF drivers can be defined as either firm-based or environmentally derived.[79] Firm-based liabilities stem from specific characteristics of the company, such as ownership structure, learning capabilities, firm-specific resources, and so on. The environmentally derived drivers can be further split into two sub-categories: those coming from the home-country environment versus those coming from host-country environment.

While LOF drivers are rarely presented in a structured way, but instead just the possible sources of LOFs are discussed,[80] certain drivers typically cause additional costs in only one of the LOF categories (Table 11.1).

Table 11.1 LOF (liability of foreignness) drivers by category

LOF category	LOF drivers
All hazards	1 Distance between home and host countries 2 Cultural sensitivity 3 Economic development and stress of host market 4 Firm characteristics 5 Industry characteristics
Unfamiliarity hazards	1 Lack of international experience 2 Lack of embeddedness in networks 3 Lack of specific host-market knowledge
Relational hazards	1 Network integration level 2 Lack of trust 3 Corporate culture differences
Discrimination hazards	1 Negative nationalistic tendencies 2 Lack of local legitimacy 3 Limited access to resources 4 External conformity pressures

Source: Denk, Kaufmann and Roesch 2012, p. 326

What impact does LOF have?

Industry effects

As mentioned previously, there are industry-specific liabilities (or costs) to expanding abroad. Parameters such as the level of competition (or rivalry), the intensity of knowledge or capital or labor inputs and the level of globalization all have an influence on the degree of LOF. These industry parameters have an impact on the LOF a company will face, its drivers, its intensity and the possible mitigation strategies.[81]

The first parameter that directly influences the firm's international strategy and performance is the *rivalry level*.[82] Entering a host-country market with a high level of competition among domestic players will increase the pressure on the foreign subsidiary, since it will have to conduct a more detailed, pre-entry market analysis. Furthermore, higher competition will generally imply lower margins. Add on the higher costs due to LOF, and one has a recipe for disaster: the company might soon exit the host country.[83]

The second factor is *resource availability*. Here the main question is whether a company will have an access to this key resource in the host market, and whether it will be able to use it as efficiently as at home. This is crucial to developing competitive advantage in the new host country.[84]

Labor-intensive industries rely mostly on readily available and relatively cheap workforce, both semi-skilled and unskilled, depending on precise company needs. Normally, it is quite easy to clone the business models across borders, either by hiring local staff, and sometimes by transferring expatriate experts (especially in key positions). The effectiveness of the company's transplant depends on the ability to create an appealing employer brand to attract local staff, or the ability to persuade home staff to transfer to foreign postings.

In the case of knowledge-intensive industries (e.g. software or financial services), competitiveness is supported by knowledge-based assets and intangible resources such as intellectual property rights (e.g. patents and licenses) and by the tacit knowledge accumulated over years of experience.[85] Such intangible assets take longer and greater effort to develop in new host countries, or to transfer from the headquarters. Here the use of expatriates or temporary postings of local staff to home-country facilities may prove the most effective ways to transfer knowledge successfully.[86]

Capital-intensive industries require substantial initial investments in assets (e.g. equipment and infrastructure) before operations can commence. This may imply large sums of tied-up capital for foreign subsidiaries. Additional LOF costs (e.g. of cultural or legal nature) that occur after market entry may result in a higher risk of failure due to insufficient funds.[87]

The third industry-specific liability is the *industry globalization level*. The issue at stake here is the necessary degree of local adaptation of the product or service. Understanding local customer needs or market requirements (remember Geely vehicles in Russia?) may require substantial investment in market research. Global industries with relatively standardized products may only need to establish a sales and distribution network, and start sales immediately.[88] By contrast, extensive localization would require developing a host-country strategy from scratch, based on market specifics, meaning additional funding and time for the local subsidiary.[89]

Emerging-developed market duality effect

Emerging multinationals experience greater problems in developed countries, where they have higher exit rates, than they do in developing markets.[90] Certain factors influence this outcome. One key factor is the difference in the levels of development of the economies themselves, and of the various institutions inside the countries. This directly influences the typical business practices, applied business models, and so on.

As for industry-level parameters, the level of industry competitiveness usually negatively affects the LOF. In other words, the more competitive an industry, the more difficult emerging multinationals will find entry. As for the global-local dimension, developed economies tend to be more global, and meaningless localization efforts are required for a foreign entrant to adjust to the local demand. In this sense, for relatively globalized industries it makes it easier to internationalize into advanced economies.[91]

Is there one important implication for companies from emerging markets? A need to verify the host-country perception regarding products from the home country from which the company hails. In this sense, most products and services from emerging countries used to be virtually automatically considered as of lesser quality. However, recently this reputation gap has been decreasing, with some top Western countries losing points (American cars in the 1970s), and some EEs gaining them (Chinese mobile handsets from ZTE, see case in Chapter 8).

Since emerging multinationals operate in environments with underdeveloped institutions, they develop specific sets of capabilities which enable them to succeed. They organize strong business groups and networks, which often serve as a starting point for their internationalization efforts into other emerging markets.[92] Emerging multinationals also benefit from high entrepreneurial motivation,[93] high learning capabilities and fast adaptiveness, in large part due to the unstable environment of their home markets.[94] However, most of these factors are of greater help in other developing markets, as opposed to developed markets.

Another institutional aspect is industry transparency. From this point of view, developed countries present much lower risk and more accessible market research than developing markets, meaning lower unfamiliarity hazards for new entrants.[95]

When venturing into developed markets, emerging companies naturally face some typical problems: their lack of international experience, and lack of technological expertise, leading to inferior quality, and of managerial capabilities, influencing, among other factors, the employer brand of EMF in the host market.[96]

Emerging multinationals that lead in strategically important sectors (and sometimes have government ownership) can have an easier time expanding into other emerging markets: they benefit from better access to resources and lower LOFs. The coin does have a reverse side though: their expansion into developed markets may experience higher resistance if they are associated with the government, since for stakeholders in developed markets this might imply lower market orientation, and higher political risks.[97]

LOF and market entry strategies

For a company to succeed to a new host-country investment, its critical first step is choosing the right entry mode. The entry method should maximize firm-specific advantages and yet accommodate risks which arise from foreign market uncertainties. Companies that choose an intermediary ownership strategy in foreign markets (e.g. joint venture) can overcome some LOF costs. These middle ground entry modes provide access to local resources and business networks. On the other hand, some argue that wholly owned subsidiaries decrease transaction costs[98] and help firms to utilize their unique capabilities (or competitive advantages) to the maximum extent possible.[99]

However, from a dynamic perspective, contemporary firms should go beyond the trade-off of exploitation versus exploration, to develop their competitive advantages over time.[100] They should deploy their own resources while extracting benefits from the external environments. Yet even sophisticated models that attempt to predict which entry mode a company should select based on production costs abroad, transaction costs, production technology adaptation and information costs,[101] often ignore socio–institutional costs.

The choice of entry mode largely relies on trade-off between local responsiveness and global integration.[102] Export-based entry strategies help to achieve the highest host-country adaptation, while wholly owned subsidiaries usually conform to parent company practices.

The higher the institutional distance between home and host country, the more likely a low ownership strategy will succeed due to twin challenges of achieving external legitimacy and parent company isomorphism.[103] The cost of doing business abroad (CDBA) caused by institutional and geographic distances is reflected in the ownership strategy pursued. Normally, multinationals select the entry method which minimizes CDBA, taking into account both economic costs and qualitative LOF costs.[104] Since activity-based costs can be easily identified and quantified, the evaluation of the more subjective LOF costs can become decisive and determine the firm's entry mode. As institutional distance increases, so does the likelihood that a multinational will choose a lower level of ownership.

Big normative institutional distance makes it difficult for a multinational to obtain external legitimacy and to transfer corporate practices effectively. Joint projects with a local partner help offset these unfamiliarity hazards. The same logic works in case of increasing cognitive institutional distance arising from consumer ethnocentrism: products are perceived through the distorted lens of consumer habits, culture and experience. Relying on a local partner can also help attenuate discriminatory risks, especially in the case of unfavorable perceptions of foreign firms. When "Made in China" vehicles are not well perceived, slap on a Volvo label!

Deep-pocketed multinationals can take advantage of their financial strength, brand recognition, bargaining power and risk establishing a wholly owned subsidiary, but this can prove risky in countries with high ethnocentrism. Thankfully, as globalization progresses, negative stereotypes are slowly fading away.

Some multinationals benefit from positive a "home-country aura." Think of fashion from France, software from the United States, cars from Germany, or agro-food from Italy. For multinationals that can profit from such benefits, low-equity strategies such as licensing may be the solution. The resource commitment in this case is low, but knowledge of the host-country market is still transferred by the company.

In countries where economic transactions are relationship-driven and where affiliation to the business network is crucial, it is preferable for an outsider to choose an intermediate entry mode. Cognitive institutional distance is increasing if the social embeddedness is high, thus raising unfamiliarity hazards for the MNE. But if not only host-country environment exhibits high embeddedness but also home-country environment as well, than an MNE is more likely to prefer low ownership strategy as it can effectively transplant such relationship-focused practices to other countries, reducing the need for supervision, facilitating communication and building trust easily.

Institutional distance is also affected by the ratio of foreign to local firms. As this ratio increases, sensitive national industries may become concerned and may enforce protective measures, thus preventing some forms of foreign investment.

Cultural distance contributes greatly to increased unfamiliarity LOF hazard. This is where a local partner can help meet the challenge. After incurring the one-time cost of understanding the local environment, the foreign investor can buy out its local partner. This is why companies are often reluctant to incur double-layered acculturation and to adapt to each other. However, if the cultural distance results not from cognitive institutional differences (based on observation or on past experience) but rather from normative differences (values or beliefs that exist in the society), then cooperation with a local partner makes more sense.

Public sector corruption is another component of LOF costs. There are two characteristics of corruption: pervasiveness and arbitrariness.[105] Pervasiveness refers to the likelihood that a company will face corruption in its government relationships, while arbitrariness implies uncertainty in corruption outcomes. In countries with pervasive corruption, the custom is considered socially acceptable and quite regular, just like tipping in a restaurant. In this case an intermediate ownership strategy will neither influence the likelihood of bribery, nor reduce the amount of the bribe. However, in cases of arbitrary corruption, an intermediate strategy using a local partner can reduce the uncertainty. Such corruption usually exists in countries with weak formal regulations and relations-driven economic transactions, so a local partner can be valuable to gain access to local social networks.[106]

Emerging multinationals that possess sustainable firm-specific advantage (FSA) are able to offset the foreignness handicap (LOF),[107] and so full ownership is the best option, and preferred entry mode. Another option to diminish the LOF is by exploring local resources,[108] one solution that joint ventures with local partners readily offer.

The key to overcome the foreignness handicap (LOF) is to establish local production in the host market. This becomes even more critical if the industry is highly competitive and mature, and the room for product innovation or differentiation is limited. Although local responsiveness can be achieved through JV with local partner, a local production facility improves the firm's own capabilities. What's more, for companies looking at regional options, a wholly owned subsidiary can act as the operational hub.[109] In countries with high social embeddedness, full ownership also helps to decrease communication costs with local companies and to manage these relationships more effectively.

Alas, a foreign subsidiary will never possess all the assets of its mother company back home. That is why it is utmost important to reinforce them when entering a foreign market, for example by establishing partnerships with local companies who possess complementary resources. Second-tier local companies are often more approachable than market leaders. Wholly owned subsidiaries help to avoid high transaction costs. Local alliances and joint ventures incur higher monitoring costs, although partners can be changed when required.

Both LOF and rule of law influence the choice of the joint venture partner (either state-owned or private), depending on the strategic motivations of the investor.[110] Joint ventures can attenuate the LOF, and protect the investor from undeveloped rule of law and institutions: abuse of property rights, corruption and insufficient legal recourse.[111] Such international joint ventures present many advantages to the entering firm: economies of scale or scope, immediate access to the host-country market, knowledge and technology spillovers, etc.[112]

Should the incoming investor choose a state-owned company or a private company? Different strategic motivations influence the decision: the level of motivation for the investment, the level of LOF and the legal background. If the strategic goals are efficiency-driven, private partners are preferable as they share similar aspirations in terms of cost optimization and corporate governance. For investors with market-driven strategies, government partnerships can provide sufficient resources and opportunities for achieving greater presence, gaining access to cheaper financing and knowledge about host-country institutions and business practices. Companies with knowledge-seeking motives can find fertile cooperation with SOEs, as both parties are interested in know-how and managerial skills transfer in order to increase efficiency of operations and develop core competencies.

Investors should beware of SOE partnerships in countries where the rule of law is weak. It is extremely challenging to confront state-owned companies on legal issues as the latter always have an advantageous position. In cases involving the risk of intellectual property rights infringement, companies should be doubly careful.[113]

Overcoming the liability of foreignness

With emerging economies becoming increasingly attractive for investment, yet displaying high uncertainty and unpredictability due to geographic, cultural and institutional distance, how can multinationals find effective mechanisms to curtail the LOF costs?

Research has pinpointed both defensive and offensive mechanisms.[114] The defensive strategies aim to reduce a company's interactions with foreign markets, thus diminishing the company's vulnerability to environmental changes. Offensive mechanisms, to the contrary, advocate deeper market understanding and penetration by establishing tighter connections in order to increase returns.

The benefits of defensive mechanisms include:

1   Contract protection: protects rights and benefits, safeguards resources committed to foreign operations and reduces the threat of environmental changes
2   Parental control: the control and support of the subsidiary reduces firm's dependence on host-market resources and its vulnerability to environmental hazards
3   Parental service: operational and economic support limits the exposure to host-market risks

4   Output standardization: lack of product (or service) adaptation leads to lower host-market influence

Offensive mechanisms provide the following advantages:

1   Local networking: improves flexibility and provides the opportunity to take advantage of interpersonal connections and creates opportunities for adaptation and localization
2   Resource commitment: increases bargaining power with the business community and government
3   Legitimacy improvement (local needs responsiveness): builds trust with local community and reduces discriminatory hazards
4   Input localization: improves reputation due to commitment to local needs, encourages knowledge transfer and decreases foreign exchange risk

In order to mitigate LOF costs, emerging multinationals have several options (Figure 11.1). First, preventive measures may be taken, in particular properly assessing market potential and conditions. Establishing connections with local potential partners is important: they provide insights regarding operations in the host country. During its entry phase, an incoming multinational should strengthen its connections, build up brand awareness and collect information about the environment. It can then decide on gradual commitment to the host country, or establish a joint venture or strategic alliance with a local partner. A full-blown localization strategy would include product adaptation to local consumer needs and preferences.[115]

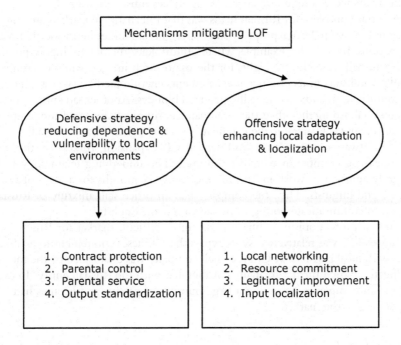

Figure 11.1 Mechanisms to overcome the liability of foreignness (LOF)

Source: Luo, Y., Shenkar, O. and Nyaw, M.K. (2000). 'Mitigating liabilities of foreignness: Defensive vs offensive approaches'. *Journal of International Management*, 8(3), p. 285

How Russian software firms handled the LOF challenge

The concept of LOF may seem quite abstract to some readers. Let us make things more concrete, by using the example of how Russian software firms – the object of my (and my colleagues) studies within last few years – handled their international expansion.[116] Several issues are especially important for emerging multinationals burdened by the emerging market pedigrees: cultural issues that require strategy localization, protectionism that inhibits some international expansion, forging relationships with international counterparts and country of origin (COO) effects consequences.[117]

Cultural integration issues

Multinationals take different approaches to their localization needs. Some follow a standardized global approach; their localization consists of simple translations for product descriptions into other languages (IKEA even skimps on this by using pictograms!). Others are highly customer-oriented, aiming to provide high levels of localization. The importance of local knowledge and of cultural aspects in the success of internationalization efforts is absolutely necessary for Russian firms.

For many companies, each new host country requires certain fine-tuning of the products to the unique characteristics (both legal requirements by authorities, and market expectations, such as payment options for customers). For manufacturing firms, the localization in terms of product and technology is often important due to cultural reasons.

The majority of Russian software firms have not met any serious problem with localization, having products developed using standardized coding programs. Obviously, some linguistic assistance was required, since user interfaces must be localized.

An important problem for Russian firms was that international markets are fragmented. Permissions to use intellectual property and copyrights are sometimes associated with non-market reasons. In India for example, where Hindu deity themes are highly popular, one Russian firm had to secure the rights for the use of such images. Another company that used Bollywood stars in its product advertisements encountered lousy customer response: it turns out the local audience actually preferred blondes. Another sad episode in Mexico: a year after establishing the office, the local manager simply disappeared after emptying the corporate accounts. Thereafter, the candidate selection process was reviewed!

For one software company that was fluent in CIS expansion, Turkey was the first non-Russian-speaking country in which it ventured. The underlying technology had to be significantly adjusted to work in Turkish, requiring six months for a team of few dozen developers and linguists. Then the company had an office staff mixture of Russians and Turks, and to communicate both groups had to rely on English.[118]

In terms of protectionism, China was the most difficult market for Russian software firms. However, it was relatively easy to bypass the Chinese requirement to establish joint ventures with local partners. A Chinese shell company was established by the future managing director, which further formally collaborated with the Russian entity. To overcome protectionism companies possessing a large number of patents and licenses had an easier time operating in the market.

Establishing relationships

Although this may seem self-evident, the very first and most critical step for expansion is to set up a local office. Proper relationships with customers often depend on an absence of language and time zone differences. The ability to meet face-to-face is one of the key elements in building up trust, and hence reducing LOF hazards.

Sometimes it is impossible to provide extensive quality services without a large number of partners, some of which are global, but many of which are local, especially the ones advertising with Russian company. This is the reason of why some firms start seeking for partners prior to entry. Although, finding reliable partners in foreign markets may be challenging, it can influence the whole business model for the company.

Many multinationals maintain ongoing connections with major players in their markets. Since many of these companies are also global operators (e.g. advertising agencies, headhunters, audit firms), this simplifies communication in the various host countries. Multinationals may even abandon their home-country image, adjusting their names, slogans or advertisement styles.

Mitigation strategies

To sum up, the LOF mitigation strategies and related actions of Russian IT firms can be split into three main groups, according to the phase of internationalization process of the company (Table 11.2).

Preventive measures are taken prior to entry, in order to increase company knowledge of the host-market; secure the ability to enter the local network; and achieve a positive legitimacy level. These measures include conducting an in-depth market analysis in order to identify market characteristics, determining its attractiveness and checking the company's ability to generate a profit. A sure method to accomplish this is via a partner, who already has an access to the market, and all the relevant knowledge. Many Russian software manufacturers would not be able to find their niche abroad without having a strategic partner to "guide" them.

During *entry phase* actions, firms continue gathering market knowledge, establishing connections and improving brand recognition and acceptance (if the company is involved in consumer goods). Firms start with the least capital-intensive mode: export through partners or distributors, then setting up a partnership abroad, and finally establishing local headquarters or local production facilities if needed. This was the pattern followed by small IT firms in speech recognition and payment systems technologies, as well as large search engine or anti-virus firms.

Table 11.2 Findings on the LOF mitigation strategies

Internationalization stage	Mitigation strategy
Before entry	In-depth market assessment through existing partners
	Use of existing networks and partners/intense networking with potential partners
Market entry	Phased entry to establish partnerships and build up market knowledge and brand recognition
	Joint projects– /strategic partnerships–based entry
	Creating a brand image separate from Russia (local/Western)
Ongoing operations	For companies with high level of localization – support of a localized brand image with relevant products/services/marketing

Smaller IT firms normally go for a joint project or strategic partnership, which ensures an internal data-source. For example, when an IT service company strikes a deal with a major client (e.g. Intel or Microsoft), the company piggybacks on the contract into one of the markets where the client is active. This action directly addresses the issue of negative country of origin effects, with two ways to overcome it: to establish foreign headquarters, or to differentiate subsidiary as a local company, with a corresponding value proposition and strategy.

After entry, the investing company exerts *ongoing efforts* to establish legitimacy during localization strategy. The focus is on product (or service) customization, by tailoring to market specifications. If required, a marketing campaign can stress these features.

11.4 Political connections as a part of strategy

Political connectedness of emerging multinationals

In much of the academic literature devoted to the impact of institutional environments on business, scholars emphasize that emerging economies frequently experience a legacy of substantial governmental or political involvement in business affairs,[119] which is usually considered as a constraint. However, the influence of politics on internationalization has not been sufficiently explored yet, with two main shortcomings:

First, prior studies on politically connected firms have examined the role of institutions in the corporate internationalization process.[120] The empirical knowledge of how internationalization and political connections are interrelated has mostly been studied in China,[121] and less so in the other BRIC countries.

Second, a framework using three different levels of analysis (firm, industry and country) has been applied to internationalization studies, while political influence has been mostly examined only from the perspective of institutional theory.[122] Some scholars have also used a resource-based view on political connectedness, and its impact on a firm's value.[123]

In this section, the existing theories are integrated and on this basis a framework is proposed to give a more comprehensive approach to the political connectedness theory.

Can political connections provide a competitive advantage?

A company is considered to be politically connected if at least one of its significant shareholders or top managers is a parliament member, a minister, a head of state or someone closely related to top government officials.[124] More specifically, for Chinese companies this means that the CEO is a present or former officer of the central government, local government, or the military.[125] A French company is politically connected if its CEO attended one of the so-called "grandes écoles" universities: École Nationale d'Administration or École Polytechnique, and had a position in government.[126] In Germany, executives or supervisory board members who were close to the main political party in the early 1930s provided political clout.[127] Both present and former politicians provide political connections to firms, if they maintain and exploit their connections, even after resignation or loss of office.[128]

Most of the recent academic empirical studies are single country studies, which makes findings less universal and only relevant to that country's specific environment. Two types of evidence have been found. The first evidence suggests that companies with political connections also have to apply significant resources to such rent-seeking activities, which possibly cancels any benefit gained from the political clout.[129] The aims of such lobbying can be either government intervention (favorable legislation), or an intention to satisfy the social objectives.

The second set of evidence suggests that political connections carry various corporate benefits. One positive effect may be on the company's value and performance. Several scholars claim it is easier to gain access to credit,[130] as well as land government contracts more frequently,[131] and even pay fewer taxes.[132] Furthermore, connections with politicians help companies to lobby for favorable regulatory policies, which may be important to sectors such as pharmaceuticals or energy.[133] Government bailouts are also bestowed on connected companies.[134] In addition, politically connected firms obtain benefits when going public[135] and advance their financial performance.[136] Finally, government connections may assist companies to diversify into different areas, with this link depending on the institutional support companies receive.[137]

Most of the studies are cross-national or focused only on emerging economies. However, one series of studies (in the United States and Denmark) uncovered substantial benefits that companies gain from government connections. This relationship is particularly important for companies bidding on state procurement contracts.[138] Furthermore, in the low-corruption Danish environment, a large positive effect of political connectedness on company profitability was identified.[139]

Empirical studies prove that political connections bring value to companies in terms of their performance, access to credits and other benefits. As a logical next step, some scholars have developed hypotheses about an indirect influence of political connections on company internationalization.

In early studies focusing on the political role of outside directors, a correlation was established between the number of directors with political experience and the extent of company export activities.[140] Later studies of Chinese outbound FDI patterns showed that government support is positively correlated to the degree of OFDI.[141] A more recent study of Chinese firms has proposed that the degree of governmental control has the following effect: increased profitability through internationalization is more common in companies with higher government affiliation, than in companies with lower governmental connections.[142]

Different perspectives on political connectedness

The ability of companies to understand their environment and see the "big picture" has a direct influence on their strategic decisions. Internationalization can be considered as a response to specific internal or external factors. In the academic literature, a broad range of these factors is classified and combined in one framework.[143] Within emerging economies, three important motivations justify a firm's strategic move toward internationalization: resource-based; industry-based; and institution-based motivations. This triple-pillar framework has been applied in several empirical studies[144] to understand the internationalization process and provide a holistic approach to understanding strategic decision making in transitional environments.

When analyzing political connections and their corporate impact, scholars mostly use the framework of institutional theory.[145] As a result, political connections are generally considered purely as an institutional factor, even though some scholars have analyzed political connections from a resource-based perspective.[146]

Resource-based view on PC

Can political connections be viewed as an important intangible asset that multinationals can use as a competitive advantage in their international expansion? Several scholars argue that political connections are a unique type of managerial resource in emerging economies,[147] particularly in host countries where the formal institutional framework is not well developed. Here political connections play a more important role in facilitating business.[148] In such economies, the government frequently holds the power to allocate strategic resources, to approve projects, and to interfere or assist in business operations. Therefore, executives with political savvy are critical in soliciting favorable government treatment,[149] such as providing information about relevant policies, the granting of valuable resources or administrative approvals.[150]

Alas, although they may constitute a competitive advantage political connections are not transferable. Each country has its own government and institutions, and even though some countries may be interconnected, the lobbying network must be rebuilt in each new host country.[151] Specifically, market imperfections in the form of recognition, disclosure and team organization in the labor market make the transfer costly.[152] To complicate matters further, top managers in emerging markets are often reluctant to move between companies,[153] and all the more so when their professional success has been built on creating localized political connections.

Scholars provide evidence that the presence of current and former politicians on company boards can bring substantial benefits to companies such as performance improvement,[154] larger bank loans[155] or larger export volumes.[156] The presence of politicians on the board of directors can provide significant support for internationalization. Academic research also shows that emerging market firms are frequently aggressive in hiring former state representatives, proof of their resource-seeking value.[157]

Institutional context for PC

How politically connect are company managers? This is a function both of the institutional context and of the managers' interest, and therefore its impact on internationalization changes from company to company. The role of institutions is more critical in emerging markets where institutional environments are changing fast.[158] These changes can have a significant impact on expansion strategies, both for local firms and for subsidiaries of multinationals.[159] Simple, consistent and liberal regulatory policies adopted by a home-country government encourage companies to engage in foreign expansion.[160] Otherwise, poor institutional policies in the home environment such as regional protectionism, corruption, high tax rates, insufficient protection of property governmental interference can also stimulate companies to move abroad looking for more efficient institutions.[161] This type of internationalization is forced more by the exit strategy from the home country rather than a usual entry strategy into foreign markets.[162]

One unique institutional characteristic of emerging economies can be the broad presence of state-owned firms (SOEs) in the economy. Previous studies have emphasized the distinctions between SOEs and private companies in terms of their behaviors and performance.[163] Government leaders have incentives to assist SOEs since their success can enhance the political status and increase their chances for promotion.[164] In addition, because SOEs can help achieve goals such as reducing unemployment or the fiscal deficit, political leaders tend to give preferential treatment to SOEs.[165] Since government support covers issues related to operational performance, the internationalization process of SOEs is also of interest.

Government involvement in business takes place not only in the form of policies and regulations but also as government contracts (tenders).[166] Contracting is understood as the formal process by which state agencies purchase goods and services from the private sector. Using a Russian example, in 2015 more than twenty-five million government contracts representing a total value of RUB 30 trillion were issued for bids.[167] This was approximately 37% of Russian GDP, showing the importance of government in the Russian economy.

As could be expected, a positive relationship exists well-connected companies and government contract allocations.[168] Multinationals with good political clout can expect more than their fair share of government contracts. This is especially applicable in BRIC countries, known for relatively high corruption levels. In addition, companies with large shares of revenue from government contracts depend to a large extent on government decisions. In a sense, government contracts are the indirect signal of governmental support and may be considered as another PC factor.

Different business sector, different politics

As far as industrial organization theorists are concerned, a company's internationalization depends on the particular industry in which it operates – namely, how competitive it is.[169] Tough competition drives companies to look for new foreign markets,[170] and a highly concentrated industry will pressure companies to expand abroad faster.[171]

As a rule, industries have different globalization potentials,[172] which lead to differences in internationalization across industries. The degree of internationalization is higher in industries producing a standardized product or service (for example, agricultural commodities such as wheat), than in industries offering tailor-made products for each different host country (for example, processed foods). Industries with high technological opportunities are characterized by their high speed of technological renewal,[173] and they attract more investment and initiate more international ventures. Geographic expansion is therefore more common in industries with high technological content than in industries with low content. Industries are also exposed to different institutional environments, with those facing rapid deregulation having greater use for internationalization.[174]

Based on the forms of internationalization (export vs. FDI), some scholars classify industries as either sheltered industries, trading industries, multi-domestic or global industries:[175]

- *Sheltered industries* are served solely by indigenous firms. They are protected from both imports and foreign investment by regulation, trade boundaries or because of the local character of goods and services on offer.
- *Trading industries* are those where internationalization takes place mostly by import and export. When goods are transportable, not differentiated nationally and offer economies of scale in production (for example, commodities), then export from the producing locations is the most efficient means to reach overseas markets.
- *Multi-domestic industries* are those that start international activities by direct investment. This is the case when export is not feasible (for example, in service industries such as consulting or banking), or when goods are nationally differentiated (for instance, food).
- *Global industries* are those in which both export and direct investment are equally important. Nearly all large-scale manufacturing industries (consumer electronics, automobiles, pharmaceuticals) tend to develop towards this structure with high levels of both export and direct investment.

Government contracts are a clear dominant in some industries. As a result, strategy patterns of firms operating in these industries are not guided by free-market laws, but rather by the specific rules of their industry. In addition, scholars argue that a few large firms characterize very concentrated and regulated industries[176] that are more likely to engage in lobbying and political campaigning activities. This leads to the conclusion that political connectedness is unequally distributed across industries.

In search of integrated approach: the case of Russia

Firms expand abroad for many reasons, but certainly one motivating factor can be institutional pressure or assistance. Although institutional factors are independent from other factors, they can have a great impact.[177] Given the big differences in the paths of institutional and industrial development, even within emerging economies, the frameworks of the three theories (resource-based theory, industrial theory and institutional theory) need to be adjusted to each particular country.

Using the example of Russia, the most internationalized industries are oil & gas, banking and metallurgy. Because of their operational characteristics, the chemical as well as the oil & gas industries traditionally have a very high ratio of export activities. The industries with high levels of state ownership are banks, machinery and transportation. Moreover, the share of state ownership varies significantly from industry to industry.

The banking and machinery industries have the highest number of politicians and SOE representatives on their boards, demonstrating the strategic importance of these industries for the government. The oil & gas industry has a relatively low share of state ownership, but has the highest number of politicians and a relatively high number of other SOE representatives on its boards.

The industries with the highest value of government contracts relative to total company revenue are machinery and construction. Machinery is mostly represented by companies producing military and aerospace equipment, which remain under dominant government control. The construction industry also relies on state largesse, with over 40% of its contracts (by value) from the public sector.

In Russia, dynamic internationalization is mostly by companies with: direct or indirect government ownership; current or former politicians on the board of directors; and personal political connections held by top company shareholders or managers.

Since top managers in Russia have long believed that political clout makes it easier to achieve corporate goals, they apply significant effort in cultivating political connections in order to achieve growth. Clearly, for Russian executives in the concerned industries, political connectedness is a strong intangible asset, all the more so that savvy executives may end up filling powerful ministerial positions at some point in time.

Conclusion

There has long been a debate about the two sides of the managerial brain: the rational side and the emotional side. In parallel fashion, corporate internationalization has both a rational side, and an institutional side. The role of these non-market institutional factors may justify a company's internationalization, especially in the context of emerging markets. No matter whether discussing the activity of multinationals in developed markets or the internationalization of emerging multinationals, in both cases politics can be involved. Institutional determinants play a much higher role than depicted in the 'classical' picture of international strategy of multinationals, which often disregards the emerging market realities.

The role of the home-country government, which can be both encouraging and interfering towards emerging multinationals, must always be taken into account when dealing with outbound internationalization (and especially FDI) from emerging economies. The internationalization strategy of an emerging multinational must not only be judged by its rational components (e.g. capital and technology) but also by the hidden part of the iceberg: the institutional factors (e.g. government pressures, state financial assistance). When the home government is supportive of the internationalization of domestic flagship firms, this sometimes causes international ripples. What are the real goals of this international foray? Is it really for legitimate growth and profit considerations? This, in turn, causes the so-called liability of foreignness, as seen in the acquisition of MOL by Surgutneftegas, which was more specifically a symptom of the "Liability of Russianness." Since the Crimean annexation and the Ukrainian conflict (2014–2016), Russian multinationals have been victims of the "Liability of Russianness," a sharpened disapproval for Russian investments and firms.

The political underpinnings behind some of these problems are not only the poison but also the medicine. With the help of political ties, some emerging multinationals are able to overcome the handicaps of their late arrival on the international scene and reap the benefit of being important to the government.

References

1 Dunning 1979; Chakraborty and Basu 2002.
2 Buckley 2007.
3 Kalotay and Sulstarova 2010.
4 Buckley and Casson 1981.
5 Kolstad and Wiig 2012.
6 Kalotay and Sulstarova 2010.
7 Blonigen 2005.
8 Wei 2000a.
9 Kolstad and Wiig 2012.
10 Fisch 2011.
11 North 1991.
12 Peng 2013.
13 Sun, Xu and Zhou 2011.
14 Lester, Hillman, Zardkoohi and Cannella 2008; Hillman, Zardkoohi and Bierman 1999.
15 Boddewyn and Brewer 1994.
16 Panibratov 2014.
17 Dlabay and Scott 2006.
18 Zutshi and Gibbons 1998.
19 Najid and Rahman 2011.
20 Eng and Mak 2003.
21 Omar and Bakar 2012.
22 Panibratov 2015.
23 Wong and Govindaraju 2012.
24 Hilmersson and Jansson 2012.
25 Dikova, Rao Sahib and van Witteloostuijn 2010.
26 Toyne and Nigh 1998; Lewin, Long and Carroll 1999.
27 Buckley, Clegg, Cross, Liu, Voss and Zheng 2007.
28 Lewis 1955.
29 Marinova, Child and Marinov 2012.
30 Child, Lu and Tsai 2007.
31 Marinova, Child and Marinov 2014.
32 Young, Tsai, Wang, Liu and Ahlstrom 2014.

33 Hoskisson, Wright, Filatotchev and Peng 2013.
34 Gugler and Boie 2008.
35 Peng 2012.
36 Lu, Liu and Wang 2010.
37 Luo, Xue and Han 2010.
38 Yang, Jiang, Kang and Ke 2009.
39 Masiero, Ogasavara, Caseiro and Ferreira 2014.
40 Mattos 2014.
41 Masiero, Ogasavara, Caseiro and Ferreira 2014.
42 Yaprak and Karademir 2011.
43 Grace 2005.
44 Hanson and Teague 2005.
45 Lee 2003.
46 McCarthy and Puffer 2007.
47 Ledeneva 2012.
48 McCarthy, Puffer and Vikhanski 2009.
49 Ledeneva 2012.
50 McCarthy, Puffer and Vikhanski 2009.
51 Chang 2006.
52 Ibid.
53 http://www.gazprom.ru/investors/stock/structure/
54 Poussenkova 2010.
55 Panibratov 2012
56 Khrushcheva 2012.
57 Sauvant, McAllister and Maschek 2010.
58 Skolkovo 2009.
59 Seljom and Rosenberg 2011.
60 Zaheer 1995.
61 Eden and Miller 2004.
62 Denk, Kaufmann and Roesch 2012.
63 Li 1995.
64 Nachum 2010.
65 Zaheer 1995.
66 Chen, Griffith and Hu 2006.
67 Kwon and Hu 2004.
68 Denk, Kaufmann and Roesch 2012.
69 Hymer 1976.
70 Zaheer 1995.
71 Yu and Kim 2010.
72 Mezias 2002; Eden and Miller 2004.
73 Sethi and Guisinger 2002; Gammeltoft et al. 2010.
74 Zaheer and Mosakowski 1997.
75 Eden and Miller 2004.
76 Denk, Kaufmann and Roesch 2012.
77 Gaur, Kumar and Sarathy 2011.
78 Kwon and Hu 2004.
79 Gaur, Kumar and Sarathy 2011.
80 Denk, Kaufmann and Roesch 2012.
81 Gaur, Kumar and Sarathy 2011.
82 Porter 1980.
83 Garg and Delios 2007.
84 Gaur, Kumar and Sarathy 2011.
85 Zaheer 1995.
86 Gaur, Kumar and Sarathy 2011.
87 Ibid.
88 Garg and Delios 2007.
89 Gaur, Kumar and Sarathy 2011.

90 Garg and Delios 2007.
91 Gaur, Kumar and Sarathy 2011.
92 Garg and Delios 2007.
93 Latukha et al. 2011.
94 Elango 2009.
95 Gaur, Kumar and Sarathy 2011.
96 Elango 2009.
97 Panibratov 2015.
98 Dunning 1988.
99 Hymer 1976.
100 Hamel and Prahalad 1990.
101 Buckley and Casson 1998.
102 Davis, Desai and Francis 2000.
103 Xu and Shenkar 2002.
104 Eden and Miller 2004.
105 Rodriguez, Uhlenbruck and Eden 2005.
106 Peng 2003.
107 Chen 2006.
108 Hennart 1988.
109 Castellani and Zanfei 2002.
110 Gaur, Kumar and Sarathy 2011.
111 Eden and Miller 2004.
112 Hitt, Dacin, Levitas, Arregle and Borza 2000.
113 Gaur, Kumar and Sarathy 2011.
114 Luo, Shenkar and Nyaw 2002.
115 Panibratov 2015.
116 Jormanainen, Latukha and Panibratov 2013; Panibratov and Latukha 2013; Panibratov and Latukha 2014b; Panibratov 2015.
117 Panibratov 2015.
118 Panibratov 2015.
119 Meyer and Peng 2005; Luo, Xue and Han 2010; Panibratov 2015.
120 Child and Rodrigues 2005; Luo, Xue and Han 2010.
121 Wang, Hong, Kafouros and Boateng 2012; Xiao, Jeong, Moon, Chung and Chung 2013.
122 Wang, Hong, Kafouros and Boateng 2012.
123 Li, He, Lan and Yiu 2011; Sheng, Zhou and Li 2011.
124 Faccio 2006.
125 Fan, Wong and Zhang 2007.
126 Bertrand et al. 2006.
127 Ferguson and Voth 2008.
128 Boubakri, Cosset and Saffar 2012.
129 Fan, Wong and Zhang 2007; Faccio 2010.
130 Khwaja and Mian 2005; Leuz and Oberholzer–Gee 2006; Claessens, Feijen and Laeven 2008; Boubakri, Cosset and Saffar 2012.
131 Goldman, Rocholl and So 2013.
132 Faccio 2010.
133 Agrawal and Knoeber 2001.
134 Faccio 2006.
135 Francis, Hasan and Sun 2009.
136 Cooper, Gulenand and Ovtchinnikov 2010.
137 Li, He, Lan and Yiu 2011.
138 Goldman, Rocholl and So 2013.
139 Amore and Bennedsen 2013.
140 Agrawal and Knoeber 2001.
141 Wang, Hong, Kafouros and Boateng 2012.
142 Xiao, Jeong, Moon, Chung and Chung 2013.
143 Peng 2003.
144 Yamakawa, Peng and Deeds 2008; Hoskisson, Eden, Lau and Wright 2000.

145 Wang, Hong, Kafouros and Boateng 2012; Xiao, Jeong, Moon, Chung and Chung 2013.
146 Li, He, Lan and Yiu 2011; Sheng, Zhou and Li 2011.
147 Li, He, Lan and Yiu 2011; Sheng, Zhou, and Li 2011.
148 Fan, Huang, Morck and Yeung 2014.
149 Tsang 1998.
150 Peng, Lee and Wang 2005.
151 Li, He, Lan and Yiu 2011.
152 Farjoun 1994.
153 Khurana 2002.
154 Boubakri, Cosset and Saffar 2012.
155 Yang, Lian and Liu 2012.
156 Agrawal and Knoeber 2001.
157 Xiao, Jeong, Moon, Chung and Chung 2013.
158 Kim et al. 2010.
159 Hoskisson et al. 2000.
160 Buckley et al. 2007.
161 Luo, Xue and Han 2010; Yamakawa, Peng and Deeds 2008.
162 Boisot and Meyer 2007.
163 Fan et al. 2007.
164 Li et al. 2011.
165 Fan et al. 2007.
166 Goldman et al. 2013.
167 http://zakupki.gov.ru/epz/main/public/home.html?placeOfSearch=fz223
168 Goldman et al. 2013.
169 Boter and Holmquist 1996.
170 Yang et al. 2009.
171 Delios et al. 2008.
172 Yip 1992.
173 Klevorick, Levin, Nelson and Winter 1995.
174 Salamon and Siegfried 1977.
175 Grant 2010.
176 Salamon and Seigfried 1977.
177 Wang et al. 2012.

12 The irrational side of internationalization

Are emerging multinationals at an advantage vis-à-vis their developed brethren? Is there a competitive advantage to being from a BRIC country?

The debate amongst academics rages on, with some arguing that emerging multinationals are no different, while other researchers point out the continuing labor cost advantage, easier access to government support and capital or better relationships with "brothers in arms" in less-developed countries.

Yet one fact cannot be argued: more and more companies from emerging markets are expanding outside their borders, thus joining the ranks of multinationals. Recently not only oil & gas or metallurgy firms but also banks and high-tech companies from emerging economies have achieved global success and recognition.

Calling intensively on examples from Russian companies to illustrate, this chapter shows how intangible assets and capabilities are assuming increasing importance for emerging multinationals. More specifically, this chapter elaborates on three important themes:

- why differences exist between the internationalization of natural resource–based and technology-oriented companies;
- how these companies develop specific internationalization know-how in the context of their respective absorptive capacities; and
- how emerging multinationals implement organizational and cultural integration in their cross-border acquisitions.

12.1 From oil to chips: moving from natural resources to technology

Multinational companies from developed economies concentrate on advanced technology and marketing skills for their product (or service) differentiation.[1] Part of their competitive advantage derives from the variety of assets, and the integration of operations across borders.[2] Airbus builds its plane components in many European countries, and then flies the bits and pieces to France for assembly. On the other hand, emerging multinationals have relied extensively on mature technologies, originally developed in developed markets. The competitive advantage of these companies appears to stem from the application of "emerging" managerial skills in less-developed country environments.[3] A pecking order of sorts has been established.

FDI flows towards less-developed countries have not always resulted in the long-term growth outcomes expected.[4] Emerging economies face the fundamental problem of having few alternatives to these external injections of capital, knowledge and network resources. It is also questionable whether local firms benefit much from the technological change introduced by foreign investors, although this is usually the case for developed countries.[5] Emerging multinationals in the BRIC area have been able to overcome this gap. How? In the case of natural resource companies (e.g. Russian Gazprom and Lukoil,[6] Brazilian Vale[7]), they have overcome by becoming vertically integrated and absorbing industrial activities either upstream or downstream from the traditional core business.

Although the extractive industries have been the main incubator of emerging multinationals, the surprise is that technology-based firms have also joined the club. This section will explain the differences in the internationalization process and outcomes of these two categories of multinationals. Although the industrial sectors will seem familiar to readers from the previous chapters, the companies are new.

Internationalization of Russian natural resource–based companies

Oil & gas

Lukoil is the largest Russian private oil company. The main activities of the company are the exploration and production of oil & gas, the production of petroleum products and petrochemicals, and the sale of these outputs. Lukoil has around 1.1% of global oil reserves and 2.3% of global production.

Although Lukoil began its international expansion in the mid-1990s with exploration and refinery projects in Azerbaijan, Bulgaria, Egypt, Iraq, Kazakhstan, Romania and Ukraine, the company's most noticeable deals were made in 2000s. Lukoil carried out a range of acquisitions, including in Colombia, Ghana, Iran, Italy, the Ivory Coast, Saudi Arabia, Uzbekistan and Venezuela. Lukoil is not only focused on upstream exploration for new deposits; an important focus of foreign investments is in downstream petrochemicals. The company owns plants in Belarus, Bulgaria, Finland and Ukraine. The majority of the company's retail gas stations are located in more than twenty markets abroad.

Compared to its Russian competitors, Lukoil has a more market-oriented and profit-seeking approach. As a result, its international forays are more motivated by economic and strategic reasons than by geopolitical governmental influence, even though sometimes these factors overlap.

Lukoil has historically been the Russian leader in oil production. Thanks to the bankruptcy of main rival Yukos, Lukoil managed to strengthen its leadership in the domestic market. This enabled the company to start its internationalization some years ago.

Lukoil's core market remains Russia – and to some extent oil-producing CIS countries – despite recent significant investments abroad. Although Lukoil leads in Russia, its significant oil & gas reserves are being depleted. If the company does not manage to identify replacement deposits, for example in new regions such as the Russian Far East, it will have to accelerate its geographic expansion in order to secure new oil patches. Regarding its downstream activities (refining, marketing and distribution), Lukoil is likely to pursue its strategy of inexpensive retail acquisitions, plus franchising, plus strategic partnerships such as its refining joint venture in Sicily.

Unfortunately for Lukoil, its most profitable activities (production and exploration) are the less internationalized, while the less profitable (marketing, refinery) are already highly internationalized. This implies that internationalization in the oil & gas industry does not necessarily introduce higher profit margins.

Electricity supply and power generation

A decade ago, RAO UES (Unified Energy System of Russia) was a power holding monopoly engaged in the generation, dispatching, transmission, and retailing of electricity and heat. RAO UES was engaged in power production via nuclear, hydroelectric and coal power plants. The company primarily operated in Russia and employed about half million people. After its lengthy reorganization at the end of 1990s and in 2000s, the original RAO UES ceased to exist, given birth to several smaller power companies. One of these new firms was Inter RAO UES established in 1997 as a power distributor for foreign markets. Inter RAO UES inherited a considerable portion of the original company's assets, as well as sizeable market share.

In the early 2000s, Inter RAO generated excess capacity, and since electricity can be exported to neighboring countries (via high-tension lines), the company began exporting its electricity from Russia. The company's foreign investments were made in various forms (mostly greenfield and acquisition) in the 2000s. In 2002, RAO Nordic Oy (greenfield investment) was established in Finland, and in the same year Inter RAO Lietuva was set up in Lithuania. In Armenia and Georgia, Inter RAO has distribution and retail companies, and power generation centers in Armenia, Kazakhstan, Georgia, Moldova and Turkey. Its main investment destinations abroad were Armenia, Georgia, Finland, Kazakhstan, Lithuania, Moldova, Tajikistan and Turkey. At the end of the 2000s, Inter RAO's foreign portfolio included over twenty companies, based in fourteen countries. By acquiring foreign assets, the company consolidated its position in the electricity markets in Europe, the South Caucasus, the Far East and Central Asia.

The company's main export destinations in 2015 were Finland, China and Lithuania, accounting for more than 55% of all exports (19.3%, 18.8%, 17% respectively). Electricity was also supplied to Azerbaijan, Georgia, Ukraine, Latvia, Lithuania, Mongolia and Norway.

In 2009, Inter RAO joined a $1 billion investment pool including the government, state-owned VTB bank, and Kuwait's Alghanim & Sons to invest in power production projects in Russia, the CIS, the UAE and Jordan. The consortium was also bidding, in partnership with Rosatom, on a contract for a nuclear power plant in Turkey.

Competition is very strong in the area of energy sales: some distributors work on a regional basis, while others specialize in specific target segments (e.g. corporate vs. industrial vs. residential). Competition is either price-based or service-based (offering more profitable and convenient energy supply conditions).

The privatization of the former electricity state monopoly in 2001 has meant an immense change in Russian mentalities. The success of the reform will hinge on consumer's acceptance of the idea that energy is not a social benefit, but carries a cost, just like bread and vodka. On the supply side, power generation will require pragmatic strategies and healthy competition, as opposed to political intrigues.

Metallurgy

UC Rusal (United Company Russian Aluminium) was formed in March 2007 by the merger of Rusal (Russian Aluminium) with Sual (Siberian-Urals Aluminium Company), along with the alumina assets of Swiss Glencore, but in fact, the company's history began much earlier.

Russian aluminium production started in 1932, when the Volkhov aluminium smelter fired up. During World War II, the Russians dismantled the equipment to protect it from

Nazi invasion and shipped out to the Urals and Western Siberia. In the 1950s, growth continued with new facilities built across the country. By the early 1980s, Russia became the world's second-largest producer of aluminium after the United States.

During the 1990s privatization wave, control of the largest Russian aluminium producers passed to Trans World Group (TWG) of the United Kingdom. The company implemented the so-called Tolling Scheme, whereby it financed imports of raw materials, processing and operating costs, in exchange for which it became the owner of the outputs.

This scheme allowed Russian companies to survive during the recession of the early 1990s. However, soon enough the directors of the Russian aluminium plants understood that the arrangement was beneficial mostly for Western traders who received the bulk of profits. This led to the so-called aluminium wars of the mid-1990s.

As a result, and with the support of the state, the Tolling Scheme was abolished by 2000. Western traders were expelled, and the country's aluminium assets were concentrated under the control of Rusal. Rusal consolidated various production facilities, including Sibal and Millhouse Capital (belonging to oligarchs Oleg Deripaska and Roman Abramovich respectively). Thus, about 70% of the Russian aluminium production was focused within a single company.

The remaining 30% of the aluminium industry was mostly in the hands of Viktor Vekselberg's Sual, established in 1996 by the merger of the stock capital of Irkutsk and Ural aluminium smelters and other smelters.

Consolidation in the Russian metallurgy sector continued, with the 2007 merger of two main rivals in the Russian aluminium sector: market leader Rusal (75% of the market), and Sual (about 25%). In 2006, Sual was among the ten biggest aluminium companies, but its primary specialization was bauxite production (the ore that is refined into the aluminium metal), while Rusal's strategic future was in primary aluminium.

Today, UC Rusal is the world's largest producer of aluminium (7% of world production) and alumina (7%). The company has approximately 61,000 employees. A set of foreign subsidiaries was developed in the early 2000s via acquisitions in Armenia, Guinea, Romania and Ukraine. Later foreign deals included companies in transport machinery (the United Kingdom and Canada) and construction (Austria and Switzerland). Its expansion was interrupted by the financial crisis of 2007/2008, which suspended several deals under consideration.

UC Rusal primarily operates in Russia, the United States, China, Japan and Singapore, although its activities span nineteen countries, including Australia, Guyana, Mongolia, Nigeria, Sweden, Jamaica, and more. One of the priority destinations for the company is Guinea, where the company operates three production facilities, acquired from 2001 to 2006. Key customers are in the automotive, construction and packaging industries.

In addition to its aluminium and alumina divisions, UC Rusal also operates bauxite and nepheline ore mines, cathode for production of alloys, mills to produce metal foils (thin sheets), production of packaging materials and power plants (for its industrial facilities). The operations are divided into six business divisions: aluminium, alumina, packaging, raw materials, energy and engineering and construction.

The company typically relies on M&A transactions for its foreign expansion, with the caveat that it avoids hostile deals, trying to strike win-win compromises with its partners instead. The company also uses licensing deals, such as the case of Compagnie des Bauxites de Kindia in Guinea. Naturally, export is a key international business mode for UC Rusal, accounting for some 80% of company revenues.[8]

Internationalization of Russian technology-oriented companies

Banking

The VTB Group has developed over the past two decades into a universal financial and banking institution with a leading position in Russia and an expanding presence in the CIS, Western Europe, Africa and Asia through organic growth and a series of strategic acquisitions.

VTB holds a secure second place in the Russia banking sector in terms of assets, capital, funding base, corporate and retail lending, with authorized capital of RUB 104.6 billion (around $3.6 billion). As of 2014, VTB's equity reached RUB 1,131 billion, and its assets are RUB 12,191 billion (around $600 billion). According to 2012 results, VTB was ranked ninety-two among the top worldwide banks (by asset size), and 210 in the ranking of the 500 largest companies in Europe in 2014, as well as 127 in the FT Emerging 500. The bulk of VTB's loan portfolio is to the construction, metallurgy, machine building and trading sectors, as well as the vast oil & gas and energy complex.

In Russia, VTB operates two subsidiary banks and a number of financial companies (VTB Leasing, VTB Insurance, VTB Capital, etc.). Abroad, the company has subsidiary banks in Ukraine, Armenia, Georgia, Belarus and Azerbaijan, as well as six banks in Western Europe (Great Britain, France, Austria, Germany, Cyprus and Switzerland), a subsidiary bank in Angola and a financial company in Namibia. The company also has representative offices in Italy, Kazakhstan, the Kyrgyz Republic and China, and operates a subsidiary in Singapore via VTB Capital plc (United Kingdom).

Being a state-owned bank, VTB acquired some of its foreign banking assets with the help of the Russian government. For example, 85% of Donau-Bank in Vienna, originally controlled by the Central Bank of Russia, were transferred to VTB bank. In order to expand its foreign banking network, VTB was allowed to establish Russian Commercial Bank in both Zurich (Switzerland) and Limassol (Cyprus).

Later on, VTB became a shareholder of East-West United Bank (Luxembourg) and Ost-West Handelsbank (Frankfurt), and increased its participation in Donau-Bank (Vienna). Since VTB's acquisitions of European banks can facilitate FDI inflows into Russia, there was government support for the company's European expansion. At the same time, VTB continues to consolidate its Western Europe subsidiaries.

VTB also holds the distinction of being the first Russian bank to obtain banking licenses for India and China, and to open branches there. Aside from taking an active part in developing trade and economic relations between Russia and China, VTB started servicing bank cards of UnionPay, the Chinese national payments processor.

Telecoms

VimpelCom is the Russian leader in mobile telecoms, with over a quarter of the national subscriber market. VimpelCom Group provides voice and data services through a range of mobile, fixed and broadband technologies, using Beeline as its brand name.

One of the company's first international acquisitions was in 1998, when it acquired a 30% stake in Norwegian Telenor. Yet VimpelCom did not neglect its CIS neighbors, where mobile coverage was still at a relatively low level, offering opportunities for profitable future expansion. Flush with cash from its Russian business, VimpelCom accelerated its international growth in the 2000s, entering Armenia, Cambodia, Georgia, Kazakhstan,

Tajikistan, Ukraine, Uzbekistan, and Vietnam. Acquisitions always played the most important entry mode for the company in foreign markets.

After Norway, in 2004, the company acquired the Kazakhstan mobile operator Kar-Tel.
By the end of the 2000s, the company turned its attention further east, towards Asia where
it strived to buy and to build mobile networks (greenfield). In 2008, it established a joint
venture with GTEL-Mobile in Vietnam, in which it held a 40% stake, and then acquired
a 90% stake in Cambodia's Sotelco.

With Russian market penetration already at 136% (i.e. quite saturated), and dim prospects for ARPU (average revenue per user, telecoms KPI) growth, the company's strategic
planners examined Cambodia and Vietnam (total population of 100 million people and
only 55% penetration rate) with envy.

What does the future hold? Saturation levels in mobile telecoms are being reached in the
CIS countries where competition has increased, so domestic fixed-line and broadband markets might be the key to future growth. For countries with low population densities, the next
generation of mobile services including high-speed mobile broadband might be the solution.

Internet

Kaspersky Lab is a Russian computer software security company, founded in 1997 in
Moscow. The company is market leader in anti-virus software. Kaspersky Lab offers anti-
spyware, anti-spam, and anti-intrusion products. Its most famous and most important
product is Kaspersky Anti-Virus, which is well praised within the industry and by thankful customers. The product has won several awards over the years and has been ranked top
anti-virus software multiple times.

By the mid-2000s, Kaspersky Lab had grown into an international company, employing over 1,500 computer specialists. The company is present all around the globe, in more
than 100 countries. Headquarters are in Moscow and the company has regional offices in
Europe (Netherlands, Germany, France, United Kingdom, Poland, Romania, Sweden), Asia
(Japan, China, South Korea) and the United States.

Software companies grow primarily through operational performance improvements
and technological innovations. While the majority of software companies grow via transactions (mergers and acquisitions), Kaspersky has followed a path of organic development.
This has not limited its geographic ambitions: its strategy focus remains on new enter-
prise-oriented solutions, projects for regional expansion, and increased partnerships. Since
the web is worldwide, companies operating in this area automatically enjoy a worldwide
vitrine. For its global presence, Kaspersky established relationships with foreign distributors, starting its international expansion via export (back in the days when software was
sold on diskettes and not downloaded online).

One of the company's first international steps was in the U.S. market, where it engaged
in partnerships. In 2001, Kaspersky Lab announced its partnership with Itamigo, a developer of Internet security services. This enabled the company to introduce its anti-virus
products to American customers. Partnerships offer the advantage of low costs and shared
risks, important traits for a young company, not yet fully established in the market and
having limited capital.

Also in 2001, Kaspersky Lab entered the European market. The company first used
local retail and distribution networks in order to supply the European market, and then
proceeded to open regional offices. For emerging markets, the company waited until
2003, when it inaugurated its regional office in Beijing. This was the beginning of its

exploration of emerging and less-developed markets. After Asia, the company set foot in the African markets.

Kaspersky Lab has established multiple strategic partnerships with top players in the software industry. Among its strategic partners are Microsoft, Intel, IBM, Novell, Check Point and Linux Solutions.

High-tech

Established in 2002, Sitronics is one of the largest Russian players in the high-tech industry. Initially set up as a scientific center, Sitronics specializes in both hardware (microelectronics and telecoms equipment), and software. In 2004, the company established a business unit providing IT services. The company acquired stakes in several companies, among which Kvazar-Mirco, the largest IT company in Ukraine. Sitronics now claims to be the largest high-tech company in Eastern Europe.

The company's rapid success comes from public sector business. Sitronics is a key partner for governmental bodies in the field of infrastructural transformations, both in Russia and the CIS countries. Sitronics succeeded in implementing strategy of public-private partnership, taking part in scientific research supported by the governments.

The company has subsidiaries in over 30 countries and employs over 10,000 people. Sitronics was ranked as a top-three Russian IT company. Major national competitors are Luxoft, Argussoft and BCC. International competitors include Microsoft, IBM and SAP.

With over 3,500 clients around the globe, the company exports to over 60 countries worldwide. Hardware manufacturing is carried out in facilities located in Russia, Greece, the Czech Republic, Romania and China. The major Sitronics plants are located in Prague and Athens (telecoms solutions), in Kiev (IT) and in Zelenograd and Moscow (microelectronics). Key customers are both local companies (e.g. MTS, Comstar-UTS and MTT), and international firms (e.g. OTE, Cosmote, Vodafone, Ericsson, Arcelor Mittal and TCL).

In the telecoms field, Sitronics participates in a range of joint projects with well-known international companies: for example Ericsson for 3G network designs, and Cisco Systems for network solutions for fixed and mobile communications.

The company's expansion strategy is based on strong partnerships with key global and regional players. Sitronics has developed strategic alliances with Cisco Systems, STMicroelectronics, Infineon and Giesecke & Devrient in relation to several important products and services. Sitronics maintains vendor relationships with Siemens, Ericsson, Motorola, Oracle, Intel, Sun Microsystems and Microsoft.

To enter attractive new markets, Sitronics uses strategic partnerships and joint venture as entry modes, enjoying the benefits of existing business networks and lower risks. It does not need to re-invent the wheel each time. One recent strategic partnership was signed with Nokia Siemens Networks, a global provider of communications services, in which Sitronics Microelectronics becomes the official global supplier of analogue power management electronic components for NSN.

Technology versus resources: why such differences in internationalization?

International diversification has advantages, and Russian companies, like their Western predecessors, realize what these benefits are. One important advantage is to provide Russian multinationals with the capabilities to match the moves of their foreign competitors. Given the Russian endogenous advantages – domestic economic growth, large human potential and closer ties with global economy – the trend of Russian business expanding abroad is bound to continue.

The differing features of the expansion of Russian multinationals are synthesized below. By examining entry modes, expansion strategies and government roles, the discrepancies between the two industrial categories (resource based vs. technology focused) can be determined.

Oil & gas companies

Foreign destinations

Mainly CIS, the Baltic States, Europe and the United States. Rarely countries of Africa, Asia, Latin America and some Arab countries

Entry modes

Exporting, turnkey projects, IJVs and wholly owned subsidiaries. Acquisitions in trading business

Expansion strategy

Market-oriented and profit-seeking approach. Greenfield projects with EU partners. Acquisition of companies in profitable downstream segments

Role of state

Generally high state involvement, varying depending on the companies' historical and political roots

Electricity firms

Foreign destinations

Mainly CIS countries. Also Northern Europe and the Baltic states. Other destinations are less attractive

Entry modes

Export, acquisitions, greenfield

Expansion strategy

Acquisition of foreign assets, the consolidation of the position in the electric power markets in foreign markets

Role of state

Very high. State support provided for large contracts and projects

Steel companies

Foreign destinations

The United States, Australia, the United Kingdom, China, Japan and Singapore, countries of Europe, CIS, and Africa. Highly diversified presence over the world

Entry modes

Acquisitions with few exceptions (such as licensing or greenfield)

Expansion strategy

Aggressive acquisitions of low performing enterprises in the strategic countries of CIS, Europe and North America

Role of state

Varies according to government relations with owners and CEOs

Banks

Foreign destinations

Mainly CIS, but also selected countries of Western Europe, the United Kingdom and the United States. Slow interest to the countries of Africa, to China, and Singapore

Entry modes

First representative offices, then subsidiaries via control of foreign companies

Expansion strategy

Expansion through organic growth and strategic acquisitions. Mostly active in active trading partner countries with Russia

Role of state

High supported for state-owned banks; relatively low otherwise

Telecoms

Foreign destinations

CIS countries, Eastern Europe, Middle East, South-East Africa and Asia (with the focus on India)

Entry modes

Acquisition of market leaders and strategic partnerships, international JVs and licensing in rare cases

Expansion strategy

"Follow the customer" strategy: expansion to CIS countries and even further to Asia and Europe, in various forms. Manufacturing in cheap labor areas

Role of state

Close government attention, with varying extent of interference. Support for expansion to CIS countries

High-tech firms

Foreign destinations

Europe and Asia in anti-virus and PC solutions, CIS for search engine platforms

Entry modes

Exporting, strategic partnerships with software industry and "virtual" entry

Expansion strategy

Opening regional offices in European countries and CIS

Role of state

Sector more independent of state intervention than other industries

(List adapted from A. Panibratov and M. Latukha, 2014. Foreign expansion of Russian firms based on natural resources and technology, in M. Marinov and S. Marinova (eds.), *Successes and Challenges of Emerging Economy Multinationals*. Palgrave Macmillan: New York: 128–57.)

The earlier classification points to some clear conclusions.

In electricity, mining, and oil & gas (resource-based sectors), the competitive advantages of the internationally active multinationals are based on:

*   the domestic monopoly position of these firms; and
*   the prevention of domestic competition and protection of the foreign operation through political tools. Government representatives often participate in the boards of these companies, which provide these firms with direct 'contact' with the state.

Both these factors render this group of firms too lazy to seek real (radical) innovations, given their confidence in their protected, strong position over time.

In the technology-intensive banking, IT and telecoms sectors, competitive advantages are based on the attempt to develop (or rather initiate self-development) of firms in these sectors, and the limited government support (financial or technological) where possible. The government factually guarantees non-intervention domestically and the relatively free market at home. Since these firms demonstrate the most obvious international results, moving abroad of their own free will, the state does not prevent their expansion, since their global integration is in line with state policy, yet does not provide significant support. These firms therefore must be active in technology development and acquisition, in marketing and branding innovations, which grounds their true multinational status.

12.2 Developing absorptive capacity

The ability to create and transfer knowledge internally is one of the most significant advantages of companies, defining what academics call a 'differentiated network':[9] knowledge is created in different parts of the company, yet travels to any interrelated unit. The right hand learns from the left, so to speak, and this ability is called absorptive capacity.

Within knowledge transfer studies, it has been suggested that the absorptive capacity of a particular company unit (division, department, subsidiary, etc.) is the most important parameter in understanding the knowledge transfer architecture within the company.[10] Alas, absorptive capacity levels are not born equal within companies, especially large multinationals. Thus different units have different levels of internal knowledge transfer. Can organizations enhance their abilities to create and absorb? Most researchers believe so, saying that these processes are endogenous (i.e. internally developed) to the company.[11] What's more, organizational learning closely correlates to human resources management,[12] implying that investments in staff training and development can enhance awareness and knowledge, and also absorptive capacity.

Both companies and nations have absorptive capacities

In 1989 Cohen and Levinthal defined absorptive capacity as "the fraction of knowledge in the public domain that a firm is able to assimilate and exploit."[13] This suggests a link between external technological opportunities and a company's capabilities to adapt them to develop new products. Hence, absorptive capacity determines a firm's ability to exploit external knowledge in order to improve its technological knowledge, an intangible but important asset.

Another important theoretical consideration is that absorptive capacity (AC) ceases to exist when a firm reaches its technological frontier.[14] In other words, this concept measures only the knowledge, which is currently available to be privatized. When a firm expands abroad, the limits of its knowledge are more significant. It can be difficult to renew and update knowledge when in a unknown environment, and assess uneven or unreliable information sources. Furthermore, available knowledge is harder to assimilate while doing business abroad, meaning that companies can only increase their absorptive capacities by investing in R&D.

In such cases, international knowledge transfer and national technological capabilities, as well as human capital development, became keys for successful international strategy (which in reality refers to the Location advantage). That is why absorptive capacity is also determined by technological capabilities. For international firms, creating new knowledge is possible by investing in it, allowing to search for the most attractive and useful technology and its acquisition in order to be adapt to the foreign technological environment.

National absorptive capacity (NAC) is more related to the international knowledge transfer and national technological capabilities, as well as overall human capital development (e.g. educational levels of the population). Technological capabilities are not only the ability to search and select the best suited technologies among the available ones, but also the ability to create of technologies and knowledge through targeted R&D expenditures.

NAC consists of the possibilities to create new knowledge through proper investment, and the opportunity to search for the most opportune technologies, and then select those to be assimilated in the national market. NAC is a complex variable to define, since there are numerous, combinatory and multiplier effects to be taken in consideration at the national level. Once this is done, the impact of NAC on economic efficiency and growth as well as employment, can be understood.

Across all industries, countries follow the principle of technological accumulation. Lagging economic units (companies or macro institutions) must have the ability to absorb and assimilate knowledge that is potentially open to them. If agencies and organizations are missing, and market mechanisms for knowledge acquisition are underdeveloped, multinationals will not be able to absorb and effectively assimilate knowledge.

There are two groups that we consider economic actors. The first group consists of private and public companies, which are involved in innovative activity. The second group includes non-firms, which, however, do impact the knowledge infrastructure significantly. The knowledge infrastructure is defined as "generic, multi-user and indivisible"[15] and consists of public research institutes, universities, organizations for standards, intellectual property protection, etc. This is the infrastructure which enables and promotes science and technological development.

Absorptive capacity has a crucial importance for development because it allows domestic economic players to internalize knowledge found elsewhere (either in the national economy or abroad). This capture of knowledge from international markets can be either in a direct manner (e.g. by purchasing know-how) or in an indirect manner (e.g. by getting closer to customers).

Technology flows occur in several ways.[16] One of them is by arms-length relations, for instance through licensing or trading processes, through plant and equipment acquisitions or purchasing of products or services. Technology flows may also occur within hierarchies, for example between affiliates and branches within a multinational, or as consequences of FDI. Spillovers from FDI are also considered to be one of the most practical and efficient ways of technological exchange, which promote the industrial development and upgrading.[17] Many past studies cover this particular topic, but few studies concern the more controversial aspect of how nations can improve their NAC by transferring knowledge from foreign companies.

When can spillovers be fruitful? Obviously the first condition is that they must be able to occur. Less evidently, they must happen in receptive territory: the absorptive capacity must be sufficient to enable true knowledge transfer. If the host-entity is "too dumb," then the spillover will never happen. In the case of national economies with low NACs, technological assets might be obtained (either through licensing or through spillovers from inward FDI indirectly), yet the capability to use and adopt these assets and knowledge may not exist, alas. FDI bears a positive impact on the development of the host economy only in those emerging and developed countries that have reached a particular level in the sphere of NAC.[18] The knowledge accumulation process is faster and more effective after an initial threshold of NAC has been acquired. Thankfully, due to economic progress, countries "learn to learn": NAC evolves exponentially, having direct implications on spillover familiarization.[19]

As a country's economy approaches its technological frontier, the cost of absorbing foreign competitive advantage increases, which implies that the quantity of technologies potentially available for imitation decreases. The returns on marginal increases in technology are dropping as the technological gap diminishes.[20] The frontier is defined as the set of all production methods that are the most efficient in the world at one particular point of time. This holds not only for the production technology but also for organizational and other administrative resources that contribute to the efficiency of the production and products realization processes.

Hence, the technological flows are not enough for development without the presence of domestic actors that contribute to industrial development. As mentioned previously, the sine qua none condition for knowledge transfer is that the host country possess the required level of NAC.

Absorptive capacity and knowledge transfer

Absorptive capacity is defined as the ability of a company to acquire new knowledge, to recognize its value, and then to assimilate this new knowledge, and apply it to commercial ends. To illustrate this abstract concept, think of a company as a sponge, that absorbs water (knowledge) to transform this into new matter (for example competitive advantage).

A transfer thus occurs between two main parties: a "sender" and a "receiver." Both parties play an important role in making the knowledge transfer successful. However, the burden of a successful transfer lies with the receiver – namely, its absorptive capacity (AC). Why this term? Because, like a sponge, a good knowledge receiver must absorb contents and then transform it for growth, just like a sponge in the ocean absorbs water and nutrients to grow. A good receiving party will be absorptive enough "to absorb inputs in order to generate outputs."[21]

The core point is not the underlying knowledge transfer process, but the degree to which the receivers acquire potentially useful knowledge and use this knowledge in their own operations.[22] In fact, companies are bombarded daily with information and knowledge from various senders, but only a company with the right AC will identify and recognize the valuable inputs, and then make productive use of them.[23]

To a certain degree, a company's AC depends on its prior knowledge of its operational areas,[24] and this helps the company look out for useful knowledge transfer opportunities. Learning from foreign markets is one very fertile area for useful knowledge transfers. On an individual basis, sponginess is helped by related educational backgrounds and expertise. For example, banking security experts from different countries (e.g. Russia and the United States) will be able to learn more from each other than say, a textile sourcing manager and a telecoms systems engineer. But once again, it is the AC of the receiving side that will establish how profitable a knowledge transfer is. To use a gardening analogy, no matter how good your seed, if the soil is not fertile, it will not grow.

What is the relevance to international business, you may be wondering? Well, absorptive capacity, or sponginess, has been determined to be the most important determinant of successful knowledge transfer within multinationals.[25] AC determines how well a company can innovate, and thus how well it can either protect its existing competitive advantages, or develop new ones (before its competitors do). A business unit with high AC is generally more capable to acquire and apply new knowledge in order to improve its performance.

Knowledge transfer can be decomposed into two stages. Stage one covers outbound knowledge flows, in other words the sender's half of the transfer. Which factors facilitate or prohibit knowledge transfer? Cross-industry network ties and employment changes have been ascertained as two important factors that facilitate the diffusion of knowledge. The stronger the network ties, the greater the willingness to share knowledge, and additional channels are available for knowledge sharing. This explains why professional conferences and exhibits are important knowledge transfer opportunities. On the other hand, fear of competition is an obstacle to knowledge transfer. Lips become sealed when fear of losing a competitive advantage arises. The recipe for Coca-Cola stills lies in a secret vault!

The second stage of knowledge transfer concerns the receiving side. What factors facilitate the inbound flow of knowledge? When the knowledge is shared, it depends on the receiving industry, how well it is possessed to exploit the knowledge. AC is important in terms of how well the "receiving" parts absorb, adapt and exploit the available knowledge. What makes for a good knowledge receiver? A company that keeps its eyes, ears and nose open, that communicates internally about market developments, that operates its own business intelligence antennae, all these are just a few practical examples.

Industrial cluster development is also highly useful for absorptive capacities. Clusters clarify how well knowledge is exploited within an industry. Since knowledge, especially experiential knowledge, often is transferred between individuals, it is essential for companies in the same industry to be capable of sharing, in order to obtain full advantage. The broader the particular cluster, the better knowledge and information will float between the industrial participants.

In practice, absorptive capacity is well seen at the inter-firm cooperation level. Strategic alliances and joint ventures, when two or more parties collaborate are not only mutual investments but also illustrate knowledge exchange. Otherwise, firms would simply borrow money and hire subcontractors to explore large-scaled or difficult projects, instead of inviting other firms to collaborate.

Knowledge transfer in cross-cultural alliances

When expanding internationally, a company finds itself bombarded by knowledge transfers, both on the sending and on the receiving ends. The company must understand the market it is entering, and therefore be absorptive on the receiving end.[26] Yet the company also needs to exert leadership in order to establish its operations, whether by greenfield investment, or by transaction; so the company must also be a knowledge sender.

Cross-cultural issues are inherent to internationalization, since the international alliances formed by partners from different countries, coalesce parties often possessing different historical customs, political norms, and cultural backgrounds. These differences may lead to considerable diversity in firm-specific characteristics, which in turn could engender cultural misunderstandings.[27] Cultural differences (for instance: national and organizational culture) impact a series of issues in alliance set up, from negotiations on setting, to first performance and further survival.

The process of knowledge transfer within alliances is a subject to cultural deflection.[28] For example, international joint ventures typically transfer knowledge by sharing of technology and know-how, by interaction between operating divisions of the partner companies, and by rotations and transfers of key personnel.[29] The success of the JV depends on these transfers, yet they can be affected by national cultural differences. International alliances can see their potential either diminished or even sabotaged completely by cultural differences that hinder the partner's ability to work together.[30] Although companies hailing from multicultural home countries may have a natural disposition for easier knowledge transfer, the transfer will require more management effort in monocultural countries.

India is attractive for many EMFs in contrast to, say Brazil, not necessarily because it has better market prospects, but because it is easier to network with Indian counterparts. Russian high-tech firms in different emerging economies (e.g. KGK in Brasil[31] and MTS in India[32]) show that better integration occurs in multicultural India, allowing MTS to extend its brand outside the CIS in 2008 through an agreement with Shyam Telelink. In monocultural Brasil, KGK felt less comfortable with establishing an office and managing a team mixing Russians and Brazilians.

International collaborations between mixed partners (i.e. from developed and developing economies) are usually very troublesome.[33] These "north-south" cultural differences may cause delays in the distillation of an effective and cohesive managing group. Only when managers can interpret one another's assessments correctly (e.g. sales team forecasts, delivery commitments of production managers, the budget or forecast estimates from financial controllers), has the alliance truly morphed into a cohesive unit. At this stage, every single cog in the alliance machinery is working towards a common objective.[34]

Organizational cultures may also act as obstacles when companies with diverse cultures merge or decide to form a third-party venture.[35] The managers and staff from the initiating firms tend to bring cultural luggage with them. Their company values may prove useful, but then again they may have to be discarded, which might not be so easy. The ironing-out of cultural wrinkles may not cause poor corporate performance, but it can lead to various tensions or frustrations in routine business operations.

Research has identified three different levels of knowledge transfer within partnerships: technical, systemic and strategic levels.[36] Knowledge transfer at the strategic level is a core challenge, which is greatly affected by cultural and personality factors. After all, in the end, strategy is decided by the company head, and most companies cannot function with two heads, if they disagree on strategy. China's shift from state-owned enterprises to private capitalism offers a telling example. During the SOE period, strategy was supervised and directed by governmental apparatchiks, and hence strategic decisions were not made at company level. Since the 1978 economic reforms, Chinese managers underwent "brain liberation" (the contrary of brainwashing), changed their ways of thinking and confronted the competitive nature of doing business with foreign companies. Proof of the absorptive capacities of Chinese managers was that they moved quickly from simple exporters taking advantage of low labor costs, to creators of world-class emerging multinationals, and not just in simpler natural resource–based sectors.[37]

Awareness of possible obstacles to knowledge transfer is critical. A healthy and productive alliance depends on good sponginess on both sides: senior managers from both international partners must communicate intensely and cooperate with their counterparts. The evolution and transformation of organizational cultures appears to be a slow process, even though the forces of free-market westernization are relentlessly at work to create one global homogenized business culture.[38]

To sum up, cross-cultural distance has a direct impact on knowledge transfer. Aspects of cultural similarity, collective or individualistic management approaches, and the relative attitudes of managers in the cross-border alliance are all relevant in making the mayonnaise succeed. Knowledge acquisition and knowledge development are undeniably affected by cultural differences. Why is this important? Because effective cross-cultural knowledge transfer is a source of competitive advantage, since this mutual learning makes the alliance stronger than the sum of its parts. If our readers should retain one message, it is that cultural differences have to be appreciated upfront, so that knowledge transfer processes can occur. Without those transfers, cross-borders deals are doomed.[39]

Some researchers argue that knowledge transfer also depends on NAC: how good is a country at making its companies absorptive? Some studies show that firms in some countries are better at discovering and exploiting knowledge spillovers caused by inward investments. NAC is sometimes considered as an essential prerequisite for the process of knowledge transfer between parties. If a host country has a high NAC level, then that can be a preliminary indicator of potential success for knowledge transfer from inbound FDI.

Ilim Timber case

The case study on Ilim Timber illustrates the process of knowledge transfer among companies, but also indirectly, among nations. By its expansion from Russia, its headquarters, to Germany and then the United States, the company demonstrates its sponginess in absorbing best practices and technology from both host countries. The miracle with Ilim Timber is that there is also reverse absorption, with the host-country subsidiaries absorbing knowledge from the mother company.

Ilim Timber is currently the best Russian performer in its industry (timber production and transformation into various downstream products such as pulp, paper, plywood, boards, etc.), and one of the European leaders in terms of production volumes, revenues and international coverage. What's more, Ilim Timber was recently involved in acquisition deals. Since the integration of the foreign acquisitions can be assessed as productive, this allows us to verify alignment with knowledge transfer theory. The case explains which core actions that were undertaken by Ilim Timber establish a smooth and efficient knowledge transfer infrastructure.

Company background

Ilim Pulp was established in 1992, resulting from the consolidation of various Russian assets in pulp and paper production, timber harvesting, wood transformation and packaging materials. After fifteen years of development, the company grew into Russia's largest vertically integrated forest industry company with annual sales over $1.5 billion.

In 2007, the group underwent a radical restructuring, in part to accommodate a new joint venture with International Paper, one of the largest pulp and paper producers in the world. Ilim Pulp split into two parts. One part (pulp and paper, timber harvesting and support holdings) went into Ilim Group, the JV with International Paper. The remaining part became Ilim Timber (including timber, plywood and panel production facilities in Eastern Siberia and northwest Russia), which became the holding group.

In 2008, Ilim Timber started its export activities, choosing China as its first international market. The company opened an office in Beijing. Soon thereafter, a wave of foreign acquisitions started. In 2010, Ilim Timber acquired two large wood processing facilities in Germany from Klausner Group,[40] making Ilim Timber one of top ten privately held wood processing companies globally. Then, in 2011, Ilim Timber acquired Tolleson Lumber, an American company.[41] Business was booming in China, with Ilim Timber becoming Russia's major timber exporter, so a second office in Shanghai was opened.

Currently the company's production facilities are located in Russia, Germany and United States. Ilim Timber's products are sold in Russia, Europe, the Middle East, North Africa and Asia. The total annual production output of the company amounts to 3.9 million m³ of sawn timber and 200,000 m³ of plywood.

The company employs about four thousand people, and has its headquarters in St. Petersburg.

International acquisitions

In 2010, Ilim Timber signed an agreement for the acquisition of two sawmills in Germany from the Klausner Group: Klausner Holz Bayern (Bavaria) and Klausner Nordic Timber (Mecklenburg-Vorpommern). Annual production capacities were 0.8 and 1.1 million m³ of sawn wood, respectively. The deal also included the acquisition of Linck sawmill equipment with additional capacity of 0.6 million m³ per year.

Ilim Timber restored business in Germany to its full capacity. The unused Linck equipment was dispatched to a facility in Eastern Siberia (Irkutsk region) before the end of

2011. The acquisition of this first-class asset qualitatively strengthened Ilim Timber's presence in Europe, and the new equipment in Eastern Siberia could help deliver product into the Chinese market. The company's total production capacity reached a level of about 2,650 million m³ of sawn timber and 220,000 m³ of plywood.[42]

In 2011, Ilim Timber agreed to acquire the U.S. sawn goods producer Tolleson Lumber Company, based in Georgia, in partnership with company management. Ilim Timber supported Tolleson's expansion strategy, meaning further acquisitions in the United States, thus setting Ilim up to become a global leader with presence in key markets in Asia, Europe and America. The two additional Tolleson sawmills increased Ilim Timber's overall production capacity to 3.9 million m³ of timber per year, and broadened the range of products to include American yellow pine. Ilim was now one of the top ten producers of lumber worldwide.

The partnership with Tolleson's management, headed by CEO Rusty Wood, helped strengthen Ilim's international management team. The management of Tolleson was commendable, as it weathered the major American industrial downturn without incurring losses.

Effect of acquisitions on knowledge transfer

The benefits that Ilim Tiber achieved from its foreign acquisitions can be synthesized as being sixfold:

- First, access to new markets and their national customer bases.
- Second, access to existing foreign supply chains and sales networks – namely, the notable access to customers from third nations.
- Third, opportunities for internal production capacity swaps, and the correlated possibility to diversify or re-assign production destinations.
- Fourth, establishment of new quality-control standards, and the avoidance of further formalities, which enables price reductions.
- Fifth, access to new technologies and services, meaning that existing capacity can be maintained at relatively low costs, as compared to acquiring new facilities or equipment.
- Sixth, the "acquisition" of human talent, in alignment with the investment objectives, with the ability to easily transfer technical or managerial knowledge from one subsidiary to another.

One of the most valuable (intangible) assets from Ilim's German and American acquisitions was the access to domestic customers in the host-country economies. Both these markets possess the highest amounts of timber customers in the world. This was particularly important in the American market, which is very autonomous for timber, with very few imports from outside (and also few exports). Furthermore, the domestic timber prices in Europe and the United States are higher than in Russia, meaning good margins, and also potential for low-cost Russian timber exports.

In the process of discovering the host-country markets, knowledge transfer plays a significant role. The key success factors are the creation of the inbound infrastructure, mainly achieved by rejigging the organizational structure, and eliminating cultural barriers. For Ilim Timber, these processes started shortly after the German Klausner Group acquisition in 2010. Top managers were selected, and then offered free language courses and cultural integration classes. Klausner managers had been using English for their international business dealings, but poor English mastery on the Russian side was a barrier to communication, and therefore to integration. Ilim decided to tackle the bull by the horns, offering a special internal program to learn German, even going so far as to offer promotions to germanophone staff.

The 2011 American acquisition confronted a similar situation, but the focus was primarily on language education. Moreover, the U.S. timber products remained under the Tolleson name, given the lack of awareness for the Ilim brand in the U.S. market. Changes in management structure accompanied the post-acquisition period, since further knowledge integration could not be achieved without the centralization of processes. That also led to shifts within the structure.

Although it might seem strange, financial management was consolidated in Russia. Hence the financial accounting (RAS, American Generally Accepted Accounting Principles, German GAAP) was mostly shifted to Russian standards to the extent possible. The structure of management is as follows: German and U.S. affiliates are united into two independent business units, both with headquarters in St. Petersburg, all of them reporting directly to the CEO.

The first step for knowledge transfer between the foreign subsidiaries was to create standard reports covering core business operations: for example, logistics, finance, accounting, and the development of communication channels between similar departments. Adapting and translating documents and reports to the different national and cultural standards was a top core priority. The contribution of knowledge sharing here was obvious: gaining sales and market share in new markets. Another important task: identifying or acquiring new human resources in alignment with the production facilities, and to help manage the new facilities, additional HQs personnel for coordination. Stricter selection criteria were enforced, and some managers from foreign business units were posted in Russia (and vice-versa).

The knowledge on existing supply chains in the market and access to sales market located abroad was another important achievement for Ilim Timber.

Since both in Germany and the United States, export volumes exceeded imports, this allowed Ilim Timber to exploit the existing export structures and networks that had been established. Moreover, that enabled an enlargement of the group's product palette, so that some markets gained access to new goods. One obvious example is Ilim Timber's supply to the Chinese market, which was serviced from Irkutsk, thanks to the unwanted Linck machinery from the Klausner deal.

Access to technology also deserves special attention. Since the United States and EU markets have strong existing technology, by entering these host countries, Ilim Timber obtained access to new production technologies and closer links to equipment manufacturers. Another side effect was reduction in maintenance expenses, since almost all of the manufacturers of timber and wood processing equipment are located in the same areas (e.g. German firms Holzma, IMA, Kraft, Raute of Finland, and others). Given the limited number of Russian timber firms operating in foreign markets, this may develop as a competitive advantage for Ilim Timber.

In this case, the knowledge identification process appears to be more complicated and more time-consuming. During the acquisition processes, no radical replacement of existing facilities took place, but significant amounts were spent on maintenance and technical upgrades. As a result, Ilim Timber had access to many European equipment manufacturers, which enabled some lower-cost equipment swaps between plants.

With a portfolio of three countries and many different productive facilities (and therefore quite a selection of machinery for different purposes), Ilim Timber decided in 2013 to establish a New Investment Department (NID). Its purpose was to analyze and enhance operational efficiency via better industrial engineering and productivity improvements. NID was set up as an independent branch in the organizational structure, reporting directly to the CEO. Opportunities for equipment swaps were considered by NID. This new department, with its mission to accelerate relations between business units, in particular for high capex equipment purchases that has important bottom line impacts, was a giant step to increase Ilim's absorptive capabilities.

A final benefit from its foreign investments was Ilim Timber's ability to reduce or even avoid formalities and expenses that greenfield entrants would face – namely, licensing and quality-control formalities. Most sawn wood products are distributed abroad through an existing distribution network of sales agents, who have to provide customers with information on product features and reliability. Ilim Timber had the ability to supply quantities of cheap Russian round wood, using its suppliers-contractors in forested areas, and then providing these raw materials to its European affiliate.

The extent of knowledge transfer within Ilim Timber was impressive: differences in local legislations and staff treatment were abolished or reduced; operational principles were standardized (e.g. in relations with suppliers and customers, in reporting and accounting principles). During its acquisitions, Ilim Timber hired consulting companies, which also provided a source of knowledge during the acquisition process.

To sum up, the main changes that Ilim Timber introduced that have directly or indirectly affected its absorptive capabilities AC were: organizational structure by division, internal rotation of top managers, standardized document flows, switch to homogenous accounting standards, cultural and language training, establishment of the NID investment department, greater involvement of expatriates, and the reinforcement of headquarter staffing.

After accumulating expertise in its U.S. operations, Ilim Timber sold Tolleson to International Forest Products (Interfor), one of the largest Canadian timber producers.[43] Ilim made a healthy capital gain in the process, having bought Tolleson in 2011 for an estimated $50–60 million, and then sold the business in 2014 for at least three times that amount. Overall, to acquire Tolleson, Interfor paid $130 million in cash and retained liabilities, plus 3.68 million Class A subordinate voting shares.[44] However, the sales agreement stipulated that part of the price was paid in Interfor shares, thus making Ilim Timber a strategic shareholder, with 5.5% of Interfor's capital.[45] Ilim thus nominates its representative to the board of directors of one of the largest sawmill companies in North America.[46]

Yet Ilim Timber has no plans to abandon the North American market. Its sale of Tolleson was linked, according to company representatives, to very specific hurdles: different standards of managerial accounting, different planning approaches, even different product formats, all significant obstacles to full unification and group-wide standardization.

12.3 Integrating organizations into cultures

What constitutes culture?

The issue of national cultural identity was addressed by many researchers and is reflected in several concepts. According to one of the earliest models, the values orientation theory,[47] humankind has a limited number of problems with a limited number of solutions to them. The values shared by a certain group or society, form the dominant value system, value orientation, which influences decision making and behavior more generally.

Another fundamental theory, that of high and low-context culture, assumes that people from different cultures and societies communicate and behave differently, depending on gaps in "context" (circumstances) and "code" (message).[48] Asian and Arab nations are examples of high context cultures, with their peoples deeply involved with each other, a hierarchical society, feelings not publicly displayed, and typically simple ways of sharing information. By contrast, the European and American nations are considered to be low-context cultures. They are characterized by less social hierarchy and more impersonal communication. People in these cultures are highly individualized, alienated and fragmented, and have relatively little involvement with each other.[49]

Hofstede made the subsequent adaptation of these general sociological theories to the business world; he also proposed to measure and compare different cultures by means of four dimensions: power distance, individualism versus collectivism, masculinity versus femininity, and uncertainty avoidance.[50] Later on, two additional dimensions were suggested: long-term orientation[51] and indulgence versus restraint.[52]

Further developing Hofstede's concept, a model was proposed[53] consisting of seven dimensions for interpreting cultural differences based on a ten-year study of Shell's management. The GLOBE (Global Leadership and Organizational Behavior Effectiveness) study identified nine cultural dimensions, two of which were unique: gender egalitarianism and performance orientation.[54] In the more recent studies, five cultural dimensions were suggested, with the argument that they suffice to evaluate and measure culture and compare national differences: hierarchy-egalitarianism, individualism-collectivism, mastery-harmony, monochronism-polychronism and universalism-particularism.[55]

How culture affects deal-making

Naturally, of great interest to researchers was the impact of culture on business transactions. To explain this impact, literature divides it into separate elements, such as cultural compatibility,[56] cultural convergence,[57] cultural fit,[58] management practices,[59] and more. The list is virtually endless, since so many components constitute culture, making it a comprehensive and multi-level notion.

With reference to FDI and transactions, a correlation between cultural specificities (level of individualism/collectivism, masculinity/femininity, power distance, uncertainty avoidance) and the entry mode was established.[60] It is therefore important for companies wishing to carry out deals to understand beforehand which discrepancies caused by national culture, may interfere. This cultural due diligence is critical.

The role of cultural differences in transactions is high, with national culture possibly playing a role in the nationalistic bias within negotiations.[61] To complicate matters further, negotiators must deal with culture at various levels: the countries, the organizations and the top managers themselves.[62] In cases where national cultures are highly different (e.g. Europe and Asia) the deal integration may involve substantial efforts on cultural integration.[63]

It is widely believed that cultural differences also impose additional threats on the realization of synergies in cross-border deals, as compared to domestic ones. Companies tend to perceive cultural differences as potential obstacles to integration plans.[64] Cultural differences or the "clash-of-cultures" are often cited as key reasons for failed transactions.[65]

However, some researchers believe otherwise, and hypothesize that cultural challenges have a positive impact on synergy realization,[66] or argue that cultural difficulties improve post-merger results.[67]

Summing up, "It seems that one has to be careful with predicting the impact of organizational, national or other cultures on M&A. There seem to be diverse sources of complexity that currently prevent us from answering 'yes' or 'no' to the relationship between culture and M&A performance."[68] Given current knowledge, the least that top management at emerging multinationals can do is to be aware of cultural impacts and take these into account during decision-making, due-diligence and post-deal integration processes of cross-border M&A projects.

Cultural integration process

Empirical studies prove that firms that give priority to resolving cultural differences and generating a shared identity during the post-transaction integration phase – namely, of human resources – are more likely to be successful.[69]

How should the buyer integrate the seller into his universe? Various approaches and classifications of integration exist. One proposed classification includes three integration strategies: preservation, absorption and symbiosis. The first strategy, preservation, means that the acquired company preserves its former culture, with the lowest level of change due to integration. Absorption implies that the acquired firm is fully merged into the new structure, while symbiosis refers to changes in both companies.[70]

Another integration model suggests a five-strategy matrix by introducing two new elements: *reverse acquisition*, when the acquired company faces changes, and *best of both*, the light version of symbiosis. However, the two firms do not need to integrate 100%: they can choose the appropriate and sufficient degree of integration and stop there.[71]

One other classification of integration is made according to its directions or motives. The first set of motives refers to *task*,[72] *operational*,[73] *structural*,[74] and *organizational*[75] integration. It implies consolidation of organizational structures, working processes, assets, and departments. It also influences the achievement of operational synergies. The second set of motives mostly deals with intangibles, such as *socio-cultural*,[76] *social*,[77] and *human*[78] integration. The purpose of this type of integration is to integrate human resources.

In the short-term cultural differences affect both socio-cultural integration (shared identity, positive attitude and trust) and task integration (capacity transfer, resource sharing and learning between firms). In the long-term cultural differences can affect performance, in particular, realization of synergies (in accounting-based terms) and increase in shareholders' values (in terms of superior returns).[79]

High attention in often focused not only on the type but also on the speed of cultural integration,[80] defined as the time between deal closing and completion of the integration.[81] Fast human integration is not only beneficial for a shared identity and for mutual trust but also provides a basis for effective task integration.[82]

Cultural differences do not a priori lead to cultural clashes in cross-border deals, if the integration strategy is well conceived. It seems that cultural differences per se may be less problematic; more relevant is how the socio-cultural integration process is managed.[83] A high level of integration results in better performance and synergy realization through knowledge codification,[84] and simultaneously the higher level of integration may decrease staff resistance, especially for middle management.[85]

Both academics[86] and practitioners[87] believe that too high a level of integration causes deal failures, because of low performance. The complex character of the integration process can also create uncertainty and ambiguity,[88] and certainly raises worries among employees[89] of both companies. "What will my future be in the new set-up?" they ask.

The complexity of cultural integration is conditioned by its unique character in every case, because of the combination of cultural peculiarities. Therefore, there is no single approach to follow in cross-border deals. In trying to find the best way to integrate, companies often make common mistakes. The top six reasons for unsuccessful cultural integration are:[90] culture risks not identified during due diligence (48%), lack of agreement among leadership on desired culture (48%), lack of leadership support (44%), lack of skills/ training (27%), inconsistent/ insufficient employee communications (23%), and insufficient resources (19%).

Unnoticed problems associated with cultural differences may strongly affect the integration process and create unexpected bottlenecks. The same survey identified five key pitfalls that companies should avoid:[91] organization distraction & loss of productivity (80%), loss of key talent (78%), failure to achieve critical milestones or synergies (77%), decreased employee engagement (73%), and delayed integration (60%).

Since these issues involve employee satisfaction and their understanding of the ongoing integration process, the HR department plays a key role in cross-border M&A deals. Without the full involvement of human resource partners in the deal integration, the chances of successful deal completion drop.[92] In cooperation with the integration team (when there is one), the HR department should implement specific tools and methods to ensure effective cultural integration. In particular, HR should measure cultural differences, correlate culture to the strategy chosen and manage the integration process.[93]

Since cultural integration requires ongoing measurement and adjustments to the action plan, it is important to monitor changes during the post-deal period. After deal completion, when the buyer gets more control and direct access to employees and customers, it should use different integration measurement benchmarks, which enable higher accuracy and involvement.

In the cases that follow, we abandon the thin air of theory, to take a closer look at the cultural integration in various cross-border deals made by Chinese and Russian firms. To provide grounding and comparisons, the cases of acquisitions made by two banks will be considered.

HSBC-Midland: merging cultures

Deal background

HSBC has a very rich history, dating back to 1865. Multi-nationalism characterized the bank from the very beginning, with Scotsman Thomas Sutherland establishing it in Hong Kong. Moreover, multi-nationalism is reflected in the bank's long-term strategy, also known as a "three-legged stool" strategy.[94] Each leg links to one of the three regions of main concern: the Asia-Pacific region, the United States and the United Kingdom.

Implementation of this strategy started in 1980 with the acquisition of the American bank Marine Midland Bank (United States). When HSBC targeted the UK market for further expansion, it faced a choice: either Royal Bank of Scotland or Midland Bank. Finally, in 1987 HSBC acquired a 14.9% stake in Midland Bank, and five years later completed the acquisition, becoming full owner.[95] As a result, HSBC headquarters moved to

Table 12.1 HSBC results in the United Kingdom, United States and Hong Kong

Region	Total assets ($ bill.)	Profit before tax ($ mill.)
HSBC UK	1,045,600	4,267
HSBC US	199,062	755
HSBC HK	896,411	15,118

Source: HSBC annual reports

London, to guarantee the balance among the three legs (see Table 12.1). Moreover, in 1999, as a part of the integration, Midland Bank was rebranded HSBC. At the end of 2014, HSBS had a total workforce of 266,000 employees, with most employees (48,000) employed in the United Kingdom, followed by India (32,000), Hong Kong (30,000), and Mainland China and Brazil (around 21,000).

Cultural integration

HSBC is an example of a company combining the origins of two cultures on different corporate levels: Western culture in leadership and local culture in staff. Despite its extensive Asian footprint – the bank was established by a Scotsman – it has remained the rule throughout its history that the majority of the bank's executive board have been Occidentals.

An in-depth analysis of the multicultural bank would involve fours cultures: China, Hong Kong, the United States and the United Kingdom. Although the Hong Kong culture is unique, this is largely based on China's mercantilism, so the focus here is on the Chinese and British cultures, the mostly influential in business dealings.

The acquisition of Midland Bank in 1987 did not encounter significant cultural difficulties. The corporate governance of the bank had already consisted of executives from the Anglo-Saxon sphere, thus making leadership integration smooth.

As far as the new governance of the bank sharing the same values and beliefs, employees of British departments did not suffer any transitional problems or cultural discrepancy. Bank executives took care to keep staff aware of its different countries of operation, by stimulating education and business exchange. Efforts were also made to enrich employees by explaining social and business practices, rules for communication, and by providing travel recommendations.[96]

To help preserve the cultural differences of its foreign subsidiaries, HSBC introduced the "Culture Wizard" Internet platform, including cultural awareness e-learning courses, virtual team training, global leadership assessment tools, and culturally focused country profiles on over 140 countries.[97]

Moreover, the bank sponsored intercultural exchanges for children and youngsters in more than fifty countries.[98] This program enabled students to live in different cultures with a host family, go to a local school or university; in other words, to broaden their minds and become acquainted with different nations. Another initiative proposed by HSBC in 2003 encouraged children from all over Great Britain to learn the Mandarin Chinese language, as well as Chinese culture basics. With the support of the British Council, HSBC conducts an annual Chinese Speaking Competition,[99] whose winners are awarded a weeklong trip to Beijing.

In 2009, possibly motivated by the negative reaction to a sumo wrestler advertisement, HSBC launched a marketing campaign using the motto: "The more you look at the world, the more you recognize that people value things differently."[100] The campaign consisted of a series of photos with different associations. It was made to show the company's respect of cultural differences, inevitable occurrences in our globalized business environment.

Consequences

The acquisition of Midland Bank enabled HSBC to drop anchor in a key financial market, the United Kingdom, and to better integrate itself in another critical financial center – the United States. Historically, senior HSBC management originated from Western molds, so therefore the company did not bear any liability of foreignness when merging with Midland Bank. The cultural integration of the UK office into the international network was smooth and fast. Thus employees did not suffer from cultural earthquakes, with the overall integration mostly about specific tasks and business operations. Moreover, the HSBC takeover was beneficial for Midland employees and managers, since they gained access to an extensive and outstanding international network, via special training sessions and business exchanges.

Sberbank–Denizbank: seeking for cultures' combination

Deal background

Sberbank is the largest bank of Central and Eastern Europe, with a 2015 market capitalization of $26.9 billion (#124 in the Forbes ranking of the world's biggest public companies).[101] The bank holds almost one-third of aggregate Russian banking sector assets, and is the key lender to the national economy and the biggest deposit taker in Russia. The Russian Central Bank is the founder and principal shareholder of Sberbank, owning 50% of the Sberbank's authorized capital, plus one voting share, with the remaining 50% held by domestic and international investors. Sberbank has more than 135 million individual customers and more than 1 million corporate clients in twenty-two countries.[102] Sberbank has the largest branch network in Russia with almost 17,000 agencies, and its international operations include the United Kingdom, the United States, CIS, Central and Eastern Europe, Turkey and other countries.

In its strategic vision of 2008, the bank highlighted three key priorities:

- the importance of entering global markets, especially India and China;
- increasing market share in CIS countries; and
- raising its profit from international operations to 5%–7% of total profits.

The bank also set the very challenging target of becoming one of the leading worldwide financial institutions by 2014.[103] In its updated strategy for 2014–2018 Sberbank aims to strengthen its leading positions and to double its profit and assets by 2018.

Carrying through its stated objectives, in 2013, Sberbank acquired 99.85% of Deniz-Bank, a leading Turkish commercial bank. As it was officially stated, it was a major step in the transformation of Sberbank into international financial institution, since it was the largest acquisition ever made by any Russian bank.

Before completing the deal, Sberbank conducted preliminary analysis of the Turkish economy, as well as comprehensive due diligence on DenizBank itself (due diligence is the process of fully analyzing the financial and operational data of the seller). Cultural and social issues were a part of Sberbank's initial observation. As mentioned in presentations to investors,[104] DenizBank's corporate governance met the highest international standards, combining cautious banking development (namely respect for reserve ratios), and social responsibility. DenizBank was an active participant in regional economic projects, as well as Turkish social and cultural development more generally.

One issue that Sberbank was aware if was an overarching national difference: Russians are more pragmatic than Turks, and they are much less indulgent. In other words, Russians tend to control their desires and impulses. Another national difference relates to slightly different perceptions of power: even though the Turkish culture remains dependent and hierarchical, the power distance in Turkey is lower than in Russian society.

Cultural integration

With both banks having long histories, their corporate cultures were deeply ingrained, well before the acquisition. Both banks had distinct corporate identities, corporate values and strategies. Yet, thankfully, the key corporate principles at DenizBank[105] did not contradict the values of Sberbank.[106] In fact, when combined, they could create a solid basis for mutual growth and further development.

Sberbank preserved the Turkish brand, simply adding "Member of Sberbank Group," thereby proving its intention to preserve DenizBank's corporate standards. The degree of integration between the two banks was very low and mostly involved learning from each other by exchanging experience: "We adopt Sberbank's best practices, while our shareholders take over all the best that we have" is the way one DenizBank executive put it.[107]

Sberbank followed these principles during the first period of the post-merger integration. Particularly, only one Russian executive enlarged the Executive Board of DenizBank and the CEO, Hakan Ateş, held his position. Sberbank management was represented only in the board of directors with Herman Gref as a chairman.

Operational integration

Soon after the deal, Sberbank launched several projects to boost the integration of its Turkish subsidiary, "including initiatives in risk management, operational efficiency and personnel training."[108] According to the Sberbank budget,[109] the company assigned RUB 70.8 million (around $2.2 million) in 2013 for the integration strategy.

The short-term integration plan for DenizBank takes into account leadership and governance, as well as down-to-earth operational factors, as well as those related to management continuity of DenizBank allow for culture preservation and smooth transition; management retention (always a problem after an acquisition); and continued operational separation from the parent company. Sberbank and DenizBank will develop a full-scale integration program, governance structure and joint business planning.

In connection with its Turkish acquisition, Sberbank decided it needed to define a common strategy, applicable to all foreign businesses the bank might try to acquire in the future. For this purpose, Sberbank organized a competition among consulting firms, in order to choose the most appropriate.

Thereafter Sberbank launched its new development strategy for the 2014–2018 period, wherein it confirmed its intent to focus on existing assets, and improve communications with foreign partners on the basis of an integrated platform. Moreover, the company aimed to

- develop a new system of managing the international business;
- strengthen the transnational team working in the main functional areas;
- adapt internal processes and the corporate culture so as to build systemic mechanisms for integrating foreign assets; and
- maximize potential synergies offered within a unified financial group.[110]

Conclusion

To sum up, in both the HSBC and Sberbank cases, the integration had positive effects on the companies. In the case of HSBC, cultural integration was smooth and fast, which could be expected given the Anglo-Saxon commonality between buyer and seller. Overall integration was mostly about tasks and business operations, which was easy to achieve due to the nature of the UK-based bank with a great history of financial operations and high reputation.

In case of Sberbank, the degree of integration was lower, since both parties decided to preserve the Turkish corporate culture, which was important given the long-established culture. The two differing strategies – merging and assimilating cultures in the case of HSBC and Midland, and keeping cultures safe in the case of Sberbank and DenizBank – have led to equally successful results for both transactions.

References

1　Wells 1983.
2　Bartlett and Ghoshal 1989.
3　Elenkov 1995.
4　Tsang and Yip 2007.
5　Blomström, Kokko and Globerman 2001.
6　Panibratov 2012.
7　Ramamurti 2009.
8　http://www.gazprombank.ru/upload/iblock/f9a/gpb_rusal_initiation_rus.pdf
9　Hedlund 1986.
10　Gupta and Govindarajan 2000.
11　Foss and Pedersen 2002.
12　Lado and Wilson 1994.
13　Cohen and Levinthal 1990.
14　Ibid.
15　Smith 1997.
16　Narula 2003.
17　Narula and Dunning 2000.
18　Borensztein, De Gregorio and Lee 1998.
19　Criscuolo and Narula 2002.
20　Narula 2003.
21　Cohen and Levinthal 1990.
22　Minbaeva, Pedersen, Bjørkman, Fey and Park 2003.
23　Zahra and George 2002.
24　Cohen and Levinthal 1990.
25　Gupta and Govindarajan 2000.
26　Ding, Akoorie and Pavlovich 2009.
27　Ibid.

28 Ibid.
29 Inkpen and Dinur 1998.
30 Ding et al. 2009.
31 Latukha, Panibratov and Safonova-Salvadori 2011.
32 Panibratov 2012.
33 Killing 1983.
34 Ding et al. 2009.
35 Ibid.
36 Child 1994.
37 Child 1994.
38 Ding et al. 2009.
39 Ibid.
40 Илим Тимбер объявляет о покупке двух лесопильных заводов Klausner Group на территории Германии: http://www.ilimtimber.com/news/more/?id=8.
41 www.ilimtimber.com/en/news/more/?id=14
42 http://www.ilimtimber.com/en/company/
43 Илим Тимбер продает свои лесопильные заводы в Северной Америке компании Interfor: http://lesprominform.ru/news/branch/4979-ilim-timber-prodaet-svoi-lesopilnye-zavody.html
44 http://www.marketwired.com/press-release/interfor-completes-acquisition-of-tolleson-tsx-ifp.a-1889143.htm
45 http://www.ilimtimber.com/en/news/more/?id=40
46 Sidorova 2014.
47 Kluckhohn and Strodtbeck 1961.
48 Hall 1976.
49 Ibid.
50 Hofstede 1980.
51 Hofstede and Bond 1988.
52 Minkov 2007.
53 Trompenaars 1993; Trompenaars and Hampden-Turner 1998.
54 House, Hanges, Javidan, Dorfman and Gupta 2004.
55 Nardon and Steers 2009.
56 Cartwright and Cooper 1996.
57 Birkinshaw, Bresman, and Håkanson 2000.
58 Weber, Shenkar and Raveh 1996.
59 Datta, Grant and Rajagopalan 1991; Larsson and Finkelstein 1999.
60 Weber, Tarba and Reichel 2011.
61 Olie 1990.
62 Teerikangas and Very 2006.
63 Chakravarty and Chua 2012.
64 David and Singh 1994.
65 Lupina-Wegener, Schneider and van Dick 2011.
66 Larsson and Finkelstein 1999.
67 Krishnan, Miller and Judge 1997.
68 Teerikangas and Very 2006.
69 Bansal 2015.
70 Haspeslagh and Jemison 1991.
71 Mirvis and Marks 1992.
72 Birkinshaw, Bresman and Håkanson 2000.
73 Björkman, Stahl and Vaara 2007.
74 Puranam, Singh and Chaudhuri 2009.
75 Waldman and Javidan 2007.
76 Stahl and Voigt 2008.
77 Björkman, Stahl and Vaara 2007.
78 Birkinshaw, Bresman and Håkanson 2000.
79 Stahl and Voigt 2008.
80 Homburg and Bucerius 2006; Bauer and Matzler 2014.
81 Cording, Christman and King 2008.

82 Bauer and Matzler 2014.
83 Lupina-Wegener, Schneider and van Dick 2011.
84 Zollo and Singh 2004.
85 Meyer 2008; Larsson and Finkelstein 1999.
86 Hennart, Dess, Gupta and Hill 1995.
87 Vestring, King, Rouse and Critchlow 2003.
88 Vaara 2003.
89 Syrjälä and Takala 2008.
90 Aon Hewitt 2011.
91 Ibid.
92 Latukha and Panibratov 2013.
93 Ibid.
94 HSBC 2014.
95 Lohr 1987.
96 Notarianni 2010.
97 HSBC Culture Wizard 2014.
98 HSBC 2014.
99 Ali 2013.
100 Wong 2009.
101 Forbes The World's Biggest Public Companies.
102 Sberbank 2016.
103 Sberbank 2008.
104 Sberbank 2012.
105 DenizBank 2012.
106 Sberbank 2014.
107 Akesh 2013.
108 Gref 2013.
109 Sberbank 2013a.
110 Sberbank 2013b.

Bibliography

Abalkina, A.A. (2014) 'Formy i metody ekspansii rossiiskih bankov za rubezh,' *Dengi i Kredit*, 3: 22–26.

Agarwal, A. and Knoeber, C. (2001) 'Do some outside directors play a political role?,' *Journal of Law and Economics*, 44(1): 179–98.

Agarwal, S. and Ramaswami, S.N. (1992) 'Choice of foreign market entry mode: Impact of ownership, location, and internalization factors,' *Journal of International Business Studies*, 23: 1–27.

Aharoni, Y. (1999) 'Internationalization of professional services: Implications for accounting firms,' in D. Brock, M. Powell and C.R. Hinings (eds.) *Restructuring the Professional Organization*, London: Routledge.

Ahsan, M., and Musteen, M. (2011) 'Multinational enterprises' entry mode strategies and uncertainty: A review and extension,' *International Journal of Management Reviews*, 13: 376–92.

Aizenman, J. and Spiegel, M.M. (2006) 'Institutional efficiency, monitoring costs and the investment share of FDI,' *Review of International Economics*, 14(4): 683–97.

Akerlof, G. (1970) 'The market for lemons: Quality uncertainty and the market mechanism,' *Quarterly Journal of Economics*, 84: 488–500.

Akesh, H. (2013) 'The purchase of Citibank assets in Turkey would strengthen Sberbank and DenizBank,' *Voice of Russia Radio*, June 21, http://rus.ruvr.ru/2013_06_21/223344510/

Aleksynska, M. and Havrylchyk, O. (2013) 'FDI from the South: The role of institutional distance and natural resources,' *European Journal of Political Economy*, 29: 38–53.

Alfa-Bank (2014) Annual Report, http://alfabank.com/f/1/investor/financial_reports/annual_reports-ifrs/ab_report2014.pdf

Alfa-Bank (2015) https://alfabank.ru/

Alfa-Bank Kazakhstan (2014) Annual Report, http://alfabank.com/f/1/investor/financial_reports/annual_reports-ifrs/ab_report2014.pdf

Alfa Group (2015) History. http://www.alfagroup.org/about-us/history/

Alfaro, L., Kalemli-Ozcan, S. and Volosovych, V. (2005) 'Capital Flows in a Globalized World: The Role of Policies and Institutions,' NBER Working Paper 11696, Cambridge, Massachusetts: National Bureau of Economic Research.

Ali, N. (2013) 'China: HSBC/British Council Mandarin speaking competition,' *British Council*, February 6, https://www.britishcouncil.org/education/schools/support-for-languages/partnerships-courses-resources/chinese-speaking-competition

Amal, M., Raboch, H. and Tomio, B. (2009) 'Strategies and determinants of Foreign Direct Investment (FDI) from developing countries: Case study of Latin America,' *Latin American Business Review*, 10: 73–94.

Amal, M. and Tomio, B.T. (2015) 'Institutional determinants of outward foreign direct investment from emerging economies,' in S. Marinova (ed.) *Institutional Impacts on Firm Internationalization*, New York: Palgrave Macmillan.

Amal, M., Tomio, B. and Raboch, H. (2010), 'Determinants of foreign direct investment in Latin America,' *Globalization, Competitiveness and Governability*, 4(3): 116–33.

Amighini, A.A. (2012) 'China and India in the international fragmentation of automobile production,' *China Economic Review*, 23(2): 325–41.

Amighini, A., Rabellotti, R., Sanfilippo, M. (2013) 'Do Chinese state-owned and private enterprises differ in their internationalization strategies?' *China Economic Review*, 27: 312–25.

Amore, M.D. and Bennedsen, M. (2013) 'The value of local political connections in a low – Corruption environment,' *Journal of Financial Economic*, 110: 387–402.

Amsterdam Trade Bank (2001) Annual Report, http://www.atbank.nl/

Amur plant in New Ural launched the first car with Chinese past 'Geely Otaka'. 05.06.2007. News agency. http://www.apiural.ru/news/economy/30895/?print

An interview with Lixin Cheng. 2016. Leaders Online, http://www.leadersmag.com/issues/2016.2_Apr/ROB/LEADERS-Lixin-Cheng-ZTE-USA.html

Andersen, O. (1993), 'On the internationalization of the firm: A critical analysis,' *Journal of International Business Studies*, 24(2): 209–31.

Anderson, E. and Gatignon, H. (1986) 'Modes of foreign entry: A transaction cost analysis and proposi-tions,' *Journal of International Business Studies*, 17: 1–26.

Andersson, S. and Victor, I. (2003) 'Innovative internationalization in new firms: Born globals – The Swedish case,' *Journal of International Entrepreneurship*, 1: 249–76.

Andersson, T. and Svensson, R. (1994) 'Entry modes for direct investment determined by the composition of firm-specific skill,' *Scandinavian Journal of Economic*, 96 (4): 551–60.

Andreff, W. (2002) 'The new multinational corporations from transition countries,' *Economic Systems*, 26(4): 371–79.

Andreff, W. (2003) 'The newly emerging TNCs from economies in transition: A comparison with Third World outward FDI,' *Transnational Corporations*, 12(2): 73–118.

Ang, S. and Michailova, S. (2008) 'Institutional explanations of cross-border alliance modes: The case of emerging economies firms,' *Management International Review*, 48(5): 551–76.

Angwin, D.N. (2007) 'Motive archetypes in mergers and acquisitions (M&A): The implications of a configurational approach to performance, advances in mergers and acquisitions,' *JAI Press*, 6: 77–106.

Annushkina, O. and Colonel, R.T. (2013) 'Foreign market selection by Russian MNEs – Beyond a binary approach?,' *Critical Perspectives on International Business*, 9(1/2): 58–87.

Ansoff, I. (1989) *Corporate Strategy, Revised Edition*, Harmondsworth: Penguin.

Aon Hewitt (2011) 'Survey findings: Culture integration in M&A,' http://www.aon.com/attachments/thought-leadership/M_A_Survey.pdf

Argyres, N.S. (1995). 'Technology strategy, governance structure and interdivisional coordination,' *Journal of Economic Behavior and Organization*, 28: 337–58.

Arregle, J., Naldi, L., Nordqvist, M. and Hitt, M. A. (2012) 'Inter- nationalization of family-controlled firms: A study of the effects of external involvement in governance,' *Entrepreneurship: Theory and Practice*, 36(6): 1115–143.

'Arunachal, RusHydro seal hydropower deal' (2014) *The Times of India*, December 13, http://timesofindia.indiatimes.com/city/guwahati/Arunachal-RusHydro-seal-hydropower-deal/articleshow/45498049.cms

The Atlas of Economic complexity (2016) http://atlas.cid.harvard.edu/explore/stacked/export/ind/show/all/1995.2014.2/

Aulakh, P. (2007). 'Emerging multinationals from developing economies: Motivations, paths and perfor-mance – editorial,' *Journal of International Management*, 13(3): 235–40.

Aulakh, P., Kotabe, M. and Teegen, H. (2000) 'Export strategies of service companies emerging markets,' *The Academy of Management Journal*, 43(3): 342–61.

Austen, I. (2006) 'Brazilian mining company to buy Inco of Canada,' *The New York Times*, September 25, http://www.nytimes.com/2006/09/25/business/worldbusiness/25canada.html?_r=0

Axelrod, R. (2004) 'Theoretical foundations of partnership,' in A. Liebenthal, O. Feinstein and G. Ingram (eds.) *Evaluation and Development: The Partnership Dimension*, New Brunswick, NJ: Transaction Publishers.

Bahree, M. (2013) 'Walmart's troubles continue in India,' *Forbes*, July 1, http://www.forbes.com/sites/meghabahree/2013/07/01/walmarts-troubles-continue-in-india/#5e5cbb6117e6

'Baidu gains more search market share in Q3' (2010, October) *China Daily*, http://chinadaily.com.cn/business/2010-10/19/content_11430298.htm

Balbutskaya, E. 2014. Russian transport infrastructure development. Russian Journal of Logistics and Transport Management, 1(2): 21-30. http://cyberleninka.ru/article/n/russian-transport-infrastructure-development

Balcet, G. and Bruschieri, S. (2010). 'Acquisition of technologies and Multinational enterprise growth in the automotive and the pharmaceutical industries: Drivers and strategies,' in K. Sauvant et al. (eds.) *The Rise of Indian Multinationals: Perspectives on Indian Outward Foreign Direct Investment*, New York: Palgrave Macmillan.

Balcet, G., Wang, H. and Richet, X. (2012), 'Geely: A trajectory of catching up and asset-seeking multinational growth,' *International Journal of Automotive Technology and Management*, 12(4): 360–75.

Baldwin, J.R. and Gu, W. (2003) 'Export market participation and productivity performance in Canadian manufacturing,' *Canadian Journal of Economics*, 36: 634–57.

The Banker (2015) http://www.thebanker.com/

Bansal, A. (2015) 'Understanding the integration mechanisms practiced during organizational change: Evidence from five M&A transactions,' *Journal of Organizational Change Management*, 28(1): 929–47.

Barassi, M.R. and Zhou, Y. (2012) 'The effect of corruption on FDI: A parametric and non-parametric analysis,' *European Journal of Political Economy*, 28(3): 302–12.

Barkema, H.G. and Vermeulen, F. (1998) 'International expansion through start-up or acquisition: A learning perspective,' *Academy of Management Journal*, 41(1): 7–26.

Barney, J.B. (1986a) 'Strategic factor markets: Expectations, luck and business strategy,' *Management Science*, 32(10): 1231–41.

Barney, J.B. (1986b) 'Organizational culture: Can it be a source of sustained competitive advantage?,' *Academy of Management Review*, 11(3): 656–65.

Barney, J.B. (1991) 'Firm resources and sustained competitive advantage,' *Journal of Management*, 17(1): 99–120.

Barney, J.B. (2001) 'Is the resource-based theory a useful perspective for strategic management research? Yes,' *Academy of Management Review*, 26(1): 41–56.

Bartlett, C. and Ghoshal, S. (1989) *Managing Across Borders*, Boston, MA: Harvard Business School Press.

Bartlett, C. and Ghoshal, S. (1995) 'Changing the role of top management: Beyond systems to people,' *Harvard Business Review*, 73(3): 132–143.

Bartlett, C.A. and Ghoshal, S. (1989) *Managing Across Borders: The Transnational Solution*. Boston, MA: Harvard Business School Press.

Bauer, F. and Matzler, K. (2014) 'Antecedents of M&A success: The role of strategic complementarity, cultural fit, and degree and speed of integration,' *Strategic Management Journal*, 35(2): 269–91.

Beamish, P.W. (1990). 'The internationalization process for smaller Ontario firms: a research agenda,' in: Rugman, A. M. (ed.), Research in Global Strategic Management International Business Research for the Twenty-First Century: Canada's New Research Agenda, Greenwich: JAI Press Inc., pp. 77–92.

Behan, R. (2004) 'All the tourists in China,' *The Telegraph*, October 23, http://www.telegraph.co.uk/travel/731518/All-the-tourists-in-China.html

'Behind the deal: Vodafone takes over Hutchison Whampoa's Indian unit' [Electronic resource] (2007, June) *Asian Law, Mumbai*, http://www.asialaw.com/Article/1971024/Search/Results/Behind-the-Deal-Vodafone-Takes-Over-Hutchison-Whampoas.html?Keywords=linklaters

Beijing Review (2009) May 2, 52(5): 14–16.

Bell, D. (2004) *Silent Covenants: Brown v. Board of Education and the Unfulfilled Hopes for Racial Reform*. New York: Oxford University Press.

Bellak, C. (2001) 'The Austrian investment development path,' *Transnational Corporations*, 10(2): 107–34.

Bénassy-Quéré, A., Coupet, M. and Mayer, T. (2007) 'Institutional determinants of foreign direct investment,' *The World Economy* 30(5): 764–82.

Bengoa, M. and Sanchez-Robles, B. (2003) 'Foreign direct investment, economic freedom and growth: New evidence from Latin America,' *European Journal of Political Economy*, 19(3): 529–45.

Bennett, J. and Jayes, S. (1995) 'Trusting the team: The best practice guide to partnering in construction,' Centre for Strategic Studies in Construction, Reading.

Bernard, A.B. and Jensen, J.B. (1999) 'Exceptional exporter performance: Cause, effect or both?,' *Journal of International Economics*, 47: 1–25.

Berning, S.C. and Holtbrügge, D. (2012) 'Chinese outward foreign direct investment – A challenge for traditional internationalization theories?,' *Journal Für Betriebswirtschaft*, 62(3/4): 169–224.

Bertrand, M., Kramarz, F., Schoar, A. and Thesmar, D. (2006) 'Politicians, firms, and the political business cycle: Evidence from France,' Unpublished working paper. University of Chicago, 2006.

Bevan, A.A. and Estrin, S. (2004) 'The determinants of foreign direct investment into European transition economies,' *Journal of Comparative Economics*, 32(4): 775–87.

Beverelli, C. and Mahlstein, K. (2011) 'Outsourcing and competition policy,' *Journal of Industry, Competition and Trade*, 11(2): 131–47.

Bhaumik, S.K., Driffield, N. and Pal, S. (2010) 'Does ownership structure of emerging-market firms affect their outward FDI? The case of the Indian automotive and pharmaceutical sectors,' *Journal of International Business Studies*, 41: 437–50.

Bilkey, W and Tesar, G. (1977) 'The export behaviour of smaller-sized Wisconsin manufacturing firms,' *Journal of International Business Studies*, 8: 93–98.

Birkinshaw, J., Bresman, H. and Håkanson, L. (2000) 'Managing the post-acquisition integration process: How the human integration and task integration processes interact to foster value creation,' *Journal of Management Studies*, 37(3): 395–425.

Birkinshaw, J.M. (1996) 'How multinational subsidiary mandates are gained and lost,' *Journal of International Business Studies*, 27(3): 467–96.

Birkinshaw, J.M. (1997) 'Entrepreneurship in multinational corporations: The characteristics of subsidiary initiatives,' *Strategic Management Journal*, 18(3): 207–29.

Björkman, I., Stahl, G.K. and Vaara, E. (2007) 'Cultural differences and capability transfer in crossborder acquisitions: The mediating roles of capability complementarity, absorptive capacity, and social integration,' *Journal of International Business Studies*, 38: 658–72.

Blitz, J. and Barber, L. (2013) 'India sees end to Vodafone tax dispute,' *Financial Times UK*, January 29, http://www.ft.com/intl/cms/s/0/94e4608e-6a3a-11e2-a7d2-00144feab49a.html#axzz2w 1HBEL8x

Blomström, M., Kokko, A. and Globerman, S. (2001) 'The determinants of host country spillovers from foreign direct investment: Review and synthesis of the literature,' in N. Pain (ed.) *Inward Investment, Technological Change and Growth*, London: Palgrave.

Blonigen, A.B. (2005) 'A review of the empirical literature on FDI determinants,' *Atlantic Economic Journal*, 33: 383–403.

Bloomberg (2014) 'Russia's Severstal sells U.S. plants for $2.3 billion,' July 22, http://www.bloomberg. com/news/articles/2014-07-21/mordashov-s-severstal-to-sell-u-s-steel-plants-for-2-3-billion

Boddewyn, J.J. and Brewer, T.L. (1994) 'International-business political behavior: New theoretical directions,' *Academy of Management Review*, 19: 119–43.

Boddewyn, J.J., Halbrich, M.B. and Perry, A.C. (1986) 'Service multinationals: Conceptualization, measurement and theory,' *Journal of International Business Studies*, 17(3): 41–57.

Boddewyn, J.J., Soehl, R. and Picard, J. (1986) 'Standardization in international marketing: Is Ted Levitt in fact right?,' *Business Horizons*, 6: 69–75.

Boeh, K.K. and Beamish, P.W. (2007) *Mergers and Acquisitions: Text and Cases*, Thousand Oaks, CA: Sage Publications.

Boisot, M. and Meyer, M.W. (2007) 'Which way through the open door? Reflections on the internationalization of Chinese firms,' *Management and Organization Review*, 4(3): 349–65.

Bonaglia, F., Goldstein, A. and Mathews, J.A. (2007) 'Accelerated internationalization by emerging markets multinationals: The case of the white goods sector,' *Journal of World Business*, 42: 369–83.

Borensztein, E., De Gregorio, J. and Lee, J.W. (1998) 'How does foreign direct investment affect economic growth?,' *Journal of International Economics*, 45(1): 115–35.

Boter, H. and Holmquist, C. (1996) 'Industry characteristics and internationalization process in small firms,' *Journal of Business Venturing*, 11(6): 471–87.

Boubakri, N., Cosset, J.-C. and Saffar, W. (2012) 'The impact of political connections on firms operating performance and financial decisions,' *Journal of Financial Research*, 35(3): 397–423.

Brada, J.C., Drabek, Z. and Perez, M.F. (2012) 'The effect of home-country and host-country corruption on foreign direct investment,' *Review of Development Economics*, 16(4): 640–63.

Brainard, S.L. (1997) 'An empirical assessment of the proximity-concentration trade-off between multinational sale and trade,' *American Economic Review*, 87(4): 520–44.

Brookes, M. and Roper, A. (2010) 'The impact of entry modes on the organizational design of international hotel chains,' *Service Industries Journal*, 30(9): 1499–512.

Brouthers, K., and Bamossy, G. (1997) 'The role of key stakeholders in international joint venture negotiations: Cases from eastern Europe,' *Journal of International Business Studies*, 28(2): 285–308.

Brouthers, K., and Brouthers, L. (2000) 'Acquisition or greenfield start-up? Institutional, cultural and transaction cost influences,' *Strategic Management Journal*, 21: 89–97.

Brouthers, K. and Hennart, J.M.A. (2007) 'Boundaries of the firm: Insights from international entry mode research,' *Journal of Management*, 33(3): 395–425.

Brouthers, K.D., Brouthers, L.E. and Werner, S. (2008) 'Resource-based advantages in an international context,' *Journal of Management*, 34: 189–218.

Buckley, P.J. (2007) 'The strategy of multinational enterprises in the light of the rise of China,' *Scandinavian Journal of Management*, 23(2): 107–26.

Buckley, P.J. (2014) 'Forty years of internalisation theory and the multinational enterprise,' *Multinational Business Review*, 22(3): 227–45.

Buckley, P.J. and Casson, M. (1981) 'The optimal timing of a foreign direct investment,' *Economic Journal*, 91: 75–87.

Buckley, P.J. and Casson, M.C. (1976) *The Future of the Multinational Enterprise*, London: Macmillan.

Buckley, P.J. and Casson, M.C. (1998) 'Analyzing foreign market entry strategies: Extending the internalization approach,' *Journal of International Business Studies*, 29(3): 539–61.

Buckley, P.J. and Casson, M.C. (1998) 'Models of the multinational enterprise,' *Journal of International Business Studies*, 29: 21–44.

Buckley, P.J. and Casson, M.C. (2009) 'The internalization theory of the multinational enterprise: A review of the progress of a research agenda after 30 years,' *Journal of International Business Studies*, 40, 1563–580.

Buckley, P.J. and Casson, M.C. (2010) *The Multinational Enterprise Revisited*, New York: Palgrave Macmillan.

Buckley, P.J., Clegg, L.J., Cross, A.R., Liu, X., Voss, H. and Zheng, P. (2007) 'The determinants of Chinese outward foreign direct investment,' *Journal of International Business Studies*, 38(4): 499–518.

Buckley, P.J., Clegg, L.J., Cross, A.R. and Voss, H. (2008) 'Emerging countries' policies on outward FDI – lessons from advanced countries,' Presentation at the Five-Diamond International Conference Cycle: Thinking Outward: Global Players from Emerging Markets, April 28–29, Columbia University, NY.

Buckley, P.J. and Ghauri, P. (eds.) (1999) *The Internationalization of the Firm: A Reader, 2nd ed.*, London: International Thomson Business Press.

Buckley, P.J. and Hashai, N. (2009) 'Formalizing internationalization in the eclectic paradigm,' *Journal of International Business Studies*, 40(1): 58–70.

Buckley, P., Yu, P., Liu, Q., Munjal, S. and Tai, P. (2015) 'Institution and location strategies of multinationals corporations from emerging economies: Evidence from China cross-border merger and acquisitions,' Conference proceeding, AIB UK and Ireland Chapter.

Bulatov, A., (1998) 'Russian direct investment abroad: Main motivations in the post-Soviet Period,' *Transnational Corporations* 7(1): 69–82.

Burgers, P., Hill, W. and Kim, C. (1993) 'A theory of global strategic alliances: The case of the global auto industry,' *Strategic Management Journal*, 14(6): 419–32.

Bushell-Embling (2015) 'ZTE increases marketing budget for SEA,' February 4, http://www.telecomasia.net/content/zte-increases-marketing-budget-sea

Business Monitor International (2014) Russia Commercial Banking Report, http://www.bmiresearch.com/sites/default/files/BMI_Catalogue_2014.pdf

Business Standard (2014) 'DoT notifies M&A guidelines,' http://www.business-standard.com/article/economy-policy/dot-notifies-m-a-guidelines-114022100011_1.html

Calomiris, C.W. (2005) 'Capital flows, financial crises, and public policy,' in M.M. Weinstein (ed.) *Globalization: What's New*, New York: Columbia University Press.

Campanario, M.A., Stal, E. and da Silva, M.M. (2012) 'Outward FDI from Brazil and its policy context,' May 10, Columbia FDI Profiles, Vale Columbia Center on Sustainable International Investment, Columbia University. http://ccsi.columbia.edu/files/2014/03/Profile-_Brazil_OFDI_10_May_2012_-_FINAL.pdf

Cantwell, J. and Barnard, H. (2008) 'Do firms form emerging markets have to invest abroad? Outward FDI and the competitiveness of firms,' in K. Sauvant (ed.) *The Rise of Transnational Corporations from Emerging Markets*, Cheltenham, UK and Northampton, MA: Edward Elgar.

Cantwell, J.A., Dunning, J.H. and Lundan, S.M. (2010) 'An evolutionary approach to understanding international business activity: The co-evolution of MNEs and the institutional environment,' *Journal of International Business Studies*, 41(4): 567–86.

Cardone-Riportella, C. and Cazorla-Papis, L. (2001) 'The internationalisation process of Spanish banks: A tale of two times,' *International Journal of Bank Marketing*, 19(2): 53–68.

Carman, J. and Lengeard, E. (1980) 'Growth strategies of service firms,' *Strategic Management Journal*, 1(1): 7–22.

Carneiro, J. and Brenes, E.R. (2014) 'Latin American firms competing in the global economy,' *Journal of Business Research*, 67(5): 831–36.

Cartwright, S. and Cooper, C.L. (1996) *Managing Mergers, Acquisitions, and Strategic Alliances: Integrating People and Cultures*, 2nd ed., Oxford, UK: Butterworth & Heinemann.

Casanova, L. and Kassum, J. (2013) 'Brazilian emerging multinationals: In search of a second wind,' Working paper, INSEAD, 2013/68/ST. http://www.insead.edu/facultyresearch/research/doc.cfm?did=52564

Casson, M. (1984) 'The theory of vertical integration: A survey and synthesis,' *Journal of Economic Studies*, 11(2): 3–43.

Castellani, D. and Zanfei, A. (2002) 'Multinational experience and the creation of linkages with local firms: Evidence from the electronics industry,' *Cambridge Journal of Economics*, 26(1): 1–25.

Caves, R.E. (1971) 'International corporations: The industrial economics of foreign investment,' *Economica*, 38(149): 1–27.

Caves, R.E. (1982) *Multinational Enterprise and Economic Analysis*, New York: Cambridge University Press.

Caves, R.E. (2007) *Multinational Enterprise and Economic Analysis, 3rd ed.*, Cambridge, UK: Cambridge University Press.

Caves, R.E. and Bradburd, R.M. (1988) 'The empirical determinants of vertical integration,' *Journal of Economic Behaviour and Organisation*, 9(3): 265–79.

Caves, R.E. and Mehra, S.K. (1986) 'Entry of foreign multinationals into the US Manufacturing Industries,' in M.E. Porter (ed.) *Competition in Global Industries*, Cambridge, MA: Harvard Business School Press.

Cavusgil, S.T. and Knight, G. (2009) *Born Global Firms: A New International Enterprise*, New York: Business Expert Press.

Cervantes, M. (1998) 'Public – Private partnerships in science and technology: An overview,' *Technology and Industry Review*, 23: 7–22.

Chakraborty, C. and Basu, P. (2002) 'Foreign direct investment and growth in India: A cointegration approach,' *Applied Economics*, 34: 1061–73.

Chakravarty, V. and Chua, S.G. (2012) *Asian Mergers and Acquisitions: Riding the Wave*, Hoboken, NJ: John Wiley & Sons.

Chan, C., Isobe, T., and Makino, S. (2008) 'Which country matters? Institutional development and foreign affiliate performance,' *Strategic Management Journal*, 29(11): 1179–205.

Chang, D. (2006) 'The politics of privatization in Russia: From mass privatization to the Yukos affair,' *Pacific Focus*, 21(1): 201–41.

Chang, S.-C. (2014) 'The determinants and motivations of China's outward foreign direct investment: A spatial gravity model approach,' *Global Economic Review*, 43(3): 244–68.

Chatterjee, S., Lubatkin, M., Schweiger D.M. and Weber, Y. (1992) 'Cultural differences and shareholder value in related mergers: Linking equity and human capital,' *Strategic Management Journal*, 13: 319–34.

Chen, H., Griffith, D.A. and Hu, M.Y. (2006) 'The influence of liability of foreignness on market entry strategies: An illustration of market entry in China,' *International Marketing Review*, 23(6): 636–49.

Chen, T.J. (2006) 'Liability of foreignness and entry mode choice: Taiwanese firms in Europe,' *Journal of Business Research*, 59(2): 288–94.

Cheng, L. K. and Ma, Z. (2008) 'China's outward foreign direct investment,' paper presented at the Indian Statistical Institute, 12 December 2008, http://www.isid.ac.in/~pu/seminar/12_12_2008_Paper.doc

Cheng, P. (2005, September) 'Baidu's six years,' *China Tech Story*, http://chinatechstory.blogspot.com/2005/09/baidus-six-years4.html

Cheng, Y.-M. (2006) 'Determinants of FDI mode choice: Acquisition, brownfield, and greenfield entry in foreign markets,' *Canadian Journal of Administrative Science*, 23: 200–20.

Child, J. (1994) Management in China during the age of reform. Cambridge: Cambridge University Press.

Child, J., Lu, Y. and Tsai, T. (2007) 'Institutional entrepreneurship in building an environmental protection system for the People's Republic of China,' *Organizational Studies*, 28: 1013–34.

Child, J. and Rodrigues, S.B. (2005) 'The internationalization of Chinese firms: A case for theoretical extension?,' *Management and Organization Review*, 1(1): 381–418.

'China approves Disney theme park in Shanghai' (2009) *The New York Times*, November 3, http://www.nytimes.com/2009/11/04/business/global/04disney.html?_r=0

'China' automotive industry expands to Russia. October 2008. 'Autostat' analytical agency. | www.autostat.ru

'China story' (2011) *Tata Review*, May, http://www.tata.com/pdf/tata_review_may_11/review_china_story.pdf

'China to flood Russia with its low-quality cars over 5 years' (2007) *Pravda.RU*, November 22, http://english.pravda.ru/business/companies/22-11-2007/101408-china_low_quality_cars-0/

Chinese Geely from Belarus are expected in Russia on summer. 01.02.2013. Avtostat: analytical agency. www.autostat.ru/news/view/12620

Chittoor, R. (2009) 'Internationalization of emerging economy firms – need for new theorizing,' *Indian Journal of Industrial Relations*, 45(1): 27–40.

Chog, C. (2009) 'China agrees to build Disneyland in Shanghai,' *BBC*, November 4, http://www.bbc.co.uk/russian/business/2009/11/091103_shanghai_disney.shtml

Chowdhury, J.R. (2014) 'Telecom merger rules in place,' *The Telegraph Calcutta*, http://www.telegraphindia.com/1140221/jsp/business/story_18005458.jsp#.UyV_Ivl_vAk

Chung, H. and Enderwick, P. (2001) 'An investigation of market entry strategy selection: Exporting vs foreign direct investment modes – a home-host country scenario,' *Asia Pacific Journal of Management*, 18: 443–60.

'Citi completes sale of Citigroup Technology Services Ltd.' India (2014) *CitiGroup*, http://www.citigroup.com

Claessens, S., Feijen, E. and Laeven, L. (2008) 'Political connections and preferential access to finance: The role of campaign contributions,' *Journal of Financial Economics*, 88(3): 554–80.

CNN Money (2011) 'World's most admired companies,' http://money.cnn.com/magazines/fortune/mostadmired/2011/index.html

Coase, R.H. (1937) 'The nature of the firm,' *Economica*, 4(16): 386–405.

Coase, R.H. (1960) 'The problem of social cost,' *Journal of Law and Economics*, 3: 1–44.

Cohen, W.M. and Levinthal, D.A. (1990) 'Absorptive capacity: A new perspective on learning and innovation,' *Administrative Science Quarterly*, 35(1): 128–52.

Collis, D.J. (1994) 'Research note: How valuable are organizational capabilities?,' *Strategic Management Journal*, 15: 143–52.

Commons, J.R. (1931) 'Institutional economics,' *American Economic Review*, 21: 648–57.

Conner, J.T. and Milford, L.P. (2008) *Out of the Red: Investment and Capitalism in Russia*, 1st ed., Hoboken, NJ: Wiley.

Contractor, F.J., Lahiri, S., Elango, B. and Kundu, S.K. (2014). 'Institutional, cultural and industry related determinants of ownership choices in emerging market FDI acquisitions,' *International Business Review*, 23(5): 931–941.

Cooper, M.J., Gulenand, H. and Ovtchinnikov, A.V. (2010) 'Corporate political contributions and stock returns,' *Journal of Finance*, 65(2): 687–724.

Cording, M., Christman, P. and King, D.R. (2008) 'Reducing causal ambiguity in acquisition integration: Intermediate goals as mediators of integration decision and acquisition performance,' *Academy of Management Journal*, 51(4): 744–67.

Coulter, M. (2009) *Strategic Management in Action*, 5th ed., Upper Saddle River, NJ: Prentice Hall.

Coviello, N. and Munro, H. (1997) 'Network relationships and the internationalization process of small software firms,' *International Business Review*, 6(4): 361–86.

Criscuolo, P. and Narula, R. (2002) 'A novel approach to national technological accumulation and absorptive capacity: Aggregating Cohen and Levinthal,' *MERIT Research Memorandum*, 2002–16.

Cristini, M. and Amal, M. (2006) 'Investimo direto externo no MERCOSUL: o papel da Europa,' Rio de Janeiro: Konrad-Adenauer-Stiftung.

Crook, T.R., Ketchen, D.J., Combs, J.G. and Todd, Y. (2008) 'Strategic resources and performance: A meta-analysis,' *Strategic Management Journal*, 29(11): 1141–54.

Cuervo-Cazurra, A. (2006) 'Who cares about corruption?,' *Journal of International Business Studies*, 37(6): 803–22.

Cuervo-Cazurra, A. (2007) 'Sequence of value-added activities in the internationalization of developing country MNEs,' Journal of International Management, 13(3): 258–77.

Cuervo-Cazurra, A. (2008) 'Better the devil you don't know: Types of corruption and FDI in transition economies,' *Journal of International Management*, 14(1): 12–27.

Cuervo-Cazurra, A. and Genc, M. (2008) 'Transforming disadvantages into advantages: Developing-country MNEs in the least developed countries,' *Journal of International Business Studies*, 39(6): 957–79.

Cuervo-Cazurra, A. and Un, A. (2005) 'Top managers and the product improvement process,' *Advances in Strategic Management*, 22: 319–48.

Cui, L. and Jiang, F. (2010) 'Behind ownership decision of Chinese outward FDI: Resources and institutions,' *Asia Pacific Journal of Management*, 27(4): 751–74.

Cui, L. and Jiang, F. (2012) 'State ownership effect on firms FDI ownership decisions under institutional pressure: A study of Chinese outward-investing firms,' *Journal of International Business Studies*, 43(3): 264–84.

Czinkota, M. and Ronkainen, I. (2004) *International Marketing*, 7th ed., Australia: Thomson Leraning.

Dai, C. and Lahiri, S. (2011) 'International business alliance under asymmetric information: Technology vis-à-vis information advantage,' *Southern Economic Journal, Southern Economic Association*, 77(3): 599–622.

Damania, R., Fredriksson, P.G. and Mani, M. (2004) 'The persistence of corruption and regulatory compliance failures: Theory and evidence,' *Public Choice*, 12: 363–90.

Da Motta Veiga, P. (2014) 'Brazilian multinational companies: Investing in the neighborhood,' *Issue Brief*, Rice University's Baker Institute for Public Policy, May 11, http://www.bakerinstitute.org/files/8426

Daniel, F. (2010) 'Head of Wal-Mart tells WFU audience of plans for growth over next 20 years', *Winston-Salem Journal*, September 29, http://www.journalnow.com/business/head-of-wal-mart-tells-wfu-audience-of-plans-for/article_5ad539d5-d616-55ba-ab27-aeaf45b06074.html

Daniel, T.A. (2001) *The Management of People in Mergers and Acquisitions*, Westport, CT: Quorum Books.

Datta, D.K., Grant, J.H. and Rajagopalan, N. (1991) 'Management incompatibility and post-acquisition autonomy: Effects on acquisition performance,' *Strategic Management Journal*, 7: 157–82.

David, K. and Singh, H. (1994) 'Sources of acquisition cultural risk,' in G. Von Krogh, A. Sinatra and H. Singh (eds.) *The Management of Corporate Acquisitions*, London: Macmillan.

Davidson, W. (1980) 'The location of foreign direct investment activity: Country characteisitics and expereince effects,' *Journal of International Business Studies*, 11(2): 9–22.

Davies, K. (2010) *Inward FDI from China and Its Policy Context, Columbia FDI Profiles*, New York: Vale Columbia Center on Sustainable International Investment.

Davis, P.S., Desai, A.B. and Francis, J.D. (2000) 'Mode of international entry: An isomorphism perspective,' *Journal of International Business Studies*, 31(2): 239–58.

Dealers trust in Chinese. Incom-Avto decided to become the owner of 25% of Amur plant who assembly chinese Geely. 31.08.2007. Vedomosti. http://www.vedomosti.ru/newspaper/articles/2007/08/31/dilery-veryat-v-kitajcev

De Beule, F. and Duanmu, J. (2012) 'Locational determinants of internationalization: A firm-level analysis of Chinese and Indian acquisitions,' *European Management Journal*, 30(3): 264–77.

De Beule, F., Elia, S. and Piscitello, L. (2014). 'Entry and access to competences abroad: Emerging marker firms versus advances market firms,' *Journal of International Management*, 20: 137–52.

Delacroix, J. (1993) 'The European subsidiaries of American multinationals: An exercise in ecological analysis,' in S. Ghoshal and E. Westney (eds.) *Organizational Theory and theMultinational Enterprise*, New York: St. Martin's Press.

Delios, A., Xu, D., Beamish, P.W. (2008) 'Within-country product diversification and foreign subsidiary performance,' *Journal of International Business Studies*, 39: 706–24.

Del Sol, P. and Kogan, J. (2007) 'Regional competitive advantage based on pioneering economic reforms: The case of Chilean FDI,' *Journal of International Business Studies*, 38(6): 901–27.

Demirbag, M., Glaister, K. and Tatoglu, E. (2007) 'Institutional and transaction cost influences on MNEs' ownership strategies of their affiliates: Evidence from an emerging market,' *Journal of World Business* 42: 418–34.

Demirbag, M., Tatoglu, E. and Glaister, K.W. (2009) 'Equity-based entry modes of emerging country multinationals: Lessons from Turkey,' *Journal of World Business*, 44(4): 445–62.

Deng, P. (2009) 'Why do Chinese firms tend to acquire strategic assets in international expansion?,' *Journal of World Business*, 44(1): 74–84.

Deng, P. (2012) 'The internationalization of Chinese firms: A critical review and future research,' *International Journal of Management Reviews*, 14(4): 408–27.

Deng, P. and Yang, M. (2015). 'Cross-border mergers and acquisitions by emerging market firms: A comparative investigation,' *International Business Review*, 24: 157–72.

DenizBank (2012) 'Human resources.' DenizBank.com.

Denk, N., Kaufmann, L. and Roesch, J.-F. (2012) 'Liabilities of foreignness revisited: A review of contemporary studies and recommendations for future research,' *Journal of International Management*, 18: 322–34.

De Wit, B. and Meyer, R. (2010) *Strategy – Process, Content, Context: International Perspective*, 4th ed., London: Cengage Learning.

Dib, L.A., da Rocha, A. and da Silva, J.F. (2010) 'The internationalization process of Brazilian software firms and the born global phenomenon: Examining firm, network, and entrepreneur variables,' *Journal of International Entrepreneurship*, 8(3): 233–53.

Di Giovanni, J. (2005) 'What drives capital flows? The case of cross-border M&A activity and financial deepening,' *Journal of International Economics*, 65: 127–49.

Dikova, D., Rao Sahib, P. and van Witteloostuijn, A. (2010) 'Cross-border acquisition abandonment and completion: The effect of institutional differences and organizational learning in the international business service industry, 1981–2001,' *Journal of International Business Studies*, 41(2): 223–45.

Dikshit, A. (2011, August 12) 'The uneasy compromise – Indian retail,' *The Wall Street Journal*, http://online.wsj.com/article/SB10001424053111903461104576461540616622966.html

Ding, Q., Akoorie, M. and Pavlovich, K. (2009) 'A critical review of three theoretical approaches on knowledge transfer in cooperative alliances,' *International Journal of Business and Management*, 4(1): 47–56.

Dixit, A.K. and Stiglitz, J.E. (1977) 'Monopolistic competition and optimum product diversity,' *The American Economic Review*, 67(3): 297–308.

Dlabay, L.R. and Scott, J.C. (2006) *International Business, 3e*, Mason City, OH: Thomson, South-Western.

Dollar, D., Hallward-Driemeier, M. and Mengistae, T. (2006) 'Investment climate and international integration,' *World Development*, 34(9): 1498–516.

Dong, B., Evans, K.R. and Zou, S. (2008) 'The effects of customer participation in co-created service recovery,' *Journal of the Academy Marketing Science*, 36: 123–37.

Drabek, Z, and Warren, P. (1999) 'The impact of transparency on foreign direct investment,' Staff Working Paper ERAD-99-02, Geneva, World Trade Organization.

Driga, I. and Dura, C. (2013) 'New trends regarding OFDI from Russia,' *Annals of the University of Petrosani, Economics*, 13(2): 41–50.

Driscoll, A.M. and Paliwoda, S.J. (1997) 'Dimensionalizing international market entry mode choice,' *Journal of Marketing Management*, 13: 57–87.

Drouvot, H. and Magalhaes, C. (2007). 'As vantagens competitivas das empresas dos países emergentes,' *Gestão & Regionalidade*, 23: 21–33.

Du, M. and Boateng, A. (2012) 'Cross-border mergers and acquisitions by emerging market firms: A review and future direction,' *ACRN Journal of Entrepreneurship Perspectives*, 1(2): 24–54.

Du, M. and Boateng, A. (2015) 'State ownership, institutional effects and value creation in cross-border mergers & acquisitions by Chinese firms,' *International Business Review*, 24(3): 430–42.

Dunning, J.H. (1958) *American Investment in British Manufacturing Industry*, London: George Allen & Unwin.

Dunning, J.H. (1973) 'The determinants of international production,' *Oxford Economic Papers*, 289–336.

Dunning, J.H. (1977) 'Trade, location of economic activity and the MNE: A search for an eclectic approach,' in B. Ohlin, P.O. Hesselborn and P.M. Wijkmon (eds.) *The International Location of Economic Activity*, London: Macmillan.

Dunning, J.H. (1979) 'Explaining changing patterns of international production: In defense of the eclectic theory,' *Oxford Bulletin of Economics and Statistics*, 41(2): 269–95.

Dunning, J.H. (1981) *International Production and the Multinational Enterprise*, London: George Allen & Unwin.

Dunning, J.H. (1988) 'The eclectic paradigm of international production: A restatement and some possible extensions,' *Journal of International Business Studies*, 19: 1–31.

Dunning, J.H. (1993) *Multinational Enterprises and the Global Economy*, Wokingham, UK: Addison-Wesley Publishing.

Dunning, J.H. (1998) 'Location and the multinational enterprise: A neglected factor?,' *Journal of International Business Studies*, 29(1): 45–66.

Dunning, J.H. (2000) 'The eclectic paradigm as an envelope for economic and business theories of MNE activity,' *International Business Review*, 9: 163–90.

Dunning, J.H. (2001) 'The eclectic (OLI) paradigm of international production: Past, present and future,' *International Journal of the Economics of Business*, 8(2): 173–90.

Dunning, J.H. (2006) 'Towards a new paradigm of development: Implications for the determinants of international business,' *Transnational Corporations*, 15(1): 173–227.

Dunning, J.H. (2009) 'Location and the multinational enterprise: John Dunning's thoughts on receiving the Journal of International Business Studies 2008 Decade Award,' *Journal of International Business Studies*, 40: 20–34.

Dunning, J.H. and Lundan, S.M. (2008a) 'Institutions and the OLI paradigm of the multinational enterprise,' *Asia Pacific Journal of Management*, 25: 573–93.

Dunning, J.H. and Lundan, S.M. (2008b) *Multinational Enterprises and the Global Economy*, 2nd ed., Cheltenham, UK and Northampton, MA: Edward Elgar.

Dunning, J.H. and Narula, R (1996) 'The investment development path revisited: Some emerging issues,' in J.H. Dunning and R. Narula (eds.) *Foreign Direct Investment and Governments: Catalysts for Economic Restructuring*, London and New York: Routledge.

Duysters, G., Saebi, T. and Dong, O. (2007) 'Strategic partnering with Chinese Companies: Hidden motives and treasures,' *Journal of Chain and Network Science*, 7(2): 109–19.

Eco, L., Kumar, A. and Yao, Q. (2011) 'Google this: The great firewall of China,' *Journal of Internet Law*, http://web.ebscohost.com.ezproxy.gsom.spbu.ru:2048/ehost/pdfviewer/pdfviewer?vid=8&hid=25&sid=3b85263c-816c-44e9-a548-7984a5643746%40sessionmgr112

Economic and Trade Information on China (2015) http://china-trade-research.hktdc.com/business-news/article/Fast-Facts/Economic-and-Trade-Information-on-China/ff/en/1/1X000000/1X09PHBA.htm

Economic Structure of China (2013) *Economy Watch*, China, June 4, http://www.economywatch.com/world_economy/china/structure-of-economy.html

Eden, L. and Dai, L. (2010) 'Rethinking the O in Dunning's OLI/eclectic paradigm,' *Multinational Business Review*, 18(2): 13–34.

Eden, L. and Miller, S.R. (2004) 'Distance matters: Liability of foreignness, institutional distance and ownership strategy,' *Advances in International Management*, 16: 187–221.

Egger, P. and Winner, H. (2005) 'Evidence on corruption as an incentive for foreign direct investment,' *European Journal of Political Economy*, 21(4): 932–52.

Egger, P. and Winner, H. (2006) 'How corruption influences foreign direct investment: A panel data study,' *Economic Development and Cultural Change*, 54(2): 459–86.

Ekeledo, I. and Sivakumar, K. (1998) 'Foreign market entry mode choice of service firms: A contingency perspective,' *Journal of the Academy of Marketing Science*, 26: 274–92.

Elango, B. (2009) 'Minimizing effects of "liability of foreignness" response strategies of foreign firms in the United States,' *Journal of World Business*, 44: 51–62.

Elango, B. and Pattnaik, C. (2007) 'Building capabilities for international operations through networks: A study of Indian firms,' 38: 541–55.

Elenkov, D.S. (1995) 'Russian aerospace MNCs in global competition: Their origin, competitive strengths and forms of multinational expansion,' *The Columbia Journal of World Business*, Summer: 30(2): 66–78.

Elmuti, D. and Kathawala, Y. (2001) 'An overview of strategic alliances,' *Management Decision*, 39(3): 205–18.

Embraer (2015) 'Who we are,' http://www.embraer.com.br/en-US/ConhecaEmbraer/TradicaoHistoria/Pages/default.aspx

'Embraer Executive Jets announces new service center in France' (2015) *Press-Release*, May 19, http://www.embraer.com/en-us/imprensaeventos/press-releases/noticias/pages/embraer-aviacao-executiva-anuncia-novo-centro-de-servicos-na-franca.aspx

Eng, L.L. and Mak, Y.T. (2003) 'Corporate governance and voluntary disclosure,' *Journal of Accounting and Public Policy*, 22(4): 325–45.

Ernst & Young (2012) 'Brazil Attractiveness Survey,' http://emergingmarkets.ey.com/report-title-2012-attractiveness-survey-brazil-2/

Ernst & Young (2013a) 'Africa attractiveness survey,' http://www.ey.com/Publication/vwLUAssets/Africa_Attract_2013_-_Getting_down_to_business/$FILE/Africa_attractiveness_2013_web.pdf

Ernst & Young (2013b) 'An overview of the Russian and CIS automotive industry,' http://www.ey.com/Publication/vwLUAssets/An_overview_of_the_Russian_and_CIS_automotive_industry/$FILE/An_overview_of_the_Russian_and_CIS_automotive_industry-March_2013.pdf

Erramilli, M.K. (1990) 'Entry mode choice in service industries,' *International Marketing Review*, 7(5): 50–62.

'Expansion of Accor in Moscow with the signing of 3 hotels that will add 700 rooms to the Group's portfolio' (2013) *Press Release*, September 2, http://www.russia-cisconference.com/downloads/130905_PR_Signature_of_700_new_rooms_Moscow_en.pdf

Faccio, M. (2006) 'Politically connected firms,' *American Economic Review*, 96(1): 369–86.

Faccio, M. (2010) 'Differences between politically connected and non-connected firms: A cross country analysis,' *Financial Management*, 39(3): 905–27.

Faeth, I. (2009) 'Determinants of foreign direct investment – A tale of nine theoretical models,' *Journal of Economic Surveys*, 23(1): 165–96.

Fan, J.P., Wong, T.J. and Zhang, T. (2007) 'Politically connected CEOs, corporate governance, and post – IPO performance of China's newly partially privatized firms,' *Journal of Financial Economics*, 84: 330–57.

Fan, J.P.H., Huang, J., Morck, R. and Yeung, B. (2014) 'Institutional determinants of vertical integration in China,' *Journal of Corporate Finance*. CORFIN-00810.

Fan, Y., Anantatmula, V. and Nixon, M.A. (2012) 'Impact of national culture on the trust-building process: Case study of an Arab-Chinese joint venture,' *International Journal of Management*, 29(3–2): 332–46.

Fang Li. (2010) Service innovation: convergence and openness. An interview with Lu Ping, President of ZTE's Communication Services R&D Institute. *ZTE Technologies*, 12(8): 3–5. http://wwwen.zte.com.cn/endata/magazine/ztetechnologies/2010/no8/201008/P020100816386246916260.pdf

Farashahi, M. and Hafsi, T. (2009) 'Strategy of firms in an unstable institutional environment,' *Asia Pacific Journal of Management*, 26(4): 643–66.

Farjoun, M. (1994) 'Beyond industry boundaries: Human expertise, diversification and resource – Related industry groups,' *Organization Science*, 5: 185–99.

Ferguson, T. and Voth, H. (2008) 'Betting on Hitler – The value of political connections in Nazi Germany,' *Quarterly Journal of Economics*, 123(1): 101–37.

The first Geely model made in Belarus will be SC7, 30 May 2012, www.n1.by/news/2012/05/30/324191.html

Fisch, J.H. (2011) 'Real call option to enlarge foreign subsidiaries – The moderating effect of irreversibility on the influence of economic volatility and political instability on subsequent FDI,' *Journal of World Business*, 46: 517–26.

Fisman, R. (2001) 'Estimating the value of political connections,' *American Economic Review*, 91: 1095–102.

Fisman, R. and Svensson, J. (2007) 'Are corruption and taxation really harmful to growth? Firm level evidence,' *Journal of Development Economics*, 83: 63–75.

Fleury, A. and Fleury, M.T.L. (2009) 'Brazilian multinationals: Surfing the waves of internationalization,' in R. Ramamurti and J. Singh (eds.) *Emerging Multinationals in Emerging Markets*, New York: Cambridge University Press.

Fleury A., & Fleury M.T.L. (2011) Brazilian Multinationals: Competences for Internationalization, Cambridge, MA: Cambridge University Press.

Fligstein, N. and Zhang, J. (2011) 'A new agenda for research on the trajectory of chinese capitalism,' *Management and Organization Review*, 7(01): 39–62.

'Foreign direct investment between the European Union and BRIC,' (2014, July) *Eurostat*, http://ec.europa.eu/eurostat/statistics-explained/index.php/Foreign_direct_investment_between_the_European_Union_and_BRIC

Fortescue, S. (2013) 'The Russian steel industry, 1990–2009,' *Eurasian Geography and Economics*, 50(3): 252–74.

Foss, N. and Pedersen, T. (2002) 'Transferring knowledge in MNCs: The roles of sources of subsidiary knowledge and organizational context,' *Journal of International Management*, 8: 49–67.

Francis, B., Hasan, I. and Sun, X. (2009) 'Political connections and the process of going public: Evidence from China,' *Journal of International Money and Finance*, 28(4): 696–719.

Froot, K. and Stein, J. (1991) 'Exchange rates and foreign direct investment: An imperfect capital markets approach,' *Quarterly Journal of Economics*, 196: 1191–1218.

Fung, A. and Lee, M. 2009. 'Localizing a global amusement park: Hong Kong Disneyland,' *Continuum: Journal of Media & Cultural Studies*, 23(2): 197–208.

Fung, K.C. and Garcia-Herrero, A. (2012) 'Foreign Direct Investment Outflows from China and India,' *China Economic Policy Review*, 1(1): 1–15.

Gabrielsson, M. and Manek Kirpalani, V.H. (2004) 'Born globals: How to reach new business space rapidly,' *International Business Review*, 13(5): 555–71.

Gammeltoft, P., Barnard, H. and Madhok, A. 2010. 'Emerging multinationals, emerging theory: Macro- and micro-level perspectives,' *Journal of International Management* 16: 95–101.

Gandolfo, G. (1998) *International Trade Theory and Policy*, Heidelberg: Springer-Verlag Berlin.

Ganitsky, J. (1989) 'Strategies for innate and adoptive exporters: Lessons from Israel's case,' *International Marketing Review*, 6(5): 51–65.

Garcia-Herrero, A. and Deorukhkar, S. (2014), 'What explains India's surge in outward direct investment?,' BBVA Working Paper 14/16.

Garg, M. and Delios, A. (2007) 'Survival of the foreign subsidiaries of TMNCs: The influence of business group affiliation,' *Journal of International Management*, 13: 278–95.

Gatignon, H. and Anderson, E. (1988) 'The multinational corporation degree of control over subsidiaries: An empirical test of a transaction cost explanation,' *Journal of Law, Economics and Organization*, 4: 305–66.

Gaur, A.S. Delios, A. and Singh, K. (2007). 'Institutional environments, staffing strategies and subsidiary performance,' *Journal of Management*, 33(4): 611–36.

Gaur, A.S., Kumar, V. and Sarathy, R. (2011) 'Liability of foreignness and internationalisation of emerging market firms,' *Advances in International Management*, 24: 211–33.

Gaurav, S. (2015) 'Ripple effect of Petrobras scandal on Brazilian investment,' April 21, http://www.forbes.com/sites/gauravsharma/2015/03/20/ripple-effect-of-petrobras-scandal-on-brazilian-investment/

Gazprom (2011) 'Gazprom opens a representative office in Rio de Janeiro,' November 3, Press Release, http://www.gazprom.com/press/news/2011/november/article122451/

Gazprom (2014) Gazprom Neft Annual Report, http://ar2014.gazprom-neft.com/

Geely Moors Rus: About the company, Official Web page, http://www.geely-motors.com/o-kompanii

'Geely speeds up overseas expansion, considering building plants in Brazil, India and Iran' (2012) *Global Times*, September 24, http://www.globaltimes.cn/content/734955.shtml

Gerds, J. and Strottmann, F. (2010) 'Post merger integration: Hard data, hard truths,' *Deloitte Review*, 6: 70–83.

Ghanatabadi, F. (2005) 'Internationalization of small- and medium-sized enterprises in Iran,' *Industrial Marketing*, 9: 36–61.

Ghemawat, P. (2001) 'Distance still matters,' *Harvard Business Review*, 79(8): 137–47.

Ghemawat, P. and Khanna, T. (1998), 'The nature of diversified business groups: A research design and two case studies,' *Journal of Industrial Economics*, 66(1): 35–61.

Globerman, S. and Shapiro, D. (2002) 'Global foreign direct investment flows: The role of governance infrastructure,' *World Development*, 30(11): 1899–919.

Goergen, M. and Renneboog, L. (2003) 'Value creation in large European mergers and acquisitions,' *Advances in Mergers and Acquisitions*, 2: 97–146.

Goerzen, A. and Beamish, P. (2003) 'Geographic scope and multinational enterprise performance,' *Strategic Management Journal*, 24: 1289–306.

Goh, S.K. and Wong, K.N. (2011) 'Malaysia's outward FDI: The effects of market size and government policy,' *Journal of Policy Modeling*, 33(3): 497–510.

Goldman, E., Rocholl, J. and So, J. (2013) 'Politically connected boards of directors and the allocation of procurement contracts,' *Review of Finance*, 17(5): 1617–48.

Goldman Sachs (2003) 'Dreaming with BRICs,' *Global Economics Paper*, no. 99, http://avikdgreat.tripod.com/InterestingReads/BRIC_GoldmanSachs.pdf

Goldman Sachs (2005) 'How solid are the BRICs,' *Global Economics Paper*, no. 134, http://www.goldmansachs.com/our-thinking/archive/archive-pdfs/how-solid.pdf

Gomes-Casseres, B. (1990) 'Firm ownership preferences and host government restrictions: An integrated approach,' *Journal of International Business Studies*, 21(1): 1–22.

Govindarajan, V. and Gupta, A. (1999) 'Taking Wal-Mart global: Lessons from retailing's giant,' *Fourth Quarter*, 17, http://www.strategy-business.com/archives/?issue=13665

Govindarajan, V. and Ramamurti, R. (2010) 'Reverse innovation, emerging markets, and global strategy,' paper prepared for inaugural issue of *Global Strategy Journal* and GSJ Conference, Chicago, July 2010.

Grace, J.D. (2005) *Russian Oil Supply: Performance and Prospects*, Oxford: Oxford University Press.

Granstrand, O. and Sjolander, S. (1990) 'The acquisition of technology and small firms by large firms,' *Journal of Economic Behavior & Organization*, 13: 367–86.

Grant, R.M. (2010) *Contemporary Strategy Analysis: Text and Cases*, 7th ed., New York: John Wiley & Sons.

Greenaway, D., Gullstrand, J. and Kneller, R. (2005) 'Exporting may not always boost firm productivity,' *Review of World Economics*, 141(4): 561–82.

Gref, G. (2013) 'Message from the Chairman,' DenizBank Annual Report, https://www.denizbank.com/en/about-us/_pdf/annual-reports/DenizBankAnnualReport2013.pdf

Greenaway, D. and Kneller, R. (2004) 'Does exporting increase productivity? A microeconometric analysis of matched firms,' *Review of International Economics*, 12(5): 855–66.

Griffin, R., and Pustay, M. (1995) *International Business: A Managerial Perspective*, New York: Addison-Wesley.

Grossman, G.M., Helpman, E. and Szeidl, A. (2006) 'Optimal integration strategies for the multinational firm,' *Journal of International Economics*, 70(1): 216–38.

Growth Strategies for 2012 and Beyond (2014) Wipro Limited, http://www.wipro.com

Gubbi, S., Aulakh, P., Ray, S., Sarkar, M.B., Chittoor, R., 2010. 'Do international acquisitions by emerging economy firms create shareholder value? The case of Indian firms,' *Journal of International Business Studies* 41(3), 397–418.

Gugler, P. and Boie, B. (2008) 'The emergence of Chinese FDI: Determinants and strategies of Chinese MNEs,' Paper presented at the Conference 'Emerging Multinationals: Outward Foreign Direct Investment from Emerging and Developing Economies,' Copenhagen Business School, Copenhagen, Denmark.

Gumbel, P. (2012) 'The not so magic kingdom,' *Time*, 19(8), http://content.time.com/time/magazine/article/0,9171,2127790,00.html

Guo, W., Wei, K.C., Li, X. and Wang, F. (2000) 'A decision support system for automotive product planning and competitive market analysis,' *International Transactions in Operational Research*, 7(6): 509–23.

Gupta, A. and Govindarajan, V. (2000) 'Knowledge flows within MNCs,' *Strategic Management Journal*, 21: 473–96.

Habib, M. and Zurawicki, L. (2001) 'Country-level investments and the effect of corruption – Some empirical evidence,' *International Business Review*, 10(6): 687–700.

Habib, M. and Zurawicki, L. (2002) 'Corruption and foreign direct investment,' *Journal of International Business Studies*, 33: 291–308.

Halepete, J., Seshadri Iyer, K.V. and Park, S.C. (2008) Wal-Mart in India: a success or failure? *International Journal of Retail and Distribution Management*, 36(9): 701–713.

Haleblian, J., Devers, C.E., McNamara, G., Carpenter, M.A. and Davison, R.B. (2009) 'Taking stock of what we know about mergers and acquisitions: A review and research agenda,' *Journal of Management*, 35: 469–502.

Halibozek, E. and Kovacich, G. (2005) *Mergers and Acquisitions Security: Corporate Structuring and Security Management*, Oxford: Elsevier Butterworth-Heinemann.

Hall, E.T. (1976) *Beyond Culture*, New York: Anchor Books.

Hamel, G. (2003) 'Innovation as a deep capability,' *Leader to Leader*, 27: 19–24.

Hamel, G. and Prahalad, C.K. (1983) 'Managing strategic responsibility in the MNC,' *Strategic Management Journal*, 4(4): 341–51.

Hamel, G. and Prahalad, C.K. (1990) 'The core competence of the corporation,' *Harvard Business Review*, 68(3): 79–91.

Hamilton, G. (ed.) (1986) *Red Multinationals or Red Herrings? The Activities of Enterprises from Socialist Countries in the West*, London: Frances Pinter.

Hamm, S. 'Bangalore Tiger: How Indian tech upstart Wipro is rewriting the rules of global competition/ Books 24*7/-2007.-ch.1 Why Wipro matters. http://library.books24x7.com.ezproxy.gsom.spbu.ru:2048/assetviewer.aspx?bookid=18167&chunkid=195396212&rowid=23

Hanson, P. (2013) 'Fear of the future: Russia in the global economy in the next few years,' *The International Spectator*, (48)3: 34–49.

Hanson, P. and Teague, E. (2005) 'Big business and the state in Russia,' *Europe-Asia Studies*, 57(5): 657–80.

Harris, S. and Wheeler, C. (2005) 'Entrepreneurs relationships for internationalization: Functions, origins and strategies,' *International Business Review*, 14(2): 187–207.

Harzing, A.W. (2002) 'Acquisitions versus greenfield investments: International strategy and management of entry modes,' *Strategic Management Journal*, 23: 211–27.

Hashai, N. (2011) 'Sequencing the expansion of geographic scope and foreign operations of "Born Global" firms,' *Journal of International Business Studies*, 42(8): 994–1015.

Hashai, N. and Almor, T. (2004) 'Gradually internationalizing "born global" firms: An oxymoron?' *International Business Review*, 13(4): 465–83.

Hashai, N. and Buckley, P. (2014) 'Is competitive advantage a necessary condition for the emergence of the multinational enterprise?,' *Global Strategy Journal*, 4(1): 35–48.

Haspeslagh, P.J. and Jemison, D.B. (1991) *Managing Acquisitions, Creating Value through Corporate Renewal*, New York: The Free Press.

He, W. and Lyles, M.A. (2008) 'China's outward foreign direct investment,' *Business Horizons*, 51(6): 485–491.

Hedlund, G. (1986) 'The hypermodern MNC – A heterarchy?,' *Human Resource Management*, 25(1): 9–35.

Held, K. and Berg, N. (2015) 'Facing discrimination by host country nationals – Emerging market multinational enterprises in developed markets,' in A. Verbeke, R. Van Tulder and S. Lundan (eds.) *Multinational Enterprises, Markets and Institutional Diversity*, Progress in International Business Research, 9. Emerald.

Helft, M. and Barboza, D. (2010) 'Google shuts China site in dispute over censorship,' *The New York Times*, http://www.nytimes.com/2010/03/23/technology/23google.html

Helpman, E. (1984) 'A simple theory of international trade with multinational corporations,' *Journal of Political Economy*, 32(3): 451–71.

Helpman, E., Melitz, M.J. and Yeaple, S.R. (2004) 'Export versus FDI with heterogeneous firms,' *The American Economic Review*, 94(1): 300–16.

Hennart, J.-F. (1982) *A Theory of Multinational Enterprise*, Ann Arbor: University of Michigan Press.

Hennart, J.-F. (1988) 'A transaction costs theory of equity joint ventures,' *Strategic Management Journal*, 9(4): 361–74.

Hennart, J.-F. (1991) 'Control in multinational firms: The role of price and hierarchy,' *Management International Review*, 31: 71–96.

Hennart, J.-F. (2012) 'Emerging market multinationals and the theory of the multinational enterprise,' *Global Strategy Journal*, 2(3): 168–87.

Hennart, J.-F., Dess, G., Gupta, A. and Hill, C. (1995) 'Conducting and integrating strategy research at the international, corporate, and business levels: Issues and directions,' *Journal of Management*, 21(3): 357–93.

Hennart, J.-F. and Park, Y.-R. (1993) 'Greenfield vs. acquisition: The strategy of Japanese investors in the United States,' *Management Science*, 39(9): 1054–70.

Hennart, J.-F. and Reddy, S. (1997) 'The choice between mergers / acquisitions and joint ventures: The case of Japanese investors in the United States,' *Strategic Management Journal*, 18: 1–12.

Hill, C. (2001) *International Business: Competing in the Global Marketplaces*, Boston: McGraw-Hill.

Hill, C.W.L., Hwang, P. and Kim, W.C. (1990) An eclectic theory of the choice of international entry mode, *Strategic Management Journal*, 11(2): 117–128.

Hille, K. and Crabtree, J. (2015) 'Rosneft buys stake in Essar Oil refinery in India,' *Financial Times*, July 8, http://www.ft.com/intl/cms/s/0/e7ab46cc-2593-11e5-bd83-71cb60e8f08c.html#axzz42nbICpAu

Hillman, A., Zardkoohi, A. and Bierman, L. (1999) 'Corporate political strategies and firm performance: Indications of firm-specific benefits from personal service in the US government,' *Strategic Management Journal*, 20(1): 67–81.

Hilmersson, M. and Jansson, H. (2012) 'Reducing uncertainty in the emerging market entry process: On the relationship among international experiential knowledge, institutional distance, and uncertainty,' *Journal of International Marketing*, 20(4): 96–110.

'The Hindu News update service' (2009) June 8, http://www.thehindu.com

Hitt, M.A., Hoskisson, R.E., Kim, H. (1997). 'International diversification: Effects on innovation and firm performance in product-diversified firms,' *Academy Management Journal*, 40(4): 767–98.

Hitt, M. and Tyler, B. (1991) 'Strategic decision models: Integrating different perspectives,' *Strategic Management Journal*, 12(5): 327–51.

Hitt, M.A., Dacin, M.T., Levitas, E., Arregle, J.L. and Borza, A. (2000) 'Partner selection in emerging and developed market contexts: Resource-based and organizational learning perspectives,' *Academy of Management Journal*, 43(3): 449–67.

Ho, C., Ahmad, N. and Dahan, H. (2013) 'Economic freedom, macroeconomic fundamentals and foreign direct investment in fast emerging BRICS and Malaysia,' *International Journal of Banking and Finance*, 10(1): 4.

Hofstede, G. (1980) *Culture's Consequences: International Differences in Work-Related Values*, Beverly Hills, CA: Sage.

Hofstede, G. (1991) *Cultures and Organizations: Software of the Mind*, London: McGraw-Hill.

Hofstede, G. (1994) The Business of International Business is Culture. *International Business Review*, 3(1): 1–14.

Hofstede, G. and Bond, M.H. (1988) 'The Confucius connection: From cultural roots to economic growth,' *Organizational Dynamics*, 16(4): 4–21.

Hollensen, S. (2001) *Global Marketing: A Market-Responsive Approach*, Essex, UK: Prentice Hall.

Hollensen, S., Boyd, B. and Dyhr Ulrich, A. M. (2011) 'The choice of foreign entry mode in a control perspective,' *The IUP Journal of Business Strategy*, 8(4): 7–31.

Holson, L. (2005) 'Disney bows to feng shui,' *New York Times*, April 25, http://www.nytimes.com/2005/04/24/business/worldbusiness/24iht-disney.html?pagewanted=all&_r=0

Homburg, C. and Bucerius, M. (2006) 'Is speed of integration really a success factor of mergers and acquisitions? An analysis of the role of internal and external relatedness,' *Strategic Management Journal*, 27(4): 347–67.

Horstmann, I. (1992) 'Endogenous market structures in international trade,' *Journal of International Economics*, 32: 109–29.

Hoskisson, R.E., Eden, L., Lau, C.M. and Wright, M. (2000) 'Strategy in emerging economies,' *Academy of Management Journal*, 43(3): 249–67.

Hoskisson, R.E., Wright, M., Filatotchev, I. and Peng, M.W. (2013) 'Emerging multinationals from mid-range economies: The influence of institutions and factor markets,' *Journal of Management Studies*, 50(7): 1295–321.

House, R.J., Hanges, P.J., Javidan, M., Dorfman, P.W. and Gupta, V. (2004) *Culture, Leadership and Organizations: The GLOBE Study of 62 Societies*, Thousand Oaks, CA: Sage Publications.

Hoy, F., and Stanworth, J. (2003) *Franchising: An International Perspective*, New York: Psychology Press.

HSBC (2014a) 'AFS intercultural exchange.' HSBC.com.

HSBC (2014b) 'HSBC's history.' HSBC.com.

Hung, M., Wong, T.J. and Zhang, T. (2008) 'Political relations and overseas stock exchange listing: Evidence from Chinese state-owned enterprises,' Available at SSRN: http://ssrn.com/abstract=1224162

Huxham, C. and Vangen, S. (2005) *Managing to Collaborate: The Theory and Practice of Collaborative Advantage*, London: Routledge.

Hymer, S.H. (1976) *The International Operations of National Firms: A Study of Foreign Direct Investment*, Cambridge, MA: MIT Press.

Hyun, H.J. and Kim, H.H. (2010) 'The determinants of cross-border M&As: The role of institutions and financial development in the gravity model,' *World Economy*, 33(2): 292–310.

IMF World Forum Outlook (2015) 'World Economic Outlook Database,' International Monetary Fund, April 2016, http://www.imf.org/external/pubs/ft/weo/2016/01/

'Incom-Avto' opened representative offices of Chinese car manufacturers Geely, Zhong Xing and JMC in Russia. 03.04.2007. http://www.finmarket.ru/news/586396

'Incom' and 'Elex' did not share Geely. 12.12.2006. RBC daily http://www.rbcdaily.ru/industry/562949979053261

Inkpen, A. and Dinur, A. (1998) 'Knowledge management processes and international joint ventures' *Organization Science*, 9: 454–68.

Irwin, A. and Gallagher, K. (2014) 'Exporting national champions: China's OFDI finance in comparative perspective,' GEGI Working Paper Series.

Ito, T. and Krueger, O.A. (2001) *Regional and Global Capital Flows: Macroeconomic Causes and Consequences*, Chicago, IL: University of Chicago Press.

Jadhav, P. (2012) 'Determinants of foreign direct investment in BRICS economies: Analysis of economic, institutional and political factor,' *Procedia – Social and Behavioral Sciences*, 37: 5–14.

James, S. (2009) *Incentives and Investments: Evidence and Policy Implications, Investment Climate Advisory Services*, World Bank Group, Washington, DC.

Jansson, H. (2008) *International Business Strategy in Emerging Country Markets: The Institutional Network Approach*, Cheltenham, UK: Edward Elgar.

Jarratt, D. (1998) 'A strategic classification of business alliances: A qualitative perspective built from a study of small and medium-sized enterprises,' *Qualitative Market Research*, 1(1): 39–49.

Javalgi, R. and Martin, C. (2007) 'Internationalisation of services: Identifying the building blocks for future research,' *Journal of Services Marketing*, 21(7): 391–97.

Javorcik, B.S. and Wei, S.J. (2009) 'Corruption and cross-border investment in emerging markets: Firm-level evidence,' *Journal of International Money and Finance*, 28(4): 605–24.

Jemison, D.B. and Sitkin, S.B. (1986) 'Corporate acquisitions: A process perspective,' *Academy of Management Review*, 11(1): 145–63.

Jensen, M.C. and Meckling, W.H. (1976) 'Theory of the firm: Managerial behavior, agency costs and ownership structure,' *Journal of Financial Economics*, 3(4): 305–60.

Johanson, J. and Vahlne, J.-E. (1977) 'The internationalization process of the firm: A model of knowledge development and increasing foreign market commitments,' *Journal of International Business Studies*, 8(1): 23–32.

Johanson, J. and Vahlne, J.-E. (1990) 'The mechanism of inernationalization,' *International Marketing Review*, 7(4): 11–24.

Johanson, J., and Vahlne, J.-E. (2009) 'The Uppsala internationalization process model revisited: From liability of foreignness to liability of outsidership,' *Journal of International Business Studies*, 40: 1411–431.

Johanson, J. and Wiedersheim, P. (1975) 'The internationalization of the firm? Four Swedish cases,' *Journal of Management Studies*, 12: 305–03.

Jormanainen, I., Latukha, M. and Panibratov, A. (2013) 'International competitiveness of Russian IT firms: Strong rivals or survivors at the edge?', in C. Mukhopadhyay, K.B. Akhilesh, R. Srinivasan, A. Gurtoo and P. Ramachandran (eds.) *Driving the Economy through Innovation and Entrepreneurship: Emerging Agenda for Technology Management*, New Delhi: Springer India.

Jormanainen, I., Panibratov, A. and Latukha, M. (2012). 'International competitiveness of Russian IT firms: Strong rivals or survivors at the edge?' in Ch. Mukhopadhyay, K.B. Akhilesh, R. Srinivasan, A. Gurtoo and P. Ramachandran (eds.) *Driving the Economy through Innovation and Entrepreneurship: Emerging Agenda for Technology Management*, New Delhi: Springer India: 849–58.

Juan, Z. (2007) 'Disneyland – Hong Kong's newest cash cow,' *China Today*, July, 56(7): 28–30.

Jullens, J. (2013) 'How emerging market giants can take on the world,' *Harvard Business Review*, 91(13): 121–25.

Kaleka, A. and Berthon, P. (2006) 'Learning and locale: The role of information, memory and environment in determining export differentiation advantage,' *Journal of Business Research*, 59(9): 1016–24.

Kalotay, K. (2003) 'EU enlargement: More FDI? The challenges for accession countries and the "new frontier",' Presentation at the Eastern European Investment Summit, October 14–15, Bucharest, Romania.

Kalotay, K. (2005) 'Outward foreign direct investment from Russia in a global context,' *Journal of East-West Business*, 11(3/4): 9–22.

Kalotay, K. (2008) 'Russian transnationals and international investment paradigms,' *Research in International Business and Finance*, 22(2): 85–107.

Kalotay, K. and Panibratov, A. (2013) 'Developing competitive advantages of Russian multinationals through foreign acquisitions,' in P.J. Williamson, R. Ramamurti, A. Fleury and M.T.L. Fleury (eds.) *The Competitive Advantage of Emerging Market Multinationals*, New York: Cambridge University Press.

Kalotay, K. and Sulstarova, A. (2010) 'Modelling Russian outward FDI,' *Journal of International Management*, 16(2): 131–42.

Kamal, M., Li, Z., Akhmat G., Bashir M. and Khan, K. (2014) 'What determines China's FDI inflow to South Asia?,' *Mediterranean Journal of Social Sciences*, 5(23): 254–63.

Kamaly, A. 2007. Trends and determinants of mergers and acquisitions in developing countries in the 1990s. *International Research Journal of Finance and Economics*, 8: 16–30.

Kaminsky, G. and Schumukler, S. (2002) 'Short-run pain, long-run gain: The effects of financial liberalization,' *World Bank Working Paper*, http://www.nber.org/papers/w9787.pdf

Kang, B. (2014) 'The innovation process of a private-owned enterprise and state-owned enterprise in China,' IDE Discussion Paper 470.

Kanter, R.M. (1994) 'Collaborative advantage: Successful partnerships manage the relationship, not just the deal,' *Harvard Business Review*, July-August: 96–108.

Kang, Y. and Jiang, F. (2012) 'FDI location choice of Chinese multinationals in East and Southeast Asia: Traditional economic factors and institutional perspective,' *Journal of World Business*, 47: 45–53.

Katrishen, F., and Scordis, N. (1998) 'Economies of scale in services: A study of multinational insurers,' *Journal of International Business Studies*, 29: 305–23.

Khanna, T. and Palepu, K. (1997) 'Why focused strategies may be wrong for emerging markets,' *Harvard Business Review*, July/August: 41–51.

Khrushcheva, O. (2012) *The Controversy of Putin's Energy Policy: The Problem of Foreign Investment and Long-Term Development of Russia's Energy Sector*, CEJISS, 6(1): 164–88.

Khurana, R. (2002) 'Market triads: A theoretical and empirical analysis of market intermediation,' *Journal for the Theory of Social Behavior*, 32: 239–62.

Khwaja, A.I. and Mian, A. (2005) 'Do lenders favor politically connected firms? Rent provision in an emerging financial market,' *Quarterly Journal of Economics*, 120(4): 1371–411.

Kiernan, P. (2014) 'Vale may consider settling suit over Guinea mining rights,' *WSJ*, December 5, http://www.wsj.com/articles/vale-may-consider-settling-suit-over-guinea-mining-rights-1417814246

Killing, J.P. (1983) *Strategies for Joint Venture Success*, New York: Praeger Publishers.

Kim, D. (2003). 'The internationalization of US Internet portals: Does it fit the process models of internationalization?' *Marketing Intelligence and Planning*, 21(1), 23–36.

Kim, D., Basu, C., Naidu, G.M. and Cavusgil, E. (2011) 'The innovativeness of born-globals and customer orientation: Learning from Indian born-globals,' *Journal of Business Research*, 64(8): 879–86.

Kim, H., Kim, H. and Hoskisson, R.E. (2010). 'Does market-oriented institutional change in an emerging economy make business group-affiliated multinationals perform better? An institution-based view,' *Journal of International Business Studies*, 41: 1141–60.

Kindelberger, C.P. (1969) *American Business Abroad: Six Lectures on Direct Investment*, London: Yale University Press.

Kindleberger, C.P. (1984) *Multinational Excursions*, Cambridge, MA: MIT Press.

King, D.R., Dalton, D.R., Daily, C.M. and Covin, J.G. (2004) 'Meta-analyses of post-acquisition performance: Indications of unidentified moderators,' *Strategic Management Journal*, 25(2): 187–200.

Kiss, A.N., Danis, W.M. and Cavusgil, S. (2012). 'International entrepreneurship research in emerging economies: A critical review and research agenda,' *Journal of Business Venturing*, 27(2): 266–90.

Klein, B., Crawford, R.G. and Alchian, A.A. (1978) 'Vertical integration, appropriable rents, and the competitive contracting process,' *Journal of Law and Economics*, 21(2): 297–326.

Klevorick, A.K., Levin, R.C., Nelson, R.R. and Winter, S.G. (1995) 'On the sources and significance of interindustry differences in technological opportunities,' *Research Policy*, 24(2): 185–205.

Kluckhohn, F.R. and Strodtbeck, F.L. (1961) *Variations in Value Orientations*, Evanston, IL: Row Peterson.

Knight, G. and Cavusgil, S.T. (1996) 'The born global firm: A challenge to traditional internationalization theory,' *Advances in International Marketing*, 8: 11–26.

Knight, G.G., Madsen, T.T. and Servais, P.P. (2004) 'An inquiry into born-global firms in Europe and the USA,' *International Marketing Review*, 21(6): 645–665.

Kogut, B., and Singh, H. (1988) 'The effect of national culture on the choice Of entry mode,' *Journal of International Business Studies*, 19(3): 411–32.

Kolstad, I. and Wiig, A. (2012) 'What determines Chinese outward FDI?,' *Journal of World Business*, 47(1): 26-34.

Kostova, T. and Roth, K. (2002) 'Adoption of an organizational practice by subsidiaries of multinational corporations: Institutional and regional effects,' *Academy of Management Journal*, 45(1): 215–33.

Kostova, T. and Zaheer, S. (1999) 'Organizational legitimacy under conditions of complexity: The case of the multinational enterprises,' *Academy of Management Review*, 24(1): 64–81.

Kotabe, M., Jiang, C.X. and Murray, J.Y. (2010) 'Managerial ties, knowledge acquisition, realized absorptive capacity and new product market performance of emerging multinational companies: A case of China,' *Journal of World Business*, 46(2): 166–76.

Kraats, S. (2000) 'Gaining a competitive edge through airline alliances: Competitiveness review,' *International Business Journal Incorporating Journal of Global Competitiveness*, 10(2): 56–64.

Krishna, J. (2014) 'India's new telecom M&A rules could deter deals,' *The Wall Street Journal*, http://online.wsj.com/news/articles/SB10001424052702304914204579396611740464266

Krishnan, H.A., Miller, A. and Judge, W.Q. (1997) 'Diversification and top management team complementarity: Is performance improved by merging similar or dissimilar teams?,' *Strategic Management Journal*, 18(5): 361–74.

Krkoska, L. and Korniyenko, E. (2008) 'China's investments in Russia: Where do they go and how important are they?,' *China and Eurasia Forum Quarterly*, 6(1): 39–49.

Kröger, F., and Von Zeisel, Stefan (2004) 'Das Endspiel gewinnen,' *Harvard Business Manager*, 82(11): 2–5.

Krugman, P., (1979) 'Increasing returns, monopolistic competition, and international trade,' *Journal of International Economics*, 9: 469–79.

Krugman, P.R. (2000) 'Fire-sale foreign direct investment,' in S. Edwards (ed.) *Capital Flows and the Emerging Economies*, Chicago: University of Chicago Press.

Kuada, J. and Sorensen, O. (2000) 'Internationalization of companies from developing countries,' New York: Haworth International Business Press.

Kuada, J. and Sorensen, O.J. (2013) *Internationalization of Companies from Developing Countries*, New York: Routledge.

Kumar, V., Jones, E., Venkatesan, R. and Leone, R.P. (2011) 'Is market orientation a source of sustainable competitive advantage or simply the cost of competing?,' *Journal of Marketing*, 75(1): 16–30.

Kuznetsov, A. (2011) 'Outward FDI from Russia and its policy context, update 2011,' Vale Columbia Center on Sustainable International Investment.

Kvint, V. (2009) *The Global Emerging Market: Strategic Management and Economics*, New York/London: Routledge.

Kweh, L.J. (2015) *Hong Kong Disneyland: When Big Business Meets Feng Shui, Superstition and Numerology*, Science, University of South Australia, http://www.studymode.com/essays/Hong-Kong-Disneyland-When-Big-Business-71747800.html

Kwon, Y.-C. and Hu, M.Y. (2004) 'Influences of liabilities of foreignness on firm's choice of internationalization process,' *Journal of Global Marketing*, 17(2/3): 45–54.

Kyrkilis, D. and Pantelidis, P. (2003) 'Macroeconomic determinants of outward foreign direct investment,' *International Journal of Social Economics*, 30: 827–36.

Lado, A. and Wilson, M.C. (1994) 'Human resource systems and sustained competitive advantage: A competency-based perspective,' *Academy of Management Review*, 19(4): 699–727.

Lall, S. (1983) *The New Multinationals*. New York: Wiley.

Lambsdorff, J. (2007) *The Institutional Economics of Corruption and Reform – Theory, Evidence, and Policy*, New York: Cambridge University Press.

Langberg, M. (2006) 'China entry raises issues of morals vs. money,' Between Heaven and Earth, January 25, http://ahdu88.blogspot.ru/2006/01/china-google-dont-be-evil.html

La Porta, R., Lopez-de-Silanes, F., Shleifer, A. and Vishny, R. (1999) 'The quality of government,' *Journal of Law, Economics, and Organization*, 15(1): 222–79.

Larsson, R. and Finkelstein, S. (1999) 'Integrating strategic, organisational, and human resource perspectives on mergers and acquisitions: A case survey of synergy realization,' *Organization Science*, 10(1): 1–26.

Larimo, J. (2003) 'Form of investment by Nordic firms in world markets,' *Journal of Business Research*, 56(10): 791–803.

Larson, A. (1992) 'Network dyads in entrepreneurial settings: A study of the governance of exchange relationships,' *Administrative Science Quarterly*, 37: 76–104.

Latukha, M. (2015) 'Talent management in Russian companies: Domestic challenges and international experience,' *The International Journal of Human Resource Management*, 26(8): 1051–75.

Latukha, M. and Panibratov, A. (2013) 'Is the role of HRM strategic in M&A success? Exploring the involvement of HRM in due-diligence process,' *Journal of General Management*, 39(1): 27–54.

Latukha, M. and Panibratov, A. (2015) 'Top management teams' competencies for international operations: Do they influence a firm's result?,' *Journal of General Management*, 40(4): 45–68.

Latukha, M., Panibratov, A. and Safonova-Salvadori, E. (2011) 'Entrepreneurial FDI in emerging economies: Russian SME strategy for Brazil,' *International Journal of Entrepreneurship and Innovation*, 12(3): 201–12.

Lawrence, T., Hardy, C. and Phillips, N. (2002) 'Institutional effects of interorganizational collaboration: The emergence of proto-institutions,' *Academy of Management Journal*, 45(1): 281–90.

Le, T.V. and O'Brien, J.P. (2010) 'Can two wrongs make a right? State ownership and debt in a transition economy,' *Journal of Management Studies*, 47(7): 1297–316.

Ledeneva, A. (2012) 'Cronies, economic crime and capitalism in Putin's sistema,' *International Affairs*, 88(1): 149–57.

Lee, G.K. and Lieberman, M.B. (2010) 'Acquisition vs. internal development as modes of market entry,' *Strategic Management Journal*, 31: 140–58.

Lee, I. (2003) 'The state-business relations in the era of globalization: The case of Russia,' *Pacific Focus*, 18(2): 59–78.

Lee, K. and Carter, S. (2005) *Global Marketing Management: Changes, Challenges and New Strategies*, Oxford: Oxford University Press.

Lee, L. and Gongming, Q. (2008) 'Partnership or self-reliance entry modes: Large and small technology-based enterprises strategies in overseas markets,' *Journal of International Entrepreneurship*, 6: 188–208.

Lee, M. (2016) 'China's nearly 700 million Internet users are hot for online finance,' *Forbes Asia*, January 25, http://www.forbes.com/sites/melanieleest/2016/01/25/chinas-nearly-700-million-internet-users-are-hot-for-online-finance/#6c6fe6411391

Lester, R.H., Hillman, A., Zardkoohi, A. and Cannella, A.A. (2008) 'Former government officials as outside directors: The role of human and social capital,' *Academy of Management Journal*, 51(5): 999–1013.

Leuz, C. and Oberholzer–Gee, F. (2006) 'Political relationships, global financing, and corporate transparency: Evidence from Indonesia,' *Journal of Financial Economics*, 81(2): 411–39.

Levine, R., and Renelt, D. (1992) 'A sensitivity analysis of cross-country growth regressions,' *The American Economic Review*, 82(4): 942–63.

Lewin, A.Y., Long, C.P. and Carroll, T.N. (1999) 'The coevolution of new organizational forms,' *Organization Science*, 10(5): 535–50.

Lewin, A.Y. and Volberda, H.W. (1999) 'Prolegomena on coevolution: A framework for research on strategy and new organizational forms,' *Organization Science*, 10(5): 519–34.

Lewis, A. (1955) *The Theory of Growth*, London: Allen and Unwin.

Lewis, J.I. (2011) 'Building a national wind turbine industry: Experiences from China, India and South Korea,' *International Journal of Technology and Globalisation*, 5(3): 281–305.

Li, J. (1995) 'Foreign entry and survival: Effects of strategic choices on performance in international markets,' *Strategic Management Journal*, 16(5): 333–51.

Li, W., He, A., Lan, H. and Yiu, D. (2011) 'Political connections and corporate diversification in emerging economies: Evidence from China,' *Asia Pacific Journal of Management*, 29(3): 799–818.

Li, L. (2009) Disney Dreamland? Plan to build Shanghai theme park met with applause and doubts. Beijing Review. February 5. http://www.bjreview.com.cn/nation/txt/2009-02/01/content_176305.htm

Lima, L.A. and De Barros, O. (2009) 'The growth of Brasil's direct investment abroad and the challenges it faces,' Columbia FDI Perspectives on topical foreign direct investment, Vale Columbia Centre on Sustainable International Investment, August 17, http://www.vcc.columbia.edu/pubs/documents/BrazilOFDI-Final.pdf

Liu, J. and Scott-Kennel, J. (2011) 'Asset-seeking investment by Chinese multinationals: Firm ownership, location, and entry mode,' *Asia Pacific and Globalization Review*, 1(1): 16–36.

Liuhto, K. and Majuri, S.S. (2014) 'Outward foreign direct investment from Russia: A literature review,' *Journal of East-West Business*, 20: 198–224.

Loeb, W. (2013) 'Walmart: What happened in India?,' *Forbes*, October 16, http://www.forbes.com/sites/walterloeb/2013/10/16/walmart-what-happened-in-india/#4d139551c49f

Lohr, S. (1987) 'Big Hong Kong bank to buy 14.9% of Midland,' *New York Times*, November 14, http://www.nytimes.com/1987/11/14/business/big-hong-kong-bank-to-buy-14.9-of-midland.html?rref=collection%2Fbyline%2Fsteve-lohr&action=click&contentCollection=undefined&region=stream&module=stream_unit&version=search&contentPlacement=3&pgtype=collection

London, B. and Ross, R. (1995) 'The political sociology of foreign direct investment: Global capitalism and global mobility 1965–1980,' *International Journal of Comparative Sociology*, 36(3): 98–119.

Loree, D.W. and Guisinger, S.E. (1995) 'Policy and non-policy determinants of U.S. equity foreign direct investment,' *Journal of International Business Studies*, 26(2), 281–99.

Lossan, A. 2015. Is Gazprom cutting the Turkish Stream in half? Russia Beyond the Headlines, July 17, http://rbth.com/business/2015/07/17/is_gazprom_cutting_the_turkish_stream_in_half_47821.html

Lu, J. and Beamish, P. (2001) 'The internationalization and performance of SMEs,' *Strategic Management Journal*, 22(6/7): 565–86.

Lu, J., Liu, X. and Wang, H. (2010) 'Motives for outward FDI of Chinese private firms: Firm resources, industry dynamics, and government policies,' *Management and Organization Review*, 7(2): 223–48.

Lu, J., Liu, X., Wright, M. and Filatotchev, I. (2014) 'International experience and FDI location choices of Chinese firms: The moderating effect of home country government support and host country institutions,' *Journal of International Business Studies*, 45(2): 428–49.

Lu, Y., Zhou, L., Bruton, G. and Li, W. (2010) 'Capabilities as a mediator linking resources and the international performance of entrepreneurial firms in an emerging economy,' *Journal of International Business Studies*, 41: 419–36.

Luo, Y. and Rui, H. (2009) 'An ambidexterity perspective toward multinational enterprises from emerging economies,' *Academy of Management Perspectives*, 23(4): 49–70.

Luo, Y., Shenkar, O. and Nyaw, M.K. (2002) 'Mitigating liabilities of foreignness: Defensive versus offensive approaches,' *Journal of International Management*, 8(3): 283–300.

Luo, Y. and Tung, R.L. (2007) 'International expansion of emerging market enterprises: A springboard perspective,' *Journal of International Business Studies*, 38(4): 481–98.

Luo, Y. and Wang, S. L. (2012) 'Foreign direct investment strategies by developing country multinationals: A diagnostic model for home country effects,' *Global Strategy Journal*, 2(3): 244–61.

Luo, Y., Xue, Q. and Han, B. (2010) 'How emerging market governments promote outward FDI: Experience from China,' *Journal of World Business*, 45(1): 68–79.

Lupina-Wegener, A., Schneider, S. and van Dick, R. (2011) 'Different experience of socio-cultural integration: A European merger in Mexico,' *Journal of Organizational Change Management*, 24(1): 65–89.

Majkgård, A. and Sharma, D. (1998) 'Client-following and market-seeking strategies in the internationalization of service firms,' *Journal of Business-to-Business Marketing*, 4(3): 1–41.

Makino, S. and Neupert, K. (2000) 'National culture, transaction costs, and the choice between joint ventures and wholly owned subsidiary,' *Journal of International Business Studies*, 31(4): 705–13.

Malhotra, D.K., Russow, L. and Singh, R. (2014) 'Determinants of foreign direct investment in Brazil, Russia, India, and China,' *International Journal of Business, Accounting, and Finance*, 8: 130–48.

Manea, J. and Pearce, R. (2006) 'MNEs strategies in Central and Eastern Europe: Key elements of subsidiary behaviour,' *Management International Review*, 46(2): 235–55.

Mani, S., Antia, K. D. and Rindfleisch, A. (2007) 'Entry mode and equity level: A multilevel examination of foreign direct investment ownership structure,' *Strategic Management Journal*, 28(8): 857–66.

Mann, J.A., Jr. (2014) 'Brazilian aircraft manufacturer Embraer oversees North America operations from Fort Lauderdale,' *Miami Herald*, November 2, http://www.miamiherald.com/news/business/biz-monday/article3526642.html

Marinova, S., Child, J. and Marinov, M. (2012) 'Institutional field for outward foreign direct investment: A theoretical expansion?,' in L. Tihanyi, T.M. Devinney, and T. Pedersen (eds.) *Institutional Theory in International Business and Management, Advances in International Management*, Bingley, UK: Emerald Group Publishing Limited, 25: 233–62.

Marinova, S., Child, J. and Marinov, M. (2014) 'The role of home governments in outward foreign direct investment,' in S. Marinova (ed.) *Institutional Impacts on Firm Internationalization*, New York: Palgrave Macmillan.

MarketLine industry profile: New cars in Russia. Datamonitor, December 2012.

Markusen, J.R. (1984) 'Multinationals, multi-plant economies, and the gains from trade,' *Journal of International Economies*, 16: 205–26.

Markusen, J.R. and Maskus, K. (2002) 'Discriminating among alternative theories of the multinational enterprise,' *Review of International Economics*, 10(4): 694–707.

Markusen, J.R. and Venables, A.J. (1998) 'Multinational firms and new trade theory,' *Journal of International Economics*, 46(2): 183–203.

Martins, T. (2012) 'Emerging MNE from emerging economies: OFDI from Brazil, http://gdex.dk/ofdi12/Taina%20Martins%20-%20Emerging%20MNE%20from%20Emerging%20Economies%20OFDI%20from%20Brazil.pdf

Masiero, G., Ogasavara, M., Caseiro, L. and Ferreira, S. (2014) 'Financing the expansion of Brazilian multinationals into Europe: The role of the Brazilian Development Bank (BNDES),' in A. Nolke (ed.) *State Capitalism 3.0*, Hampshire: Palgrave Macmillan.

Mason, R. (2011) 'Gazprom wins long Kovykta battle over TNK-BP gas,' March 2, *The Telegraph*, http://www.telegraph.co.uk/finance/newsbysector/energy/oilandgas/8355472/Gazprom-wins-long-Kovykta-battle-over-TNK-BP-gas.html

Mathews, J.A. (2006), 'Dragon multinationals: New players in 21st century globalization,' *Asia Pacific Journal of Management*, 23: 5–27.

Mattos, P. (2014) 'Institutions for industrial development: The state as a risk taker in Brazil,' FGV-RJ Workshop, October 14, Rio de Janeiro, Brazil.

Mauro, P. (1995) 'Corruption and growth,' *The Quarterly Journal of Economics*, 110(3): 681–712.

McCarthy, D.J. and Puffer, S.M. (2007) 'Can Russia's state-managed, network capitalism be competitive? Institutional pull versus institutional push,' *Journal of World Business*, 42(1): 1–13.

McCarthy, D.J., Puffer, S.M. and Vikhanski, O.S. (2009) 'Russian multinationals: Natural resource champions,' in R. Ramamurti and J.V. Singh (eds.) *Emerging Multinationals in Emerging Markets*, Cambridge: Cambridge University Press.

Melitz, M. (2003) 'The impact of trade on intra-industry reallocations and aggregate industry productivity,' *Econometrica*, 71(6): 1695–725.

Mengistu, A.A. and Adhikary, B.K. (2011) 'Does good governance matter for FDI inflows? Evidence from Asian economies,' *Asia Pacific Business Review*, 17(3): 281–99.

Meyer, C.B. (2008) 'Value leakage in merger and acquisitions: Why they occur and how they can be addressed,' *Long Range Planning*, 41: 197–224.

Meyer, K.E., Estrin, S., Bhaumik, S. K. and Peng, M. W. (2009) 'Institutions, resources and entry strategies in emerging economies,' *Strategic Management Journal*, 30(1): 61–80.

Meyer, K.E. and Peng, M.W. (2005) 'Probing theoretically into central and eastern Europe: Transactions, resources and institutions,' *Journal of International Business Studies*, 36(6): 600–21.

Mezias, J.M. (2002) 'How to identify liabilities of foreignness and assess their effects on multinational corporations,' *Journal of International Management*, 8: 265–82.

Michailova, S., McCarthy, D.J. and Puffer, S.M. (2013) 'Russia: As solid as a BRIC?,' *Critical Perspectives on International Business*, 9(1/2): 5–18.

Mihailova, I. and Panibratov, A. (2012) 'Determinants of internationalization strategies of emerging market firms: A multilevel approach,' *Journal of East-West Business*, 18(2): 157–84.

Miles, T. (2013) 'Russia was most protectionist nation in 2013: Study,' *Thomson Reuters*, December 30, http://www.reuters.com/article/us-trade-protectionism-idUSBRE9BT0GP20131230

Miller, S.R., Thomas, D.E., Eden, L. and Hitt, M. (2008) 'Knee deep in the big muddy: The survival of emerging market firms in developed markets,' *Management International Review*, 48(6): 645–65.

Minbaeva, D., Pedersen, T., Bjørkman, I., Fey, C.F. and Park, H.J. (2003) 'MNC knowledge transfer, subsidiary absorptive capacity, and HRM,' *Journal of International Business Studies*, 34: 586–99.

Mining Weekly (2015) 'Severstal needs partner to bring Liberian iron-ore mine online,' April 13, http://www.miningweekly.com/article/severstal-needs-partner-to-bring-liberia-iron-ore-mine-online-2015-04-14

Ministry of Economic Development of the Russian Federation (2015) http://www.ved.gov.ru

Ministry of Economic Development of the Russian Federation (2014) http://economy.gov.ru

Minkov, M. (2007) *What Makes Us Different and Similar: A New Interpretation of the World Values Survey and Other Cross-Cultural Data*, Sofia, Bulgaria: Klasika i Stil.

Mirvis, P.H. and Marks, M.L. (1992) *Managing the Merger: Making It Work*, Upper Saddle River, NJ: Prentice Hall.

Mishra, A. and Daly, K. (2007) 'Effect of quality of institutions on outward foreign direct investment,' *The Journal of International Trade & Economic Development*, 16(2): 231–44.

Moghaddam, K., Sethi, D., Weber, T. and Wu, J. (2014) 'The smirk of emerging market firms: A modification of the Dunning's typology of internationalization motivations,' *Journal of International Management*, 20: 359–74.

Moran, A. and Keane, M. (2013) *Cultural Adaptation*, London: Routledge.

Morck, R., Yeung, B., & Zhao, M. (2007). Perspectives on China's Outward Foreign Direct Investment. *Journal of International Business Studies*, 39(3): 337–50.

Morck, R., Yeung, B.Y. and Zhao, M. (2008) 'Perspectives on China's outward foreign direct investment,' *Journal of International Business Studies*, 39(3): 337–50.

Morosini, P., Shane, S. and Singh, H. (1998) 'National cultural distance and cross border acquisition performance,' *Journal of International Business Studies*, 29(1): 137–58.

Mroczek, K. (2014) 'Transaction costs in institutional environment and entry mode choice,' *International Journal of Social, Behavioral, Educational, Economic, Business and Industrial Engineering*, 8(4): 1121–26.

Mudambi, R. and Navarra, P. (2002) 'Institutions and international business: A theoretical overview,' *International Business Review*, 11(6): 635–46.

Munjal, S., Buckley, P., Enderwick, P. and Forsans, N. (2014) 'The growth trajectory of Indian multinational enterprises,' in C. Brautaset and C.M. Dent (eds.) *The Great Diversity: Trajectories of Asian Development*, Wageningen, Netherlands: Wageningen Academic Publishers.

Musteen, M., Francis, J. and Datta, D.K. (2010) 'The influence of international networks on internationalization speed and performance: A study of Czech SMEs,' *Journal of World Business*, 45(3): 197–205.

Nachum, L. (2010) 'When is foreignness an asset or a liability? Explaining the performance differential between foreign and local firms,' *Journal of Management*, 36(3): 714–39.

Nachum, L. and Zaheer, S. (2005) 'The persistence of distance? The impact of technology on MNE motivations for foreign investment,' *Strategic Management Journal*, 26(8): 747–67.

Nadolska, A. and Barkema, H.G. (2007) 'Learning to internationalise: The pace and success of foreign acquisitions,' *Journal of International Business Studies*, 38(7): 1170–86.

Nagaraj, R. (2006) 'Indian investments abroad,' *Economic and Political Weekly*, November 18, 2006: 4716–718.

Najid, N.A. and Rahman, R.A. (2011) 'Government ownership and performance of Malaysian government-linked companies,' *International Research Journal of Finance and Economics*, 61: 42–56.

Nardon, L. and Steers, R.M. (2009) 'The culture theory jungle: Divergence and convergence in models of national culture,' in R.S. Bhagat (ed.) *Cambridge Handbook of Culture Organizations and Work*, Cambridge: Cambridge University Press.

Narula, R. (2003) *Globalisation and Technology: Interdependence, Innovation Systems and Industrial Policy*, Cambridge: Polity Press.

Narula, R. (2010) 'Keeping the eclectic paradigm simple,' *Multinational Business Review*, 18(20): 35–50.

Narula, R. and Dunning, J.H. (2000) 'Industrial development, globalisation and multinational enterprises: New realities for developing countries,' *Oxford Development Studies*, 28(2): 141–67.

Narula, R. and Dunning, J.H. (2010) 'Multinational enterprises, development and globalisation: Some clarifications and a research agenda,' *Oxford Development Studies*, 38(3): 263–87.

Narula, R. and Kodiyat, T.P. (2013). 'The growth of outward FDI and the competitiveness of the underlying economy: The case of India,' UNU-MERIT Working Paper 2013–042.

Narula, R. and Kodiyat, T.P. (2014) 'How home country weaknesses can constrain further EMNE growth: Extrapolating from the example of India,' Discussion Paper JHD-2014-01, Henley Business School, John H. Dunning Centre for International Business.

Nicholson, R. and Salaber, J. (2013) 'The motives and performance of cross-border acquirers from emerging economies: Comparison between Chinese and Indian firms,' *International Business Review*, 22: 963–80.

NIS Annual Report (2013) http://www.nis.eu/ru/wp-content/uploads/sites/4/2013/07/nis_godisnji_izvestaj_2013_ru.pdf

Niu, C. and Liu, J. 2016. Positioning China's Aid to Educational Development in Africa: Past, Present, and Post-2015, in Shoko Yamada (ed.) Post-Education-For All and Sustainable Development Paradigm: Structural Changes with Diversifying Actors and Norms (International Perspectives on Education and Society, Volume 29) Emerald Group Publishing Limited: 269–299.

Nocke, V. and Whinston, M. (2013) 'Merger policy with merger choice,' *American Economic Review*, 103(2): 1006–1033.

North, D.C. (1990) *Institutions, Institutional Change and Economic Performance*, Cambridge: Cambridge University Press.

North, D.C. (1991) 'Institutions,' *Journal of Economic Perspectives* 5(1): 97–112.

North, D.C. (1994) 'Economic performance through time,' *American Economic Review*, 84(3): 359–68.

North, D.C. (2005) *Understanding the Process of Economic Change*, Princeton, NJ: Princeton University Press.

Notarianni, R. (2010) 'Knowledge stops culture clash,' *South China Morning Post*, October 30, http://www.scmp.com/frontpage/international

Nunnenkamp, P., Sosa Andrés, M., Vadlamannati, K., Waldkirch, A. (2012). What drives India's outward FDI? *South Asian Journal of Macroeconomics and Public Finance*, 1(2): 245–279.

Olie, R. (1990) 'Culture and integration problems in international mergers and acquisitions,' *European Management Journal*, 8(2): 206–15.

Omar, N. and Bakar, K.M.A. (2012) 'Fraud prevention mechanisms of Malaysian government-linked companies: An assessment of existence and effectiveness,' *Journal of Modern Accounting and Auditing*, 8(1): 15–31.

O'Neill, J. (2001) 'Building better global economic BRICS,' Global Economics Paper No. 66, Goldman Sachs Asset Management, November 30.

'An overview of the Russian and CIS automotive industry in Russia and CIS' (2013) http://www.ey.com/Publication/vwLUAssets/An_overview_of_the_Russian_and_CIS_automotive_industry/$FILE/An_overview_of_the_Russian_and_CIS_automotive_industry-March_2013.pdf

Oviatt, B. and McDougall, P. (1994) 'Toward a theory of international new ventures,' *Journal of International Business Studies*, 25(1): 45–64.

Pan, Y., Teng, L., Supapol, A.B., Lu, X., Huang, D. and Wang, Z. (2014) 'Firms FDI ownership: The influence of government ownership and legislative connections,' *Journal of International Business Studies*, 45: 1029–43.

Pandey, Manjit Kumar, Sharma, Parul Shailendra, Saboo, Utsav A. (PGDIE, NITIE) and Narayana Rao, K.V.S.S. (2007) 'Acquisition of Hutchinson Essar by Vodafone – Case study,' http://nrao-m-a-handbook.blogspot.ru/2007/10/acquisition-of-hutchinson-essar-by.html

Panibratov, A. (2009) 'Internationalization process of Russian construction industry: Inward investments perspective,' *Journal for East European Management Studies*, 2: 210–28.

Panibratov, A. (2010) *Russian Multinationals: Entry Strategies and Post-Entry Operations*, Electronic Publications of Pan-European Institute, 15/2010 www.tse.fi/pei.

Panibratov, A. (2012) *Russian Multinationals: From Regional Supremacy to Global Lead*, London: Routledge.

Panibratov, A. (2015) 'Liability of foreignness of emerging market firms: The country of origin effect on Russian IT companies,' *Journal of East-West Business*, 21(1): 22–40.

Panibratov, A. and Kalotay, K. (2009) 'Russian outward FDI and its policy context,' *Columbia FDI Profiles*, Vale Columbia Center on Sustainable International Investment. Columbia University, October 13, http://issuu.com/gsom/docs/fdi/1?e=0.

Panibratov, A. and Latukha, M. (2013) 'Servicing local customers for entering foreign markets: Internationalization of Russian IT firms,' in M. Marinov and S. Marinova (eds.) *Emerging Economies and Firms in the Global Crisis*, New York: Palgrave Macmillan.

Panibratov, A. and Latukha, M. (2014a) 'Foreign expansion of Russian firms based on natural resources and technology,' in M. Marinov and S. Marinova (eds.) *Successes and Challenges of Emerging Economy Multinationals*, New York: Palgrave Macmillan.

Panibratov, A. and Latukha, M. (2014b) 'Obtaining international results through partnerships: Evidence from Russian MNEs in the IT sector,' *Journal for East European Management Studies*, 19(1): 31–57.

Panibratov, A. and Verba, C. (2011) 'Russian banking sector: Key points of international expansion,' *Organizations and Markets in Emerging Economies*, 2(1/3): 63–74.

Parker, A. (2007) 'Vodafone acquires Hutchison Essar stake,' *Financial Times UK*, http://www.ft.com/intl/cms/s/2/0c6cb68a-fdb1-11db-8d62-000b5df10621.html#axzz2w1HBEL8x

Patibandla, M. (2009) 'Globalization of Tata Motors,' http://tejas-iimb.org/articles/31.php

Pauwels, P. and Ruyter, K. (2005) 'Research on international service marketing: Enrichment and challenges,' in K. de Ruyter and P. Pauwels (eds.) *Research on International Service Marketing: A State of the Art (Advances in International Marketing, Volume 15)*, Bingley, UK: Emerald Group Publishing Limited.

Peng, M.W. (2001) 'The resource-based view and international business,' *Journal of Management*, 27: 803–29.

Peng, M.W. (2002) 'Towards an institution-based view of business strategy,' *Asia Pacific Journal of Management*, 19(2/3): 251–67.

Peng, M.W. (2003) 'Institutional transitions and strategic choices,' *Academy of Management Review*, 28(2): 275–96.

Peng, M.W. (2012) 'The global strategy of emerging multinationals from China,' *Global Strategy Journal*, 2(2): 97–107.

Peng, M.W. (2013) *Global Strategy*, South-Western: Cengage Learning.

Peng, M.W., Lee, S.H. and Wang, D.Y. (2005) 'What determines the scope of the firm over time? A focus on institutional relatedness,' *Academy of Management Review*, 30: 622–33.

Peng, M.W., Wang, D.Y.L. and Jinag, Y. (2008) 'An institution-based view of international business strategy: A focus on emerging economies,' *Journal of International Business Studies*, 39(5): 920–36.

Peng, M.W. and Zhou, J.Q. (2005) 'How network strategies and institutional transitions evolve in Asia,' *Asia Pacific Journal of Management*, 22(4): 321–36.

Penrose, E. (1966) *The Theory of the Growth of the Firm*, Oxford, UK: Basil Blackwell.

Peteraf, Margaret, (1993) 'The cornerstones of competitive advantage: A resource-based view,' *Strategic Management Journal*, 14(3): 179–91.

Petrou, A.P. and Thanos, I.C. (2014) 'The "grabbing hand" or the "helping hand" view of corruption: Evidence from bank foreign market entries,' *Journal of World Business*, 49: 444–54.

Pfeffer, J. and Salancik, G. (2003) The External Control of Organizations: A Resource Dependence Perspective, 2nd ed., Standard, CA: Stanford University Press.

Pfeffer, J. and Salancik, G.R. (1978) *The External Control of Organizations: A Resource Dependence Perspective*, New York: Harper & Row.

Phan, M., Styles, C. and Patterson, P. (2005) 'Relational competency's role in Southeast Asia business partnerships,' *Journal of Business Research*, 58(2): 173–84.

Porter, M.E. (1980) *Competitive Strategy: Techniques for Analyzing Industries and Companies*, New York: Free Press.

Porter, M.E. (1985) *Competitive Advantage*, New York: Free Press.

Porter, M.E. (1990) 'The competitive advantage of nations,' *Harvard Business Review*, March/April: 73–93.

Poussenkova, N. (2010) 'The global expansion of Russia's energy giants,' *Journal of International Affairs*, 63(2): 103–24.

Powers, T.L. and Loyka, J.J. (2010) 'Adaptation of marketing mix elements in international markets,' *Journal of Global Marketing*, 23: 65–79.

Pradhan, J.P. (2008) 'Rise of Indian outward FDI: What implications does it hold for host developing countries?,' *Economia: Teoria y Practica*, 29, http://www.scielo.org.mx/scielo.php?script=sci_arttext&pid=S0188–33802008000200002

Pradhan, J.P. (2011) 'Emerging Multinationals: A Comparison of Chinese and Indian Outward Foreign Direct Investment.' *International Journal of Institutions and Economies*, 3(1): 113–148.

Prahalad, C.K. and Hamel, G. (1990) 'The core competence of the corporation,' *Harvard Business Review*, 68(3): 79–91.

Prahalad, C.K. and Lieberthal, K. (1998) 'The end of corporate imperialism,' *Harvard Business Review* 76(4): 68–79.

Prime (2015) 'Nordgold в рамках buy back погасила 0,776% акций уставного капитала,' April 22, http://1prime.ru/companies/20150422/808319225.html

Public Eye nominations (2012) 'Company responses & non-responses,' *Business and Human Rights Resource Centre*, http://business-humanrights.org/en/documents/public-eye-nominations-2012-company-responses-non-responses

Puig, F., Gonzalez-Loureiro, M. and Ghauri, P. N. (2014) 'Internationalization for survival: The case of new ventures,' *Management International Review*, 54(5): 653–73.

Puranam, P., Singh, H. and Chaudhuri, S.R. (2009) 'Integrating acquired capabilities: When structural integration is (un)necessary,' *Organization Science*, 20(2): 313–28.

PWC (2015) 'Auto market report,' https://www.pwc.ru/ru/automotive/publications/assets/auto-market-feb-16l.pdf

Qiu, L.D. and Wang, S. (2011) 'FDI policy, greenfield investment and cross-border mergers,' *Review of International Economics*, 19(5): 836–51.

Quazi, R. (2007) 'Economic freedom and foreign direct investment in East Asia,' *Journal of the Asia Pacific Economy*, 12(3): 329–44.

Quer, D., Claver, E. and Rienda, L. (2011) 'Political risk, cultural distance, and outward foreign direct investment: Empirical evidence from large Chinese firms,' *Asia Pacific Journal of Management*, 29(4): 1089–104.

Rabbiossi, L., Stefano, E. and Bertoni, F. (2012) 'Acquisitions by EMNCs in developed markets: An organizational learning perspective,' *Management International Review*, 52: 193–212.

Radosevic, S. and Sadowski, B. (2004) *International Industrial Networks and Industrial Restructuring in Central and Eastern Europe*, Boston: Kluwer academic publisher.

Ramamurti, R. (2009) 'What have we learned about emerging-market MNEs?,' in R. Ramamurti and J.V. Singh (eds.) *Emerging Multinationals in Emerging Markets*, Cambridge: Cambridge University Press.

Ramaswamy, K., Li, M. and Veliyath, R. (2002) 'Variations in ownership behavior and propensity to diversify: A study of the Indian corporate context,' *Strategic Management Journal*, 23(4): 345–58.

Ramsinghani, M. (2012) 'The trouble with India's people's car,' *MIT Technology Review*, 115(1): 69–70.

Ravenscraft, David J. and Scherer, F.M. (1987) *Mergers, Sell-Offs and Economic Efficiency*, Berkeley, CA: The Brookings Institution.

Raz, A.E. (2000) 'Domesticating Disney: Onstage strategies of adaptation in Tokyo Disneyland,' *Journal of Popular Culture*, 33(4): 77–99.

Reid, S.D. (1981) 'The decision-maker and export entry and expansion,' *Journal of International Business Studies*, 12(2): 101–12.

Rennie, M. (1993) 'Global competitiveness: Born global,' *McKinsey Quarterly*, 4: 45–52.

Review (2007) 'The cost of Google's collaboration with China: The dilemma of political censorship in online business,' *Strategic Direction*, 23(10): 15–17.

Richet, X. and Ruet, J. (2008) 'The Chinese and Indian automobile industry in perspective: Technology appropriation, catching-up and development,' *Transition Studies Review*, 15: 447–65.

Rienda, L., Claver, E. and Quer, D. (2013) 'The internationalization of Indian multinationals: Determinants of expansion through acquisitions,' *Journal of the Asia Pacific Economy*, 18(1): 115–32.

Rio Tinto (2012) 'Rio Tinto announces further investment in the development of Simandou,' June 20, http://www.riotinto.com/media/media-releases-237_6223.aspx

Rio Tinto (2014) 'Simandou South: Signature of the investment framework marks a significant move forward,' May 26, http://www.riotinto.com/media/media-releases-237_10508.aspx

Rodrigues, B.S. and Dieleman, M. (2014) 'Co-evolution of internationalization strategies: The case of Vale,' http://www.anpad.org.br/admin/pdf/2014_EnANPAD_ESO1598.pdf

Rodriguez, P., Uhlenbruck, K. and Eden, L. (2005) 'Government corruption and the entry strategies of multinationals,' *Academy of Management Review*, 30(2): 383–96.

Rodrik, D. (2005) 'Feasible globalizations,' in M.M. Weinstein (ed.) *Globalization: What's New*, New York: Columbia University Press.

Rolf Group Annual Report (2007) http://www.rolfgroup.com/files/rolf-group-annual-report-2009.pdf

Rolf Group Annual Report (2008) http://www.rolfgroup.com/files/rolf-group-annual-report-2008.pdf

Rolf Group Annual Report (2009) http://www.rolfgroup.com/files/rolf-group-annual-report-2009.pdf

'Rolf' pushed 'Incom' 1 August 2008, RBC weekly – South. http://www.rbc.ru/

Romanelli, E. and Tushman, M.L. (1986) 'Inertia, environments and strategic choice: Quasi-experimental designs for comparative research,' *Management Science*, 32(5): 608–21.

Root, F. (1994) *Entry Strategies for International Markets*. New York: Lexington Books.

'Rosneft completes acquisition of TNK-BP' (2013) *The New York Times*, http://www.nytimes.com/2013/03/22/business/global/rosneft-finalizes-acquisition-of-tnk-bp.html?_r=0

'Rosneft completes TNK-BP takeover paving way for BP to return cash to shareholders' (2015) *The Telegraph*, http://www.telegraph.co.uk/finance/newsbysector/energy/oilandgas/9946328/Rosneft-completes-TNK-BP-takeover-paving-way-for-BP-to-return-cash-to-shareholders.html

'Rosneft pays out in historic TNK-BP deal completion' (2013) *The Reuters*, http://www.reuters.com/article/2013/03/21/us-rosneft-tnkbp-deal-idUSBRE92K0IZ20130321

Ross, W. (2014) 'Is Nigeria serious about tackling corruption?,' *BBC News, Lagos*, March 12, http://www.bbc.com/news/world-africa-26535530

Rothenbuecher, J., Schrottke, J. and Niewiem, S. (2008) 'All mergers are not alike,' *A.T. Kearney*, http://jerrysoverinsky.com/pdfs/Articles/AllMergersAreNotAlike.pdf

Rothkopf, D. (2009). The BRICs and what the BRICs would be without China. *Foreign Policy* June 15.

Rouse, T. and Frame, T. (2009) 'The 10 steps to successful M&A integration,' *Bain & Company*, http://www.bain.com/publications/articles/10-steps-to-successful-ma-integration.aspx

Rugman, A. (1979) *International Diversification and the Multinational Enterprise*, Lexington, MA: Lexington Books.

Rugman, A., Oh, C. and Lim, D. (2012) 'The regional and global competitiveness of multinational firms,' *Journal of the Academy of Marketing Science*, 40(2): 218–35.

Rugman, A.M. (1981) *Inside the Multinationals: The Economics of Internal Markets*, New York: Columbia Press.

Rugman, A.M. (1982) *New Theories of Multinational Enterprises*, New York: St. Martin's Press.

Rugman, A.M. (2009) 'Theoretical aspects of MNEs from emerging countries,' in R. Ramamurti and J.V. Singh (eds.) *Emerging Multinationals in Emerging Markets*, Cambridge: Cambridge University Press.

Rugman, A.M., & Verbeke, A. (1992). A note on the transnational solution and the transaction cost theory of multinational strategic management. *Journal of International Business Studies*, 23(4): 761–771.

Rugman, A.M. and Verbeke, A. (2001) 'Subsidiary-specific advantages in multinational enterprises,' *Strategic Management Journal*, 22(3): 237–50.

Rugman, A.M. and Verbeke, A. (2008) 'A regional solution to the strategy and structure of multinationals,' *European Management Journal*, 26(5): 305–13.

Rugman, A.M., Verbeke, A. and Nguyen, Q.T.K. (2011) 'Fifty years of international business theory and beyond,' *Management International Review*, 51(6): 755–86.

Rui, H. and Yip, G.S. (2008) 'Foreign acquisitions by Chinese firms: A strategic intent perspective,' *Journal of World Business*, 43(2): 213–26.

Rumelt, R.P. (1987) *Theory, Strategy and Entrepreneurship – In The Competitive Challenge*, New York: Harper & Row.

Russia-China Investment Fund (2013) 'Russia China investment fund secures 42% stake in RFP group,' http://www.rdif.ru/Eng_fullNews/290/

'Russia leads the world in protectionist trade measures, study says' (2014) *The Moscow Times*, January 12, http://www.themoscowtimes.com/business/article/russia-leads-the-world-in-protectionist-trade-measures-study-says/492550.html

'Russian food embargo an opportunity for Latin America' (2014) *Live Mint*, August 17, http://www.livemint.com/Politics/1daSEGCi4KklQ5X98tWJkK/Russian-food-embargo-an-opportunity-for-Latin-America.html

Sabi, M. (1988) 'An application of the theory of foreign direct investment to multinational banking in LDCs,' *Journal of International Business Studies*, 19(3): 433–47.

Safarian, A.E. (2003) 'Internalization and the MNE: A note on the spread of ideas,' *Journal of International Business Studies*, 34: 116–24.

Salamon, L.M. and Siegfried, J.J. (1977) 'Economic power and political influence: The impact of industry structure on public policy,' *American Political Science Review*, 71(3): 1026–43.

Salehizadeh, M. (2007) 'Emerging economies' multinationals: Current status and future prospects,' *Third World Quarterly*, 28(6): 1151–66.

Salvan, P. (2011) 'Growth and internationalization: The case of Tata Motors,' *The Indian Journal of Industrial Relations*, 47(1): 1983–93.

Sanchez-Peinado, E. and Pla-Barber, J. (2006) 'A multidimensional concept of uncertainty and its influence on the entry mode choice: An empirical analysis in the service sector,' *International Business Review*, 15: 215–32.

Sarala, R.M. and Vaara, E. (2010) 'Cultural differences, convergence, and cross convergence as explanations of knowledge transfer in international acquisitions,' *Journal of International Business Studies*, 41(8): 1365–90.

Satyanand, P. and Raghavendran, P. (2010) 'Outward FDI from India and its policy context,' in *Columbia FDI Perspectives on topical foreign direct investment*, Vale Columbia Centre on Sustainable International Investment, September 22, http://hdl.handle.net/10022/AC:P:9622.

Sauvant, K. and Chen, V. (2014a) 'China needs to complement its 'going-out' policy with a 'going-in' strategy,' *Columbia FDI Perspective*, 121 May 12, http://ccsi.columbia.edu/files/2013/10/No-121-Sauvant-and-Chen-FINAL.pdf.

Sauvant, K. and Chen, V.Z. (2014b) 'China's regulatory framework for outward foreign direct investment,' *China Economic Journal*, 7(1): 141–63.

Sauvant, K.P., McAllister, G. and Maschek, W.A. (2010) *Foreign Direct Investments from Emerging Markets – The Challenges Ahead*, London: Macmillan.

Sauvant, K.P. and Nolan, M.D. (2015) 'China's outward foreign direct investment and international investment law'. *Journal of International Economic Law*, 18(4): 893–934.

Sberbank (2008) 'Sberbank's development strategy up to 2014,' October 21, http://www.sberbank.ru/en/about/about_sberbank/sberbank_strategy_2014.

Sberbank (2012) 'Acquisition of DenizBank AS building Sberbank's international platform,' *Report*, June 13, https://www.google.ru/url?sa=t&rct=j&q=&esrc=s&source=web&cd=1&ved=0ahUKEwj7956j qaLPAhWDJSwKHUJ0AhcQFggeMAA&url=http%3A%2F%2Fwww.sberbank.com%2Fcommon%2 Fimg%2Fuploaded%2Fir%2Fdocs%2FAnalyst_presentation_DenizBank_acquisition.pdf&usg=AFQjC NGp5hxAYJXMFO63sYwjSVfyIUSACw&sig2=xFHu2p6gJQ1DSWBi44MCjQ&cad=rjt

Sberbank (2013a) 'Plan of purchases,' https://www.google.ru/url?sa=t&rct=j&q=&esrc=s&source=web &cd=4&cad=rja&uact=8&ved=0ahUKEwjv86HPqaLPAhUHDywKHe6UDTUQFgguMAM&url= https%3A%2F%2Fwww.sberbank.ru%2Fcommon%2F_en%2Fimg%2Fuploaded%2Ffiles%2Fpdf%2Fn ormative_docs%2Fsberbank_strategy_presentation.pdf&usg=AFQjCNEKSJOMFby2De1v8n50DQPf f1bLlQ&sig2=lYDY53mXaA594s05sJRGxQ

Sberbank (2013b) Sberbank development strategy 2014–2018, http://www.sberbank.ru/en/about/about_sberbank/sberbank_strategy_2014-2018

Sberbank (2014) 'Codex of corporate cultural ethics of Sberbank co-worker' [In Russian]. Sberbank.ru.

Sberbank (2016) Press release, 13 January, http://data.sberbank.ru/moscow/en/press_center/all/index.php?id114=200010638

Schneider, F. and Frey, B.S. (1985) 'Economic and political determinants of foreign direct investment,' *World Development*, 13(2): 161–75.

Schumpeter, J. (1954) *History of Economic Analysis*. New York: Oxford University Press.

Scott, W.R. (1995) *Institutions and Organizations: Ideas, Interests and Identities*, New York: Sage.

Scott, W.R. (2002) 'The changing world of Chinese enterprise: An institutional perspective,' in A.S. Tsui and C.M. Lau (eds.) *The Management of Enterprises in the People's Republic of China*, New York: Springer Science-Business Media.

Segan (2015) 'Can Huawei and ZTE Conquer the U.S.?,' http://www.pcmag.com/article2/0,2817,2474884,00.asp

Seljom, P. and Rosenberg, E. (2011) 'A study of oil and natural gas resources and production,' *International Journal of Energy Sector Management*, 5(1): 101–24.

Serbia signs strategic energy deal with Russia (2008) http://uk.reuters.com/article/2008/01/25/uk-russia-serbia-idUKL2515142420080125

Sethi, D. and Guisinger, S. (2002) 'Liability of foreignness to competitive advantage: How multinational enterprises cope with the international business environment,' *Journal of International Management*, 8(3): 223–40.

Sethi, D. and Judge, W. (2009) 'Reappraising liabilities of foreignness within an integrated perspective of the costs and benefits of doing business abroad,' *International Business Review*, 18: 404–16.

Severstal. Annual Reports: 2000–2013, http://www.severstal.com/eng/ir/results_and_reports/annual_reports/index.phtml

Seyoum, B. (2009) 'Formal institutions and foreign direct investment,' *Thunderbird International Business Review*, 51(2): 165–81.

Shan, W., Walker, G. and Kogut, B. (1994) 'Interfirm cooperation and startup innovation in the biotechnology industry,' *Strategic Management Journal*, 15(5): 387–94.

Sheng, H.H. and Carrera Júnior, J.M. (2016) 'Leading Brazilian multinational enterprises: Trends in an era of significant uncertainties and challenges,' *Columbia Center on Sustainable Development*, January 20, http://ccsi.columbia.edu/files/2013/10/EMGP-Brazil-Report-2015-Jan-27-final.pdf.

Sheng, S., Zhou, K.Z. and Li, J.J. (2011) 'The effects of business and political ties on firm performance: Evidence from China,' *Journal of Marketing*, 75: 1–15.

Shirokova, G. and Tsukanova, T. (2013) 'Impact of the domestic institutional environment on the degree of internationalization of SMEs from transition economies,' *International Journal of Entrepreneurship and Innovation*, 14(3): 193–204.

Shleifer, A. and Vishny, R. (1993) 'Corruption,' *The Quarterly Journal of Economics*, 108: 599–617.

Shrivastava, P. (1986) 'Postmerger integration,' *Journal of Business Strategy*, 7(1): 65–76.

Sidorova, M. (2014) Интервью генерального директора Ilim Timber, Лесная Индустрия, March, http://www.lesindustry.ru/issues/li_n71/Intervyu_generalnogo_direktora_Ilim_Timber_830/

Simeone, J. (2013) 'Russia's forestry sector and international trade in forest products,' *Vestnik, the Journal of Russian and Asian Studies*, 55(1): 37–70.

Skolkovo (2009) *Global Expansion of Emerging Multinationals: Post-Crisis Adjustment*, Skolkovo Institute of Emerging Market Studies, https://iems.skolkovo.ru/downloads/documents/SKOLKOVO_IEMS/Research_Reports/SKOLKOVO_IEMS_Research_2009-05-10_en.pdf.

Smith, K. (1997) 'Economic infrastructure and innovations systems,' in C. Edquist (ed.) *Systems of Innovation: Technologies, Institutions and Organizations*, London: Pinter.

Smith, T. (2013) 'Krakatau Steel to enlarge blast furnace project,' *Steel Times International*, August 7, http://www.steeltimesint.com/news/view/krakatau-steel-to-enlarge-blast-furnace-project

SMMT (2012) Motor industry facts, http://www.smmt.co.uk/wp-content/uploads/SMMT_FACTS_2012_WEBv.pdf

SMMT (2015) Motor industry facts, http://www.smmt.co.uk/wp-content/uploads/sites/2/100049_SMMT-Facts-Guide-2015.pdf

Stahl, G.K. and Voigt, A. (2008) 'Do cultural differences matter in mergers and acquisitions? A tentative model and examination,' *Organization Science*, 19(1): 160–76.

Standard and Poor's (2014) http://www.standardandpoors.com/en_EU/delegate/getPDF?articleId=1498249&type=COMMENTS&subType=REGULATORY

Stoian, C. (2013) 'Extending Dunning's investment development path: The role of home country institutional determinants in explaining outward foreign direct investment,' *International Business Review*, 22(3): 615–37.

Stoian, C. and Filippaios, F. (2008) 'Dunning's eclectic paradigm: A holistic, yet context specific framework for analysing the determinants of outward FDI,' *International Business Review*, 17(3): 349–67.

Stuart, T. (2000) 'Interorganizational alliances and the performance of firms: A study of growth and innovation rates in a high-technology industry,' *Strategic Management Journal*, 21: 791–811.

Stucchi, T. (2012) 'Emerging market firms' acquisitions in advanced markets: Matching strategy with resource-, institution- and industry-based antecedents,' *European Management Journal*, 30(3): 278–89.

Summary, R. and Summary, L. (1995) 'The political economy of United States foreign direct investment in developing countries: An empirical analysis,' *Quarterly Journal of Business and Economics*, 34(3): 80–93.

Sun, P., Xu, H. and Zhou, J. (2011) 'The value of local political capital in transition China,' *Economics Letters*, 110(3): 189–92.

Sun, S.L., Peng, M.W., Lee, R.P. and Tan, W. (2015) 'Institutional open access at home and outward internationalization,' *Journal of World Business*, 50(1): 234–46.

Svetlicic, M. (2003a) 'Outward foreign direct investment by enterprises form Slovenia,' *Transnational Corporations*, 16(1): 55–88.

Svetlicic, M. (2003b) 'Theoretical context of outward foreign direct investment from transition econo-mies,' in M. Svetlicic and M. Rojec (eds.) *Facilitating Transition by Internationalization: Outward Direct Investment from European Economies in Transition*, Aldershot: Ashgate.

Syrjälä, J. and Takala, T. (2008) 'Ethical aspects in Nordic business mergers: The case of electro-business,' *Journal of Business Ethic*, 80: 531–45.

Tanzi, V. and Davoodi, H.R. (2001) 'Corruption, growth, and public finances', in A.K. Jain (ed.) *Political Economy of Corruption*, Routledge.

Tata Motors Annual Reports, 2011–12, www.tatamotors.com.

'Tata Motors ready to pull plug on UK launch' (2010) *Birmingham Post*, http://www.birminghampost.net/birmingham-business/birmingham-business-news/automotive-business/2012/05/04/tata-motors-ready-to-pull-plug-on-uk-launch-of-indica-vista-electric-car-65233-30897221/

Teerikangas, S. and Very, P. (2006) 'The culture-performance relationship in M&A: From yes/no to how,' *British Journal of Management*, 17: 31–48.

Terpstra, V. and Yu, C.M. (1988) 'Determinants of foreign investment of U.S. advertising agencies,' *Journal of International Business Studies*, 19: 33–46.

Te Velde, D.W. and Bezemer, D. (2006) 'Regional integration and foreign direct investment in developing countries,' *Transnational Corporations*, 15(2): 41–70.

The Japan Times (2016) Visitors to USJ increased to record 13.9 million in fiscal 2015. http://www.japantimes.co.jp/news/2016/04/01/national/visitors-to-usj-increased-to-record-13-9-million-in-fiscal-2015/#.WBS1_cl8O2k

Thomas, D.E., Eden, L. Hitt, M.A. and Miller, S.R. (2007) 'Experience of emerging market firms: The role of cognitive bias in developed market entry and survival,' *Management International Review*, 47(6): 845–67.

Thompson, A.A. and Strickland, A.J. (1999) *Strategic Management: Concepts and Cases*, Boston: Irwin McGraw-Hill.

Thompson, C. (2006) 'Google's China problem (and China's Google problem),' *New York Times*, April 23, http://www.nytimes.com/2006/04/23/magazine/23google.html?pagewanted=all

Tian, R. G. (2009). 'Cross-cultural issues in the 21st century marketing,' http:// www.studyoverseas.com/america/used/crosscultural.htm

'Timeline: Alaska pipeline chronology' (2006) *PBS*, April 4, http://www.pbs.org/wgbh/amex/pipeline/timeline/index.html

Tolentino, P.E. (2010) 'Home country macroeconomic factors and outward FDI of China and India,' *Journal of International Management*, 16(2): 102–20.

Toth, J.M. (2008) 'Cross-border M&A deals: National security and interest reviews raise flags,' *Inside Counsel*, 18: 20–21.

Toyne, B. and Nigh, D. (1998) 'A more expansive view of international business,' *Journal of International Business Studies*, 29: 863–75.

'Trade with Brazil gains momentum' (2011) *The Moscow Times*, April 20, http://www.themoscowtimes.com/sitemap/free/2011/11/article/trade-with-brazil-gains-momentum/447186.html

Transnationality Ranking of Brazilian Companies (2012) http://www.fdc.org.br/pt/Documents/2012/ranking_transnacionais_brasileiras2012.pdf

Transparency International (2014) http://www.transparency.org/country#BRA_DataResearch

Trompenaars, F. (1993) *Riding the Waves of Culture: Understanding Cultural Diversity in Business*, London: Economists Books.

Trompenaars, F. and Hampden-Turner, C. (1998) *Riding the Waves of Culture: Understanding Diversity in Global Business*, London: Economists Books.

Tsai, H. and Eisingerich, A.B. (2010) 'International strategies of emerging market firms,' *California Management Review* 53(1): 114–35.

Tsang, E.W.K. (1998) 'Can guanxi be a source of sustained competitive advantage for doing business in China?,' *Academy of Management Executive*, 12: 64–73.

Tsang, E.W.K. and Yip, P.S.L. (2007) 'Economic distance and the survival of foreign direct investments,' *Academy of Management Journal*, 50(5): 1156–68.

Tse, D., Pan, Y. and Gang, Au K. (1997) 'How MNCs choose entry modes and form alliances: The China experience,' *Journal of International Business Studies*, 28(3): 779–S805.

Turnbull, P. (1987) 'Interaction and international marketing: An investment process,' *International Marketing Review*, 4(4): 7–19.

UNCTAD (1998) 'Trends and determinants,' in *World Investment Report*, New York/Geneva: United Nations.

UNCTAD (2011) World Investment Report, http://unctad.org/en/PublicationsLibrary/wir2011_en.pdf

UNCTAD (2013) 'The rise of BRIC FDI and Africa,' in *Global Investment Trends Monitor*, http://unctad.org/en/PublicationsLibrary/webdiaeia2013d6_en.pdf

UNCTAD (2014) 'Investing in the SDGs: An action plan,' in *World Investment Report*, New York/Geneva: United Nations.

UNCTAD (2015) 'Reforming international investment governance,' in *World Investment Report*, New York/Geneva: United Nations.

U.S. Department of State (2014) Investment Climate Statement, http://www.state.gov/documents/organization/227130.pdf

US giant Walmart quits India after venture ends (2013) *The Express Tribune*, October 9, http://tribune.com.pk/story/615742/us-giant-walmart-quits-india-after-venture-ends/

Vaara, E. (2003) 'Post-acquisition integration as sensemaking: Glimpses of ambiguity, confusion, hypocrisy, and politicization,' *Journal of Management Studies*, 40(4): 859–94.

Vahtra, P. and Liuhto, K. (2005) 'Russian corporations abroad – Seeking profits, leverage or refuge?,' in K. Liuhto and Z. Vincze (eds.) *Wider Europe*, Turku: Turku School of Economics and Business Administration.

Vale across the world (2016) http://mundo.intranetvale.com.br/EN/Unidade/Content/Oman

Vale Annual Report (2013) http://www.vale.com/EN/investors/information-market/annual-reports/20f/20FDocs/20F_2013_i.pdf

Vale Annual Report (2014) http://www.vale.com/EN/investors/information-market/annual-reports/20f/20FDocs/Vale%2020-F%202014_i_novo.pdf

Vale History Book (2012) http://www.vale.com/EN/aboutvale/book-our-history/Pages/default.aspx

Vale History, www.vale.com

van Tulder, R. (2015) 'Getting all motives right: A holistic approach to internationalization motives of companies,' *The Multinational Business Review*, 23(1): 36–56.

Vascellaro, J.E., Dean, J. and Gorman, S. (2011) 'Google warns of China exit over hacking,' *Wall Street Journal*, January 13, http://online.wsj.com/article/SB126333757451026659.html

Vasilaki, A. and O'Regan, N. (2008) 'Enhancing post-acquisition organisational performance: The role of the top management team,' *Team Performance Management*, 14(3/4): 134–45.

Vedimosti (2015) Alfa-Bank sells business in USA to BKS Group, http://www.vedomosti.ru/finance/articles/2015/10/01/611042-alfa-bank-prodal-biznes

Velde, D.W. (ed.) (2006) *Regional Integration and Poverty*. Aldershot: Ashgate.

Verbeke, A. and Yuan, W. (2010) 'A strategic management analysis of ownership advantages in the eclectic paradigm,' *Multinational Business Review*, 18(2): 89–108.

Verma, N. and Sharma, R. (2014) 'Impact of mergers and acquisitions on firms' long term performance: A pre and post cost analysis of the Indian telecom industry,' *International Journal of Research in Management and Technology*, February, 4(1), http://www.iracst.org/ijrmt/papers/vol4no12014/2vol4no1.pdf

Vernon, R. (1966) 'International investment and international trade in the product cycle,' *Quarterly Journal of Economics*, 80(2): 190–207.

Vestring, T., King, B., Rouse, T. and Critchlow, J. (2003) 'Merger integration: Why 'soft issues' matters most,' *European Business Forum*, Spring(13): 69–71.

Vijayakumar, N., Sridharan, P. and Rao, K.C.S. (2010) 'Determinants of FDI in BRICS countries: A panel analysis,' *International Journal of Business Science and Applied Management*, 5(3): 1–13.

Villalonga, B. (2004) 'Intangible resources, Tobin's q, and sustainability of performance differences,' *Journal of Economic Behavior and Organization*, 54(2): 205–30.

Vodafone applies to buy out India partners for $1.7 billion (2013) *Bloomberg*, http://www.bloomberg. com/news/2013–10–29/vodafone-applies-to-buy-out-indian-unit-stake-for-1–65-billion.html

Vogiatzoglou, K. (2007) 'Vertical specialization and new determinants of FDI: Evidence from South and East Asia,' *Global Economic Review*, 36(3): 245–66.

Voyer, P.A. and Beamish, P.W. (2004) 'The effect of corruption on Japanese foreign direct investment,' *Journal of Business Ethics*, 50: 211–24.

Wach, K. (2014) 'Market entry modes for international business,' in E. Horská (ed.) *International Marketing: Within and Beyond Visegrad Borders*, Kraków: Wydawnictwo Episteme.

Waldman, D.A. and Javidan, M. (2007) 'Alternative forms of charismatic leadership in the integration of mergers and acquisitions,' *Leadership Quarterly*, 20: 130–42.

Waldron, G. (2015) 'ABACE: Embraer has 'no plan B' for Harbin joint venture,' *Flightglobal*, April 13, https://www.flightglobal.com/news/articles/abace-embraer-has-no-plan-b-for-harbin-joint-vent-411118/

Walmart Annual Report (2014) https://cdn.corporate.walmart.com/66/e5/9ff9a87445949173fde56316 ac5f/2014-annual-report.pdf

Walsh, J.P. and Yu, J. (2010) 'Determinants of foreign direct investment: A sectoral and institutional approach,' IMF Working Paper WP/10/187 Asian Pacific Department.

Wang, C., Hong, J., Kafouros, M. and Boateng, A. (2012) 'What drives outward FDI of Chinese firms? Testing the explanatory power of three theoretical frameworks,' *International Business Review*, 21(3): 425–38.

Warner, M., Hong, N.S. and Xu, X. (2004) 'Late development' experience and the evolution of transnational firms in the People's Republic of China,' *Asia Pacific Business Review*, 10(3/4): 324–45.

Weak Russian Ruble Pushes Severstal's Q1 Margin to Record High (2015) *The Moscow Times*, April 23, http://www.themoscowtimes.com/business/article/weak-russian-ruble-pushes-severstals-q1-margin-to-record-high/519620.html

Weber, Y., Shenkar, O. and Raveh, A. (1996) 'National and corporate cultural fit in mergers and acquisitions: An exploratory study,' *Management Science*, 42(8): 1215–27.

Weber, Y., Tarba, S.Y. and Reichel, A. (2011) 'A model of the influence of culture on integration approaches and international mergers and acquisitions performance,' *International Studies of Management and Organization*, 41(3): 9–24.

Wei, S. (2000a) 'How taxing is corruption on international investors?,' *Review of Economics and Statistics*, 82(1): 1–11.

Wei, S. (2000b) 'Local corruption and global capital flows,' *Brookings Papers on Economic Activity*, 31(2): 303–46.

Wei, S. and Wu, Y. (2002) 'Corruption, composition of capital flows, and currency crises,' in S. Edward and J.A. Frankel (eds.) *Preventing Currency Crises in Emerging Markets*, Chicago, IL: University of Chicago Press.

Wei, W. (2000) 'China and India: Any difference in their FDI performances?,' *Journal of Asian Economics*, 16(4): 719–36.

Weinstein, A.K. (1977) 'Foreign investments by service firms: The case of the multinational advertising agency,' *Journal of International Business Studies*, 8: 83–91.

Weitzel, U. and Berns, S. (2006) 'Cross-border takeovers, corruption, and related aspects of governance,' *Journal of International Business Studies*, 37: 786–806.

Welch, L.S. and Luostarinen, R. (1988). Internationalization: evolution of a concept. *Journal of General Management*, 14(2): 34–55.

Wells, L.T. (1983) *Third World Multinationals: The Rise of Foreign Direct Investment from Developing Countries*, Cambridge, MA: MIT Press.

Wells, T. (2010) 'Baidu profits from Google's China exit,' *Seochat.com*, July, http://seochat.com/c/a/ Search-Engine-News/Baidu-Profits-From-Googles-China-Exit

Wernerfelt, B. (1984) 'A resource-based view of the firm,' *Strategic Management Journal*, 5(2): 171–80.

Wheatley, J. (2010) 'Globalization: Companies must expand to prosper,' *Financial Times*, November 14, https://www.ft.com/content/a9288530-edfe-11df-8616-00144feab49a

Wheeler, D. and Mody, A. (1992) 'International investment location decisions: The case of U.S. firms,' *Journal of International Economics*, 33: 57–76.

Wilkinson, T. J. (2006) 'Entrepreneurial climate and U.S. state foreign trade offices as predictors of export success,' *Journal of Small Business Management*, 44(1): 99–113.

Williamson, O.E. (1971) 'The vertical integration of production: Market failure considerations,' *American Economic Review*, 61: 112–23.

Williamson, O.E. (1985) *The Economic Institutions of Capitalism*, New York: Free Press.

Williamson, O.E. (1989) 'Transaction cost economics,' *Handbook of Industrial Organization*, 1: 135–82.

Williamson, O.E. (2000), 'The new institutional economics: Taking stock, looking ahead,' *Journal of Economic Literature*, 38: 595–613.

Williamson, O.E. (2008) 'Outsourcing transaction cost economics and supply chain management,' *Journal of Supply Chain Management*, 44: 5–16.

'Wipro is now decentralising like crazy' (2014) *Times of India*, http://timesofindia.indiatimes.com

'Wipro's CFO Suresh Senapathy on current changes' (2014) *Business Today*, http://businesstoday.intoday.in

'Wipro's new strategy: Outsource locally' (2014) *The New York Times*, http://bits.blogs.nytimes.com

Wipro to acquire SAIC's global oil and gas information technology services business (2014) http://finance.boston.com

Wohl, J. (2012) 'RPT-Wal-Mart employees to pay more for health care plans,' November 12, *Reuters*, http://www.reuters.com/article/walmart-healthcare-idUSL3E8MC18E20121112

Wong, C.-Y. and Govindaraju, V.G.R.C. (2012) 'Technology stocks and economic performance of government-linked companies: The case of Malaysia,' *Technological and Economic Development of Economy*, 18(2): 248–61.

Wong, E. (2009) 'Why HSBC wants New Yorkers to get on a soapbox,' *Adweek*, July 14, http://www.adweek.com/news/advertising-branding/why-hsbc-wants-new-yorkers-get-soapbox-106108

World Bank (2013) Ease of Doing Business Report, http://www.doingbusiness.org/~/media/GIAWB/Doing%20Business/Documents/Annual-Reports/English/DB13-full-report.pdf

World Bank (2016) Gross domestic product. http://databank.worldbank.org/data/download/GDP.pdf

World Bank (2016) India's overview, http://www.worldbank.org/en/country/india/overview

World Bank (2016) Indonesia's overview// http://www.worldbank.org/en/country/indonesia/overview

World Bank (2016) Mexico's overview// http://www.worldbank.org/en/country/mexico/overview

World Bank (2016) Russia's overview// http://www.worldbank.org/en/country/russia/overview

World Bank (2016) Turkey's overview// http://www.worldbank.org/en/country/russia/overview

World Development Indicators Database, http://databank.worldbank.org/ddp/home.do?Step=12&id=4&CNO=2

World Investment Report (2015). UNCTAD. http://unctad.org/en/PublicationsLibrary/wir2015_en.pdf

World Steel Association (2014) World Steel in Figures, http://www.worldsteel.org/dms/internetDocumentList/bookshop/World-Steel-in-Figures-2014/document/World%20Steel%20in%20Figures%202014%20Final.pdf

Wortzel, L. and Vernon-Wortzel, H. (1988) 'Globalizing strategies for multinationals from developing countries,' *Columbia Journal of World Business*, Spring: 27–35.

Xia, J., Ma, X., Lu, J.W. and Yiu, D.W. (2014) 'Outward foreign direct investment by emerging market firms: A resource dependence logic,' *Strategic Management Journal*, 35: 1343–63.

Xiao, S.S., Jeong, I., Moon, J.J., Chung, C.C. and Chung, J. (2013) 'Internationalization and performance of firms in China: Moderating effects of governance structure and the degree of centralized control,' *Journal of International Management*, 19: 118–37.

Xinhua (2012) 'India's Tata Motors aiming at Chinese market,' *China Daily*, http://www.chinadaily.com.cn/bizchina/2012-08/20/content_15690130.htm

Xu, D. and Shenkar, O. (2002) 'Institutional distance and the multinational enterprise,' *Academy of Management Review*, 27(4): 608–18.

Yamakawa, Y., Peng, M.W. and Deeds, D.L. (2008) 'What drives new ventures to internationalize from emerging to developed economies?,' *Entrepreneurship Theory and Practice*, 32(1): 59–82.

Yang, J., Lian, J. and Liu, X. (2012) 'Political connections, bank loans and firm value,' *Nankai Business Review International*, 3(4): 376–97.

Yang, X., Jiang, Y., Kang, R. and Ke, Y. (2009) 'A comparative analysis of the internationalization of Chinese and Japanese firms,' *Asia Pacific Journal of Management*, 26(1): 141–62.

Yaprak, A. and Karademir, B. (2011) 'The emerging market multinationals' role in facilitating developed country multinationals' regional expansion: A critical review of the literature and Turkish MNC examples,' *Journal of World Business*, 46(5): 438–46.

Yeaple, S.R. (2003) 'The complex integration strategies of multinationals and cross country dependencies in the structure of foreign direct investment,' *Journal of International Economics*, 60(2): 293–314.

Yeung, H.W. and Liu, W. (2008) 'Globalizing China: The rise of mainland firms in the global economy,' *Eurasian Geography and Economics*, 49(1): 57–86.

Yin, X. and Shanley, M. (2008) 'Industry determinants of the "Merger versus Alliance" decision,' *Academy of Management Review*, 33(2): 473–91.

Yip, G.S. (1992) *Total Global Strategy: Managing for Worldwide Competitive Advantage*, Englewood Cliffs, NJ: Prentice – Hall.

Young, M., Tsai, T., Wang, X., Liu, S. and Ahlstrom, D. (2014) 'Strategy in emerging economies and the theory of the firm,' *Asia Pacific Journal of Management*, 31(2): 331–54.

Yu, J. and Kim, S.S. (2010) 'Liability of foreignness and the growth of an industry: A dynamic approach,' *Academy of Management Annual Meeting Proceedings*, 1–6.

Yung, Ch. (2014) 'Hong Kong Disneyland to invest in third hotel,' *The Wall Street Journal*, February 17, http://online.wsj.com/news/articles/SB10001424052702304899704579387931316825784

Zaheer, S. (1995) 'Overcoming the liability of foreignness,' *Academy of Management Journal*, 38(2): 341–63.

Zaheer, S. and Marakhan, S. (2001) 'Concentration and dispersion in global industries: Remote electronic access and the location of economic activities,' *Journal of International Business Studies*, 32(4): 667–86.

Zaheer, S. and Mosakowski, E. (1997) 'The dynamics of the liability of foreignness: A global study of survival in financial services,' *Strategic Management Journal*, 18: 439–63.

Zahra, S.A. and George, G. (2002) 'Absorptive capacity: A review, reconceptualization, and extension,' *Academy of Management Review*, 27(2): 185–203.

Zejan, M. (1990) 'New ventures of acquisitions: The choices of Swedish multinational enterprises,' *Journal of industrial Economics*, 38(3): 349–55.

Zhang, K. (2001) 'How does foreign direct investment affect economic growth in China?,' *Economic of Transition*, 9(3): 679–93.

Zhang, J., Zhou, C. and Ebbers, H. (2011) 'Competition of Chinese overseas acquisitions: Institutional perspectives and evidence,' *International Business Review*, 20: 226–38.

Zhang, X. and Daly, K. (2011) 'The determinants of China's outward foreign direct investment,' *Emerging Markets Review*, 12(4): 389–98.

Zheng, A. and Murphy, C. (2015) 'Chinese car maker Geely's profit plunges 46% in 2014,' *The WSJ*, March 18, http://www.wsj.com/articles/geely-2014-profit-drops-46-in-part-on-sales-decline-1426663433

Zhou, L. and Leung, D. (2015) 'China's overseas investments, explained in 10 graphics,' *The World Resources Institute*, http://www.wri.org/blog/2015/01/china%E2%80%99s-overseas-investments-explained-10-graphics

Zollo, M. and Singh, H. (2004) 'Deliberate learning in corporate acquisitions: Post-acquisition strategies and integration capability in US bank merger,' *Strategic Management Journal*, 25: 1233–56.

ZTE (2004) Annual reports, http://www.zte.com.cn/mi_imgs/global/investor_relations/352960/P020120918590182744369.rar

ZTE (2005) Annual reports, http://www.zte.com.cn/mi_imgs/global/investor_relations/352961/P020120918590186321174.rar

ZTE (2012) Annual reports, http://www.zte.com.cn/mi_imgs/global/investor_relations/395164/P020130414667427851218.pdf

ZTE (2013) Annual reports, http://wwwen.zte.com.cn/en/about/investor_relations/corporate_report/annual_report/201404/P020140408599365909862.pdf

ZTE (2014) Annual reports, http://wwwen.zte.com.cn/en/about/investor_relations/corporate_report/annual_report/201504/P020150408612617327250.pdf

ZTE (2015) Annual reports, http://www.zte.com.cn/MediaFiles/5/3/8/%7B538634A7-5C16-45C2-9FA0-39901F83657D%7DP020160406712290589315.pdf

ZTE (2015) Corporate website, http://www.zte.com.cn/global

Zutshi, K.R. and Gibbons, P.T. (1998) 'The internationalization process of Singapore government-linked companies: A contextual view,' *Asia Pacific Journal of Management*, 15(2): 219–46.

Index